Tyndale Old Testament Commentaries

Volume 20

TOTC

Isaiah

Tyndale Old Testament Commentaries

Volume 20

Series Editor: David G. Firth
Consulting Editor: Tremper Longman III

Isaiah

An Introduction and Commentary

Paul D. Wegner

An imprint of InterVarsity Press
Downers Grove, Illinois

Inter-Varsity Press, England
36 Causton Street, London SW1P 4ST, England
Website: www.ivpbooks.com
Email: ivp@ivpbooks.com

InterVarsity Press, USA
P.O. Box 1400, Downers Grove, IL 60515, USA
Website: www.ivpress.com
Email: email@ivpress.com

Inter-Varsity Press, England, publishes Christian books that are true to the Bible and that
communicate the gospel, develop discipleship and strengthen the church for its mission in the world.

IVP originated within the Inter-Varsity Fellowship, now the Universities and Colleges Christian
Fellowship, a student movement connecting Christian Unions in universities and colleges throughout
Great Britain, and a member movement of the International Fellowship of Evangelical Students. That
historic association is maintained, and all senior IVP staff and committee members subscribe to the
UCCF Basis of Faith. Website: www.uccf.org.uk.

InterVarsity Press®, USA, is the book-publishing division of InterVarsity Christian Fellowship/
USA® and a member movement of the International Fellowship of Evangelical Students. Website:
www.intervarsity.org.

First published 2021

Set in Garamond 11/13pt
Typeset in Great Britain by Avocet Typeset, Bideford, Devon
Printed and bound in Great Britain by Ashford Colour Press Ltd, Gosport, Hampshire

UK ISBN: 978-1-78359-966-0 (print)
UK ISBN: 978-1-78359-967-7 (digital)

US ISBN: 978-0-8308-4268-1 (print)
US ISBN: 978-0-8308-4269-8 (digital)

British Library Cataloguing-in-Publication Data
A catalogue record for this book is available from the British Library.

Library of Congress Cataloging-in-Publication Data
A catalog record for this book is available from the Library of Congress.

CONTENTS

Excurses

GENERAL PREFACE

The decision to completely revise the Tyndale Old Testament Commentaries is an indication of the important role that the series has played since its opening volumes were released in the mid 1960s. They represented at that time, and have continued to represent, commentary writing that was committed both to the importance of the text of the Bible as Scripture and a desire to engage with as full a range of interpretative issues as possible without being lost in the minutiae of scholarly debate. The commentaries aimed to explain the biblical text to a generation of readers confronting models of critical scholarship and new discoveries from the Ancient Near East while remembering that the Old Testament is not simply another text from the ancient world. Although no uniform process of exegesis was required, all the original contributors were united in their conviction that the Old Testament remains the word of God for us today. That the original volumes fulfilled this role is evident from the way in which they continue to be used in so many parts of the world.

A crucial element of the original series was that it should offer an up-to-date reading of the text, and it is precisely for this reason that new volumes are required. The questions confronting readers in the first half of the twenty-first century are not necessarily those from the second half of the twentieth. Discoveries from the Ancient Near East continue to shed new light on the Old Testament, while emphases in exegesis have changed markedly. While remaining true to the goals of the initial volumes, the need for contemporary study of the text requires that the series as a whole be updated. This updating is not simply a matter of commissioning new volumes to replace the old. We have also taken the opportunity to update the format of the series to reflect a key emphasis from linguistics, which is that texts communicate in larger blocks rather than in shorter segments such as individual verses. Because of this, the treatment of each section of the text includes three segments. First, a short note on *Context* is offered, placing the passage under consideration in its literary setting within the book as well as noting any historical issues crucial to interpretation. The *Comment* segment then follows the traditional structure of the commentary, offering exegesis of the various components of a passage. Finally, a brief comment is made on *Meaning*, by which is meant the message that the passage seeks to communicate within the book, highlighting its key theological themes. This section brings together the detail of the *Comment* to show how the passage under consideration seeks to communicate as a whole.

Our prayer is that these new volumes will continue the rich heritage of the Tyndale Old Testament Commentaries and that they will continue to witness to the God who is made known in the text.

David G. Firth, Series Editor
Tremper Longman III, Consulting Editor

AUTHOR'S PREFACE

It was at the beginning of my doctoral studies, when I began to study Isaiah in earnest, that a deep appreciation and reverence for the book developed. It is amazing how God uses Isaiah to inspire, confound and provide hope in the way that he does. Throughout history each generation has found hope and encouragement within the pages of this book. It is our desire in the commentary to help today's reader understand its continuing relevance.

The book of Isaiah presents a number of challenges to those who study it. Are there multiple authors? Which of its passages are narratives or prophecies? New Testament authors frequently quote Isaiah – how did they apply it to their own historical circumstances? These and other questions serve to make the book immensely more intriguing. Even though it is a long book, it is never dull or boring. Its gems, hiding just under the surface, always invite and encourage us to dig deeper.

This commentary uses the popular NIV translation, with some modifications in wording where necessary. Because Isaiah is a lengthy book, it will be important to have a good grasp of its structure, as this will have an impact on our understanding. Notably, we will take time to examine where there are clear seams that join the book.

Isaiah is an extraordinary prophet whose message was often directed towards the king and his people. He seems never to tire of correcting misplaced faith in power or false gods – a message we still need today. Isaiah's vision of God's holiness and glory in chapter 6 permanently influenced his message and prophecies. Our prayer is that Isaiah's vision will correct our faulty understanding of God and open our eyes to the sovereign creator of the world who inspired Isaiah to write this remarkable book.

Paul D. Wegner
Highland, California

ABBREVIATIONS

AB	Anchor Bible
ABD	*Anchor Bible Dictionary*, ed. D. N. Freedman, 6 vols. (New York: Doubleday, 1992)
AJSL	*American Journal of Semitic Languages and Literatures*
ANEP	*The Ancient Near East in Pictures Relating to the Old Testament*, ed. J. B. Pritchard, 2nd edn (Princeton, NJ: Princeton University Press, 1969)
ANET	*The Ancient Near East Texts Relating to the Old Testament*, ed. J. B. Pritchard, 3rd edn (Princeton, NJ: Princeton University Press, 1969)
AOAT	Alter Orient und Altes Testament
ARAB	*Ancient Records of Assyria and Babylonia*, ed. D. D. Luckenbill, 2 vols. (Chicago: University of Chicago Press, 1926)
b.	Babylonian Talmud
BAR	*Biblical Archaeologist Review*
BDB	F. Brown, S. R. Driver and C. A. Briggs, *The Brown–Driver–Briggs Hebrew and English Lexicon* (1907; Peabody, MA: Hendrickson, 1998)
BETL	Bibliotheca Ephemeridum Theologicarum Lovaniensium
BHS	*Biblia Hebraica Stuttgartensia*, ed. K. Elliger and W. Rudolph (Stuttgart: Deutsche Bibelgesellschaft, 1983)

BZAW	Beihefte zur Zeitschrift für die alttestamentliche Wissenschaft
CC	Continental Commentaries
ConBOT	Coniectanea Biblica: Old Testament Series
EAEHL	*Encyclopedia of Archaeological Excavations in the Holy Land*, ed. M. Avi-Yonah, 4 vols. (Englewood Cliffs, NJ: Prentice-Hall, 1976)
ExpTim	*Expository Times*
FOTL	Forms of the Old Testament Literature
ft	feet
GKC	*Gesenius' Hebrew Grammar*, ed. E. Kautzsch, tr. A. E. Cowley, 2nd edn (Oxford: Clarendon, 1910)
HALOT	*The Hebrew and Aramaic Lexicon of the Old Testament*, ed. L. Koehler, W. Baumgartner and J. J. Stamm, tr. and ed. under the supervision of M. E. J. Richardson, 5 vols. (Leiden: Brill, 1994–2000)
Herodotus, *Hist.*	Herodotus, *The Histories*
HKAT	Handkommentar zum Alten Testament
HTR	*Harvard Theological Review*
IBD	*The Illustrated Bible Dictionary*, ed. J. D. Douglas and N. Hillyer, 3 vols. (Downers Grove, IL: InterVarsity Press, 1998)
ICC	International Critical Commentary
IEJ	*Israel Exploration Journal*
Int	*Interpretation*
JAOS	*Journal of the American Oriental Society*
JBL	*Journal of Biblical Literature*
JETS	*Journal of the Evangelical Theological Society*
Josephus, *Ant.*	Josephus, *The Antiquities of the Jews*
JSOT	*Journal for the Study of the Old Testament*
JSOTSup	Journal for the Study of the Old Testament: Supplement Series
JSS	*Journal of Semitic Studies*
JTS	*Journal of Theological Studies*
KHC	Kurzer Hand-Commentar zum Alten Testament

LCL	Loeb Classical Library
lit.	literally
m.	metres
NAC	New American Commentary
NCBC	New Century Bible Commentary
NICOT	New International Commentary on the Old Testament
NIDOTTE	*New International Dictionary of Old Testament Theology and Exegesis*, ed. W. A. VanGemeren, 5 vols. (Grand Rapids: Zondervan, 1997)
OTE	*Old Testament Essays*
OTL	Old Testament Library
OTS	*Oudtestamentische Studiën*
SBL	Society of Biblical Literature
SBLSymS	Society of Biblical Literature Symposium Series
SBT	Studies in Biblical Theology
TBü	Theologische Bücherei
TOTC	Tyndale Old Testament Commentaries
VT	*Vetus Testamentum*
VTSup	Supplements to Vetus Testamentum
WBC	Westminster Bible Companion
Williams	R. J. Williams, *Williams' Hebrew Syntax: An Outline*, 3rd edn, revised and expanded by J. C. Beckman (Toronto: University of Toronto Press, 2007)
ZAW	*Zeitschrift für die alttestamentliche Wissenschaft*
ZBK	Zürcher Bibelkommentare

Texts and Bible versions

1QIsaᵃ	The Great Isaiah Scroll: the first copy of the book of Isaiah found in Cave 1
1QIsaᵇ	The second copy of the book of Isaiah found in Cave 1
ESV	Scripture quotations from the ESV Bible (The Holy Bible, English Standard Version), copyright © 2001 by Crossway, a publishing

SELECT BIBLIOGRAPHY

Ackroyd, P. R. (1978), 'Isaiah I – XII: Presentation of a Prophet', in *Congress Volume: Göttingen 1977*, VTSup 29 (Leiden: Brill), pp. 16–48.

—— (1982), 'Isaiah 36 – 39: Structure and Function', in W. C. Delsman et al. (eds.), *Von Kanaan bis Kerala: Festschrift für Prof. Mag. Dr. J. P. M. van der Ploeg O.P. zur Vollendung des siebzigsten Lebensjahres am 4. Juli 19*, AOAT 211 (Kevelaer: Verlag Butzon & Bercker; Neukirchen-Vluyn: Neukirchener Verlag), pp. 3–21.

Adams, L. L. and A. C. Rincher (1973), 'The Popular View of the Isaiah Problem in Light of Statistical Style Analysis', *Computer Studies* 4: 149–157.

Allen, L. C. (1976), *The Books of Joel, Obadiah, Jonah and Micah*, NICOT (Grand Rapids: Eerdmans).

Alt, A. (1953), 'Jesaja 8,23 – 9:6: Befreiungsnacht und Krönungstag', in *Kleine Schriften zur Geschichte des Volkes Israel*, 2 vols. (Munich: Beck), pp. 206–225.

Anderson, G. W. (1962), 'Isaiah XXIV – XXVII Reconsidered', in *Congress Volume: Bonn 1962*, VTSup 9 (Leiden: Brill), pp. 118–126.

Avigad, N. (1953), 'The Epitaph of a Royal Steward from Siloam Village', *IEJ* 3: 137–153.

Barthélemy, D. (ed.) (1986), *Critique textuelle de l'Ancien Testament*, Orbis Biblicus et Orientalis 50.2 (Göttingen: Vandenhoeck & Ruprecht, 1986).

Beardslee, J. W. (1903), *Outlines of an Introduction to the Old Testament* (Chicago: Fleming H. Revell).

Beckwith, R. (2008), *The Old Testament Canon in the New Testament Church and Its Background in Early Judaism* (Eugene, OR: Wipf and Stock).

Beuken, W. A. M. (1989), 'Servant and Herald of Good Tidings: Isaiah 61 as an Interpretation of 40 – 55', in J. Vermeylen (ed.), *The Book of Isaiah*, BETL 81 (Leuven: Peeters), pp. 411–442.

—— (1992), 'Isaiah 34: Lament in Isaianic Context', *OTE* 5: 78–102.

Blenkinsopp, J. (2000), *Isaiah 1 – 39*, AB 19 (New York: Doubleday).

—— (2002), *Isaiah 40 – 55*, AB 20 (New York: Doubleday).

—— (2003), *Isaiah 56 – 66*, AB 21 (New York: Doubleday).

Bright, J. (2000), *A History of Israel*, 4th edn (Louisville / London: Westminster John Knox).

Brownlee, W. H. (1964), *The Meaning of the Qumran Scrolls for the Bible* (New York: Oxford University Press).

Budde, K. (1928), *Jesaja's Erleben: Eine gemeinverständliche Auslegung der Denkschrift der Propheten (Kap 6,1 – 9,6)* (Gotha: L. Klotz, 1928).

Calvin, J. (1850), *Commentary on the Book of the Prophet Isaiah*, tr. W. Pringle, 4 vols. (Edinburgh: Calvin Translation Society; repr. Grand Rapids: Eerdmans, 1948).

Cannon, W. W. (1929), 'Isaiah 61, 1–3 an Ebed-Jahweh Poem', *ZAW* 47: 284–288.

Chafer, L. S. (1948), *Systematic Theology*, 10 vols. (Dallas: Dallas Seminary Press).

Charlesworth, J. H. (1992), 'Pseudepigrapha, OT', in *ABD* 5.539.

Childs, B. S. (1967), *Isaiah and the Assyrian Crisis*, SBT 2.3 (London: SCM; Naperville, IL: Allenson).

—— (2001), *Isaiah*, OTL (Louisville: Westminster/Knox).

Clements, R. E. (1980a), *Isaiah 1 – 39*, NCBC (Grand Rapids: Eerdmans).

—— (1980b), *Isaiah and the Deliverance of Jerusalem: A Study of the Interpretation of Prophecy in the Old Testament* (Sheffield: JSOT).

—— (1980c), 'The Prophecies of Isaiah and the Fall of Jerusalem', *VT* 30: 421–436.

—— (1982), 'The Unity of the Book of Isaiah', *Int* 36: 117–129.

Cline, E. H. (2005), *Jerusalem Besieged: From Ancient Canaan to Modern Israel* (Ann Arbor, MI: University of Michigan).

Coggins, R. J. (1978–9), 'The Problem of Isa. 24 – 27', *ExpTim* 90: 328–333.

Davidson, A. B. (1903), *Old Testament Prophecy* (Edinburgh: T&T Clark).

Delitzsch, F. (1980), *Commentary on the Old Testament*, vol. 7: *Isaiah*, tr. J. Martin (Edinburgh: T&T Clark).

Dillard, R. B. and T. Longman (2006), *An Introduction to the Old Testament*, 2nd edn (Grand Rapids: Zondervan).

Döderlein, J. C. (1775), *Esaias* (Norimbergae et Altdorfi: Apud Georg. Petr. Monath).

Driver, S. R. (1913), *Introduction to the Literature of the Old Testament*, 9th edn (New York: Scribner's).

Duhm, B. (1922; orig. 1892), *Das Buch Jesaja*, 4th edn, HKAT 3.1 (Göttingen: Vandenhoeck & Ruprecht).

Eichhorn, J. G. (1780–3), *Einleitung ins Alte Testament*, 5 vols. (Leipzig: Weibmanns, Erden und Reich).

Emerton, J. A. (1969), 'Some Linguistic and Historical Problems in Isaiah 8:23', *JSS* 14: 151–175.

—— (1977), 'A Textual Problem in Isaiah 25:2', *ZAW* 89: 64–73.

—— (2001), 'Some Difficult Words in Isaiah 28:10 and 13', in A. Rapoport-Albert and G. Greenberg (eds.), *Biblical Hebrew, Biblical Essays: Essays in Memory of Michael P. Weitzman*, JSOTSup 333 (Sheffield: Sheffield Academic Press), pp. 39–56.

Erlandsson, S. (1970), *The Burden of Babylon*, ConBOT 4 (Lund: Gleerup).

Finkelstein, I. et al. (2013), 'Has King David's Palace in Jerusalem Been Found?', *Tel Aviv* 34.2: 142–164.

Firth, D. G. and P. D. Wegner (2011), *Presence, Power and Promise: The Role of the Spirit of God in the Old Testament* (Nottingham: Apollos).

Fleming, W. B. (1915), *The History of Tyre*, Columbia University Oriental Studies 10 (Lancaster, PA: Columbia University Press).

Goldingay, J. and D. Payne (2006), *Isaiah 40 – 55: A Critical and Exegetical Commentary*, vol. 1, ICC (London: T&T Clark).

Gottwald, N. K. (1958), 'Immanuel as the Prophet's Son', *VT* 8: 36–47.

Grudem, W. (2020), *Systematic Theology: An Introduction to Bible Doctrine* 2nd edn (London: Inter-Varsity Press; Grand Rapids: Zondervan).

Harrison, R. K. (1969), *Introduction to the Old Testament* (Grand Rapids: Eerdmans).

Hess, R. S. (2007), *Israelite Religions: An Archaeological and Biblical Survey* (Grand Rapids: Baker).

Hoffmeier, J. (1999), *Israel in Egypt: The Evidence for the Authenticity of the Exodus Tradition* (Oxford: Oxford University Press).

—— (2003), 'Egypt's Role in the Events of 701 BC in Jerusalem: A Rejoinder to J. J. M. Roberts', in A. G. Vaughn and A. F. Killebrew (eds.), *Jerusalem in Bible and Archaeology: The First Temple Period*, SBLSymS 18 (Atlanta: Society of Biblical Literature), pp. 219–234.

Holladay, J. (1970), 'Assyrian Statecraft and the Prophets of Israel', *HTR* 63: 29–51.

Kaiser, O. (1983), *Isaiah 1 – 12*, tr. J. Bowdon, OTL, 2nd edn (Philadelphia: Westminster).

Kaiser, W. C. and P. D. Wegner (2016), *A History of Israel: From Bronze Age through the Jewish Wars*, rev. edn (Nashville: B&H Academic).

Ladd, G. E. (1959), *The Gospel of the Kingdom: Scriptural Studies in the Kingdom of God* (Grand Rapids: Eerdmans).

LaSor, W. S., D. A. Hubbard and F. W. Bush (1996), *Old Testament Survey: The Message, Form, and Background of the Old Testament*, 2nd edn (Grand Rapids: Eerdmans).

Lobell, J. A. and E. Powell (2010), 'Sacrificial Dogs', *Archaeology* 63.5 (Sept.–Oct.): 26–35.

Machinist, P. (1982), 'Assyria and Its Image in the First Isaiah', *JAOS* 103: 719–737.

McKenzie, J. L. (1968), *Second Isaiah*, AB 20 (Garden City, NJ: Doubleday).

Marti, K. (1900), *Das Buch Jesaja*, KHC 10 (Tübingen: Mohr).

Montgomery, J. A. and H. S. Gehman (1951), *A Critical and Exegetical Commentary on the Books of Kings*, ICC (Edinburgh: T&T Clark).

Motyer, J. A. (1993), *The Prophecy of Isaiah: An Introduction and Commentary* (Leicester: Inter-Varsity Press; Downers Grove, IL: InterVarsity Press).

—— (1999), *The Prophecy of Isaiah: An Introduction and Commentary*, TOTC (Leicester: Inter-Varsity Press; Downers Grove, IL: InterVarsity Press).

Muilenburg, J. (1956), 'The Book of Isaiah, Chapters 40–66', in G. A. Buttrick et al. (eds.), *The Interpreter's Bible*, vol. 5 (Nashville: Abingdon), pp. 381–776.

Oswalt, J. N. (1986), *The Book of Isaiah Chapters 1–39*, NICOT (Grand Rapids: Eerdmans).

—— (1998), *The Book of Isaiah Chapters 40–66*, NICOT (Grand Rapids: Eerdmans).

Oulton, J. E. L. (tr.) (1942), Eusebius of Caesarea, *Ecclesiastical History*, LCL, 2 vols. (Cambridge, MA: Harvard University Press).

Pope, M. (1952), 'Isaiah 34 in Relation to Isaiah 35, 40 – 66', *JBL* 71: 235–243.

Posner, R. (1963), 'The Use and Abuse of Stylistic Statistics', *Archivum Linguisticum* 15: 111–139.

Radday, Y. T. (1973), *The Unity of Isaiah in the Light of Statistical Linguistics* (Hildesheim: H. A. Gerstenberg).

Rendtorff, R. (1991), 'The Book of Isaiah: A Complex Unity; Synchronic and Diachronic Reading', in E. H. Lovering, Jr (ed.), *SBL 1991 Seminar Papers*, 30 (Atlanta: Scholars Press), pp. 8–20.

Ridderbos, J. (1986), *Isaiah*, tr. J. Vriend, Bible Student's Commentary (Grand Rapids: Zondervan).

Roberto, M. (2013), *Why Great Leaders Don't Take Yes for an Answer*, 2nd edn (Upper Saddle River, NJ: FT Press).

Roberts, J. J. M. (1979), 'A Christian Perspective on Prophetic Prediction', *Int* 33: 240–253.

—— (2015), *First Isaiah: A Commentary*, Hermeneia (Minneapolis: Fortress).

Rowley, H. H. (1965), 'The Servant of the Lord in Light of Three Decades of Criticism', in *The Servant of the Lord* (Oxford: Blackwell), pp. 7–20.

Saggs, H. W. F. (1959), 'A Lexical Consideration for the Date of Deutero-Isaiah', *JTS* 10.1: 84–87.

Sasson, J. M. (1976), 'Isaiah LXVI 3–4a', *VT* 26: 199–207.

Schaff, P. and H. Wace (eds.) (1991), *A Select Library of Nicene and Post-Nicene Fathers of the Christian Church*, 2nd series, 14 vols. (Grand Rapids: Eerdmans).

Schneider, T. (1991), 'Six Biblical Signatures: Seals and Seal Impressions of Six Biblical Personages Recovered', *BAR* 17.4 (July/Aug.): 26–33.

Scott, R. B. Y. (1933), 'The Relation of Chapter 35 to Deutero-Isaiah', *AJSL* 52: 178–191.

—— (1952), 'Isaiah XXI 1–10: The Inside of a Prophet's Mind', *VT* 2: 278–282.

Seitz, C. R. (1991), *Zion's Final Destiny: The Development of the Book of Isaiah; A Reassessment of Isaiah 36 – 39* (Minneapolis: Fortress).

—— (1993a), 'Account A and the Annals of Sennacherib: A Reassessment', *JSOT* 58: 47–57.

—— (1993b), *Isaiah 1 – 39*, Interpretation: A Bible Commentary for Teaching and Preaching (Louisville: Westminster/John Knox).

Smelik, K. A. D. (1986), 'Distortion of the Old Testament Prophecy: The Purpose of Isaiah XXXVI and XXXVII', *OTS* 24: 70–92.

Smith, G. V. (2007), *Isaiah 1 – 39*, NAC 15a (Nashville: Broadman & Holman).

—— (2009), *Isaiah 40 – 66*, NAC 15b (Nashville: Broadman & Holman).

Snaith, N. (1944–5), 'The So-called Servant Songs', *ExpTim* 56: 79–81.

Stade, B. (1886), 'Miscellen: Anmerkungen zu 2 Kö. 15 – 21', *ZAW* 6: 156–192.

Sweeney, M. A. (1988), *Isaiah 1 – 4 and the Post-Exilic Understanding of the Isaianic Tradition*, BZAW 171 (Berlin: de Gruyter).

—— (1996), *Isaiah 1 – 39 with an Introduction to Prophetic Literature*, FOTL 16 (Grand Rapids/Cambridge: Eerdmans).

Thiele, E. R. (1994), *Mysterious Numbers of the Hebrew Kings*, rev. edn (Grand Rapids: Kregel).

Thompson, J. A. (1980), *The Book of Jeremiah*, NICOT (Grand Rapids: Eerdmans).

Watson, W. G. E. (1994), *Classical Hebrew Poetry* (Sheffield: JSOT Press).

Watts, J. D. W. (2005a), *Isaiah 1 – 33*, WBC 24, rev. edn (Waco: Word).

—— (2005b), *Isaiah 34 – 66*, WBC 25, rev. edn (Waco: Word).

Wegner, P. D. (1991), 'Another Look at Isaiah viii 23b', *VT* 41: 481–484.

—— (1992a), *An Examination of Kingship and Messianic Expectation in Isaiah 1 – 35* (Lewiston, NY: Edwin Mellen).

—— (1992b), 'A Re-examination of Isaiah ix 1–6', *VT* 42: 103–112.

—— (2006), *A Student's Guide to Textual Criticism of the Bible* (Downers Grove, IL: InterVarsity Press).

—— (2010), 'Seams in the Book of Isaiah: Looking for Answers', in R. Heskett and B. Irwin (eds.), *The Bible as a Human Witness to Divine Revelation: Hearing the Word of God through Historically Dissimilar Traditions*, Library of Hebrew Bible/Old Testament Studies 469 (New York/London: T&T Clark), pp. 62–94.

—— (2011), 'How Many Virgin Births Are in the Bible? (Isaiah 7:14): A Prophetic Pattern Approach', *JETS* 54.3: 467–484.

Westermann, C. (1967), *Basic Forms of Prophetic Speech*, tr. H. White (Philadelphia: Westminster; repr. 1991).

—— (1969), *Isaiah 40 – 66*, OTL (Philadelphia: Westminster).

Whybray, R. N. (1975), *Isaiah 40 – 66*, NCBC (Grand Rapids: Eerdmans).

Wildberger, H. (1991), *Isaiah 1 – 12: A Commentary*, tr. T. H. Trapp, CC (Minneapolis: Fortress).

—— (1997), *Isaiah 13 – 27: A Commentary*, tr. T. H. Trapp, CC (Minneapolis: Fortress).

—— (2002), *Isaiah 28 – 39: A Commentary*, tr. T. H. Trapp, CC (Minneapolis: Fortress).

Wilken, R. L. (2007), *Isaiah Interpreted by Early Christian and Medieval Commentators*, The Church's Bible (Grand Rapids: Eerdmans).

Williamson, H. G. M. (1978), '"The Sure Mercies of David": Subjective or Objective Genitive?', *JSS* 23: 31–49.

—— (1986), 'Isaiah 40,20: A Case of Not Seeing the Wood for the Trees', *Biblica* 67.1: 1–20.

—— (1994), *The Book Called Isaiah: Deutero-Isaiah's Role in Composition and Redaction* (Oxford: Clarendon).

—— (2003), 'Isaiah 1 and the Covenant Lawsuit', in
A. D. H. Mayes and R. B. Salters (eds.), *Covenant as Context:
Essays in Honour of E. W. Nicholson* (Oxford: Oxford University
Press), pp. 393–406.

—— (2006, 2018), *A Critical and Exegetical Commentary on Isaiah 1
– 27*, 3 vols. ICC (London: T&T Clark).

—— (2009), 'Recent Issues in the Study of Isaiah', in D. G. Firth
and H. G. M. Williamson (eds.), *Interpreting Isaiah* (Nottingham:
Apollos; Downers Grove, IL: InterVarsity Press), pp. 21–29.

Yadin, Y. (1972), *Hazor*, Schweich Lectures, 1970 (London:
Oxford University Press).

Young, E. J. (1965–72), *The Book of Isaiah*, vols. 1–3 (Grand Rapids:
Eerdmans).

Zimmerli, W. (1950), 'Zur Sprache Tritojesaja', *Schweizerische
theologische Umschau* 20: 110–122; repr. (1963) in *Gottes
Offenbarung: Gesammelte Aufsätze zum Alten Testament*, TBü 19
(Munich: Chr. Kaiser Verlag), pp. 217–233.

GLOSSARY

alliterations repetition of letters fairly close together (e.g. Isa. 28:10, 13)

apocalyptic literature literature that details the author's visions of the end times, leading up to and following the destruction of the present world; often is revealed to the author by a heavenly messenger

chiasm a symmetrical literary feature in which parallel lines or phrases are repeated in reverse order, a b b′ a′ (e.g. 1:18; 7:15–16)

diptych a literary structure that contains two contrasting but complementary units

dittography a textual critical term for the unintentional repetition of a letter or word

ellipsis omission of a word or words that must be determined from the context

hendiadys the expression of a single idea by two words connected with 'and', often used for emphasis (e.g. 30:7)

kĕthîb reading that which is written in the Hebrew text

merism using two opposite ends of a spectrum to refer to everything in between also (e.g. 1:2; 7:11)

metathesis a textual critical term that means two letters that have been reversed due to a copyist error (e.g. 38:11 where ḥādel [lit. 'ceasing'] should read ḥāled ['world'])

metonymy the substitution of the name of an attribute for that of the thing meant (e.g. 'arm' for 'power' in 51:5)

palistrophe an extended chiasm that revolves around a key central unit, a b c **d** c′ b′ a′ (1:21–26; 5 – 12)

pivot parallelism a word or phrase that ends one parallel unit while simultaneously beginning the next

***qērê* reading** that which is to be read instead of what appears in the Hebrew text

***rîb* oracle** an oracle that pleads a case, similar to what occurs in a courtroom (e.g. 1:2–20)

stair-step parallelism the starting of each new unit with a similar phrase and then adding another that builds upon the former (e.g. 25:9)

synecdoche a figure of speech in which part of something represents the whole or vice versa (e.g. where 'the Name of the LORD' represents the LORD in 18:7)

INTRODUCTION

1. Nature of the book of Isaiah

Isaiah is arguably the most important book of the prophets and has been called the 'centerpiece of the prophetic literature' (LaSor, Hubbard and Bush 1996: 276). Within its sixty-six chapters lie the foundations for numerous themes, prophecies and promises. The book is an interesting combination of oracles of judgment and promise in which God, through his chosen servants, attempts to draw the nation of Israel back to himself. While there was little hope that the eighth-century Israelites would turn back to God, Isaiah's task was not entirely hopeless, for he foresaw a time when God would rule over a restored nation containing a remnant of both Jews and Gentiles who were wholly devoted to him.

The book of Isaiah is sometimes referred to as the Bible of the Old Testament, with thirty-nine chapters in the first section and twenty-seven chapters in the second, corresponding to the numbers of books in the Old and New Testaments, respectively. Additionally, a portion of Isaiah often called 'the Little Apocalypse'

(Isa. 24 – 27) contains themes similar to those of the New Testament book of Revelation (see Figure 0.1). Isaiah's primary purpose is theological – to proclaim God's message to the errant Israelites in hopes that they might change their ways.

THE BOOK OF ISAIAH	
ISAIAH 1 – 39	**ISAIAH 40 – 66**
OT = 39 BOOKS	NT = 27 BOOKS
LITTLE APOCALYPSE (24 – 27)	BOOK OF REVELATION

Figure 0.1 The book of Isaiah

The book is written in semi-poetic form, addressing issues pertinent to the Jewish nation from the eighth century BC onwards. Isaiah is the prophetic book most quoted by New Testament writers (at least 69x), who saw its continuing relevance to the New Testament church. It is one of the earliest books to speak of a remnant (Isa. 10:20–22; etc.) and a future deliverer, from which developed the concept of a 'Messiah' (9:1–7; etc.).

2. Origin, date and characters

a. Origin
Besides the oracles themselves, 2 Chronicles 26:22 says that Isaiah wrote the *events* (lit. 'words') of Uzziah, in which case he may have been a royal scribe.

b. Date
If Isaiah lived between the late eighth to early seventh centuries BC, he lived during one of the most turbulent times in Israel's history. According to Isaiah 6:1, the prophet was called to be God's spokesperson in the *year that King Uzziah died*, which was about 739 BC.

The last specific historical event mentioned is the accession of Esarhaddon to the throne (c.681 BC; Isa. 37:38). If indeed Isaiah recorded this event, then this places Isaiah's ministry between approximately 740 and 680 BC. Given the length of this sixty-year ministry, Roberts suggests that we should not expect the book to have the same homogeneity as those of other prophets whose ministries were significantly shorter (2015: 12).

Tradition says that Isaiah was put to death during the reign of King Manasseh, who ordered him to be sawn in two (*Martyrdom of Isaiah*, chapter 5; also the possible background for Heb. 11:37), a story that is undoubtedly embellished.

c. Characters

Jewish tradition also states that Isaiah was a cousin of Uzziah or a nephew of Amaziah (b. Meg. 10b). He most probably lived in or near Jerusalem, where he could easily confront both king (7:3) and priest (8:2) when necessary.

Isaiah's wife was called a prophetess (8:3) in the sense that God used her to bear children who served as visible signs for specific prophecies. Isaiah had at least two children: Shear-Jashub ('a remnant will return', 7:3) and Maher-Shalal-Hash-Baz ('soon [will be] the spoil; quickly [comes] the plundered', 8:1–4). Some have suggested that Immanuel ('God [is] with us', 7:14) was the name of yet another son (Gottwald 1958: 36–47).

Isaiah was a ready messenger who received his prophetic call (6:8–9) at a critical period in Israel's history; the Assyrian army was advancing on Israel as its leadership was steering the nation away from God. Isaiah felt his own unworthiness as God's messenger (6:5) and his prophecies were often discouraging (6:9–13), for Israel would remain unrepentant. A ray of hope for the prophet lay in the knowledge that God would reserve for himself a righteous remnant to serve as a light to other nations, leading them to God.

3. Historical background and setting

The book of Isaiah is closely tied to the historical context of both Isaiah's lifetime and the post-exilic period (after 539 BC). From 834 to 745 BC Assyria's expansion slowed dramatically, which allowed for Judah and Israel to enjoy a period of prosperity not experienced since the days of Solomon. However, renewed prosperity lulled both nations into a sense of complacency (Isa. 2:6–8). They assumed God was pleased with their religious observances, yet this was far from the case. Their wealth had been gained at the expense of the poor, sexual promiscuity was becoming rampant, and Baal worship was increasing in the land.

Respite from Assyrian expansionism would end abruptly with the accession of Tiglath-pileser III to the throne (745–727 BC; Pul of 2 Kgs 15:19). As he sought to expand westwards, smaller countries such as Lebanon, Israel and Judah that lay in his path were forced to either fight (and probably be destroyed) or surrender and pay a heavy annual tribute. Assyria's territory eventually reached from the Persian Gulf to the Mediterranean Sea, including the rich soil in the Mesopotamian Basin and trade routes along the River Euphrates.

The empire flourished under successive kings, from the reign of Shalmaneser V (727–722 BC) to Ashurbanipal (669–633 BC), after whose death the nation quickly declined. Isaiah's prophetic ministry was during Assyria's final period of greatness.

a. The Syro-Ephraimite War (733–732 BC)

As Assyria pressed relentlessly westwards under Tiglath-pileser III, Rezin (king of Syria) and Pekah (king of Israel) formed a coalition to resist them. In an effort to build military strength, Syria and Israel called on King Ahaz of Judah to join forces.

When Ahaz refused, the coalition sought to depose him to place the son of Tabe'el (possibly a Tyrian ally) on the throne (see Figure 0.2). Ahaz called on Assyria for help, sending a hefty tribute to back his request. Tiglath-pileser was only too willing to oblige, a situation Oswalt describes as 'one mouse asking a cat for help against another mouse. Only the cat could be the winner in such an arrangement' (1986: 7).

Tiglath-pileser returned to this area in 733–732 BC to attack Damascus and fight against the coalition of Israel and Syria, thus sparing Judah. By 732 BC, Tiglath-pileser had destroyed Damascus and ended the rebellion; Pekah was assassinated shortly thereafter (2 Kgs 15:30). Ahaz had accomplished his goal, but at a drastic cost.

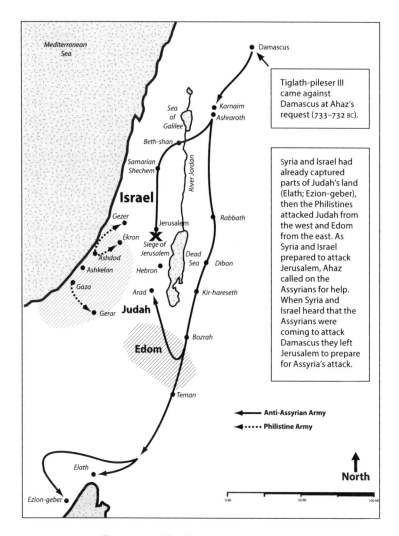

Figure 0.2 The Syro-Ephraimite War

b. Destruction of Samaria (722/21 BC)

After the death of Tiglath-pileser III in 727 BC, several insurrections broke out, one of them led by Hoshea, king of Israel. Shalmaneser responded by sending troops to Samaria. Hoshea quickly sent a tribute payment but was nevertheless forced to fight, unaided by Egypt, which was embroiled in troubles of its own.

Shalmaneser threw Hoshea in prison and began a three-year siege of Samaria that ultimately ended in its defeat.

c. Sennacherib's invasion (701 BC)

Marduk-Baladan (Babylon; sometimes called Merodach-baladan) appears to have made a special trip to Judah to elicit Hezekiah's assistance (Isa. 39) against the Assyrians. Hezekiah consented and helped pull together a coalition of Judah, Philistia, Edom, Moab and Egypt. Sennacherib proved to be more powerful than expected, subjugating Babylon and securing his eastern border before marching west to meet the coalition (see Figure 0.3).

Sennacherib marched his army to the Mediterranean coast and then turned southwards, besieging Sidon, Tyre and other cities. He then continued south along the coast to the Philistine strongholds of Ekron and Ashkelon, before moving inland to capture the cities of the Shephalah region.

There has been considerable discussion regarding the capture of Jerusalem (Childs 1967; Clements 1980b). Sennacherib's annals imply but do not actually state that he captured the city, yet the biblical text offers a significantly different account of the events (see specifically 2 Kgs 18 – 19; Isa. 36 – 37; *ANET* 288). Thus, some scholars question the biblical account and suggest dividing it into two separate stories (A = 2 Kgs 18:14–16; and B = 2 Kgs 18:17 – 19:37). The first part (A) corresponds fairly closely with the Assyrian records wherein Jerusalem surrenders and continues to pay tribute, but the second (B) is redactional activity that turns a defeat into a divine victory.

Childs believes that there are two levels in the second part (B1 and B2; 2001: 262–264), while Clements argues it is a later midrashic expansion (1980b). Bright suggests that Scripture records a series of events separated by several years that are combined into a single account (2000: 298–309).

Adding to the puzzle are two other circumstances: (1) contrary to Assyrian policy and Sennacherib's practice, Hezekiah remained on the throne after having been a major proponent of the rebellion; and (2) reliefs depicting the conquest of Lachish, a fortress city, adorn Sennacherib's palace at Nineveh (*ANEP*

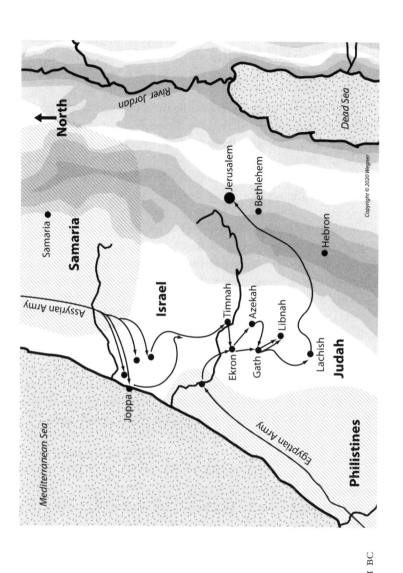

Figure 0.3
Sennacherib's
invasion of 701 BC

131).[1] If Jerusalem had also been conquered, it seems more likely that the capture of Israel's capital, instead of a less significant fortress city, would have been depicted on the walls of his palace (see Smith 2007: 32–33).

In our view, the biblical account and the account in Sennacherib's annals can be harmonized: (1) After Sennacherib begins his assault on Judah, Hezekiah submits and pays Sennacherib tribute (2 Kgs 18:14–16; *ANET* 288); (2) Sennacherib sends his messengers to Jerusalem the first time to demand from them unconditional surrender in addition to the tribute they have already sent (2 Kgs 18:17–37; Isa. 36:2–22); (3) Hezekiah sends for Isaiah to request prayer on behalf of Jerusalem, and God responds that Sennacherib will return to Assyria, where he will die (2 Kgs 19:1–7; Isa. 37:1–7); (4) Sennacherib, receiving word that Egypt is advancing against him, again sends messengers to Jerusalem with a letter demanding Hezekiah's complete surrender (2 Kgs 19:8–13; Isa. 37:8–13); (5) Hezekiah takes this letter to God, who responds that Sennacherib will not harm the city but will return home the same way he came (2 Kgs 19:14–34; Isa. 37:14–35); (6) Sennacherib defeats Egypt, led by Tirhakah, at Eltekeh (2 Kgs 19:9; Isa. 37:9), then brings his troops to Jerusalem; and (7) God sends his angel to kill 185,000 Assyrian soldiers, whereupon Sennacherib returns to Assyria. After this defeat, Sennacherib never undertook another campaign to the west and died in 681 BC (Isa. 37:36–38).

When recounting these events, the Assyrian record and the biblical record had two very different purposes in view. The Assyrian record sought to elevate the king by highlighting accomplishments and leaving out setbacks. This would explain why the capture of a significant number of prisoners and plunder at Lachish was memorialized, whereas there was silence regarding the deaths of 185,000 Assyrian soldiers. The biblical account of the narrative serves to draw attention to Yahweh's protection and victory.[2]

---

1. The rock reliefs from Lachish depicting the capture of Lachish are housed in the British Museum in London.

2. Herodotus (*Hist.* 2.141) records that Sennacherib marched on the city of Pelusium on the northern border of Egypt, where field mice nibbled

d. Destruction of Jerusalem by the Babylonians (605–586 BC)

The Babylonians marched against Assyria in 612 BC to destroy Nineveh, though it took two more battles to finally secure Assyria's defeat (Battle of Haran, 609 BC; Battle of Carchemish, 605 BC). Nabopolassar, Nebuchadnezzar's father, died shortly after this final battle, whereupon Nebuchadnezzar returned to Babylon to ascend the throne. He then returned to Jerusalem to subdue any hint of rebellion and force Judah into subservience.

Jehoiakim, king of Judah at the time, shifted allegiance from Egypt to Babylon, thereby remaining on the throne and averting the destruction of Jerusalem. After about three years, however, Jehoiakim rebelled and aligned himself once again with Egypt. Nebuchadnezzar returned to lay siege to Jerusalem, but Jehoiakim died before Nebuchadnezzar arrived, and his son Jehoiachin ascended the throne. Nebuchadnezzar soon took Jehoiachin captive and installed Zedekiah in his place.

When Zedekiah eventually rebelled (c.588 BC), the Babylonians dealt more severely with Judah, destroying both Jerusalem and the temple (586 BC) and deporting many of its inhabitants. These events left the Israelites both discouraged and doubtful that God still cared about them. The book of Isaiah warns that the people would be deported by Babylon (Isa. 39:6–7), but that a remnant would later return to Israel.

e. Exiles return from Babylon (c.538 BC)

The Babylonian Empire gradually declined until its capital, Babylon, was ultimately conquered by the Persian Empire in 539 BC. Prior rulers of Assyria and Babylon had used deportation as a means of controlling the people. The foreign policy of Cyrus, the Persian king, was just the opposite. He contended that by letting nations return to their homelands and use imperial funds to rebuild their gods' temples, they would be more amenable to their new ruler (Ezra 1:1–4; *ANET* 316).

(note 2 *cont.*) away his soldiers' bowstrings, causing their defeat. However, according to the royal annals, Sennacherib never went to Egypt, thus it could be a modified rendition of the biblical account.

As a result, Zerubbabel, a royal descendant, and Joshua, the high priest, led almost fifty thousand exiles from Babylon to Israel (see Ezra 2:64–65). The returning exiles were motivated, at least initially, to purify themselves from the errors that had landed them in Babylon in the first place and to restore proper Yahweh worship.

However, rebuilding the temple turned out to be a much more difficult task than imagined. Within a couple of years, the foundations had been laid, but the returnees were hindered in their work by the 'people of the land' who were outraged that they had not been allowed to work on the project as well. Discouraged, the returnees stopped building the temple and turned their attention to their own personal affairs to survive. About sixteen years later (*c.*520 BC) two prophets, Haggai and Zechariah, were sent by God to encourage the people to resume work on the temple, which was finally completed around 516/15 BC, though not to the same grandeur as Solomon's temple (Ezra 3:12; Hag. 2:3).

4. Theology and purpose

The name Isaiah (*yěšaʿyāhû*) means 'Yahweh is Salvation' (as do the names Joshua and Jesus), which is one of the key themes of the book. God is repeatedly said to be Israel's *Redeemer* (44:6, 24; etc.). The primary purpose of the book of Isaiah is to encourage the Israelites to turn away from their wickedness and back towards God, so that they can be a light to other nations.

Isaiah calls God *the Holy One of Israel* twenty-five times, another key theme of the book (see Figure 0.4). In using the word *qādôš*, 'holy, set apart, separate', Isaiah underscores how far Israel's wickedness had removed them from their God.

Holy One of Israel
Isa. 1 – 39
Isa. 1:4; 5:19, 24; 10:20; 12:6; 17:7; 29:19; 30:11, 12, 15; 31:1; 37:23
Isa. 40 – 66
Isa. 41:14, 16, 20; 43:3, 14; 45:11; 47:4; 48:17; 49:7; 54:5; 55:5; 60:9, 14

Figure 0.4 Holy One of Israel

a. God is working out his purpose

Isaiah portrays a time when Israel, after a period of purging, will be refined until a holy remnant emerges that not only follows God, but leads others to him as well. God's plan to use his people to draw all nations to himself is simple yet almost impossible to believe.

b. God will judge the wicked

The message of judgment for the wicked is likewise clear throughout the book (e.g. 1:28–31; 4:6). From the outset of his call when the seraphim cried *Holy, holy, holy is the LORD Almighty* (6:1–3), Isaiah was deeply impressed with both his own sin and that of the nation. God's righteousness demanded judgment, yet it was also his intention to use this judgment to produce for himself a righteous remnant referred to as *the holy seed* (6:13).

c. All nations will desire to know about Yahweh (universal appeal)

Throughout Isaiah, Yahweh is clearly depicted as Israel's God and redeemer, but he will draw a remnant from other nations as well, a message that Israel most probably did not want to hear. In one of the most striking passages of Isaiah, God is portrayed as having a personal relationship with people from other nations, all people having been created by him (see 19:24–25).

d. A remnant

God does not force faith or obedience, so if Israel as a nation chooses to wander away from him, he can still fulfil his promises by working with individuals who do obey him – a remnant (see 10:21–22). While at times in Israel's history this remnant appears as a lowly *hut in a cucumber field* (1:8–9) or a *stump in the land* (6:13), they will be the ones to benefit from God's promises (61:3–7).

e. Servant of the LORD

The word *servant* has a variety of referents in Isaiah: (1) the nation of Israel (41:8–9; 44:1–2, 21; etc.); (2) Isaiah (20:3; 44:26); (3) a remnant (41:8–9; 43:10; 48:20); and the suffering servant (49:5–7; 50:5–10; 52:13 – 53:12). In the latter part of the book the servant of the LORD takes on special significance as God's messenger and the one who will be used to deliver his people.

The concept of the servant of the LORD ultimately goes beyond the ability of Israel, for they would never be able to purge the nation of its sins and live in obedience to God. God therefore had to supply his own 'suffering servant', the Messiah, to give his life to purify the nation and restore them to God (52:15; 53:4–12).

5. Canonical status

The book of Isaiah has traditionally been an integral part of the Old Testament canon and was accepted as authoritative almost immediately, based upon the character of the prophet and the numerous direct statements in Isaiah suggesting its divine authority (e.g. *the Lord . . . the Mighty One of Israel, declares* [1:24]; *declares the Lord, the LORD Almighty* [3:15]).

Other evidence for its canonicity comes from early Jewish tradition (b. *Baba Bathra* 14b; Sirach 48:24), material from Qumran, and writings of the early Church Fathers (Origen, *c.* AD 184–254 [Eusebius, *Ecclesiastical History* 6.25.1–2, in Oulton 1942: 2.72–74]; Athanasius, *c.* AD 296–373 [Schaff and Wace 1991: 4.551–559]; etc.).

To date, twenty-one manuscripts of Isaiah have been found at Qumran, which is the third-largest number of Qumran manuscripts for a biblical book (Psalms, forty MSS; Deuteronomy, thirty) and the largest number of manuscripts for any of the prophets. While not proof in and of itself of its authority, the number is indicative of its importance to the Qumran community. A nearly complete scroll, 1QIsa^a, is dated to around 100 BC or earlier; 1QIsa^b, dated about the same time, is not as well preserved.

a. Position within the canon

Modern canons of the Old Testament and many of the early canons (e.g. MT, LXX, Jerome; see Figure 0.5) typically place Isaiah first among the Latter Prophets (Isa., Jer., Lam., Ezek.). Vaticanus and Alexandrinus place the twelve Minor Prophets before Isaiah. Likewise, Athanasius, bishop of Alexandria in AD 367, listed the Minor Prophets before Isaiah (Schaff and Wace 1991: 4.551–552).

However, stability in the order of canonical books is, as Roger Beckwith points out, 'a relatively modern phenomenon, and owes a good deal to the invention of printing' (2008: 181).

Text	Order	Date
Common order: MT, LXX, Jerome, Josephus, Vulg., etc.	Isa., Jer., Lam., Ezek.	350 BC–5th century AD
Babylonian Talmud Baba Bathra 14b	Jer., Ezek., Isa.	6th century AD (but probably contains earlier material)
Melito, Bishop of Sardis	Isa., Jer., the twelve Minor Prophets, Dan., Ezek.	c. AD 170
Origen	Isa., Jer. with Lam., Dan. and Ezek.	AD 185–254

Figure 0.5 Order of books

b. Relationship to the rest of the canon

The closest book to Isaiah chronologically and thematically is Micah, the two books even sharing a highly similar passage – Isaiah 2:2–4 and Micah 4:1–3. The few differences between these two passages (about thirty letters) suggest either that one may have copied the other or, more likely, that they are separate copies of a third source (Wegner 2006: 32–34).

Of the approximately sixty-nine times the New Testament quotes the book of Isaiah, most often the same wording as the MT and LXX is reflected (e.g. Rom. 9:29; Heb. 2:13a).

6. Literary issues

For the last several decades, scholars have been more willing to take into consideration the final form of the Old Testament text, and the book of Isaiah is no exception. Many scholars now realize that the book conveys an overall message, whether it was written by a single author, multiple authors, or was redacted.

a. Prophecy

Some scholars argue that prophecy is occasioned by some con-temporaneous historical event, but we consider this limitation far too restrictive. Sometimes prophetic oracles can refer to historical events at that time ('forth-telling') and sometimes they speak of events far into the future ('foretelling'). Biblical prophecy is broad enough to include both types. Short-term prophecies (e.g. Isa. 7 – 8) served to confirm the authenticity of a prophet; long-term prophecies (e.g. Isa. 40 – 66) served to encourage and inform God's people, as well as confirm Yahweh's sovereignty. A prophet had a responsibility to prophesy about future events to help inform the nation of what was coming. These predictions, clearly reaching beyond the human abilities of a prophet to foretell the future, also served to exalt God.

b. Literary techniques

The book contains a variety of literary techniques, including chiasms (e.g. 1:18; 7:15–16), palistrophes (e.g. 1:21–26; 5 – 12), merisms (e.g. 1:2; 7:11), *rîb* oracles (e.g. 1:2–20) and wordplays (e.g. 5:7). These literary devices are used to highlight the message of the book and add interest for the reader.

c. Genres

Prophetic material can be a mixture of poetic material interspersed with narrative material and often includes direct discourse from God through the prophet. It is sometimes difficult to know exactly who is speaking, God or Isaiah, but in one sense the result is the same: God's message is declared.

d. An anthology

While some have suggested that the book is basically chronological (e.g. Watts 2005a; etc.), it is best to understand the book as an anthology (i.e. collection) of Isaiah's writings. The arrangement of the book is intended to highlight certain themes as opposed to a chronological flow through the prophet's lifetime.

7. Structure

Since Bernhard Duhm's commentary in 1892, it has become common to divide Isaiah 40 – 66 into a Second (40 – 55) and Third (56 – 66) Isaiah, but this is no longer as widely accepted as it once was (Williamson 2009: 21). We would suggest the following overarching structure for the book of Isaiah (see also Wegner 2010: 62–94).

a. Introduction and conclusion of the book

Many scholars view chapter 1 as an introduction to Isaiah as a whole, often asserting that it was added later to help unify the message of the book. We agree with those who argue that the vocabulary and themes in Isaiah 1 and 65 – 66 form an *inclusio* (Sweeney 1988: 97–98; etc.). Chapters 65–66 are clearly a much fuller discussion of the themes of chapter 1, even following the same flow of thought as in the book's introduction. They highlight how God worked out his plan throughout the book: a stubborn and rebellious nation will be severely punished; only a humble and contrite remnant will be spared and return to Jerusalem to be protected by their God; and those who continue to rebel against God (i.e. the wicked) will be punished.

b. Arrangement of the book

i. Introductions

Typically, three introductions, thought to reflect some type of editorial activity, are recognized in the book of Isaiah (1:1; 2:1; 13:1). Because Isaiah's full name, *Isaiah son of Amoz*, is mentioned in each introduction, scholars believe that the book was compiled from multiple sources (see Zech. 1:1, 7; 7:1 which has a similar structure) that circulated separately for some time – a view that goes back at least as far as John Calvin (1850 1.xxxii).

There is some evidence, however, that the form of the book took shape early, sometime in the pre-exilic period: (1) the initial introductions to Amos and Micah, traditionally thought to be eighth-century prophets, are similar in wording to the book of Isaiah; (2) only pre-exilic prophets use the word *ḥāzâ*, 'to see or envision', to describe how they received their prophecies (Amos 1:1;

Mic. 1:1; Hab. 1:1), the same term Isaiah uses in each of his introductions; and (3) only Isaiah, Obadiah and Nahum are called a *vision* (*ḥāzôn*) in their introductions, and Obadiah and Nahum are generally considered pre-exilic prophets.

ii. Refrains
There are also three refrains (48:22; 57:21; 66:24), corresponding to the three introductions, that appear to divide the second part of the book. It is interesting that these refrains do not correspond to the divisions commonly made by modern scholars.

iii. Book divisions
A major division is traditionally identified between Isaiah 39 and 40, though in more recent years some scholars have proposed a division between Isaiah 35 and 36 (Clements 1980a: 277–280; Childs 2001: 260–266; etc.) or 37 and 38 (Motyer 1993: 287–288).

The narrative of chapter 39 records the visit of the Babylonian king Marduk-Baladan to Hezekiah slightly before 701 BC, after which Hezekiah is told that Jerusalem's wealth along with some of his descendants will be carried off to Babylon. However, the context of the next chapter, Isaiah 40, appears to jump in time about 150 years and depicts a remnant returning from Babylon about 539/538 BC.

iv. Seams
We argue that seams which unite the book can be identified at the end of each section. While the seams appear to some as awkwardly placed secondary additions, we view them as integral to its unity, serving two key purposes: (1) to summarize the major themes of the book; and (2) to link the unit to the next section which will describe the themes in more detail (see Figure 0.6).

v. Sections of the book

1. First section (chapter 1)
The first verse of chapter 1 introduces the *vision* (*ḥāzôn*) seen by *Isaiah son of Amoz*, which goes on to describe the punishment that Israel deserves for wandering away from God (see Figure 0.7).

OVERALL STRUCTURE OF ISAIAH

1ST INTRO-DUCTION 1:1	2ND INTRO-DUCTION 2:1	3RD INTRO-DUCTION 13:1	MAJOR HISTORICAL BREAK – 150 YEARS BETWEEN ISA. 39 AND 40	1ST REFRAIN 48:22	2ND REFRAIN 57:21	3RD REFRAIN 66:24
Seam: 1:27–31	Seam: 4:2–6	Seam: 36 – 39		Seam: 48:17–22	Seam: 57:14–21	Seam: 65 – 66

Figure 0.6 Structure of Isaiah

CHAPTER 1

1ST INTRODUCTION (1:1)

'The vision concerning Judah and Jerusalem that Isaiah son of Amoz saw during the reigns of Uzziah, Jotham, Ahaz and Hezekiah, kings of Judah.'

ISRAEL, LISTEN TO REASON	GOD HAS HAD ENOUGH	ZION WILL BE REDEEMED 'FAITHFUL CITY' PALISTROPHE	SEAM: 1:27–31
		City has become a harlot (v. 21)	1. Israel will be judged (vv. 28–31)
		Murderers dwell there (v. 21)	2. A righteous remnant will be saved (v. 27)
		Silver become dross (v. 22)	3. The wicked will be punished (vv. 28–31)
		Everyone is corrupt (v. 23)	4. Zion will be delivered (v. 27)
		CLIMAX: THE LORD DECLARES (v. 24)	
		God's foes are destroyed (v. 24)	
		Dross is removed (v. 25)	
		Righteousness has returned (v. 26)	
		Faithful city (v. 26)	
1:1–9	1:10–15	1:21–26	1:27–31

Figure 0.7 Structure of Isaiah 1

The chapter reaches its climax when Jerusalem is called *the City of Righteousness, the Faithful City* (v. 26), yet the section ends with judgment on the wicked. Why would the chapter build to a climax of God restoring Jerusalem and then sink back into judgment? We suggest the final verses 27–31 form a seam that summarizes the main themes of this unit: (1) Israel will be judged (1:28–31); (2) a righteous remnant will be delivered (1:27); (3) the wicked will be punished (1:28–31); and (4) Zion will be delivered (1:27). This seam links to chapters 2–12 which repeat these main themes, only in much greater detail. The judgment is pictured as a fire that will not be quenched in both 1:31 and 66:24.

2. Second section (chapters 2–12)

The wording of the second introduction (2:1) is highly consistent with similar introductions in Micah and Amos. Chapters 2–12 consist of two separate units. One unit (Isa. 2 – 4) begins and ends with a glorious future for Israel (e.g. 2:1–4; 4:2–6), but in the middle (2:5 – 4:1) we see the present wickedness that Yahweh needs to purge (4:4; see Figure 0.8). The second unit is a palistrophe consisting of chapters 5–12.

Chapters 5–12 form a palistrophe that begins with the Song of the Vineyard (5:1–7) describing Israel's reprehensible condition and ends with the Song of Thanksgiving (12:1–6) wherein God is praised for his great deliverance of Israel (Wegner 1992a: 88–89). The palistrophe is structured as follows:

A: Song of the Vineyard (5:1–7)
    B: Six woe oracles (5:8–23)
        C: An uplifted-hand oracle (5:24–30)
CLIMAX: D: The Isaianic memoir (6:1 – 9:7)
        C′: Four uplifted-hand oracles (9:8 – 10:4)
    B′: A woe oracle (10:5 – 11:16)
A′: Song of Thanksgiving (12:1–6)

This palistrophe depicts God bringing about great deliverance through the punishment portrayed in the woe oracles and the uplifted-hand oracles. The theme recalls earlier passages where God says he will use fire to purge away their dross (1:25) and will

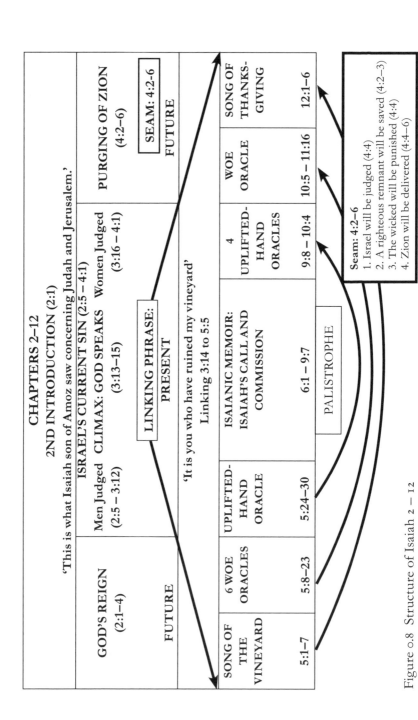

Figure 0.8 Structure of Isaiah 2 – 12

The content within the figure:

CHAPTERS 2–12

2ND INTRODUCTION (2:1)

'This is what Isaiah son of Amoz saw concerning Judah and Jerusalem.'

ISRAEL'S CURRENT SIN (2:5 – 4:1)

GOD'S REIGN (2:1–4)	Men Judged CLIMAX: GOD SPEAKS (2:5 – 3:12) (3:13–15)	Women Judged (3:16 – 4:1)	PURGING OF ZION (4:2–6)
FUTURE			SEAM: 4:2–6 FUTURE

LINKING PHRASE: PRESENT

'It is you who have ruined my vineyard' Linking 3:14 to 5:5

SONG OF THE VINEYARD	6 WOE ORACLES	UPLIFTED-HAND ORACLE	ISAIANIC MEMOIR: ISAIAH'S CALL AND COMMISSION	4 UPLIFTED-HAND ORACLES	WOE ORACLE	SONG OF THANKS-GIVING
5:1–7	5:8–23	5:24–30	6:1 – 9:7	9:8 – 10:4	10:5 – 11:16	12:1–6

PALISTROPHE

Seam: 4:2–6
1. Israel will be judged (4:4)
2. A righteous remnant will be saved (4:2–3)
3. The wicked will be punished (4:4)
4. Zion will be delivered (4:4–6)

wash away their filth (4:4). Right at the heart of the palistrophe is the Isaianic memoir where God asks, *Whom shall I send?* and Isaiah answers, *Here am I. Send me.* The Isaianic memoir then goes on to explain how God will deliver his people.

If this structure is correct, then it poses two significant problems for our theory of seams in the book of Isaiah. First, the introduction (2:1) indicates that this section continues to chapter 12, but as we have noted there are two clear units in this section. Second, there does not appear to be a seam at the end of chapter 12. Isaiah 12 is a 'song of thanksgiving' thanking God for the amazing deliverance he has brought about, but there is no mention of Israel being judged or of a remnant who would be spared, as there was in the first seam (1:27–31). What makes matters even worse is that the seam we would expect at the end of the section in chapter 12 appears instead in 4:2–6. These verses summarize the main themes of this unit (i.e. Israel will be judged, 4:4; a righteous remnant will be saved, 4:2–3; the wicked will be punished, 4:4; and Zion will be delivered, 4:5–6) and form a link to the next section that describes these concepts in greater detail.

If 2:2–4 and 4:2–6 are to be understood together, then nations will stream to Zion to hear about Israel's God. The reader is thus prepared for the next section where God will purge not only Israel but all the nations, from which a remnant will emerge.

But why are chapters 5–12 included with chapters 2–4 to form a section? The answer appears to lie in the central part of Isaiah 2 – 4. Up until 3:13, the sins of Israel's leaders are being described, but at verse 13 *he* [Yahweh] *rises to judge* the leaders of his *people*. The charge that God has against the leaders forms two parallel units:

> v. 14 *It is you who have ruined* [consumed] *my vineyard;*
> *the plunder from the poor is in your houses.*
> v. 15 *What do you mean by crushing my people*
> *and grinding the faces of the poor?*

This charge ends with the phrase *declares the Lord, the LORD Almighty.* Then the passage goes on to describe the punishment for the *women of Zion* – a new section.

Verses 13–15 serve as a climax: the judgments that God is about to pour out on his people focus first on the leaders and princes (2:5 – 3:12), and then on the women of Zion (3:16 – 4:1). In the midst of God's declaration, a grievous charge against the leaders is that they have *ruined* (*bāʿar*, lit. 'burned or consumed') God's vineyard (3:14). This wording is picked up in 5:5 when the vineyard owner says that he will allow his vineyard to be *destroyed* (*bāʿar*). The terminology 'consuming the vineyard' is not used anywhere else in the book of Isaiah. We therefore understand Isaiah 5 – 12 to be a further description of how the leaders have devoured the vineyard and of what God is going to do about it. It uses the phrase *you have ruined* [consumed] *my vineyard* (3:14) as a link to the Song of the Vineyard beginning the next section. So rather than disrupting the flow of thought that the author had already created by encapsulating the present situation (2:5 – 4:1) within the glorious future for Israel (2:2–4; 4:2–6), the author chose to complete that structure and then make the link to the further development of God's plan with the palistrophe (Isa. 5 – 12) that describes the punishment and then the restoration of his vineyard (cf. 27:2–5). The Isaianic memoir (6:1 – 9:7) is the central portion of the palistrophe (chs. 5–12), because when God rises to judge his people (3:13), Isaiah will be the first witness God calls; he will be God's spokesperson to explain his awe-inspiring plan to his people.

3. Third section (chapters 13–39)
The third introduction (13:1) is similar in wording, though not in order, to the second, except that this time Isaiah *saw* (*ḥāzâ*) an oracle (*maśśāʾ*).

What follows is a series of oracles against the nations, similar to those found in other prophetic books (Jer. 46 – 51; Ezek. 25 – 32; Amos 1:3 – 2:6). There is once again some disagreement as to the length of this section, but we argue that Isaiah 13 – 39 forms a palistrophe like those found in each of the earlier sections (see Figure 0.9). Isaiah's message to Hezekiah in chapter 39 regarding the Babylonian seizure of his offspring and his wealth opens the door to the events occurring in Isaiah 40 – 66.

CHAPTERS 13–39
3RD INTRODUCTION (13:1)
'A prophecy against Babylon that Isaiah son of Amoz saw.'

ORACLES AGAINST THE NATIONS	THE LITTLE APOCALYPSE	WOE ORACLES FOLLOWED BY RESTORATION		FINAL JUDGMENT AND RESTORATION	ISAIANIC NARRATIVES
		JUDGMENT	RESTORATION		
Babylon	Tribulation (24:1–23)	1. Woe (Drunkards) (28:1–4)	1. Restoration (28:5–6)	Great Battle (34)	Sennacherib invades Jerusalem (36)
Assyria (finished)	Great Feast (25:6–8)	2. Woe (Leaders) (28:7–15)	2. Restoration (28:16–17)	Sky Rolled Up Like Scroll (34:4)	Hezekiah Calls Out to God (37)
Philistia	Great Battle (25:9 – 26:10)	3. Woe (Leaders) (28:18–22)	3. Restoration (28:23–29)	The Lord's Day of Vengeance (34:8)	Assyrians Are Destroyed (38)
Moab	Defeat of Leviathan (27:1)	4. Woe (Ariel + Others) (29:1–4)	4. Restoration (29:5–8)	God's Rule (35)	Babylonian Envoys Come (39)
Damascus [Aram/Syria]		5. Woe (Prophets) (29:9–16)	5. Restoration (29:17–24)		
Ethiopia [Cush]		6. Woe (Rebellious ones) (30:1–17)	6. Restoration (30:18–33)		
Egypt		7. Woe (Unbelieving ones) (31:1–3)	7. Restoration (31:4 – 32:8)		
Babylon		8. Woe (Women) (32:9–14)	8. Restoration (32:15–20)		
Judah		9. Woe (Destroyer) (33:1)	9. Restoration (33:2–24)		
Tyre					
13 – 23	24 – 27	28 – 33		34 – 35	36 – 39
					SEAM: 36 – 39

PALISTROPHE

Seam:
1. Israel is judged (36 – 37; 39:5–7); 2. A righteous remnant is saved (37:4, 31–32); 3. The wicked will be punished (36:1–20; 37:36–38; 39:5–7); 4. Zion will be delivered (37:22, 29–38)

Figure 0.9 Structure of Isaiah 13 – 39

1) Isaiah 13 – 23//Isaiah 36 – 39

The Oracles against the Nations (chs. 13–23) are a well-defined unit. God's message is one of judgment for Israel's neighbours, yet several among them will have, like Israel, a remnant that turns to God (e.g. Cush, 18:7; Egypt, 19:19–25; Tyre, 23:17–18). The shortest oracle (14:24–27[28?]), directed against Assyria, is pictured as having already taken place (v. 24, lit. 'so it has happened'), and probably refers back to 10:24–28 and the events surrounding 701 BC. This short oracle is also the most prominent because it provides the rationale for all the rest; there will be punishment for each nation that goes against God's people (v. 26).

The last unit in this section comprises what are known as the Isaianic Narratives (chs. 36–39) which describe in great detail the events surrounding 701 BC and correspond to the Oracles against the Nations in the palistrophe. The theme of Assyria's destruction briefly highlighted in the Oracles against the Nations is further described in chapters 36–39. If any nation wanted proof of future divine judgment for having caused harm to Israel, it could merely look at the thorough description of Assyria's punishment in the Isaianic Narratives.

The largest seam (chs. 36–39) serves as a bridge between the two major sections of the book (Seitz 1991: 6–9; Sweeney 1996: 42, 454–511; etc.). It contains the same four key themes as other seams: (1) Israel is judged (36 – 37; 39:5–7); (2) a righteous remnant is saved (37:4, 31–32); (3) the wicked will be punished (36:1–20; 37:36–38; 39:5–7); and (4) Zion will be delivered (37:22, 29–38).

(2) Isaiah 24 – 27//Isaiah 34 – 35

Isaiah 24 – 27 is sometimes called 'the Little Apocalypse' – certainly an overstatement (see Wildberger 2002: 317), but it does describe the destruction of the earth in terms similar to those of the New Testament book of Revelation. As several scholars have noted, Isaiah 24 – 27 is well positioned after the Oracles against the Nations, for after describing their destruction by God, this section begins, *See, the LORD is going to lay waste the earth* (24:1).

Elements of this future time in chapters 24–27 are continued in chapters 34–35, thus connecting the two sections. Isaiah 27 ends with God 'threshing' (lit. 'to beat out') the nations while collecting his children (i.e. the remnant). Isaiah 34 picks up the theme of judgment on the nations, then in chapter 35 combines it with a description of God's final kingdom. This final kingdom will be a place of joy and gladness, where people are safe in the presence of wild animals (35:9), reminiscent of 11:6–9 and 65:25.

Scholars have attempted to highlight the strong connection between chapters 34–35 (often called a 'diptych pattern' since the work of Beuken 1992: 78–102) and the material that precedes (chs. 6; 13; 24; 27) and follows (chs. 40; 43; 51; 62; 63; 65). We suggest that the themes of chapters 24–27 and their further development in chapters 34–35 should be viewed as parallel units in the palistrophe of chapters 13–39.

(3) Isaiah 28 – 33
The middle unit of this palistrophe is composed of nine sets of woe oracles paired with restoration oracles (see Figure 0.9). These oracles are primarily concerned with events in the context of 701 BC. Their key theme is that the wicked will be punished, but a righteous remnant will be spared – the same message that is found in each of the major sections of Isaiah. This unit of woe–restoration oracles ends with a declaration of God's protection, prosperity and health being poured out on Zion (33:17–24a) and the iniquity of God's people being forgiven (33:24b).

4. Fourth section (chapters 40–48)
Chapter 40 moves away from the period of Assyrian conquest primarily covered in chapters 1–39 to the return from the Babylonian exile (539/538 BC). Yet there are striking correlations between the two sections of Isaiah. One of the most compelling arguments for this relationship is the *former/latter* terminology used by the author in chapters 40–48 where God's latter works are portrayed as fulfilments of his former ones (42:9; 46:9; etc.; see Figure 0.10).

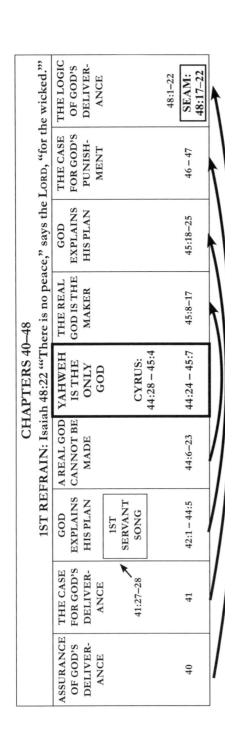

CHAPTERS 40–48

1ST REFRAIN: Isaiah 48:22 "'There is no peace,' says the LORD, 'for the wicked.'"

ASSURANCE OF GOD'S DELIVER-ANCE	THE CASE FOR GOD'S DELIVER-ANCE	GOD EXPLAINS HIS PLAN	A REAL GOD CANNOT BE MADE	YAHWEH IS THE ONLY GOD	THE REAL GOD IS THE MAKER	GOD EXPLAINS HIS PLAN	THE CASE FOR GOD'S PUNISH-MENT	THE LOGIC OF GOD'S DELIVER-ANCE
	41:27–28	1ST SERVANT SONG		CYRUS: 44:28 – 45:4				48:1–22
40	41	42:1 – 44:5	44:6–23	44:24 – 45:7	45:8–17	45:18–25	46 – 47	SEAM: 48:17–22

NOT IDOLS:
40:18–20; 41:5–7; 41:21–24; 41:29; 42:17; 44:9–20

GOD BROUGHT CYRUS:
41:2–4; 41:25–26; 42:1–9

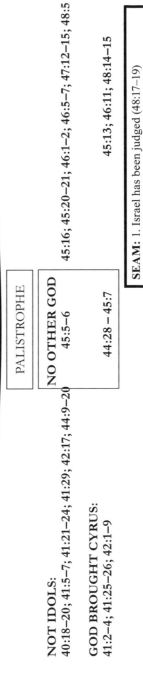

PALISTROPHE

NO OTHER GOD
45:5–6

44:28 – 45:7

45:13; 46:11; 48:14–15

45:16; 45:20–21; 46:1–2; 46:5–7; 47:12–15; 48:5

SEAM: 1. Israel has been judged (48:17–19)
   2. Israel will be delivered (48:20–21)
   3. The wicked will be punished (48:18–19, 22)

Figure 0.10 Structure of Isaiah 40 – 48

There are two major breaks in Isaiah 40 – 66 marked by the recurring refrain *'There is no peace,'* says the LORD, *'for the wicked'* (or slight variations; 48:22; 57:21) and a finale (66:24). These refrains divide Isaiah 40 – 66 into three nearly equal sections (each nine chapters long) that in our view correspond to the three introductions in the first part of the book.

Isaiah 44:24 – 45:7, the centre unit of this palistrophe, makes it clear that God claims to be the only God (45:5–7) and that idols could never have delivered Israel. Twelve other passages in Isaiah also claim that idols could never have effected this great deliverance: six are before the central passage of Isaiah 44:24 – 45:7 (40:18–20; 41:5–7; 41:21–24; 41:29; 42:17; 44:9–20) and six appear after it (45:16; 45:20–21; 46:1–2; 46:5–7; 47:12–15; 48:5). The ultimate proof that Yahweh is the only true God is that he can use the pagan king Cyrus to deliver his people. Seven passages in this section speak about this great deliverance through Cyrus: one in Isaiah 44:28, three before it (41:2–4; 41:25–26; 42:1–9) and three afterwards (45:13; 46:11; 48:14–15). After chapter 48, Cyrus is not mentioned again in the rest of the book.

We believe that Isaiah 48:17–22 functions as a seam. This seam both begins and ends with the phrase *the LORD says (ʾāmar yĕhwâ)*, and includes similar key elements to the other seams: (1) Israel has been judged (48:17–19); (2) Israel will be delivered (48:20–21); and (3) the wicked will be punished (48:22).

However, because of their different historical settings, there are two crucial differences between the seams in the second half of the book and those of the first half: (1) the punishment of the nation is seen as already having taken place; and (2) a remnant is no longer highlighted, since that is all that is left of true Israel at this point. Still, God's plan for delivering Israel continues as they are told to depart from Babylon and prepare for the ideal servant pictured in the following section.

5. Fifth section (chapters 49–57)

Since the time of Bernhard Duhm, it has been common for scholars to identify a break after chapter 55, which is considered the end of so-called Second Isaiah (or Deutero-Isaiah); however, this overlooks the obvious refrain at the end of chapter 57.

This section contains three of the so-called Servant Songs and an ending refrain *'There is no peace,' says my God, 'for the wicked'* (57:21), similar to 48:22. The most important developments in the Servant Songs in this section are the identity change from Israel to the Messiah in the second Servant Song (i.e. 49:1–6) and the detailed description of the substitutionary death of the servant in the last song (i.e. 52:13 – 53:12).

Isaiah 49 – 57 builds to a climax of Zion's glorious future (ch. 54) and God's gracious mercy (chs. 55–56), yet once again the section ends with punishment for the wicked (Isa. 57; see Figure 0.11).

The section could have ended at Isaiah 57:13, but the passage lacks further details about God's deliverance – about who will be delivered and why. The seam in 57:15–21, which addresses these questions, begins with the introduction *For this is what the high and exalted One says*, and ends with the refrain *'There is no peace,' says my God, 'for the wicked.'* It includes the same themes as the other seams: (1) Israel has been judged (vv. 16–17); (2) Israel will be delivered (vv. 18–19); and (3) the wicked will be punished (vv. 17, 20–21).

Again, the punishment of the nation is seen as already having taken place (v. 17), and now it is time to heal them (vv. 18–19). A hint of repentance is also suggested in this seam where God is said to dwell with the *contrite* (lit. 'crushed') and *lowly in spirit* (v. 15), implying those who are truly sorry for their iniquity. The indefinite nature of this verse (i.e. *the one who is . . .*) opens the possibility that the remnant could include more than Israelites alone.

6. Sixth section (chapters 58–66)
This section contains what is sometimes called the fifth Servant Song (61:1–3) and ends with a particularly lengthy and detailed description of judgment on the wicked (66:24). The structure is depicted in Figure 0.12.

This final section of Isaiah begins with a call for true repentance from Israel (ch. 58), which is then followed by a national confession of sins (ch. 59). This confession allows God to bring his deliverance to Zion (chs. 60–62), which will include destruction of its enemies (pictured as Edom) in Isaiah 63, as well as restoration of his people (chs. 65–66).

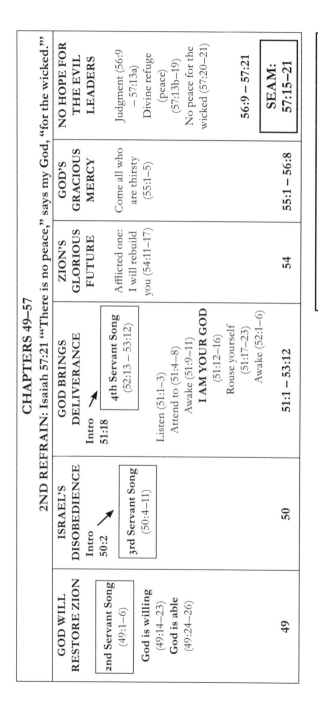

	CHAPTERS 49–57				
	2ND REFRAIN: Isaiah 57:21 "There is no peace," says my God, "for the wicked."				
GOD WILL RESTORE ZION	ISRAEL'S DISOBEDIENCE	GOD BRINGS DELIVERANCE	ZION'S GLORIOUS FUTURE	GOD'S GRACIOUS MERCY	NO HOPE FOR THE EVIL LEADERS
2nd Servant Song (49:1–6) **God is willing** (49:14–23) **God is able** (49:24–26)	Intro 50:2 **3rd Servant Song** (50:4–11)	Intro 51:18 **4th Servant Song** (52:13 – 53:12) Listen (51:1–3) Attend to (51:4–8) Awake (51:9–11) **I AM YOUR GOD** (51:12–16) Rouse yourself (51:17–23) Awake (52:1–6)	Afflicted one: I will rebuild you (54:11–17)	Come all who are thirsty (55:1–5)	Judgment (56:9 – 57:13a) Divine refuge (peace) (57:13b–19) No peace for the wicked (57:20–21)
49	50	51:1 – 53:12	54	55:1 – 56:8	56:9 – 57:21
					SEAM: 57:15–21

SEAM: 1. Israel has been judged (57:16–17)
2. Israel will be delivered (57:18–19)
3. The wicked will be punished (57:17, 20–21)

Figure 0.11 Structure of Isaiah 49 – 57

CHAPTERS 58–66
3RD REFRAIN (66:24) 'The worms that eat them will not die.'

CALL FOR TRUE REPENTANCE	CONFESSION THEN GOD COMES TO DELIVER	ZION WILL BE GLORIFIED	YAHWEH'S DAY OF VENGEANCE	GOD'S GREAT GLORY	GOD'S ANSWER: HIS ULTIMATE PLAN
	INTRO-DUCTION: GOD WILL ? BRING DELIVERANCE 59:15b–16	THE SPIRIT OF THE LORD IS UPON ME (61:1–3)			
58	59	60 – 62	63:1–6	63:7 – 64:12	65 – 66
					SEAM: 65 – 66

SEAM: 1. Israel has been judged (65:1–7, 11–15; 66:3–6)

2. Israel will be delivered (65:8–15, 17–25; 66:7–14a, 18–23)

3. The wicked will be punished (65:6–7, 11–15; 66:3–6, 14b–17, 24)

Figure 0.12 Structure of Isaiah 58 – 66

The final seam of the book (i.e. chs. 65–66) concludes with an extended refrain on the theme 'there is no peace for the wicked' in verse 24: *And they will go out and look on the dead bodies of those who rebelled against me; . . . and they will be loathsome to all mankind.* This seam concludes the whole book with themes similar to those of the other seams: (1) Israel has been judged (65:1–7, 11–15; 66:3–6); (2) Israel will be delivered (65:8–15, 17–25; 66:7–14a, 18–23); and (3) the wicked will be punished (65:6–7, 11–15; 66:3–6, 14b–17, 24).

The punishment of the nation is merely alluded to since the new-found joy that has come from the restoration far surpasses the agony of the punishment. Again, God highlights the obedience of the righteous remnant by indicating that he will have favour on *those who are humble and contrite in spirit*, and *tremble* at his word (66:2). But the most interesting development in this seam is that the righteous remnant will come from all nations and not just Israel (66:19–21).

The message that began in chapter 1 and was summarized in 1:27–28 has been realized in this final seam (66:23–24).

c. Conclusion

Over the past hundred years, the book of Isaiah has typically been divided into smaller and smaller units. By contrast, we have argued that the author created an overall structure to the book that is unified by three introductions (1:1; 2:1; 13:1) and three refrains (48:22; 57:21; 66:24). This design may have been overlooked because of older, out-of-date assumptions as to how the book was constructed.

8. Style

The author sometimes uses a narrator to set the scene and introduce the characters, but most of the book is poetic in style. Many of the oracles are written in the first person, yet it can be difficult at times to determine whether God or the prophet is speaking.

a. Characterization

We learn significantly more about God, who is extremely patient and merciful towards his people, than we do about the various characters in the book. This focus appears intentional, so as not to distract from the important warnings that God gives to unrepentant Israel.

b. Language

The language and style of Isaiah are consistent with other prophetic books in the Bible (e.g. *rîb* oracles, ch. 1; vision, ch. 6; covenant language, 24:5; 33:8; etc.). There are multiple examples of wordplays (5:7), alliterations (28:10, 13), chiasms (7:15–16), *inclusios* (chs. 2–4), climactic and repetitive parallelism (1:3, 8), and repetition of words beginning oracles (primarily in the second part: 29:1; 51:9, 17; 52:1, 11; etc.). Of the approximately 1,300 words that occur only once in the Old Testament, 201 appear in the book of Isaiah.

c. Mood

The stern mood and tone of the first part of the book of Isaiah is created through repeated descriptions of Israel's rebellion against God and the impending judgment that results. The mood then lightens considerably in the second part of the book, as optimism is reignited through anticipation of God's deliverance and restoration of his people from Babylon. Out of judgment we glimpse the hope of a new heaven and earth, and a new Jerusalem that draws people from all nations.

d. Tension

The book is loaded with tension, primarily between a righteous God and a nation that has chosen to go its own way. The tension is heightened by the juxtaposed descriptions of Israel's sinful state and complacency and impending judgment.

9. Unity/authorship

Historically, this has been one of the most contentious issues in connection with the book of Isaiah. Whybray succinctly summarizes the critical consensus:

> All but the most conservative scholars now accept the hypothesis put forward by Doederlein in 1775, but already anticipated by Ibn Ezra in

the twelfth century, that the prophecies contained in chapters 40–66 of
the book of Isaiah are not the words of the eighth-century prophet
Isaiah but come from a later time. The further hypothesis of B. Duhm
(1892) that chapters 56–66 must equally be distinguished from chapters
40–55 has met with less unanimous agreement but is nevertheless very
widely accepted.

(1975: 20)

This direction in scholarship has led to the division of the book
into smaller and smaller units with little consideration as to how
they relate to the larger message of the book.

Peter Ackroyd's concept of the 'presentation of a prophet' (1978:
16–48) influenced a shift in the direction of biblical studies. This
approach allows for an editor to shape material not only within a
section, but across sections in order to portray a more unified
message of a text. Christopher Seitz comments that 'Ackroyd is not
so much interested in the historical prophet . . . he is interested in
the prophet *as he has been presented to us*' (Seitz 1993b: 22). This
development provided the foundation for redaction criticism,
which attempts to demonstrate larger layers of editorial shaping
within biblical books. Clements applied this methodology to the
book of Isaiah in his influential article entitled 'The Unity of the
Book of Isaiah' (1982) in which he argued that Isaiah's unity was
created by at least four distinct redactions from eighth-century BC
(pre-exilic), seventh-century BC (Josianic: King Josiah, 641/640–
609 BC), exilic and post-exilic periods.

Childs explains that 'Whereas earlier form critics tended to see
the creative periods lying within the oral stage, later critics have
discovered a continuing process of reinterpreting the written text'
(2001: 2). These scholars argue that the text continued to evolve as
it interacted with various historical influences.

Largely due to canonical and redaction criticisms, there has
more recently been a renewed interest in examining the redactional
unity of the text. Williamson summarizes the direction of this
study:

The most noteworthy development in the study of the book of Isaiah
over the past two decades or so has been the rediscovery of the book's

unity . . . This does not in the least mean, however, that scholars have
reverted to a view that the book was all written by a single individual.
While that position is still defended from time to time, it is more
normal for a view of overall literary unity to be held in conjunction with
a (sometimes quite radical) analysis of the history of the book's growth
over two or more centuries with many hands contributing to it.
(2009: 21)

When taking the seams of Isaiah into consideration, it seems less
likely that the book could be the product of multiple redactors that
grew over time into its present shape. However, the structure could
allow for two possibilities: (1) either it was written by an eighth-
century prophet, or (2) it was written or redacted sometime
following the return from the Babylonian exile. The wording and
structures of the introductions (1:1; 2:1; 13:1) are like those of other
pre-exilic prophets, which lends support to an eighth-century
author. Yet the historical context of Isaiah 40 – 66 seems to suggest
a time following the Israelites' return from Babylon, particularly
the mention of Cyrus, king of Persia, about 150 years before he
lived (45:1). The book itself acknowledges the extraordinary nature
of its prophecies and accounts for this by asserting that Yahweh,
the God who made creation, also knows and controls the future,
so people can trust him (see 41:21–24). Thus, the heart of this
dilemma is a theological issue, not simply a literary one: can Israel's
God know and control the future?

a. Arguments for multiple authorship of Isaiah

Some have suggested that Ibn Ezra (AD 1092–1167), a Jewish
scholar, was one of the earliest to question Isaianic authorship of
the book; however, this is debatable. Certainly by the eighteenth
century AD, scholars under the influence of rationalistic thinking
began to seriously consider the idea of a Deutero-Isaiah (i.e.
Second Isaiah [material from a second author]). Near the end of
the eighteenth century, with J. C. Döderlein (1775) and
J. G. Eichhorn (1780–3), and into the nineteenth century, with
B. Duhm and K. Marti, the opinion developed that (1) chapters
40–55 were composed by Second Isaiah in Babylon before the
liberating decree of Cyrus in 538 BC; and (2) Trito-Isaiah (i.e.

Third Isaiah [material from a third author]) wrote chapters 56–66, most probably from Israel sometime after 538 BC. Others have argued for an original Isaianic core which was reworked and augmented by a variety of editors/redactors (Clements 1980a: 3–8; Rendtorff 1991: 8–20).

Generally, the arguments for multiple authorship of the book of Isaiah include the following:

i. Historical context

1. Events suggesting the exilic period
Chapters 40–48 deal with the Israelites' return from Babylon after 539 BC and would have had little relevance to people living in Israel in the eighth century BC. S. R. Driver dates the book between 549 and 538 BC because the conquest of Babylon is still in the future and the union of the Medes and the Persians appears to already have taken place (e.g. 41:25, *from the north* [Media] and *from the rising sun* [Persia]) (1913: 236–244). The text also describes Jerusalem as ruined and deserted (44:26b; 58:12; 61:4; 64:10–11); the temple as having long been in ruins (58:12; 61:4, *ancient ruins*); and the Jewish nation in exile in Babylonia (47:6; 48:20), despairing of ever being released (40:27; 49:14, 24). When considering these events, scholars generally argue that it is unlikely that Isaiah could have taken such a lengthy, futuristic standpoint to address people over a century in the future. They conclude, therefore, that the exile is presupposed rather than predicted.

2. Cyrus is mentioned
Some argue that the mention of Cyrus the Persian king specifically by name about 150 years before he lived (44:28; 45:1), as well as references to Babylon (43:14; 47:1, 5; 48:14, 20) as a major empire nearly a hundred years before its rise to power, has very few parallels in the rest of Scripture (see, however, Mic. 5:2).

3. Knowledge of Babylon
The detailed references to Babylon and its gods suggest to some scholars that the author is writing from Babylon during the time of the exile or later. Sometimes even specific events, such as the

return from Babylon, are referred to in the past tense as though having already happened.

ii. Unique literary style, themes and vocabulary
Scholars have pointed out the differences in vocabulary and style between the various parts of the book (for a good summary of these issues see Driver 1913: 238–246). The words or phrases that are said to be found repeatedly in Isaiah 40 – 66 but not in Isaiah 1 – 39 include the following:

1. 'To choose', *bāḥar* (41:8, 9; 43:10; 44:1, 2; etc.); however, see 1:29; 7:15, 16; and 14:1.
2. *Praise, těhillâ; hālal* (42:8, 10, 12; 43:21; 48:9; 60:6, 18; etc.); however, see 38:18.
3. 'To shoot or spring forth', *ṣāmaḥ* (44:4; 55:10; 61:11a; etc.); however, the noun form appears in 4:2.
4. 'To break out', *pāṣaḥ* (into singing) (44:23; 49:13; 52:9; 54:1; 55:12); however, see 14:7.
5. 'Pleasure', *ḥēpeṣ* (44:28; 46:10; 48:14; 53:10; etc.); however, the verb form of this word is found in 1:11; 13:17.
6. 'Good will, acceptance [God's]', *rāṣôn* (49:8; 56:7; 58:5; 60:7, 10; 61:2).
7. 'To rejoice', *śôś* (61:10; 62:5; 64:5; 65:18, 19; 66:10, 14); however, see 35:1.
8. 'I am Yahweh, and there is none else [or besides]' (45:5, 6, 18, 21, 22).
9. *I am the first and I am the last* (44:6; 48:12).

Of these terms which are said to be unique to Isaiah 40 – 66, only three are not found earlier in the book. And of these three, the last two phrases (i.e. 'I am Yahweh, and there is none else [or besides]' and *I am the first and I am the last*) may result more as a function of the content of the second part of Isaiah than of the date of this section.

Isaiah 40 – 48 is said to be characterized by the following stylistic features:

1. The duplication of words signifying the impassioned ardour of the preacher (40:1; 43:11, 25; etc.). While this type of repetition is rare in Isaiah 1 – 39, it can be seen in 29:1.
2. Differences in the structure of sentences; for example, the relative particle is omitted with much greater frequency than in the earlier chapters of Isaiah.
3. In Isaiah 40 – 66, a much more flowing style, warm and impassioned rhetoric, and the prophet often bursting into a lyrical strain (42:10–11; 44:23; etc.) (Beardslee 1903: 78).
4. In chapters 40–66, a literary style that is sometimes argued by scholars to be marked by personification of cities and nature, a dramatic depiction of the fortunes of individuals and nations, whereas Isaiah 1 – 39 is very terse and compact.

Using computer analysis to evaluate the linguistic style and language of Isaiah, Y. Radday concluded that the book was not a unity (1973: 274–277). However, his work also suggested different divisions for the latter part of Isaiah than are commonly assumed (chs. 40–48; 49–66), which would significantly alter many other scholars' views of the theology of Second Isaiah. Later, using different literary criteria, the computer analysis of L. L. Adams and A. C. Rincher concluded that the book was a unity (1973: 149–157). These conflicting findings can be attributed to differences in methodologies, the limited amount of Hebrew vocabulary examined, and the inherent difficulties in developing algorithms to analyse the complex language (see Posner 1963: 111–139); thus, computer analysis is probably of little assistance here.

iii. Theological concepts
Another basis for dividing Isaiah into at least two parts involves theological concepts.

1. Isaiah 1 – 39 speaks of God's majesty, while Isaiah 40 – 66 speaks of his uniqueness and eternality.
2. The remnant of the first part of Isaiah refers to those who had been left behind in Jerusalem, whereas in the second part the exiled Judeans who returned to Israel form the

remnant. However, it is a misunderstanding of the identity of the remnant to say that they are those who were left in Jerusalem (cf. Jer. 24).

3. The messianic king in Isaiah 1 – 39 is replaced by a servant concept in Isaiah 40 – 66, though these concepts may simply be two aspects of the same future deliverer.

Several presuppositions go into dividing a book based upon theological concepts, making it difficult to confirm such determinations.

iv. The author's assumed context
In the early 1900s, S. R. Driver proposed one of the strongest arguments against single authorship of Isaiah:

> In the present prophecy there is no *prediction* of exile: the exile is not announced as something still future; it is *presupposed*, and only the *release* from it is *predicted*. By analogy, therefore [that is, with Jeremiah and Ezekiel], the author will have lived in the situation which he thus presupposes, and to which he continually alludes.
> (Driver 1913: 237)

His argument has significant weight, yet some evidence argues against it: (1) The final form of the text itself suggests that it was written by Isaiah, the eighth-century prophet; no other prophet is mentioned. One reason the book was considered authoritative is based upon its having been authored by Isaiah (see Beckwith's argument for the deceptiveness of pseudonymous texts, 2008: 354; and Harrison 1969: 764–795). (2) It would seem unusual for an anonymous author to have been able to join his work with that of the eighth-century prophet without there being any hint of this author. This is especially true since the second part of Isaiah has such a significantly different style and context; generally pseudonymous works try to copy the original author's style and content. (3) It would have been deceptive for an author to add the fulfilment of the return from exile in order to give the impression that Isaiah had foretold this return; this would even impinge upon God's character, given his claim in 41:21–24 that only he can foretell the future, if indeed he did not really foretell these events. (4) While

Isaiah 40 – 66 pictures in detail issues the Israelites will face in the exile, some of the descriptions fit a pre-exile time period better – see discussion below under 'Arguments for single authorship of Isaiah'. (5) There is a significant reason why the exile is assumed: Isaiah 39:5–7 clearly prophesies the exile and its ramifications for the nation of Israel, but Isaiah's purpose in chapters 40–66 is to describe the period of restoration. In order to create a vivid description of this restoration, he needs to picture them in the exile from which they will be delivered.

It must also be pointed out that Driver is not consistent in applying his argument 'from analogy'. According to his logic the Pentateuch, which presupposes a second-millennium setting, must come from that period; yet he argues for source criticism (i.e. the JEDP sources) and that the works were written later.

b. Arguments for single authorship of Isaiah
Traditionally, arguments for a single author of the book come largely from (1) early Jewish sources (b. *Baba Bathra* 15a states that Hezekiah and his men 'wrote' [but probably means 'edited' or 'compiled'] the book of Isaiah; Josephus says 'the prophets, who were after Moses, wrote down what was done in their times in thirteen books', *Against Apion* 1.8); and (2) Christian sources (see specifically John 12:38–41 where John introduces his quotes from 53:1 and 6:10 with 'This was to fulfil the word of Isaiah the prophet' and 'Isaiah says elsewhere', respectively). Figure 0.13 sets out some of the early Church Fathers who believed the book to come from Isaiah.

Eusebius of Caesarea	*c.* AD 260/265–339/340
Jerome	*c.* AD 347–420
Augustine of Hippo	*c.* AD 345–430
John Chrysostom	*c.* AD 349–407
Cyril of Alexandria	*c.* AD 376–444
Isidore of Seville	*c.* AD 560–636

Figure 0.13 Church Fathers and Isaiah

As already noted, one of the most intriguing developments over the past twenty years is that many scholars are arguing for a literary or redactional unity of the book of Isaiah. Even though a single author is still not given serious consideration (Williamson 2009: 21), it is at least feasible to begin asking questions concerning the meaning of the text as a whole.

i. Theological reasons

Traditionally Isaiah 40 – 66 has been understood as God's revelation to the nation of Israel concerning their future, given in order to encourage them that, (1) even though they will experience adversity, God will ultimately keep his promises to them; and (2) God knows what is happening and will protect them through adversity. It is interesting that one aspect by which God chooses to differentiate himself from all other gods is his ability to determine the future, something no other god can do (see 41:21–24).

It is ironic that one of the strongest arguments for a Second Isaiah put forth by Williamson does not question that God can foretell the future. Instead he argues that if a prophet claims that things prophesied in the past have been accurately fulfilled, then it 'presupposes the validity of the predictive prophecy, and also demands that the speaker should himself be located after the fulfillment of those predictions' (1994: 2). For example, God says to the nation of Israel that they will be his witnesses after these predicted events are fulfilled (43:10, 12; 44:8–9).

Williamson would be correct if God were merely speaking to an individual; however, God is speaking to a nation. Those in the nation who first heard the initial prophecies would not need to be the same ones to later confirm that the prophecies were accurately fulfilled. The prophecies first given by Isaiah would be kept alive by the nation and when they were fulfilled could be confirmed by future generations of the nation.

Isaiah 41:15–20 may help to further explain our argument for predictive prophecy. Verses 15–16 claim that God has made Israel a *threshing-sledge, new and sharp* that will *thresh the mountains and crush them*, but this surely has not yet happened. Verse 20 states that when fulfilled, all nations will know that it was God who accomplished it and will learn from it. Isaiah's original listeners did not see the fulfilment of these verses, but those Israelites who are alive when they are fulfilled will be able to confirm their fulfilment and know that God has done it.

ii. Similar wording or phrases

Some scholars have argued for a single author based on similar wording across the book (e.g. the title *Holy One of Israel*). However, it could be just as reasonably argued that a redactor imitated Isaiah's vocabulary and modes of expression. It has also been suggested that an 'Isaianic school' kept Isaiah's ideas alive (Ackroyd 1978: 29), yet there is surprisingly little evidence for this. As Clements has pointed out, why would a school form around Isaiah and no other prophet (1980c: 434–435)?

Just as using similar vocabulary/phrases to argue for a single author is tenuous, so arguments that unique vocabulary across various parts of the book (as discussed above) points to multiple authors are equally insufficient. One author could employ different wording depending upon the content of the message or adopt new vocabulary and literary styles over time (see Roberts' caution, 2015: 12). Isaiah could also have used an amanuensis (like Baruch in Jeremiah) in his later writings, which may account for significant differences in wording and style.

iii. Similarities with other pre-exilic prophets

As mentioned earlier, the headings in the book of Isaiah are similar in wording and structure to those of other pre-exilic books. Several Isaianic passages also correspond closely to the book of Micah, generally considered an eighth-century prophet (see Isa. 2:4–6// Mic. 4:1–4; Isa. 41:15//Mic. 4:13a; Isa. 48:2//Mic. 3:11b; etc.). While scholars have also questioned the dating of parts of Micah, we have attempted to use only those passages that demonstrate significant evidence as pre-exilic materials (see Allen 1976: 241–253). Notice that these similarities are not limited to the early part of Isaiah.

iv. Canonicity of the book

Traditionally, Isaianic authorship was assumed by witnesses, both Jewish (Josephus, Babylonian Talmud) and Christian (Matt. 1:23; John 12:38–41; etc.). Two critical criteria of canonicity are that a book is written by a prophet and that it claims to come from God. Modern scholars have been fairly willing to accept the possibility that other authors or redactors added to prophetic works without jeopardizing their authoritative stature (see Charlesworth 1992: 5.539), but there is evidence to suggest otherwise (Beckwith 2008: 351–354). Despite these debates, there has never been any serious question concerning the canonicity of the book of Isaiah, largely due to the importance of the prophet who is associated with it.

v. Nature of prophecy

Many modern scholars typically argue that biblical prophecy was intended to modify the behaviour of those who first received it. While we agree that this is one of the purposes of prophecy (i.e. 'forth-telling'; Deut. 18:18–22), we do not limit prophecy so narrowly. Habakkuk 2:2–3 and Isaiah 30:8 suggest that another purpose is to serve as a witness to future events. We believe that predictive prophecy can also have important relevance to a nation. In the case of Isaiah 40 – 66 it provides hope that God has not finished with the nation of Israel, even though they were to be purged by the Babylonian exile (Oswalt 1986: 46–49). One of the most difficult problems for modern scholars is the mention of Cyrus specifically by name about 150 years before his birth. Yet it is not without precedent in prophecy: the birthplace of Messiah in Bethlehem was announced about seven hundred years before Jesus' birth (Mic. 5:2; Matt. 2:6).

vi. Content of Isaiah

Several concepts in Isaiah 40 – 66 fit a pre-exilic context, not an exilic one: (1) The term used for new wine (ʿāsîs) appears to be a grape product, but wine in Babylon would most probably have been made from dates. (2) It seems odd that Israel's oppressors mentioned in 52:4 are Egypt and Assyria, but not Babylon. (3) Egypt and Cush are used in parallel units in 45:14, but Psamtik I took control of Thebes in 656 BC and all ties were severed between the two shortly after his death in 610 BC. (4) The Sabeans mentioned in 45:14 were at their peak under Karib'il Water (620–610 BC), after which little is known about them. (5) The idolatry mentioned in 57:5–7 is clearly pre-exilic Canaanite, a form of idolatry for which there is little evidence in the post-exilic period. Some have argued that the idolatry in Isaiah 40 – 55 refers to that of Babylon, which would have been alluring to the Israelites. However, the wood mentioned in 44:14, the classic idolatry passage, did not naturally grow in Babylonia (see also 41:19 and 55:13). (6) The terms commonly used for Babylonian idolatry (sorceries, spells, astrologers, etc. [47:9, 12–13]) are not generally used for idolatry (graven images, molten images, etc.) in Isaiah 40 – 55.

Motyer also argues that some of the wording fits a Palestinian and not a Babylonian setting:

> The idolater goes out into the woods to cut a tree for carving (44:14), not possible in Babylonia! The trees are those a Palestinian knows; the oils are those of West Asia (41:19; 55:13); the landscapes and climates are those of the west – mountains, forests, sea, snow and land refreshed by rain, not by irrigation.
> (Motyer 1999: 32)

vii. New Testament evidence
Several New Testament authors quote from various parts of Isaiah and acknowledge that the words were those of Isaiah the prophet. Some of these passages may simply refer to the book that bears Isaiah's name, but others imply more than this; for example, Acts 28:25 states, 'The Holy Spirit spoke . . . when he said through Isaiah the prophet' (see also: 'It is just as Isaiah said previously', Rom. 9:29; 'All this took place to fulfil what the Lord had said through the prophet', Matt. 1:22; etc.).

viii. Evidence from Qumran
The Isaiah scroll from Qumran (1QIsaᵃ) does not give evidence of a break between chapters 39 and 40; there is, however, a small three-line space between chapters 33 and 34. W. H. Brownlee argues that the length of the book of Isaiah would have been prohibitive for a single scroll, so it was divided into two parts between chapters 33 and 34 (Brownlee 1964: 247–259); yet 1QIsaᵃ contains the whole book on a single scroll. The break may rather reflect literary balance (each part contains about an equal number of words) than literary origin.

c. Conclusion

As Smith correctly observes, it is not crucial to know with certainty
who had the pen in his hand, Isaiah or a scribe (Smith 2007: 43).
The introductions in the book of Isaiah suggest that Isaiah had the
visions, but not necessarily that he recorded them all (see b. *Baba
Bathra* 15a). It should be noted, however, that Isaiah is said to have
been a royal scribe and therefore would have been skilled at both
reading and writing (2 Chr. 26:22); also, the chronicler later refers
to the book as 'the vision of the prophet Isaiah' (2 Chr. 32:32).

10. Textual issues

The text of the book of Isaiah is remarkably well preserved, with a
significant number of manuscripts and versions available for
comparison. Primary witnesses include LXX, Targum and several
Qumran scrolls (e.g. 1QIsa^a, 1QIsa^b). There are a few places where
the text is somewhat obscured and may reflect textual corruptions,
but these are remarkably few in comparison with other Old Testament books.

ANALYSIS

ISAIAH: WILL GOD'S PEOPLE EVER OBEY?

1. CONDEMNATION (1:1 – 39:8)
  A. Introduction (1:1–31)
    i. Israel, listen to reason (1:1–9)
      a. Superscription (1:1)
      b. God levels charges against Israel (1:2–4)
      c. Israel has not learned from its punishment (1:5–9)
    ii. God despises their artificial worship (1:10–15)
    iii. God demands true repentance (1:16–20)
    iv. Zion will be redeemed; 'faithful city' palistrophe (1:21–26)
    v. A remnant will be delivered; **SEAM** (1:27–31)
  B. Oracles concerning Judah and Israel (2:1 – 12:6)
    i. Contrast between present and future Jerusalem (2:1 – 4:6)
      a. Future Jerusalem will lead nations to the true God (2:1–4)
      b. Present Jerusalem is extremely sinful and without good leadership: Zion is in need of purging (2:5 – 4:1)

(1) Exhortation to Israel (2:5–11)

(2) God is against all pride and wickedness (2:12–22)

(3) A future time of anarchy (3:1–12)

(4) Yahweh pronounces judgment upon the leaders (3:13–15)

(5) Jerusalem's proud women are also under judgment (3:16 – 4:1)

(6) A future glorification of Jerusalem; **SEAM** (4:2–6)

ii. God's plan for restoring his people (5:1 – 12:6)

  a. The Song of the Vineyard (5:1–7)

  b. Six woe oracles announced upon his nation (5:8–23)

    (1) Woe to those who buy up houses and land (5:8–10)

    (2) Woe to those who love pleasure and drink (5:11–17)

    (3) Woe to those who are deceived by lies (5:18–19)

    (4) Woe to those who pervert the truth (5:20)

    (5) Woe to those who consider themselves clever (5:21)

    (6) Woe to drunkards and swindlers (5:22–23)

  c. Judgment is coming: uplifted-hand oracle (5:24–30)

  d. Isaianic memoir: God calls his prophet for Judah (6:1 – 9:7)

    (1) Isaiah's call and commission (6:1–13)

    (2) Isaiah's first sign (7:1–25)

      (a) Isaiah's message to King Ahaz (7:1–9)

      (b) A second message (7:10–17)

      (c) Isaiah's further explanation (7:18–25)

    (3) Isaiah's second sign (8:1 – 9:7)

      (a) A dramatic oracle (8:1–15)

      (b) Isaiah's further explanation (8:16 – 9:7)

        (1′) Isaiah waits for God's punishment (8:16–22)

        (2′) A future deliverance (9:1–7)

  e. God delineates his punishment: four uplifted-hand oracles (9:8 – 10:4)

    (1) God will punish arrogant Israel (9:8–12)

    (2) God will destroy the leaders and false prophets (9:13–17)

    (3) Wickedness devours Israel like fire (9:18–21)

    (4) Woe to evil rulers (10:1–4)

  f. A woe oracle (10:5 – 11:16)

(1) God will also judge Assyria (10:5–34)
  (a) The reason for Assyria's judgment (10:5–14)
  (b) The boastful nation's judgment (10:15–19)
  (c) Both Israel and Judah will be reduced to a mere
      remnant (10:20–27)
  (d) The Assyrian advance upon Jerusalem and
      Assyria's destruction (10:28–34)
(2) God promises his deliverance (11:1–16)
  (a) A shoot from the stump of Jesse (11:1–9)
  (b) The remnant of God's people will return
      (11:10–16)
g. A song of thanksgiving (12:1–6)
C. Oracles of judgment and restoration (13:1 – 39:8)
  i. Oracles against foreign nations (13:1 – 23:18)
    a. Babylon (13:1 – 14:23)
    b. Assyria (14:24–27)
    c. Philistia (14:28–32)
    d. Moab (15:1 – 16:14)
    e. Aram (ancient Syria) and Ephraim (17:1–14)
    f. Cush (18:1–7)
    g. Egypt (19:1 – 20:6)
    h. The wilderness of the sea, Babylonia (21:1–10)
    i. Edom (21:11–12)
    j. Arabia (21:13–17)
    k. The valley of vision (22:1–25)
    l. Tyre (23:1–18)
  ii. God's purpose in judgment (so-called 'Little
      Apocalypse') (24:1 – 27:13)
    a. Judgment on the nations (24:1–23)
    b. Salvation for God's people (25:1–12)
    c. A song of trust (26:1–21)
    d. Deliverance for Israel that spreads to the world
       (27:1–13)
  iii. Prophecies concerning Judah: judgment and restoration
       oracles (28:1 – 33:24)
    a. First judgment–restoration cycle: woe to the
       drunkards of Ephraim (28:1–4); deliverance for a
       remnant of his people (28:5–6)

(1) Judgment oracle (28:1–4)

(2) Restoration oracle (28:5–6)

b. Second judgment–restoration cycle: punishment for the spiritual leaders (28:7–15); deliverance for the remnant (28:16–17)

(1) Judgment oracle (28:7–15)

(2) Restoration oracle (28:16–17)

c. Third judgment–restoration cycle: punishment for the political leaders of Judah (28:18–22); deliverance for the remnant illustrated by the parable of the wise farmer (28:23–29)

(1) Judgment oracle (28:18–22)

(2) Restoration oracle (28:23–29)

d. Fourth judgment–restoration cycle: punishment on Ariel (i.e. Jerusalem; 29:1–4); also deliverance for Ariel from her enemies (29:5–8)

(1) Judgment oracle (29:1–4)

(2) Restoration oracle (29:5–8)

e. Fifth judgment–restoration cycle: judgment on the blind nation (29:9–16); regeneration for Israel (29:17–24)

(1) Judgment oracle (29:9–16)

(2) Restoration oracle (29:17–24)

f. Sixth judgment–restoration cycle: woe against the rebellious children (30:1–17), but God will bring a day of salvation (30:18–33)

(1) Judgment oracle (30:1–17)

(2) Restoration oracle (30:18–33)

g. Seventh judgment–restoration cycle: woe to the unbelieving nation (31:1–3), but God will protect Jerusalem and set up a righteous king to rule over Israel (31:4 – 32:8)

(1) Judgment oracle (31:1–3)

(2) Restoration oracle (31:4 – 32:8)

h. Eighth judgment–restoration cycle: judgment against complacent women (32:9–14); blessing promised in the future (32:15–20)

(1) Judgment oracle (32:9–14)

(2) Restoration oracle (32:15–20)

i. Ninth judgment–restoration cycle: judgment on the destroyer (33:1); restoration for a remnant (33:2–24)

    (1) Judgment oracle (33:1)

    (2) Restoration oracle (33:2–24)

iv. The coming judgment and restoration (34:1 – 35:10)

    a. Yahweh's day of vengeance (34:1–17)

    b. Zion's future blessing (35:1–10)

v. The Isaianic Narratives; **SEAM** (36:1 – 39:8)

    a. The deliverance of Jerusalem (36:1 – 37:38)

    b. Hezekiah's sickness and recovery (38:1–22)

    c. The envoys from Babylon (39:1–8)

2. COMFORT (40:1 – 66:24)

A. The promise of deliverance (40:1 – 48:22)

i. A message of comfort to the exiles (40:1–31)

    a. The announcement of God's return with his remnant (40:1–11)

    b. God is able and willing to restore his chosen nation and bring them home (40:12–31)

        (1) The greatness of God (40:12–17) (first disputation oracle)

        (2) God has no rivals (40:18–26) (second disputation oracle)

        (3) God watches over his people (40:27–31) (third disputation oracle)

ii. The case for God's deliverance (41:1–29)

    a. God will use Cyrus to bring back the Israelites (41:1–4) (first trial speech)

    b. God will bring about an extraordinary deliverance (41:5–16)

    c. The homeward march of the exiles (41:17–20)

    d. God's final argument: he is the true God, for he predicts the future (41:21–29) (second trial speech; see 41:1–4)

iii. God explains his plan (42:1 – 44:5)

    a. First Servant Song (42:1–9)

        (1) Description of the servant (42:1–4)

(2) The servant is used to reveal God's greatness
   (42:5–9)
b. Two oracles of salvation (42:10 – 44:5)
   (1) First oracle of salvation (42:10 – 43:13)
      (a) Sing to the LORD a new song (42:10–13)
      (b) God has long been silent, but now he will come
         in power (42:14–17)
      (c) The prophet rebukes Israel, hoping to turn them
         back towards Yahweh (42:18–25)
      (d) God will deliver Israel (43:1–13; contains third
         trial speech, 43:8–13)
   (2) Second oracle of salvation (43:14 – 44:5)
      (a) God will deliver Israel (43:14–21)
      (b) Israel's disobedience and her punishment
         (43:22–28)
      (c) Israel's deliverance: a salvation oracle (44:1–5)
iv. A true God cannot be created by people (44:6–23)
   a. The LORD, not idols (44:6–8)
   b. The futility of idolatry (44:9–20)
   c. Wake up, Israel (44:21–23)
v. The LORD is sovereign (44:24 – 45:7)
   a. Jerusalem will be inhabited (44:24–28)
   b. God uses Cyrus to deliver his people (45:1–7)
vi. The true God is the creator (45:8–17)
   a. God's supreme power (45:8–13)
   b. Because Yahweh has proven himself to be the true
      God, the wise will turn to him (45:14–17)
vii. God further elaborates his plan (45:18–25)
viii. The case for God's punishment: the gods of Babylon
   versus the God of Israel (46:1 – 47:15)
   a. The example of the Babylonian gods (46:1–4)
   b. Yahweh has no equals (46:5–13)
   c. A taunt song regarding Babylon (47:1–15)
ix. Israel's faithlessness is rebuked, but deliverance is
   promised (48:1–22)
   a. Israel's obstinacy (48:1–11)
   b. The promise of deliverance (48:12–16)

   c. A message of remorse and restoration; **SEAM** (48:17–
   22) (Refrain: *'There is no peace,' says the* LORD, *'for the
   wicked'*)
 B. Zion is restored through Yahweh's servant (49:1 – 57:21)
  i. God will restore Zion (49:1–26)
   a. The second Servant Song (49:1–13)
    (1) Yahweh's servant is a light to the nations (49:1–6)
    (2) Two further oracles concerning the servant
     (49:7–13)
   b. Zion's restoration (49:14–26)
    (1) God has not forgotten his people Israel (49:14–21)
    (2) Yahweh has restored Zion's children (49:22–26)
  ii. Israel's disobedience (50:1–11)
   a. Yahweh did not reject Israel, but Israel rejected
    Yahweh (50:1–3)
   b. The third Servant Song (50:4–11)
  iii. God brings deliverance (51:1 – 53:12)
   a. Yahweh will bring comfort to Zion (51:1–16)
    (1) Look to your past (51:1–3)
    (2) Remember God's promises (51:4–6)
    (3) Remember God's character (51:7–8)
    (4) Trust your redeemer (51:9–16)
   b. Yahweh delivers his people (51:17 – 52:12)
    (1) Yahweh's cup of wrath has been appeased
     (51:17–23)
    (2) Prepare for deliverance (52:1–12)
   c. The fourth Servant Song: the servant of the LORD is
    humiliated then exalted (52:13 – 53:12)
  iv. Zion's glorious future (54:1–17)
   a. Yahweh's covenant of peace with Zion (54:1–10)
   b. The new Jerusalem (54:11–17)
  v. God's gracious mercy (55:1 – 56:8)
   a. Yahweh offers an everlasting covenant (55:1–5)
   b. A solemn invitation (55:6–13)
   c. The true people of God (56:1–8)
  vi. No hope for evil leaders (56:9 – 57:21)
   a. The sins of the nation of Israel (56:9 – 57:14)

COMMENTARY

1. CONDEMNATION (1:1 – 39:8)

At the end of the twentieth century, the primary goal of Isaian scholars was to distinguish, insofar as possible, the authentic parts of the book from later secondary additions. In more recent years, opinion has shifted towards the importance of the final form of the text (i.e. generally considered the MT text), the only certain form passed down from the scribes (Childs 2001: 16). While there continues to be significant disagreement as to when and by whom the book was brought together, we use the three introductions (1:1; 2:1; 13:1) already present in the book's final form as markers that delineate major sections of chapters 1–39.

The structure of Isaiah is less chronological than it is thematic; for instance, Isaiah's call does not appear until chapter 6. The primary theme/message of chapters 1–39, repeated in each of its three major sections, increases in detail with each repetition. The frequent messages of impending punishments raise the question 'Will Israel ever repent?' The answer is a qualified 'yes'. On a day much farther into the future than Isaiah would ever expect, a remnant will repent and faithfully serve God.

A. Introduction (1:1–31)

The content of chapter 1 and the second introduction at the beginning of chapter 2 suggest that chapter 1 serves as an introduction to the book as a whole (Roberts 2015: 11; etc.). Structurally, chapter 1 resembles a 'covenant lawsuit' whereby God formally accuses Israel of sin and finds them guilty (Williamson 2003: 393–406). Israel's constant rebellion prompts God's punishment – so much so, that the land is devastated. Verses 7–9 suggest that these events took place around 701 BC when Assyria destroyed much of the land until God stepped in to spare Jerusalem.

Following a brief introductory superscription (1:1), Yahweh summons Israel to court to hear the case presented against them. The heavens and earth stand as witnesses against them as God himself testifies to the ingratitude of their wayward acts. The climax is reached in a palistrophe that describes God's restoration of Jerusalem. It is time for him to act and purge the nation of its sin. The section is then closed by a seam that summarizes God's overarching plan (vv. 27–31; see Figure 0.7 on p. 18).

Several scholars have suggested that the seam in verses 27–31 is a post-exilic insertion largely because its placement after the climax of verse 26 seems awkward. We argue instead that verses 27–31 form one of the seams that join the book with the recurring themes (1) Israel will be judged (note the *you* [pl.] referring to those being punished; vv. 28–31); (2) a remnant (i.e. *penitent ones*) will be saved (v. 27); (3) the wicked will be punished (vv. 28–31); and (4) Zion[1] will be delivered (v. 27; see discussion of seams in the Introduction). The seam also prepares the reader for the next section, which begins with another introduction (2:1).

---

1. *Zion* (47x in Isa.; 17x in Jer.; 15x in Lam.; 9x in Mic.; and 28x in Pss) commonly refers to the religious capital of Israel, in contrast to Jerusalem the political capital.

i. Israel, listen to reason (1:1–9)

Context

Yahweh has a right to expect more from his nation since he delivered them from Egypt, protected them in the wilderness and led them to the Promised Land. However, instead of showing gratitude, they turned their back on him to pursue false gods. God will therefore punish them in an attempt to draw them back to himself, but they will refuse Yahweh's advances and incur even greater punishment. The semi-poetical style of Isaiah helps to drive home the points he is making.

Comment

a. Superscription (1:1)

1. This superscription includes the subject, author and date. The book is called *the vision* (*ḥāzôn*) [of] *Isaiah son of Amoz* (*'āmôṣ*; not the prophet Amos, *'āmôs*). The name *Isaiah* (*yĕša'yāhû*) means 'Yahweh[2] is (my) salvation' or 'Yahweh has saved' (Williamson 2006: 12). We are never told why he was given this name, though it fits the context of the book well. According to Jewish tradition Isaiah's father, *Amoz*, was the brother of King Azariah, father of Uzziah (*Pesiqta de Rab Kahana* 117b; b. Meg. 10b; etc.).

A *vision* is divine communication given through a dream or trance, though the word may also refer to prophetic revelation in general. The only formal vision in Isaiah appears in chapter 6. In chapter 1 the vision is said to concern *Judah and Jerusalem*, reflecting the order in which they will be mentioned in the chapter.

This verse places Isaiah's vision during a highly turbulent time in Israel's history. Since chapter 1 is probably dated after the fall of Samaria in 722 BC, it lists only kings from Judah (Uzziah, 792/791–739 BC; Jotham, 740/739–732/731 BC; Ahaz, 735–716/15 BC; Hezekiah, 729/28–687/86 BC), though some passages later in the book refer to the northern kingdom.

---

2. Yah is a shortened form for Yahweh and El is the shortened form of Elohim. Both are commonly used in names.

The nation began the eighth century BC politically strong, prospering under the reigns of Jeroboam II (793–753 BC) in the northern kingdom and Uzziah (792/791–739 BC) in the southern kingdom. However, by the end of the century Israel had been taken into Assyrian captivity (722 BC) and not long afterwards Judah was nearly destroyed by Sennacherib (701 BC). It was into this critical period that Isaiah was called to prophesy for God.

b. God levels charges against Israel (1:2–4)

2–4. This charge is directed specifically against the wayward nation of Israel. Notice that Isaiah uses the term *Israel* to refer to the whole nation even though about 722 BC the northern kingdom had been deported to Assyria. We will continue to use Isaiah's terminology unless a passage clearly refers specifically to the northern or southern kingdom.

The legal terminology (i.e. *hear, listen, rebelled, forsaken*), as well as the personal aspect of the charges (i.e. Israel has rejected the kind mercies of Yahweh), suggest that this passage is a 'covenant lawsuit' oracle (like Deut. 32:1–43; Williamson 2003: 393–406).

The terms *heavens* and *earth* (v. 2) are a common merism for 'the whole of creation' and are also echoed at the end of the book (65:17; 66:1, 22), where they refer to a new creation. Here they are called upon to *listen* as witnesses because (*kî*) God, the plaintiff, is ready to bring charges against Israel, the defendant. The *heavens* and *earth* had seen all the numerous acts of God since creation and were considered impartial and reliable witnesses.

The nation turned away from Yahweh despite his special relationship with them (v. 2; see Exod. 4:22). God uses two terms to describe Israel's 'growing up' – reared (*gādal*) and *brought them up* (*rûm*) – to convey his care and nurturing as they gained stature. Even though God had protected and nurtured Israel, they still *rebelled* against him. Williamson notes that the rejection of parental authority is 'of great social significance in a society where the family unit was the chief means of support' (2006: 33).

Isaiah declares that even dumb animals display more gratitude than did Israel. The contrast is striking: the animals *know*, though they would not be expected to, in contrast to Israel who *does not know*, though it ought to. God mourns that *Israel* does *not understand* that he is the one who has cared for them all this time. The continual care of feeding domesticated animals from a *manger* forms a certain bond or attachment between the animals and their owners, whereas God's constant care for Israel produced only growing contempt.

Isaiah cries *Woe* (v. 4), a cry of grief and sorrow, as he declares the people's sins before the *heavens* and *earth* (v. 2). The multiple harsh phrases of verse 4 underscore the hardness of Israel's heart: *sinful nation* (lit. 'nation of sinners'); *whose guilt is great* (lit. 'heavy with iniquity'); *brood of evildoers*; *children given to corruption*; *forsaken the LORD*; and *spurned the Holy One of Israel*. To have *spurned the Holy One of Israel* is contemptible in view of how much God had done for them; the people made a wilful, stubborn choice when they *turned their backs on him*.

The name *the Holy One of Israel* (v. 4) is a distinctive title for Yahweh in the book of Isaiah that stresses the aspect of his holiness, in contrast to the wickedness of the nation (even though he is supposed to be their God; see Figure 0.4 on p. 10).

c. Israel has not learned from its punishment (1:5–9)

5–9. With graphic imagery, God addresses Israel, his wayward children, who have been punished with 'beatings' that correspond to famine, drought, war and ultimately exile: *From the sole of your foot to the top of your head / there is no soundness* ('nothing healthy'; v. 6). Yet the *children* still refuse to obey and persist in *rebellion*. God, pictured as a father who is weary and sorry for his unruly children, appeals to them, *Why should you be beaten any more?* (lit. 'Where else can you be punished?' v. 5).

Israel is a pitiable sight, with *wounds*, *bruises* and *open* [lit. 'fresh'] *sores* (v. 6) that have received no medical attention. These images are an apt description of the ravages suffered in a war-torn land. Even though God is justified in punishing his ungrateful, wicked nation, he is a loving father whose heart aches to see his children persist in their sin and reap judgment as the consequence.

Verses 7–9 turn next to the reality behind this imagery: *foreigners* have devastated Israel's cities by fire, a description consistent with the Assyrian march against Judah in 701 BC when it destroyed forty-six 'strong' cities before God stepped in to deliver Jerusalem (2 Kgs 18:1 – 19:35; see Figure 0.3 on p. 7).

Jerusalem is likened to a *shelter* sticking out high above a *vineyard*, or a *hut* which rises over a 'melon field' (*miqšâ*; NIV *cucumber field*). The designation for Jerusalem, *Daughter Zion* (v. 8), emphasizes what should be their close relationship to Yahweh, in sad contrast to where they find themselves. However, they are still alive by the graciousness of the LORD *Almighty* (lit. 'LORD of hosts', a name that emphasizes God's sovereignty; 'hosts' refers to 'heavenly hosts').

Israel is pictured as a remnant (*some survivors*) that has narrowly survived total destruction (v. 9), unlike the unfortunate cities of Sodom and Gomorrah (see Gen. 19:24–25) with whom they are compared.

Meaning

God is pictured as a loving father who has been spurned by his children. The gravity of the situation is compounded by the fact that he had made every effort to provide for his nation. Isaiah will faithfully prophesy with little apparent success during one of the most difficult periods of the nation's history. Isaiah's audience is remarkably similar to our generation – hard-hearted and oblivious to God's work. Yet God's ultimate goal continues: he will one day secure for himself a righteous remnant.

Jerusalem's miraculous deliverance from Sennacherib's invasion was a wonderful demonstration of God's grace. They deserved no better treatment than Sodom and Gomorrah, yet they did not receive what they deserved – the very definition of 'grace'. This gracious, merciful God is the same God whom we serve.

ii. God despises their artificial worship (1:10–15)

Context

After the sad illustration of Israel's punishment, God describes how even their worship is detestable to him. The people thought that their diligence in keeping the rituals of the law pleased God when in fact it angered him, for they continued to outwardly observe religious rituals while inwardly harbouring corrupt hearts. Other prophets declared similar condemnations of their worship: Jeremiah 7:2–12, 21–34; Hosea 6:4–11; Amos 4:4–5; 5:14–25; Micah 6:6–8.

God's laws regarding sacrifices were meant to remove sin that formed a barrier to a close relationship with him. The wording and imagery here would have elicited angry disbelief from the people: surely they were not to be compared with reprehensible Sodom and Gomorrah (v. 10). Historically, this is the first prophet to equate Israel with Sodom and Gomorrah in terms of the depth of their corruption and wickedness.

Comment

10–11. The prophet's sharp rebuke should gain Israel's attention: *Hear the word of the LORD, you rulers of Sodom . . . you people of Gomorrah!* For centuries Sodom and Gomorrah were denounced for their wickedness and debauchery (see Deut. 29:23); now Isaiah points out that Israel's sins demand similar punishment. Israel's sins had blinded them to the deplorable situation that Isaiah describes.

The great quantity of their *sacrifices – burnt offerings, fat of fattened animals* and *blood of bulls and lambs and goats –* is no substitute for a genuine heart attitude. God has *no pleasure in* (v. 11) their heartless worship.

12–15. Their outward forms of worship lacked a heart attitude of true worship (see 29:13). *When you come to appear before me* (v. 12) refers to their attendance at the annual pilgrimages (see Exod. 23:14–17), as well as to their many festivals: *New Moons, Sabbaths, convocations* and *assemblies* (v. 13). When God enquires *who has asked this of you . . . ?* (lit. 'seeks this from your hand'), the Israelites would surely have replied, 'You did.' But their actions were missing the most important ingredient: a repentant heart (see Ps. 51:16–17). Without this their worship was merely a *trampling of my* [God's] *courts,* a figurative expression for 'a meaningless stomping on God's glory and honour'.

God commands them to *stop bringing meaningless* [lit. 'empty'] *offerings.* Even their *incense,* which was meant to be a pleasing aroma to God (see Lev. 6:15), was *detestable* (lit. 'an abomination') to him, one of the strongest words for disgust and abhorrence (see Deut. 7:25).

Observances that God required had become *worthless assemblies* (lit. 'iniquity and assembly', v. 13), which he was *weary* of putting up with (see Amos 5:21–24). God cannot literally become weary; it is anthropomorphic language for the point at which God will no longer tolerate meaningless repetitions or contempt for his glory. Their actions are said to weigh upon God; they are a *burden* (*tōraḥ* [2x; see Deut. 1:12], v. 14), which is a wordplay on the similar-sounding word 'law' (*tōrâ*).

When you spread out your hands [lit. 'palms', as in open palms turned up towards God] *in prayer*, a typical posture for prayer, Yahweh would no longer listen (lit. 'hide his eyes'; v. 15). Even multiplying their prayers, like the pagans who thought that their many words could appease their gods, would have no effect.

The next phrase explains why: their *hands are full of blood* (*dāmîm*, lit. 'bloodshed'). This may refer to the blood of their worthless sacrifices or to the blood of the weak and defenceless victims of their violent crimes (vv. 16–17). The plural form of the word translated *blood* in this verse suggests 'blood shed violently'.

Meaning

Meaningless ritual is deceptive at its core, for God knows the innermost thoughts and desires of our hearts. It is foolish to try to deceive him. God puts a high priority on true worship: (1) ritualistic actions (even though prescribed by God) that are devoid of a proper heart attitude of repentance are not acceptable worship; and (2) sinful action or inaction (e.g. not helping the oppressed) negates our worship. James similarly develops the concept of true faith (Jas 2:18b): true worship entails both heart attitude and right action. God detests heartless worship as much today as he did in Isaiah's time.

iii. God demands true repentance (1:16–20)

Context

After confronting the nation about their outward and empty compliance with the forms of religion, God now turns to the root of the problem: the need for true acts of worship that are characterized by repentance and that seek justice for the poor and oppressed.

Comment

16–17. God has declared his weariness of the people's hypocritical worship while harbouring sin in their lives. The progression of true repentance is laid out in verses 16–17: *wash and make yourselves clean* (i.e. the acknowledgment of 'dirt' or sin is implied), then turn away from sin, *stop doing wrong*, and *learn to do right* (vv. 16b–17a). True repentance has both a negative aspect of ceasing from sin or removing sin through washing or cleansing (v. 16), and a positive aspect of learning to do right (v. 17) and seeking justice for those who are oppressed/defenceless (see Exod. 22:22–24).

To *seek justice* means to pursue it intently, implying that it does not happen naturally. The phrase *defend the oppressed* (lit. 'make straight the ruthless') means to direct the oppressor into a 'straight or right path'. To *take up the cause of the fatherless* and *plead the case of the widow* are active demonstrations of righteousness. God's people were to stand out for their generosity and helpfulness (see Deut. 24:17–22). Their example of love and fairness would demonstrate God's nature before the other nations.

18–20. In this rhetorical climax to chapter 1, Yahweh offers a new beginning after his powerful call to repentance. With a note of urgency, *Come now*, God insists that Judah come and meet with him to *settle the matter* (lit. 'work out, arbitrate'). God's offer sounds almost too good to be true – the stain of sin as indelible as *scarlet* and *crimson* (*tôlāʿ*, 'worm from which a red dye comes', 2x; see Lam. 4:5) can be changed to the pure white of snow or wool.

In this vivid illustration, God's forgiveness requires that they make the choice to be *willing* and *obedient*. The verbs here should be understood in a hypothetical sense. The people have a choice to make, which is highlighted by a wordplay (words underlined). They can either (1) <u>obey</u> God's laws and *<u>eat</u> the good things of the land* (v. 19); or (2) <u>disobey</u> and <u>be eaten</u> *by the sword* (i.e. war; v. 20). What seems like an easy choice has far-reaching consequences.

There is a delicate balance between divine sovereignty and human responsibility in these verses. God longs for them to repent, but he will not force them to do so. This section, which begins with a stern call to *listen* (v. 10), ends with the certainty of God's verdict, *for the mouth of the LORD has spoken* (v. 20).

Meaning

The people of Israel have a clear choice to make: they can either receive forgiveness and blessing by turning to God in repentance, or they can experience further punishment for continued rebellion. God, the sovereign of the universe, is in earnest that Israel must change their ways; if not, punishment is coming. The choice seems easy, but turning from our sin is never without a cost.

iv. Zion will be redeemed; 'faithful city' palistrophe (1:21–26)

Context

Verses 21–26 form a palistrophe that opens with a lament over the deplorable condition of Jerusalem. At the centre (v. 24a) Yahweh, *the Lord, the* LORD *Almighty, / the Mighty One of Israel, declares* that he will hold back no longer. It is time for him to act and purge the nation of its sin. The palistrophe ends with the declaration that Jerusalem will once again be called *the Faithful City*.

Comment

21–23. The opening words of the palistrophe, *See how*, lead into a dirge lamenting the deplorable condition of Jerusalem: she is a *prostitute* surrounded by *murderers* and *thieves* (vv. 21, 23). In Hebrew it is not unusual to personify cities or countries as female, for they were thought to give rise to their inhabitants (see 1:8). It is the actions of the city's inhabitants that make her either righteous or wicked.

The stark contrasts of verse 21 depict the extent of her downfall: the *faithful city* is now a *prostitute*; her *rulers* were once *full of justice* but are now *thieves* and *murderers*. Notice that verse 23 criticizes the *rulers* and not simply the king, implying that wickedness had filtered down through all its leaders.

The imagery in verse 22, *your silver has become dross*, depicts how Jerusalem has been made worthless by impurities (the plural form of dross implies multiple impurities). Jerusalem's worthlessness is portrayed by the additional metaphor of *choice wine* that has been ruined by dilution (lit. 'weakened'; i.e. no longer has its intended effect).

Verse 23 then describes how greed had corrupted the nation's rulers so that they no longer *defend* the weak of society – *the fatherless* (lit. 'they do not judge the orphans') and *the widow*. They are called *rebels* and *partners with thieves* who *love bribes* and *chase after gifts* (lit.

'pursuing rewards'). Her leaders, having wandered away from God, have little motivation to defend the weak of society. Money can buy influence and power, but at a high cost to society.

24–26. Verse 24 functions as a hinge at the centre of the palistrophe: the action is about to turn (signalled by *therefore*), for God will bring change. The three names for God – *the Lord*, *the* LORD *Almighty* (lit. 'of hosts') and *the Mighty One of Israel* – emphasize his ability to effect this change. The latter two names highlight God's power and his relationship to Israel. Who would dare to defy this mighty God who controls the heavenly hosts?

The announcement beginning with *Ah!* (lit. 'woe') in verse 24 is directed against Israel; they will be the object of God's purging. This is not a vengeful God lashing out in anger to strike his enemies, but a just God who has restrained his anger towards his people's sin for years, and now it is time for cleansing. God *will vent* [*his wrath*] (*nāḥam*, 'to gain satisfaction or consolation from my enemies'), a verb which is very similar in sound and meaning to the next verb, *avenge* (*nāqam*).

Two phrases indicate the thoroughness of the cleansing: *I will thoroughly purge away your dross*, and *I will . . . remove all your impurities* (lit. 'separations'). Just as the high heat of the smelting process removes *dross* to purify metal, so God will use affliction to purify his people. The word *kabbōr* (NIV *thoroughly*) in the second phrase of verse 25 may be translated several ways: (1) 'like the lye', a comparison with the thoroughness of cleaning with lye; (2) 'like the lye', referring to lye used in the smelting process; or (3) 'like the pureness', thus resulting in the NIV reading. This last reading seems preferable because of the article on 'pureness' in the Hebrew text.

God will halt the downward spiral of his people through the renewal of their *rulers* (v. 23) in both wisdom and integrity. This profound reversal process is underscored in the repeated vocabulary of this section. The corrupt city of the beginning of this section (v. 21) has been restored into the *City of Righteousness, / the Faithful City* by the section's end (v. 26). The emphasis here is entirely theocentric: God is the one who accomplishes this cleansing (Childs 2001: 21).

Meaning
The palistrophe summarizes a recurring theme of the first part of
the book: God uses the crucible of suffering to cleanse his children.
The refining process, like the intense heat of smelting, will be
painful to endure and will take a significant toll on Jerusalem. But
those who successfully come through will be cleansed of sin and
made righteous. Society will again be restored, with judges and
counsellors who no longer seek bribes instead of justice and who
defend the cause of the marginalized. This is a change that only
God can produce.

v. A remnant will be delivered; SEAM (1:27–31)

Context
Verses 27–31 highlight the contents of chapter 1 and form the first
of the seams that join the book together. Each of the seams will
contain the following themes: (1) Israel will be judged (note the
plural *you* referring to those being punished, vv. 28–31); (2) a
remnant (the *penitent ones*) will be saved (v. 27); (3) the wicked will
be punished (vv. 28–31); and (4) Zion will be delivered (v. 27). The
seam prepares the reader for a fuller description in the next section.

Comment
27–31. The restoration of *the Faithful City* described in the
palistrophe is reiterated in this seam. *Zion will be delivered with* [lit.
'because of'] *justice* and *righteousness.* God mercifully buys her back
(lit. 'to ransom, redeem') from those he had used to punish her.

There are differing views as to whose *righteousness* will deliver
Zion: the righteousness of her inhabitants (Roberts 2015: 31), of
God (Childs 2001: 22), or of both (Oswalt 1986: 110). The context
certainly favours God's righteousness: the verb *will be delivered*
suggests a passive sense in which Zion is receiving the action.
Conceptually it is also more reasonable that God would deliver
those who are penitent than that those who are penitent would
deliver themselves.

Yet it is clear that God will preserve only a remnant of his people
(i.e. *her penitent ones*, lit. 'returning ones'). The rest (*rebels and sinners*,
v. 28) who have rebelled against the LORD will be *broken* (lit.

'crushed ones together') and *perish* (lit. 'they will be finished').
Verse 29 speaks of a time when these *sinners* will realize that their
false gods cannot save them and thus they (*you* [pl.] highlighting
Israel's own sin) *will be ashamed* of the oaks and gardens (i.e. cultivated sanctuaries) they had planted. Oswalt (1986: 111) points out
that 'to be ashamed' is commonly used in the Old Testament of
someone whose trust has been misplaced. The Israelites had
abandoned their trust in the maker of trees and trusted the trees
themselves – a foolish choice.

Three images from their pagan worship are used to depict their
own ruin: (1) *an oak with fading leaves*, in contrast to the oaks in their
sacred gardens; (2) *a garden without water*, in contrast to the well-
watered gardens where they worshipped; and (3) burning wood
(*tinder*), in contrast to their pagan wooden idols. The destruction of
trees is a common image in Isaiah that represents the destruction
of the wicked (see 10:33–34).

The apex of the seam is reached in verse 31, where a strong man
is pictured as feeble as flax fibres that burst into flame and are gone.
The word translated *tinder* (*ně'ōret*, 2x; see Judg. 16:9) refers to the
small strands combed off flax that are useless for spinning into
thread and are highly flammable. The wicked, pictured as a strong
man, will not escape this destruction orchestrated by God; there
will be *no one to quench the fire* (see 66:24).

The seam looks towards the future cleansing, as did the
palistrophe of verses 21–26. It describes the restoration of Zion
mentioned in 1:27 in much greater detail and prepares the reader
for chapters 2–12.

Excursus: Baal worship

Baal worship was often conducted in gardens planted on the
mountaintops. Baal, the storm god, was an important deity to
appease so that the land would be fertile. The Canaanites believed
that Baal and Asherah (i.e. deities of fertility) could be manipulated
through rituals to make the land fertile (see 1 Kgs 14:23); thus, high
places were planted with lush gardens and trees (e.g. oaks). Certain
trees were popular with fertility cults because they appeared to die
in the winter and come back to life in the spring. They were also

easy to carve into Asherah poles resembling the fertility goddess. Because of the need for rain in order to grow crops on such arid land, the people were continually tempted into syncretistic worship of Yahweh and Baal.

Meaning
The primary focus of chapter 1 is on Yahweh and his plan to bring Israel back to himself. His people continued to offer sacrifices and conduct solemn assemblies as if they were obedient, but their worship was often syncretistic, attempting to appease both Yahweh and Baal. How quickly the nation had forgotten God's mighty acts in their history: delivering them from Egypt and bringing them to the land flowing with milk and honey. How easy it is for us to take our eyes off God and put our trust in lesser, inadequate things.

Nevertheless, God's plan is not thwarted. It is true that Israel reaped suffering as a consequence of their rebellion. Yet a remnant of Israel will be left – those who will serve God with a renewed commitment and renewed righteousness.

B. Oracles concerning Judah and Israel (2:1 – 12:6)

Isaiah 2 – 12 is made up of two smaller units, chapters 2–4 and 5–12, each describing in greater detail how God will bring about the deliverance of Israel mentioned in chapter 1. Isaiah 1 briefly describes God's plan for restoring Israel, then chapters 2–4 develop the theme much more fully by means of an interesting *inclusio* structure that begins (2:1–4) and ends (4:2–6) with a future, glorified Zion. In between these two glimpses of restored Zion is a description of Israel's current state, as well as the purging judgment that will be necessary to transform them into a righteous nation – a process that would take much longer and be more painful than anyone could have imagined.

The middle unit (2:5 – 4:1) opens with four consequences that God has determined for the wicked leaders of Israel, each beginning with the Hebrew word *kî*, 'for' (2:6, 12; 3:1, 8). The climax is reached in Isaiah 3:13 when Yahweh rises to judge *the elders and leaders of his people* who are guilty of plundering his vineyard and crushing the poor (vv. 14–15). Then God judges the women of

Judah (3:16 – 4:1) who will suffer punishment like that of the male leaders (2:6 – 3:12).

Chapters 5–12 form a lengthy palistrophe at the centre of which is the section commonly referred to as the 'Isaianic memoir' (or *Denkschrift*). Isaiah's call and commission begins the memoir; he is God's primary agent to tell the nation of his plan for them.

These two sections are joined by the word-link *bāʿar* (lit. 'burned or consumed'): *It is you who have ruined* [*bāʿar*] *my vineyard* (3:14); then in the Song of the Vineyard God *will take away its hedge, / and it will be destroyed* [*bāʿar*] (5:5; see Figure 0.8 on p. 20). These are the only two instances in the book of Isaiah that speak of the vineyard being *bāʿar*.

Instead of interrupting the *inclusio* structure of chapters 2–4 in order to further describe how Yahweh will restore the nation, the author finishes that structure and then joins it by means of the linking word *bāʿar* to the next section (chapters 5–12), which describes God's plan of restoration. Thus, the seam that appears at the end of Isaiah 4 (vv. 2–6) speaks of a time when nations will go up to Zion to learn about Israel's God. Chapters 13–39 then describe judgments on various nations that will give rise to a multinational remnant who will be obedient to God.

i. Contrast between present and future Jerusalem (2:1 – 4:6)

Scholars are generally agreed that Isaiah 2 – 4 is a unit within the final form of the book of Isaiah, but there is much disagreement regarding the relationship of its smaller units because of differences in genres, speakers and subject matter (Williamson 2006: 238). Despite this, we learn that God will ultimately restore his people (2:1–4; 4:2–6) and will hold Israel's elders and leaders responsible for destroying his vineyard. How this works out is explained in more detail in the next section, chapters 5–12.

a. Future Jerusalem will lead nations to the true God (2:1–4)

Context

Many scholars argue that Isaiah 2:1–4 is a post-exilic addition. There are several indicators, however, of a pre-exilic date. While this passage certainly looks forward to a future restoration, the restoration appears to be a renewal of the present world and not its destruction and recreation, as is often found in later eschatological thought. Micah 4:1–3, a book that also claims to be pre-exilic, has nearly the same wording as Isaiah 2:1–4 (see Introduction). If Isaiah 2:2–4 and 4:2–6 originate from Zion theology (as seems plausible) and if *descendants of Jacob* (2:5) and/or 'house of Jacob' (2:6) refer to the northern kingdom, then both these two passages could be dated before 722 BC when the northern kingdom was deported.

Theologically there is no doubt that Isaiah 2:2–4 and 4:2–6 would have provided hope and encouragement that God was not yet finished with Israel, although hope would more easily have arisen after the miraculous deliverance of Jerusalem in 701 BC (and thus a pre-exilic date) than after its destruction in 586 BC.

Comment

1. This new introduction that claims to be a message from *Isaiah son of Amoz* is usually thought to be a redactional heading for either chapters 2–4 or 2–12 and is generally considered later than the introduction in 1:1. The wording of this introduction is similar to that of 1:1 except that it speaks of 'the word' (*haddābār*; NIV *this is what*) instead of *the vision* (*ḥāzôn*, 1:1) that Isaiah saw, and there is no mention of when this 'word' was given. The repetition of Isaiah's full name here, although somewhat unusual, is similar to the introductions in Zechariah 1:1 and 1:7 (see also 7:1). Again this 'word' concerns the fates of *Judah and Jerusalem* (same name order as 1:1), which are intimately connected.

2–3. The *inclusio* pattern of chapters 2–4 begins with a description of the future glory of Zion, setting the stage with the key phrase *in the last days* (or 'the future days', v. 2). This oracle (2:2–4) pictures *the mountain of the LORD's temple* (lit. 'house'; i.e. Zion) in two parallel phrases: (1) it *will be established / as the highest of the mountains*; and (2) it *will be exalted above the hills*.

In the Ancient Near East the *mountains* or *hills* were considered the abode of the gods. Zion was the primary abode of Yahweh (see Ps. 48:1–3). Resuming the *faithful city* theme of 1:21–26, the *nations will stream to it* (v. 2; i.e. Mt Zion) to learn about Yahweh and his ways (v. 3).

Mount Zion is located 2,510 ft above sea level, so to say that *all nations will stream* [lit. 'flow'] *to it* disregards natural laws of gravity. The literal meaning suggests that people from various nations would walk up to Zion, but it should more probably be read figuratively as a description of Zion's importance and authority.

Interest in learning about Yahweh and his ways will no longer be confined to the Israelites, but rather *all nations* (v. 2) and *many peoples* (v. 3) will be drawn to Zion. The next phrase, *He will teach us his ways*, literally reads 'and he will be teaching us from his ways', conveying continual action. Notice that this teaching will come directly from God and that the nations will want to be guided by and obedient to him (to *walk in his paths*).

Israel will serve as a beacon to the other nations (see Exod. 19:5–6), leading them to God, a role in which the nation largely failed during Isaiah's lifetime. Yahweh will rule from *Zion* and his *law* (*tôrâ*) or 'instruction' *will go out from* there. The use of the name *Zion* emphasizes the religious aspects of the Jewish nation that will be promulgated to the other nations. The word *tôrâ* suggests God's overarching justice and teaching that instructs the nations how to live moral, upright lives.

4. Verse 4 depicts God's assertion of his rightful rule as the *nations* and *many peoples* acknowledge Yahweh's sovereignty and learn his ways. He *will settle* their *disputes*, and universal peace will ensue (see 11:6–9).

Because *nation will not take up sword against nation*, weapons will be made into more useful tools. The peoples *will beat their swords into ploughshares* (the cutting blades at the front of a plough) and *their spears into pruning hooks* (a hooked blade used for pruning grapevines and trees). These weapons of war will be permanently repurposed, a reversal of the imagery in Joel 3:10.

This clearly figurative language portrays Jerusalem's special role in bringing peace and blessings to many nations. A kingdom of peace is also seen in 9:1–7; 11:1–9; and 32:1–8; however, those passages picture a Davidic king ruling as God's regent, whereas this passage emphasizes God's reign. The future envisioned in 2:4 and 4:2–6 is like that described in the New Testament book of Revelation (see Rev. 20 – 22).

Meaning

This second introduction leads into a glorious vision of God's plan for the nations of the world, with Zion as his special dwelling place (see Pss 87; 93; etc.). Nations will be drawn to Zion, wanting to find out about Israel's great God of wisdom and peace. He will rule justly, and nations will gladly accept his judgments, resulting in peace and security throughout his kingdom. The New Testament envisions the future very similarly (Rev. 20 – 22): God will rule over a righteous nation in which peace, justice and security prevail.

b. Present Jerusalem is extremely sinful and without good leadership: Zion is in need of purging (2:5 – 4:1)

Here the *inclusio* pattern of Isaiah 2 – 4 turns from the glorious future of Israel to Israel's deplorable current condition (2:5 – 4:1; see Figure 0.8 on p. 20). The first part of the description (2:5 – 3:12) contains four sections, each beginning with the Hebrew word *kî*, 'for' (2:6, 12; 3:1, 8), and each describing consequences Israel will experience for turning away from their God. A woe oracle declaring Israel's punishment follows (3:11–12), then Yahweh rises to contend with his nation (3:13). In a law-court scene God declares a guilty verdict first upon the leaders of Israel, and then upon the women of Israel (3:16 – 4:1). At the heart of Yahweh's verdict regarding the leaders, God declares that they have 'devoured [*bāʿar*] the [God's] vineyard', a theme that reappears in the next section (chs. 5–12).

Many scholars agree with Duhm that Isaiah 2:5–22 is, formally speaking, the most textually corrupted material in the book, with verses that appear to be missing a word or phrase (see v. 5), abrupt openings (vv. 5, 9, 13–16, 18, etc.) and the appearance of editorial reconstructions (vv. 18, 20–21, 22). Nevertheless, there is little textual evidence for these suggested corruptions and the MT makes reasonable sense as it stands. We therefore agree with Oswalt that the text should be read as it is (1986: 121).

Williamson (2006: 207) points out that at least part of the section is structured as a chiasm (strictly, palistrophe):

A *Go into the rocks, hide in the ground* (2:10)
    B *The eyes of the arrogant will be humbled* (2:11)
        C [Middle Core] *a day in store / for all the proud and lofty*
            (2:12–16)
    B' *The arrogance of man will be brought low* (2:17)
A' *flee to caves in the rocks / and to holes in the ground* (2:19)

The emphasis of the passage is twofold: (1) God condemns human pride and self-sufficiency; and (2) he will pour out his judgment during the Day of the LORD.

(1) Exhortation to Israel (2:5–11)

Context
Following the description of Israel's amazing future hope (2:2–4) is an exhortation to live up to that hope: *let us walk in the light of the LORD* (2:5). The author includes himself (*let us*) in this exhortation. The phrase *descendants of Jacob* may refer to the northern kingdom (see 9:8) but is more likely to refer to the whole nation (see 1:3–4), given the warning in 3:1 that the southern kingdom of Judah will also undergo cleansing by God. This phrase is not only in the emphatic position here, it is also repeated in the next verse to capture their attention and impress upon them their great privilege.

Comment
5. The exhortation beginning verse 5 suggests that the author hoped Israel could avert the coming judgment which their actions deserved, yet the mention of a future hope in the preceding section did not in any way excuse their present behaviour; if anything, it heightened their culpability.

The abrupt beginning of verse 5 suggests to some scholars that something is missing, but Childs is correct in his observation that verse 5 looks both forwards and backwards (2001: 31), thereby joining the two sections. *Let us walk in the light* [*'ôr*] *of the LORD* implies an about-turn, turning their backs on the darkness and wickedness in which they were then walking. The concept of walking in God's light entails both the laws that he had given, as well as all the blessings that would result from following those righteous directives.

6–7. The Hebrew particle *kî*, 'for', in 2:6, 12; 3:1, 8 introduces four consequences of turning away from God. The first consequence is that Israel's sins had caused a rift with their God: ['for', *kî*] *you, LORD, have abandoned your people.* The second person singular form emphasizes the direct connection Israel could have with God: they are *your* [God's own] *people.*

We can see from the list of transgressions in verses 6–11 that Israel had adopted the sins of other countries (see Deut. 18:9–14). Verse 6b lists three of these sins: (1) *They are full of superstitions from the East* (lit. 'they are full from the east'). Some translate *from the East* as 'diviners' (*qōsĕmîm*), but significant modification is needed for this reading, with little textual evidence. The idea is that they are strongly influenced by Eastern ideas and/or customs (see Josh. 7:21, where Achan lusted after the beautiful robe from Shinar [in the East]). (2) *They practise divination like the Philistines* (lit. 'and diviners like the Philistines'; see 2 Kgs 1:2). Diviners were thought to communicate with the deity; thus, this powerful group of people were outlawed in Israel (Deut. 18:10–14). (3) They *embrace pagan customs* (lit. 'they clasp the sons of foreigners').

As their money and treasures increased (see the prohibition in Deut. 17:16–17), so did their iniquities. God is not opposed to money, horses and chariots when used in the right way; but Israel had taken their eyes off God and sought to buy protection through alliances with powerful foreign nations.

8. Israel and Judah were especially prosperous under Jeroboam II (2 Kgs 14:25) and Uzziah (2 Chr. 26:5–16), but their spiritual condition was exceedingly depraved. Verse 8 describes *their land* as being *full of idols* (*'ĕlîlîm*, 'worthless ones') which *their fingers have made* (see 44:10–17). There is a wordplay here between God (*'ĕlōhîm*) and idols (*'ĕlîlîm*), driving home the futility of trusting in something made by human hands.

9–11. Israel had everything that would make them great according to human wisdom, but it all led to pride. God will therefore humble them (vv. 9–11). The two words for 'man' in verse 9 draw a distinction between 'mankind' (*'ādām*) in general and individuals (*'îš*). Verses 9 and 11 use similar vocabulary to state that all humanity (*'ādām*/ *'îš* [pl.]) will be *humbled* and *brought low*, in contrast to *the* LORD *alone* [who] *will be exalted in that day* of punishment. Scholars have struggled over the final phrase of verse 9, *do not forgive them* (lit. 'do not lift them up now'). The form suggests a temporary prohibition (Williams §186); that is to say, the author's desire is that God withhold forgiveness at this moment because their sins demand justice.

Verse 10 points out that people will attempt to evade God's mighty power (*the splendour of his majesty*) by hiding in caves in the hills or digging holes in the ground (see vv. 19–21; Rev. 6:15–17), all to no avail. *In that day* (v. 11) anticipates the Day of the LORD, when people will flee and unsuccessfully attempt to hide from God (see Amos 9:2–4). In the end they will be destroyed, human pride and arrogance will be a thing of the past, and Yahweh alone will be exalted – the one who truly deserves it.

Meaning

Israel had wandered far from their God, but Isaiah offers them a chance to return (v. 5). They had turned to everything but God for their protection, filling the land with horses, chariots, silver, gold and foreign gods. God will indeed humble and punish them so that they can learn that only he is to be exalted.

(2) God is against all pride and wickedness (2:12–22)

Context

The word 'for' (*kî*) introduces the second consequence of turning away from God: there will be a day of reckoning. This section is a poetic expansion of the Day of the LORD (lit. 'a day belonging to the LORD') described in verses 9–11. In that day, all who foolishly challenge Yahweh's supremacy – *the proud and lofty* and *all that is exalted* – will be punished and God alone will be exalted.

Comment

12–16. The imagery here features many tall objects that reach towards the heavens as metaphorical expressions of humankind's proud and arrogant mindset: *cedars of Lebanon, oaks of Bashan, towering mountains*, and 'ships of Tarshish' (NASB, NRSV) with their tall sails.

The LORD Almighty [lit. 'of hosts'] *has a day* of reckoning or judgment when all the proud who have rebelled against him and chosen their own way will be humbled. This day, commonly referred to as the Day of the LORD in other passages, is a day of God's judgment. His authority to judge is emphasized by the title *LORD Almighty*.

17–21. God will allow no rivals (v. 17). The sin of *pride* (*gabbût* [2x]; see 2:11) is developed in the book of Isaiah as human attempts to live out and control their lives without God. The warning that *the arrogance of man will be brought low and human pride humbled* is repeated four times in these two sections (2:9, 11, 12, 17), clearly bringing home the point that God alone *will be exalted*.

In that day (vv. 17, 20) refers to the day of reckoning mentioned in verse 12. The emphatic structure of verse 18 underscores that idols will no longer be present anywhere in Israel (lit. 'the idols completely pass away'). Verses 10, 19 and 21 are similar: those who were once lofty and proud will rightly flee to *caves*[3] and *holes* to escape the *fearful presence of the LORD* and *his majesty*. The phrase *when he rises to shake the earth* (vv. 19, 21) is a figurative expression meaning to cause humankind's foundations, the people and things upon which they have relied, to crumble. This 'shaking' also looks forward to the ultimate Day of the LORD (Rev. 6:12, 15–17).

Verses 19 and 21 flank verse 20 to form an *inclusio* that describes how people will abandon their *idols* (*'ĕlîlîm*, lit. 'worthless ones') in the Day of the LORD, having seen how insignificant they are compared to a sovereign God who can shake the earth. When the true God arises, idols will be thrown where they belong – to the *moles* (*laḥpōrpērôt*; occurs only here) and *bats* (*'ăṭallēpîm*, 3x; see Lev. 11:19).

22. Based upon this terrifying picture of the Day of the LORD, Yahweh says to *stop trusting in mere humans* whose death is only one breath away (lit. 'his breath is in his nose'). *Why hold them in esteem?* The prophet is challenging them to adjust their priorities. It is not through hope in humans that Israel will be secure nor their glorious future be accomplished, but through hope in the all-powerful God.

---

3. Israel has over 1,200 registered caves today.

Meaning

God uses images of high and lofty things to impress upon the Israelites that he has no equals – he can humble them all. When the Day of the LORD comes, humankind will clearly see the power and majesty of God and attempt to flee from him. The climax is reached when the prophet charges the Israelites to stop fearing humans whose next breath is uncertain, and rely instead upon God who controls the universe. There will be an awe-inspiring correction of power and authority when God takes his throne.

(3) A future time of anarchy (3:1–12)

Context

The structure of chapter 3 is one of the most difficult in the first part of Isaiah, leading to a wide variety of opinions on the matter. We suggest that the *kî*, 'for', beginning verse 1 is continued from the earlier chapters to introduce the third consequence of turning away from God: he will remove their *supply and support*. This passage continues the theme regarding the folly of trusting in human power and achievement. The first seven verses detail imminent future action, then verse 8 turns the focus onto Israel's present state.

Comment

1–3. *See* [*kî*, 'for'] *now, the Lord, the LORD Almighty, is about to take from Jerusalem and Judah both supply and support.* This sovereign Lord is Yahweh, *the LORD Almighty* (lit. 'hosts', 11x in Isaiah to emphasize his power). The details of God's judgment on Jerusalem and Judah (named in reverse order from the two earlier occurrences in 1:1 and 2:1) become more specific. Because of their sin (see 2:6–9), he is about to remove from Judah both *supply* and *support*.

The word *supply* (*maš'ēn*, occurs only in this verse) refers to *all supplies of food and . . . water* that sustain them. The word *support* (*maš'ēnâ*, occurs only here) refers to the backbone or supporting structure of the nation, including military, political and religious leaders, and even skilled artisans. The important point is that all customary sources of guidance and advice will no longer be available to the people, causing widespread confusion. It is interesting that there is no mention of a king.

God even removes *the diviner* (v. 2) and *clever enchanter* (often of 'those who charm snakes'; v. 3), those from whom the people sought guidance even though they were ungodly. This is exactly what the Assyrians and Babylonians did when they conquered a nation: they removed anyone who could pose a potential threat or cause a rebellion (see 2 Kgs 24:14–17).

4–5. The image here is of what is called a 'topsy turvy society' (*ANET* 441–445), wherein those who are unsuited rule over those more qualified. In a culture where age was thought to bring wisdom, honour and the ability to lead well (see Lev. 19:32), this nation will be governed by *youths* [*naʿar*] and *children* (lit. 'capricious, mischief-maker'). The word *naʿar* can range anywhere from about three months old (Exod. 2:6) to an adult male of about thirty years old (Jer. 1:6). The point is that these leaders will be inexperienced, fickle, inconsistent or worse – tyrannical and malicious.

Tyranny, emphasized in verse 5, will be just one portion of God's punishment; another part will be general upheaval or anarchy (lit. 'person against person'). People will be self-serving to the extent that they will oppress others to lay hold of what they want or need. Societal norms will be shattered: the *young* will usurp the *old*, and *the nobody* (*niqleh*, lit. 'one lightly thought of') will rise up *against the honoured* (*nikbād*; these two similar-sounding words are used for effect).

6–7. In the void left by those who have been removed from power, others with no particular qualifications will be coerced to rule, some for the most trivial of reasons – because the man has a *cloak* in which to make a public appearance. Williamson observes that the person with a *cloak* has managed to come through God's punishment with something of value, similar to 'the shirt off one's own back' (2006: 250); nevertheless, the emphasis is on his incompetence.

Verse 6 drips with irony: those coerced do not want to be in *charge* (lit. 'under your hand', a reference to power or authority) of a *heap of ruins* (*makšēlâ*, 2x; see Zeph. 1:3), nor do they have resources to remedy the situation (*I have no remedy. / I have no food or clothing in my house*, v. 7). Only God can provide restoration.

The *heap of ruins* could picture the Assyrian destruction of Israel in 722 BC, the later destruction of Judah (all but Jerusalem) in 701

BC, or the Babylonian destruction of Judah in 586 BC (though the last is less likely, since the conquering Babylonians chose Israel's next leaders).

8–9. The *kî* ('for', v. 8) introduces the fourth consequence of turning away from God: *Jerusalem* and *Judah* (same order as in v. 1) are *falling* and *have brought disaster upon themselves* (v. 9). The picture is that of a person who has fallen headlong and remains lying on the ground. The reason for this destruction will be obvious to all: *their words* [lit. 'tongue'] *and deeds* are against their God (lit. '[they have] rebelled against the eyes of his glory').

Verse 9 begins with *hakkārat* (occurs only here), which some have translated as *look* (i.e. some type of facial expression; NIV, NASB, ESV), from *kārâ* (uncertain meaning, but suggesting 'look, appearance'). However, it is more likely that *hakkārat* derives from the common north-west Semitic root *kārat*, 'to cut', and thus 'the cut' *on their faces testifies against them.* This may refer either to cuts made on their faces to appease Baal (see 1 Kgs 18:28) or to their mouths (i.e. the 'cut' of their faces) which visibly express their anger or distaste for Yahweh.

Either way the phrases *testifies against* (lit. 'answer against them') and *they parade* [lit. 'declare'] *their sin* are probably legal terms indicting them of sin. Jerusalem has shamelessly paraded her ungodliness, demonstrating her wilful rejection of Yahweh. *Woe to them!* (lit. 'to their souls') is most likely to be a reference to the leaders in verse 6 who deserve the fate that will befall them and have only themselves to blame (*they have brought disaster upon themselves*).

10–12. There is an abrupt change in the flow of thought in verse 10, which may be a common wisdom saying. It serves to confirm that God will not treat the righteous in the same way as the wicked, an idea that goes back at least as far as Abraham's discussion with God about Sodom and Gomorrah (Gen. 18:20–32).

Ungodliness and wickedness cannot go unpunished, but because God is just and fair there is still hope for the righteous. Even while punishing evildoers, God can protect the righteous ones: *it will be well* [lit. 'good'] *with them, / for they will enjoy* [lit. 'eat'] *the fruit of their deeds.* Similarly, the wicked will also receive the fruit of their wickedness – *they will be paid back / for what their hands have done* – which the author calls *disaster* (*rā'*, lit. 'evil, disaster').

Verse 12 further describes these evil leaders: (1) *youths oppress my people*; (2) *women rule over them*; (3) *your guides lead you astray*; and (4) *they turn you from the path*. Both *youths* (lit. 'to act like a child') and *women* were seen as inexperienced, thus as leaders they were prone to falling into excesses and abuses. The youths are said to *oppress* their people, a word generally used of a foreign nation lording it over a subservient nation. The phrase *women rule over them* suggests domination; here the author could be remembering the sad consequences of Athaliah's ruthless rule (2 Kgs 11:1–20).

A unique two-term combination is used for *path* (*wĕderek 'ōrĕḥōteykā*, lit. 'the direction of your path', v. 12b), referring to the godly paths that the people should walk in, as opposed to the ungodly leaders who were leading them astray (*tāʿâ*) and confusing them (*bālaʿ*). This same verb pairing is also found in 28:7.

Meaning
God will use the powerful Assyrian nation to remove any semblance of safety and order so that the people will learn that God is the only one in whom they should place their trust. They had foolishly sought protection by forming alliances with neighbouring nations that were often the means of their undoing. Safety comes only from having the almighty God on one's side.

God's long-suffering patience caused Israel to believe they would escape punishment. Their callousness towards sin led their leaders to sin boldly, not realizing that God holds leaders even more responsible when they lead their nation into sin. Yet God will differentiate between the righteous, who will be blessed, and the wicked, who will be punished.

(4) Yahweh pronounces judgment upon the leaders (3:13–15)

Context
The climax of verses 2:5 – 3:12 is now reached: God stands to judge the leaders who have so brutally and corruptly performed their responsibilities. He must call them to account (see Ps. 82).

Comment

13–15. Yahweh has been exceedingly patient, but it is now time for him to judge: he *takes his place in court* [lit. 'stands to contend'] and *rises to judge the people*. The term *people* (lit. 'peoples') often refers to multiple nations, but in this context is most likely to refer to specific groups of people within his nation. Serving as both prosecutor and judge, God declares his charges against the *elders* and *leaders*, terms that can refer to both religious and political leaders.

The first charge is weighty: they have *ruined* [lit. 'consumed'] *my vineyard* (v. 14b). God had chosen these leaders to watch over, protect and take care of his vineyard; instead they had trampled and destroyed it (see 5:1–7). Many people would have had first-hand knowledge of pruning and related work; here the vineyard represents the people God had been nurturing and pruning. This vineyard was destroyed by the very leaders God had appointed to care for it. The second, equally damaging charge is that *the plunder* [*gĕzēlâ*, typically taken in war but here from their own people] *from the poor is in your houses* (v. 14c). They had not even tried to hide it.

They had misused their offices to enrich themselves, plundering instead of protecting those who were poor and in need of assistance. Yahweh passionately questions the leaders (v. 15): What made them think they could treat God's people in such a manner? How could they be so cruel, *crushing my people* and *grinding the faces of the poor* [in the dirt] (see Prov. 22:22–23)? The imagery continues the vineyard theme, with people being crushed by their leaders as grapes are crushed for wine; but God never intended leaders to treat those under them in this way.

The verse ends with *declares the Lord, the Lᴏʀᴅ Almighty* (lit. 'of hosts'), the same title used in 3:1. This title emphasizes the fact that God alone, 'the sovereign of all the hosts', has every right to judge the leaders because he is the Lord of everything. There is an interesting overlap between God's speech and the prophet's: at the beginning of verse 13 the prophet speaks, then in the middle of verse 14 God speaks. This shift in person is not unusual in the prophetic books, particularly in Isaiah, who is clearly God's spokesperson and often speaks the very words of God.

Meaning
God will not tolerate such corruption and callousness from these
wicked leaders. The evidence is clear: the leaders have hoarded in
their houses plunder taken from the poor, who have been reduced
to abject poverty. The leaders have forgotten that it is God who
placed them in their positions and holds them responsible for how
they administer their offices. At the climax of this passage we see
God ready to judge and mete out punishment, a picture that
should deter us from letting greed and power take control of our
lives.

(5) Jerusalem's proud women are also under judgment (3:16 – 4:1)

Context
This section is commonly thought to be an independent oracle but
it fits the context well, mirroring the earlier oracle of judgment on
the men of Israel. This oracle of judgment upon the proud *women of
Zion* (lit. 'daughters of Zion' = the wealthy women of Jerusalem)
begins in 3:16 with God's accusation, followed by an explanation
given in the third person of what God intends to do.

Comment
    16–17. The designation *women of Zion* corresponds to the phrase
descendants of Jacob in 2:5. The proud attitude (*gābah*, 'to be high,
exalt') of these women of Israel, who were no better than the men
already mentioned, is described in four phrases. They went
(1) *walking along with outstretched necks* (a vivid picture of someone
trying to impress others); (2) *flirting* [*mĕśaqqĕrôt*, occurs only here]
with their eyes (suggestive of eye make-up and/or winking); (3) *strut-
ting along with swaying hips* [lit. 'mincing steps or tripping along']; and
(4) wearing *ornaments jingling* [*ʿākas*, occurs only here] *on their ankles.*
These women unabashedly used their looks, adornments and
suggestive movements to attract the attention of and exert influence over the leaders of society.
    The grammar of verses 16–17 indicates a cause-and-effect rela-
tionship between the two verses; in other words, their punishment
will be fitting. When people look at them, they will be appalled or
stunned. God will cause the women to be covered with *sores* (*śippaḥ*,

occurs only here) and will make *their scalps bald* (lit. 'their forehead')
– universal signs of disgrace and humiliation.

18–24. An extensive list of finery will be removed *in that day*:
bangles, *headbands* (occurs only here), *crescent necklaces* (see Judg. 8:21),
earrings, *bracelets* (occurs only here), *veils* (occurs only here), *head-
dresses*, and so on. The exact nature of some of the items is unknown,
but the context conveys that all were used to make the women
more attractive.

To highlight the severity of the punishment, five ghastly
reversals are cited, beginning in verse 24: *fragrance* is turned to
stench; a *sash* to *rope* (i.e. as a belt); *well-dressed hair* (*miqšeh*; initially
referred to fancy metal work [see Exod. 25:18], but later referred to
any type of artistry) to *baldness*; *fine clothing* (occurs only here) to
sackcloth; and *beauty* to *branding* (occurs only here). *Fragrance* refers
to resin from the balsam tree (a type of fir tree) which has a
delightful fresh scent that was used in ointments and healing
agents. Their smell, sores, bald spots and sackcloth will make
them repulsive to others.

The reading of the final phrase in verse 24 is problematic. The
NIV reads the word *kî* as *branding*; however, there are two difficulties
with this: (1) it requires a change in the word order of the phrase,
and (2) there are no other examples of the word with this meaning.
Either a word at the end of the phrase is missing (1QIsaᵃ reads
'shame'), or *kî* is used to summarize the previous list (i.e. all this
instead of beauty). Humiliation is a fitting outcome for those who
put their trust in the wealth and influence of people instead of in
God. Clements points out that these types of reversals would have
been commonly experienced by those taken into exile (1980a: 51).
The final blow will be the slaughter of their males in battle (v. 25),
leaving the women without protection and support.

25–26. The parallel units in verse 25 convey great devastation:
Your men will fall by the sword (a common figure of speech for battle);
even the nation's strong *warriors* will die in *battle*. The city *gates . . .
will lament* [*ʾānâ*] *and mourn* [*ʾābal*], two verbs very similar in meaning.
The reason for weeping is that the city is deserted. The term
'openings' is not the typical term for *gates*; it may be a more general
term for various types of openings to the city, or it may mean that
the walls themselves had openings in them.

Zion, although not mentioned by name in the Hebrew text, is probably pictured here as a woman weeping over her children who have been severely punished by God. Childlessness was a serious curse in the Ancient Near East, for children provided labour, protection and care of elderly parents, and kept the memory of departed parents alive after their deaths (see Ps. 127:3).

This punishment will cause great distress in the city. Under normal conditions the city's males would congregate around its gates, but these verses picture Jerusalem's gates as a young woman sitting and mourning the loss of her husband who has been killed.

4:1. The chapter division at 4:1 is unfortunate, this verse being better suited to the curses of chapter 3 than to the restoration of chapter 4 (even though the MT divides it here as well). Verse 1 is the natural outcome of the decimation of the male population described in 3:25–26: *in that day seven women / will take hold of one man. Seven* is not necessarily to be taken literally, but rather is a number that indicates the 'full' or 'complete' severity of the situation (see the curses in the Sefire treaty, *ANET* 659).

These women are in an appalling state. Driven to desperation by childlessness and/or widowhood, they *will take hold of one man*, asking only for marriage (*only let us be called by your name* suggests marriage) to remove any stigma associated with singleness and barrenness (see Williamson 2006: 229).

The women even waive the customary responsibility of the husband to provide the necessities of life, including *food* and *clothes* (see Exod. 21:10), pleading, *Take away our disgrace!* (lit. 'gather away our reproach'). The humiliation and desperate circumstances that the women of Israel will experience are a far cry from the pride and opulence to which they were once accustomed. Avoiding *disgrace* is a powerful motivator in many cultures.

Meaning

Just as we saw the male leaders of Israel brought low for having been corrupted by power and greed (2:5 – 3:12), so now the proud women of the nation will be similarly humiliated (3:16 – 4:1). All that the women took pride in – wealth, prosperity, beauty and extravagance – will be stripped away. In rags, bald and disfigured, these women will be destitute, having no husbands to remove their disgrace. God is no respecter of persons; both men and women will experience the consequences of their pride and corruption. God's punishments fit the crime; the things that they desired most will be removed.

(6) A future glorification of Jerusalem; **SEAM** (4:2–6)

Context

This section is positioned at the end of an *inclusio* pattern in which a unit that describes the sinful state of the nation lies between and in striking contrast to two descriptions of a glorious future for a believing remnant of God's people (2:1–4; 4:2–6). Its content is a theological reflection upon the passage just prior that describes Israel's sad condition: if God, who is just and righteous, has a plan for his people, then he must purge the nation so that they can be restored to their proper standing. Its overall style is not poetic, as some have suggested, even though there are several parallel phrases in the unit.

While the passage is eschatological in nature, it does not contain apocalyptic elements that would later appear (e.g. the destruction of the present world order and the setting up of a new). Thus, it is not the failed hopes of the post-exilic period that provide the context for the righteous kingdom that God will set up; it is instead the purging of Israel's wickedness highlighted in chapters 1–4.

Isaiah 4:2–6 is another seam with the same elements as the earlier seam in 1:27–31: (1) Israel will be judged (4:4); (2) a remnant will be saved (4:2–3); (3) the wicked will be punished (4:4); and (4) Zion will be delivered (4:4–6). This seam prepares us for the next section (Isa. 13 – 39) in that God will not only purge Israel and bring from them a believing remnant, but the nations will also be drawn to Israel's God, and a believing remnant will arise from them as well (see esp. 19:24–25).

Comment

2. The phrase *in that day* corresponds to some future time period which is more clearly specified by the phrase *in the last days* (2:2). The final outcome for Jerusalem is not only purging, but deliverance and transformation into a glorious city, as mentioned in Isaiah 1. *In* *that* [future] *day the Branch* [*ṣemaḥ*, 'sprout, growth'] *of the LORD will be beautiful and glorious* (v. 2a).

The Targum of this passage interprets the 'branch' as the Messiah; however, in this context the phrase *the Branch of the LORD* is parallel to the next phrase, *the fruit of the land*. Read in a literal sense, the 'branch' conveys the bountifulness of the produce that the remnant from Israel will enjoy during this time of deliverance (see Williamson 2006: 306–309). Or it may be understood in a metaphorical sense, where *the fruit of the land* (or earth) is a remnant gathered from the nations of the earth that will bring *pride and glory* to a remnant from Israel; that is, this remnant gathered from the nations will be brought to Israel to enhance the number of its *survivors* (lit. 'the escaped ones').

3–4. The phrase *those who are left in Zion* and its parallel phrase refer to those who will remain after the nation undergoes major cleansing of sin. These people will finally demonstrate the character of their God (Lev. 19:2) and *will be called holy* (v. 3). The ones God has chosen to deliver will be *recorded among the living* [better translated as 'recorded for life'] *in Jerusalem*.

Verse 4 describes the cleansing implied in verse 3, after which God will come and dwell on Mount Zion. While there will indeed be several lesser purgings throughout the history of Israel (e.g. 701 BC and 586 BC), this verse speaks of an ultimate cleansing of *the filth of the women of Zion* (v. 4) which will culminate in the arrival of God's presence; it is thus an eschatological statement of what will happen only in the last days.

The filth [*ṣō'â*, 'excrement' (see 36:12) or 'vomit' (see 28:8)] *of the women of Zion* could refer back to 3:16 – 4:1; the word *bloodstains* (lit. 'bloodshed' [pl.]) would then refer to the sin of the leaders mentioned in 2:5 – 3:12. However this phrase is to be understood, Zion is purged by *a spirit of judgment and a spirit of fire* (v. 4). Both are necessary: God's justice demands that judgment be poured out because of their sin, and fire pictures the cleansing that results. God's power will perform the cleansing (i.e. 'the spirit of judgment and the spirit of fire').

5–6. This thorough cleansing now allows for God's presence to be manifested within Jerusalem itself. *The LORD will create over all* [lit.

'over the whole site'] *of Mount Zion . . . a cloud of smoke . . . and a glow of flaming fire* – terms that indicate God's presence that are reminiscent of the exodus (see Exod. 13:21–22). However, unlike in the exodus, these appear to be permanent symbols of God's protection of Zion.

The word 'assembly' is used in the Pentateuch twenty times to refer to a holy gathering or convocation where sacrifices and offerings are made before the LORD. The conditions of daily life in this restored Jerusalem are radically different, with Yahweh providing protection from all danger. A *canopy* (*ḥuppâ* [a term used for the covering in a modern Jewish wedding], v. 5) and a *shelter* (v. 6) will cover Zion to protect its inhabitants from the elements – *heat* and *rain*. Verse 6 echoes Psalm 91:1: those who abide 'in the shelter of the Most High' have nothing to fear.

Meaning
This section portrays God's glorious plan for Israel. During Isaiah's time the nation was not living up to the great privileges they had been given. The good news is that one day God will purify the nation and a righteous remnant will emerge to live in Zion, which will be ruled and protected by God. As mentioned in chapter 2, we believe that this time of cleansing and restoration is best suited to the millennial reign of Christ (Rev. 20:1–7), as suggested by G. E. Ladd (1959).

One of God's goals for Israel was that they would live in such a way that other nations who looked upon them would be drawn to the God who protected and watched over them (see Exod. 19:5–6). However, because of Israel's sin, God continued to pour out judgment and punishment upon them. As a result, few nations were drawn to a God who continually punished his people. Yet there is hope. Pictured in this section is a time when Israel will fulfil their initial calling as a light to the nations, so much so that nations will stream to Zion to hear about their God. This restoration will not be achieved in Israel's near future but will be realized *in the last days*.

ii. God's plan for restoring his people (Isa. 5:1 – 12:6)

Context

The dating and structure of this section (chs. 5–12) have been much debated, but it is our view that these chapters form a palistrophe that describes more fully God's plan for the nation of Israel (see Figure 0.8 on p. 20). The nation will undergo a series of purgings and deliverances which will then result in a final restoration.

Right at the heart of this structure is the so-called *Denkschrift* (or Isaianic memoir, 6:1 – 9:7), a classic view that came on the scene as early as K. Budde (1928). This section is primarily a first-person account, except for chapter 7 which reads like a historical annal (possibly written by Isaiah when he was a scribe for Uzziah; see 2 Chr. 26:22) that recounts events from the Syro-Ephraimite War (733–732 BC) to 701 BC. While some have since questioned the *Denkschrift* theory, we consider it the focal point of the palistrophe, serving to lay out the rationale of God's plan for the nation, as well as Isaiah's call to inform the nation of that plan.

When Isaiah asks *how long* the nation will be blind and deaf (6:11) to this message, God responds that it will be until the cities are destroyed and the land is left uninhabited. He further explains that there will be two destructions, giving rise to a 'holy seed' (i.e. a righteous remnant).

a. The Song of the Vineyard (5:1–7)

Context

This song is a carefully constructed judicial parable that would have resonated strongly with its readers, who were familiar with vineyards and the disappointment of a poor yield. It draws the listeners in and excites their sympathy for the frustrated vineyard owner (e.g. the author uses the Hebrew *na'* particle of entreaty ['I pray, now'] three times: vv. 1, 3, 5). In an unexpected twist at the end, the verdict is levelled against the listeners, who are accused of being the 'villains' of the song.

Comment

1. The *song* is preceded by a brief introduction that provides a setting (v. 1a) and introduces the singer as someone who knows the vineyard owner intimately, calling him *my loved one* (i.e. 'close friend' in this context). The vineyard is planted on a *fertile hillside* (lit. 'a horn of a son of fatness'; only instance where 'horn' is used figuratively of a hillside projecting from the earth). Hillsides were often terraced and planted with vineyards or other crops. The word *fertile* (lit. 'son of fatness [oil]') suggests it is 'oozing' with productivity.

2–3. Sparing no expense to provide everything needed to produce a bumper crop, the owner of the vineyard (1) chose *a fertile hillside*; (2) *dug it up* ('*āzaq*, occurs only here); (3) *cleared it of stones*; (4) *planted it with the choicest vines* (*śōrēq*); (5) *built a watchtower* for protection; (6) *and* [lit. 'and even'] *cut out a winepress* for wine production (two troughs of rock connected by a channel or pipe served as wine vats; juice from grapes crushed in the upper trough ran down into the lower trough). The words 'and even' suggest the wine vat was extravagant, in that shared winepresses were probably more common.

The word *śōrēq* (2x) means a choice plant and may refer to either a rich red colour, or to an area such as the Sorek Valley, known for good vines. After investing so much of his time and resources, the owner is sorely disappointed when the vineyard produces only worthless, sour grapes (*bĕ'ušîm* [2x]) or 'rotten, stinking' grapes (from *bā'aš*).

The words 'and now' (v. 3) mark a shift as the song takes on a legal character and the vineyard owner now speaks for himself. The readers become active participants in judging the case of the errant vineyard, similar to when the elders of a city were called upon to settle a dispute (see Deut. 22:15–18). After hearing the evidence presented by the owner, he asks them *to judge between me and my vineyard* and then adds, *What more could have been done for my vineyard . . . ?* (v. 4).

4–6. The author helps his listeners to empathize with the anger and frustration of the vineyard owner. Surely the owner is not to blame for the sad condition of the vineyard; the blame must lie with the vineyard itself. The second 'and now' (v. 5) signals that a decision has been reached. It is the owner's prerogative to decide its fate, for he is the one who has invested all the time, money and energy (i.e. similar to God who had taken the initiative to call Israel as his people and provide for them).

Judgment begins almost immediately with the removal of protection: *I will take away its hedge* and *break down* (an infinitive, suggesting continual or repetitive action) the stone wall so that *it will be trampled*. The word *hedge* (*mĕśukkâ*, occurs only here) is possibly a type of thornbush. By removing it and the wall, sheep and goats could enter to trample and devour (*bāʿēr*) the vineyard, turning it into a *wasteland* (v. 6; *bātâ*, occurs only here) fit only for *briers and thorns*, a phrase consistently used in the book of Isaiah to designate a useless, wasted area (see 7:23–25). At the peak of his wrath, the vineyard owner commands *the clouds / not to rain* on the vineyard (v. 6b), a curse that is either a simple expression of his anger or a hint that this is no ordinary vineyard owner.

7. In the chiasm of verse 7 the judgment takes a sudden turn (beginning with *kî*, 'for') when we learn the identities of the vineyard owner and the vineyard:

> A [For] *the vineyard of the* LORD *Almighty*
>   B *is the nation of Israel*
>   B' *and the people of Judah*
> A' *are the vines he delighted in.*

The poem ends with two startling wordplays featuring pairs of similar-sounding words. God waited for *justice* (*mišpāṭ*) as a farmer waits for a bountiful crop, but 'behold', he found *bloodshed* (*miśpāḥ*, occurs only here) instead (see Wildberger 1991: 172–173). In the parallel unit he waited for *righteousness* (*ṣĕdāqâ*) but instead found *cries of distress* (*ṣĕʿāqâ*).

The song was intended to entrap the listeners. Just as Nathan's parable led King David to unwittingly condemn himself (2 Sam. 12:1–10), so any objective listener to this song would say that the owner was fully justified in destroying the vineyard. The woe oracles that follow in the rest of the chapter are the direct outcome of the promised judgment on the vineyard.

Meaning

This song compellingly pictures Israel's condition: God had given his chosen people (i.e. the *vineyard*) preferential treatment, yet they still rebelled against him (i.e. yielding the *bad fruit* of *bloodshed* instead of *justice*, and *cries of distress* instead of *righteousness*). In a matter of a few centuries Israel had gone from a mighty nation led by godly King David to a divided nation led by the weak and ungodly King Ahaz. Sorely disappointed, God would withdraw his protection from Judah and allow them to be trampled and destroyed by the Gentiles. The parable is intended to awaken Israel to their terrible predicament (similar to Matt. 21:33–46).

b. Six woe oracles announced upon his nation (5:8–23)

Context

During the reigns of Jeroboam II (793–753 BC) in Israel and Uzziah (792/791–739 BC) in Judah, both nations experienced significant growth and prosperity which led to the moral decay described in Isaiah 5. However, with the ascension of Tiglath-pileser III (745–727 BC) to the Assyrian throne, this prosperity came to an end.

The second unit of the palistrophe describes the punishment that God will pour out on his nation. These 'worthless grapes' chose to pursue greed (vv. 8–10), debauchery (vv. 11–17), arrogance (vv. 18–19), perversion (vv. 20–21), injustice (vv. 22–23), and so on, instead of following God. Yahweh will go to extreme measures to eventually bring the nation back to himself, but in the short term they would be ineffective.

A woe oracle generally announces judgment (Oswalt suggests that it combines a lament and a threat, 1986: 157) upon a person or nation. The woe oracles here are reminiscent of the rebellious child in 1:5–6 who continues to receive punishment but does not know why or how to make it stop (see woe oracles in Amos 5:18–24; 6:1–8).

Comment

(1) Woe to those who buy up houses and land (5:8–10)

8–10. This *woe* refers to those who had accumulated large cultivated estates by absorbing neighbouring property (lit. 'touching house to house and field to field'). These rich landowners had acquired so much land, often through unjust means (see Mic. 2:1–5), that their nearest neighbours were far away. It was almost as if they lived *alone in the land* (lit. 'so that *you* are caused to *live alone*'; implied is that this loneliness is a judgment from God, v. 8). The land was to be evenly divided among the tribes (see Num. 33:54) so that each person could make a living; land rights were to be returned to the original owners in the Year of Jubilee (see Lev. 25:23–28). Thus, God's people were to view themselves as temporary tenants of the true landowner, the LORD Almighty.

Verse 9 emphatically declares with an oath the judgment to be poured out on these wealthy landowners: their fine houses will be abandoned, something that came to pass when wealthy landowners were exiled during the Assyrian and later the Babylonian captivity. The judgment continues in verse 10 with an exceptionally scant harvest: (1) a *ten-acre vineyard* (lit. 'a ten-team vineyard', perhaps the amount of land that ten pairs of oxen could plough in a day) will yield only *a bath* [approximately 22 litres] *of wine*; and (2) *a homer* [about 6 bushels][4] *of seed* will yield *only an ephah* [approximately two-thirds of a bushel] *of grain*. Those who tend the land will not be able to survive long on such meagre returns, a sure sign that God has removed his blessing (see Lev. 26:14–20).

(2) Woe to those who love pleasure and drink (5:11–17)

11–12. The second *woe* oracle is directed against the wealthy, whose lifestyle of luxuriant feasting at the expense of the poor was an affront to God. They spent their days becoming intoxicated (lit. 'pursuing strong drink'), drinking from *early in the morning* (i.e. this was unheard of; see Acts 2:15) till *late at night*. A wordplay in verse

---

4. A homer was originally the volume of grain that a donkey could carry (Williamson 2006: 355).

11 indicates how difficult it would be to extricate themselves from this lifestyle: initially they 'pursued' (NIV *run after*) strong drink, but now *wine* 'pursues hotly after' (NIV *inflamed with*) them. Both alcohol and self-indulgence have deadened their spiritual sensitivity. As their desire for pleasure increases, their need and passion for God diminishes: *but they have no regard for the deeds of the LORD*. Unfortunately, becoming oblivious to God's actions is as easy for us today as it was for the Israelites.

13–14. *Therefore* signals the logical result of turning from God and not heeding his guidelines: the *people will go into exile* because of their *lack of understanding*. The consequence of disobedience according to Leviticus 20:22 is that the land will 'vomit [them] out'.

The latter part of verse 13 is less clear: *those of high rank will die of hunger* (lit. 'its glory [is] men of famine'). Oswalt alters 'men' (*mĕtê*) to 'wasted' (*mĕzê*; see Deut. 32:24), translating the phrase as 'wasted with famine' (1986: 156). It is preferable, however, to read the phrase 'men of famine' (*mĕtê rāʿāb*) as 'are dying of famine' (*mĕtê rāʿāb* = the participle of *mût* with only a vowel change), following the versions and 1QIsaᵃ. The parallel units are then translated as *those of high rank will die* [lit. 'are dying'] *of hunger / and the common people will be parched with thirst*. Hunger and thirst are common images of privation, but here the two may signify a lack of spiritual sustenance which the first part of the verse suggests. There is a direct cause-and-effect relationship between verses 11–12 and verse 13: because they have missed God's warnings, they will be carried off into captivity.

In verse 14 this thorough destruction is pictured as a personified Sheol (i.e. the place of the dead in the OT) expanding *its jaws* (lit. 'its soul') and *opening wide* [lit. 'without limit'] *its mouth*, this last phrase conveying the thoroughness of this destruction. The joy and merriment of all Jerusalem's inhabitants, its *nobles* [lit. 'her splendour'] *and masses*, *brawlers* [lit. 'uproar'] *and revellers* (lit. 'the jubilant [ʿālēz, occurs only here] within her'), will soon be forgotten in the caverns of Sheol.

15–17. The nation will be *humbled* and all its inhabitants put on an equal footing, using the terms *ʾādām*, 'mankind' (all humanity), and *ʾîš*, 'man' (specific human), to convey its comprehensiveness (see 2:9, 11, 17). This humbling did in fact happen as a result of major attacks by the Assyrians and the Babylonians.

The conjunction beginning verse 16 marks a clear contrast between verses 15 and 16. God will punish these wicked people and thereby prove himself to be a *holy* and *righteous* judge – thus the statement *the* LORD *Almighty will be exalted by his justice* (v. 16). The exiles of Samaria in 722 BC and Jerusalem in 587 BC did not demonstrate the powerlessness of God, but rather his holiness and righteousness.

Following these exiles, the sheep of nomads will eat *as in their own pasture* (*kĕdobrām*, 2x; see Mic. 2:12), the implication being that they are making themselves at home in Israel while the Israelites are in exile. However, the parallel phrase, *lambs will feed among the ruins of the rich*, is more difficult to translate. We suggest reading the phrase *mēḥîm* [2x; see Ps. 66:15] *gārîm* as two nouns in apposition (i.e. 'foreigners' fatlings', Williams §70), thus the reading 'foreigners' fatlings will feed among the ruins'; this has the fewest emendations, maintains parallelism with the prior phrase, and creates a chiastic structure.

(3) Woe to those who are deceived by lies (5:18–19)

18–19. The third *woe* is directed against the shameless mockers who are so entangled by their sins that they drag them along wherever they go. The words 'iniquity' and 'sin' are a common word pair in the book of Isaiah (see 6:7): *woe to those who draw sin* [lit. 'the iniquity'] *along with cords of deceit* [*šāwĕ*, 'emptiness, vanity, worthless'], / *and wickedness* [lit. 'sin'] *as with* [lit. 'the'] *cart ropes* (v. 18). Roberts observes that Isaiah's audience 'puts more strenuous effort into sinning than most people put into honest work' (2015: 82).

The people boldly ridicule Isaiah's prophecy, repeatedly challenging God to act: *let him hasten his work*; *the plan of the Holy One of Israel –* / *let it approach* (i.e. draw near). Their contemptuous use of the epithet for God *the Holy One of Israel* shows how mistaken they are concerning his character. They are convinced of the inviolability of Jerusalem and wilfully disregard Isaiah's warnings concerning God's judgment.

Isaiah ironically turns the word pair *see* (*rā'â*) and *know* (*yāda'*) of their mocking challenges against them in 6:9: *be ever seeing* [*rā'â*], *but never perceiving* [*yāda'*]. The three woe oracles that follow are effectually Isaiah's response to their taunt.

(4) Woe to those who pervert the truth (5:20)

20. The fourth *woe* is addressed to those who in effect were rewriting God's moral code: *to those who call evil good / and good evil*. The three polar-opposite word pairs – *evil/good; darkness/light; bitter/sweet* – convey how far the people had turned from God's standards. Not content merely to remain wicked, they seek to justify themselves by convincing others to follow in their wickedness, stating that God's commands are evil, while the sin they want to do is good. Redefining sin to make it more palatable is still with us today.

(5) Woe to those who consider themselves clever (5:21)

21. The fifth *woe*, flowing from verse 20, is directed against those who rely upon their own wisdom (*are wise in their own eyes*) to circumvent God's punishments. Believing the governmental policies which they pursue so vigorously to be a sign of great skill and wisdom, they will discover too late that they are not as clever as they had supposed. The author turns the common word pair 'wise ones' and *bîn*, 'to discern', into an accusation: they are only *wise in their own eyes / and clever* [*bîn*] *in their own sight* (lit. 'before their faces'), the implication being that they have neither true wisdom nor insight.

(6) Woe to drunkards and swindlers (5:22–23)

22–23. The sixth *woe* is directed against unjust leaders. The terms *heroes* and *champions*, generally used of military leaders, are applied to those who excel at *drinking wine* or *mixing drinks*. The drinks were not mixed with water, as was common in the Ancient Near East, but with spices or other, more potent alcoholic beverages.

Excessive drinking both blunts their sense of justice and heightens their need for money, thus they *acquit the guilty for a bribe* and *deny justice to the innocent* (lit. 'they turn aside the righteousness of the righteous ones'). Kaiser points out that 'Nothing shakes the confidence in state and society more deeply than the public corruption of justice and the removal of the certainty of fair treatment' (1983: 102–103). It is no wonder that God's *vineyard* is full of 'sour grapes': the leaders have used their positions to corrupt the nation.

Meaning
It is incredible how low the nation of Israel had already sunk by the
end of the eighth century BC. Warning after warning had done little
to put them on a path of repentance. But God loves his people too
much to let them continue in sin (see Heb. 12:6); he therefore will
apply more pressure in the next section, warning of even more
severe punishment.

c. Judgment is coming: uplifted-hand oracle (5:24–30)

Context
Chapter 5 opened with the Song of the Vineyard (5:1–7) describing
Israel as *bad fruit*, followed by the woes that are pronounced upon
them (5:8–23). Here in 5:24–30 the description of punishment is
even more explicit.

Verses 24–30 form an 'uplifted-hand oracle' (a type of oracle
found only in Isaiah): since Israel has not yet responded with
repentance to the punishments God has already sent, he warns that
his hand is still stretched out, ready to come down with continued
punishment. This refrain, appearing in 9:12, 17, 21; 10:4, serves to
mark parallel units in the palistrophic pattern (see Figure 0.8 on p.
20). The transitional verse 24 links verses 8–23 to 25–30 by
summarizing the resulting judgments (*therefore*) of verses 8–23 and
declaring the reason for the continued judgments in verses 25–30.

Comment
24. The word *therefore* signals the consequence of the behaviour
described in the oracle which precedes. Their punishment is illustrated in two ways: (1) *fire* (lit. 'a tongue of fire' [phrase occurs only
here]) that instantly and thoroughly consumes stubble and chaff
(*ḥăšaš*, 2x; see 33:11); and (2) rottenness (*māq*, 2x; 3:24) that destroys
both the roots and the flower of a plant (i.e. a merism to describe
the whole plant). The parallel units in the last half of the verse link
their punishment to their disdainful rejection of God's laws.

25. This second *therefore* further clarifies the results of their
continued disobedience, which had already brought down one
wave of suffering as a consequence (possibly the Syro-Ephraimite
War). In spite of this (v. 25), Israel continued to reject God's laws.

God's hand therefore remains ready to come down again in punishment: *his anger is not turned away, / his hand is still upraised* (v. 25b). The imagery of mountains quaking and bodies lying strewn about *like refuse* [*sûḥâ*, occurs only here] *in the streets* (lit. 'open spaces') could be the consequence of war, famine or even an earthquake.

26. Despite punishment, Israel still refused to repent. Yahweh therefore raises a *banner* (*nēs*, 'standard') to signal to Assyria (*distant nations*) to continue Judah's punishment. Having risen to world dominance in the eighth century BC, the Assyrians were a ruthless and effective tool in God's hands. The Assyrian army comprised many nations, utilizing in wartime both mercenaries and conscripted soldiers from conquered nations. This they did in both 722 and 701 BC.

As great and ruthless as Assyria was, we see that God merely *whistles* and they come, their speed emphasized by the adjectives *swiftly* and *speedily*. This image of the LORD sovereignly controlling the movements of nations is a key theme in the book of Isaiah (see the Oracles against the Nations). The Assyrians would travel over five hundred miles to reach Judah; yet they would be eager to do so, as they were already in the process of expanding their empire in that direction.

27–29. These verses provide a vivid description of the fierceness and strength of the professional, well-trained Assyrian army: *not one of them grows tired . . . [nor] slumbers . . . [nor is] a sandal strap . . . broken. / Their arrows are sharp, / all their bows are strung.* Unpreparedness in any one of these areas could prove fatal in warfare; the Assyrians are indeed ready for combat. By contrast, Israel's force was largely an untrained militia called upon to serve in time of war.

Assyria's horses and chariots allowed them to descend upon their enemies quickly. Their horses' hooves, hard as *flint*, would not only be able to withstand the journey but could trample soldiers in battle. Their chariot wheels spun as fast as a *whirlwind*. The image of lions (v. 29) carrying off their prey is an apt portrayal of Assyria, which was well known for deporting peoples who rebelled or refused to pay tribute.

30. The destructive power of the Assyrian army is pictured in figurative terms. It covers the land, *roaring* like *the sea* and bringing *darkness and distress*. There is also a literal aspect to this imagery:

their movement would cause considerable noise and their massive army would kick up dust clouds as it descended upon Jerusalem; and after the attack, the sky would be *darkened* by smoke (*'ărîpîm*, 'clouds of smoke', occurs only here) from the burning city, even in bright daylight. According to verses 29–30, the wealth and glory that Israel once enjoyed would now be gone.

Meaning

This uplifted-hand oracle is important to the entire book of Isaiah. In it we see God's remarkable forbearance and patience towards Israel, having given them multiple warnings and ample time to return to him; yet they refuse and wilfully continue in their disobedience. When he does punish them, it is calculated and with a view towards their redemption. Yahweh is indeed a gracious God.

d. Isaianic memoir: God calls his prophet for Judah (6:1 – 9:7)

Scholars have suggested that Isaiah 6:1 – 9:7 constitutes Isaiah's *Denkschrift* or 'memoir' since much of its material is written in the first person singular (see 6:1, 5; etc.) and refers to the last part of the eighth century BC when Isaiah, according to the biblical material, conducted his ministry (see Figure 0.8 on p. 20). The third-person forms in chapter 7 may reflect material taken from a royal annal, possibly written, or at least collected, by Isaiah himself; what appear to be later additions are indeed Isaiah's further prophetic elaborations of these events.

These questions aside, Isaiah 6:1 – 9:7 is undoubtedly the centre of the palistrophe of Isaiah 5 – 12. Just as Isaiah 1 and 2 – 4 inform readers that God will orchestrate a stunning restoration of the nation of Israel, so we learn here that God will use Isaiah to bring a message of deliverance and an exhortation to obey God in hopes of averting the coming judgment.

(1) Isaiah's call and commission (6:1–13)

Context

Historically, this chapter is at a crucial turning point in the life of the nation of Judah. Under the long reign of Uzziah (*c.*792/791– 739 BC), the nation had prospered, but by the time of Ahaz (*c.*735–715 BC) the country had become an Assyrian vassal. Morally and politically the nation had experienced a deplorable decline. God sends Isaiah at this difficult time as a prophetic voice to the nation.

In chapter 6 Isaiah receives his call and commission that serves as the foundation for the rest of the Isaianic memoir (see Figure 6.1).

PERSON	REFERENCE	ELEMENTS
Moses	Exod. 3:1 – 4:17	1. Call
Joshua	Josh. 1	2. Reasons for refusal
Isaiah	Isa. 6	3. Reasons overcome (sometimes by a sign)
Jeremiah	Jer. 1:4–19	4. Commissioned as God's spokesman
Ezekiel	Ezek. 1 – 3	

Figure 6.1   Call narratives

The call narrative of Isaiah 6 also contains elements of a judgment oracle. God again informs Isaiah of grim punishments that are on the horizon for the nation of Israel: the northern kingdom would be exiled to Assyria during Isaiah's lifetime, and the southern kingdom would be severely subdued by the Assyrians in 701 BC. Most call narratives appear early in the book; however, the placement of Isaiah's call in chapter 6 is more a function of its message and the palistrophe – the prophet Isaiah's call is right at the heart of the palistrophe and he will be part of God's plan to ultimately bring Israel back to God.

Comment

  1. Isaiah's call is dated to *the year that King Uzziah died* (about 739 BC). Isaiah saw his vision of the true king at an important transition time of human kingship (from Uzziah to Jotham). Uzziah had been a strong and able king throughout most of his lifetime, but indiscretion towards the end of his life cost him dearly (2 Chr. 26:19). God's punishment was a forceful reminder that he is the true king.

  The names for God (*the Lord*, v. 1; *the LORD Almighty*, lit. 'Lord of hosts', vv. 3, 5) and the vision of God *seated on a throne, high and exalted* (vv. 1b–4), emphasize his royal authority and power, as the true sovereign over all creation.

The train of his robe filled the temple, though it is uncertain whether God's royal garments filled the heavenly temple or stretched down to the earthly temple (the latter makes a nice connection to God's sovereignty over this earth). Two terms for the temple are used here: *hahêkāl* ('the temple', v. 1) and *habbayit* ('the house', v. 4); both are common terms for God's dwelling place.

This is one of the rare glimpses into heaven in the Old Testament (see Job 1 – 2 [uncertain location, but assumed to be heaven]; 1 Kgs 22:19–23; Zech. 3). It is interesting that in this scene a throne rather than the ark (see Num. 7:89) represents the seat of God's presence, yet the term 'throne' better pictures God's sovereignty.

2–3. Yahweh is attended by at least two *seraphim* (lit. 'burning ones'; see *ANEP* 212–213, 358) who are standing *above him* (if God is seated, the seraphim would indeed be standing above him) and praising him antiphonally (lit. 'and this called to this'). They continually announce God's holiness (the threefold repetition suggests completeness or emphasis), which is precisely what God wanted Isaiah to understand. God's very nature is holiness, and he expects his people to be holy (see Lev. 19:2). Holiness refers to his separateness from evil, a characteristic of God emphasized in the book of Isaiah. God's laws set the standard for what holiness is.

God's glory fills the *whole earth*; creation itself demonstrates God's glory (see Ps. 19:1), and part of that glory is his holiness, which people can mirror only to a small degree (see v. 5). God's glory will also be demonstrated in his judgment of Israel: because he is holy he will not allow Israel's wickedness to go unpunished.

Even the details regarding the seraphim's use of their *six wings* is insightful (see Rev. 4:8). *With two wings they covered their faces* suggests that even angelic beings who reside in heaven are not worthy to gaze upon God's holiness (see Exod. 33:18–23). *With two they covered their feet⁵* most probably means that their whole bodies were covered for modesty.

---

5. *Feet* may be a euphemism for genitals (1 Sam. 24:3; Isa. 7:20) or synecdoche, in which a part stands for the whole.

4–5. The collective voices of the seraphim caused the *doorposts and thresholds* (lit. 'the sockets of the thresholds') of the temple to shake as it *filled with smoke*, a common representation of God's presence (see 1 Kgs 8:10–13). Isaiah gets to see an entirely different dimension of reality: God's perspective.

As God's presence fills the temple, Isaiah is overawed by his glory and, in recognition of his own unworthiness, utters *Woe to me! . . . I am ruined!* (lit. 'I am silenced [struck dumb]'). He is also acutely aware of his unholiness in the presence of a perfectly holy God and exclaims, *I am a man of unclean lips, and I live among a people of unclean lips.* This is not only an admission of general sinfulness, but also suggests that Isaiah feels unfit to use his mouth for God's purposes, in contrast to the seraphim who were able to declare God's glory. We, too, should feel the same depth of unworthiness when we get a true picture of who God is.

6–7. Isaiah feels the hopelessness of his situation, but in grace God sends *one of the seraphim . . . with a live coal* (*rispâ*, once with this meaning; see masculine form in 1 Kgs 19:6) taken *from the altar* to cleanse Isaiah's lips. The searing hot charcoal, carried in *tongs* (*melqāḥayim*, 6x; see 2 Chr. 4:21) to Isaiah, symbolizes cleansing, just as fire and burning do elsewhere in the book (see 4:4). Isaiah's *guilt* (lit. 'iniquity') is *taken away* and his *sin* is *atoned for* (*kipper*, 'covered'). Notice that it took something from the very presence of God to cleanse Isaiah's lips; surely this symbolizes total cleansing. His sin was an obstruction, but once cleansed he was free to be the messenger God needed. Isaiah never lost that perspective of speaking for God.

8–10. Finally, the LORD speaks, enquiring for a messenger: *Who will go for us?* The plural pronoun for God appears three other times in the Old Testament (Gen. 1:26; 3:22; 11:7; see Figure 6.2). In this context God appears to be speaking to the angels, whom he regularly sends to do his bidding (see Ps. 103:20). Notice that God (*I*) does the sending, but Isaiah is being sent for all of them (i.e. angels).

Isaiah can volunteer for this important but difficult job. He is better qualified for this role than the angels because he lives among the Israelites and can continually inform and remind them of God's messages. Isaiah's eager willingness to be a spokesperson for God is seen in his quick response, *Here am I. Send me!* (lit. 'behold me').

This plural form has been explained in a variety of ways:
1. **Divine plurality:** God is speaking to other members of the Trinity.
2. **Heavenly court:** God is speaking to the angels.
3. **Plural of majesty:** God is too great to be spoken of in the singular, thus the plural is used.
4. **Grammatical plural:** since Lord (*'ădōnāy*) is plural, grammatically it must take a plural.
5. **Plural of deliberation:** God deliberating within himself.

Figure 6.2 Plural pronouns for God

God's command to Isaiah to *tell this people* lacks the warmth of 'tell *my* people' and hints that their hearts were already partially hardened. Isaiah's message will actually further harden their hearts: *Be ever hearing* [lit. 'continue to hear'], *but never understanding* [lit. 'but you will not understand', temporary prohibition]; / *be ever seeing* [lit. 'continue to see'], *but never perceiving* [lit. 'but you will not perceive', temporary prohibition]. The meaning here is not that they will never understand, but only that they will not understand at the time they hear Isaiah's message. God's message to Isaiah highlights the contrasts between Isaiah's message and its outcome in the palistrophic pattern of verses 9–10:

Be ever hearing,
         but never understanding;
be ever seeing,
         but never perceiving.
    A *Make the heart of this people calloused;*
      B *make their ears dull*
        C *and close their eyes.*
      Otherwise
        C' *they might see with their eyes,*
      B' *hear with their ears,*
    A' *understand with their hearts,*
and turn, and be healed.

Even though God desires their repentance, he does not force his will upon anyone. In this case, Israel's sin will lead them away from, not towards, him. Just as God used Pharaoh, who had hardened his heart against God, to show his power and have his name 'proclaimed in all the earth' (Exod. 9:16), so too Israel's hard-heartedness will serve a purpose for a time until some finally turn back to him.

11–12. Unable to accept that this message of hardening is God's final word, Isaiah asks, *For how long?* The question demonstrates the prophet's care for his people. God responds, *Until the cities lie ruined / and without inhabitant.* Their hardness of heart would cause Israel to be exiled from the land (see Deut. 29:25–28). This was fulfilled in 722 BC for the northern kingdom and in 586 BC for the southern kingdom.

13. Here at the end of chapter 6 we see the fulfilment of the Song of the Vineyard wherein God removes the protective hedge and the vineyard is destroyed. Verse 13 details the sequence of this destruction. After the first destruction, *a tenth remains in the land*; this corresponds to Judah (i.e. the one tribe remaining in the land after the northern kingdom's exile in 722 BC). A second devastation would follow: *it will again be laid waste* (lit. 'for burning'), referring to the Babylonian exile in 586 BC. After the latter destruction, a *stump* (*maṣṣebet*, 3x; see 2 Sam. 18:18) will remain.

To ensure that the readers understand the image, he likens it to the *terebinth* or *oak*, two of the most common trees in Israel that leave a stump when cut down. This stump is called *the holy seed* and corresponds to the righteous remnant preserved by God. Thus, while the nation must undergo significant punishment, it is not entirely without hope.

Meaning
After Isaiah willingly volunteers to prophesy on God's behalf, God informs the prophet of his plan for Israel. Just as the nation had spurned God up to this point, so too they would spurn Isaiah; his messages would actually have the effect of hardening the nation even more. Yet this hardening of Israel's heart would not frustrate God's plan. Indeed, a righteous remnant would come forth from the nation.

About the time of Isaiah and Micah (see Mic. 2:12), God determined to work with a righteous remnant – those who were willing to serve him. God continued to develop this concept through the rest of the Old Testament and into the New Testament. Believers today are a continuation of this righteous remnant that began in the Old Testament.

(2) Isaiah's first sign (7:1–25)

Context

Isaiah 7:1–17 further explains the message that Isaiah was given at his commissioning. The first two oracles are closely associated with the Syro-Ephraimite War in 733–732 BC (see Introduction) and centre around symbolic names given to Isaiah's children, *Shear-Jashub* (7:3), *Maher-Shalal-Hash-Baz* (8:1) and perhaps *Immanuel* (7:14).

Isaiah 7 first describes the imminent threat to Judah from the Syro-Ephraimite alliance and then confirms that Syria and Israel will be defeated. When Ahaz refuses a sign from the LORD, we learn that Judah will be punished by Assyria (i.e. the events of 701 BC). A crucial theme in this section is trust in God. If Judah relies on God, they will succeed; if they rely on their own strength or the strength of their allies, they will fail miserably.

Comment

(a) Isaiah's message to King Ahaz (7:1–9)

1–2. The setting of this oracle is just prior to the Syro-Ephraimite War (733–732 BC) when Ahaz was preparing for an attack by Rezin king of Syria and Pekah king of Israel (see 2 Kgs 16:5–19). Ahaz had just become co-regent with his father (about 735 BC) and was young and inexperienced.

Verse 1 jumps ahead in time to give the reader the outcome – God already had everything under control. Pekah and Rezin would be unsuccessful in their goal to capture Jerusalem (i.e. *not overpower it* [Jerusalem], lit. 'not able to fight against her'). We assume that Ahaz had not yet called upon Assyria for help, otherwise the ensuing sign would be superfluous. At some point he does call on Assyria, although that alliance would put Israel under their authority until the conquest of Assyria by Babylon over a hundred years later.

Ahaz and all the house of David were terrified (*the hearts of Ahaz and his people were shaken* [*nûaʿ*]) because Pekah and Rezin were preparing to attack Judah, settling (*nûaḥ*, 'to rest', using a wordplay here) their troops into the highlands of Ephraim, less than a day's march from Jerusalem (about 12 miles; see Figure 0.2 on p. 5).

Syria was much stronger than Judah, having acquired most of the surrounding lands, including much of Israel which it controlled as a puppet country. Humanly speaking Ahaz had every right to be fearful.

3–4. When Isaiah came to King Ahaz with a message from God, he brought his son *Shear-Jashub* (lit. 'a remnant will return'), who appears to somehow serve as a sign to Ahaz, although the exact meaning of the name and how it relates to Ahaz is never stated. The child's name may be either a positive sign ('at least a remnant will return') or a negative one ('only a remnant will return'). The ambiguity could have been intentional and dependent upon Ahaz's response. They found King Ahaz outside the city by *the aqueduct of the Upper Pool*, quite probably checking the vulnerable water supply in anticipation of the coalition's attack. The pool is said to be located *on the road* [lit. 'highway' = 'raised roadway'] *to the Launderer's Field.*

Ahaz is told, *don't be afraid. Do not lose heart* (lit. 'do not let your heart be weak') because the coalition is merely *two smouldering stubs of firewood*, an image portraying that their power is dying out. In this passage Pekah is contemptuously referred to three times as *the son of Remaliah* because he killed Pekahiah, the legitimate ruler (2 Kgs 15:25), to usurp the throne of Israel.

5–6. The coalition *plotted your* [i.e. Ahaz's] *ruin* (lit. 'evil'). Pekah had allied himself with the more powerful country of Syria, intending to force Ahaz to join their coup against Assyria. If Ahaz refused, they would replace him with the unknown *son of Tabeel*, 'God is good', but the Hebrew reads 'Good for nothing'; this wordplay shows the author's disdain for Tabe'el.[6]

---

6. Roberts thinks that the name should be Tubail (= Ittobaʿl, king of Tyre; 2015: 111).

7–9. God uses 'permanent prohibitions' to assure Ahaz that this will never happen. It nevertheless took faith to believe this message since the circumstances looked hopeless from a human point of view. The reason why (*kî, for*, beginning v. 8) the coalition's plan will not succeed is because it was created by two men, Pekah and Rezin. The author also uses a circumlocution to help Ahaz see that a country is only as strong as its leader and that God can surely manage two mere men (cf. 2:22; see Figure 7.1).

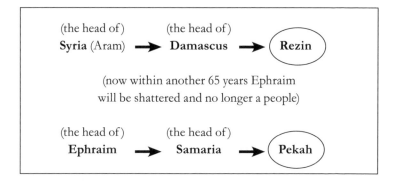

Figure 7.1   Circumlocution in 7:7–9

Ahaz is not known for his faith, so verse 9 contains an interesting play on the word *'āman*, 'to believe', that is meant to encourage his and the nation's faith: *If you* [pl.] *do not stand firm in your faith* ['*āman* (*hiphil* form) = 'to believe'], / *you* [pl.] *will not stand at all* ('*āman* [*niphal* form] = 'to be established').

Interpreting the phrase *within sixty-five years / Ephraim will be too shattered to be a people* has been problematic for two reasons: (1) Damascus, along with Israel's army, was conquered in 732 BC, only about two to three years after this prophecy; and (2) Israel was conquered and deported in 722 BC, only about twelve or thirteen years after the prophecy. Some have suggested that the six and five should be added since eleven years would be a much more reasonable estimate, but this would require significant reconstruction of the text.

Most scholars think that this phrase refers to a later deportation by Esarhaddon in 670 BC (i.e. sixty-five years after the Syro-Ephraimite War; see Ezra 4:2). While this leaves the text intact, it

does not follow Isaiah's flow of thought, which is why some translations put the phrase in parentheses. It is most plausible that the
phrase was first added in the margin by a copyist after 670 BC and
was subsequently incorporated into the text.

(b) A second message (7:10–17)

10–11. *Again the LORD spoke to Ahaz*: here Isaiah claims to speak
directly for God, giving Ahaz the opportunity to request a *sign*
from *the LORD your God*. The sign could be anything at all, from *the
deepest depths* to *the highest heights* (a merism that includes everything
in between). A sign can be either a natural occurrence (Exod. 3:12)
or a supernatural one (Exod. 4:7–8). Ahaz is invited to see whether
God can be trusted to deliver them, as opposed to calling upon
Assyria for help.

12–13. Ahaz rejects the offer of a sign under the guise of pseudo-
faith: *I will not put the LORD to the test*. Ironically, by refusing to
request a sign, Ahaz not only shows his unwillingness to believe
but also tests the LORD's patience. Isaiah is understandably angered
at Ahaz's blatant lack of faith.

The prophet states that the *house of David* (whom Ahaz repre-
sents) had tried *the patience of humans*, a probable reference to his
indecisiveness during the threat of invasion by Pekah and Rezin.
But now he is trying *the patience of my God also* (v. 13) by declining
God's offer. Notice that it is now Isaiah's God (*my God*), not the
God of Ahaz, since he has demonstrated his unbelief.

14. The LORD will still give a sign, not to encourage Ahaz's faith
but to confirm God's truthfulness. The sign, directed to Ahaz and
the entire nation (the *you* in v. 14 is plural), has both positive and
negative aspects. The welcome news is that the Syro-Ephraimite
coalition will soon be destroyed (vv. 14–16); however, Assyria will
also attack Judah (701 BC; v. 17). Thus the sign (i.e. the child
Immanuel) will remind the whole nation of God's message and its
consequences.

In the style of a common birth announcement (see Gen. 16:11),
Ahaz hears that *the virgin* ('almâ, 'young woman') is pregnant and
about to *give birth to a son, and will call him Immanuel*. The article on
the word 'almâ suggests that this is a specific woman. The name
'Immanuel' ('immānû'ēl) can mean 'God is with us' ('im = 'with'

preferred; see Matt. 1:23) or 'God is against us' ('*im* = 'against'; see Ps. 94:16); the ambiguity here may be intentional.

Excursus: young maiden (*'almâ*) and virgin (*bĕtûlâ*)

There is significant overlap in these words, for an *'almâ*, 'young maiden', who is unmarried would also probably be a virgin (an unmarried young woman who was not a virgin was to be stoned according to Deut. 22:23–24). But there are also differences, since an older woman could also still be a virgin. Thus, while *'almâ* and *bĕtûlâ* have some degree of overlap, they have two clearly different nuances: *'almâ* emphasizes 'youngness' and *bĕtûlâ* emphasizes 'virginity'. Several other passages add the word 'young' to the word *bĕtûlâ*, either to be specific or because the idea of youth is not necessarily inherent to the word *bĕtûlâ*, but the phrase 'a young *'almâ*' never occurs.

Isaiah 7:14 is the only passage where most literal translations of the Bible read *'almâ* as 'virgin' (see NASB, ESV, KJV). This passage also states that the *'almâ* is pregnant (*hārâ* is most probably a predicate adjective suggesting 'in a state of pregnancy'; Williams §75); thus, it is unlikely that *'almâ* without further qualifiers would mean 'virgin'.

Of the many suggestions regarding the identity of the *'almâ* and the child, the two most plausible are (1) the queen or royal consort/ Ahaz's child; or (2) the prophet's wife/the prophet's son. The crucial point is that the sign make sense to Ahaz and the nation of Israel. Immanuel was alive in the land of Judah in 701 BC according to Isaiah 8:8: *Its* [Assyria's] *outspread wings will cover the breadth of your land, / Immanuel!* (i.e. *your land* must refer to Judah).

New Testament's Use of Isaiah 7:14
There are various views as to how Isaiah 7:14 is fulfilled in Matthew 1:22–23. We argue that Isaiah 7:14 forms 'a prophetic pattern' which Matthew picks up and then, utilizing the Greek word *plēroō* ('to make full, fill up, complete'), fills with more meaning (see Matt. 2:15, 17, 23; etc.). Isaiah 7:14 can be fully understood in its context as a sign to Ahaz and the house of Israel, but Matthew takes up this pattern of a young woman giving birth to a son named Immanuel and fills it with more meaning by applying it to Jesus (see Wegner 2011: 467–484).

15–16. The subject *he* beginning verse 15 refers to the *son* just mentioned (v. 14); thus verses 15–17 are a further elaboration of the sign, constructed as a chiasm:

15 A *He will be eating curds and honey*
    B *when he knows enough to reject the wrong and choose the right,*
    B′ *for before the boy knows enough to reject the wrong and choose the right,*
  A′ *the land of the two kings you dread will be laid waste.*

The middle two units are nearly identical in Hebrew. The first and last units of the chiasm also represent parallel ideas: the child *will be eating curds and honey* when *the land of the two kings you* [i.e. Ahaz (sing.)] *dread* [i.e. Syria and Israel] *will be laid waste.* Thus the child living in Judah will be able to sustain himself even after the destruction of Syria and Israel. The arrival of Syria and Israel in 735 BC would have halted the harvesting of crops, but curds and honey could still be obtained fairly quickly (see also v. 22).

Verse 16 confirms that the destruction of Syria and Israel will take place by the time the child can *reject the wrong* [lit. 'bad'] *and choose the right* [lit. 'good']. These phrases could refer to various times in the life of the child. It is relatively easy to determine when the parts of this sign were fulfilled:

Verse 16: The land . . . Ahaz dreads will be laid waste = Syro-Ephraimite War (*c.*733–732 BC) when Damascus was conquered and most of Israel's army was killed or taken prisoner.
Verse 16: By 722 BC both nations had been destroyed by Assyria.
Verse 17: The king of Assyria will come upon Judah (701 BC).

If this oracle was given about 735/734 BC, shortly before the start of the Syro-Ephraimite War, then the child would have been approximately two to three years of age when the coalition was defeated in 732 BC by Assyria. At this age he would begin to differentiate harmful things (i.e. 'bad') from good things in the environment. Historically, by 701 BC everything described in this sign had been fulfilled. By this time the child would have been an adult (about thirty-four or thirty-five years old) capable of moral discrimination between good and evil things. Once Ahaz saw the birth of this child, he would know that the rest of the sign would take place.

17. Ahaz should not expect an entirely positive sign after his lack of faith – in reality it would prove to be far worse. *Ephraim broke away from Judah* (i.e. division of the kingdom) under wicked King Rehoboam (about 931 BC); but as severe a blow as this was to the nation, the arrival of the Assyrian king Sennacherib in 701 BC would be even more devastating.

The syntax of verse 17, which places the direct object as far as possible from the verb, highlights the dread that the coming of the Assyrian king should instil. Thus, Ahaz is warned that the very instrument he will call upon for protection will instead bring destruction.

Meaning

God graciously gives Ahaz multiple opportunities to trust him, but because Ahaz refuses, the sign given to both Ahaz and the house of David includes both positive and negative elements. The immediate threat of attack by Syria and Israel will be removed when they are conquered by Assyria; however, God will later use Assyria to punish Judah as well (701 BC). Ahaz's lack of trust in God led Judah down a destructive road from which they never recovered. From that point on Judah would always be in a position of subservience. Lack of faith can sometimes have disastrous, even permanent consequences.

(c) Isaiah's further explanation (7:18–25)

Context

Continuing the theme of punishment in verse 17, each of the four units here (vv. 18, 20, 21, 23) describes the thorough destruction of Judah's fertile land when the Assyrians came against Judah in 701 BC, despite the aid of Tirhakah, king of Ethiopia/Cush (see 2 Kgs 19:9; Isa. 37:9; *ANET* 287). The phrase *in that day* does not signal a new oracle as many scholars suggest. It simply introduces a new aspect of or perspective on a previously described event, which is the case here.

Comment

18–19. *In that day* refers to the judgment mentioned in the preceding verses. In this first unit (vv. 18–19) Yahweh *will whistle* (cf. 5:26)[7] for flies (i.e. incessantly biting flies such as horseflies or deer flies), which represent Egypt, and bees, which represent Assyria, to infiltrate the land. Although both are swarming pests, bees are more dangerous (see Deut. 1:44). Their vast armies will flood Judah, infiltrating *the steep ravines* [*battōt*, occurs only here] *and . . . all the thorn-bushes* [*naʿăṣûṣîm*, occurs only here] *and . . . all the water holes* (*nahălōl*, occurs only here).

Israel is pictured as a very rough and forbidding land with flies and bees extending even into the barren parts of the land. The flies originate from the extremity of the Nile (see v. 18), most probably the area near Khartoum in Sudan where the Blue and White Niles meet, and not *the Nile delta in Egypt* as the NIV suggests. This corresponds to the region from which Tirhakah came (i.e. Cush). The word *yěʾōr* typically refers to the River Nile in the Old Testament; its plural form in verse 18 appears much less frequently (14x out of 64x).

20. The second unit describes Assyria as *a razor hired from beyond the River* (i.e. Euphrates). Assyria's desire to utterly devastate and humiliate is shown in the fact that all Judah's hair is shaved, from the *head* to the *private parts* (lit. 'the hair of the feet', a euphemism for genitals; see Judg. 3:24) to the *beards*.

That the LORD only 'rents' or 'hires' Assyria to do his work (see similar terms used for Babylon in Ezek. 29:19–20) is in marked contrast to his special relationship with Israel. Historically, it was Hezekiah who felt the 'clean shave' of the Assyrians (i.e. Sennacherib).

21–22. The third unit graphically depicts Judah's depopulation. Far from living in abundance, the meagre remnant left in the land

---

7. Commentators commonly reference beekeepers who whistle to summon their bees (see Cyril of Alexandria, *Commentarius im Isaiam prophetam, ad loc.*; see also Virgil, *Georgics*, 4.64).

will have their needs met, but not much more. *A young cow and two goats* (*ṣōʾn*, either 'sheep' or 'goats', here goats; see Lev. 1:10) will provide enough so that *all who remain in the land will eat curds and honey*. The *razor* (v. 20) will so lay waste the people and their fields that the few who remain will need to survive on naturally occurring *honey*, and *curds* made from the milk their animals provide (a cow and two goats could produce about 26 litres of milk a day, enough for one large family).

23–25. The last unit continues the description of Judah's thorough devastation, with an allusion to the Song of the Vineyard of chapter 5. The land which was once rich and cultivated with *a thousand vines worth a thousand silver shekels* (implied is the high-quality vines valued at one silver shekel each) will revert back to wilderness.

Several phrases emphasize how useless and unproductive the land will become: (1) *briers* [*šāmîr*, occurs only in Isaiah with this meaning] *and thorns* [*šayit*, a common term for thornbush] is repeated in each verse; (2) *hunters* will come there to hunt wild game; (3) those who seek land to cultivate will avoid it *for fear of the briers and thorns*; and (4) it will be fit only for cattle and sheep to roam. If only Israel had obeyed their God.

Meaning

This section further describes the punishment mentioned in Isaiah 7:17 that Yahweh will inflict upon his people. God will hire the Assyrians to punish his wicked nation, thoroughly depleting the population and destroying the land. Because of Ahaz's lack of faith in calling on the Assyrians for help, the nation of Israel would lose its independence from 701 BC until AD 1947, when Israel once again became an independent state. Ahaz and his nation paid dearly for their lack of trust in God.

(3) Isaiah's second sign (8:1 – 9:7)

(a) A dramatic oracle (8:1–15)

Context

This section also refers to events surrounding the Syro-Ephraimite War (733–732 BC), as did most of chapter 7. It is interesting how similar the signs are in these two chapters, which is why some conclude that the two oracles refer to the same child (Oswalt 1986: 213). However, the fall of Damascus is more probably about three years after the birth of the child of chapter 7, whereas the events of chapter 8 are only about one year after the child's birth (i.e. before he can say *My father* or *My mother*), which suggests this is a different child. If the fall of Damascus is about one year after the child's birth (as in chapter 8), then the primary purpose of this sign is to warn Judah since the northern kingdom would already have been engaged in the Syro-Ephraimite War (733–732 BC).

Chapter 8 begins with a sign (vv. 1–4) which is then explained (vv. 5–8). As in chapter 7, the sign contains elements both positive (vv. 3–4) and negative (vv. 5–8). The last part of the passage goes into further detail about the destruction originally mentioned in 6:11–13.

Comment

1–2. Isaiah is told to *take a large scroll* (*gillayôn*, 2x; see 3:23; possibly a 'clay tablet', 'bronze mirror' or 'piece of papyrus'), something large enough to be easily seen by the witnesses and which could be sealed; a piece of papyrus seems most likely (8:16; see *ANEP* 265). Isaiah is told to *write on it with an ordinary pen* (lit. 'stylus of man'). The *ordinary pen* of that day could have been a stylus or reed, but here may simply refer to 'writing'.

The two-part name *Maher-Shalal-Hash-Baz* (see on v. 3) is to be a sign that punishment is coming, first for the northern kingdom, then continuing on into Judah. Two *reliable witnesses* are to confirm this sign: *Uriah the priest* (see 2 Kgs 16:10–16) and *Zechariah son of Jeberekiah* (possibly Ahaz's father-in-law; see 2 Kgs 18:2). Once the sign was fulfilled, they could serve as eyewitnesses of the power of God in bringing about the events of chapter 8. It would thereby be impossible for anyone to argue that the oracles were prophesied 'after the fact', apparently a tendency in Isaiah's day as it is now.

3–4. Then Isaiah *made love* [lit. 'drew near'] *to the prophetess* (i.e. his wife, called a *prophetess* for her integral role in the message to the nation), and she gave birth to a son whom Isaiah named *Maher-Shalal-Hash-Baz* ('soon [will be] the spoil; quickly [comes] the plundered'). Verse 4 explains the meaning of the name in this way:

For before the boy knows how to say 'My father' or 'My mother', the wealth of Damascus and the plunder of Samaria will be carried off by the king of Assyria (i.e. Tiglath-pileser III; see *ANET* 283). More than likely this is the very king with whom Ahaz had made an alliance.

5–8. Verses 5–15 form a separate oracle that employs flood imagery (vv. 6–7) to describe the punishment mentioned in verses 3–4 that would come to *this people* (i.e. the northern kingdom) for having rejected *the gently flowing waters of* [the] *Shiloah*. The Hebrew word *Shiloah* means 'sent' and corresponds to the Greek word *Siloam* with the same meaning (see John 9:7–11). It refers either to a pool (*bĕrēkat haššelaḥ*, Neh. 3:15) near the king's palace, or more probably to a pool filled from the Gihon Spring. Either way it is a reference to Judah where *Shiloah* is located.

The northern kingdom is at fault for allying with a foreign power and turning against Judah: Israel *rejoices over Rezin* [i.e. king of Syria] *and the son of Remaliah* [i.e. Pekah]. By stating Pekah's lineage instead of his name, the author is highlighting that Pekah is not the legitimate heir to the throne of Israel.

Therefore (lit. 'Now therefore behold', v. 7) signals a message of judgment on Israel, which is stated as a play on words: because they had *rejected the gently flowing waters of* [the] *Shiloah* (i.e. they chose to ally themselves with a foreign power instead of Judah), they will be washed away by *the mighty floodwaters of the Euphrates* (i.e. Assyria). While the Gihon Spring (i.e. *Shiloah*) is a significant source of water for Judah (up to 1.2 million cubic feet of water per year), it is nothing in comparison to the mighty River Euphrates (990 billion cubic feet of water per year).

The powerful River Euphrates, described by two plural Hebrew adjectives, 'mighty' and 'great', is an excellent image of the power of the Assyrian army that would 'flood' and conquer both Israel and Judah (v. 8). The phrase *reaching up to the neck* (i.e. a dangerous level, v. 8) is a fitting picture of the events of 701 BC when Assyria destroyed nearly all the land of Judah before God miraculously saved the capital city of Jerusalem (see 36:1 – 37:37).

Assyria is also pictured as a bird whose wingspan (*outspread wings*, v. 8) *will cover the breadth of your land, Immanuel*; in other words, the entire nation would be affected. This declaration implies that

Immanuel will be alive in the land of Judah where he was born when the Assyrian destruction takes place.

9–10. The command to the nations to *prepare for battle* (lit. 'gird oneself') does not readily flow from what immediately precedes. Verse 9 is structured in parallel units, as follows:

A   B   C
Raise the war cry,[8] *you nations, and be shattered!*
　　A   B
Listen, all you distant lands.
　　　　　　　　　　　　　　　　　　　　C
Prepare for battle, and be shattered!
Prepare for battle, and be shattered!

The message is clear: the nations that go against Judah will be shattered. Verse 10 further describes that no plan formed against God's people will stand, no matter how carefully conceived it may be.

This may refer to the Syro-Ephraimite coalition's plan or the later attack by Assyria in 701 BC; both are in the immediate context. Neither plan will succeed, for God will protect Judah (*'immānû'ēl, God is with us*; i.e. will protect us, v. 10b; the meaning in 7:14 is therefore positive). The phrase *it will not stand* is similar to the description in 7:7 that the coalition's plan *will not take place*. These phrases most probably express the author's confidence that Jerusalem will be delivered.

11–13. While many scholars have questioned it, there does appear to be a flow of thought in verses 11–15. Isaiah addresses the misguided thinking of the people, warning that difficult times are ahead if they do not listen to God.

The 'for' (*kî*) beginning verse 11 marks the beginning of another unit that is linked to verses 9–10. God powerfully exhorts Isaiah *not to follow the way of this people* (i.e. *with his strong hand upon me*, v. 11). This is the only time in the book of Isaiah when God speaks

---

8. While the meaning of *rō'û* is uncertain, it is most likely to be a corruption of *dě'û* ('to give ear'; see LXX and the parallel unit).

in this manner. Isaiah needs to be strong and exercise faith in God's plan so that he does not fall into the trap of the Israelites' flawed reasoning.

Verses 12–13 mirror each other, explaining to Isaiah and his followers (i.e. second person plural forms) who they are not to fear or dread versus who they are to fear. The people would have considered Isaiah's messages of impending judgment to be a traitorous *conspiracy*. They feared the might of the other nations instead of fearing the LORD *Almighty* (lit. 'the LORD of hosts'). He is the only one capable of protecting them from such threats.

14–15. The phrase *He will be a holy place* completes the thought of the preceding verse: to those who fear God, he will be a 'sanctuary' (NASB), a place where they can be under his protection. The parallel structure of verse 14b can be shown as follows:

for both **Israel and Judah** *he will be a* **stone** *that causes people to stumble*
and [he will be] *a* **rock** *that makes them fall.*
And for **the people of Jerusalem** *he will be a* **trap**
and [he will be] *a* **snare.**

Both Israel and Judah will stumble and ultimately fall because they did not rely on God. The image of the *trap/snare* implies that the people will not be able to escape from it.

Using many of the same words as verse 14, verse 15 portrays a downward progression: (1) *stumble*; (2) *fall*; (3) be *broken*; (4) be *snared*; and (5) be *captured*. Because *many of them will . . . fall*, the believing remnant will indeed be small.

Meaning

God gives another sign, the child *Maher-Shalal-Hash-Baz*, that contains both positive and negative elements: (1) the near problem of Syria and Israel will soon be resolved, but (2) the bigger problem is that both Israel and Judah will be overwhelmed by the Assyrians. God once again demonstrates his mercy and kindness by warning both houses of Israel of their impending punishment, so that they can escape if they repent. He is the only one who can truly be their sanctuary, if only they would trust him. We too tend to hide in pseudo-sanctuaries and rely on things other than the one who is our true sanctuary.

(b) Isaiah's further explanation (8:16 – 9:7)

(1′) Isaiah waits for God's punishment (8:16–22)

Context
While some see a major break between 8:16–22 and the unit that precedes (vv. 11–15), there is a natural progression from the sign and its explanation to the act of sealing it up and waiting until it occurs. The change in verse 19 from the first person to the second and third persons is context driven and does not indicate later additions.

Isaiah and his children serve as *signs and symbols* in a dark time to help point people back to God. However, as 6:9–10 states, Israel will continue in their hard-heartedness and soon find that God follows through on his word. This section leads up to God's answer to Israel's hard-heartedness in 9:1–7, where he sends a deliverer.

Comment
16–18. Following the proclamation of God's message, Isaiah waits for its fulfilment. The *testimony* is to be bound up and sealed *among my* [Isaiah's] *disciples*. In Ruth 4:7, the word 'testimony' (*tĕʿûdâ* [3x]) refers to the physical means by which a legal transaction is symbolically confirmed. Thus, it is likely that the written prophecy regarding *Maher-Shalal-Hash-Baz* was to be sealed and witnessed by *Uriah* and *Zechariah* (vv. 2–4) until it was fulfilled, at which point it could be opened. The confirmation of this short-term prophecy would be proof that Isaiah was a true prophet whose long-term prophecies would also come true.

The word *instruction* (*tôrâ*) refers to the prophetic explanation of the document that Isaiah gave to his *disciples* (lit. 'learners'; i.e. those who had been told the meaning of the sign in v. 2). There is little evidence to suggest an Isaianic school as some have proposed (see Clements 1980a: 4).

Isaiah will then *wait* [i.e. in hope] *for the* LORD to turn his face back towards the nation. The image of God *hiding his face* indicates that the people may no longer expect his protection and guidance. During this waiting period, Isaiah ('Yahweh is salvation'), *Maher-Shalal-Hash-Baz* ('soon [will be] the spoil; quickly [comes] the plundered') and *Shear-Jashub* ('a remnant will return') will stand as *signs and symbols* (lit. 'wonders') to the nation. Notice that God still dwells with the people on Zion; he has not moved despite Israel's wickedness. Isaiah expects, and even eagerly awaits, the time when God will turn his face back towards his nation with all of his blessing and protection.

19–20. Verses 19–22 refer to a time of great national distress and crisis. *When* [*kî*] *someone* (lit. 'they') comes to Isaiah and his children (pl. *you*) for guidance, asking them to *consult mediums and spiritists* (both were thought to be able to communicate with the dead; see 1 Sam. 28:13) to ascertain how to appease the gods in order to alleviate their suffering, Isaiah is to send them back to *God's instruction* [*tôrâ*] *and the testimony* [*tĕʿûdâ*] that had already been given to them (v. 16). These are the only authoritative sources of divine revelation.

If they could understand that God had already prophesied these events, then perhaps they would turn to him for help. However, *if* (*ʾim-lōʾ*, a conditional statement) they do not heed Yahweh's message, they will have no way of escape (*no light of dawn* [*šāḥar*], i.e. 'deliverance').

21–22. During the terrible punishment that the nation endures, the people will be *distressed* and *hungry* as they *roam through the land* (lit. 'through it'). Then they will *curse their king* for getting them into this crisis, and *their God* for not delivering them from it. People have a tendency to blame God even when they themselves are the cause of their difficulties. The last phrase in the Hebrew text of verse 21, *looking upwards*, is difficult to translate: 'then they [lit. 'he'] will turn upwards' (i.e. they die); or 'will turn to unfaithful acts' (i.e. they blaspheme God). Both interpretations fit the context, but the first one appears to better explain the progression in verse 22: they will be distressed and hungry, will curse their king and their god, and will ultimately die. Some of them *will be thrust into utter darkness*, meaning that they will be exiled.

Meaning

The Israelites' hearts are so hardened that they are willing to search for revelation from nearly any source other than God himself. Their persistent rebellion simply confirms the justice of God's continued punishment. The further we distance ourselves from God, the more desperate we become to find 'revelation' that we find more palatable, even if it is wrong.

(2') A future deliverance (9:1–7)

Context

This passage is the climax to the Isaianic memoir in 6:1 – 9:7 and is the fulfilment of 6:13b which refers to a righteous remnant (or *holy seed*) who will be spared. Having turned away his face during the nation's time of punishment, God now turns back towards his people to restore them.

The author, without fully understanding the timing of events, does grasp the sequence of punishment then restoration. Isaiah 9:1–7 pictures a complete reversal of the preceding circumstances, often using the same (or very similar) words to highlight this contrast. The liberation of the northern kingdom (9:4) from *the yoke that burdens them* (i.e. Assyria) is mentioned first. Then we see a future deliverer sitting on the throne of David (i.e. the southern kingdom), who sets up a kingdom of peace (9:7). The section ends with a dramatic statement: *The zeal of the LORD Almighty will accomplish this*. Thus the prophet sees a startling defeat of Assyria (i.e. the divine defeat of the Assyrians in 701 BC) that advances into the complete deliverance of the nation; but this deliverance would be much further into the future than Isaiah realized. This is an example of the 'prophetic perspective' that allows Isaiah to envision future events in the light of contemporaneous ones.

Comment

1.[9] Many scholars consider verse 1 a redactional addition of a later editor that joins the two passages; however, we agree with Alt (1953: 206–225) that it was added by the author himself (see Matt. 4:14–16). The context is very likely to be the Assyrian incursions around 734 BC to 722 BC.

Nevertheless [*kî*], *there will be no more gloom for those* [lit. 'for her'] *who were in distress*. The *kî* draws a contrast between what came before and what is now happening. The vocabulary of 9:1 essentially mirrors that of 8:22 (especially the rare words) in order to stress contrast: *māʿûp*, *gloom* (occurs only in v. 22)/*mûʿāp*, *gloom* (occurs only in v. 23); and *ṣûqâ*, *distress* (3x; v. 22)/*mûsāq*, *distress* (2x; v. 23). This contrast continues in the antithetical parallelism of verse 1b, which serves as a clear transition into the poem that follows (vv. 2–7).

The apparent lack of agreement in gender between the word 'time' which is typically feminine (see 18:7) and the adjective 'former' which is masculine in verse 1 has caused significant translational issues (see Emerton 1969: 151–175). However, even within the book of Isaiah itself, the masculine form of the word 'time' (*ʿēt*) occurs (see 13:22). Also, the articles on the noun and adjective suggest the adjective is modifying the noun. Therefore, we believe that the parallel units of this part of the verse should be translated as follows:

> *In the past* [lit. 'according to the former time']
>   he [God] *humbled the land of Zebulun and the land of Naphtali,*
> *but in the future* [lit. 'according to the latter time']
>   he [God] *will honour Galilee of the nations, by the Way of the*
>   *Sea, beyond the Jordan.*

The contrast is between an 'earlier time' when God treated with contempt the lands of *Naphtali* and *Zebulun* (i.e. two major tribal units in the northern kingdom) and a 'later time' when God will

---

9. This poorly placed chapter division is in the middle of a literary unit; it is labelled 8:23 in the MT, but 9:1 in the English translations.

honour *the Way of the Sea, beyond the Jordan*, and *Galilee of the nations* (according to Alt, following 732 BC most of the northern kingdom was divided into these three Assyrian administrative centres; 1953: 206–225); these are thus overlapping geographical areas.

This time of contempt for the northern kingdom begins with the Syro-Ephraimite War (733–732 BC) and continues to 722/721 BC when Israel is taken into captivity. Little is known about the northern kingdom following 722/721 BC, but the most plausible context for this deliverance is when Jesus the Messiah arose from this area; he was the deliverer who would bring righteousness and peace to the nation (Wegner 1992a: 152–177). This is certainly how Matthew 4:12–17 understands the passage.

2–3. The author delivers a poetic salvation oracle (vv. 2–7) with elements of both a birth announcement and a coronation ritual that announce the deliverance God will bring to this area. *The people* must in this context refer to at least the northern kingdom; but by the end of the poem (v. 7) Judah is also included in the restoration since the child will sit on the throne of David.

Those who had been in dire straits (*in darkness, land of deep darkness* [*salmāwet*, lit. 'shadow of death'; popular folk etymology suggests it is probably from *sal*, 'shadow', and *māwet*, 'death']) will experience deliverance that is likened to a *great light* shining into a dark land (58:8, 10). *Light* in this context refers to the saving action of God.

In verse 3 we see Yahweh increasing the nation (lit. 'increase to it'; probably referring to population growth) and bringing a *joy* to this area that is likened to the nation's happiest occasions: (1) during *harvest*, when food is plentiful; and (2) when dividing the spoils of war after a victorious battle.

4. In verses 4–7 Isaiah gives three reasons for this great joy, each beginning with *for* (*kî*); the NIV uses *for* only twice (vv. 4, 6). The first reason is deliverance from their oppressors, pictured as breaking *the yoke that burdens them* (lit. 'yoke of his [i.e. the nation's] burden'; see 10:27). The Assyrian kings were proud of the heavy burden (*yoke*, referring to tribute, forced labour and taxes) that they placed on their vassals (*ANET* 287–288).

The triumph pictured here by the breaking of this yoke is likened to *Midian's defeat* during the time of Gideon, when God intervened to deliver Israel with only three hundred soldiers (Judg. 7). The historical event most similar to this was in 701 BC when the angel of the LORD destroyed 185,000 Assyrian warriors in a single night (see 2 Kgs 19:35//Isa. 37:36).

5. The second reason for this great rejoicing is the destruction of battle gear, which speaks of a time of peace. The word *sĕʾôn*, *warrior's boot*, occurs only here, but probably refers to the Assyrian battle boot and highlights its relevance to the Assyrian army. Typically boots and clothing were taken as spoil and reused (1 Sam. 31:8), but in this case the military equipment is destroyed. Either the author is using highly figurative language or he is referring to a time of peace and safety hitherto unknown.

6–7. The third reason (*kî*) for joy is that *a child is born*. He will rule over the nation of Israel but is never called a 'king', probably because Isaiah considers God the true King (6:5). In addition, *the government* [*hammisrâ*, 2x; see vv. 6–7] *will be on his shoulders*, which signifies his legitimate right to rule and may be derived from the fact that the king's sceptre was often resting on his shoulder.

He will bear a name (singular) that incorporates expectations or wishes somehow associated with him. The first appellation, *Wonderful Counsellor*, conveys great wisdom and ability, as when a king relies upon a counsellor for advice in time of battle.

The second appellation, *ʾEl gibbôr, Mighty God*, is applied to Yahweh in 10:21. How could the *Mighty God* be born, as described in 9:6?

The third title, *ʾăbî ʿad, Everlasting Father*, may be understood as (1) the child's nature (i.e. 'my father [is] eternal'); (2) his role (i.e. 'father of eternity'); or (3) the length of his rule (i.e. 'eternal father').

The word *śar* in the fourth appellation, *śar šālôm, Prince of Peace*, is never used of the king in Israel, but rather is applied to leaders under the authority of the king (see 1 Sam. 17:55). *Peace* is a characteristic of royal ideology (see Mic. 5:5) but was also a common wish for the reign of any king throughout history (Ps. 122:7).

We propose that the name be divided into two parallel units that form a chiastic structure. Each contains one theophoric element (i.e. a name for God), as follows:

And his name will be called:
    a *wonderful counsellor*   [is] the *mighty God*
                                 [theophoric element]

    the *everlasting father*   [is] a *prince of peace*
    [theophoric element]

This interpretation is suggested by (1) its similarity to the parallel structure of the name *Maher-Shalal-Hash-Baz* ('soon [will be] the spoil; quickly [comes] the plundered'); (2) the singular form of the name; (3) the Masoretic pointing which places a major accent on the middle of the name; and (4) the usual translation of theophoric names (e.g. the name Isaiah means 'Yahweh saves': his name says something about God and is not stating that he is God; see Wegner 1992b: 103–112).

In this context the name emphasizes that God is a *Wonderful Counsellor* whose plans to deliver his nation are remarkable (vv. 1–6). He is *a Prince of Peace*, for he will bring about a peace that will have no end (v. 7). Yahweh the true *Counsellor* and *Prince* forms a contrast to the despicable counsellors and rulers of Israel who have been leading the nation into shame and defeat.

The greatness[10] *of his government* (*hammiśĕrâ*) will not end (v. 7), and it is characterized by justice, righteousness and peace. The author understands that this child's rule will extend into the unending future when he states *from that time on* [lit. 'from now'] *and for ever*. He will be the final king, the ideal Davidic monarch. The readers are assured that this will come to pass because *the zeal of the LORD Almighty* [lit. 'of hosts'] *will accomplish this*, a phrase that concludes both this section (i.e. 9:1–7) and the Isaianic memoir (i.e. 6:1 – 9:7).

Meaning
This passage describes the remarkable divine deliverance of Israel from the Assyrians and the establishment of a kingdom of peace

---

10. The Masoretes placed a final *mêm* on the word *lĕmarbēh* to indicate that they believed it should read: 'to them the government will be great'.

and righteousness, ruled by a Davidic king whose reign extends into the unending future (*there will be no end*). Amos (9:11–15), Hosea (3:5) and Micah (5:1–6), all eighth-century prophets, also pictured a deliverance culminating with a ruler (often a Davidic king) who would rule over Israel without any perceptible end to his reign.

We suggest that this passage has combined royal ideology with the events following God's deliverance of Jerusalem in 701 BC to give rise to the concept of a 'future deliverer' who would release the nation from Assyrian bondage. This concept would continue to develop over time into the traditional concept of Messiah. At this point the concept of a 'future deliverer' has a teleological intent without the encumbrance of the eschatological elements it later developed.

e. God delineates his punishment: four uplifted-hand oracles (9:8 – 10:4)

Context
In the first half of the palistrophe there was only one 'uplifted-hand oracle' (see Figure 0.8 on p. 20), whereas in the second half there are four (i.e. 9:12b, 17b, 21b; 10:4b). These oracles are a progression of judgments that focus first on decimating property (9:9–10), then on the leadership (9:14–17), then on the people themselves (9:19–21), until finally the Assyrians arrive and exile the people (10:3). Isaiah 9:21 indicates that destruction will begin in Israel with Manasseh and Ephraim, and then progress into Judah.

Comment

(1) God will punish arrogant Israel (9:8–12)
   8–9. The northern kingdom (i.e. *Jacob/Israel*) has been punished by Yahweh, but instead of repenting and turning to God, the people boast that it was merely a small setback from which they will emerge stronger than ever. The *message against Jacob* concerns judgment that *will fall on Israel*, implying a harsh outcome. Verse 9 states that *all the people will know it* (i.e. they will experience this punishment), but in *pride and arrogance* [lit. 'greatness'] *of heart* they will continue to rebel against God. Their arrogance causes them to run headlong into an angry God whom they have spurned.

10–12. The people of Israel have been punished and their houses destroyed, but boastfully they claim that they will rebuild even better than before. Inexpensive mud *bricks* baked in the sun will be replaced with *dressed stone*[s] (lit. 'cut'), which were typically reserved for fine, expensive structures (see 1 Kgs 5:17). Buildings formerly constructed of common *fig-trees* will be rebuilt with highly prized *cedars* (see 1 Kgs 10:27).

Some have suggested emendations to the phrase *Rezin's foes* or have tried to remove the name *Rezin* altogether, but the phrase needs no emendation if we understand that it refers to the Assyrians. It is also possible that these are adversaries who belong to Rezin (i.e. subjective genitive) who have come against Judah (see 2 Kgs 16:6).

The punishment will come by means of both *Arameans* (i.e. Syria) and the *Philistines* (see 2 Kgs 18:8). Israel will be surrounded by enemies (*from the east* [lit. 'before'] *and . . . from the west* [lit. 'behind']) who will gobble up parts of Israel's land. These punishments prove to be ineffective in turning the people towards repentance, thus the refrain: *Yet for all this, his anger is not turned away, / his hand is still upraised* (lit. 'stretched out'), ready to come down again.

(2) God will destroy the leaders and false prophets (9:13–17)

13–16. These verses reiterate the purpose of the uplifted-hand oracles: the people of Israel still do not turn back to Yahweh, who therefore must continue to punish them. The images of *head/tail* and *palm branch/reed* are merisms that indicate that all of Israel's leaders will be cut off in a single day. These images vividly portray the leaders in society: the *elders* or *dignitaries* (lit. 'ones with lifted-up faces' = *head/palm branch*), and the *prophets who teach lies* (*tail/reed*). Isaiah considers false prophets to be the lowest of the low, for they pretend to speak for God but, in reality, lead many away from him.

The nation's leaders have led them further into sin; poor leadership begets corrupt people. There are several interesting twists in verse 16: (1) *those who guide* (lit. 'the ones going straight') *mislead them*; and (2) *those who are guided are led astray* (lit. 'are swallowed up'). The people are easy prey.

17. This verse forms the conclusion: *Therefore the Lord will take no pleasure in* (lit. 'not rejoice over') their *young men* (i.e. those upon

whom the nation's legacy depends) nor in their *fatherless and widows*
(i.e. those who are God's special charge), because all of them are
ungodly and *wicked* and speak *folly*. Therefore, the solemn refrain
warns that *his hand is still upraised*.

(3) Wickedness devours Israel like fire (9:18–21)

18–20. *Wickedness* is pictured as a *fire* consuming relatively small
and insignificant *briers and thorns*, then rapidly increasing until it
consumes the whole land, leaving only a towering *column of smoke*.
This is a poignant picture of how *wickedness* can begin on a small
scale then rapidly increase until it permeates a society. At some
point God's patience runs out and his justice must be meted out.

In time the degenerate person does not care who gets hurt; even
friends and relatives are exploited (*they will not spare one another*; lit.
'his brother'). The wicked will never be satisfied. Israel will even
feed on the flesh of their own offspring (lit. *zĕrōʿô*, 'arm', but NIV's *offspring*,
zĕrʿô, is probably correct), which may suggest cannibalism (see 2
Kgs 6:28–29), but it is more likely to be read in the figurative sense
of devouring the land and resources of another even though he is
a brother.

21. Ephraim and Manasseh attack each other even though they
are brother tribes descended from Joseph. Only momentarily do
they stop fighting one another long enough to strike Judah (i.e. the
Syro-Ephraimite War). Like a death knell, the refrain sounds once
again: *his hand is still upraised*.

(4) Woe to evil rulers (10:1–4)

1–2. After the initial *woe*, we learn that these reprehensible rulers
make unjust laws (lit. 'statutes of iniquity') and *issue oppressive* [lit.
'troubling, laborious'] *decrees*. Oswalt states that the final manifestation of human pride is oppression (1986: 258).

These rulers prey upon the most vulnerable of society who need
their protection (those who are *poor*, *oppressed*, *widows* and *fatherless*).
The rich manipulated the legal system in order to seize their lands
and property (i.e. thus the terms 'spoil' and 'plunder'; cf. NASB); they
have effectively declared war on their own people.

3–4. *On the day of reckoning* (lit. 'day of visitation' = punishment)
they will be treated as they have treated others. God will not help

them. The question *Where will you leave your riches?* implies that even their offspring will be killed. The *disaster* which *comes from afar* refers to the punishment meted out by the Assyrians: exile. It would be directed primarily towards those who deserved it the most (i.e. the rich who plundered the poor), whereas the poor (who were not a threat to Assyria) were typically left in the land to work property that the rich had taken from them, though they would still have to pay tribute and submit to Assyrian rule.

Nothing will remain (lit. 'nothing but'): the vast majority of Israelites will be either taken into captivity (lit. 'he bowed in the place of the prisoners') or killed, both dismal options. Wealth, status and power mean nothing when God pours out his wrath. Again, the solemn refrain is sounded: *his hand is still upraised.*

Meaning

The uplifted-hand oracles make it clear that God punishes only as much as necessary; he can cease at any point if Israel repents. It is reprehensible that the nation was so thoroughly wicked that even the poor and disenfranchised refused to turn to God for help. When leaders and judges do not maintain justice, then in time society crumbles. God is fair and patient, but at some point his justice must be administered.

f. A woe oracle (10:5 – 11:16)

(1) God will also judge Assyria (10:5–34)

Context

This woe oracle corresponds to the six woes in the first half of the palistrophe (see Figure 0.8 on p. 20), the difference being that while the earlier oracles were directed against the nation of Israel, this one is directed against the Assyrians who are devastating Israel. Just as Israel became proud and took advantage of its relationship with God by wandering into sin, so the Assyrians grew proud and overstepped the boundaries God had put in place for them. Both nations would be punished.

The oracle, given before 701 BC when Assyria was at its peak, describes punishment which would soon occur. Isaiah 10:5–34 comprises three smaller sections: (1) verses 5–19 confirm that God will use Assyria as his tool over which he has ultimate control; (2) verses 20–27 declare that a remnant of Israel will be delivered; and (3) verses 28–34 describe Assyria's destruction. Several scholars question the unity of this passage, but we argue that much of the perceived awkwardness is due to (1) the author's choice of direct discourse style; and (2) his choice to include explanatory segments interspersed between the poetic parts.

Comment

(a) The reason for Assyria's judgment (10:5–14)

5–6. This woe oracle includes both positive and negative elements concerning the Assyrians, who are called the *rod* of God's *anger*. The phrase *I send him against a godless nation* indicates that Yahweh used Assyria as his tool to punish his own sinful people (both Israel and Judah). The imperfect form *send* suggests iterative action; he repeatedly sent the Assyrians against unruly Israel, a reference to the events of at least 733–732, 722 and 701 BC. God is the one moving history; nations can do nothing unless Yahweh, the sovereign God of all creation, allows it. This is at least part of the punishment on Israel inflicted by *distant nations* that was promised in 5:26.

In verse 5b, the construct chain, *the club of my wrath*, which generally is never divided, has been separated by the clarifying phrase 'it is in their hands'. This unusual syntax emphasizes that God's wrath is being poured out by means of the Assyrians. God is justified in his *anger* against Israel for their blatant rebellion and expresses his *wrath* at being treated unjustly.

It is ironic that God should refer to Israel, his chosen people, as a *godless nation* and then commission Assyria, an equally if not more godless nation, to defeat and humiliate Israel. The phrase *to seize loot and snatch plunder* is reminiscent of Isaiah's son Maher-Shalal-Hash-Baz ('soon [will be] the spoil; quickly [comes] the plundered'), whose name predicted this event.

7–9. Assyria's goal was not simply to *trample* Israel, but to destroy and annihilate it along with many other nations (lit. 'cut off nations not a few', v. 7). Pride caused the nation of Assyria to overreach God's limits. This pride is seen clearly in verse 8 where the Assyrian king reasons that his *commanders* are more powerful than the other nations' *kings*. This could be a play on words in that the Hebrew word *commanders* (*śāray*) sounds like the Assyrian word for 'king' (*śarru*).

Prior to attacking Israel, Assyria's list of victories was impressive: *Kalno* (738 BC; possibly Akkadian *Kullâni* or Kalneh); *Carchemish* (717 BC); *Hamath* (720 BC); *Arpad* (738 and 720 BC); *Samaria* (722 BC); *Damascus* (732 BC). In the minds of the Assyrians, one defeated nation was the same as any other (i.e. *Hamath like Arpad, / and Samaria like Damascus*).

10–11. As the Assyrian king builds his argument in verses 10–11, the word *ka'ăšer* ('just as') introduces each reason: (1) just *as my hand seized* [lit. 'has found'] *the kingdoms of the idols*; and (2) just *as I dealt with Samaria and her idols*. He then concludes, *shall I not deal with Jerusalem and her images . . . ?* Notice that Jerusalem likewise has idols.

It was a common Ancient Near Eastern assumption that the strongest gods were on the side of the nation that won. Assyria had already defeated Samaria (722 BC) which had the same God as Judah (v. 11). Another assumption of the Assyrians is that nations that honour their gods with numerous temples, *idols* and *images* will receive greater assistance from these gods in time of war (see *ANET* 316). Judah's God, who had only one temple, must have little power or importance; here is where the Assyrians' pride turns to blasphemy.

12–14. Because this verse begins in the third person (*When the Lord has finished all his work* – that is, inflicts the full measure of judgment upon Judah) then abruptly changes to the first person (*I will punish the king of Assyria*), some modification of the text seems necessary. The NIV resolves the issue well by adding to the text the phrase *he will say*, after which the punishment (lit. 'I will visit') of the arrogant nation of Assyria is described.

Verses 13–14 are written as if spoken by the Assyrian king, who boasts that his own great strength (*the strength of my hand*) and wisdom have made him a wealthy world power (see Sennacherib's boastful account of his third campaign; *ANET* 287). But God is the true sovereign with the power to limit and destroy Assyria.

Removed the boundaries of nations probably refers to the growth of the Assyrian Empire as it conquered nations and reconfigured boundaries. The Assyrian king arrogantly asserts that conquering nations is as easy as gathering *abandoned eggs*; a country may have *flapped a wing* or *opened its mouth to chirp*, but in the end it was easily overpowered (e.g. Syria and Israel). In verse 13, the Assyrian says that he has *subdued their kings* (lit. 'inhabitants') like 'the Mighty One'. By including the article here, he elevates himself to deity (a similar description is given of Yahweh in 1:24; 49:26; etc.).

(b) The boastful nation's judgment (10:15–19)

15–19. To put God's sovereignty into perspective, the author poses two rhetorical questions followed by two statements of absurdity. Is the axe to 'glorify itself' or the saw (*maśśôr*, occurs only here) to 'make itself great' (i.e. an inanimate tool boasts that it is greater than the person wielding it). Similarly absurd is it to think that a rod can exercise control over the person who holds it. At this point God steps in to show that it is he who truly controls nations.

Therefore (v. 16) signals a transition to God's judgment of his tool, Assyria. The names *the Lord, the* LORD *Almighty* emphasize God's authority and ability to control all nations. This punishment (vv. 16–19) corresponds to the events of 701 BC when God sends a *wasting disease* (lit. 'leanness') among Assyria's *sturdy* [lit. 'fat'] *warriors* and lights a *blazing flame* under their *pomp* (lit. 'glory'; see 2 Kgs 19:35–37; Isa. 37:36–38). Fever (i.e. *fire, blazing flame*) is a symptom of plague, and *wasting disease* may signify a plague spread by field mice (see Herodotus, *Histories* 2.141). Some conjecture that Hezekiah's boil may also have been caused by this plague (Isa. 38).

God, *the Light of Israel . . . their Holy One*, will destroy Assyria's army (i.e. *his thorns and his briers*, v. 17) *in a single day*, either literally or in the figurative sense of 'rapidly'. The unusual wording of the phrase *one who is ill wastes away* (lit. 'melting away') pictures someone 'becoming weak to the point of death'. Assyria's soldiers *will be so few that a child* (i.e. one too young to know large numbers yet) will be able to record their number (v. 19).

(c) Both Israel and Judah will be reduced to a mere remnant (10:20–27)

Isaiah 10:20–27 has two units: (1) verses 20–23 announce that Israel's destruction will give rise to a remnant who will return to

God (see 6:13); and (2) verses 24–27 confirm that this remnant will be delivered from Assyria, just as the people were earlier delivered from the vast number of Midianites in Gideon's day and from Egypt in Moses' day. The author, prompted by the catchword *remaining* (*šĕʾār*, v. 19), returns to the theme of the sign Shear-Jashub (*šĕʾār yāšûb*; 'a remnant will return') used in 7:3.

20–23. *In that day* (v. 20), which must refer to the day of Assyria's defeat just mentioned, a *remnant of Israel* who had survived God's punishment experience a change of heart. They *will no longer rely on him / who struck them down* (i.e. Assyria, 10:5–19), but instead *will truly rely* ['to lean, support'] *on the LORD, / the Holy One of Israel* (see Figure 0.4 on p. 10).

Recalling earlier patriarchal prophecies, Israel is described as being as numerous as *the sand by the sea* (see Gen. 22:17), yet only *a remnant will return . . . to the Mighty God* (*ʾēl gibbôr*; see 9:6). The *destruction* (*killāyôn* [2x]; see Deut. 28:65, 'weary with longing') that gives rise to this remnant is said to be 'complete' and 'righteous' (NASB), and sweeps through *the whole land*. These verses describe the outcome of the two signs given in Isaiah 7 and 8: both Israel and Judah are decimated; only Jerusalem remains (fulfilled in 701 BC); and a remnant returns to God (a future fulfilment).

24–25. The word *therefore* beginning verse 24 marks either a climax or a conclusion. Yahweh speaks comfort to those remaining in Zion, the religious capital of Israel, calling them *my people* and telling them *not* to *be afraid of the Assyrians* who struck them *as Egypt did* (Exod. 1:8–22). The good news is that there is a time limit to Israel's punishment: *very soon* [lit. 'for yet a very little'] *my* [God's] *anger*, which had been directed towards his people, will be satisfied and *will be directed to their* [Assyria's] *destruction* (*tablît*; occurs only here).

26–27. Following the purification of God's nation by the Assyrians, he now turns to punish the latter. *The LORD Almighty*, a name that underscores his sovereignty and power, encourages the people of Jerusalem that he can destroy Assyria. He reminds them of two previous occasions when he miraculously destroyed their enemies: (1) he *will lash them* [the Assyrians] *with a whip, / as when he struck down Midian* in Gideon's time (v. 26); and (2) the pursuing Egyptians were engulfed and drowned by the waters of the Reed

Sea[11] when Moses brought down his staff. Both images suggest thorough defeat.

The *burden* and the *yoke*, signs of servitude, *will be lifted from your* [i.e. the remnant's] *shoulders* (v. 27). The burden of Assyria's domination was relieved in 701 BC but was not removed until the Babylonians usurped their power. The unusual image (*the yoke will be broken / because you have grown so fat* [lit. 'because of fatness']) suggests that the Assyrian yoke will burst because of Israel's strength and abundance. Some have suggested emending 'fatness' (*šāmen*) to either Rimmon (*rimmôn*) or Samaria (*šōmĕrôn*) and joining it to the next verse ('from Rimmon or Samaria he has come'). Yet there is no textual evidence for these emendations, and the first part of verse 27 suggests it is meant to be an optimistic statement. However one understands the phrase, the context suggests God's tool Assyria will be punished and fall, whereas the remnant of his precious people will be blessed.

(d) The Assyrian advance upon Jerusalem and Assyria's destruction (10:28–34)

28–29. Isaiah 10:28–34 is a section that does not flow naturally from the context that precedes and there has been much debate regarding to whom it refers. The 'he' (NIV *they*) beginning verse 28 is most probably a reference to the Assyrians, similar to verse 27 in which 'his' (NIV *their*) burden and 'his' (NIV *their*) yoke also refers to them; however, the northern advance upon Jerusalem here does not coincide with the south-western march of the Assyrians up to Jerusalem in 701 BC.

We suggest the passage refers to a march of reinforcements and supplies for the Assyrian army in preparation for the attack on Jerusalem in 701 BC, following their depletion at the battle of Lachish. The army will march down through the Benjaminite Plateau, taking the smaller strongholds of Judah (*Aiath, Migron*) but bypassing the fortress city of Mizpah and the even stronger cities

---

11. Traditionally identified as the 'Red Sea', its literal name is the 'Reed Sea'. It may have referred to different locations at different points in history (Hoffmeier 1999: 214).

of Gibeon, Ramah and Gibeah. The path follows a more rugged trail through the Wadi Es-Suwenit instead of the usual route from Bethel to Jerusalem (Figure 10.1) (see Childs 2001: 96).

However one reads this section, the outcome is clear: the Assyrians (*the lofty trees*, v. 33) will be toppled by the Mighty One.

30–32. The meaning of the word *ǎnîyâ* (NIV *poor*, v. 30) is somewhat uncertain. We suggest retaining the MT's reading *Poor Anathoth!* as a play on words (see 51:21), for the other readings have insufficient evidence. *Nob*, the final stop before Jerusalem, is just one mile north and overlooks Jerusalem (modern-day Mt Scopus).

Looking down on the city, the Assyrian (i.e. the king or the one in charge) waves his hand (NIV *they . . . shake their fist* – but more probably a backward wave of the hand) towards Jerusalem, a gesture of disgust, as if to say 'away with the Daughter of Zion' (lit. 'house of Zion', but does not occur elsewhere), for he plans to destroy it. The parallel terms here distinguish the religious capital *Zion* from the political capital *Jerusalem*.

33–34. The word *See* marks a climactic event: *the Lord* steps in to destroy the Assyrian army, pictured as *lofty trees*. They will be brought down (see vv. 15–19) *with great power* (*maʿǎrāṣâ*, occurs only here; signifies either a terrifying power or a loud, thundering crash).

The parallel phrases of verse 34 form a merism: everything from the lower *thickets* to the towering cedars of *Lebanon* (see Ezek. 31:3) will be brought down by *the Mighty One*. There is a play on words here: the Assyrian who called himself *a mighty one* (*ʾabbîr*, 10:13) is as nothing before God who has proved himself to be the true *Mighty One* (*ʾaddîr*). The devastation of Assyria pictured here stands in marked contrast to the new shoot that will sprout up from Israel in the next verse (11:1).

Meaning

Assyria is only a tool used by God to accomplish judgment on Israel. When they overstep the boundaries intended by God with their harsh treatment of Israel, he will step in to 'punish the punisher'. This is an interesting example of human responsibility working under the auspices of divine sovereignty.

The destruction in this section is similar to the historical events of Assyria's humiliation in 701 BC, when proud Sennacherib was

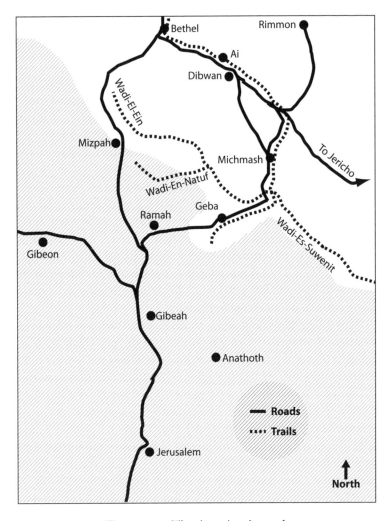

Figure 10.1 The Assyrians' march

forced to return home without having taken Jerusalem. Pride carries a great cost when it seeks to elevate itself above God. This section (10:5–34) should serve as an encouragement to Israel: God has an overall plan that will not be thwarted, not even by the mighty Assyrians.

(2) God promises his deliverance (11:1–16)

Context

While the Assyrian army is decimated, a new shoot will sprout back in Israel. As we have seen in an earlier passage (9:1–7), God will use a future royal son to restore his people and bring justice and righteousness to the land. This passage provides significantly more details concerning the nature of this Davidic ruler and the type of kingdom he will bring. The Davidic covenant (2 Sam. 7:8–17) confirmed that the kings of Judah would come from the line of David and that his throne would be established for ever. It was therefore important that the Messiah descend from the line of David in order that it continue for ever (see Matt. 1:1–17). The New Testament understands this deliverer to be Jesus Christ (see Rom. 15:12), and this time of peace and safety may picture the future Millennium (Rev. 20:4–6; Ladd 1959).

Isaiah 11 is usually divided into two sections, verses 1–9 and verses 11–16, linked by verse 10. Isaiah 11:1–9 is further subdivided into two parts: (1) verses 1–5 refer to the character of this ruler; and (2) verses 6–9 refer to his rule. Many scholars have dated the concepts in verses 6–9 a post-exilic development. However, the theme of harmony in nature appears in the Sumerian text 'Enki and Ninḫursag', dated to the first half of the second millennium (*ANET* 37–41).

The prose section (vv. 10–16) provides further details concerning the events initiated by the ruler described in the poetic parallel units of verses 1–9. There are two oracles, both introduced by the phrase *in that day*: the first prophesies that the nations (pl.) will seek the *Root of Jesse* (v. 10), and the latter that a remnant of Israelites scattered across the world will return to the land (vv. 11–12).

Comment

(a) A shoot from the stump of Jesse (11:1–9)

1. Parallel units describe the hope that springs from David's family: *a shoot* (*ḥōṭer*, 2x, 'new growth of a plant or tree'; Prov. 14:3, 'lashes out' [lit. 'is a <u>rod</u> for his back']) will spring up *from the stump* or stock (*geza'*, 3x; see 40:24) *of Jesse* and *a Branch* [*nēṣer*, 4x; see 60:21] *will bear fruit*. As long as someone from David's family is alive, there is hope for a future ruler, a theme seen earlier in 9:6–7. The connection to Jesse highlights David's humble beginnings and possibly that the deliverer precedes David.

Childs believes the 'stump' image refers to the wicked house of Ahaz being cut off (2001: 102). Clements (1982: 122) and others believe it more accurately pictures the Davidic nation being cut off in the Babylonian exile (586 BC). However, similar tree imagery was used in 10:33–34 to describe God's defeat of the Assyrian army, though Assyria remained in control of their empire. Thus this image could describe the punishment inflicted on Israel by Assyria in 701 BC, when the water reached *up to the neck* (8:8), or when Jerusalem looked like a hut in the middle of a cucumber field (1:8).

We see it as representing the events of 701 BC, when all that remained of Judah was Jerusalem (*reaching up to the neck*, 8:8) and the deliverance of the nation would probably have fostered hopes of restoration.

To *bear fruit* (*pārâ*) means to be productive and abundantly blessed. The suggested emendation to *pāraḥ*, 'to sprout forth', is unnecessary.

2–3. Verses 2–5 describe the character of this Davidic ruler. First, *the Spirit of the LORD will rest on him* (v. 2). In the Old Testament the spirit of God came upon kings (1 Sam. 10:6), leaders (Deut. 34:9), prophets (Num. 24:2) and judges (Judg. 3:10) to enable them to fulfil a role, accomplish a task or prophesy (Firth and Wegner 2011: 15–21).

Three word pairings list what this king receives from the Spirit of the LORD: *wisdom* and *understanding*; *counsel* and *might*; *knowledge* and the *fear of the LORD*. *Wisdom* is often associated with a technical skill or experience and shrewdness (see *NIDOTTE* 2.133). *Understanding* is insight, discernment or good judgment (see *NIDOTTE* 1.653). Wise *counsel* is advice given to help determine a judicious plan or course of action and is crucial when going into battle or making difficult decisions (see *NIDOTTE* 2.490). The *fear of the LORD* is a genuine reverence for God and his sovereignty and is foundational to the other five characteristics.

The phrase *he will delight* [*rāwaḥ*; perhaps a play on the word 'spirit', *rûaḥ*] *in the fear of the* LORD implies that he will be pleased to be guided by the LORD. Oswalt comments that human judges can do no better than to rely upon their natural faculties, but this king will see beyond appearances to discern the truth (1986: 280–281).

4–5. Verse 4 contains two doublets, the first describing his fairness, and the second, the power of his judgments. He will judge righteously and render fair decisions for the *needy* and *poor* who cannot afford to buy his favour. The phrase *the poor of the earth* may suggest his rule extends beyond Israel. His authority is such that he need only speak (*the breath of his lips*) to bring judgment and subsequent punishment on the wicked.

The *sash*, either a 'waist cloth' (a close inner garment) or *belt*, pictures *righteousness* and *faithfulness* as among his essential characteristics. Upholding truth and justice for the poor and afflicted was a standard commonly espoused throughout the Ancient Near East (*ANET* 161–197) but was seldom practised. Certainly the kings in Isaiah's time did not display the qualities described here, but the people could look forward to one day having a fair and just king.

6–9. This king ushers in a kingdom of peace that extends over every aspect of creation. Doublets picture natural enemies at peace with one another: *the wolf* and *the lamb*; *the leopard* and *the goat*; and *the calf* and *the lion*. The transformation of these formerly dangerous wild animals into safe, gentle creatures is demonstrated in the fact that a *little child* will lead them around without fear.

This peace in the animal kingdom will be extended to the people: *the infant* (lit. 'nursing child') or *young child* (lit. 'weaned child') will be able to *play near* the *den* (*ḥur*, 2x; see 42:22) of the *cobra* or *viper* (*ṣipʿônî*, 4x; see 59:5) without fear, something that would greatly relieve any loving parent. This picture of peace and safety has been unknown since the time of paradise (Gen. 1 – 2).

The peace and harmony summarized in verse 9 exists *on all my holy mountain* (referring to at least Zion, 66:20) and is attributed to the fact that *the knowledge of the* LORD will saturate the earth, just as *waters cover the sea*. The image portrays how the peace and safety this ruler brings will change the world.

(b) The remnant of God's people will return (11:10–16)

10. The phrase *in that day* looks to a future time when this kingdom of peace is established and other nations will come to learn more about the *Root of Jesse*. Jesse's family, from which David came, will bring forth another Davidide to once again unify his nation and place it in the world's spotlight (2 Sam. 7:8–17; see Jesus' lineage, Matt. 1:1–17).

That the ruler originates from the line of David is not surprising, but that he should be a *banner* (*nēs*, 'standard', in the sense of a 'rallying point') for the *peoples* or *nations* outside Israel is extraordinary. Nations will *rally to* (lit. 'seek') this Davidide, presumably to voluntarily submit to him, and *his resting-place* [i.e. Israel] *will be glorious*, as already described in verses 1–9.

11–12. In that future time (*in that day*) *the Lord will reach out . . . a second time to reclaim the . . . remnant of his people*. The verb *reclaim* (*qānâ*, 'to acquire, purchase'; also used in Exod. 15:16 when God first acquired his people) emphasizes the cost of returning a *remnant of his people*.

The first time God recovered his remnant is most probably their return from Babylon, but the second return will come from the four points of the compass: from the north (i.e. *Assyria, Hamath* [in Syria]); from the south (Egypt divided into three parts: *Lower Egypt* = the Nile Delta; *Upper Egypt* [lit. Pathros = the Nile Valley]; and *Cush* = the far south region [Nubia or Ethiopia]); from the east (*Elam* = east of Babylon; *Babylonia* [lit. *šinʿār*, 'Shinar' = an early name for Babylon]); and from the west (*the islands of the Mediterranean*). According to Genesis 10:10, Shinar (8x) is the plain between the Tigris and Euphrates rivers.

13–14. The Syro-Ephraimite War (734–732 BC) demonstrated the serious tensions that had arisen between Israel and Judah, but verse 13 pictures a future day when there will no longer be animosity between Ephraim (i.e. the northern kingdom was reduced to the highlands of Ephraim) and Judah. Together they will rule supremely over their enemies (v. 14) – the Philistines to their *west* (lit. 'to the sea') and Edom, Moab and Ammon *to the east* (lit. 'before').

This is the only occurrence of the phrase 'sons of the east' (NIV: *the people to the east*) in the book of Isaiah. Judah's enemies of the eighth century BC represent the enemies of this future Davidide's kingdom, yet the peace and prosperity of his reign will be even greater than that of any Israelite king thus far.

15–16. Just as God through Moses struck the Reed Sea and the Israelites walked across, so he will again strike *the gulf of the Egyptian sea* (lit. 'the tongue of the Sea of Egypt', a reference to the Reed Sea's shape) and *the River Euphrates* (lit. 'the river') so that they will be dry riverbeds providing easy access for his returning remnant.

The *scorching wind* (*ba'yām*, occurs only here) separates the major bodies of water into *seven streams* – seven signifies fullness or completeness. This *highway* ('raised road', never used of a city street) will bring the remnant from Egypt and even Assyria, and is likened to Israel's exodus from Egypt (Exod. 12:33–41).

Meaning

God's new deliverer, unlike any of Israel's past rulers, will rule in righteousness and justice, accept no bribes, and bring peace and safety to his nation – a time unequalled since paradise in the original creation. While Isaiah 4:2–6 and 9:1–7 also picture a time of restoration and peace, this section emphasizes to a greater extent the king's character, and the peace and safety that ensue. Only in an environment of absolute peace can true justice and safety be achieved.

During the reign of this future deliverer, God will gather his remnant from the ends of the earth, leading them victoriously against their enemies to usher in a time of world peace.

g. A song of thanksgiving (12:1–6)

Context

This final unit of the palistrophe, a song of thanksgiving by the righteous remnant, is a wonderful reversal from the sorrowful song regarding the unrighteous vineyard which appeared at the beginning of the palistrophe (see Figure 0.8 on p. 20). The poem is very similar to songs of thanksgiving in the Psalter (see Pss 65; 67) and is divided into two sections, each beginning with the phrase *in that day* (vv. 1–3, 4–6). Similar to other psalms, it moves back and forth between the second person singular and plural forms. Childs (2001: 107) argues that this is an eschatological hymn of praise, but the deliverance in 701 BC could also have fostered these types of hopes (see v. 6, *for great is the Holy One of Israel among you*).

Comment

1–3. *In that day* refers to the deliverance mentioned in the previous section. *You* [sing.] *will say* denotes either the remnant of Israel or the nation personified, who will praise God for all the great things he has done. Several of the phrases in this song are commonly found in other songs of thanksgiving (e.g. *I will praise you, LORD* [Pss 138:1; 145:2]; *God* ['*ēl*] *is my salvation* [Pss 27:9; 62:2]; *give praise* [or 'thanks'] *to the LORD* [Pss 7:17; 9:1]).

The phrase *although you were angry with me* is the only reference in the song to the distress that God had brought upon the nation, an integral part of songs of thanksgiving. The punishment was effective in yielding a remnant of purified Israelites. God's anger has now been *turned away* so that there is no longer reason to dread (v. 2). The author believes with certainty that God is present and will deliver.

In verse 3 the song switches to second person plurals. Because God has shown his greatness and justice by delivering his nation, they will now serve him readily. Drawing from God's *wells of salvation* suggests an ever-flowing, bountiful source of God's salvation that will always be available to his people.

4–6. Verse 4 also begins with *in that day*, a time when God will receive the *praise* he deserves for bringing a remnant of Israel back to himself. Yahweh's *name* (his name represents his character) is to be extolled because of his great actions. Reminding others of God's mighty deeds will cause them to appreciate this extraordinary God, especially in contrast to their powerless gods.

The remnant are to *sing to the LORD*, expressing their words and feelings in worship to their God. Declaring the *glorious things* God had done allowed Israel to become the witness for Yahweh that they were intended to be. Yahweh is enthroned upon *Zion*; but more importantly he is dwelling *among* them, which is what preserves them.

With good reason the song and this major section end with the title *Holy One of Israel*, for holiness is an attribute that separates him from humanity and underlies all that he has done in and for Israel.

Meaning
This final song is well-deserved praise to Yahweh who brought about this amazing deliverance. Israel will finally bring the light of God's salvation to the nations. When the nations hear about what God has done for his people, they too will want to serve this great and remarkable God.

C. Oracles of judgment and restoration (*13:1 – 39:8*)

The placement of these oracles is intentional, forming part of another palistrophe (Isa. 13 – 39; see Figure 0.9 on p. 23). The introduction to this section is now the third in the book of Isaiah (i.e. 1:1; 2:1; 13:1), each signalling a major literary unit.

The first section, the 'Oracles against the Nations' (chs. 13–23), contains primarily judgment oracles on various nations (similar to Jer. 46 – 51; Ezek. 25 – 32; Amos 1 – 2; Zeph. 2:4–15). There is only a single, short oracle of three to four verses regarding Assyria, which was Israel's primary enemy during Isaiah's time. However, at the heart of this oracle against Assyria are these words: *This is the plan determined for the whole world* (14:26), the implication being that anyone who goes against God's people (i.e. Israel) will be treated similarly to the Assyrians (see 14:24, lit. 'so it has happened'). A much fuller discussion of what happened to Assyria is found in the Isaianic Narratives of chapters 36–39, suggesting that these two sections are related to each other.

We suggest that chapters 24–27 (sometimes called 'the Little Apocalypse') and chapters 34–35, both of which speak of events surrounding the latter days, are corresponding units of the palistrophe. The middle section of the palistrophe (chs. 28–33) contains nine woe oracles, several of which describe the events around 701 BC; each is followed by a description of restoration. Thus, each of the three main sections of Isaiah 1 – 39 either contains a palistrophe or is structured as one.

i. Oracles against foreign nations (13:1 – 23:18)
These Oracles (*maśśā'*) against the Nations confirm that God has control over all nations, not simply Israel. The nine nations (i.e. Babylon, Assyria, Philistia, Moab, Damascus [Aram/Syria],

Ethiopia [Cush], Egypt, Judah, Tyre) addressed in these oracles are all to be punished by God, generally for harming his nation Israel; however, even Israel is included in the *Valley of Vision* oracle (22:1).

a. Babylon (13:1 – 14:23)

Context
This section comprises two poetic oracles connected by a narrative unit concerning Israel (i.e. 14:1–4a). In a future day when Israel once again enjoys relief after having suffered, the people *will take up this taunt against the king of Babylon* (14:4). Both oracles feature poetic and figurative language that describes the destruction carried out by Babylon and then on Babylon itself.

Additional note: Babylonia

Babylonia rose to prominence when Nabopolassar ascended the throne in Babylon in November 626 BC. He immediately made peace with Elam, which then joined forces with Babylonia against Assyria. As Assyria grew weaker, skirmishes continued until the summer of 612 BC when Nineveh was sacked, making Babylonia the pre-eminent world power in the Ancient Near East under the brilliant military leader Nebuchadnezzar (605–562 BC).

In 605 BC Nebuchadnezzar marched to Jerusalem to ensure their allegiance and took some of their most talented sons, including Daniel and his companions (see Dan. 1), to train them for leadership in the Babylonian Empire. Jehoiakim, king of Judah, became a vassal of the Babylonians, which lasted for several years until he transferred loyalty to Pharaoh Neco II and rebelled against Babylon (2 Kgs 24:1). Nebuchadnezzar returned to Jerusalem in 597 BC to punish the rebellious king; however, Jehoiakim had already died before his arrival, leaving his son Jehoiachin to withstand a three-year siege before surrendering and being taken captive to Babylonia. Zedekiah, installed as king in Jehoiachin's place (*ANET* 564), served Babylon for about eleven years, after which he too rebelled. Nebuchadnezzar, having had enough, followed Babylonian policy and came back to destroy the city in 586 BC and deport its people (see Jer. 52).

Comment

1–3. The third introduction in the book of Isaiah introduces an oracle (*maśśā'*) in which God initiates the destruction of Babylon (vv. 2–3; *ANET* 315–316), an event that would occur about a century after Isaiah's lifetime. Here *maśśā'* is used in the figurative sense of a 'burden' placed upon the prophet until he prophesies a particular message (see Jer. 20:7–9). Instructions are given to summon the troops: *raise a banner on a bare hilltop* (*nēs*, 'standard' = a signal around which the troops would rally; v. 1), *shout* and *beckon* [lit. 'wave a hand'; see 10:32] *to them*. The phrase *bare hilltop* (lit. 'hill of bareness' [*nišpeh*, 2x; see Job 33:21]) may refer to a hill in the north-east part of Babylon.

These troops will *enter the gates of the nobles* to conquer them. God's troops are called 'my consecrated ones' (i.e. set apart for a specific job), *my warriors*, and *those who rejoice in my triumph* (lit. 'my jubilant pride'). His warriors are carrying out 'God's wrath' on Babylon, but the reason why is not given until verse 11: they are wicked, arrogant and ruthless.

4–5. The LORD *Almighty* is mustering a great army from many nations (*faraway lands*) to *destroy the whole country* of Babylon. The comparison *like that of a great multitude* seems redundant but fits the parallel unit well. God uses these nations as *the weapons of his wrath* to punish Babylonia for their severe treatment of God's people when they were sent into exile. God's wrath is justified and he will not hold back – the entire land will be affected. God executed this judgment on Babylonia through Cyrus and the Medo-Persian Empire in 539 BC.

6–10. Wailing will be heard in anticipation of this *day of the* LORD, the day when *destruction* (*śōd*) comes *from the Almighty* (*śadday*). There is a wordplay here: the word for *destruction* derives from the same Hebrew letters as *the Almighty*. The splendour of the Persian army will cause extreme fear among the Babylonians: *all hands will go limp* and *every heart will melt with fear*. The *terror* and *pain* (v. 8) that will grip the people are compared to those of a *woman in labour* (lit. 'writhing in pain'). *They will look aghast at each other* in shock and horror, with *their faces aflame* (lit. 'their faces are faces of flames', indicating great anxiety). Roberts translates this phrase as 'their faces pale with fright', possibly from the colour of flames (2015: 196).

God displays *fierce anger* on *the day of the LORD* when he executes judgment. Because the Babylonians had hurt his chosen people who were dear to him, he will make their *land desolate* and decimate the Babylonian people (called *sinners*, v. 9). The *stars* and the *constellations* that do not *show their light* may be a figurative reference to the Babylonian astrologers, known for their ability to discern meanings from the heavenly bodies; they will be unable to do so because the sun and moon will refuse to give their *light* (i.e. omens).

11–12. Here the prophet sees farther into the future to a time when God extends punishment across the entire world because of wickedness and humbles all who are arrogant and haughty (see 2:12–22). The destruction will be so comprehensive that people will be rarer *than the gold of Ophir*. Gold from Ophir was renowned for its purity (see 1 Kgs 9:26–28), but the exact location of Ophir is unknown.

13–16. Signs in the heavens and on earth will demonstrate God's great anger: *the heavens tremble; / and the earth will shake*. The title *LORD Almighty* (lit. 'of hosts') emphasizes God's sovereignty and his right to punish Babylonia. The metaphors of a *hunted gazelle* and shepherdless sheep (v. 14) convey terror and confusion as the Babylonians *flee to their native land*, mistakenly thinking they will find safety. Those who are captured will be killed, *their infants will be dashed to pieces* (i.e. the same cruel treatment they had shown to Israel's children in the destruction of Jerusalem; see Ps. 137:8–9), *their houses will be looted* and *their wives violated*, all cruelties of war. The verb *dashed to pieces* (*riṭṭēš*, 6x; see Hos. 13:16) highlights the heartlessness of the slaughter of their young children.

17–18. God will use the Medes and Persians to bring down the Babylonians. The description of the Medes as those who *do not care for silver / and have no delight in gold* is ambiguous: either their attack is not motivated by a desire to plunder, or their onslaught will not be deterred by offers of gold and silver. Given the events of Cyrus's conquest, both may be true. The Persians will be ruthless, showing mercy neither to women nor children. The inverted syntax lends emphasis to the phrase *their bows will strike down the young men*.

19–22. Babylon, built to impress their gods (*ANET* 68–69), was known for its beauty and splendour. The Hanging Gardens of

Babylon have been described as one of the Seven Wonders of the Ancient World. Nevertheless, the city would fall from its status as the *jewel of kingdoms, / the pride and glory of the Babylonians* (v. 19). The prophet likens its total destruction to that of Sodom and Gomorrah (Gen. 18 – 19) seven centuries earlier, a classic picture of God's destruction. Babylon would never be rebuilt; its ruined fortresses and palaces would instead be inhabited by wild animals (*jackals* [*'ōḥîm*, occurs only here],[12] *owls* [*benôt ya'ănâ*, lit. 'daughters of ostriches'], *goats, hyenas*). The MT's reading 'widows' (*'almānôt*) should be read as 'strongholds, fortresses' (*'armānôt*) from a common dialectal interchange between languages ('l' to 'r'). The precise identification of some of these animals is uncertain, but they are all desert creatures. The *wild goats* are said to *leap about* (*rāqad*, 9x), meaning to frolic or play.

This section ends with a fateful reminder that destruction was imminent: *Her time is at hand* [lit. 'near to come her time'], / *and her days will not be prolonged* [lit. 'stretched out']. Following the death of Alexander the Great, Babylon was finally abandoned and left uninhabited (Roberts 2015: 199), as described in the preceding verses. While parts of Babylon have been reconstructed, many of its ruins can still be seen today.

14:1–4a. In the midst of this oracle against Babylon, there is a promise of restoration for Israel written in prose (contrary to the NIV). Many scholars consider this narrative section a post-exilic interpolation joining the two poetic sections of the oracle. Yet it is likely that Isaiah believed that exile would not be the last word for Israel and that at least some Israelites (a remnant) would return to Yahweh (see 6:11–13).

The *kî* ('but') beginning verse 1 marks a strong contrast with the previous section: Babylon will never again be inhabited, whereas *Israel* will return to (lit. 'settle into') their land. Their return is based upon the *compassion* the LORD shows by settling them *once again* in the land, implying that there was a former time when God had allowed them to be removed from the land (i.e. 586 BC). *Foreigners* (lit. 'the sojourners') will voluntarily join themselves to

---

12. These are not the usual words for jackals (*tannîm*) or owls (*taḥmās*).

Israel and live there as *servants*; thus, the *captives* ultimately become the *captors*.

Once their captivity (described as *suffering, turmoil* and *harsh labour*) is over, they will then *take up this taunt* (lit. 'proverb, parable'; in this context, a 'mocking song') against the king of Babylon.

4b–6. The *taunt* comprises four nearly equal sections: (1) joy at the Babylonian king's demise (vv. 4b–8); (2) amazement in Sheol at his downfall (vv. 9–11); (3) his pride (vv. 12–15); and (4) his ultimate disgrace (vv. 16–20). The exclamation *how* (*'êk*) is common in laments (vv. 4, 12). The lament metre (i.e. 3/2 beats per unit) appears consistently throughout the taunt. However, instead of mourning there is great rejoicing over Babylon's demise. There is also a sense of surprise that such a powerful king has fallen, for the LORD has ensured that *the oppressor* and *his fury* [*madhēbâ*, occurs only here; scholars commonly emend it to *marhēbâ*, 'fury', a slight change of a Hebrew letter that looks similar in square script] are no more: *the LORD has broken the rod of the wicked, / the sceptre of the rulers*.

Verse 6 describes the uncontrolled cruelty of Babylon, who punished their adversaries far more than was necessary: in anger they *struck down peoples / with unceasing blows* (lit. 'a blow without turning aside'). The parallel phrase states *with relentless aggression* (lit. 'punishment without withholding').

7–11. The Babylonian reign of terror has been cut off, allowing the whole world (lit. 'all the land') to breathe a sigh of relief and break out into shouts of joy. Even the trees *gloat* that they will no longer be cut down, for Babylon will no longer demand cedars of Lebanon for their building projects (*ANET* 306–307). *The realm of the dead* (i.e. Sheol; v. 9) raises the *departed* (*rĕpā'îm*, 'shades') *leaders* [*'attûdê*, lit. 'male goats'] *in the world* (many of whom the Babylonians had killed) *from their thrones* to meet him. These thrones probably represent the 'thrones of power' they once held.

The kings delight in the fact that Babylon's king, whose immense power had made him seem almost immortal, is indeed mortal and has become as *weak* as they are. *You have become like us* (*nimšāltā*) is probably a play on the word *māšal*, which can mean either 'to rule' or 'to be like'. The ruler has now become like the dead who are pictured in a weakened state, unable to affect what is happening in life on earth. All the Babylonian king's great splendour and the *noise* [*hemyâ*, occurs only here] *of* [his] *harps* (*nĕbāleykā* = a type of harp or lute, v. 11) enter the grave as well, soon to be forgotten. There is a grisly reference to the deterioration of the king's body: he who once seemed invincible is now food for *maggots* (*rimmâ*, 7x; see Job 25:6) and *worms* (*tôlēʿâ*, 8x), confirmation that everyone, no matter how powerful, meets death, the great leveller.

12–14. These verses express surprise or disbelief as they focus again on the downfall (lit. 'hewn down to the earth') of this great king: *How* [could] *you* [sing.] *have fallen from heaven, / morning star, son of the dawn?* LXX and the Vulgate read 'Lucifer' for *morning star* (lit. 'shining one'); the name was then picked up by the KJV and became a popular designation for Satan. However, the parallel terms *morning star* and *son of the dawn* are most likely to refer to the planet Venus, sometimes called the 'morning star' because it rises in the early morning, then appears to tumble from the sky without completing a true elliptical orbit. Marduk, the patron deity of Babylon, was believed to guide Jupiter through the heavens, which in turn guided the other stars and planets. Similarly, the Babylonian king who had risen to his exalted position in *the heavens* and *the utmost heights of Mount Zaphon* (*ṣāpôn*, 'north', v. 13) by defeating nations (*laid low the nations*) has been *cast down* [lit. 'cut down'] *to the earth* (see Ezek. 28:16–18). Verse 12 may also allude to the Canaanite myths of lesser gods being cast out of the pantheon of deities (some close parallels come from the Canaanite myths found at Ugarit, but there are no direct parallels).

The proud ambitions of the Babylonian king's heart are laid bare for all to see in verses 13–14: (1) *I will ascend to the heavens* (i.e. the abode of the gods). (2) *I will raise my throne* [i.e. 'seat of honour' or 'royal throne'] / *above the stars of God* (*ʾēl*, shortened form of Elohim and a common name for divinity throughout the Ancient Near East; note that he does not say 'above God'); *stars* refers to other leaders or lesser deities. (3) *I will sit enthroned on the mount of assembly*, parallel to the *heights of Mount Zaphon* (= Jebel Aqra in Northern Syria). In context he boasts that he intends to sit with the deities. (4) *I will ascend above the tops* [*bāmŏtê*, lit. 'backs/high places'] *of the clouds* (the gods dwelt above the clouds in heaven). The Babylonian's desire is similar to that of those who attempted to build the tower in Shinar ('Come, let us build ourselves . . . a tower that reaches to the heavens', Gen. 11:4). (5) *I will make myself like the Most High* ('*elyôn*). In the Babylonian pantheon of gods, there was one god who ruled over the others. The Babylonian is claiming that in time he could rival this most high god. The name 'El Elyon' is also frequently used for Yahweh in the Old Testament to emphasize his sovereignty (see Gen. 14:19–20).

This may be a description of Nebuchadnezzar, who was chastened by God for boasting that he had made Babylon great by his own power and might (Dan. 4:29–33). At no other time in the biblical record does God step in to chasten the pride and arrogance of a Babylonian king. Alternatively, it may compile the traits of more than one Babylonian king, since Nabonidus appears to have fulfilled verses 19–21.

Additional note: fall of Satan

Some scholars have suggested that verses 12–14 refer to the fall of Satan, arguing that the actions described go beyond mere human ability. But this understanding demands lifting these verses out of their context, which clearly refers to a human king (see v. 16). In Ancient Near Eastern thought a god was only somewhat more powerful than humans. It is therefore reasonable that a Babylonian king might hope to rival the gods, perhaps even supplanting the highest god.

The word *śāṭān* ('adversary') occurs thirty-three times in the Old Testament; but generally it emphasizes the action of being an adversary and is not a proper name. However, there are three passages where a specific adversary accuses one of God's messengers; in the first two of these passages an article appears on the word *śāṭān* (i.e. 'the adversary'; Job 1 – 2; Zech. 3:1–2). In 1 Chronicles 21:1, the article does not appear, which suggests that by this time (*c.*400 BC) *śāṭān* had become a proper name. Thus, towards the end of the Old Testament, the Israelites appear to have developed the concept that a specific adversary accuses God's people. This does not rule out the possibility that the same entity does the accusing each time, but simply means that they would not have understood this concept until later. The New Testament provides significantly more revelation about Satan (e.g. 2 Cor. 11:14; Eph. 2:2; 1 Pet. 5:8).

15–17. Despite the Babylonian king's boastful claims, the biblical text states emphatically that he will die and enter Sheol, just like any other human: *But you are brought down to the realm of the dead* (Sheol). Instead of ascending to where the gods dwell *on the utmost heights of Mount Zaphon* (v. 13), he will be brought down *to the depths* [lit. 'remotest parts'] *of the pit* (v. 15). There, too, other departed spirits will ask, *Is this the man [hā'îš] who shook the earth . . . ?* Notice that the other kings rightly consider him a man, not a god.

The Babylonians were known for overthrowing cities, depopulating other nations (lit. 'made the world like the wilderness') and deporting captive peoples to other Babylonian holdings (indicated by the phrase *would not let his captives go home* [lit. 'his prisoners he did not open to home']. Yet he is no better than others in Sheol, having been unable to take any of his former power and influence with him beyond the grave.

18–21. Kings usually erected a royal *tomb* (lit. 'house') or honoured family grave where they could *lie in state* (lit. 'lie down in honour'; see *ANET* 505). But the Babylonian king will be *cast out* of his grave, *like a rejected branch* (lit. 'an abhorred shoot'; see 22:15–23). Graves were typically protected and not harmed in Ancient Near Eastern societies; even enemies typically received the honour of a burial (2 Kgs 9:34). Not so for the Babylonian king. Instead of receiving special recognition upon his death, his body is tossed into a pile of corpses (i.e. 'clothed with the slain'), ending up at the bottom of the heap (*stones of the pit* suggests the bottom of the pit, v. 19). The parallel phrase *like a corpse trampled underfoot* suggests humiliation after death. Not only is the king punished for devastating other nations, he is also punished for ruining his own country (*killed your people* is probably a reference to the king sending troops to war and thus to their deaths). He will therefore suffer the deep humiliation of not being allowed to rest with his ancestors, a common blessing for the dead (see Gen. 15:15).

Verse 20 ends with a curse: *Let the offspring of the wicked / never be mentioned again.* Instead of inheriting a good name and the land, the Babylonian king's children will be slaughtered. None of his descendants will be left to build more cities (i.e. to extend the Babylonian Empire) as their fathers once did. Persia fulfilled this prophecy. In the Ancient Near East the end of an out-of-favour dynasty often meant the dismantling of temples, palaces and buildings so that their memory would be forgotten.

22–23. The taunt against Babylon ends with the LORD *Almighty*'s (lit. 'of hosts') confirmation of their destruction: *I will rise up against them* [and] *will wipe out Babylon's name and survivors.* The plural pronoun in the phrase *against them* refers either to multiple Babylonian kings or to the king and his people. The certainty of their destruction is underscored three times in these verses (*declares the* LORD, vv. 22a, 22b, 23b). The phrase *declares the* LORD *Almighty* that occurs at the beginning and end forms an *inclusio* (vv. 22–23).

The destruction will also be unusually thorough: *Babylon's name* ('reputation, fame') will be wiped out, along with any *survivors, offspring* (*nîn*, 3x; see Gen. 21:23) or *descendants* (*neked*, 3x; see Job 18:19). It will become a place for *owls* (*qippôd*, 3x; perhaps 'owl' or 'hedgehog'?; see 34:11) and a *swampland* (*'agmê* [8x]-*māyim*, 'muddy pool of water'), being thoroughly swept away with *the broom* [*maṭ'ăṭē'*, occurs only here] *of destruction*, just as one would sweep away dust.

This destruction and humiliation began with Nabonidus, the last king of Babylonia, who suffered the humiliation of hearing the cheering of Babylonian citizens in the streets when he was removed from office by Cyrus (*ANET* 315–316). But the nation was not entirely terminated until after the death of Alexander the Great.

Meaning

God makes it clear that he will hold the Babylonian kings responsible for their pride, arrogance and cruelty towards other people. Babylon would be thoroughly destroyed and no longer inhabited. Just as Babylonia had deported peoples, so will the Babylonian king be cast out of his own land. Even the blessing of a final resting place, lying in a tomb with his ancestors, would be withheld from him. God chose to use these wicked people as his tool to discipline his own people, yet he ultimately punishes them as well.

b. Assyria (14:24–27)

Context

The prevailing view in nineteenth-century scholarship was that Isaiah 14:24–27 should be joined to the Assyrian section in 10:5–15; then in the twentieth century some scholars began to consider it part of a Josaianic redaction (Clements 1980a: 146). Some have also argued that because this message against Assyria does not have a title, it is part of the earlier oracle against Babylon. However, there are other examples of untitled oracles in this section (Isa. 18; 20; 21:16–17; 22:15–25). This short oracle is directed against Assyria, Israel's enemy at the time, but also provides the rationale for judgment against all the other nations (v. 26).

Comment

24–25. *The LORD Almighty* ('of hosts') now confirms with an oath the truth of what he declares in verses 24–25. The oath formula was considered one of the strongest means of assurance in the Ancient Near East. The text implies that God's plan to punish the Assyrians was accomplished just as he said it would be: *Surely, as* [*kaʾăšer*, 'just as'] *I have planned, so* [*kēn*] *it will be* [lit. 'so it has happened'], */ and as I have purposed, so it will happen* (v. 24).

Verse 25 describes Assyria's destruction: (1) *I will crush the Assyrian in my land*; (2) *I will trample him down*; (3) *his yoke will be taken from my people* (see 9:4); (4) *and his burden* [will be] *removed*. The Assyrian yoke of oppression eased in 701 BC when God punished Sennacherib and wiped out 185,000 of his soldiers outside Jerusalem (see 2 Kgs 19; Isa. 37:36), but it would not be fully removed until Assyria's final demise at the hands of the Babylonians in 605 BC.

26–27. These verses apply the punishment Assyria received to any nation that attempts to harm God's people. God's judgment will be worked out on all the earth and cannot be frustrated. Once he has determined to act, no-one can retract God's 'outstretched hand' (*the hand stretched out*), a phrase similar to that used in other judgments (see 5:25).

Meaning
We learn that God keeps his promises even in regard to destruction. The little land that the Assyrians thought would be easy to conquer would be the very land where they would be defeated by God. The context suggests that the readers would be able to both witness and confirm the punishment on Assyria. We also learn of God's sovereign plan to judge any nation that seeks to harm his people.

c. Philistia (14:28–32)

Context
It is not entirely clear whether verse 28 concludes the preceding oracle or introduces the next. Given that prophetic oracles do not typically conclude with information about when they were declared, we view it as the introduction to the next oracle (vv. 29–32) in which God forewarns of Philistia's destruction. Even though debate concerning the dating and occasion of this oracle has led a number of scholars to suggest significant emendations, the text itself is fairly stable across the various ancient versions and makes good sense as it stands.

Additional note: Philistia

The Philistines inhabited the south-west corner of Palestine in land that God originally gave to Israel, who had difficulty gaining control over the area. The Pentapolis (i.e. five governing cities) that constituted Philistia were Gaza, Ashkelon, Ashdod, Ekron and Gath.

Multiple waves of sea peoples settled in this region, most having migrated around 1200 BC from the area around the Aegean Sea to land in the region between Egypt and Canaan after having been repulsed by the Egyptians. Several times during the divided kingdom there were border skirmishes between Philistia and Israel, one of the more serious being during the reign of Ahaz (9:8–12).

Comment
28–30. The prophecy *came in the year King Ahaz died* – most probably about 715 BC (2 Kgs 16:19–20; Thiele 1994: 133–138). Since

dates are not generally included in introductions to the oracles to the nations, we can assume that this date has significance. The Philistines made frequent raids into Israel at the beginning of Ahaz's reign (2 Chr. 28:18), but these assaults stopped when Sargon II made Philistia a fully fledged vassal of Assyria about 711 BC.

The Philistines (*kullēk*, lit. 'all of you', perhaps because they ruled as a group [i.e. a Pentapolis]) are told not to rejoice because *the rod that struck you is broken* (i.e. the death of Ahaz). At the beginning of his reign Ahaz had called on Assyria (i.e. Tiglath-pileser III) for help against Damascus, Syria, Edom and Philistia (2 Chr. 28:5–18; see *ANET* 283), so his death would have been welcome news. However, God cautions the Philistines that *from the root* [figurative for 'offspring', i.e. Hezekiah] *of that snake* [i.e. Ahaz] *will spring up a viper* [*ṣepaʿ*, 'viper or some type of poisonous snake', occurs only here; i.e. Hezekiah's rebellion will cause Sennacherib to come, *ANET* 287–288], / *its fruit will be a darting* [lit. 'flying'], *venomous serpent* [lit. 'burning serpent'; i.e. Esarhaddon, *ANET* 291]. The imagery of progressively more dangerous animals is intended to convey that respite from Ahaz would be only temporary; ultimately the Assyrians would inflict even greater damage.

Two phrases in verse 30 give hope to Israel, who at this point were struggling under Ahaz, that better days lay ahead: *the poorest of the poor* (lit. 'firstborns of the poor ones') will eat and *the needy will lie down in safety*. Their current plight is contrasted with the mighty Philistines, who are to be destroyed (*your root* [i.e. 'the Philistines' offspring'] *I will destroy by famine*). In time the destruction of the Philistines would leave no survivors (v. 30), whereas a remnant would one day be brought back to Israel.

31–32. These verses refer to the failed rebellion of Ashdod, Gath and Asdudimmu against Assyria in 711 BC (*ANET* 286–287). The images of the wailing city gate and city speak of destruction. City gates were crucial targets to capture in battle, with many often dying in the process.

The verb *wail* is common in laments. Once again, the Philistines are warned of their coming destruction (lit. *Melt away, all you* [*kullēk*] *Philistines!*). The *cloud of smoke* [that] *comes from the north* refers either to the clouds of dust kicked up by an advancing large army, or to the smoke from cities burned in their wake. The Assyrians are pictured as an efficient, well-disciplined army: *there is not a straggler in its ranks* (lit. 'not one separated from his appointed place'; see 5:26–30). Unlike the envoys of Philistia who have nowhere to turn (i.e. *What answer shall be given / to the envoys of that nation?*), Zion will be protected by the LORD and will be a refuge for the afflicted Israelites (v. 32; see 4:2–6).

Additional note: Zion theology

A key concept in Zion theology is that God will protect Zion because he established his temple there. Initially this positive concept encouraged his people to trust God (see Pss 46; 48; etc.). However, it gradually became distorted, so that by Jeremiah's time the people believed God would protect them no matter how they lived, simply because God's temple was in their midst (Jer. 7:2–7). The Babylonian exile proved this distortion to be false.

Meaning
The Philistines hoped for better days since Ahaz, their nemesis, had died, but God informs them that their joy is ill-founded. Assyria will inflict much worse damage than Judah. They will have no place to turn, there will be no survivors; by contrast, Israel will be protected by the LORD, the true Sovereign.

d. Moab (15:1 – 16:14)

Context
Moab (Isa. 15 – 16) is the fourth nation that will feel the dreaded punishment of God. There is little offer of hope here – only a clear message of destruction and disaster. Contrast this with the Mesha Inscription which claimed that Moab would be delivered and Israel destroyed for ever (*ANET* 320). The date of this oracle is debated since the punishments are general in nature and little is known of Moab's geography and history, but the time frame may be between 715 and 711 BC when Sargon was consolidating his empire just before coming to punish the Moabites (see *ANET* 287).

Scholars generally agree that this oracle can be divided into four parts: (1) a lament concerning a recent attack on Moab (15:1–9); (2)

a prophetic command to provide protection for Moab's fugitives (16:1–5); (3) a further lament because of Moab's pride (16:6–12); and (4) an announcement of judgment on Moab that was about to take place (16:13–14).

Additional note: Moab

According to biblical history, the Moabite people originated from the incestuous relationship between Lot and his elder daughter (Gen. 19:37). They were generally located east of the Dead Sea between the Arnon and Zered rivers, but often extended beyond these boundaries. Their less-defined eastern border probably included the arable land up to the Arabian Desert, for a total land region of about 900 square miles.

Moses was warned not to attack the Moabites, for they were relatives and God had given them their land (Deut. 2:9). However, because the Moabites had refused to let the Israelites pass through their land during the exodus, they were never to be part of the assembly of God (Deut. 23:3–6). Several kings of Israel (e.g. David, Omri) controlled parts of Edom, but following Ahab's death, Moab broke free. With the help of Jehoshaphat and the king of Edom, Jehoram punished Moab and regained control over it (2 Kgs 1:1; 3:4–27). The Assyrians conquered Moab, forcing them to pay tribute under Tiglath-pileser III, Sennacherib, Esarhaddon and Ashurbanipal.

This oracle against Moab was merited for two important reasons: (1) Nebuchadnezzar had used Moabite mercenaries to help conquer Jerusalem (2 Kgs 24:2); and (2) Ezekiel 25:8 states that the Moabites had mocked Israel's God by saying that Israel was just like the other nations (i.e. denying God's special relationship with them).

Comment

1–3. This long oracle against Moab describes the quick (lit. *in a night*) conquest of its major cities: *Ar* (possibly Aroer), *Kir*, *Dibon*, *Nebo* and *Medeba*. In the MT the name Moab is attached to each of the city names, which is unusual, thus Oswalt connects Moab with the next verb (e.g. 'Ar is desolated; Moab is cut off'; 1986:

334). While this makes sense in the context, the accenting in the first phrase in the MT and the *maqqeph* in the second clearly go against this reading. The same two terms are used of both Moab's major cities, Ar and Kir; they will be *ruined* and *destroyed* (lit. 'cut off').

The grammar of verse 2 is awkward but appears to read: 'He [i.e. Moab] went up [to] the temple [lit. 'the house'], [to] Dibon, [and to] the high places to weep' (thus indicating three places to weep). The NIV's translation *Dibon goes up to its temple* seems unlikely given the *wāw* on *Dibon*. The destruction stretched from *Dibon*, Mesha's capital city in the middle of the country, to *Nebo* and *Medeba*, which were located in the far north. Mount Nebo was one of Moab's defensive strongholds, built on a high mountain (see *ANET* 320).

Signs of mourning abound: *every head is shaved*; *every beard* [is] *cut off*; and *they wear sackcloth*. These signs can be seen everywhere: *in the streets*, *on the roofs* and *in the public squares* (lit. 'broad places, plazas'). Everyone will feel the pain and will be wailing and weeping (lit. 'going down in weeping').

4–5. These verses emphasize the fear and distress caused by this destruction. Weeping extends to even more Moabite cities, from *Heshbon* and *Elealeh* in the far north to *Jahaz* near its eastern border. Their strong and *armed men* cry out and tremble in fear. Even the author himself feels pain over the severity of Moab's destruction, which is so extensive that survivors flee as far south as *Zoar*, *Eglath Shelishiyah*, *Luhith* and *Horonaim*, mourning as they go. *Zoar* was south-west of the Dead Sea, probably in the land of Edom, but the other cities are unknown.

6–7. A *kî* ('for') begins verses 6, 8 and 9 to introduce the reasons for the author's grief over Moab's woes. The first reason is that *the waters of Nimrim are dried up* / *and the grass is withered*, although we are not told whether this is due to drought or to overuse by either the advancing army or the refugees. The word *nimrîm*, 'pure water', occurs only in Isaiah 15:6 and Jeremiah 48:34, both of which are oracles against Moab. It may refer to the Wadi Numeira on the south-eastern shore of the Dead Sea, whose waters are said to be *dried up* (lit. 'desolate') so that *nothing green is left*.

The abundance (*yitrâ*, 2x; see Jer. 48:36) of the Moabites has been carried off over the *Ravine of the Poplars* (v. 7) by the invading armies. The location of this wadi is uncertain; it could be Wadi el-Ḥesā at the southern end of the Dead Sea.

8–9. The second reason (indicated by *kî*) for distress is that destruction has spread throughout *Moab*, even to the border towns of *Eglaim* and *Beer Elim* (lit. 'well of heroes'; exact locations unknown). The word *Dimon* (v. 9) occurs only here and is probably a reference to *Dibon* (see comment on v. 2). The slight change in spelling to *Dimon* creates a wordplay on *blood* (*dām*) in the phrase *The waters of Dimon are full of blood*, which serves as a fitting end to this lament. The important message of verse 9 is that the punishment is not over: *I will bring still more upon Dimon*. The *fugitives* and *those who remain* from Moab will encounter a *lion*, a metaphor for either the Babylonians or the Assyrians.

16:1–2. This chapter, an apparent response to the prior lament, reads like the interaction between Israel and a delegation sent from Moab to request asylum in the *Daughter* [of] *Zion*. The author appears to be giving advice, first to the fleeing Moabites (v. 1) and then to the Israelites (vv. 3b–4).

In hopes of making peace with Israel, Moab is told to send *lambs* (lit. 'lamb' [sing.]) as an offering (NIV reads *tribute*) to appease the ruler of Israel (see 2 Kgs 3:4). The tribute comes *from Sela* (lit. 'a rocky crag or cliff'), often associated with Petra, and is sent *across the desert* to Mount Zion (lit. 'to the hill of the daughter of Zion').

The Moabites are pictured as *fluttering birds* [lit. 'fleeing birds'] / *pushed from the nest*, imagery that depicts their vulnerability even though they thought themselves secure, living in the cliffs of Petra. They will pass through *the fords* [*maʿbārōt*, 8x; see Josh. 2:7] *of the Arnon* (i.e. on their northern border) on their way to Israel.

3–5. The *fugitives* (lit. 'outcasts') request sanctuary in Israel saying: (1) *Make up your mind* (lit. 'bring [us] advice') and (2) *Render a decision* (*pĕlîlâ*, occurs only here). The decision they seek is a positive offer of help so that they might be hidden and not betrayed (lit. 'uncovered'), which they say would be as refreshing as a dark shadow in the bright noonday sun (lit. 'between two noons', v. 3).

The prophet (or God) tells the Israelites to give the refugees asylum (lit. 'let them sojourn with you') and shelter (lit. 'a hiding place') *from the destroyer* (*šôdēd*), a possible reference to Assyria. The reason (*kî*) why they should do so (v. 4b) is described in three parallel phrases: because (1) their *oppressor* [*hammēṣ*, occurs only here] *will come to an end* [*'āpēs*, lit. 'has come to an end'; 5x]; (2) *destruction* [*šōd*] *will cease* [lit. 'has ceased']; and (3) *the aggressor* [*rōmēs*] *will vanish from the land*. Each of these phrases makes it clear that the punishment God has sovereignly allowed is now completed. Thus, Israel is to extend a much more hospitable hand to Moab than the Moabites had offered them in their trouble (see Num. 22 – 25).

Part of the reason why Israel can extend a gracious hand to the Moabite fugitives is because they will be shown mercy. A contrast is drawn between the destruction that is happening in Moab and the establishment of a Davidic ruler in Zion (*from the house* [lit. 'tent'] *of David*). The author looks forward to a time when the Moabites, who have run into the arms of Israel for protection, will also seek the *justice* and *righteousness* brought to Israel by this Davidic ruler. This time period is characterized by a cluster of terms used in other messianic passages: 'lovingkindness' (NIV *love*), *faithfulness*, *justice* and *righteousness* (see 9:7; 11:1–9; etc.) Again, the author looks past the current circumstances to a future time when a righteous king will rule on the throne of David, and nations will come to find justice and righteousness in Israel (commonly known as the 'prophetic perspective').

6–8. The Israelites protest that those from Moab do not deserve their help: *We* [Israel] *have heard of Moab's pride . . . her arrogance* and her empty boasts. *Moab's pride* and *arrogance* may refer to their presumed security, living in the cliffs of Petra, but their *boasts are empty* (lit. 'his idle talk [is] not so'). Just as Israel must undergo punishment to purge out pride and arrogance, so Moab must go through similar punishment: *Therefore the Moabites wail . . . Lament and grieve / for the raisin cakes of Kir Hareseth* (v. 7).

The vineyards of *Kir Hareseth* that provided raisins for the *raisin cakes* (*'ăšîšâ*, 5x; Hos. 3:1; i.e. a delicacy made by pressing together raisins) offered to their god Chemosh are now gone, as are *the fields of Heshbon* and the vineyards of *Sibmah*. The vineyards of Kir Hareseth (lit. 'city of earthenware') and Sibmah were expansive; they *once reached Jazer / and spread towards the desert . . . and went as far as the sea* (most probably the Dead Sea). The phrase *Their shoots* [*šĕluḥôt*, 'tendrils', occurs only here] *spread out / and went as far as the sea* (lit. 'they went over a sea') suggests the exportation of wine and raisins from Moab to Judah; or, less likely, it may suggest the Mediterranean Sea. Their enemies, which the author calls *the rulers of the nations*, have trampled all their vast, fruitful vineyards.

9–10. The joy and shouting that are ordinarily part of celebrating the harvest (see 9:3) are absent since Moab is invaded at a crucial time just before the harvest (i.e. from early August's *ripened fruit* [lit. 'summer fruit'] into late September). Moab's devastation has been so extensive and distressing that even God weeps: *I drench you with tears!* (lit. 'I will weep in weeping' = 'bitter weeping'). The word ʾărayyāwek (with uncertain meaning) probably has transposed letters and should be read ʾărawwāyek, 'I will drench you [with tears]'. Verse 10 helps us know that it is God speaking in the first person – only he could have *put an end to the shouting*. These two verses highlight two aspects of God: (1) his love (*So I weep, as Jazer weeps*, v. 9); and (2) his sovereignty in bringing the punishment (*for I have put an end to the shouting*, v. 10).

11–12. God is also saddened by Moab's idol worship. His *heart* (lit. 'internal organs') mourns for her *like a harp* playing a sad tune (v. 11). Moab's worship was relentless and useless, as she continually presented herself to her gods, either at *her high place* or at *her shrine*. She *wears herself out* in repetitive pagan rituals, including dancing, cutting/self-mutilation and other frenzied actions, to appease her god Chemosh – all to no avail since she refuses to turn to Yahweh, the only true God.

13–14. The words *already* [mēʾāz] *spoken* imply that there was a previous oracle against Moab and not that these verses are a reinterpretation of the oracle against Moab, as Childs suggests (2001: 132). They clarify that these events will soon take place: *Within three years, as a servant bound by contract would count them* [i.e. very carefully], *Moab's splendour . . . will be despised* and its great population reduced to a small (lit. 'a little few'), powerless remnant.

Meaning
Moab refuses to turn to Yahweh even though it has had several interactions with Israel's God. Moab's wealth and prosperity had made the people proud and blind to the true God. Because of their rejection of Yahweh and their excessive pride and arrogance (16:6), punishment and consequent shame are on the near horizon, much

closer than they think. They would soon feel the shame and punishment that come with choosing the wrong god.

e. Aram (ancient Syria) and Ephraim (17:1–14)

Context

With Judah's southern enemies, Philistia and Moab, having been dealt with, the fifth Oracle against the Nations now turns to their two enemies in the north, Aram and Ephraim (i.e. the northern kingdom being reduced to the highlands of Ephraim). While most Oracles against the Nations (chs. 13 – 23) are directed against countries, this one is directed against the city of Damascus, the capital of Aram. By this time, Aram had largely overpowered the northern kingdom and thus is included in the oracle against Damascus.

There has been significant discussion regarding chapters 17 (directed against Aram) and 18 (directed against Cush) since there is no separate title for the oracle against Cush. Most scholars, however, identify them as separate oracles (Clements 1980a: 163; Wildberger 1997: 211–212).

Additional note: Aram (Damascus)

Syria was bounded on the north by the River Euphrates, on the west by the Mediterranean Sea, on the east by the Syrian desert, and on the south by Israel. The region's history dates back to Palaeolithic times, but only with the Syro-Ephraimite War in 733–732 BC did it gain importance for the book of Isaiah (see 'The Syro-Ephraimite War' in the Introduction). In 732 BC Tiglath-pileser III (745–727 BC) destroyed Damascus and deported the greater part of its population to Assyria, after which little is known of its history until the Greek and Roman periods.

Comment

1–3. This oracle begins with a common title (*maśśā'*), declaring that *Damascus* will soon be destroyed and *become a heap of ruins* (*mě'î*, occurs only here). There is probably a wordplay between *mě'îr*, 'from a city', and *mě'î*, 'a ruin'. This was fulfilled during the

Syro-Ephraimite War which ended with the destruction of Damascus and the deportation of its people (*ANET* 283).

The destruction would affect more than the capital since *the cities of Aroer will be deserted*, but there is no record to date of a Syrian city/district known as Aroer. The phrase *cities of Aroer* (*ʾārê ʿărōʿēr*) is a wordplay in that *cities* and *Aroer* have the same Hebrew consonants. The cities will be of little value except as pastureland for flocks, which will graze in safety since there will be no-one to chase them off (lit. *no one to make them afraid*, v. 2).

Ephraim will suffer the same fate as the *royal power* (lit. 'sovereignty') of Damascus (their *fortified city will disappear*), suggesting that they were in alliance. In 732 BC Assyria conquered Damascus and deported or killed soldiers from both countries. This judgment comes from the LORD *Almighty* (lit. 'of hosts') who has the power and authority to use a foreign nation, if necessary, to bring it about.

4–6. Because the outcomes for Syria and Israel are intrinsically linked (*in that day* = the time of punishment), the fading of Syria's glory will also mean that Jacob's glory *will fade* (*dālal*, 'be brought low', 8x; v. 4). The parallel phrase further describes Israel's gradual decline: *the fat* [*mišmān*, 4x] *of his body will waste away* [*rāzâ*, 'to make lean', 2x; see Zeph. 2:11).

Jacob's fading glory is compared to a field after *reapers* (repointing *qāṣîr*, 'harvest', to *qōṣēr*, 'the one who harvests' or 'a reaper') have come through. Just as harvesting leaves a field nearly bare, so will Israel's population be depleted. The *Valley of Rephaim* (lit. 'dead spirits'), a rich and productive area lying south-east of Jerusalem, was frequently taken by the Philistines in their recurring skirmishes with Israel. Israel would suffer severely yet not be entirely destroyed, for a remnant would remain in the land, just as *gleanings* are left after the *olive tree is beaten* (*nōqep*, 'shaken', 2x), the most common harvesting method. This is an accurate picture of the events of 732 BC when Assyria destroyed Damascus as well as Israel's army, leaving Israel in a significantly weakened condition.

7–8. Again the phrase *in that day* refers to the day of judgment just mentioned (i.e. the Syro-Ephraimite War) that will cause the people (lit. 'the person') of Israel to *look to* (lit. 'have regard for') the one true God, signified by the phrases *the Holy One of Israel* and *their Maker.* It will be fairly obvious that their false gods did not help them, so they *will not look to the altars, the Asherah poles* and *the incense altars* [*ḥammān*, 8x] *their fingers have made.*

Fertility rites were often associated with Baal worship in which carved poles often represented Asherah, a mother-goddess who was a consort of Baal. The Israelites were to cut down or burn these (see Deut. 12:3).

9–10. These verses return to a description of the punishment: *In that day their* [lit. 'his' = Syria and Israel linked together, since they have an alliance] *strong cities* (lit. 'fortress cities') will be *abandoned . . . And all will be desolation.* The middle part of this verse is indeed difficult: *BHS* suggests significantly emending the phrase *thickets and undergrowth* (*haḥōreš* [3x] *wĕhāpāmîr* [occurs only here]) to 'Hivites and Amorites', which has little textual support.

A better translation would be: 'In that day his fortified cities will be like the abandoned wooded heights and treetops, which they abandoned from before the sons of Israel.' This last phrase calls to mind several occasions when Judah captured Israel or Syria's cities (e.g. 1 Kgs 15:22), even though it was more common for Israel or Syria to capture Judah's cities.

The referent for *you* (fem. sing.) in the context of verses 10–11 is the northern kingdom, as countries are commonly referred to in the feminine. The prophet reminds them that they have abandoned Yahweh, their *Saviour,* and turned away from *the Rock,* [their] *fortress* (v. 10; see Ps. 31:3), who had so frequently delivered them in the past. As a result, God will not bless the harvest.

The last part of verse 10 is difficult to interpret, but the context suggests two negative actions: (1) planting *the finest plants* (occurs only here, but probably are high-quality plants dedicated to other gods); and (2) planting *imported vines* (lit. 'foreign shoots', probably plants dedicated to foreign gods).

11–14. Israel carefully tends and protects the plants as they grow (*tĕsagsēgî, you make them grow,* occurs only here), but the harvest will be dismal (*nēd,* 'a heap', 6x), coming as it does in a *day of disease and incurable* [*kĕ'ēb,* 7x] *pain* [*'ănûš,* 8x]. Another interpretation of 'heap of harvest' is that they will reap a great harvest of sin, which will bring sickness and incurable pain. In any case, either God has not blessed the growth or destruction comes before the harvest.

The author emphasizes in verse 12 that Aram, and later Israel, will be overcome by many nations. The Assyrians hired mercenaries from other nations and thus were a powerful and merciless enemy. They are pictured as a great wave overflowing and drowning the nations, *like the roaring* [*šānâ*, used only here and in the next verse] *of great waters!*

The first phrase of verse 13 is similar to the last phrase of verse 12, the only difference being that the more common word 'many' (*rabbîm*; 'many waters', NASB) occurs in verse 13 instead of the less common *kabbîrîm* ('great, mighty'). The intentional repetition forms a necessary balance to the contrast drawn in the second phrase of the verse when God rebukes the nations (lit. 'him') and *they* [lit. 'he'] *flee far away.*

Assyria's ultimate downfall is pictured next. After the Babylonians conquered Nineveh (612 BC), the flight of the Assyrians to Haran (609 BC) and finally to Carchemish (605 BC) was like *chaff on the hills* or *tumble-weed* (*galgal*) driven by the wind (v. 13). In ancient times the best location for a threshing-floor was on a hilltop so that the wind could carry away the chaff from the grain during winnowing. The word *galgal* (NIV *tumble-weed*; 2x; see Ps. 83:14), sometimes translated as 'whirlwind' (see BDB), carries the idea of 'wheel' or 'to roll'. Their final destruction would not come about until a hundred years later, but then it would happen swiftly: *In the evening . . . Before the morning, they are gone!* (*ANET* 304–305).

Most of this oracle is delivered in the third person; however, at the end it changes to the first person plural as it affirms that those who *plunder* Israel will incur the same outcome. By using the first person, Isaiah includes himself among God's people; what a remarkable statement of trust in God's protection.

Meaning

For much of the ninth and eighth centuries BC, Aram repeatedly attacked Israel and on occasion Judah. Then towards the middle of the eighth century BC, the Israelites formed an alliance with them in order to attack Judah. Consequently, God would use the Assyrians to punish both Aram and the northern kingdom for harming his people. In fact, verse 14 confirms that similar punishment will happen to anyone who harms his people. Like other oracles in Isaiah, there is a ray of hope in the fact that a small remnant of those who turn to God will be preserved and their enemies punished.

f. Cush (18:1–7)

Context

It is unusual that a new oracle begins without an introduction, although 14:24–27 and 14:28–32 do not have one either. Chapter 17 and this sixth oracle against Cush are probably linked because they both refer to the events of 701 BC. Isaiah 17 initially refers to the Syro-Ephraimite War (733–732 BC), but the chapter ends (vv. 13–14) with the destruction of Assyria in 701 BC, which is when Hezekiah called on Tirhakah, pharaoh of Egypt and Cush, for help (2 Kgs 19:9; Isa. 37:9).

Chapter 18 also links Cush to the events of 701 BC. The inclusion of Cush in this pronouncement is probably due to their role in assisting the Egypt–Israel alliance against Assyria, the country God had sent to punish Israel.

Additional note: Cush

Cush was the land of Nubia or northern Sudan, an area that classical writers call 'Ethiopia'. Initially it referred to the district between the Second and Third Cataracts of the Nile (*IBD* 1.349), but later it was used as a general name for the entire region of Nubia.

In the late eighth century BC, specifically during Isaiah's lifetime, the 25th 'Ethiopian' dynasty comprised both Egypt and Cush (*IBD* 1.350). After 660 BC, Cush regained independence from Egypt, although they occasionally were hired as mercenaries in the Egyptian army.

Comment

1–2. The phrase *land of whirring wings* most probably refers to locusts, a pest that can devour virtually all vegetation in its path (see Joel 1:4). Locust plagues often came across the deserts from the south, *along the rivers of Cush* where the Blue Nile and White Nile rivers originate.

The oracle suddenly shifts in verse 2 from a general description of Cush which *sends envoys by sea / in papyrus boats* (see *ANEP* 109) to a command that messengers go quickly down to Cush for help: *Go, swift messengers, / to a people tall and smooth-skinned* (i.e. the Cushites). The people of Cush are described in four phrases. (1) They were *tall and smooth-skinned*. While the word *tall* (lit. 'ones drawn out') is fairly common, this is the only passage where it refers to a person (vv. 2, 7). The word *smooth* means smooth of skin (i.e. 'without both hair and beard'). (2) They were *feared far and wide* (lit. 'feared from himself and outward'). (3) They were an *aggressive* [lit. 'trampling', 3x; see 22:5] *nation of strange speech* (*qaw-qaw*, occurs here and in 28:10–13; probably an onomatopoeic nonsense word meant to sound like an unintelligible foreign language). (4) Their nation was *divided by rivers* (i.e. the Blue Nile and White Nile).

3–6. The message given to the prophet (*to me*, v. 4) concerns regions far beyond Cush, extending to all *people of the world* (*tēbēl*, v. 3). God expects the whole world to watch when the *banner* [*nēs*] *is raised* (see 5:26) and the *trumpet sounds*. All will see God's punishment poured out on Cush.

This punishment is described in two causal clauses (*kî*, vv. 4–5). (1) It is certain because God is sovereignly watching over the entire situation undisturbed *from* [his] *dwelling-place* (v. 4). God's oversight is pictured as *shimmering* [*ṣaḥ*, 3x; see Jer. 4:11] *heat in the sunshine*, emphasizing its intensity, and *a cloud of dew in the heat of harvest*, emphasizing its swiftness. Both images also hint that God's oversight is barely perceptible, until he suddenly acts. (2) It will inflict maximal damage. At the necessary time, pictured as just before harvest when the grapes are still unripe (*bōser*, 5x), God will step in to seal the judgment (i.e. the image of pruning the nation): he will *cut off the shoots* [*zalzal*, occurs only here] *with pruning knives* [*mazmērâ*, 4x; 2:4], / *and cut down* [*tāzaz*, occurs only here] ... *the spreading branches* (*nĕṭîšâ*, 3x; Jer. 5:10).

So many people will die that their bodies will remain unburied. The *mountain birds of prey* (i.e. eagles, buzzards) and *wild animals* will feed on their remains from summer to winter, a graphic portrayal of the extent of this destruction. Israel's plan to ally with Cush to fight the Assyrians in 701 BC would prove unsuccessful, with devastating consequences for Cush (see *ANET* 287–288).

7. This verse parallels verse 2 regarding the Israelites' request for help from the Cushites. Both verses refer to the Cushites indirectly in a four-phrase description. *At that time* may refer to the messengers in verse 2 who were sent with a request for help, thus meaning that the Cushites will indeed come to their aid. But it is more likely to refer to a future time of destruction of Cush that will purge the people and bring forth a remnant (similar to what happens to the Israelites).

The author sees not only a near-term destruction, but one far into the future that ushers in a time of restoration when a remnant of the Cushites will bring *gifts* (*šay*, 'a gift [of homage]', 3x; see Ps. 76:11) to *Mount Zion, the place of the Name of the LORD Almighty* ('of hosts'; 'place of his name' suggests ownership). Just as we have seen elsewhere in Isaiah (2:1–4; 4:1–6), a remnant of people from other nations come to pay homage to and worship God on Mount Zion (the ultimate fulfilment of Zion theology).

Meaning

Judah sent messengers to Cush for assistance; however, they were of little help. Tirhakah and his army were soundly defeated by Assyria (701 BC). Rather than relying on the Egyptians for help, Israel should have relied on their God who is truly the one who oversees history, sovereignly controlling these events. God's sovereignty will also be on display much further in the future when powerful nations, such as Cush, one day come to Jerusalem to learn about Israel's mighty God. This may correspond to the Millennium (Rev. 20:1–6) when God and his saints rule over all nations.

g. Egypt (19:1 – 20:6)

Context

The seventh oracle is directed against the ancient country of Egypt, whose history overlapped significantly with that of Israel. Initially God used Egypt to protect his people, but later Egypt either plundered or dominated Israel. Even though God demonstrated his great power and might to the Egyptians (especially during the Israelites' exodus from Egypt), they rejected Yahweh and chose to serve their many gods, to their own demise. However, this oracle confirms that in the future a remnant from Egypt will come to worship Yahweh.

The authorship and dating of the oracle against Egypt (19:1 – 20:6) are debated because Egyptian chronology during the seventh and eighth centuries BC is uncertain. The thorough discussions of this time period by Roberts (2015: 252–253) and Hoffmeier (2003: 219–234) suggest that this passage fits within Isaiah's lifetime. The identity of *a cruel master, and a fierce king* (v. 4) is likewise difficult to determine; suggestions range from the Ethiopian Piankhy (715 BC) to Antiochus Epiphanes (170 BC). However, it may simply be a metaphorical description of Egypt's demise.

Scholars generally agree that this oracle against Egypt is made up of at least three parts: 19:1–15; 19:16–25; 20:1–6. The first section (19:1–15) consists of three nearly equal parts: (1) the consequences of God's judgment on Egypt's people (vv. 1–4); (2) the consequences of God's judgment on Egypt's land (vv. 5–10); and (3) the consequences of following human wisdom (vv. 11–15). The second section (19:16–25) is composed of five short *in that day* declarations that describe the restoration of the land following God's judgment. The last section (20:1–6) is a separate oracle against Egypt and Ethiopia describing their conquest by Assyria about 713–711 BC.

Additional note: Egypt

Egypt, one of the most populous nations in Africa, has a long and glorious history spanning well over five thousand years. Ninety-nine per cent of the population lives within 5 miles of the River Nile, which is the only arable land in Egypt and the source of its wealth and prosperity.

Egypt's Third Intermediate Period (*c.*1069–332 BC) was largely one of decline, with a few respites along the way. During this time, Egypt and Israel had several significant interactions: (1) Pharaoh So (probably Osorkon IV, *c.*730–715 BC) was of little help to Hoshea against the mighty Assyrians. (2) Shebitku, an inexperienced pharaoh, sent his brother Tirhakah to help Hezekiah fight the Assyrians in 701 BC but was quickly defeated. (3) Judah had a major confrontation with Neco II (*c.*610–595 BC), but Neco was soon defeated by the Babylonians. (4) When Zedekiah called upon Egypt for help in his rebellion against Babylon, Hophra (*c.*589–570 BC) came to his aid but was decisively defeated by Nebuchadnezzar; he then fled, leaving Jerusalem to be conquered.

Comment

1–2. Verses 1–25 are *a prophecy* [*maśśā'*, 'oracle'] *against Egypt*; verses 1–15 are poetic and 16–25 are narrative. The common name for *Egypt* (*miṣrayim*) contains a dual ending that refers to 'two lands', Upper Egypt and the delta region of Lower Egypt (see the rarer singular form in v. 6, *māṣôr*). The interjection *hinnēh* is used to introduce something unexpected to the reader: *See, the* LORD *comes riding on a swift cloud*[13] *. . . to Egypt*, demonstrating his sovereignty over nature (see Deut. 33:26). This could be an intentional contrast with the highly valued Egyptian horses that were dedicated to Ra, the Egyptian sun god. Yahweh is the true sovereign whose mere presence causes the *idols of Egypt* to tremble *and the hearts of the Egyptians* [to] *melt with fear.*

During Isaiah's lifetime, Egypt was in a downward spiral due to internal strife that caused political weakness – so much so that Cush, under its leader Shabaka (*c.*716–702 BC), took control of Egypt. The words *stir up* [*sûk*, 2x; see 9:11] *. . . kingdom against kingdom* may be a reference to this. Internal struggles were not new to Egypt, but this direct confrontation of God affected every echelon of society: *brother, neighbour, city, kingdom* (v. 2).

3–4. As the Egyptians continue to weaken, they *will lose heart* (lit. 'their spirits will be emptied' [*bāqaq*, 7x; see 24:3]), suggesting fear, depression and discouragement. In desperation they will call out to their *idols* (*'ĕlîlîm*, 'worthlessness, idols') and to departed spirits (*'iṭṭîm*, occurs only here), all to no avail. The two words at the end of verse 3 pertain to people who communicate with the dead: (1) *hā'ōbôt*, 'necromancer, medium' (occurs only here); and (2) *hayyiddĕ'ōnîm*, 'soothsayer, spiritists'.

God *will bring their plans to nothing* (lit. 'swallow up their plans', v. 3) and give them over (*sākar*, occurs only here) to a *cruel master* (lit. 'harsh lords') and *a fierce king* (v. 4), most probably a reference to

---

13. The storm god Baal was also titled 'the rider of the clouds'.

Ashurbanipal (*c.*669–633 BC), the Assyrian king who conquered
Thebes in 664/663 BC and took control of the nation (*ANET* 295).
Note the irony here: the nation that imposed servitude on Israel
will receive similar treatment from a *cruel master.* The accuracy of
this prophecy is verified by *the Lord, the* LORD *Almighty* (lit. 'of
hosts'); he sovereignly controls even the heavenly hosts. This title
for God should have been highly convincing to Egypt, since one
of the primary gods in their hosts of heaven was Ra, the sun god.

5–8. The first-person pronouns cease after verse 4 as new
images emerge, prompting some to suggest that a new oracle
begins. A more straightforward view is that these next verses
merely describe in more detail the consequences of the destruction
mentioned in verses 1–4 and the horrific outcome for Egypt (v. 6).
Verse 6 uses the singular form *māṣôr* (30x, and 681x with dual
ending) for *Egypt*, perhaps to refer mainly to the Nile Delta.

The *streams of Egypt* represent the branches or irrigation ditches
of the River Nile itself, since no streams feed into it. The Nile's lack
of water would affect all of Egypt, including *the plants* ['*ārôt*,
'bulrushes', occurs only here] *along the Nile* that die, *the fields* that
wither away, and *the fishermen* (*dayyāgîm*, only occurrence with this
spelling; see *dawwāgîm* in Jer. 16:16) who catch no fish.

Because rainfall is negligible in Egypt, being only 0.1 to 0.2 in.
per year, irrigation is necessary to grow crops. The Nile's annual
flooding deposits a new layer of rich silt over nearby farmland that
allows crops to grow. But when the Nile (lit. 'the sea', v. 5; the
parallel unit has *nāhār*, 'river, stream') is low (*nāšat*, 'exhausted or
dried up', 4x; see Jer. 18:14), there is no means to irrigate the soil.

As the water plants die (*qāmal*, 'wilt, wither away', 2x; see 33:9),
the canals will stink (*wĕheʾeznîḥû*, occurs only here) of mud and rotting
fish and plants. All those who fish, whether they fish with *hooks*
(*ḥakkâ*, 3x; see Hab. 1:15) or *nets* (*mikmōret*, 3x; Hab. 1:16; see *ANEP*
34), will mourn, not being able to make their living from the Nile.

9–10. Even *those who work with combed* [*śārîq*, occurs only here] *flax*
and *linen* (*ḥôrāy*, 'white stuff', occurs only here) *will despair* (lit. 'be
ashamed'). Key Egyptian industries – agriculture, fishing, textiles
(*šātōteyhā*, 'the pillars [of Egypt]', not *workers* as in NIV, v. 10) – will
be crushed and the people who work in those industries *will be sick
at heart* (*ʾagmê*, 'grieved', occurs only here).

Additional note: flax

Flax is one of the oldest cultivated crops in the world. Fibres from the bast, or skin, of the plant are stronger than cotton but less elastic. Soft, high-quality fibres are used in the production of linen, a fabric often worn in warm climates. Courser fibres are used to make twine and rope. Flaxseed is used as a nutritional supplement and in the production of linseed oil.

11–13. A new unit, marked by the emphatic particle 'surely' (*'ak*; translated as *nothing but* in the NIV), shifts focus from the effects of drought to the leaders of Egypt. *Zoan* (Tanis) was the capital of Lower Egypt and the first major city in the Nile Delta that travellers from the East would encounter. These *officials of Zoan* are called *fools* and the *counsellors of Pharaoh* 'stupid' (*bāʿar*, 7x; see Jer. 10:8) in a country that was known for its great wisdom (see 1 Kgs 4:30).

The prophet marvels that these leaders can tell Pharaoh, *I am one* [*ben*, 'a son'] *of the wise men, / a disciple* [*ben*, 'a son'] *of the ancient kings* [lit. 'former kings'], when they cannot recognize the clear judgment of God. The phrase 'a son of the wise men' does not refer to physical descendants but to members of a guild of wise men (see 'sons of the prophets', 2 Kgs 2:3, ESV).

The *officials of Zoan* and *Memphis* (lit. 'Noph', the capital of Upper Egypt) were unable to foresee and avert this destruction (lit. 'they have acted foolishly . . . they are beguiled', v. 13). These leaders who should have been the *cornerstones* (i.e. the anchors of Egypt) have led their country astray.

14–15. Widespread confusion (a *spirit of dizziness* [*ʿiwʿîm*, occurs only here]) sets in because these leaders chose to follow false gods. Yahweh allows once-proud Egypt to stagger around pathetically like drunkards who vomit all over themselves (lit. *staggers around in his vomit* [*qîʾ*, 3x; see 28:8]). The effects of this judgment will reach everyone, from Egypt's *head* and high *palm branch* (*kappa*, 4x = highest leaders) to its *tail* and low bulrushes (*'agmôn*, 5x = the lowest-ranked persons). After the New Kingdom period (1550–1069 BC), the nation of Egypt never again enjoyed a period of greatness.

16–17. The last part of this chapter (vv. 16–25) shifts from poetry to prose and contains five declarations, all beginning with *in that day*, that progress from judgment upon Egypt to its deliverance. It is difficult to determine whether the events in these declarations are sequential.

In the day of God's punishment (*In that day*) the Egyptians *will become weaklings* (lit. 'like women'), overcome with dread (*they will shudder with fear*). He will merely wave (NIV = *uplifted*) his hand over them and the judgment will begin (see 10:32 where Assyria waves its hand over Jerusalem). Notice the title for God: he is *the LORD Almighty* (lit. 'of hosts'), who has the power to command the heavenly hosts.

Even the land of Judah will become an object of *terror* (*ḥāggā*ʾ, occurs only here), because they serve the God whose plans are against Egypt (lit. 'he is counselling against her'). The Egyptians once again dread the Israelites (or their God), just as they did in the time leading up to the exodus (Exod. 12:31–33).

18. This second *in that day* declaration bears a positive message: five Egyptian cities will speak Hebrew (lit. 'the lip of Canaan'; this phrase occurs only here) and *swear allegiance to the LORD Almighty*. It is unclear whether the cities change their allegiance from the gods of Egypt to *the LORD Almighty* or whether this refers to Jewish colonies in Egypt after the exile (possibly Migdol, Tahpanhes, Memphis, Pathros and Elephantine; see Jer. 44:1; *ANET* 491) that swear allegiance to Yahweh; the latter seems more likely given the unlikelihood that entire Egyptian cities would change so dramatically as to worship Yahweh. The fact that there are five cities out of approximately 30,000 in the nation of Egypt (Oswalt 1986: 376) also points to the concept of a remnant, which is the theme of the next several oracles.

The final phrase *City of the Sun* (*ḥeres* = 'Heliopolis') occurs in several witnesses (e.g. 1QIsaᵃ, fifteen Hebrew manuscripts, Targum, Vulg.), but the MT reads *ḥeres*, 'destruction'. Even though the change of *ḥēth* to *hē* is minor in Hebrew square script, MT's reading 'city of destruction' is most probably the original, for it fits the context well and is the more difficult reading (meaning it is more likely that a scribe would change it to 'City of the Sun' [= Heliopolis] than change it from 'City of the Sun' to 'City of Destruction'). 'City of Destruction' may refer to Thebes, capital of Upper Egypt (destroyed by Ashurbanipal in 664/63 BC; see Nah. 3:8), or possibly to Memphis, capital of Lower Egypt (captured by Esarhaddon, 671 BC, and Ashurbanipal, 664 BC).

19–22. This third, somewhat longer *in that day* declaration describes a time when an *altar* will be built *in the heart of Egypt* and a *monument* (lit. 'pillar') on their border that are dedicated to the LORD. These will stand as a *sign* and a *witness* to the LORD in the land of Egypt. Some suggest the altar was at Leontopolis (or Elephantine, which had a Jewish temple about 410 BC; *ANET* 491–492). However, since Egypt has not yet demonstrated its dedication to God, the altar at Leontopolis or Elephantine may be only a partial fulfilment that looks forward to a fuller completion in the future.

Verse 20 describes a time when Egypt calls out to the LORD and he sends a deliverer (*saviour and defender*). This may have been initially fulfilled by Psammetichus I (664–610 BC) who, by uniting all of Egypt, brought stability and prosperity. The *oppressors* were the Nubians, Libyans and Assyrians. Psammetichus won Egyptian independence from Assyria during his reign; however, he did not lead the Egyptians to Yahweh, thus these words would ultimately look forward to a future deliverer.

The last part of this declaration (vv. 21–22) describes God's punishment of Egypt (*The LORD will strike Egypt*); the NIV adds the phrase *with a plague*, reminiscent of the exodus, though the MT simply reads 'striking' Egypt. This punishment also has a redemptive element to it, for it adds *he will strike them and heal them*. Similar to God's treatment of Israel, God will punish Egypt then later heal them. Egypt will demonstrate repentance and allegiance to God by offering *sacrifices* (a general term for many types of sacrifices) and *grain offerings* (lit. 'gifts, offerings'), and by making (lit. 'performing') vows. The Egyptians' response to Yahweh's punishment suggests that they would experience spiritual healing that would mark the beginning of a relationship with Yahweh.

23. These two final declarations bring the oracle to a climax. The fourth *in that day* declaration describes God's plan to include Egypt and Assyria as part of his kingdom (see 2:2–4).

A *highway* (most likely to be a roadway elevated above the surrounding landscape) will run from Egypt to Assyria, promoting free access and harmony between the two countries to *worship* (lit. 'serve') the one true God together. The primary importance of this verse is to highlight the harmony and goodwill within God's kingdom.

24–25. The fifth *in that day* declaration continues the fourth declaration's theme of God's future kingdom, comprising Israel, Egypt and Assyria. Not only does God's plan include the restoration of the known world in Isaiah's time, but these countries will be used by him to bring a blessing upon the entire earth (see Gen. 12:3).

Terminology that was once restricted to Israel is now applied to Egypt and Assyria: *Egypt my people, Assyria my handiwork, and Israel my inheritance*. The phrase *my inheritance* is retained for Israel since it was the initial channel of his revelation (see Exod. 19:5–6). Each of these nations is on a par with the others; each receives special treatment from God based on a relationship with him. Throughout their history, Israel often wanted to keep God to themselves, but God's plan is much bigger.

20:1–2. This untitled oracle is dated and linked with the previous one in that it concerns Egypt and Cush (during much of Isaiah's lifetime these two countries were allied). Almost immediately after the Ethiopian pharaoh Shabako combined Upper and Lower Egypt in 714 BC, he unwisely rebelled against Assyria, despite the fact that Sargon II was beginning to consolidate his strength.

The setting of this oracle is most probably around 713–711 BC when Sargon sent his *supreme commander* (*tartān*) to defeat the Philistines at Ashdod (*ANET* 286). The word *tartān* is an Assyrian loanword referring to the highest official next in authority to the king (see 2 Kgs 18:17). Some consider verse 1 a later addition since the sign in the verses that follow is directed to Egypt and Cush, not Ashdod (v. 1). However, the setting of verse 2 links it with the previous events: *at that time the* LORD *spoke through* [lit. 'by the hand of'] *Isaiah son of Amoz* (his full name is given thirteen out of the thirty-two times he is mentioned in the OT). Thus, we believe that the capture of Ashdod is to serve as a sign that Egypt and Cush will suffer the same fate.

Isaiah is told to *Take off* [lit. 'open or loosen'] *the sackcloth from your body* [lit. 'loins']. *Sackcloth* (i.e. a rough jute fabric) was worn as a sign of mourning; its removal suggests that the time for mourning is past and that exile (represented through his being *stripped and barefoot*, v. 2) would soon begin.

3–4. The humbling of Isaiah (i.e. *stripped and barefoot* [*yāḥēp*, 5x; see 2 Sam. 15:30]) for *three years* (1) signified that Egypt and Cush's humbling would take place in three years (this option is preferred); (2) signified that it would last for three years (i.e. the amount of time it would take to be carried off to Assyria); or (3) was a figurative reference to a 'complete' amount of humbling. In any case, the purpose of the sign is to confirm that it will happen (i.e. reason for a *sign*, *ʾōt*, and a 'wonder', *môpēt*) and to give Egypt and Cush the opportunity to avoid destruction by surrendering to Assyria. The punishment would be both thorough, affecting both *young and old*, and humiliating (they would be 'stripped [*ḥăśûpay*] to the buttocks' [*šēt*, 4x; see 2 Sam. 10:4]). The word *ḥăśûpay*, most probably a spelling error, should be read *ḥăśûpê* with the same meaning.

Isaiah's symbolic actions are rare in the book, although prophets such as Jeremiah and Ezekiel were also required to perform symbolic actions. Some scholars consider the final phrase of verse 4, *to Egypt's shame* (lit. 'the nakedness of Egypt'), to be a gloss placed awkwardly at the end of the verse; we argue that it is a summary of the previous statements.

5–6. *Those who trusted in Cush* [lit. 'from Cush [is] their hope' (*mabbāṭ*), 3x; see Zech. 9:5] *and boasted in Egypt* [lit. 'from Egypt [is] their splendour'] will likewise be put to shame. *The people who live on this coast*, a reference to Philistia and Judah, will realize just how misplaced their hope in Egypt/Cush has been: *How then can we escape?* (see *ANET* 287–288). This refers either to Ashdod's dependence on Egypt in 711 BC or to Hezekiah who sought an alliance with Cush in 701 BC; both proved to be disastrous. Only God can provide true help and hope.

Meaning

The oracles against Egypt (and Cush) warn of an approaching disaster, but God's desire is that the destructions carried out by Sargon II and Sennacherib will cause them to turn to Yahweh. The first oracle contains five *in that day* declarations that describe how Egypt will turn to God. He will send a 'deliverer' (possibly Psammetichus I) to rescue them, but this deliverance pales in comparison with the deliverance that the author sees when even Assyria, Egypt's enemy, will one day serve Yahweh alongside Egypt. The prophet may be seeing Egypt's deliverance under Psammetichus I alongside God's ultimate deliverance farther into the future, a day when God's kingdom will include nations that historically were fierce enemies – Israel, Egypt and Assyria.

The second oracle is much more limited in scope. A sign is given to all who rely on Egypt (Cush) for help: they will be defeated just as Ashdod was by the Assyrians in 713–711 BC. If only Israel could have learned from Ashdod's mistake.

h. The wilderness of the sea, Babylonia (21:1–10)

Context

The eighth Oracle against the Nations (21:1–10) is poetic, more obscure, and directed against Babylonia (see vv. 2, 9), though the nation is called *the Desert by the Sea*. Babylonia, known for its seagoing vessels, was about to become a wilderness. While the details at the beginning of the oracle are vague, verse 9 clarifies that *Babylon has fallen*.

Babylonia was defeated by Assyria several times. Smith (2007: 369–370), Roberts (2015: 274–275) and others think the destruction refers to the Assyrian defeats of Babylon in 710, 702 or 689 BC and thus hold to Isaianic authorship. But verses 2 and 9 appear to point to the final destruction administered by the Persians in 539 BC, prompting others to suggest a post-exilic date (Clements 1980a: 177; Wildberger 1997: 310–314). Verse 2 does seem to suggest Babylon's destruction in 539 BC, yet we still maintain its Isaianic authorship based upon his prophetic role. Isaiah is warning of the dangers Babylon will cause and that God has decreed an ending to the pain they will inflict on others (v. 2); this end comes in verse 9.

Two phrases in verse 10 imply that this oracle is written to encourage God's remnant in exile: *my people who are crushed*, and *I tell you what I have heard from the LORD*. However, there were other times when God's people were crushed and needed encouragement (e.g. 722 BC and before 701 BC). Some have suggested that verse 10 applies to Babylon (see Scott 1952: 278–282), but it seems unlikely that God would call Babylon 'my people', especially when he reinforces in the verse that he is the *God of Israel*. In addition, the riders come from Babylon in verse 9; thus the sentinels in verse 8 must be located somewhere else.

However one understands verse 10, the oracle serves as a warning to Judah not to rely upon Babylon against Assyria, for Babylon is said to be a *traitor* that *betrays* and a *looter* that *takes loot* (v. 2), and will be punished.

Comment

1–2. Scholars have suggested several emendations for the ambiguous reference to *the Desert* [*midbar*, 'wilderness, desert'] *by the Sea* in verse 1. The phrase may be a wordplay for southern Mesopotamia, either because the Sealand Dynasty was in this region or because it was a religious wilderness (see Oswalt 1986: 391) – their many gods were useless. Babylonia (i.e. *the Desert*) churns out windstorms such as the well-known windstorms of the Negev Desert. These represent Babylon's persistent rebellion against Assyria when they ruled over them; thus they are called *a land of terror.*

Isaiah received this *dire* [lit. 'harsh, severe'] *vision* of punishment because Babylon persisted in their wickedness: *the traitor* [*habbôgēd*, 'the treacherous one'] *betrays* (*bôgēd*, 'acts treacherously') and *the looter* (*haššôdēd*, 'destroyer') continues to *loot* (*šôdēd*, 'destroy'). Babylon, who had caused severe suffering, will receive their well-deserved punishment. God will allow *Elam* and *Media* (both were incorporated into Persia by 539 BC) to pour out his punishment on Babylonia, which will bring an end to *all the groaning she caused.*

3–5. This *dire vision* of intense judgment has an effect on the prophet himself, causing him trembling (*ḥalḥālâ*, 4x) and physical pain (*ṣîrîm*, 4x; see 13:8) as acute as that of childbirth. With two similar-sounding words, the prophet describes his anguish: *I am staggered* [*naʿăwêtî*, 'I am disturbed'] *by what I hear* (lit. 'because of hearing') and *bewildered* [*nibhaltî*, 'I am terrified'] *by what I see* (lit. 'because of seeing').

His heart staggers and is gripped with horror (*pallāṣût*, 4x). The prophet had longed for light (*twilight*), but instead is filled with terror. As we can see, prophets were not impersonal messengers who remained detached and unaffected by the messages they delivered.

The arrangements to eat and drink in verse 5 were both ceremonial and conventional preparations for war. There is an abrupt call to arms, giving a sense of urgency, which correlates well with the events in Daniel 5 when Belshazzar and his nobles were feasting while the Persians surrounded the city. The command to *oil* [lit. 'anoint'] *the shields* could have been either for ceremonial purposes (i.e. an act of dedication) or to prepare them for battle (see 2 Sam. 1:21). Ancient shields, which were made of leather, skin, bronze or other metals, could be either conditioned or made slippery with oil to help deflect swords and spears.

6–8. The oracle shifts its focus to Judah with the words *This is what* [lit. 'for thus' for emphasis] *the Lord says to me* (i.e. the prophet). The *Lord* (*'ădōnāy*; the name underscores his right to control events on earth) directs the prophet to *post a lookout* (*hamṣappeh*, a different word for 'sentinel' from that used in v. 11) to watch for signs of an army going out to war (i.e. chariots, riders, etc.). Xenophon states that the Persian army marched two by two, and used donkeys and camels (*Cyropaedia* 1.6, 10; 4.3–5; etc.).

Once the signs appear, the sentinel is to be on highest alert (lit. 'and he is to be attentive with attentiveness' [*qešeb*, 4x; v. 7]). Many scholars understand Isaiah to be the sentinel in verse 8. The MT's reading *wayyiqrā' 'aryēh*, 'and the lion called', at the beginning of verse 8 is most probably a corruption that should instead read either (1) 'and the lookout called' (*wayyiqrā' hārô'eh*, the preferred reading; appearing in most English translations), assuming that two letters were corrupted; or (2) 'and he called, I will show' (*wayyiqrā' 'ar'eh*), assuming only one corrupted letter. The prophet's response emphasizes his vigilance and perhaps impatience: *Day after day* [lit. 'I am standing continuously by day'] . . . *every night* [lit. 'all the nights'] *I stay at my post* [lit. 'my watch']. The inverted syntax of this last phrase is for emphasis.

9–10. The sign that the sentinel so eagerly awaited has indeed arrived: *Look, here comes* [lit. 'behold this is coming'] *a man in a chariot / with a team of horses* (or a chariot and a pair of horse riders). This small contingent is returning from Babylon with news of its defeat (v. 9). The phrase *rekeb 'îš ṣemed pārāšîm* (lit. 'a single chariot with a couple of horses'; only occurrence of the phrase) is most likely to mean 'a person in a chariot with a team of horses'; in other words, a herald is spreading the news of victory over Babylon.

Someone replies, though it is not clear who (most probably the one in the chariot): *Babylon has fallen, has fallen* (repeated to convey certainty), and their *gods lie shattered*, a sure sign of their defeat (see *ANET* 315–316). Isaiah then relays this good news to his people *who are crushed on the threshing-floor* (lit. 'my threshed [one] [*mĕdušâ*, occurs only here and suggests a downtrodden people] and son of my threshing-floor'), a sad picture of the Israelites who had been heavily defeated and deported to Babylon. But just as grain was crushed on the threshing-floor to loosen its husks for the wind to carry off, so the devastation and exile inflicted by the Babylonians (i.e. the *threshing-floor*) would cause some Israelites to repent of sin and disobedience (i.e. the husk) to form a righteous remnant.

This judgment oracle against Babylon was intended as a message of enduring hope to encourage the Israelites to remember that God would punish those who brought harm to Israel.

Meaning

Although few details are given, Isaiah sees a time in the future when the sovereign God who holds nations accountable for their actions will repay the treacherous Babylonians for their harsh treatment of his people. Yet God also takes full responsibility for Israel's punishment (i.e. *My people who are crushed on the threshing-floor*, lit. 'my threshed [one] and son of my threshing-floor'), knowing that it would result in a righteous remnant. Even today God continues to hold nations accountable for their actions against his people and other nations.

i. Edom (21:11–12)

Context

This ninth oracle is both brief and ambiguous. Similar to the veiled title in 21:1, the opening words of this prophecy refer to *Dumah* ('silence'), which most consider an indirect reference to Edom (the parallel phrase is *from Seir*, probably Mt Seir in Edom). Also similarly to the prophecy against Babylon, a sentinel is on duty (see 21:6). These two oracles against Babylon and Edom may be placed next to each other since Babylon called on both Edom and Arabia for aid against Assyria, especially just prior to Sargon's stinging defeat of Marduk-Baladan in 710 BC.

Because the Edomites had rejoiced over the fall of Jerusalem to Babylonia (Ps. 137:7) and had killed innocent Israelites, several prophets proclaimed judgment on them (e.g. Ezek. 25:12–14; 35:15; Joel 3:19).

Additional note: Edom (lit. 'Dumah')

Edom, formerly called Seir (see Gen. 32:3), was a rugged, mountainous area stretching from Wadi Zered to the Gulf of Aqaba. Esau's descendants intermarried with the region's inhabitants and became known as the Edomites.

Israel generally prevailed in its frequent skirmishes with Edom (see 2 Sam. 8:14). However, during the invasion by the coalition forces of Pekah, Rezin and Edom, captives were carried away from Judah, an event foundational to this oracle. After 736 BC, Edom became a vassal state of the Assyrians, the Babylonians, and finally the Nabateans.

Comment

11–12. The announcement of this oracle against *Dumah* (lit. 'silence') is similar to the veiled references in Isaiah 21:1 and 22:1. *Someone* – we are not told who – *calls to me* (Isaiah, the *watchman*) from Seir. He continues to call (i.e. a participle) to the *watchman* (*šōmēr*, 'keeper'; see v. 6), the guardian of the city, asking how much of the night is left (lit. 'what from the night'); the repetition of the question conveys the insistence of the enquirer. The word *night* is most probably used here in the figurative sense of 'judgment'.

The watchman's encouraging response is that deliverance, represented by the morning 'light', is arriving: *Morning is coming*. However, the words *but also the night* that immediately follow are an unexpected warning of further judgment to come.

The watchman invites the questioner to *come back* (lit. 'return and come', a hendiadys) and *ask* (*bā'â*, 2x; see Obad. 6, 'pillaged', lit. 'sought out') again. The phrase *come back yet again* joins two finite verbs, 'to return' and 'to come'. Childs suggests that the watchman does not yet know when the events will take place, so he invites the enquirer to return and ask whether the timing has become any clearer (2001: 153). But it is more likely to mean that, depending on their actions, further judgments may be added.

The deliverance referred to may be the weakening and defeat of Assyria by the Babylonians that allowed Edom to regain limited freedom from about 736 BC. This freedom was short-lived; as the prophet foresaw, *night* was coming. In Nebuchadnezzar's fifth year he annexed Ammon and Edom (Josephus, *Ant.* 10.181); Nabonidus attacked Edom around 553 BC; later the Nabateans invaded Edom and took control of the entire country.

Meaning

God's message for Edom is that they will undergo more than one wave of judgment for their gloating reaction when Israel was led off to captivity in Babylon (586 BC; Ps. 137:7), a reaction all the more detestable considering that they were related to Israel through Esau, their ancestor. At the very least Edom should have demonstrated compassion towards Israel when the latter were struggling under the Babylonian conquest.

Edom were also negligent in worshipping and honouring Yahweh, especially in the light of the fact that Esau knew of the promises given to Abraham, Isaac and Jacob.

j. Arabia (21:13–17)

Context

The tenth oracle, directed against Arabia, requests the inhabitants of Arabia to provide sustenance to those fleeing from war and warns that soon they too will be defeated. Even though some question whether the oracle refers to Arabia (*'ărab*; 2x with this pointing), the names Dedan (Al Ula, a city and a major region along the north-eastern side of the Red Sea), *Tema* (Tayma, a prominent crossroads city 200 miles south-west of Dumah) and *Kedar* (a region in the north-western part of the Arabian Desert) are all locations on the Arabian Peninsula.

This oracle contains two units: (1) a request that aid be given to soldiers fleeing from war (vv. 13–15); and (2) a prophecy about the destruction of *Kedar* (vv. 16–17).

Additional note: Arabia

The Arabian Peninsula largely consists of the Arabian Desert and a ridge of mountains along its western border. Parts of Arabia receive ample rainfall to grow certain crops, but the bulk of the region receives only a negligible amount. While nomads and desert dwellers have survived nearly unchanged for millennia, most settlements throughout its history were in the south-western and north-western corners of the Arabian Peninsula.

During Solomon's reign, trading relationships with Arab tribes were common, especially from his port at Ezion-geber on the Red Sea. During Hezekiah's time, Arab tribes were hired as mercenaries to help defend Jerusalem against Sennacherib (Taylor Prism 3.31). By Josiah's time, Arabs were gaining prominence as traders (Ezek. 27:20–21).

Comment

13–15. This oracle (*maśśāʾ*) against *Arabia* (*ʿărāb*) commands the people of *Tema* and the *caravans of Dedanites* who were camping in the *thickets* of the western portion of the Arabian Desert where Dedan and Tema were located, to bring *water* and *food* [lit. 'bread'] *for the fugitives*. There is an interesting wordplay between *in the thickets* (*bayyaʿar*) and *Arabia* (*baʿrāb*).

The four images in verse 15 highlight that these refugees are fleeing the ravages of war: *they flee from the sword* (lit. 'swords', i.e. meaning war in general); *the drawn sword* (lit. 'an abandoned sword'); *the bent bow* (referring to a strung bow); and *the heat of battle* (lit. 'the oppression of war'). Wartime fugitives often fled to the outskirts of empires to hide; thus, Tema would have been a crucial stop for water and food before entering the Nefud desert. Few people would have braved the dangers except out of dire necessity.

16–17. God informs the prophet that not even the Arabs will be able to avert the judgment he has planned: *Within one year* [lit. 'in yet a year'], *as a servant bound by contract* [lit. 'as the years of a hired labourer'] *would count it* [i.e. meticulously, so as not to be subservient any longer than necessary], *all the splendour of Kedar will come to an end*. There is a wordplay here: *the splendour* [*kābôd*] *of Kedar* (v. 16) will fall under the *heat* [*kōbed*, lit. 'weight'] *of battle* (v. 15).

The *survivors* [lit. 'remnant'] *of the archers* and *the warriors of Kedar will be few* (v. 17). Arabia should know that this destruction is certain since *The LORD, the God of Israel, has spoken*; when Yahweh speaks, it will happen.

Meaning

God shows his sovereignty over yet another nation. Little information is given in the biblical text as to why the Arab tribes would be punished; however, failure to serve God would have been reason enough.

k. The valley of vision (22:1–25)

Context

The eleventh Oracle against the Nations begins with yet another veiled reference, this time to the *Valley of Vision*, the prophet's own people (see vv. 8–10). It bears two distinct messages: punishment on Judah (vv. 1–14) and specific punishment for Shebna (vv. 15–25). Scholars typically identify one of three historical contexts for this oracle: (1) Sargon's campaign in 711 BC (Oswalt 1986: 408); (2) Marduk-Baladan's campaign in 703 BC (Roberts 2015: 286–287); or (3) a sequence of events that led to Judah's downfall, beginning with Sennacherib's invasion in 701 BC (Wildberger 1997: 357–358) that further hardened Israel's heart (vv. 12–14) and resulted in Judah's final destruction in 586 BC. The third option makes the most sense in the light of the prophetic perspective (i.e. the prophet may see future events that take place at different points in the future).

Verses 1–11 appear to describe two periods of God's punishment: (1) 701 BC when the Assyrians advanced upon Judah (vv. 5–11); and (2) 586 BC when the Babylonians destroyed Jerusalem and deported its people (vv. 1–3). The second punishment is described first: Jerusalem's people are in an upheaval. Zedekiah and the city's leaders had fled and were subsequently captured by Nebuchadnezzar (v. 3; see Jer. 52:7–11).

It is ironic that this oracle (NIV, *prophecy*) is directed against the *Valley of Vision* when those concerned, God's chosen people, were exceptionally blind in foreseeing the consequences of their rebellion against him.

The message regarding Shebna (vv. 15–25) illustrates this on an individual level: the steward had used his office for personal aggrandizement instead of fulfilling his duty to *be a father to those who live in Jerusalem* (v. 21). God sees the actions of nations and individuals and holds them both accountable.

Additional note: Jerusalem

Old Jerusalem (i.e. the City of David), located on a ridge in the Judean highlands, is surrounded by valleys on three sides: the Kidron Valley to the east, the Hinnom Valley to the south, and the Tyropoean Valley to the west (although this last valley has been filled in by rubble over the ages). The section known as the City of David sits at an elevation of approximately 2,490 ft (760 m.).

Present-day Jerusalem is a holy city for three major religions: Judaism, Christianity and Islam. Its history spans thousands of years, with occupation levels dating back to at least 4000 BC. Jerusalem has been besieged twenty-three times, captured and then recaptured forty-four times, and destroyed twice (Cline 2005: 2). David captured it from the Jebusites about 1000 BC and declared it the capital of the United Monarchy. When the kingdom divided, Jerusalem remained the capital of Judah until its destruction by the Babylonians in 586 BC.

Comment

1–3. The *prophecy* (*maśśā'*, 'oracle') is directed against the *Valley of Vision* (vv. 1, 5), an indirect reference to Jerusalem (see vv. 9–10). The city is full of *commotion* (lit. 'noises'), *tumult* and *revelry* (*'allîzâ*, 'exultant', 7x; see 23:7), but initially it is unclear why (*What troubles you now . . . ?* , lit. 'what to you now'). The people climb to their rooftops to assess what is happening in the surrounding area. There is little doubt that a battle is taking place, but the Israelites did not die in battle; instead *All your leaders have fled together* and *have been captured without using the bow* (v. 3).

The only point at which we know that *leaders* (*qĕṣînayik*, 12x; a general term for someone in authority) fled the city during a time of war was in 586 BC when Zedekiah and his fellow leaders fled Jerusalem into the Arabah (see Jer. 39:3–7) right before the Babylonian king Nebuchadnezzar captured the city.

Verse 3 is arranged in a chiastic structure (literal translation):

A All your leaders have fled together;
  B Without [*min*] a bow they have been captured [emphatic order].
  B' All your found ones have been bound together;
A' To [*min*] distant places they have fled [emphatic order].

This structure helps clarify and even enhance the description of the outcome for those who fled. Though they tried to flee far from Jerusalem, they were captured and bound.

4–5. As a result (*therefore*) of receiving this oracle of future judgment, the prophet cannot be consoled (lit. 'do not hasten to comfort me'). He 'weeps bitterly' (lit. 'let me be bitter in the weeping') *over the destruction of my people* (lit. 'daughter of my people'). There is no comfort here; the nation will be punished and destroyed for their wickedness.

The word *kî* (lit. 'because') beginning verse 5 in the Hebrew text introduces the reason for the prophet's pain: *the Lord, the* LORD *Almighty* (lit. 'of hosts') is bringing a coming day of mass *tumult* (*mĕhûmâ*, 'panic'), *trampling* (*mĕbûsâ*, 'subjugation') and *terror* (*mĕbûkâ*, 'confusion') in the *Valley of Vision*. The similar-sounding words create emphasis.

Now we see the purpose of the title of the vision: it is a vision of judgment. The rest of this verse contains two rare words: (1) *battering down* [*mĕqarqar*, 2x] *walls* (*qir*; the letters in bold could be a wordplay); and (2) *crying* [*šôaʿ*, occurs only here] *out to the mountains* (lit. 'the mountain' = probably Mt Moriah [2 Chr. 3:1], also known as Mt Zion where Yahweh dwells).

6–7. *Elam takes up the quiver* (*ʾašpâ*, 6x; see 49:2) and prepares *her charioteers and horses* (lit. 'chariots, man [can also be read 'infantry'] and horse riders' – common divisions of an army) for war. *Kir uncovers* [lit. 'exposes'] *the shield* (i.e. removes it from its holder). Both locations are preparing for the LORD's day of battle.

Elam, located east of Babylon, was conquered by both Sennacherib and Ashurbanipal, who then conscripted the captives into the Assyrian army (see *ARAB* 2.234). Later the Babylonians utilized them as allies to help fight against the Assyrians. Because it is unlikely that the Elamites fought with Babylon against Judah, this passage fits better during the Assyrian time period. The location of *Kir* is uncertain, but, given the parallelism in the context, we can assume it is part of Elam. In addition, the Assyrians sent Syrian exiles to Kir (2 Kgs 16:9), something that Elam would have granted if they were in alliance with Assyria.

Assyrian chariots will fill the flatter areas of the valleys surrounding Jerusalem: *Your choicest valleys are full of chariots.* Horse riders are *posted* [lit. 'took fixed positions'] *at the city gates.* The Assyrians were known for surrounding a city, allowing no-one in or out until food and water supplies ran out and the inhabitants were ready to surrender.

8–11. Verses 8–11 form a chiasm that describes the efforts of the people to protect themselves instead of relying on God (literal translation):

A And he uncovered the defence [*māsak*, 'covering'] of Judah.
  B <u>In that day you looked to the weapons of the house of the forest,</u>
    C (1) and you saw that the breaches [*bāqîaʿ*, 2x; see Amos 6:11] of the city of David were indeed many;
      (2) And you collected the waters of the lower pool [see 2 Kgs 20:20].
    C′ (1) Then you counted the houses of Jerusalem and you tore down the houses to fortify the walls
      (2) and you made a reservoir [*miqwâ*, occurs only here] between the two walls for the waters of the old pool.
  B′ <u>But you did not depend on him who made it</u> [i.e. the house of the forest],
A′ <u>nor did you take into consideration him who planned it long ago.</u>

The repairs to the breaches in the city wall (line C) are described in more detail in line C′: houses were torn down so that their stones could be used in the walls. Similarly, the people were able to collect water (line C) because they constructed a reservoir between the two walls (line C′).

When *the Lord* [lit. 'he'] *stripped away* his protection, they relied on their own strength by (1) stockpiling *weapons in the Palace* [lit. 'house'] *of the Forest* (i.e. the building Solomon built as an armoury, 1 Kgs 7:2); (2) repairing Jerusalem's walls that were *broken through in many places*; and (3) storing *water in the Lower Pool* (i.e. the Pool of Siloam, called here the Lower Pool). The singular *you* in verse 8 refers to the king, who makes the decision to go to battle; verses 9–11 use second person plural forms to refer to the nation.

In that day (v. 8) signifies God's day of punishment (v. 5), which in context is 701 BC, when the many 'breaches' in Jerusalem's walls were repaired. Before Sennacherib's invasion a *reservoir between the two walls,* known today as 'Hezekiah's tunnel', was cut through solid rock for about a third of a mile to allow water to flow from the Gihon Spring outside the city walls to the Pool of Siloam within them (*ANEP* 275, 744). Jerusalem had two walls during Hezekiah's time: (1) the old Jebusite wall around Mount Zion; and (2) Hezekiah's expanded wall encircling the western hill of Jerusalem (known as 'the broad wall', discovered in 1970 by Nahman Avigad in the Jewish Quarter of modern-day Jerusalem [*EAEHL* 2.586]).

Hezekiah and the leaders of Jerusalem began by relying on their own ingenuity rather than trusting in God, *the One who made it* [this third person singular pronoun probably refers to the plan to punish Jerusalem] . . . *who planned* [lit. 'formed'] *it long ago*. Eventually, at a certain point in 701 BC, Hezekiah realized that he had nowhere else to turn but to God (see 2 Kgs 19:1–4//Isa. 37:1–4).

12–14. *On that day* (i.e. the same one mentioned in vv. 5, 8, namely 701 BC), God expected that the punishment by the Assyrian coalition and the subsequent deliverance clearly performed by him would engender gratitude and repentance in his people. He expected to see signs of repentance, such as (1) weeping, (2) wailing, (3) tearing out their *hair* (lit. 'to make bald') and (4) putting on *sackcloth* (see Nineveh's actions in Jon. 3:5–9). Instead their actions were just the opposite: *But see* [lit. 'but behold', indicating astonishment], *there is joy and revelry,* / <u>*slaughtering*</u> *of cattle and . . . sheep,* / <u>*eating*</u> *of meat and* <u>*drinking*</u> *of wine* (the underlined forms suggest continual or repetitive action). Their ingratitude and ingrained sin are demonstrated by their response: *'Let us eat and drink,'* you *say*,[14] / '*for tomorrow we* [may] *die*' (potential). However one translates this last verb (future, NIV; potential, NASB), the outcome is the same: instead of repenting and giving thanks to God for this great deliverance, they snub his great act of mercy. Their attitude is, 'Let's enjoy ourselves as much as possible today, for tomorrow it may all be over' (the height of hedonism).

Their attitude demonstrates hard-heartedness and complete disrespect for God (see 6:9–10). No wonder God's response through the prophet (*the* LORD *Almighty* [lit. 'of hosts'] *has revealed this in my hearing*, lit. 'in my ears') in verse 14 is so strong: *Till* [lit. 'surely until'] *your dying day this sin* [lit. 'guilt'] *will not be atoned for.* God's solemn declaration is confirmed by a common Old Testament oath formula (v. 14). The plural pronoun *your* (*your dying day*) refers to the people in verse 13, whom Roberts identifies as the elite leaders (2015: 290), but are more likely to be all the wicked inhabitants of Jerusalem.

If this iniquity is not forgiven during their lifetime, then it will certainly not be forgiven in the future. This is the 'unpardonable sin of the Old Testament' whose New Testament counterpart is in Matthew 12:31–32. The people of Jerusalem were so hard-hearted that even when they knew God had just miraculously delivered them, they did not respond with gratitude and reverence for God but passed it off merely as good luck. This type of ingratitude in the face of clear mercy deserves God's punishment.

15–16. Verses 15–25 contain a new section, still in the context of 701 BC, in which God sends Isaiah to *Shebna*,[15] the highest *steward* (*sōkēn*, occurs only here) over the *palace* (lit. 'the house'), with a biting reproof for his arrogance and presumption. His presumption is implied in the two-part question *what are you doing here* [lit. 'what is to you here'] and *who gave you permission* [lit. 'who is to you here'] . . . ?

---

14. The MT does not include the words *you say*, but the context suggests it and the other versions assume it.

15. *Šebna'* may be a shortened form of Shebanijah ('God has come near'; *HALOT* 4.1395–1396). There are variations in spelling in the biblical text for this name (e.g. *Šebnâ* [2 Kgs 18:18], but the parallel passage reads *Šebna'* [Isa. 36:3]).

The chastening appears to be for (*kî*) his having made himself a rock-hewn tomb in a conspicuous place. Such tombs were generally family graves, but his seems to be for himself alone (v. 16). It is located *on the height* and *in the rock* (lit. 'the cliff'): in other words, he has chosen to make the equivalent of a monument to himself by constructing a tomb in a prominent location where he has no right to be. Instead of focusing on the critical condition of the nation, Shebna seeks a way to memorialize himself when he is gone. Shebna was never buried in the tomb he created. For its possible location, see Avigad 1953: 137–153.

17–19. The consequence of Shebna's indiscretion is that he will be taken to a foreign land instead of being buried in this place of honour. The warning to *beware* (*hinnēh*, 'behold', v. 17) is meant to draw Shebna's attention to the grim prophecy concerning him. The LORD will *take firm hold of you* [lit. 'continuing to grasp you'] . . . *roll you up tightly* [*ṣānap*, lit. 'wrap you tightly a wrapping', used 3x in this verse,] *like a ball* [*dûr*, 2x] *and throw you into a large country* [lit. 'a land wide of hands' = Babylon].

Shebna will die in that land so that his wealth will be of no avail. It was considered a great curse not to be buried with one's ancestors. The *chariots you* [Shebna] *were so proud of* (lit. 'your glorious chariots') will also be taken to the foreign land. This may have been fulfilled when Sennacherib claimed that Hezekiah's elite troops, which may have included Shebna, deserted him and came to Nineveh (*ANET* 288).

His defeat would have brought shame on Shebna's *master's house*. God says he will *depose* (*hādap*, 'to thrust away, push') Shebna, signifying his forceful removal from his position; the reading *ousted* (*hāras*, 'to throw down, tear down') in the parallel phrase has a similar meaning.

20–21. *In that day* (i.e. of Shebna's downfall) God *will summon* (i.e. 'to call for duty') his servant Eliakim, whose father, Hilkiah, was the high priest during Josiah's time (*c.*641–609 BC). Hilkiah's existence has been confirmed by a clay bulla and two seals (Schneider 1991: 32–33).

The terms used in verse 21 suggest a transfer of God's authority from Shebna to Eliakim: (1) *clothe him* [i.e. Eliakim] *with your* [Shebna's] *robe* ['outer clothing, tunic']; (2) *fasten your sash* [*'abnēt*, 'waistband', 9x;

see Lev. 16:4] *around him*; and (3) *hand your authority over to him* (lit. 'I will give into his hand'). A special *robe* and *sash* may have been associated with this high-level position of leadership. This transfer of authority from Shebna to Eliakim took place before the time of Rabshakeh's first trip to Jerusalem (see 2 Kgs 18:18//Isa. 36:3); there is no evidence of Shebna's presence in Jerusalem after this.

Unlike Shebna, Eliakim *will be a father to those who live in Jerusalem and to the people of* Judah. As a true father, he would lead, protect and guide the people.

22–23. God will honour Eliakim with special authority. First, he *will place on his shoulder the key to the house of David*. The word *key* appears in Judges 3:25 and 1 Chronicles 9:27, both of which refer to a literal key. But the *key* here in verse 22 is more probably a symbolic reference to his power and authority (see Matt. 16:19), clarified by the next phrases, *what he opens no one can shut, and what he shuts no one can open*. The weight of authority is commonly pictured as being borne on the shoulder (see 9:6).

Eliakim is then likened to a peg: *I will drive him like a peg* [*yātēd*, 'tent peg'] *into a firm place* [lit. 'a reliable place'], meaning he will bring stability to the nation and honour to his family. Eliakim will establish a *seat of honour for the house of his father* (either his literal father or a figurative reference to the king), unlike Shebna who brought shame to his master (v. 18). During Eliakim's tenure God will deliver the nation (701 BC).

24–25. An official who demonstrates wisdom, justice and righteousness will bring honour to the entire kingdom and be given authority over it (i.e. the position that Shebna once had). Continuing to use the tent peg image, verse 24 says: *All the glory of his family will hang on him*. The next phrases stress the extent of this honour, which includes (1) everyone from the royal *offspring and offshoots* (these terms refer to offspring who are in direct line to the throne as well as other progeny); and (2) the rest who are in the palace, pictured as *lesser vessels* (lit. 'all the vessels of the little'). The clarifying phrase *from the bowls* ['*aggānôt*, 3x; Exod. 24:6] *to . . . jars* highlights that it includes all of them. Eliakim will be in charge over everything and bring honour to it all.

But this period of honour will be limited, for a time will come (*in that day*) when the secure peg *will give way* (lit. 'depart') and the nation will suffer a devastating blow: (1) *it will be sheared off* (lit. 'cut in two'); (2) it *will fall*; and (3) *the load [maśśaʾ] hanging on it will be cut down*. The load hanging on the peg (i.e. *it*) refers to the weight of the nation; when it falls, the whole nation will also give way. The events surrounding the Babylonian captivity in 586 BC coincide with the nation's fall, when it was uprooted from a *firm place*. This judgment is certain because it has been announced by the LORD, highlighted at both the beginning and the end of the verse (*declares the LORD*, v. 25a; *The LORD has spoken*, v. 25b).

Meaning

This oracle of judgment directed against the *Valley of Vision* (Jerusalem) concerns two important events in Israel's history (vv. 5–14, 701 BC; and vv. 1–4, 586 BC). The first event (i.e. 701 BC) sets the stage for the second (i.e. 586 BC). Following the first, not only did the Israelites fail to trust God to deliver them, but they actually mocked him after he had demonstrated great mercy by delivering them (i.e. 'Let us eat and drink for tomorrow we may die'). As a result, God promises on oath that this sin will not be forgiven them. Because of their hardness of heart and their lack of gratitude, God will bring judgment. The second part of the oracle concerning Shebna and Eliakim pictures the same message: God will remove Shebna because of his hardness of heart (i.e. largely pride and presumption) and replace him with Eliakim, who will stabilize and bring honour to the government. Nevertheless, Judah's destruction will indeed come.

Mocking God by not recognizing his kindness and mercy is a grievous sin that God cannot ignore. This kind of hardness of heart is what Romans 1:18–32 refers to when God gives the wicked over to their own devices until he justifiably pours out his wrath on them.

l. Tyre (23:1–18)

Context

The Oracles against the Nations, which began with Babylon on the far eastern edges of the Ancient Near East, now turn in this final oracle towards Tyre, the merchant capital on the far western edge of the ancient world. The oracle is divided into two major sections, the first regarding the destruction of Tyre (vv. 1–14) and the second, its restoration (vv. 15–18). The first section opens with an announcement that Tyre has been destroyed (vv. 1–7), followed by confirmation that Yahweh brought this destruction about because of her pride (vv. 8–14).

The second section specifies a period of *seventy years* in which Tyre will remain in obscurity (vv. 15, 17), after which Yahweh will 'visit' (v. 17) and restore her trade (vv. 15–18). His visit will also restore her wealth, which will be *set apart for* [lit. 'holy to'] *the LORD*. It is unclear whether Tyre's wealth is willingly offered to the LORD or is confiscated by him; either way God's worshippers (lit. *those who live before the LORD*) will greatly benefit from it.

Additional note: Tyre

This ancient major seaport of the Phoenicians consisted of two parts: an island which was the centre of commerce for the region, and the mainland suburb of Ushu (or 'Old Tyre') which supplied the island with wood, water and other necessities. The island of Tyre had two harbours, one on its north coast and the other on the south. Its sea trade brought great wealth to Tyre from around the Mediterranean world, making it the envy of nations.

Around the turn of the millennium, as Egypt's hold on the Phoenician coast weakened, Tyre became an independent city with strong ties to King David and King Solomon, supplying many resources for their construction activities (see 1 Kgs 5:1–12).

Several kings tried unsuccessfully to conquer Tyre: Sargon II in 722 BC; Ashurbanipal in 664 BC; and Nebuchadnezzar II, whose siege lasted twelve years, c.587–574 BC. Alexander the Great finally captured all of Tyre in July 332 BC by building a land bridge of rubble from the destruction of Tyre's mainland city out to the island fortress. The city recovered to some extent under Seleucid patronage, but never again regained the power and authority it had exercised in the early ancient world.

Comment

1–2. The eleventh and final Oracle against the Nations is a communal lament describing the destruction of *Tyre*. The *ships of*

Tarshish refer to Tyre's large trading vessels (see 1 Kgs 10:22) returning to their home port in Tyre with a great variety of resources from Tarshish, including gold, silver, iron, tin and lead (Ezek. 27:12). The location of Tarshish is uncertain, but it was probably on the west coast of Spain.

The ships are told to *Wail . . . For Tyre is destroyed / and left without house or harbour* (lit. 'it is devastated from house and from going'), a picture of thorough destruction such as that wrought by Alexander the Great in 332 BC. The merchant vessels hear about the destruction of Tyre from *the land of Cyprus* (lit. 'Kittim'), which was the merchants' last stop before Tyre.

The phrase *Be silent* [*dāmam* (4x); v. 2]*, you people of the island* [lit. 'coastland'] is a reference to the *merchants of Sidon* (located 22 miles further up the coast), who would have been grieved over the loss of their primary trading partner. Both cities had been greatly enriched by the seafaring merchants (lit. 'the ones crossing the sea'). The inverted Hebrew syntax places the verb at the end of verse 2 for emphasis and reads: 'the merchants [lit. 'ones going around'] of Sidon fill you [by] continuously crossing [i.e. a participle] over the sea'. In other words, the sailors were constantly replenishing Sidon.

3–4. The description of how Tyre and Sidon were replenished is continued in the chiastic structure of verse 3:

A *On the great* [lit. 'many'] *waters* [i.e. the Mediterranean Sea]
  B *came the grain of the Shihor* [probably the Nile; see Jer. 2:18];
  B' *the harvest of the Nile* [*yĕ'ôr* = Nile]
A' *was the revenue of Tyre.*

The next phrase captures Tyre's influential position: *and she became the market-place of the nations*; there is a wordplay here between *Shihor* (*šiḥōr*) and *marketplace* (*sēḥar*, 6x). The word *revenue* (*tĕbû'â*) is related to the root *bô'* ('to come, go'), implying that which is 'brought in'. Tyre so dominated the Mediterranean marketplace that she became synonymous with 'trade' (i.e. *she became the market-place of the nations*, v. 3b).

The prophet tells Sidon to *be ashamed* because (*kî*) Tyre, the *fortress of the sea*, could not duplicate its success in Sidon by raising up children with the same maritime prowess (i.e. *I have neither been in labour nor given birth*). There was no other city like Tyre.

The *fortress* [vv. 4, 11, 14] *of the sea* pictures the island of Tyre as rising high above the sea, her 150-ft-high walls and island location making her nearly inaccessible.

5–7. When news of Tyre's destruction travels, it will cause *anguish* and 'wailing' from Egypt to Tarshish, that is, from one end of the Mediterranean Sea to the other. Egypt and Tarshish would be hit hardest, since their economies were so heavily dependent upon shipping. The intensity of the word *anguish* (*ḥîl*, 'to writhe in pain', as in childbirth) is also used to describe the fear of God (e.g. Ps. 96:9) or news of impending war (e.g. Ezek. 30:16).

The rhetorical question (*Is this your city of revelry . . . ?*) expresses the surprise of the nations that this powerful, wealthy city, one that had existed for as long as anyone could remember (i.e. *the old, old city*; lit. 'from days before'), could now be gone. Tyre, over her long history, had gained significant influence among the nations; she used this influence and her trade to develop other nations. Once trade relations were established, many nations, even *far-off lands*, were enriched.

8–9. This section begins to answer the question that everyone must have been asking: *Who has planned this against Tyre . . . ?* Tyre's former honour and majesty are described in three phrases: (1) *the bestower of crowns* (lit. 'the one causing crowns [*ʿāṭar*, 7x] to be given'); (2) *whose merchants are princes*; and (3) *whose traders are renowned in the earth*. Though sailors were not always highly respected, Tyre's *merchants* (*sōḥăreyh*, lit. 'her ones who go around') and *traders* (*kinʿānyhā*, occurs only here)[16] were among the most honoured (NIV, *renowned*) leaders of the world, like wealthy and powerful *princes*.

The only one who could have planned the downfall of such a powerful merchant nation is *the Lord Almighty* (lit. 'of hosts'; v. 9), the name for God that expresses his sovereignty. He would ruin (lit. 'pollute') Tyre's *splendour*, all that she took pride in and that the

---

16. The singular form is the name 'Canaan', suggesting perhaps that this was a land of merchants.

world revered. God despises what this world honours; he will have no rivals, and Tyre is no exception.

10–11. The meaning of verse 10 largely depends upon how the rare word *mēzaḥ* is to be translated: (1) as *harbour*, from the Egyptian word *mdḥ* (NIV); or (2) as 'restraint' (NASB). The reading *harbour* suggests that Tyre will have to work (i.e. emending the verb *'ābar*, 'to pass over', to *'ābad*, 'to work [the ground]') their land as the Egyptians do, since they will no longer have a harbour to import food. However, since there is little evidence for the emendation (i.e. 1QIsaᵃ, LXX) and there is a clear meaning for *mēzaḥ* in Psalm 109:19, the reading 'restraint' is preferable. It then confirms that judgment is coming to Tyre and will no longer be withheld.

Tyre is called *Daughter Tarshish*, for its merchant activities have benefited both cities, like family members (see v. 12 where Tyre is called a 'daughter of Sidon').

When God stretches *out his hand over the sea*, an action associated with punishment, the *kingdoms tremble* in response (v. 11). The sea that the Phoenicians dominated is ultimately controlled by God, who can use it at his bidding. God's command to demolish Tyre's *fortresses* (*ma'uzneyhā*),[17] a term sometimes used for a place of shelter (see 25:4), included both the island fortress as well as one on the mainland, and may even have encompassed those around the Mediterranean Sea. Tyre is said to be in *Phoenicia* (lit. 'Canaan', *kĕna'an*, the word for *traders* in v. 8); the Egyptians referred to the entire region of Syria, Phoenicia and Palestine as Canaan.

12–14. The verdict against Tyre is sealed: destruction is certain; she will never again prosper (lit. 'you will never increase again'). The prophet envisions Tyre's future as a crushed virgin daughter of Sidon (i.e. a 'virgin' was to be treated delicately; see 47:1). The word *crushed* implies 'oppressed, exploited, ravished', possibly even 'raped'. Even if she flees to *Cyprus* (*kittîyîm*; see v. 1), she *will find no rest* (i.e. protection).

Verse 13 likens Tyre's conquest to what the Assyrians did to the Babylonians: (1) *they raised up their siege towers* (*baḥîn*, occurs only here);

---

17. The MT reads *mā'uzneyhā*, which is probably a corruption of *mā'uzzeyhā*, 'her strongholds'. 1QIsaᵃ seems to confirm this reading.

(2) *they stripped its fortresses bare* (*ʿārar*, 4x); and (3) they *turned it into a ruin* (*mappālâ*, 3x). This verse is vital in determining the meaning and date of the passage. Whereas Tyre thought that the Babylonians (lit. 'Chaldeans', a West Semitic group that migrated to Babylon about 850 BC and controlled the lower Mesopotamian region by the Neo-Babylonian period) could assist them against Assyria, God had other plans, using the Assyrians to nearly extinguish the Babylonians (i.e. *this people that is now of no account*; lit. 'was not'). When the Assyrians had finished, Babylonia was fit only for *desert creatures* (*ṣiyîm*, 6x). This is most likely to be a reference to Sennacherib's extensive attack in 689 BC, when Babylon's walls, temples and palaces were destroyed and their rubble thrown into the sea (Erlandsson 1970: 89–91). All of Tyre's hopes for assistance from the Babylonians were dashed.

Tyre's destruction is picked up again in verse 14 to form an *inclusio*, with words similar to Tyre's mention in verse 1: *Wail, you ships of Tarshish; / your* [masc. pl.] *fortress* [Tyre] *is destroyed.* The destruction of Tyre described in verses 1–14 probably includes elements from various destructions, beginning with Nebuchadnezzar in 586 BC until its final destruction by Alexander the Great in 332 BC.

15–18. The phrase *at that time* signals a new section in the oracle that moves from the judgment of the preceding verses to a time of restoration for the Phoenicians. Tyre will lie *forgotten for seventy years* (vv. 15, 17), a period likened to the normal *span of a king's life* (e.g. Nebuchadnezzar is thought to have lived for seventy-two years [634–562 BC]). The *seventy years* most probably correspond to the length of time they would be dominated by Babylon (i.e. seventy-three years, from approximately 612 to 539 BC). The similarity between Judah's captivity in Babylon for seventy years (i.e. Jer. 25:11–12) and Tyre's lying forgotten for seventy years is intentional, drawing a connection between the two countries for disregarding God. Following the siege of Tyre, the kings of Babylonia redirected so much of her trade to their country that a period of great depression ensued in the city (Fleming 1915: 43–48).

But at the end of these seventy years, it will happen to Tyre as in the song of the prostitute, a song no doubt popular at the time whose lyrics are given in verse 16. Because of her skill with harp and song, the prostitute was remembered again. In the same way, after the seventy years, *the LORD will deal with* [lit. 'visit'] *Tyre*, allowing her to return to her former 'lucrative business' (lit. 'return to her harlot's earnings and her prostitution'). However, this time her profits will be used for (lit. 'will be holy to') the LORD even though she herself will not serve him: *Her profits will go to those who live before the LORD, for abundant food* [lit. 'eating to satisfy'] *and fine* [ʿātîq, occurs only here] *clothes* (lit. 'coverings', v. 18).

Tyre's circumstances dramatically improved during the Persian period. Her royal treasuries and forests were used to build the walls of Jerusalem (Neh. 2:8) and the temple with all its accoutrements (Ezra 6:8–12).

Meaning

Tyre was a proud, wealthy and powerful merchant city that knew of Yahweh from at least the time of David and Solomon (see 2 Chr. 2:11–12) yet chose to follow other gods. As a result, God warns that she will experience a reversal from her high position in the world. Just as God promised a day of reckoning for those who are proud and lifted up in Isaiah 2:11–22, so Tyre would be destroyed and forgotten for seventy years. Only God is to be *high and exalted* (6:1).

ii. God's purpose in judgment (so-called 'Little Apocalypse') (24:1 – 27:13)

Isaiah 24 – 27 is well positioned after the Oracles against the Nations. Just as the destruction of the countries named in the oracles would have laid waste much of the known world at the time and demonstrated God's victory over evil, so too 24:1 opens with a declaration of future destruction, but on a much grander scale: *See, the LORD is going to lay waste the earth.* Chapters 24–27 also showcase Israel's role among the nations in a future age. Delitzsch (1980: 423) considers chapters 24–27 a finale to the Oracles against the Nations (chs. 13–23).

While Isaiah 24 – 27 has been referred to as the 'Little Apocalypse', most scholars agree that it is not apocalyptic material in a technical sense since there is no mention of the destruction of the present world followed by the dawn of a new heaven and earth (Anderson 1962: 123). However, it does fall into the category of eschatological material that was possibly an earlier form of apocalyptic literature in that it discusses events in the distant future within the context of the current age.

In the overall structure of Isaiah 13 – 39 (see Figure 0.9 on p. 23), chapters 24–27 are balanced against chapters 34–35. Both speak of a future time of God's judgment followed by his restoration, with chapters 34–35 providing a fuller explanation of the judgments begun in chapters 24–27. It is even possible that Isaiah 24 (speaking of destruction) and 25 (speaking of restoration) are a diptych similar to Isaiah 34 and 35, with one major difference being that Isaiah 24 and 25 are further described by four 'in that day' oracles (26:1; 27:1; 27:2; 27:12).

Because there are no clear historical indicators, there is a wide variety of opinions concerning the date and authorship of this section. The mention of Assyria and Egypt (27:13) suggests an earlier date. Some think that the general references to resurrection (25:8; 26:19) could suggest a later date; however, it is difficult to date any passage based solely upon theological concepts (see Coggins 1978–9: 328–333; Roberts 2015: 306–307).

The primary theme of chapters 24–27 is that God triumphs over all his enemies and fights for his people. Chapter 24 contrasts sweeping destruction over all the earth (i.e. *See, the LORD is going to lay waste the earth*, v. 1) with the establishment of God's glorious reign on Mount Zion (i.e. *the LORD Almighty will reign / on Mount Zion . . . with great glory*, v. 23). Chapters 25–26 are songs of praise to God for destroying the world's cities/nations and yet delivering Zion. Chapter 27 begins with God's punishment of the Leviathan (i.e. primordial evil, but in the NT seen as Satan) and ends with God's protection and deliverance of a believing remnant that is scattered across the known world (i.e. from Assyria to Egypt).

a. Judgment on the nations (24:1–23)

Context
Chapter 24 transitions from judgments upon individual countries in the Oracles against the Nations (chs. 13–23) to judgment upon the world (*tēbēl*, v. 4) as a whole for its rebellion against God. The entire earth is polluted because, according to 24:5, *they have disobeyed*

the laws, / . . . and broken the everlasting covenant (i.e. God's covenant with creation; see Gen. 9:4–6). These charges do not relate to the specific stipulations of the law that God gave to Israel, but to the conscience and to the requirements of the law that are written on the hearts of people (Rom. 2:14–15). God's punishment of the world is therefore just, yet he is merciful in retaining a remnant.

Although this chapter is typically divided into two larger sections, verses 1–13 and 14–23, it is better divided into four parts: (1) a narrative description (i.e. differing from the NIV that sees it as poetry) of the earth's punishment, ending with the phrase *and very few are left* (vv. 1–6); (2) a poetic description of the punishment, ending with a fuller description of the few who are left (vv. 7–16a); (3) a second poetic section that highlights the inability to escape judgment, ending with *it falls – never to rise again* (vv. 16b–20); and (4) a third poetic section regarding the comprehensiveness of the judgment (i.e. *the powers in the heavens above / and the kings on the earth below*), followed by the LORD Almighty's reign on Mount Zion (vv. 21–23).

Comment

1–2. The interjection *see* (*hinnēh*, 'behold!') is used to draw the reader's attention to the declaration of Yahweh's coming judgment: *the LORD is going to lay waste the earth*. The participles introduce the imminence of this destruction. The LORD will strike a severe blow to the entire earth. He will (1) lay it *waste* (*bāqaq*, 6x); (2) *devastate it* (*bālaq*, 2x; Nah. 2:10, 'stripped', lit. 'devastated'); (3) *ruin* [*'āwâ*, 'to twist'] *its face*; and (4) *scatter its inhabitants*. The first two verbs are a wordplay with similar sounds and meanings. The figurative description and the unusual phrase *ruin its face* may imply an earthquake that will damage or scar the earth's surface, causing people to flee.

The image depicts a time of complete upheaval and chaos when even religious (*priest*) and social structures (*master/servant* and *mistress/servant*) will be overturned. Devastation is a great equalizer (see 'Topsy Turvy World', *ANET* 445). The last two phrases of verse 2 are also wordplays between similar-sounding words: *for borrower* [*lāwâ*, qal participle] *as for lender* [*lāwâ*, hiphil participle; 'the one causing to borrow'], / *for debtor* [*nāšā'*, 'to be a creditor by him'] *as for creditor* [*nāšā'*].

3–5. The message of verse 1 is repeated in verse 3, except that the tone is highly emphatic (*completely laid waste* and *totally plundered*). To this point the reader has not been told how it will happen, but it will take place because (*kî*) *the* LORD *has spoken this word.*

The similar-sounding words and word repetition in verse 4 ring out like a death knell as the devastation of the earth is described: *The earth dries up* [*ʾāblâ*, 'mourns'] *and withers* [*nāblâ*], / *the world languishes* [*ʾumlĕlâ*] *and withers* [*nāblâ*], / *the heavens languish* [*ʾumlālû*] *with the earth*. The translation of this last clause depends primarily upon the vowel pointing: (1) *the heavens* [lit. 'heights'] *languish with* [*ʿim* = preposition] *the earth* (NIV); or (2) 'the exalted of the people [*ʿam* = people] of the earth fade away' (NASB). The NIV translation is probably preferred given the context of global punishment.

All three parallel phrases about the earth drying up may be an accusation against Baalism (i.e. the Canaanite deity thought to control rain), something Israel was repeatedly drawn to throughout its history because of the constant threat of drought (i.e. *dries up, withers, languishes*). Verse 3 makes it clear that only the LORD controls nature.

The parallel phrases in verses 1–4 can be understood in the general sense of destruction, or as alluding to three different catastrophes: earthquake (v. 1, *he will ruin its face*); war (v. 3, *totally plundered*); and drought (v. 4, *the earth dries up and withers*). Then verse 5 gives the reason for this judgment: *The earth is defiled* [*ḥānap*, 'polluted', 8x] *by its people*. This defilement is described in the next three phrases: (1) *they have disobeyed* [lit. 'crossed over'] *the laws*, (2) *violated* [lit. 'altered'] *the statutes* and (3) *broken the everlasting covenant*.

These verbs are similar in meaning but seem to progress until the covenant is ultimately broken. The third phrase is most likely to refer to the Noahic covenant (Gen. 9:1–17), which was simple enough in its terms: (1) 'you must not eat meat that has its lifeblood [lit. 'its life'; i.e. its blood] still in it' (Gen. 9:4); and (2) a murderer was not to be allowed to live (Gen. 9:5–6). These basic commands preceded the existence of the nation of Israel and provide a standard for all creation.

6. Curses are typically associated with a covenant. Once a covenant is broken, the punishments assuredly follow (see Deut. 27 – 28). As with the flood during the time of Noah (Gen. 6 – 9), so the earth suffers again because of the wickedness of its inhabitants. The *curse* (*'ālâ*) is divided into two parts, both beginning with *therefore*: (1) *a curse consumes the earth; / its people must bear their guilt*; and (2) *earth's inhabitants are burned up* [*ḥārâ*, 'to become hot'], */ and very few* [*mizār*, 4x, all in Isaiah] *are left.* The imagery of these parallel phrases pictures cleansing: the few who are left after the earth is 'consumed' form a purified remnant (lit. 'a few') of humanity (*'ĕnôš*).

7–9. The narrative description of the punishment in verses 1–6 now shifts to a poetic lament (vv. 7–20). Continuing the theme of drought (v. 4), *the new wine* [i.e. the juice from newly crushed grapes] *dries up* [*'ābal*, 'mourns'] *and the vine withers* [*'āmal*].

The celebration that usually accompanies harvest time is *stilled.* Would-be *merrymakers* (lit. 'all those joyful of heart'; i.e. celebrants who are happy because they have drunk to their hearts' content) now *groan.* All outward show of rejoicing has stopped: *the joyful tambourines* (see *ANEP* 211), *the noise of the revellers* (*'allîzîm*, 7x; 5x in Isaiah), *the joyful harp* (*kinnôr* = lyre, harp; *ANEP* 205–209) and the songs (vv. 8–9). The *wine* and *beer* (*šēkār* = strong drink) usually associated with celebration and rejoicing bring no joy; they are a bitter reminder of the lack of critical resources.

10–12. *The ruined* [*tōhû*, 19x; 11x in Isaiah] *city* [lit. 'city of emptiness'] *lies desolate*, with every house boarded up, either being abandoned (NASB) or because people have *barred* (NIV) themselves inside for protection. The gates of the city are *battered to pieces* (*šĕ'îyâ*, occurs only here, but is parallel to the phrase *in ruins*, lit. 'destruction'). Although many have attempted to identify this city, the text itself is purposefully vague.

There is an interesting repetition that lends emphasis to the concepts in the parallel phrases of verses 7–12, as shown in Figure 24.1.

The city's few inhabitants *cry out for wine*, an indication that the necessities of life have been exhausted. Across the entire earth, *joy turns to gloom* (*'ārĕbâ*, 'turns to evening', 2x; see Judg. 19:9). What has happened to this one city causes despair around the world (*all joyful sounds are banished from the earth*, v. 11).

13–16a. Whereas verses 7–12 describe these dire events as past events, verse 13 confirms that they are still future: *So* [lit. 'for thus']

Verses 7–10	Verses 11–12
V. 7: **new wine** [*tîrôš*] *dries up,* **merry**makers [*śāmēaḥ*] *groan*	V. 11a: *they cry out for* **wine** [*yayin*], **joy** [*śāmēaḥ*] *turns to gloom*
V. 8: **joyful** [*mᵉśôś*, 2x] *tambourines are stilled*	V. 11b: *all* **joyful** [*mᵉśôś*] *sounds are banished*
V. 10: *the ruined* [*tōhû*] **city** [*ʿîr*] *lies desolate*	V. 12: *the* **city** [*ʿîr*] *is left in ruins* [*šammâ*], *its gate is battered to pieces*

Figure 24.1   Parallel phrases in Isaiah 24:7–12

it will be. Then there is a return to the theme that a remnant will remain after this devastation. Two images emphasize just how few people are left, scattered across the earth: (1) the few olives left on a tree after the harvest (*nōqep*, 'beating', 2x); and (2) the few grapes remaining after the vines have been picked (*gleanings* [*ʿōlēlôt*, 6x]). Nevertheless, as few as the remnant are, their voices are heard *from the ends* [lit. 'extremities', v. 16] *of the earth* – from the *west* (lit. 'sea', v. 14), from the *east* (lit. 'the region of light') and *in the islands of the sea* (v. 15) – glorifying God for his *majesty* (v. 14) and righteousness (i.e. *Glory to the Righteous One*, v. 16a).

16b–20. At this point the remnant's praise to God causes Isaiah to be nearly overcome by the unrighteousness of the world around him: *But I said, 'I waste away* [*rāzî-lî*, occurs only here], *I waste away! / Woe to me!'* The first part is repeated for emphasis; the second part is similar to his response after seeing the holiness of God and realizing his own unworthiness (6:5). Like the pounding of a gavel at sentencing, Isaiah repeatedly cries out against the treachery of the world's people: *The <u>treacherous betray</u>* [*bāgad*, 'deal treacherously']*! / With <u>treachery</u> the <u>treacherous betray</u>!* Each of Isaiah's five words of condemnation (the words underlined) derives from the root *bgd*; this repetition adds emphasis to the ominous tone.

The prophet sees once again the inevitability of the punishment that awaits the world's people. In a wordplay he declares that there is no escape; only *terror* (*paḥad*), a *pit* (*paḥat*) and a *snare* (*paḥ*, v. 17) await. Then, turning nature against evil humanity, God opens *the floodgates of the heavens* (lit. 'the heights', terminology also used to

describe God's initial destruction of the earth by a flood in Gen.
7:11; 8:2), and *the foundations of the earth shake*. The details of this
destruction (v. 19) call to mind a cataclysmic earthquake: *The earth
is* [thoroughly] *broken up* / ... [utterly] *split asunder* / ... *violently
shaken* (the syntax indicates emphasis; Williams §205).

The earth reels incessantly (again the syntax is emphatic) under the
weight of its sin, swaying like a *drunkard* (*kaššikôr*, same letters as
šēkor, 'strong drink') or a rickety *hut* [*kammělûnâ*, 2x] *in the wind. The
guilt of its rebellion* is so great that when the earth finally falls, it will
never rise again – the climactic result of the judgment.

21–23. Details of the world's final fall are now given: *In that day*
(i.e. the day of punishment) God will inflict punishment (lit. 'visit')
on all wickedness, including *the powers in the heavens above* (lit. 'host of
the height', probably a reference to demonic hosts; see Dan. 10:13;
Eph. 6:12) and *the kings on the earth below*, representative of all wicked
people on earth. This merism expresses the all-inclusiveness of the
punishment: it will extend from heaven above to the earth beneath.

They will be herded together / like prisoners bound in a dungeon (*bôr*, 'pit,
cistern') or *prison*, where they will *be punished* [lit. 'visited'] *after many
days* (i.e. eschatological judgment). This could refer either to Sheol,
where the wicked wait until judgment, or the abyss where Satan will
be bound during the Millennium (Rev. 20).

The moon [lit. 'the white one', 3x; a probable reference to the full
moon] *will be dismayed* [*ḥāpar*, 'ashamed'], / *the sun* [lit. 'the hot one']
ashamed (*bôš*); for very similar, highly figurative language, see the
description of judgment before the Day of the LORD in Joel 2:31
and Matthew 24:29. These terms may have been used to demythologize the sun (*šemeš*) and moon (*yārēaḥ*). Being the brightest
lights in the sky, the sun and moon were often worshipped as gods
in the Ancient Near East; thus, the imagery represents their
cowering before the glory of God.

Once again, the prophet sees that *the LORD Almighty* [lit. 'of
hosts' = the one who controls the heavenly hosts] *will reign / on
Mount Zion* and his glory will be displayed *before its elders*. The suffix
on the word *elders* can be read as 'his [God's] elders' or 'its
[Jerusalem's] elders'; either way they will serve God as he rules in
Jerusalem. Similarly, the book of Revelation indicates a time when
elders will sit around God's throne and worship him (see Rev. 4:4).

Chapter 24, which begins with a portrayal of the earth's utter devastation, now concludes with a picture of all creation acknowledging the sovereignty and *great glory* of the one true God (v. 23).

Meaning

The earth, having been so polluted by humanity's sin and rebellion, requires thorough cleansing. God's justice demands that the pervasive evil of this world be met with an equally pervasive punishment. At the beginning of the chapter chaos and devastation reign, but this is only temporary. The prophet sees a time when God will eventually reign upon Zion, his rightful throne. No longer will anyone question why God allows sin, for sin will be removed and the wicked gathered into a pit.

Scholars have long recognized that events described in this chapter appear to correspond to future events recorded in the book of Revelation, particularly the tribulation mentioned in Revelation 4 – 18 and the culminating rule of God in Revelation 20 – 22.

b. Salvation for God's people (25:1–12)

Context

The song extolling God's greatness in chapter 25 often picks up images from the devastation just described in chapter 24 (see 24:10/25:2 and 24:16a/25:3). Could this even be one of the songs of praise mentioned in 24:16?

In response to the judgments of chapter 24, this poetic chapter follows the general form of a song of praise, citing three specific reasons to praise God, each introduced by the word *kî*: (1) he has *done wonderful things* (v. 1); (2) he has destroyed cities which *will never be rebuilt*, causing him to be revered among the nations (vv. 2–3); and (3) he has been *a refuge for the poor* and *the needy*, defending them against *the ruthless* (vv. 4–5).

The second part of the song (vv. 6–8) describes the benefits of living in a world under the sovereign control of the LORD. The final portion (vv. 9–12) tells of the joy that God's people experience having been delivered from their enemies (typified by Moab).

Comment

1–3. Verse 1 begins with a declaration of personal commitment to Yahweh: *LORD, you are my God.* Even though God relates to the nation of Israel as a whole, each individual needs to make a personal commitment to him; each person is important to God. The first reason (*kî*, 'for') why the poet praises God is because he has *done wonderful things*, a common phrase in Scripture expressive of the outstanding acts that only God can do (see Exod. 15:11).

It is difficult to determine the author's vantage point: whether he is looking back on what God has done or is speaking prophetically of what he will do. If, however, this chapter is a song of praise concerning the events accomplished in the previous chapter, then they are future events described in prophetic perfect terms (i.e. as accomplished events in the author's mind; Williams §165). These wonders had been planned from *long ago* (lit. 'from distant [time]') and will be faithfully completed (lit. 'with utmost faithfulness'). Unlike idols, not only can God be trusted to act, he also has a divine purpose for his actions. The ingenuity of those who are wicked cannot surprise or hinder him.

The second reason (*kî*, v. 2) that elicits the psalmist's praise is that no city, no matter how well fortified, will be able to avert God's punishment (see 24:10). Some have argued that the reading *You have made the city a heap of rubble* (lit. 'you have made from a city to the heap') is worded awkwardly in the Hebrew text (Emerton 1977: 64–73), but the *min* preposition is more likely to be read as an emphatic *min* (Williams §325), translated as: *You have made* even a *city* into *a heap* [of ruins]. There also appears to be a chiasm in the verse:

A *kî śamtā* [verb] **mē`îr laggāl**	*You have made the city a heap of rubble,*
B *qiryâ bĕṣûrâ lĕmappēlâ*	*the fortified town a ruin,*
B' *`armôn zārîm*	*the foreigners' stronghold*
A' **mē`îr lĕ`ōlām** *lōʾ yabbāneh* [verb]	*a city no more; it will never be rebuilt.*

Fortified cities (lit. 'an inaccessible town') and *the foreigners' stronghold* (lit. 'a citadel of strangers') will be destroyed (*mappālâ*, '[in] ruins', 3x, all in Isaiah). The *foreigners' stronghold* may refer to something similar to the palace that Eglon, the Moabite king who reigned during the time of the judges, built for himself inside the walls of Jericho after defeating Israel (Judg. 3:13–14). These cities will be destroyed, never again to be rebuilt or to rise up against God.

Verse 3 states the natural outcome (i.e. *therefore*) of the previous verse: even *ruthless nations will revere* God, realizing that they cannot compete with his power and strength. The phrases *cities of ruthless nations* (v. 3) and *foreigners' stronghold* (v. 2) are equivalent terms; they will have seen God's power and will honour him.

4–5. The final reason (*kî*, v. 4) for praise is that God helps the helpless. Not only can he destroy mighty fortified cities, but we now see his compassionate side as well. God is often referred to as *a refuge* (i.e. 'a place of safety') in hymns of praise (see Ps. 46:1). He shelters the vulnerable *poor* and *needy* from danger (*a shelter from the storm* [*zerem*, 10x; 8x in Isaiah]) and provides safety and protection (*a shade from the heat*) for them. The *breath of the ruthless* represents the power of a cruel enemy whose ability to destroy is likened to the wind and rain of a *storm driving against a wall* (lit. 'like a rainstorm of a wall') to demolish it. Several scholars add 'against' instead of 'of', noting the awkwardness of this phrase, since a construct relationship does not generally exhibit an adversative relationship; however, see the construct relationship of the titles to the Oracles against the Nations which seem to suggest this type of translation (see 15:1; etc.). Others suggest emending *qîr*, 'wall', to *qôr*, 'winter' (i.e. 'like the rain of winter') or to a proper name (i.e. 'the rainstorm[s] of Kir', a city in Moab that receives about 12 in. of rain per year). These emendations are exceptionally creative, but unnecessary.

The thought continues into verse 5 with imagery that depicts how easily God subdues his enemies – like *the shadow of a cloud* that stops the sun's blazing heat. The ruthless will have no victory celebration, for God will protect his people: *the song of the ruthless is stilled* (lit. 'he humbles the song of the ruthless person'). This is the only place where *ʿānâ* would mean 'to be stilled', but the meaning is clear: the joy is taken out of the person's song. It is interesting that the verb *kānaʿ* in the parallel phrase also has the meaning 'to be humbled'.

6–8. The main body of this song of praise describes the abundant provisions and protection that Yahweh will shower upon his remnant *on this mountain* (i.e. Mt Zion). In verse 6 the LORD himself lays out a lavish feast (*mištēh šĕmānîm*, 'feast of fats' = rich food) for a redeemed community. The feast speaks to the wealth and breadth of his kingdom: (1) Only the finest is provided: *the best of meats* [lit. 'fats full of marrow'; *mĕmuḥāyim*, dual form, occurs only here] *and the finest of wine* [lit. 'refined dregs (i.e. impurities) of wine'] are superlatives. The word for meats (*mĕmuḥāyim*) may have been chosen as a wordplay on the final word in the sentence, *mĕzuqqāqîm* (*wines*). (2) It is abundant enough *for all peoples*; that is, the multinational remnant who have survived God's purging of the nations (Isa. 24). Once again, the sound and word repetitions create a poetic rhythm in the song.

Inaugural banquets for the coronation of a king were common in the Ancient Near East. During this celebration, the king would often bestow gifts on his favoured servants (see Ps. 2:8). In this case *the Sovereign LORD* (lit. 'the Lord LORD' [*'ădōnāy yĕhwih*]) will bestow gifts far surpassing anything people have known that will usher in a new era: (1) *he will destroy* [*bāla'*, 'swallow up'] / *the shroud that enfolds all peoples* (lit. 'the surface of the covering [*hallôṭ*, 2x], the covering [*massēkâ*, 'blanket', 2x] of the nation'); (2) he will *swallow up death for ever* (see Rev. 20:14; 21:4); (3) he will *wipe away the tears / from all faces* (65:19; Rev. 7:17; 21:4); and (4) he will *remove his people's disgrace* (vv. 7–8).

The repetition of 'covering' could be (1) a gloss to explain the word *hallôṭ* (i.e. the covering of the nation); (2) to create emphasis; or (3) a corruption which some amend to *hallûṭ*, a passive participle, thus reading 'a covering that covers' (see Roberts 2015: 320). The *shroud* (*hallôṭ*) over all the nations (lit. 'nation', v. 7) is not a reference to a 'veil' of spiritual blindness (i.e. 2 Cor. 3:15–16), but to the custom of covering oneself as a sign of grief (i.e. 2 Sam. 15:30). The need to grieve has been removed because death is no more.

His people's disgrace (lit. 'reproach') refers to the special suffering and humiliation that the Jews endured during exile and dispersion when other nations looked upon them with contempt. In the end they will be vindicated by God when he gathers them back to the land and sets up his everlasting kingdom.

These gifts, which remove the disastrous consequences of sin, will indeed be bestowed, because (*kî*) *the LORD has spoken* it.

9–12. The removal of death and the disgrace of God's people *in that day* will prove that they have not trusted him in vain: *Surely* [*hinnēh*, used to get their attention] *this is our God; / we trusted* [lit. 'waited'] *in him, and he saved us.* His remnant, rejoicing in their deliverance, will give praise to God, in words written in stair-step parallelism (my translation):

> Surely this is **our God; we have waited for him**
> > that he may save us;
> This is **the LORD; we have waited for him;**
> > let us rejoice and be glad in his salvation.

The wait has been long, but God's amazing deliverance has more than compensated for it (see 25:1).

Verse 10 highlights the difference between those who waited for the LORD and those who did not: God's hand *will rest on this mountain* [i.e. Mt Zion]*; / but Moab will be trampled.* Here Moab represents any nation opposed to God; however, the Moabites did merit God's particular punishment for having mocked and plundered his people (see Zeph. 2:8). The image of being trampled down is also used of Assyria's treatment of Israel (see Isa. 10:6). *Straw* (*matbēn*, occurs only here) sounds like the word *manure* (*madmēnâ*, occurs only here). This could also be a wordplay on the city name 'Madmen' (Jer. 48:2), said to be in Moab.[18]

Moab taunted the nation of Israel for their belief in Yahweh, claiming the Israelites were no different from every other nation, even though they were God's chosen people (see Ezek. 25:8). Now the tables are turned: Israel is vindicated and Moab humiliated. Even if the Moabites were to *stretch out their hands* to *swim* (*śāḥâ*, 2x) in order to free themselves from the wave of God's punishment (v. 11), no amount of effort will avail. They will be engulfed and brought low, *despite the cleverness of their hands.* The word *cleverness* or possibly 'skill' (*'ārbôt*, occurs only here) is suggested based on the earlier part of the verse (see *HALOT* 1.83).

---

18. J. A. Thompson has suggested that the name *madmēnâ* is Dimon and that the *mēm* is a duplication of the preceding *mēm* (1980: 703).

Moab's position of pride and strength, characterized by their *high fortified walls* (lit. 'fortified stronghold' = Petra?), will suddenly be reversed when their walls are brought down. The repetition of similar words is for emphasis: *He will bring down . . . / and lay them low; / . . . down to the ground* [lit. 'touch the ground'], / *to the very dust.*

Clements indicates a post-exilic date for this passage (1980a: 210), but a much earlier date is suggested by Psalm 83 where Moab, in alliance with others (esp. Assyria, v. 8), attempts to wipe out the nation of Israel. Moab had been a significant foe in the past and continued as such for much of Judah's history, meriting God's promise of future destruction.

Meaning

This chapter is a song of praise to Yahweh for his majestic deliverance of his remnant. God's plan to deliver his people, established from long ago, will come to fruition and be evident to all, whereas those who had fought against his people will be punished.

God will provide for his remnant a lavish banquet of the choicest food and drink (v. 6; see Rev. 19:7–9). His gifts will be unparalleled: the 'covering' that had signified mourning will be removed, death will be destroyed, all tears will be wiped away, and the people's disgrace will be no more. Israel's long-standing enemies, pictured as Moab, will be destroyed, never to rise again. Several elements of this deliverance are highlighted in the book of Revelation when God draws the history of this creation to a close.

c. A song of trust (26:1–21)

Context

Whereas Isaiah 24 – 25 centres more on the future destruction of those who set themselves against God and his people, Isaiah 26 – 27 highlights the effects of God's future deliverance on his people. There is little agreement regarding the genre of Isaiah 26, but it can be characterized as a song of trust citing at least two reasons for trusting in God: (1) the LORD is the eternal Rock (v. 4); and (2) he humbles the proud and casts them to the ground (v. 5).

This song begins with the phrase *in that day* (like 27:1, 2) which describes the time of restoration mentioned in the previous chapter:

in that day this song of trust will be sung in Judah. Childs notes an interesting difference between chapters 25 and 26: 'Chapter 25 speaks of life removed from death [i.e. 25:8], while chapter 26 of the promise of resurrection to life even after the suffering of death [i.e. 26:19]' (2001: 190; my additions).

Chapter 26 is composed of two parts: (1) verses 1–6 describe the blessings of trusting in Yahweh; and (2) verses 7–21 contrast the outcomes for the righteous and the wicked. The eschatological nature of verses 20–21 tells us that these are future promises that do not have an imminent fulfilment.

Comment

1–3. The phrase *in that day* refers to the time when God delivers and protects his people, *the land of Judah* (see also 25:9). Jerusalem will be a place of security, fortified by God (i.e. a *strong city*), in contrast to the foreigners' city mentioned in 25:2. This city has walls and ramparts of salvation, for only Yahweh's presence can provide true protection that cannot be breached.

Even though the name of the city is never mentioned, the only city God had promised to protect was Zion. This city will be a place where *the righteous nation* (v. 2) can enter (i.e. *open the gates*) and remain safe (i.e. *You will keep in perfect peace*, v. 3). The last phrase in verse 2, *the nation that keeps faith* (lit. 'the one who continues to keep faithfulnesses'), highlights the continual nature of this belief. The people will enjoy security in a way they have never before experienced: *You will keep in perfect peace* [lit. 'peace, peace', the repetition suggests a superlative; Williams §16a] *those whose minds are steadfast* [lit. 'whose inclination (towards God) is firm']. This abundance of contentment is *because* [*kî*] *they trust in* him, the only one who can truly be trusted.

4–6. As a natural response to verse 3, the author turns to the community with the command *Trust in the LORD for ever* (lit. 'until for ever', v. 4) because (*kî*) he is the *Rock eternal* (lit. 'eternals' [pl.]; see Ps. 18:31–34). The word *eternal* is either an abstract plural referring to the quality, state or characteristic of the *Rock* (Williams §7), or a plural of intensity (Williams §8); either underscores the unchanging characteristic of the *Rock*. Both the shorter (*yāh*) and longer (*yāhweh*) forms of Yahweh are used here, an emphasis that the NIV translation captures well: *for the LORD, the LORD himself, is the Rock eternal.*

The second reason (*kî*) why Yahweh can be trusted is because he will humble *those who dwell on high* (i.e. 'the proud and the powerful'; v. 5), laying low *the lofty city*, even *to the dust* (see 25:12). The *lofty* [lit. 'inaccessible'] *city* is a general reference to any city thought to be inaccessible (see parallel unit *who dwell on high*).

Repetition of the word 'foot' (*regel*) in verse 6 is not an instance of dittography, but rather provides emphasis and grammatically balances the parallel final unit. Yahweh accomplishes all of this by those who are least able to conquer such powerful cities (i.e. the *oppressed* and *poor*); they are able to do so through God's intervention.

7–9. Verses 7–21 are a continuation of the song of trust as it now describes the *righteous* who rely upon God. Yahweh, *the Upright One*, makes the *path/way* (lit. 'wagon track') of the righteous both *level* (*mêšārîm*, an abstract plural; Williams §7) and *smooth* (lit. 'to clear a way', 4x). God removes any obstacle or hindrance, facilitating their return to Zion.

Verse 7 contains an interesting wordplay in which the first phrase ends with a form of the word *yāšār* (i.e. *mêšārîm*, 'upright, smooth') and the next phrase begins with a vocative of *yāšār* referring to God, literally *the Upright One.*

The people of Israel wait patiently for God's deliverance while continuing to obey his laws: *Yes* [lit. 'indeed'], *LORD, walking in the way of your laws* [lit. 'judgments'], / *we wait for you* (v. 8). They honour his *name and renown* (lit. 'remembrance'), a phrase that expresses God's very person, the object of Israel's desire. Thus, the people wait with confident hope and trust that Yahweh will deliver them because of his steadfast character.

The inverted syntax of verse 9 highlights the remnant's deep longing for God: *My soul yearns for you* [lit. '(in) my soul, I desire you'] *in the night.* The literal reading of its parallel phrase is 'even my spirit, in my midst I seek you early'. The remnant longs for God's judgments because then the world will learn the true standard of righteousness, as well as the benefits of following God's laws: *the people of the world learn righteousness.*

10–11. The wicked have rejected all the kindness that God has shown to them and continue in their rebellion against him (*when grace is shown to the wicked, / they do not learn righteousness*). The wicked often see mercy and repentance as signs of weakness. The author is convinced that even in an environment of justice and righteousness (lit. 'in the land of uprightness' [*nĕkōḥôt*, 7x]), they do not turn from sin (lit. 'they act unjustly', 3x), nor do they acknowledge *the majesty of the LORD*.

The wicked do not see that God's hand *is lifted high*, a sign of imminent judgment. It is not until they see God's deliverance of his people (lit. '[God's] zeal for a people') that they will *be put to shame*. Their eyes will be opened, but it will be too late. The author is emphatic as he states the consequence: 'surely' *let the fire reserved for your* [God's] *enemies consume them*.

12–15. These verses demonstrate a confident assurance that God will deliver his people: *you establish* [*šāpat*, 4x] *peace for us* (v. 12), a reference to their deliverance even though the word *peace* usually has a much broader meaning (i.e. 'wholeness, healthiness, completeness, prosperity, deliverance, salvation'). The author realizes that Israel is powerless, and God's plans cannot be thwarted (*all that we have accomplished you have done for us*). Yet his past deeds are but a foretaste of Israel's future.

The prophet has two reasons for this confidence. First, Yahweh has not allowed the nation of Israel to forget him. Even though *other lords* (*'ădōnîm* = Assyria, Babylon, Persia, etc.) have *ruled* (*bā'al*) over them, they still maintain that Yahweh is their God (lit. 'only in you we remember your name'). Second, Israel will continue to exist (v. 15) long after these *other lords* have been destroyed and *you* [have] *wiped out all memory of them* (v. 14).

The emphatic order of the first two phrases of verse 14 (lit. '[the] dead ones will not live; [the] spirits [*rĕpā'îm*, 'ghosts, shades of the dead'] will not arise') indicates the certainty of the outcome. The dead here refer to the nations that God had brought to ruin (v. 13). Not only will Israel outlive them all, but God will extend (prophetic perfects) its borders (lit. 'to be made distant the ends of the land', v. 15) and thereby bring glory to himself. The repetition of the phrase *you have enlarged the nation* is not dittography, but pivot parallelism (Watson 1994: 214–215). The book of Isaiah repeatedly pictures an expanded future for Israel whose population includes people from all nations, and whose power and importance dominate the world (see 54:2–3).

16–19. In contrast to Israel's glorious future, we now look back again to the time when they were punished. Frequent shifts between past, present and future are typical in Isaiah 24 – 27. When Israel turned to God in their distress, they were so weak that they could *barely* [*ṣāqûn*, occurs only here] *whisper a prayer*. The word *laḥaš* is best translated as *whisper*; however, Oswalt reads it as 'affliction/discipline', thus the translation '[in] straits they were humbled [by] your discipline upon them' (1986: 483–484).

Their suffering was intense, like that of *a pregnant woman about to give birth*, yet their efforts to bring deliverance to the world were entirely ineffectual, giving *birth to wind*. Two factors shed light on the difficult phrase *and the people of the world have not come to life* (*nāpal*, lit. 'have not fallen'): (1) the parallel phrase refers to salvation (*We have not brought salvation to the earth*); and (2) birthing stools that were customarily used in the Ancient Near East allowed the child 'to fall' into the hands of the waiting midwife. Israel failed in their task of leading nations to God (i.e. *We have not brought salvation to the earth*; see Exod. 19:6), having wandered away from him themselves rather than drawing people to him.

The ultimate answer is that God will nevertheless accomplish his purpose of delivering a remnant of his people despite their disobedience: Israel's *dead* [pl. 'ones'] *will live, . . . / their* [lit. 'my' = God's] *bodies* [*nĕbēlâ*, 'body' = collective] *will rise* (i.e. those bodies belonging to God will rise). Israel's corpses will be brought to life; but for God's ultimate purpose to be fulfilled, deliverance will need to be brought to the world (v. 18). Israel's all-powerful God who created the world and life from nothing can certainly resurrect dead bodies, even those that have turned to dust.

But what Israel could not do (i.e. bring deliverance to the world, v. 18), God will do through a remnant of Israel (v. 19), who are pictured as *the dew of the morning* (lit. 'lights') that brings life-giving moisture to the dry *dust* (i.e. the world). As in the final phrase of verse 18, the verb 'to fall' (lit. 'to cause to fall') is used again in speaking of giving birth to the earth's *dead* (*rĕpā'îm*, 'spirits', 10x). The phrase *your* [masc. sing.] *dead will live* (v. 19) must refer to a remnant of Israel that will be resurrected to live in God's restored kingdom. The earth is said to give them birth, for their bodies had returned to the dust (see Gen. 3:19).

20–21. These verses return once again to the wider punishment of the entire earth. God's true people (i.e. the remnant) receive instruction for their protection, figuratively pictured as hiding themselves indoors (i.e. *enter your rooms / and shut the doors behind you*), until God's punishment has run its course. Here we are informed of three things: (1) God will punish the wicked; (2) his people will somehow be spared/protected from this punishment; and (3) the punishment (i.e. *his wrath*) will last only *for a little while* (lit. 'according to a little moment').

Verse 21 explains why his people must hide (*ḥābâ*, occurs only here): because (*kî*) at the right time the master of the universe will return to punish the wicked. God's people are to get well out of the way of the punishment he sends on the wicked; they are to *hide* until his *wrath* (lit. 'indignation') has run its course (lit. 'passes over'; the image is reminiscent of the events of the night of Passover in Egypt).

The iniquity of the inhabitants of the earth is about to be (i.e. a participle implying imminent action) revealed. The justice of this punishment will be obvious to all because *the earth will disclose* (i.e. reveal) the *blood* (pl. = massive bloodshed) that has been shed upon it. The earth has been keeping record, like Abel's blood that called out to God, and justice will be served: *the earth will conceal its slain no longer.*

God does not want any to perish (see 2 Pet. 3:9), yet he is just and must punish the wicked. In his mercy he often preserves a remnant even in the midst of punishment (Noah, Lot, the Hebrew firstborn in Egypt, etc.).

Meaning
This song is the first of three passages (26:1; 27:1, 2) that provide more detail regarding the future time of punishment and restoration described in chapters 24–25. It is a song of trust that highlights two reasons why God is to be trusted: (1) he is an everlasting Rock to those who trust him; and (2) he will humble the proud. The first theme describes the way of the righteous (vv. 7–9), which is then

contrasted with the way of the wicked (vv. 10–14). The reason the wicked are judged is because of their unbridled cruelty and atrocious bloodshed. The earth has been keeping a record and will expose their sins to all (v. 21).

God's nation went through punishment (vv. 16–18) and in the process some realized that they had failed to bring deliverance to the whole world (v. 18). Thus, God himself would have to deliver a remnant (vv. 15, 19–20).

d. Deliverance for Israel that spreads to the world (27:1–13)

Context
The final chapter of this section (Isa. 24 – 27) continues to describe God's future plan for the world in which Israel will play a key role. The vineyard, which was destroyed and discarded in Isaiah 5, is now entirely transformed, being tended and protected by God; its flavoursome fruit will be bountiful. As in chapter 26, the phrase *in that day* is used to introduce important units in chapter 27 that speak of a future day of judgment and restoration when God will settle accounts for both the righteous and the wicked.

There is general agreement that the chapter is divided into the following units: verses 1, 2–5, 6–11 and 12–13, with most sections beginning with the phrase *in that day* (vv. 1, 2, 12, 13; used more in this chapter than in the rest of chapters 24–27 combined). 'This day' refers to the Day of the LORD when God will protect his people and punish the wicked, often repeated themes in chapters 24–27. The first-person divine speech in verses 2–5 is followed by the author's explanation of the oracle in verses 6–11. The final two verses conclude both the chapter and the entire section (Isa. 24 – 27).

Comment
1. *In that day* the *Leviathan*,[19] pictured as *the gliding* [*bāriaḥ*, 'fleeing', 4x] *serpent,* / . . . *the coiling* [*'āqallātôn*, 'writhing'; occurs only here]

---

19. Stories of a battle between a chief god and a sea/chaos monster were fairly well known throughout the Ancient Near East: in Babylonian

serpent; / ... the monster of [lit. 'which is in'] *the sea*, will also be punished. The name *Leviathan* occurs several times in the Old Testament (see Job 3:8; Pss 74:13–14; 104:26; etc.). Job 41:1 presents him as one of the mighty creatures that Yahweh created; here in verse 1 he is described as *the monster of the sea*.

Although the identity of *Leviathan* is uncertain, in Israel he came to represent wickedness, chaos, Satan, or a combination of all three. Whatever the case, God is clearly pictured as supreme in power, able to extinguish *Leviathan*, slaying him with his *great and powerful sword*. According to the book of Revelation the great dragon will be destroyed by God and cast into the 'lake of burning sulphur' (Rev. 20:2, 7–10).

2–3. The opening words *In that day* – [apparently the same day as the *Leviathan* is killed and thus an eschatological future event] *'Sing about a fruitful [ḥemed] vineyard'* introduce another song (similar to those in chs. 25 and 26) that describes a beautiful, divinely protected vineyard in contrast to the useless vineyard of 5:1–7. God's care had never left Israel, but for a time, when they were being punished, it did not feel that way.

Some scholars suggest there is a missing element, such as *yōʾmēr*, 'he will say', due to a perceived abruptness between the phrase *in that day* and the instruction to sing; however, the poetic nature of the song does not require this. More important is whether the rare word *fruitful* (*ḥemed*, 'delightful', 6x) is correct. *BHS* suggests emending *ḥemed* to *ḥemer*, 'wine' (*dālet* and *rêsh* are quite similar in Hebrew square script), but the phrase 'vineyard of wine' is hardly an improvement.

Yahweh himself (i.e. the name signifying God's personal, covenantal relationship with Israel) is protecting the vineyard: (1) *I, the LORD, watch over it*; (2) *I water it continually* (lit. 'according to the moments'); and (3) *I guard it day and night / so that no one may harm it* (lit. 'lest someone visit against it'). To guard something *day and night* is a

---

(note 19 *cont.*) tradition Marduk kills the sea monster Tiamat (*ANET* 66–68); in Ugaritic tradition Baal(?) defeats Lotan the sea monster (*ANET* 138); and in Hittite tradition the storm god kills the dragon Illuyankas (*ANET* 125–126).

merism that indicates continuous protection. Unlike the vineyard in Isaiah 5, God unceasingly cares for and protects this vineyard.

4–5. Some seek to emend God's emphatic statement *I am not angry* (lit. 'wrath there is not to me', v. 4), thinking it sounds out of place here. But the statement makes sense as it stands: in contrast to the vineyard of chapter 5, God's wrath has been appeased, leaving only love for his vineyard.

An enemy is pictured sowing harmful weeds into God's precious vineyard, a common practice in warfare: literally 'whoever would bring to me' *briers and thorns*. The phrase *briers and thorns* occurs only in Isaiah (5:6; 7:23, 24, 25; etc.) and refers to worthless weeds that steal precious nutrients and moisture from the vines. God would totally eradicate them (lit. 'I would stomp [*pāśaʿ*, occurs only here] on them and burn [*ṣût*, occurs only here] them all at once'). God takes special care of this vineyard when it is threatened, in contrast to the vineyard of 5:6 where he allows *briers and thorns* to grow.

The relationship between verses 4 and 5 is problematic. Gesenius states that the *ʾô* beginning verse 5 should be read as a shortened form of *ʾô kî*, meaning 'it would then happen that' (GKC §162a). Verse 5 would thus describe the special protection God provides as he eradicates the weeds: 'it would then happen that it [i.e. the vineyard] would be strong in my refuge [and] peace there will be with me [this phrase is repeated].' Another less likely translation of verse 5 is: 'Or [else] let him [i.e. the one to whom gave God briers and thorns to use against Israel, v. 4] turn to God for refuge and let them [lit. 'him'] make peace with me.' The logic is that any enemy who goes against God's people is an enemy of God. The first interpretation continues the theme of God's protection of Israel, while the second is an offer to any of Israel's enemies to turn to God and seek refuge in him.

The repetition of the phrase *let them make peace with me* is emphatic in nature, but each phrase has a different emphasis depending on the word order. In the first phrase, emphasis is placed on the words *with me*, whereas in the second it is on the word *peace*. The word *šālôm* is a rich concept that includes wholeness, prosperity, well-being, peace and safety.

6. One day Israel (lit. *Jacob*) will prosper, pictured as taking root, budding (*ṣûṣ*, 9x), blossoming and ultimately bearing fruit. The phrase *in days to come* (*habbā'im*, 'the coming [days]') is unusual. The editors of *BHS* suggest emending the text to *bā' hayyôm wĕ*, 'the day comes and', or *hayyāmîn bā'îm*, 'the days are coming', but there is little textual evidence for either and little difference in meaning between these emendations and the original reading.

This verse looks past the punishment Israel would undergo (see 26:16) and envisions the nation so restored that its produce will *fill all the world with fruit* (*tĕnûbâ*, 'produce of all kinds', 7x). The rare word *tĕnûbâ*, *fruit*, may be literal or figurative, but here it is most probably spiritual fruit (i.e. the remnant) that fills the earth.

7–9. Despite rare vocabulary and unexpected changes in tense, person and gender, the overarching message of verses 7–11 is clear: Israel will be punished until she is thoroughly purged of her sin.

The assumed answer to both questions in verse 7 is 'yes'. Israel had indeed gone through much of the same punishment that was inflicted on her enemies due to her rebellion and stubbornness. Words with the same roots help convey the equity of the punishment (i.e. the striker gets struck; the slayer gets slain). No wicked person is immune from divine punishment, not even if one of God's own people.

Israel's punishment according to verse 8 would be *warfare* [*bĕsa'ssĕ'â*, occurs only here] *and exile* [lit. 'sending her forth'], pictured as a *fierce blast* (lit. 'wind') driving (*hāgâ*, 'to remove', 2x) them out of the land. The phrase *as on a day the east wind blows* recalls the scorching east winds of the sirocco, a figurative reference to Assyria and Babylon, who came from the east. Alternatively, but less likely, it could mean 'blowing to the east', a reference to the direction in which Israel would be 'blown' when exiled.

The lengthy process of punishment was the means by which (lit. 'therefore by this') atonement for *Jacob's guilt* would be made. It was the 'full price' (*full fruit*, lit. 'all the fruit') to be paid before the remnant would return to God and thus accomplish his plan. This does not mean that the punishment itself paid the debt for their sin, otherwise there would have been no need for Christ's sacrifice, but the punishment produced faith in God.

Proof of their changed hearts will show itself *when he* (i.e. Jacob) destroys all the altars to false gods (*makes all the altar stones / to be like limestone* [*gir*, occurs only here] *crushed to pieces*), as well as the *Asherah poles* (representations of Asherah) and *incense altars* (see 2 Chr. 34:4, 7). The implication is that Israel will at last be whole hearted in their dedication to Yahweh; idols will no longer be worshipped.

10–11. The identity of *the fortified city* [that] *stands desolate* is never clarified. The *kî* beginning verse 10 (not translated in the NIV) signals a contrast (i.e. 'but the fortified city . . .') with the restoration described in verse 9. Verse 10 thus refers back to the pre-restoration period of Jerusalem and provides a further description of the events in verse 8 (i.e. *by warfare and exile you contend with her*). The reason for the punishment is found in verse 11 (*For this is a people without understanding; / so their Maker has no compassion on them*).

The other nations will so utterly destroy Jerusalem that it will be entirely *forsaken like the wilderness* (v. 10). It will be so desolate that grazing *calves* (lit. 'calf') strip its branches bare (lit. 'finish its branches' [*sā'ip*, 2x]) until they dry up and are fit only for firewood (i.e. so that they are taken away). There may be a subtle play on the word 'light' in the phrase *women come and make fires* [lit. 'causing them to light', an unusual term to describe burning something] *with them*. The Israelites were lacking the true light (i.e. the true knowledge of God) and thus God will remove them.

The irony of this imagery is that calves, which Israel once worshipped, now feed where Israel's capital had once been (see Oswalt 1986: 496). The nation of Israel was *a people without understanding*; therefore, their *Maker* and *Creator* shows them *no compassion* or *favour*. Yet this is not Israel's final end, as the next two verses indicate.

12–13. As a fitting conclusion to the description of the future events in Isaiah 24 – 27, a remnant will return to worship God on Mount Zion. The *wāw* beginning verse 12 suggests a contrast ('but') with the desolation of verses 10–11. *In that day* is apparently the same future eschatological day mentioned in verses 1–2 when God threshes (*yaḥbōṭ*, 'will beat out', 5x) the nation of Israel. Thus, in the future there will be a great ingathering of his people, pictured as a harvest (see similar image in Matt. 24:30–31), when God will gather a remnant *one by one*. Not one will be missing, from the border of Babylon (i.e. the stream [*šibbōlet*, only occurrence with this meaning] of the *Euphrates*) all the way to the *Wadi* [*naḥal*] *of Egypt* (i.e. the Wadi el-Arish, commonly the border between Israel and Egypt in biblical times). This delineates the furthest borders the land of Israel ever reached during the reign of Solomon when it was allied to people living in the Syria–Lebanon area.

Verse 13 pictures the same event: *in that day a great trumpet* [*šôpār,* 'ram's horn'] *will sound.* While the word *great* modifies *trumpet,* it references the loudness of its sound, not its size, for it will be heard all the way to Assyria and Egypt. This trumpet is similar to those that summoned troops to battle (Judg. 6:34). Here God is calling Israelites who have been scattered or dispersed into the bordering lands of Assyria and Egypt to return to Mount Zion (see 11:11–12).

Two factors point to a future ingathering, rather than those coming from the Babylonian exile: (1) the context is one of restoration of the righteous remnant and punishment of the wicked; and (2) the remnant is described as *those . . . perishing in Assyria and those . . . exiled in Egypt.*

Even in this future period *the holy mountain* [i.e. Mt Zion] *in Jerusalem* is the centre of Yahweh *worship* (lit. 'they will bow down to the Lord'). The emphasis here is not only on returning to Jerusalem, but on returning to Yahweh worship as well; this implies a purified, obedient people.

Meaning
God's mighty power will be displayed when he wipes out evil and even more specifically the power behind evil, represented as Leviathan. Israel, the continued focus of God's deliverance, will finally become the light to the nations that God had intended. He will use punishment for redemptive purposes in his people, causing a remnant to turn back to him. This remnant will be gathered from both Assyria and Egypt, suggesting that it is broader than the return from Babylonia.

iii. Prophecies concerning Judah: judgment and restoration oracles (28:1 – 33:24)
There has been much disagreement concerning the date and structure of chapters 28–33, but in the final canonical form they appear to be the centre of a finely crafted palistrophe (i.e. chs.

13–39) that concerns events from before the fall of the northern kingdom to around the time of Jerusalem's deliverance in 701 BC (see Childs 2001: 199). There are nine judgment oracles and nine restoration oracles that alternate back and forth in chapters 28–33 (see Figure 0.9 on p. 23). The key theme of this section is that Israel will not be spared by human alliances or their own ingenuity, but only by God's power.

Several scholars suggest that, because of its apocalyptic flavour, chapter 33 should be grouped with chapters 34–35, yet it is more closely tied to the destruction–restoration theme of chapters 28–32.

a. First judgment–restoration cycle: woe to the drunkards of Ephraim (28:1–4); deliverance for a remnant of his people (28:5–6)

Context
This section comprises two units, the first a 'woe' oracle (vv. 1–4) and the second an oracle of restoration (vv. 5–6). This first 'woe' oracle reveals that the proud leaders of Samaria will soon be overwhelmed by the formidable Assyrian army. The restoration oracle reveals that only God can deliver them.

Comment

(1) Judgment oracle (28:1–4)
1–2. This first *woe* (*hôy*) oracle describes Samaria as a *wreath* and a *fading flower* that is *set on the head of a fertile valley* (lit. 'valley of oils', plural form emphasizing its fertility). Verses 1–4 are arranged in two parallel panels (see Figure 28.1). These panels balance each other, except for two additions: (1) the phrase *of those laid low by wine* (shown in parentheses, v. 1); and (2) the phrase *will be trampled underfoot* (shown in parentheses, v. 3). Verse 2 explains that God's agent (i.e. the Assyrians), who will punish the northern kingdom, is strong and powerful as a storm. Verse 4 gives the example of how quickly they will be destroyed: as figs that are plucked and eaten *as soon as people see them* (lit. 'the seer sees it'; the wording suggests a quick, almost automatic response).

Samaria's inhabitants took great pride in their city: *the pride of Ephraim's drunkards*. *Ephraim* was a common name for Israel in the

¹ *Woe to that wreath, the pride of Ephraim's drunkards*	³ *That wreath, the pride of Ephraim's drunkards* (*will be trampled underfoot*)
to the fading flower, his glorious beauty	⁴ *That fading flower, his glorious beauty*
set on the head of a fertile valley . . . (*of those laid low by wine*)	*set on the head of a fertile valley*
² *See the Lord has one who is powerful and strong . . . he will throw it forcefully to the ground*	*Will be like the first-ripe fig . . .* *as soon as people see them and take them in hand, they swallow them.*

Figure 28.1 Parallel passages in Isaiah 28:1–4

latter seventh century BC when the northern kingdom, far reduced in size, was limited to the highlands of Ephraim.

Omri built Samaria on a hilltop at the head of *a fertile valley* (see 1 Kgs 16:24) to display the greatness of his kingdom, and this became the centre of wine and oil production. However, after the mid eighth century BC, it was a *fading* [*nōbēl*, 'sinking, drooping'] *flower* in a sad state of decline; its leaders were decadent (i.e. *drunkards . . . laid low* [*hălûmê*, 'smitten', 8x] *by wine*) and its beauty had faded.

The announcement is made (*see* [*hinnēh* = to alert the reader]) that the LORD would send Assyria, his *powerful and strong* instrument, to thoroughly destroy Samaria, which helps date this passage before 722/721 BC. Assyria's destructive power is portrayed as a violent storm (*zerem*, 9x; 7x in Isaiah) that wreaks havoc, with hail, wind, rain and flooding:

A *See, the Lord has one who is powerful and strong* [*'ammîs*, 6x].
   B *Like a hailstorm and a destructive wind,*
   B' *like a driving rain* [lit. 'downpour of water'] *and a flooding downpour* [lit. 'mighty overflow'],
A' *he will throw* [lit. 'he settled' = prophetic perfect] *it forcefully to the ground* (lit. 'by his hand' = his power).

The description of Assyria, written in the form of a chiasm, is highly accurate. As the world's first professional army, they devastated many nations.

3–4. Samaria will be *trampled underfoot*, an event fulfilled in 722/721 BC when the Assyrians destroyed the city. They are likened to *figs ripe before harvest* (*bakkûrâ*, occurs only here and resembles *bikkûrîm*, 'firstborn'). Figs can produce two crops a year: the first, breva crop (i.e. the figs mentioned here) develops in the spring from the prior year's growth; the second, main crop is the new year's growth that ripens in late summer or early autumn. Samaria is warned that it will tumble quickly unless its leaders realize the danger and call out to God.

(2) Restoration oracle (28:5–6)

5–6. *In that day* signals the beginning of the oracle of restoration that employs terms very similar to those of the woe oracle of verses 1–4: *the LORD Almighty* [lit. 'of hosts'] / *will be a glorious crown,* / *a beautiful wreath* [*ṣĕpîrâ*, occurs only here with this meaning] / *for the remnant of his people.* The rare word *ṣĕpîrâ* (*wreath*) can also mean 'doom' or 'end' (see Ezek. 7:7, 10), thus creating a wordplay: it will be an 'end' for the northern kingdom (i.e. Samaria) as mentioned in the woe oracle, but a wreath (i.e. figurative for a 'moment of glory') for God's *remnant*.

A day is coming when God will be the source of his remnant's true beauty and pride: (1) the remnant will be proud of the LORD God, pictured as their *glorious crown*; (2) they will have a fair and upright judge for those who sit before God in judgment (*He will be a spirit of justice* / *to the one who sits in* [lit. 'within' or 'before'] *judgment*); and (3) they will have a source of strength, for God will help them in battle (i.e. *who turn back* their enemy from *the gate*).

The outcome for Samaria in the previous section was destruction (i.e. 722 BC), which is contrasted with the victory in this section for Jerusalem when their enemies are turned back *at the gate* (v. 6). The glory Israel had longed for, but missed with Samaria, will ultimately be accomplished by Yahweh for a remnant.

Meaning

God will call on the mighty nation of Assyria to punish the pride and arrogance of the northern kingdom. Samaria, which was once seen as a glorious flower of Israel, has begun to fade and will soon be destroyed. However, a day is coming when God will be the source of his remnant's true beauty. He will provide true justice and absolute protection.

b. Second judgment–restoration cycle: punishment for the spiritual leaders (28:7–15); deliverance for the remnant (28:16–17)

Context

The second oracle (vv. 7–17) builds upon the first and is directed against Israel's corrupt spiritual leaders (i.e. priests, prophets), who are unable to make wise decisions. The location of these leaders, whether Israel, Judah, or both, is unclear.

Some scholars argue for a late date for this oracle because it speaks of the punishment and destruction of Jerusalem; however, this reasoning is far too simplistic, for even the pre-exilic prophets warned Judah of destruction if they did not change their ways (see Hos. 1 – 3; Amos 6:1–7; Mic. 3:12).

These religious leaders are pictured as incompetent drunkards who cannot discern God's messages. They think they can evade his punishment by their shrewd alliances, but God warns that they will not escape. Oswalt is correct in his assessment of their condition: 'There is no more hardened nor cynical person in the world than a religious leader who has seared his conscience' (1986: 509).

The oracle has two sections: (1) judgment upon the drunken prophets and priests (vv. 7–15); and (2) the restoration of true justice in Zion (vv. 16–17).

Comment

(1) Judgment oracle (28:7–15)

7–8. With a note of surprise and irony (lit. *and these also*), the author denounces the prophets and priests who are meant to be God's messengers but are too inebriated to hear from him: *they stagger when seeing visions, / they stumble [pûq, 2x] when rendering decisions* [*pĕlîlîyâ*, occurs only here]. Because they *are befuddled with wine* (lit. 'wine has swallowed [*bālaʿ*, 7x] them'), their *visions* and *decisions* are alcohol-induced meanderings instead of messages from God.

The imagery then turns graphic with the intent to shock: the tables where they hold their drinking binges are covered with both *vomit* (*qîʾ*, 3x) and excrement (*ṣôʾâ*, 7x), so much so that *there is not a spot* left clean. The shock value increases, as this seems to be a regular occurrence in the temple courts. At a time when the nation desperately needs true spiritual leadership, those who should be leading them are wallowing in their own filth.

9–10. With a tone of frustration, the author poses two rhetorical questions: (1) *Who is it he is trying to teach?* and (2) *To whom is he explaining his message?* The answer appears to be 'to children who have just been weaned' (lit. 'the one weaned from milk', a highly unusual grammatical construction in which a preposition interrupts a construct chain [GKC §130a]). The plural verbs of verses 7–8 have changed to the singular, as God teaches these inebriated leaders. In the Ancient Near East weaning generally took place between the ages of three and five years, when a child has only a rudimentary moral understanding of good and bad. With cutting irony God must give his messages to 'young children', namely the corrupt priests and prophets who should already be educated in his ways but are not.

There is little agreement on the exact meaning of verse 10: *For it is: / do this* [*ṣaw*, possibly a shortened form of *miṣwâ*, 'command'], *do that* [lit. 'for a command'; repeated twice], / *a rule* [lit. 'line'] *for this, a rule for* [lit. 'for a line'] *that* [repeated twice]; / *a little here* [lit. 'there'], *a little there*. The vocabulary may be understood as (1) gibberish to mock the prophet's divine message (Childs 2001: 207); (2) a shortened form of the word 'commands' (*miṣwâ*) to mimic divine commands (Oswalt 1986: 512; Wildberger 2002: 17); (3) the names of archaic letters (*HALOT* 3.1009); (4) the repetition of sounds in imitation of a teacher teaching children (Clements 1980a: 228); or (5) baby talk for excrement and vomit (Emerton 2001: 51–54; Roberts 2015: 351).

Either this verse is a short poem that teachers used to train their students, or the author is imitating a teacher who teaches children through repetition. Whatever the exact meaning, the point made is that God must teach the wicked prophets and priests as one does a child, 'line upon line', 'here a little, there a little', a tedious process that will be neither pleasant nor quick.

11–13. When the priests and prophets fail to do their job, much sterner measures (i.e. the cruel Assyrians) will be required for God to teach his religious leaders: *Very well then* [*kî*, 'As a result'; Williams §450]*, with foreign* [lit. 'stammering'] *lips and strange* [lit. 'other'] *tongues / God will speak to* [i.e. teach] *this people.* The Hebrew noun translated as *foreign* is used in Psalm 35:16 and Hosea 7:16 to mean 'mocking, derision'; the related verb also carries that connotation (see 2 Kgs 19:21). Here, however, the parallel phrase *and strange tongues* makes it clear that it is an unknown language.

The words *to whom* (lit. 'to them') which begin verse 12 refer to the priests and prophets who *would not listen* (lit. 'they were unwilling to hear') when God indicated a place of rest. This is probably a reference to God's laws, which were meant to bring rest to the weary of Israel (i.e. *let the weary rest* [*margēʿâ*, occurs only here]). Since the priests and prophets did not lead people in the plans that God had for Israel, he will change tactics and use carefully administered punishment.

The next phrases, repeated from verse 10, are short and choppy to emphasize the methodical nature of the punishment: *do this* [*ṣaw*, 2x in this passage]*, do that, / a rule* [*qaw*, 2x in this passage] *for this, a rule for that; / a little* [*zĕʿêr*, 3x] *here, a little there.* This time the punishment will be clear – no-one will escape. The punishment, meted out by Assyria, proceeds in a logical progression: they will *fall backwards* (i.e. be caught off guard and fall), *be injured* (i.e. be defeated) and finally be *snared* and *captured* (i.e. ultimately removed to Assyria). Assyria typically deported the peoples of the nations it captured and subjugated. If only Israel could have learned through their prophets, their path would have been much easier. Affliction is often a much harsher teacher.

14–15. The word *therefore* introduces the logical consequence of verses 7–13: since they would not listen to God's gentler message, they will hear a sterner rebuke. The rulers in Jerusalem, called *scoffers* (lit. 'men of scorn' [*lāṣôn*, 3x] who mock God's ways), will hear God's message concerning them.

Verse 15 explains how they have mocked God's message: *We have entered into a covenant* [lit. 'cut a covenant'] *with death, / with the realm of the dead* [i.e. 'Sheol'] *we have made an agreement* (*ḥōzeh*, occurs only here with this meaning). The author puts words into the mouths of the leaders to show them the truth: they have made an alliance with other nations to repel the Assyrians, but it will prove useless. Again the author speaks for the rulers, for they themselves certainly would not say: *we have made a lie our refuge / and falsehood our hiding-place*. This phrase uses two different words for these false hopes: *kāzāb*, 'a lie', and *šeqer*, 'falsehood'.

If the context of this passage is around 701 BC, then this cov-enant probably refers to the alliance that Hezekiah made with Tirhakah, king of Cush, when they fought against Sennacherib (see 2 Kgs 19:9; Isa. 37:9). This alliance gave Israel great hopes for deliverance: *When an overwhelming [šôṭēp] scourge [šôṭ*, similar-sounding words] *sweeps by, / it cannot touch us*. But Egypt would provide little help against the Assyrians whom God had sent to punish Israel. Isaiah can therefore mock them for relying on the Egyptians instead of turning to their God for protection.

(2) Restoration oracle (28:16–17)

16–17. These verses contain a message of restoration in contrast to the earlier judgment found in verses 7–15. The word *so* (*lākēn*, 'therefore') which begins verse 16 introduces the Lord's (lit. 'the Lord [*ʾădōnāy*] Lord [*yĕhwih*]') response to the leaders who have put false hopes in alliances: *See* [*hinnēh*, used to get their attention]*, I lay a stone in Zion* (lit. 'behold I, in Zion a stone is established'; the inverted syntax is for emphasis).

This *stone*, which God sets in Zion and upon which they should rely, is described as (1) a *tested* [*bōḥan*, 'proven'; occurs only here] *stone*; and (2) *a precious cornerstone* [lit. 'corner'] *for a sure foundation* (lit. 'firmly established'), one that is secure. Scholars have variously identified the stone as the coming righteous reign of God (Childs 2001: 209–210); God himself (Clements 1980a: 231); belief in God (Roberts 2015: 353–355); faith in God (Wildberger 2002: 42; etc.). The best answer would be a combination of all these ideas. The overarching theme that God continues to develop from the outset in Isaiah is that he is building his kingdom in Zion for those who believe in him.

The person who relies on this tested and secure *stone* (i.e. God and his coming kingdom) *will never be stricken with panic* (lit. 'will not be hastened'). When God builds a 'stronghold' or 'refuge' in Zion, he will use *the measuring line (qāw*; see v. 10) of *justice* and *the plumb-line (mišqelet*, 2x; see 2 Kgs 21:13) of *righteousness* (v. 17). Those who do not align with God's standards of righteousness and justice will be swept away (*yā'â*, occurs only here) from their hiding places (lit. 'your refuge of falsehood', v. 17). The image of *hail* and *water* washing away their poorly constructed refuge is a good picture of the weakness of their alliances and treaties.

Meaning
The leaders, who thought they could evade God's judgment, will not be able to outsmart him. What they considered a wise action will only trigger his punishment. Yet there is a message of hope: God will establish his kingdom (i.e. *a precious cornerstone*) in Zion. Those who rely on him will take part in this kingdom and enjoy security, while the rest will suffer his punishment.

c. Third judgment–restoration cycle: punishment for the political leaders of Judah (28:18–22); deliverance for the remnant illustrated by the parable of the wise farmer (28:23–29)

Context
The third judgment–restoration cycle, directed against God's people, describes how their covenant with death/Sheol (v. 15) will be rendered completely ineffectual, allowing the *overwhelming scourge* to come through multiple times. This oracle, coinciding closely with the preceding one, is balanced by a parable of hope (about a farmer) meant to reassure the people that God will not allow the judgment to go beyond what is necessary (vv. 23–29).

Comment

(1) Judgment oracle (28:18–22)
18–19. The covenant that Judah's leaders had boasted would avert God's judgment (v. 15) is now rendered null and void: their *covenant with death will be annulled (kuppar*), and the *agreement [ḥāzût*, 5x; only occurrence with this meaning] *with the realm of the dead* [i.e. 'Sheol'] *will not stand*. The verb *will be annulled (kuppar)* literally means

'to be covered, atoned for, exempt from punishment'; this is the only place where it is translated 'dissolved, cancelled'. Even though some suggest emending *kuppar*, this reading is supported by the parallel phrase, *your agreement . . . will not stand*. The nation which had a covenant of life with God chose instead a *covenant with death* by putting their trust in alliances with foreign nations.

Because of the leaders' misplaced trust, they will not be able to ward off God's judgment. The people will be *beaten down* (*mirmās*, 'a trampling place', 7x; 4x in Isaiah) by a *scourge* that will sweep through multiple times: *as often as, morning after morning, by day and by night*. Assyria would be the instrument of this scourge, causing *sheer* [lit. 'only'] *terror* as it invaded the land in 732, 722 and 701 BC. If the Israelites understood and believed this warning, they should have been terrified: Assyria was a cruel foe.

20–22. These verses begin with an illustration warning Israel that their times of comfort and ease are now past. Their reliance on alliances with other nations to avert God's judgment will prove ineffective, just like a *bed* (*maṣṣāʿ*, occurs only here) that is too short to sleep upon comfortably (*śāraʿ*, 'to stretch out upon', 3x) or a *blanket* (*massēkâ*, 2x; see 25:7) that is too small to provide adequate warmth (lit. 'the covering was cramped as it is gathered').

Verse 21 explains why their alliances will prove insufficient: (*kî*, 'for') *the LORD will rise up as he did at Mount Perazim*. This mount most probably refers to Baal-perazim where God defeated the Philistines (2 Sam. 5:17–25), and the *Valley of Gibeon* was where God threw down hailstones and lengthened the day so that the Canaanites could be defeated (Josh. 10:10–11). On both occasions God miraculously stepped into history to protect his people – only here he will rise to punish his people. God's action will be a *strange work*, an *alien task*, for he does not often resort to such severe measures to bring his children back.

The prophet warns that the more they mock God's discipline, the more severe the punishment must become: *Now stop your mocking* [*lîṣ*, 'to scoff, scorn, deride', 8x], / *or your chains* [*môsēr*, 'bonds', 5x = God's discipline] *will become heavier*. The people 'scorn' God by not listening to him or turning to him for help. Their actions make a mockery of his sovereignty and power. Yet the Israelites have a chance to lessen the punishment's severity by turning back to him.

This is the very reason why God issues the warning. However, the sovereign LORD (lit. 'the Lord [*'ădōnāy*] LORD [*yĕhwih*]') has informed the prophet of a *decreed* (i.e. 'determined') *destruction* that will come *against the whole land* and will illustrate how God punishes only to the extent that it accomplishes his plans. The phrase *against the whole land* ('*eres*) could also be translated 'against the whole earth', but it seems unlikely in this context.

(2) Restoration oracle (28:23–29)

23–29. In a conventional wisdom form of address, God pleads with the nation to listen to (or, more specifically consider) his wise words: *Listen and hear my voice.* Does the farmer plough and harrow *continually* (lit. 'all the day') but never plant? The author poses two related rhetorical questions to help his audience understand God's purpose for their punishment: (1) it will not go on without end, even though it may feel that way (v. 24); (2) it will not damage more than it should, even though it is severe (v. 27); and (3) it serves a purpose (vv. 25, 28a, 29).

If a farmer were to plough continually yet never plant seeds, nothing would grow – a tremendous waste of time. Ploughing is not an end in itself but a means to a more important end, that of harvesting a crop. So too, God will not continue to punish the nation of Israel, for punishment is not the end in itself, but a means to an end: that of restoring the nation.

Next the author explains how specific harvesting techniques are needed for each crop in order to avoid damaging the seed/grain: *caraway* (*qeṣaḥ*, 'black cumin', 2x, both in this passage) and *cummin* (*kammōn*, 2x, both in this passage) are scattered on the surface of the ground; *wheat* is planted in rows (*śôrâ*, occurs only here); *barley* in its place (*nismān*, occurs only here); and *spelt* (*kussemet*, 3x) in its area. The word *spelt* (*kussemet*) is probably some type of wheat. How the farmer cares for his crops is likened to how God cares for his people in using the right methods – a mixture of punishment and mercy, in just the right dose – to bring them back to himself.

But *caraway* and *cummin* seeds would be crushed if a 'threshing sledge' (*ḥārûṣ*, 3x) were used; a rod is sufficient to knock off the seeds for gathering. On the other hand, grain for bread must be crushed (*dûq*, occurs only here) and ground into flour; even then the grinding must cease at a certain point or the flour will be ruined (lit. 'or the wheel of his cart and his horses will it not destroy [*hāmam*, see Deut. 2:15] it'). The imagery of verses 24–28 is meant to highlight the farmer's good judgment in planting and raising crops, and thus educate the Israelites about the care God takes to discipline his people for their good.

Verse 29 declares that it is the LORD *Almighty* (lit. 'of hosts') who, in his wisdom, taught the farmer how to care for his crops. This wisdom *is magnificent* and follows a *plan* [that] *is wonderful*. Even then only a remnant will return; many others will lose their lives. Roberts points out that a non-farmer may find the specific care of the different crops strange, like the other nations watching God's handling of Israel (2015: 359).

Meaning
God's people will not be able to avert his punishment. Even though it will be severe and, of necessity, repeated, God will never administer more punishment than is necessary. Like the wise farmer, God will carefully and methodically administer judgment until he is able to harvest a remnant.

d. Fourth judgment–restoration cycle: punishment on Ariel (i.e. Jerusalem; 29:1–4); also deliverance for Ariel from her enemies (29:5–8)

Context
The fourth judgment–restoration cycle begins with a *woe* (*hôy*) oracle directed against *Ariel, / the city where David settled*. The city reference is initially ambiguous; most understand it to be Jerusalem (see later discussion) since it is the city where David settled and in verse 8 is identified as Mount Zion.

The 'woe oracle' warning Jerusalem of coming judgment may correspond to 28:1–6 where Ephraim (i.e. Samaria) is also denounced for not heeding God's warning. Neither Israel (ch. 28) nor Judah (ch. 29) understands why they are about to be punished. Their continuing outward adherence to the law and its religious ceremonies had become a source of pride, blinding them to what should have been a true heart attitude. This oracle of judgment again contains two parts: a woe oracle (vv. 1–4) that describes

Jerusalem's coming punishment, balanced by a message of hope (vv. 5–8) in which God turns to punish her enemies.

Notice that even though God has declared that Israel would be invaded (by Assyria), he is also pictured as the one who surrounds Israel with siege works and towers: *I will encircle you with towers / and set up my siege works against you* (v. 3). The description of both siege works/towers and deliverance aligns with the events of 701 BC when Assyria attacked Jerusalem and then God stepped in to wipe out Assyria's army. At this point the deliverance did not have the effect of drawing a purified remnant back to God; thus more punishment would be coming.

Comment

(1) Judgment oracle (29:1–4)

1–2. This 'woe oracle' opens with a warning of punishment that will come upon Ariel: *Woe to you, Ariel, Ariel, / the city where David settled!* (*ḥānâ*, 'to encamp, lay siege to'). The literal translation of the name *Ariel* (*ărî'ēl*) means 'the lion of God', but it is also plausible that *ărî'ēl* means 'altar hearth', as in Ezekiel 43:15–16,[20] or *uruel*, 'city of El' (similar to the beginning of *urusalima*, 'city of peace'). Verse 2 sheds some light: *Yet I will besiege* [*ṣûq*, 'to harass, oppress'] *Ariel; / she will mourn and lament, / she will be to me like an altar hearth* [= Ariel]. Here altar hearth signifies 'a place of burning' after a siege. It is most likely that this passage contains a play on the word *ărî'ēl* as meaning both 'lion of God' (see Gen. 49:9 where Judah, the tribe in which Jerusalem is located, is called a lion) and 'altar hearth', signifying a place of burning after the Assyrians have attacked Jerusalem.

The phrases at the end of verse 1 imply the reason for punishment. She had relied on perfunctory rituals rather than on God for her protection: *Add year to* [*'al*, 'upon'] *year / and let your cycle of festivals go on* [*nāqap*, 'revolve']. The city of Ariel is further described as the city *where David settled* (possibly where he established his capital).

---

20. Thus, the form *har'ēl* in Ezek. 43:15a would be a corruption of *ărî'ēl* found later in the verse and in the following verse.

But given the comparison in verse 3, it is more likely to refer to a place where David encamped for an attack (see LXX, 'the city against which David encamped'; i.e. David's capture of Jerusalem; 2 Sam. 5:7).

Even though the Israelites were continually offering sacrifices and celebrating religious festivals, God would nevertheless *besiege Ariel* for their empty-hearted observance of rituals. Jerusalem would *mourn* [*ta'ănîyâ*, 2x] *and lament* ('*ănîyâ*, 2x; see Lam. 2:5), two similar-sounding words with similar meanings that add intensity to the expression of their distress. In an alarming reversal, expressed as a play on words, God will turn the tables on Jerusalem: she who meticulously offered sacrifices on an altar would be made like an altar upon which to burn sacrifices (*she will be to me like an altar hearth* [*'ărî'ēl*]).

3–4. Just as David had once encamped against Jerusalem to capture her, so now Yahweh, using Assyria as his tool, will encamp against her. Assyria will surround her (*kaddûr*, 'like a circle', occurs only here) with siege towers (*mĕṣurâ*, 'fortified cities', but here clearly refers to Assyrian siege towers) and a siege wall (*muṣṣāb*, occurs only here), typical instruments of war used by the Assyrians and Babylonians in the first millennium BC.

Verse 4 pictures the city as nearly dead, having little, if any, remaining strength: (1) she will be *brought low*; (2) she *will speak from the ground*; (3) her *speech will mumble out* [*šāḥaḥ*, 2x with this meaning] *of the dust*; (4) her *voice will come ghostlike from the earth*; and (5) her *speech will whisper* (*ṣāpap*, 4x, all in Isaiah) out of the dust. Those who were once loud and boisterously arrogant will be reduced to humble whispers. These phrases also call to mind the image of a victorious warrior placing his foot on the head of a defeated foe, grinding his face into the dust (see *ANEP* 345, 393).

(2) *Restoration oracle (29:5–8)*

5–8. The woe oracle changes from judgment to hope (see *but* at the beginning of v. 5): Ariel's *many enemies* (lit. 'strangers') will be destroyed *suddenly, in an instant* (lit. 'instantly, in a moment'). They will be rendered as insignificant as *fine dust* ('*ābāq*, 5x) and *blown chaff*.

The LORD Almighty (lit. 'of hosts') will come to Ariel's defence (lit. 'you will be visited', v. 6), bringing punishment, portrayed as powerful acts of nature, on Israel's enemies: *thunder (ra'am)*; *earthquake (ra'aš)*; a *great noise*; *whirlwind (sûpâ)*; *tempest (sĕ'ārâ)*; and *flames of a devouring fire.* The grammatical structure contains two similar-sounding words, *thunder (bĕra'am)* and *earthquake (ûbĕra'aš)*, joined by a *wāw*, 'and', followed by the phrase *and great noise* that explains the previous two words. The next unit mirrors this structure.

Those who attack *Ariel* and *her fortress (mĕṣôdâ,* 3x) will expect to savour victory but will be sadly disappointed. Their disappointment is pictured as that of a person who dreams of eating and drinking, only to find upon awakening that he or she is still hungry or thirsty. The final phrase of verse 8 explains what the vision means: *So [kēn] will it be . . .* [that] *the hordes* that attack Mount Zion will come away empty-handed, not being able to defeat the city. This is in line with the events of 701 BC when Assyria, having built up its army with captives from conquered nations, thought that conquest of Jerusalem was assured until God intervened one night and snatched away this victory (see 2 Kgs 19:32–37; Isa. 37:33–38).

Meaning

The woe oracle against *Ariel* describes just one of the punishments that Jerusalem will undergo. God's tool, the Assyrians, will erect siege works and towers against her, but almost immediately God will step in to deliver her. The events of 701 BC, in which God's protection and loving care were obvious, should have prompted contrition but did not (see 22:12–14). Judah's failure to repent would bring further punishment.

e. Fifth judgment–restoration cycle: judgment on the blind nation (29:9–16); regeneration for Israel (29:17–24)

Context

In this fifth judgment–restoration cycle, which continues the theme of Israel's inability to comprehend why they are being punished, the people are judged for honouring God with their lips while their hearts are far from him. Because they have rejected the guidance that God has given, he will allow them to be blinded by their own choices. Its message is very similar to that of 28:7–13:

God is warning that judgment is coming, but they are blind and cannot read the signs. In fact, they appear to think themselves wiser than God.

This judgment oracle has two parts: (1) a judgment section which contains two poetic units (vv. 9–10 and vv. 13–14) joined by a narrative illustration (vv. 11–12), and which is followed by a climactic pronouncement of woe upon God's people for questioning his wisdom (vv. 15–16); (2) a restoration section that describes the renewal of both the land and the people (vv. 17–24). Some scholars view verses 9–16 as a combination of original text (vv. 9–10) and later additions (vv. 11–12), but Oswalt argues it is a unity such that, if the parts were separated from each other, they would become meaningless (1986: 531).

Comment

(1) Judgment oracle (29:9–16)

9–10. Because the people refuse to listen to Isaiah, they will be shocked when his oracle comes true: *Be stunned* [*māhāh*, 'be delayed' = MT] *and amazed* [*tāmāh*], / *blind yourselves* [*šāʿaʿ*] *and be sightless* [*šāʿaʿ*]. It is most likely that the first word in verse 9, *hitmahmĕhû*, 'be delayed', contains dittography of *mh* in the middle of the word and should actually read *hittammāhû*, 'be amazed' (supported by all the versions). If this is correct, then the phrase contains two wordplays: (1) 'be stunned and amazed' and (2) 'blind yourselves and be blind' are both different forms of the same Hebrew verb.

Though they stagger about like drunkards, their behaviour is not the result of wine or strong drink but rather of their lack of spiritual guidance. This blindness towards God is indicative of their hardness of heart. They would rather rely on the armies of the Egyptians, forces that can clearly be seen, than on God and his armies who cannot be seen.

Their spiritual blindness is God-induced: *The LORD has brought over you a deep sleep* (*tardēmâ*, 7x). Neither their *prophets* (figuratively referred to as their *eyes*; lit. *he has sealed* [*ʿāṣam*, 3x] *your eyes*), nor their *seers* (referred to as their *heads*) hear from God. It is disturbing to think that those who continue to harden their hearts by refusing to listen to God may at some point no longer be allowed to hear from him.

11–12. These two verses are an illustration of verse 10. Isaiah's *vision* (*ḥāzût*; 5x) will be like the words of a sealed book that no-one reads for one of two reasons: the literate (lit. 'one knowing of the book') because the *scroll . . . is sealed*, the illiterate (lit. 'one who does not know a book') because they *don't know how to read*.

A scroll was sealed by tying a piece of string or leather around it and then pressing a seal of clay or wax into the knot (see *ANEP* 265). A sealed scroll was to be opened only by the one to whom it was addressed. Even though this oracle was offered to everyone, they all found an excuse not to read and obey it.

13–14. These verses briefly describe the problem (v. 13) and the solution (v. 14). The problem is that the people are in a covenantal relationship with God, but it is one-sided. Outwardly they appear to honour him with their words (lit. *lips*), but their *hearts* betray the fact that they are *far from* him (v. 13), lacking love and trust.

Their worship, *based on merely human rules* (lit. 'learned commandments of men'), was mechanical, ritualistic and heartless. These traditions taught by the religious leaders lacked the spirit of the law. LXX's reading captures the idea well: 'their fear is empty' (reading *wĕtōhû* ['empty'] instead of *wattĕhî* ['it is']). Merely following the laws and ordinances was not enough; God expected a mutually loving relationship with his children. This should serve as a stern warning to us in our day as well.

As a solution (v. 14), God will wake up the people to show them who he truly is: *I will astound* [*pālā'*, 'display power upon'] *these* [lit. 'this'] *people / with wonder* [*pālā'*, 'shock'] *upon wonder* (*pele'*; i.e. duplication of similar words for emphasis). Watts says it well: 'God must intervene with *wondrous acts* to restore the sense of his holy and awesome presence' (2005a: 454).

The words *once more* underscore that this is not the first time God has had to step in to discipline his people. Once they get a renewed sight of God's true self, their own wisdom and knowledge will seem as nothing; their wisdom *will perish*. God has an amazing way of getting people's attention – we all seem to learn best through discipline or suffering.

15–16. *Woe* is pronounced upon those who try *to hide their plans from the LORD, / who do their work in darkness* (*maḥšāk*, 7x). Their consciences are sufficiently at work to realize that their deeds are not pleasing to God, but they are naïve to think they can actually hide them from him: *Who sees us? Who will know?* Their behaviour reflects how poorly they understand God's omnipresence (see Ps. 139:7–12) and omniscience (see 1 Chr. 28:9).

Their thought processes are upside down (*You turn things upside down* [*hapkĕkem*, 'your perversity', 2x]): they consider themselves on a par with God their creator (*as if the potter were thought to be like the clay!*, v. 16). No other god of the Ancient Near East was said to have created the entire universe; different parts of creation were thought to have been the work of different gods. By contrast, the biblical text pictures Yahweh as the sole creator who made everything for his pleasure. Instead of recognizing God's right to authority over them as their creator, they defy his authority: *Can the pot say to the potter, 'You know nothing'?* God's wayward nation will never outwit him; the potter still controls the clay.

This is quite likely a reference to the events of 701 BC when Hezekiah sent envoys to Egypt to plead for assistance against Assyria (see 30:2–7). What Israel no doubt considered a shrewd manoeuvre to repel Assyria would be turned upside down by God; he would use Assyria to destroy the Egyptian forces and punish Israel.

(2) Restoration oracle (29:17–24)

17–21. Verse 17 marks a significant shift to a future time of restoration when the weak and helpless will be released from the oppression of their wicked leaders. Since the time of Duhm, it has generally been argued that verses 17–24 are a post-exilic addition, primarily because the glowing predictions of a coming deliverance are not found in pre-exilic prophecy. And yet to restrict a prophet solely to messages of destruction ignores the fact that Zion theology was at its peak during the pre-exilic period and that other eighth-century prophets included messages of deliverance in their prophecies (see Mic. 4 – 5).

The interpretation of verse 17 is problematic: *In a very short time* [lit. 'yet a little, a few'], *will not Lebanon be turned into a fertile field* [*hakkarmel*, 'the fertile field'] / *and the fertile field* [*hakkarmel*, 'the fertile field'] *seem like a forest?* The meaning of *hakkarmel* could be (1) the *fertile field* (see 32:15–16); (2) the 'orchard' or 'tree plantation' (see 10:18); or (3) Mount Carmel (with an article it often refers to Mount Carmel, 1 Kgs 18:42). Translating the verse as 'Lebanon will be turned into the orchard [*hakkarmel*; i.e. a good orchard], and Mount Carmel [lit. 'the Karmel'] to a forest' provides a nice parallel structure and even a play on the word *hakkarmel*. But it is unlikely that *hakkarmel* should be translated two different ways in the same verse; thus we believe that the former translation is correct. Lebanon, Israel's northern neighbour, was known for its great cedars, and at certain points in history was included within Israel's territory.

The people will experience a time of spiritual renewal in contrast to the *gloom and darkness* in which they had lived (see 8:22 – 9:1): *In that day* [i.e. the day of restoration, v. 17] *the deaf* [*ḥērēš*, 9x] *will hear the words of the scroll* [lit. 'a scroll'; see v. 11], */ and out of gloom* [*'ōpel*, 9x] *and darkness / the eyes of the blind will see.* The message of Isaiah fell on dry and hard ground during his lifetime, but the time would come when it would fall on receptive soil such that formerly spiritually blind eyes would be opened.

Praise will flow as a result of the moral and social reformation resulting from this deliverance (vv. 17–18): *the humble will rejoice in* [lit. 'will increase in the joy of'] *the LORD* (v. 19). The title *the Holy One of Israel* is common in the book of Isaiah and emphasizes the justice of God's actions (see Figure 0.4 on p. 10). The reason (*kî* beginning v. 20) for this joy is that the heartless oppressors who have taken advantage of society's poor and weak will disappear: *The ruthless will vanish* [*'āpēs*, 5x], */ the mockers will disappear, / and all who have an eye for evil* (lit. 'who are lying in wait to do wickedness').

Verse 21 further describes the vileness of these oppressors: (1) they wrongly *make someone out to be guilty* (lit. *with a word*); (2) they *ensnare* (*qôš*, 'lay bait for', occurs only here) the judges (lit. 'the one who decides'; NIV, *the defender*) at the gate; and (3) they bear *false testimony* [to] *deprive the innocent of justice* (lit. 'they stretch out the righteous with emptiness'). The hearts of those who were formerly at the mercy of these oppressors will be filled with joy upon their deliverance and their new-found freedom. This joy, felt at different points in Israel's history when God sent his deliverance, is merely a foretaste of the future joy that ultimately will be ours in heaven (Rev. 22:1–5).

22–24. *Therefore* introduces the consequence of the removal of *all who have an eye for evil* (v. 20). *The LORD*, who in the past *redeemed Abraham*, will show that he is continuing his covenant with Jacob and will bring forth (i.e. *the work of my hands*) godly children for him. In times past there was reason for Jacob to *be ashamed* (or *ḥāwar*, 'grow pale'; occurs only here) of his children, but that will all change in this future day of restoration.

The *descendants of Jacob* will have truly learned to reverence God and live in a way pleasing to him: (1) *they will keep my name holy* (i.e. have true devotion for God's name); (2) *they will acknowledge the holiness of the Holy One of Jacob* (only occurrence of this title); and (3) they *will stand in awe of the God of Israel*. The phrase *the LORD, who redeemed Abraham*, is a reminder that God's plan to redeem Israel goes all the way back to their renowned forefather, Abraham.

Verse 24 describes a dramatic change of character that has taken place in Jacob's children: the ones *wayward in spirit will gain understanding; / those who complain* [*rāgan*, 7x] *will accept instruction* [*leqaḥ*, 'insight', 9x]. The erring ones will know and accept God's truth; those who are belligerent will accept instruction and thereby gain 'insight' or 'wisdom' (see 32:3–8). This renewal is entirely the opposite of their previous behaviour: (1) Formerly they could not know God's revelation (vv. 10–12), but now they know the truth. (2) Their hearts, once far from God and insincere in their worship (v. 13), now sanctify God. (3) Once lacking wisdom (v. 14), they now accept instruction.

Meaning
The oracle opened with a depiction of the nation being led further and further from God by its blind leaders until God turns the nation around, something only he can do. Initially the people were insincere and cold-hearted towards God in their worship. In the arrogance of their hearts, they thought they knew more than he. But a time of transformation will come: the land will be restored and become productive. This change will extend to the people as well: those who are ruthless will be no more, the blind and deaf will become responsive to God, and God's people will serve him in truth and righteousness.

The author uses the example of Abraham, a pagan whom God shaped over a lifetime to become the forefather of God's chosen nation (i.e. those who would have faith in God). Reversals like this can be accomplished only by an all-powerful, sovereign God.

f. Sixth judgment–restoration cycle: woe against the rebellious children (30:1–17), but God will bring a day of salvation (30:18–33)

Context

The sixth judgment–restoration cycle becomes even more specific regarding Israel's sin, denouncing their alliance with Egypt. It has the same structure as earlier oracles: denunciation (vv. 1–17) followed by restoration (vv. 18–33). The denunciation section comprises several smaller units (vv. 1–5, 6–11, 12–14, 15–17, though some divide them at slightly different points), all centred around the alliance Judah forged with Egypt, the very nation that once enslaved them, instead of relying upon Yahweh for protection. In the restoration section there are two poetic units (i.e. vv. 18 and 27–33) joined by a narrative unit describing God's deliverance (vv. 19–26). The defeat of Assyria is specifically mentioned in verse 31.

Most scholars agree that this oracle points to the historical period around the Assyrian advance on Jerusalem in 701 BC. Taharqa (or Tirhakah; 690–664 BC), the commander of the Egyptian army (and later to become pharaoh), was sent to Israel's aid but was defeated in 701 BC by the Assyrians. The irony is that the alliance between Egypt and Israel, which Israel had hoped would deliver them, was all for nought: Egypt provided little assistance in 701 BC.

The events of 701 BC were crucial to God's instruction of Israel as he clearly demonstrated to the nation his power and protection. However, the Israelites were so hardened that they did not even recognize God's mercy and compassion towards them. This clear message not to rely on Egypt for protection makes their hardness of heart all the more obvious and will also make the appearance of a believing remnant that much more remarkable.

Comment

(1) Judgment oracle (30:1–17)

1–3. This *woe* (*hôy*) oracle, addressed to the *obstinate children* (lit. 'rebelling sons'), implies that God still maintains a relationship with his people even though they were clearly disobedient. The parallel phrases *who carry out plans* (lit. 'a plan') and *forming an alliance* (lit. 'weave a covering', *massēkâ* [2x]) describe actions associated with sealing alliances. But God did not approve of their alliance with Egypt (i.e. *plans that are not mine*) and therefore could not bless it.

Despite the prophet's valiant efforts to dissuade them, they called on the Egyptians in an attempt to circumvent God's punishment, thereby (*lĕmaʿan*, but not translated in the NIV) *heaping sin upon sin*. Oswalt suggests that 'adding sin to sin' may refer first to Ahaz's alliance with Assyria that allowed their presence in Canaan, and then to Hezekiah's alliance with Egypt in an effort to try to drive out the Assyrians (1986: 545).

God's words in verse 2 drip with irony: *who look for help to* [*lāʿôz*, 'seek refuge in', 5x] *Pharaoh's protection* [*māʿôz* = a wordplay with similar-sounding *lāʿôz*], / *to Egypt's shade for refuge* (lit. 'shelter in the shadow of Egypt'). The god Horus was often depicted with wings wrapped around the pharaoh as his protector. Israel did this without consulting God (lit. 'they did not ask of my mouth'; the word 'mouth' is out of order for emphasis), perhaps because they knew they would not like his answer.

Using nearly the same words as verse 2 except that *heḥāsût* ('shelter'; missing in NIV; occurs only here) appears in place of *laḥsôt* (NIV, *refuge*), verse 3 forewarns of the outcome of their ill-placed hope: Egypt will not protect Judah from Assyria. Their carefully crafted plan will only bring them *shame* and *disgrace* (lit. 'insult').

Tirhakah, king of the unified countries of Egypt and Cush (or Nubia, 2 Kgs 19:9; Isa. 37:9), came out against Assyria but was quickly defeated, just as Rabshakeh, Sennacherib's emissary, had boasted (see Isa. 36:6). Sennacherib then resumed his march to Jerusalem. How much it must hurt God when his people turn only to fellow human beings or false gods for assistance when he, the source of all power, longs to help them. They had not learned from their predecessors, who in Joshua's day did not ask God before making an alliance and suffered dearly for it (Josh. 9).

4–5. Judah had sent envoys to Egypt to request assistance: *they have officials in Zoan / and their envoys have arrived in Hanes.* The city *Zoan*, later called Tanis, was located on the border between Egypt and Judah. It was the capital of Lower Egypt during the 21st and 22nd dynasties, *c.*1069–716 BC. *Hanes* (*ḥānēs*, occurs only here), later called Heracleopolis, was situated on an island about midway down the River Nile (i.e. close to present-day Fayyum). It was an important political city during the Third Intermediate Period, *c.*1069–747 BC.

Verse 5 reiterates the *shame* (*hōbîš*; MT reads *hib'îš*, 'to make stink') and *disgrace* that Egypt would cause Judah (see v. 3); not only would Egypt prove useless as an ally, but the alliance only further angered Sennacherib, bringing more severe punishment.

6–7. These verses are part of a restatement of the message of woe given to Judah in verses 1–5. While some view verses 6–7 as an addition because of the apparently new introduction, they are a logical continuation of the thoughts of verses 1–5. In verse 6 we glimpse the envoys as they, with their animals, make their way through the hostile Negev wilderness towards Egypt. The Assyrians may already have been in the area, cutting off the coastal route so that the emissaries were forced to travel this route.

In the phrase *a prophecy concerning the animals of the Negev* the word *prophecy* (*maśśā'*, 'burden, oracle') may be a wordplay on the 'beasts of burden' (i.e. donkey, camels) that carried the envoys' gift for Egypt. The wording is reminiscent of Israel's earlier trip through the wilderness. The doublets create emphasis: *hardship* and *distress* (*ṣûqâ*, 3x); *lions* and *lionesses* (*layiš*, 3x); *adders* (*'ep'eh*, 3x) and *darting snakes* (*śārāp*; see 14:29). The Judean emissaries were willing to endure these dangers in order to gain Egypt's assistance. Judah's treasures were taken down to Egypt, an *unprofitable nation* (lit. 'unto a people [who] will not profit [them]'). The sense here is that Judah's money would be wasted, since Egypt would provide little help against Assyria.

The words *utterly useless* (v. 7) are a hendiadys (lit. 'vanity' and 'empty') for 'utterly worthless'. For this reason, God calls Egypt *Rahab* [lit. 'raging, surging'] *the Do-Nothing* (lit. 'they are ceasing';

HALOT suggests combining the words *hem* and *šābet* to read *hammāšbāt*, 'Rahab who has lain silent' [3.1193]). There was a popular Ancient Near Eastern legend about a sea monster named Rahab that the gods struggled to subdue. It is not surprising, therefore, that the Israelites often used *Rahab* as a metaphor for (1) God's victory over the oceans or seas (see 51:9), or (2) Egypt (see Ps. 87:4).

8–9. The focus now shifts slightly from reliance upon an Egyptian alliance to the attitudes that led up to it. Isaiah is told: *Go now, write it on a tablet for them* [lit. 'in their presence'], / *inscribe it on a scroll*. By so doing, after the alliance with Egypt proves to be worthless (*that for the days to come*, lit. 'to a day after'), all will be able to see that Yahweh had already informed them of this so that it would *be an everlasting witness* (reading *'ēd* as 'witness' instead of MT's reading *'ad*, 'until').

The word *tablet* is commonly used of 'stone tablets' (see Exod. 24:12); however, in this passage it is used in parallel with 'book, scroll' (*sēper*; scrolls at the time were made of papyrus and were semi-permanent records).

For [*kî*] *these are rebellious people* (v. 9) who repeatedly have refused to listen to the prophets. Their punishment is well deserved, for they are (1) a *rebellious people*; (2) *deceitful* [*keḥāšîm*, occurs only here] *children*; and (3) *children unwilling to listen to the LORD's instruction* (*tôrâ*). Oswalt points out how unusual it is for such negative statements about a people to be recorded in their own history (1986: 551).

10–11. The people rebuke and dismiss the *seers* (*rō'îm*) and *prophets* (*ḥōzîm*, 'those who have visions' – not the common word for prophet) with the words, *Give us no more visions of what is right!* (*nĕkōḥôt*, 'straight, right, righteousness'; the syntax is emphatic). Even if the people did not make these statements outright, their actions revealed their true feelings. They had already made up their minds and did not want to be told about God's wrath or turn from their path towards destruction. They would rather that the prophets *prophesy illusions* (*maḥătallâ*, 'deceptions', occurs only here) and tell them *pleasant things* (*ḥălōqôt*, 'smooth words') about their future prospects than listen to the truth.

In parallel statements of harsh dismissal, the people tell the prophet to *stop confronting us* [lit. 'cease from our faces'] / *with the*

Holy One of Israel! The term *the Holy One of Israel* is one of the key designations the author uses for Yahweh in this book (see Figure 0.4 on p. 10). Their rejection of God could not be clearer: they want no part of him or the holiness that he requires.

12–14. *Therefore* introduces God's response to their actions of verses 9–11: *Because you* [pl.] *have rejected this message* (lit. 'word') and continued in a path that relies on (lit. 'trusting in') *oppression* (lit. 'brutality') and *deceit* (lit. 'being crooked and leaning upon it'), Israel will soon be disciplined. The title *Holy One of Israel* draws a strong contrast between God and his people: the Holy One will hold them responsible for their blatant sin.

This sin (lit. 'iniquity') that the author refers to in verse 13 is the rejection of the prophet's *message* (v. 12). Their continued rejection is pictured as *a high wall* that is *cracked and bulging* (*bāʿâ*, 2x), ready to collapse at any moment with devastating consequences. Just as a wise observer would realize the danger of a wall that is cracked and bulging, so the people should have seen the danger in their alliance with Egypt. When it *collapses suddenly* (lit. 'suddenly in an instant'), it will shatter *in pieces* [*mĕkittâ*, 'fragment', occurs only here] *like pottery*, pieces so small that they cannot even be used to carry coals (lit. 'to snatch up fire from a fireplace') or scoop up (lit. 'skim off') water from a *cistern* (*gebeʾ*, 2x; it is more likely to mean 'reservoir') – a picture of thorough destruction.

15–17. Referring to *this message* in verse 12, verses 15–18 provide the reason (*kî*, v. 15) for their punishment: they had refused to engage in the *repentance and rest* that would have resulted in their *salvation*. The word *repentance* (*bĕšûbâ*, occurs only here) is probably related to the verb *šûb*, 'to return'. God had asked his rebellious children to turn back to him in *quietness and trust*, to rely on his strength so that Judah could be spared. Notice that the names for God in verse 15 emphasize first his sovereignty (i.e. *Sovereign LORD*, lit. 'the Lord [*ʾădōnāy*] LORD [*yĕhwih*]') and then his character (i.e. *Holy One of Israel*).

The people refuse God's offer; they *would have none of it* (lit. 'but you were not willing', v. 15), defiantly telling him 'no' (v. 16). They persist in thinking they will escape his punishment by fleeing on horses (lit. 'on horses we will flee'; the word 'horses' is out of order for emphasis). They will try to escape (lit. 'upon thus [horses] you will flee') but will fail (lit. 'upon thus [i.e. equally swift horses] they [the Assyrians] will be quickly pursuing you'). The Israelites were fooling themselves in thinking they could outsmart or outmanoeuvre the expertly trained Assyrians. Their own ingenuity could not save them; only God could do that.

A thousand [Israelites] *will flee / at the threat of one* [Assyrian]. The Assyrians were masters at terrifying their enemies, and for good reason: they were ruthless in their punishments. The phrase *at the threat of five / you will all flee away* suggests that Israel's army is small (i.e. five thousand) in comparison with the Assyrian army. The main idea is that the Assyrian invasion would leave very few survivors, who are pictured as a solitary *banner on a hill*. This image nevertheless gives a measure of hope that Jerusalem, though quite small, will still remain after the destruction.

(2) Restoration oracle (30:18–33)

18. In contrast to verse 17, a message of restoration begins in verse 18: *Yet the Lord longs* [lit. 'waits'] *to be gracious to you* [pl.]. God is poised and ready to show mercy to Israel the moment they call out to him. This is the only time in the Old Testament where God is said to wait for people; generally, people are to wait for God (see Hab. 2:3). So too God sometimes waits for us until we are in a place where he can be gracious to us.

The next phrase, *For* [kî] *the Lord is a God of justice,* provides the rationale as to why God must wait to show compassion: it would be unjust to pour out blessings on a nation that is in open rebellion against him. Yet there is encouragement for those who put their trust in him: *Blessed are all who wait* [i.e. the same word used for God waiting in the first phrase of v. 18] *for him* [i.e. God].

The progression of thought in this verse is (1) the Lord's overriding desire is to show grace; (2) he will therefore act to show compassion; (3) but because he is also just, justice must first be meted out; then (4) those who surrender to him (i.e. who wait for him) will be blessed.

19–22. Verses 19–26 are a narrative explanation of the restoration promised in verse 18, beginning with *kî* ('for'; not present in the NIV) and are addressed to the *people of Zion* (i.e. the remnant in Jerusalem). The verbal forms are emphatic in the phrases *you will* [indeed] *weep no more* and *How gracious* [indeed] *he will be* [to you]. The author is certain that God is merely waiting for Israel to call out to him: *As soon as* [lit. 'when'] *he hears, he will answer you.*

Bread and *water*, two images drawn from the restricted diet of a prisoner (lit. 'bread of oppression and water of oppression' = 'sparingly'), are the means by which God seeks to teach them about himself and cause them to turn back to him: *Although the Lord* [*ʾădōnāy*; the name emphasizes God's sovereignty] *gives you the bread of adversity and the water of affliction.*

The identity of the teachers is uncertain in the phrase *your teachers will be hidden* [*kānap*, occurs only here] *no more*. Several options have been proposed: (1) God (plural of majesty, Williams §8); (2) the *bread of adversity* and the *water of affliction*; and (3) various teachers whom God will use to purify a remnant (= Isaiah, Syria, Assyria, Babylon, etc.). The last two options are most plausible and work together (i.e. the prophets prophesied about the affliction that would cause Israel to turn back to God).

The main point of the passage is that the teachers (i.e. *the bread of adversity and the water of affliction*), being no longer *hidden*, will be used to help guide the nation. They will give clear direction to the people of Jerusalem, helping them to know what God expects from them (i.e. *This is the way; walk in it*, v. 21).

Then you will desecrate [*ṭāmēʾ*, 'to consider unclean'] *your idols* [*sippûy*, 'plated idols', 5x] *overlaid with silver and . . . images* [*massēkâ*, 'cast images'] *covered* [*ʾăpuddâ*, 'overlaid', 3x] *with gold; you will throw them away like a menstrual cloth* [*dāweh*, lit. 'menstrual flow', 5x]. These false gods, which had often been the cause of leading Israel astray from following God's direction, are now viewed with revulsion (*Away with you!*) and treated as filthy objects to be discarded (i.e. menstrual cloths).

23–24. When the Israelites turn back to God, he will pour blessings on the nation once again. These blessings will be evident in the fertility of the land and rich harvests (i.e. the terms *dāšēn*, 'fat, juicy' [3x], and *šāmēn*, 'fat', highlight their productivity). There will be rain in season, abundant grain for bread, roomy (lit. 'wide') pastures (*kar*, 3x) for cattle, and plenty of food for the hard-working oxen and donkeys to eat.

The words used to describe the animals' food highlight that it is the best food: (1) it will be *fodder* [*bĕlîl*, 3x; food for livestock that includes the entire stalk] *and mash* [*ḥāmîṣ*, 'seasoned fodder', occurs only here]; (2) it will be *spread out with fork* [*raḥat*, 'winnowing fork', occurs only here] *and shovel* (*miẓreh*, 'pitchfork', 2x), meaning that the grain will be separated from the chaff. Generally, in the Ancient Near East the animals grazed the land, seeking to find enough food to eat, even if it was not the best food. The food here will be both plentiful and the best.

25–26. The nation will be victorious in battle over former enemy nations (i.e. *the day of great slaughter* [*hereg*, 6x]), destroying *towers* which are either defensive fortified towers or Assyrian siege towers. Abundant water (lit. *streams of water*) will flow on the lofty mountains (*gābōah*) and high hills (*gibʿâ*) – similar-sounding words. The hills that had formerly been sites of idolatrous worship are now cleansed and blessed by Yahweh.

Though the LORD himself inflicted both fractures (*šeber*) and wounds (*maḥaṣ* [occurs only here] *makkātô*, lit. 'the wounds of his blows'), in this new era of restoration he also heals them. The punishment that he inflicted had its desired effect, working to turn the nation back towards God (see 1:4–6). The restoration that ensues is portrayed as an enhanced universe, the figurative language here suggesting perfection: *The moon will shine like the sun, and the sunlight will be seven times brighter* ('seven' suggests fullness or the perfect amount).

The further explanation that the sun's brightness will be *like the light of seven full days* suggests extended daylight and thus enhanced productivity. Roberts explains that 'This is poetic hyperbole to indicate how glorious and happy that day will be' (2015: 395). Surrounded by these abundant blessings, the remnant will forget the sorrow of their former affliction.

27–28. The parallel units in verses 27–33 form a poetic description of God's plan for the nations (see esp. vv. 28 and 31). The theophany in verse 27 depicts Yahweh being roused from his habitation to rescue Israel: *See* [*hinnēh*; marks the beginning of judgment], *the Name of the LORD comes from afar.* The *Name of the LORD* represents God's character and his reputation coming in power. It may also refer to the Assyrian army coming in Yahweh's name to punish the nations, for that is ultimately how he punished Israel in 701 BC.

Four image pairs capture the terrifying nature of his wrath: (1) *with* [lit. 'his'] *burning anger and dense* [*kōbēd*, 'heaviness', 4x] *clouds of smoke* [*maśśā'â*, occurs only here]; (2) *his lips are full of wrath* [lit. 'indignation' = anger that arises from what is perceived as unfair treatment], / *and his tongue is* [lit. 'like'] *a consuming fire*; (3) *His breath is like a rushing* [lit. 'overwhelming'] *torrent*, / *rising up to the neck* ['and ready to drown' is implied]; and (4) *He shakes the nations in the sieve* [*nāpâ*, occurs only here] *of destruction* [lit. 'emptiness']; / *he places in the jaws of the peoples* / *a bit that leads them astray* [lit. 'causes them to wander aimlessly about'].

The last two images complement each other to form a single concept: God shakes the nations to unsettle humanity's power structures so that the *sieve of destruction* that follows can filter out a righteous remnant from the pagan nations (see Amos 9:9 for a similar image). God uses a bit to lead them into ruin in hopes that they will see their need for a deliverer. He is about to mete out justice upon the nations: *his lips are full of wrath* (v. 27).

29–31. The remnant, now freed from its yoke, will experience great joy, expressed in songs of rejoicing: literally 'the song will be to you' (pl.; the inverted syntax is for emphasis) *as on the night you celebrate a holy festival*. These festivals will be accompanied by music (*ḥālîl*, 'flute', 5x) and great joy. The people will rejoice with a proper heart attitude, gladly approaching Yahweh, whom the author calls *the Rock of Israel*, their powerful protector.

In effecting this deliverance, God directs his power, depicted as a *voice* that shatters and a *rod* that strikes (v. 31), against the Assyrians to defeat them (701 BC). The Assyrians will *hear his majestic voice* and see *his arm coming down* in fierce anger (v. 30). This anger is pictured as a *consuming fire*; a *cloudburst* (*nepeṣ*, occurs only here); a *thunderstorm*; and *hail* (lit. 'stones of hail'). Together they are a terrifying manifestation of God's power. Yahweh's power exercised in the mere sound of his voice will shatter the Assyrian army.

32–33. Judah will rejoice with tambourines and lyres as God himself fights the Assyrians: *Every stroke* [*ma'ăbār*, 'crossing of the back', 3x] *the LORD lays on them* / *with his punishing club* [lit. 'club of foundation'] / *will be to the music of tambourines and harps*. This verse figuratively underscores the fact that this punishment is just and fair: they deserve every blow they receive. However, 'club of foundation' (*mûsādâ*) makes little sense. The only other occurrence of *mûsādâ* is in Ezekiel 41:8, where it means 'forming the foundation'. The word *mûsādâ* is more probably a corruption of *mûsārâ*, 'discipline', which differs by one similar-looking letter in Hebrew square script.

God had long ago prepared the site of their destruction at *Topheth* in the Valley of Ben Hinnom, where humans had been sacrificed to the god Molech (see Jer. 7:31–32) – *it has been made ready for the king* (i.e. the Assyrian king). He will cast them into a deep and large *fire pit* (*mĕdûrâ*, 'pile of wood', 2x), filled with *an abundance of fire and wood*, ready to be lit by the *breath of the LORD*, pictured as *a stream of burning sulphur* (*goprît*, 7x).

These images, especially that of *burning sulphur*, call to mind Revelation 20:10, 15 which pictures those who rebel against God as being cast into 'the lake of burning sulphur'. Thus, the section ends as it began, with Yahweh's burning anger being poured out (i.e. vv. 27, 33).

Meaning

In defiance of God's warnings Israel chose to make alliances with Egypt rather than rely upon him. He therefore would use the Assyrians to punish the nation, as they did in 701 BC (see *ANET* 288). Yet God longed to be gracious to Israel (v. 18), waiting for them to call out to him. According to the biblical record, Hezekiah did call out to God, and because of that the angel of the LORD came to decimate Sennacherib's army (see 37:36).

Yet instead of turning to God and trusting him, the nation persists in rebellion (see 22:13–14), thinking they can rely on their own strength (portrayed as fleeing on their fast horses, v. 16). God will therefore continue to punish them till they are very few: *like a banner on a hill* (v. 17). Nevertheless, God *longs to be gracious* to them; he will hear their cries of distress and come to their rescue. This deliverance, prefigured in Israel's return from the Babylonian exile, will ultimately be accomplished in the end times (see Rev. 20:10, 15) when a remnant of Israel will praise God for his powerful deliverance. God's long-suffering love for and patience with his rebellious children is truly extraordinary.

*g. Seventh judgment–restoration cycle: woe to the unbelieving nation (31:1–3),
but God will protect Jerusalem and set up a righteous king to rule over Israel
(31:4 – 32:8)*

Context

This seventh judgment–restoration cycle in the central portion of
the palistrophe, chapters 28–33 (see Figure 0.9 on p. 23), continues
to reiterate God's plan. Like previous judgment oracles, there are
two parts: a 'woe oracle' announcing that Israel will be punished
by Assyria for relying on Egypt instead of on God (31:1–3), followed
by an extensive restoration oracle (31:4 – 32:8).

Historically, there were very few occasions when the Israelites
turned to Egypt for help; they did so just once during the eighth
and seventh centuries BC. The actions highlighted in chapter 31
correspond well to the events of 701 BC when Hezekiah called out
to God and Jerusalem was spared (see Isa. 36 – 37). Yet this is just
the beginning of God's ultimate plan which extends much further
into the future, when a remnant will return to him and he will place
over them a righteous king.

Several scholars have argued that chapter 31 is made up of
smaller oracles (i.e. at least vv. 1–3, 4–9). Childs argues that they are
closely joined (2001: 231) and Roberts contends that they were
edited by Isaiah himself (2015: 401).

Comment

(1) Judgment oracle (31:1–3)

1–3. This *woe* oracle is parallel to 30:1–5. Both describe the
events of 701 BC when Israel demonstrated a lack of faith by putting
their trust in Egypt's powerful resources: *horses; the multitude of their
chariots;* and *the great strength of their horsemen.* The Egyptians dedicated
their horses to Ra, the sun god, and Astarte, the daughter of Ra.
Second Kings 23:11 suggests that the kings of Israel had also
dedicated some chariots with horses to the Egyptian sun god, Ra.
Josiah destroyed these idols when he purged the land of the influence of foreign gods.

Israel would be punished for relying on Egypt instead of on the
LORD: *but* [they] *do not look to* [lit. 'seek'] *the Holy One of Israel* [a title

expressing God's special relationship to Israel] . . . *Yet he too is wise and can bring disaster* (v. 2). In their arrogance, they think that procuring Egypt's aid demonstrates wisdom and strategic statesmanship.

God, who is wiser, plans to *bring disaster* upon both Judah, who is called a *wicked nation* (lit. 'the house of evildoers'), and Egypt, referred to as the one who helps *evildoers* (lit. 'the workers of iniquity', v. 2). His plan most assuredly will take place, for he will *not take back his words* (lit. 'his words he will not turn aside'; the inverted syntax is for emphasis). The Egyptians, whose pharaohs claimed to achieve divinity upon death, are declared to be *mere mortals*.

Egypt will also be made to suffer under the direction of the true God (*'ēl*) for aiding Israel against Yahweh's punishment. Yahweh's power is emphasized when he merely *stretches out his hand* and they *stumble*. When God brings the Assyrians into the land, both *those who help* (i.e. Egypt) and *those who are helped* [i.e. Judah] *will fall*. Indeed, when Hezekiah called for the assistance of Tirhakah, king of Cush, in 701 BC, both nations felt Assyria's wrath (2 Kgs 19:9). It was only because of a gracious act of God that Jerusalem was spared.

(2) Restoration oracle (31:4 – 32:8)

4–5. Isaiah calls for his audience's attention: *This is what the LORD says* [lit. 'thus says the LORD'] *to me*. God states emphatically that he will not allow the Assyrians to totally annihilate his people, even though that was their desire (see 10:5–7); he therefore comes to the rescue of Jerusalem. God's protection and deliverance are likened (i.e. *ka'ăšer* ['just as'] . . . *kēn* ['so']) to two images: (1) *a great lion* (lit. 'young lion'; see Ezek. 19:5–6) that fearlessly protects *its prey* (Jerusalem), refusing to abandon it even *though a whole band of shepherds / is called together against it*; and (2) birds that hover overhead in order to *shield* [*gānan*, 7x] *Jerusalem* (i.e. similar to birds that swoop down on anything attempting to harm their young).

Clements (1980a: 257) maintains that the phrase *will come down / to do battle on Mount Zion* must be understood in a hostile sense (see 29:1–4); however, the rest of the context does not suggest this. Verse 5 says that God will <u>*shield*</u> [lit. 'defend'] *it*; <u>*deliver*</u> *it*; '*pass over*' *it*; and *rescue it*. The historical context of 701 BC when God spared Jerusalem favours this interpretation.

6–9. The prophet exhorts the Israelites who *have so greatly revolted* (lit. 'have so deeply defected') to return to God. Then he envisions a time (i.e. *in that day*) when a remnant of Israel will return to God and abandon their idols, including those they had manufactured (lit. 'which your hands had made for yourself') out of costly metals such as silver and gold. The author also links this time of returning to God with the destruction of the Assyrians: *Assyria will fall by no human sword*. Even though God spared Israel from the Assyrians in 701 BC, the Israelites did not turn back to him for any significant length of time (see 22:12–14); therefore, the phrase *that day* (v. 7) must ultimately refer to a future restoration.

God did decimate the Assyrians (by disease, not a *human sword*, as specified in v. 8) in 701 BC; however, their young people were not subjected to forced labour (v. 8) at that time. As is frequently the case in the prophets, the author's vision combines near events with events in the more distant future (see also 14:1–2).

The phrase *their stronghold will fall* (lit. 'his rock will pass away', v. 9) refers either to the Assyrians' gods or to their strength and power; either way it leaves them feeling terrified (*māgôr*, 8x). Their *commanders* panic when they see the *battle standard* (*nēs*) raised to rally God's armies (see 5:26).

This oracle is confirmed by the LORD, *whose fire* ['*ûr*, 5x with this meaning, 4x in Isaiah] *is in Zion, / whose furnace is in Jerusalem*, images of God's consuming wrath that will be directed towards his enemies (v. 9). Childs states: 'Jerusalem becomes the furnace in which the refuse is burned' (i.e. 'the refuse' represents the Assyrians; 2001: 234). The purging of Israel and then the punishment of the Assyrians will take place on Mount Zion (see 10:12).

32:1–2. There has been significant debate as to whether verses 1–8 were authored by Isaiah, and whether they are messianic or non-messianic. We argue that they were authored by Isaiah, who envisioned a future deliverer through a proto-eschatological lens (i.e. he sees this deliverer in the context of the present world, not a restored future world – more akin to Zion theology than later developed eschatology). This concept of a future deliverer will lay the groundwork for the coming Messiah.

The message of restoration continues from the earlier section linking two similar ideas here – a time of deliverance from the

Assyrians (31:8–9) and a time of restoration under a righteous king – even though there is a lengthy separation in time between them (other passages also refer to a future deliverer: 9:1–7; 11:1–9; etc.). The deliverance from the Assyrians prefigures a greater deliverance when God will set up his king who will reign righteously (32:1–8). This part of the oracle of restoration did not occur in 701 BC since Hezekiah, who was already king, remained on the throne at that time and the changes recorded in verses 4–8 did not take place.

The short interjection *see* (*hēn*) in verse 1 calls attention to the significant changes that will occur with the coming of a future deliverer. This is the first time in the book of Isaiah that this righteous deliverer is specifically called a *king*. The syntax emphasizes that he will rule according to God's righteous standards (i.e. *lĕṣedeq*), and *rulers* (pl.) under his command will *rule* [*śārar*, 6x] *with justice* (i.e. emphasizing the manner in which they will rule).

This righteous leadership will provide welcome relief from suffering, as four images suggest: (1) they will be *like a shelter* [*maḥābē*, occurs only here, but is most probably related to *ḥāba*, 'to hide'] *from the wind*; (2) *a refuge from the storm* [*zerem*, 9x; 7x in Isaiah]; (3) *streams of water in the desert* [*ṣāyôn*, 2x; but sounds similar to *ṣîyôn*, 'Zion']; and (4) *the shadow of a great rock in a thirsty* [lit. 'exhausted'] *land*.

3–4. With the arrival of this king, people will be transformed from a spiritually dull or hardened state; their *eyes* . . . *will no longer be closed* (most probably from *šā'a'*, 'to be smeared over, blinded') and their *ears* . . . *will listen* (i.e. they are fully alert; see the reverse case in 6:9–10). People whose thinking had been characterized by fear or rashness (i.e. *the fearful heart*, lit. 'hasty of heart') now *know and understand* (i.e. are now clear-minded and discerning). Those who had a *stammering* [*'illĕgîm*, occurs only here] *tongue* are now *fluent and clear* (lit. 'will hurry to speak clearly [*ṣāḥôt*, 4x]'). The word *stammering* could imply a speech impediment or the stammerings of a liar who is caught in a lie. Regardless of the cause of the stammering, the greater emphasis in this context is on their new ability to speak uprightly and with truthfulness.

5–6. The reign of this king will completely revolutionize society, bringing it back to righteous conditions: a *fool* will no longer *be called noble* / *nor the scoundrel* [*kîlay*, 2x] *be highly respected* (2x with this meaning). People will be viewed through the lens of who they truly are (see the reversal in 5:20).

The speech of a *fool* (*nābāl*) is not simply lacking in sense (v. 6); the word *folly* (*nĕbālâ*, 'foolishness') also carries an immoral aspect. Because the fool's 'heart inclines toward wickedness' (NASB), he is led to commit profane acts (*ḥōnep*, occurs only here), including speaking against God himself. A *fool* even refuses to observe common courtesies, such as giving food and drink to those in need. For example, Nabal, whose name means 'fool', would not supply David and his men with food; as a result, God later killed him (1 Sam. 25).

7–8. Under corrupt governments, moral values are quickly perverted, and fools rise to positions of leadership. There is a wordplay between *scoundrels* (*kēlay*) and the wicked *methods* (*kēlāyw*, 'weapons') they use. Their *evil schemes* (lit. 'evils') pervert justice; their slander destroys the afflicted/needy whose pleas are just. Clements describes the 'scoundrel' as an 'unscrupulous opportunist who quickly exploited his talents in a time of weak government' (1980a: 260). By contrast, the *noble* (*nādîb*) demonstrate high moral principles, for they devise *noble plans* [*nĕdîbôt*, lit. 'nobles'; from the same root word as *nādîb*, 'noble'], / *and by noble deeds they* [lit. 'he himself', emphatic] *stand*.

Meaning

God's future plans become even clearer in this section, starting with Judah's deliverance from the Assyrians (701 BC) and continuing into the future when society will be entirely transformed. At that time people will (1) attentively listen to and follow God's commands; (2) be able to discern the truth; and (3) be governed by a king who reigns with righteousness and royal officials who are just. God's future for Israel is truly glorious.

h. Eighth judgment–restoration cycle: judgment against complacent women (32:9–14); blessing promised in the future (32:15–20)

Context

This judgment–restoration cycle is directed against Israel's women who, feeling secure in their wealth, had become complacent

towards God (see similar judgment on the women of Zion, 3:16 –
4:1). Their punishment is on the horizon, coming in little over a
year. Once again, the prophet envisions near-term and far-term
events as part of one and the same punishment: the Assyrians
would invade in 701 BC, but the palace and the cities of Israel would
not be abandoned until the Babylonian captivity of 586 BC.

Several scholars agree on two points: (1) a core of this passage
(i.e. at least vv. 9–14) comes from the time period of Isaiah the
prophet, and (2) the passage should be divided into two sections,
verses 9–14 and 15–20. Roberts suggests that verses 19–20 are a
later addition that adds a 'word of judgment' after the promises in
verses 15–18 (2015: 413); but if the NIV translation is correct, then
there is no additional word of judgment.

Comment

(1) Judgment oracle (32:9–14)

9–10. These women who are *complacent* (*šaʾănannôt*, 'carefree',10x;
5x in Isaiah) and *feel secure* receive a warning that very soon (i.e. *in
little more than a year*, lit. 'days over a year') there will be a national
catastrophe (lit. 'you will tremble'), when *the grape harvest will fail* (lit.
'come to an end') and *the harvest* [*of fruit*] *will not come*.

If this passage has the same historical context as the rest of the
section, then the harvest will be devastated during the war of 701
BC and not by drought or plague. During times of war, vineyards
go untended and their fruit is not harvested.

11–14. The prophet urges the women to action, for if they truly
understood the judgment about to take place they would *tremble* and
shudder instead of lounging in complacency, thinking themselves
safe and secure. The prophet exhorts them to *strip off* (the NIV
inserts the words *fine clothes* but they are not in the Hebrew text, v.
11) and put on sackcloth (*wrap yourselves in rags*, lit. 'gird upon your
loins'). The word *rags* is not in the text, but the context of
'mourning' suggests 'sackcloth'. The phrase *beat your breasts* is figurative language for deep mourning (v. 12). There is a wordplay
between *breasts* (*šādayim*) and *fields* (*śĕdê*) in verse 12.

Gone will be *the pleasant* [*ḥemed*, 9x] *fields, the fruitful* [*pōrîyâ*, 4x]
vines. Instead of a joyful (*ʿallîzâ*, 'jubilant', 7x) city, their land will be

devastated: (1) the crowded city (lit. 'crowd of a city') and its *fortress* will be abandoned; (2) the *citadel* (*'ōpel*)²¹ and *watchtower* (*baḥan*, possibly the great tower in Neh. 3:27) will be a *wasteland* [*mĕ'ārâ*, occurs only here] *for ever*. With no-one to cultivate the fertile land, it will become overgrown with *thorns and briers* (a common image for devastation in Isaiah) and useful only for *donkeys* and *flocks* to graze.

Because this is an accurate depiction of Judah and Jerusalem after 586 BC, Wildberger locates the passage after this date (2002: 249). Yet Micah also prophesied destruction of Jerusalem in similar terms (Mic. 3:12); thus, the concept must have been in circulation in the eighth century BC.

(2) Restoration oracle (32:15–20)

15–16. The oracle of restoration that begins in verse 15 confirms that this judgment will not last for ever – only until *the Spirit is poured on us* [notice the author includes himself] *from on high*. The 'spirit' in the Old Testament is largely understood as power emanating from God (i.e. *from on high*) or an extension of his being. This would almost certainly have called to mind other occasions when the spirit of God descended – for example, on Gideon (Judg. 6:34), Jephthah (Judg. 11:29) or Samson (Judg. 15:14–15).

This manifestation of God's power results in a progressive renewal of the land, from *desert* (lit. 'wilderness') to *fertile field* (*karmel*) to *forest* (see 29:17). Not only will the land be restored physically, but the nation itself will be a place of *justice* and *righteousness* (see vv. 1–8). These images may be a figurative reference to spiritual renewal of the land, but often in the Old Testament physical blessings and spiritual blessings go hand in hand.

17–18. The *fruit* (lit. 'deeds') and *effect* (lit. 'work') of that righteousness will be *peace, quietness* and *confidence* [lit. 'security'] *for ever*. These characteristics mentioned earlier in the chapter will be a crowning touch to the age of salvation which will not end. God's people *will live in peaceful dwelling-places, / in secure homes* [lit. 'dwelling-places'], / *in undisturbed places of rest* (v. 18), similar to the peaceful security portrayed in 11:6–9.

---

21. See excavations of the Ophal: Finkelstein et al. 2013: 142–164.

19–20. Again, the prophet reminds the complacent women that judgment is coming. The phrase *though hail flattens the forest* is difficult to translate: (1) the verb *bārad*, 'to hail', occurs nowhere else in the Old Testament and therefore is most likely to be a mispointing of the noun *hail* (*bārād*; see LXX and Targum); and (2) *bĕredet* (*flattens*) should most probably be translated literally as 'even when hail brings down the forest'. This is the rationale for the translation found in the NIV.

The last part of verse 19 states that *the city is levelled completely*, literally 'in the lowness [occurs only here] the city is laid low'. 'Lowness' and 'low' are from the same root to lend emphasis; however, they do not necessarily imply total destruction as suggested by the NIV.

No matter the translation of the verse, the key point is that though Jerusalem must be humbled, those who inherit this renewed, righteous land will be blessed (v. 20). The water supply will be so abundant that it will be possible to sow grain *by every stream*. Their *cattle and donkeys* will be able to wander freely (lit. 'sending away the foot of the bull and the donkey') without fear of rustlers or predators (see 11:6–9).

Meaning

Once again, the prophet reveals that while God will severely punish his people, there will be a clear ending when God pours out his spirit upon those whom he had punished. Historically, this prophecy covers a broad span of time, from the initiation of punishment in 701 BC by the Assyrians to their final destruction by the Babylonians in 586 BC. The first steps of restoration began in 539 BC when the remnant was allowed to return to the land, but it will be fully complete only when justice and peace are the pervasive way of life in the land.

i. Ninth judgment–restoration cycle: judgment on the destroyer (33:1); restoration for a remnant (33:2–24)

Context

The final judgment–restoration cycle of this section (Isa. 28 – 33) begins with a 'woe oracle' directed against the *destroyer* (i.e. Assyria;

see 10:5–7). While the identity of the destroyer is never mentioned in the woe oracle, it can be ascertained by the description in the parallel units that begin verse 1: *destroyer,* / *you who have not been destroyed!* . . . *betrayer* [lit. 'one who deals treacherously'], / *you who have not been betrayed!* [lit. you who have not been dealt treacherously with']. No other nation had as yet attacked Assyria (i.e. 'you have not been destroyed') and yet they had, without provocation, attacked and destroyed many other nations. God would use Assyria to punish his people, but when they had finished serving God's purpose, they themselves would be punished.

After God's promise to punish the destroyer (v. 1), a long restoration section presents the Lord as Israel's king and protector. This restoration oracle, written in the form of a song of trust, reaches its climax when those in Zion ask who can dwell with a holy God (v. 14). The answer takes the form of an 'entrance liturgy' that details the righteous characteristics required in order to enter God's presence (vv. 15–16; see Ps. 15). The rest of the song presents the joys of living in a restored Zion that is filled with justice and righteousness (see v. 5). The near context is Assyria's destruction in 701 BC, an event that helped foster the idea of God's ultimate protection of Zion (i.e. Zion theology; see Roberts 2015: 419–420).

Comment

(1) Judgment oracle (33:1)

1. The judgment oracle is only one verse, and opens with the phrase *Woe to you, destroyer,* an apt description of Assyria at this time. The *destroyer* is also accused of being a *betrayer* (lit. 'one who deals treacherously'), another appropriate descriptor for Assyria, for two reasons: (1) Sennacherib at first accepted a large tribute in exchange for pulling back his forces from an attack on Jerusalem in 701 BC. But within a short time, he changed his demands, requiring the city's full surrender (see 2 Kgs 18:17–37). (2) Assyria went beyond God's intention of inflicting punishment on other nations, choosing instead to destroy them entirely; in this sense, Assyria 'betrayed' God's intent. Now those who had dealt treacherously with others (see 21:2) would likewise be treated treacherously by the Babylonians as punishment (*you will be betrayed*). Their world dominance was thus limited, for the Babylonians eventually overtook them (*When you stop destroying, / you will be destroyed; / when you stop* [*nālâ*, occurs only here] *betraying, / you will be betrayed*). The repetition of words (i.e. *destroyed* and *betrayed*) indicates that the Assyrians would receive just punishment from the Babylonians.

(2) Restoration oracle (33:2–24)

2–6. The rest of this chapter is patterned after a song of trust in which the author leads the nation in a plea, exhorting God to reveal his *strength* (lit. 'arm', a metaphor for strength) and bring *salvation in* [this] *time of distress*. The plea begins LORD, *be gracious to us; / we long for you* (lit. 'for you we wait'; the inverted syntax emphasizes their plea for God's deliverance); then the author confirms God's power: *when you rise up* [lit. 'from your uprising', *rômēmut*, occurs only here], *the nations scatter* (*nāpṣû*, 3x with this meaning). They implore him to send wicked nations fleeing, as he had done in the past. Roberts argues that verses 3–5 are a historical recitation (though admittedly one that includes figures of speech) of God's past actions, as in a song of praise (2015: 426–427).

To illustrate the speed and thoroughness with which God's army (i.e. Assyria in this case) will attack and plunder the nations, the author employs the well-known image of hungry, swarming locusts: they attack like *young locusts* (*ḥāsîl*, 6x) with voracious appetites, *like a swarm of locusts* (*maššaq gēbîm*; both words occur only here) whose vast numbers devastate crops.

No-one can compete with Yahweh. He will be exalted through his use of Assyria to inflict punishment on Zion, which in turn will bring *justice and righteousness* into the city (v. 5) so that he can dwell there. Just as God has been their firm foundation in the past, he will be the source of Israel's stability (lit. 'steadfastness') in the present (*for your times*, v. 6).

God is a wealth (*ḥōsen*, 7x) of *salvation and wisdom and knowledge*, but to access these treasures the people must demonstrate true reverence for him: *the fear of the* LORD *is the key to this treasure* (lit. 'the fear of the LORD it is his treasure').

7–9. Like most songs of trust (e.g. Pss 27; 62), this song alternates between despair and hope in God's deliverance. The author first draws the readers' attention (i.e. *hēn*, *Look*, v. 7) to Israel's time of despair, described in five phrases: (1) *Their brave men* [*'er'ellām*, occurs only here] *cry aloud in the streets*. (2) *The envoys of peace weep bitterly* (i.e. the envoys who were sent to procure peace did not obtain their goal). (3) *The highways are deserted, / no travellers are on the roads* (i.e. the effects of war make travel too perilous). (4) *The treaty is broken, / its witnesses* [*'ādîm*, 'witnesses', from 1QIsa^a instead of the MT's *'ārîm*, 'cities'] *are despised*. (5) *No one is respected* (lit. 'he does not regard man').

The situation is dire – there is hope only for those who trust in the LORD, as mentioned in verse 6. The weeping envoys (v. 7) were either (1) the men sent to secure Egypt's help against the Assyrians (i.e. they are weeping out of fear); or (2) the Israelite representatives sent to Rabshakeh and his officials, who received terms of surrender that were so harsh (i.e. total surrender and probable deportation) it caused the envoys to weep bitterly. This second option is most likely given the context and the singular forms of the verbs (lit. 'he has broken the covenant', 'he has despised the witnesses' and 'he has no regard for others'). Sennacherib at first agreed simply to exact tribute, but then reversed course and demanded total surrender.

The war-ravaged land is described by two similar-sounding words (v. 9): *dries up* (*'ābal*, 'mourns') and *wastes away* (*'umlĕlâ*). These effects are felt all the way from *Lebanon* (i.e. the northern coast) to *Sharon* (i.e. the southern coast, just above the Philistines' land), and from *Bashan* (i.e. the east coast of the Sea of Galilee) on the eastern border to Mount *Carmel* on the western border. The fortunes of the Plain of Sharon, Bashan and Mount Carmel are later reversed in Isaiah 35:2, the only other place in the Old Testament where all three names appear together.

10–12. The repetition of *now* three times in verse 10 suggests that God, who has waited patiently, is ready to defend Jerusalem. The identity of *you* (pl.) in the phrase *you conceive chaff* (*šaš*, 'dry grass', 2x; see 5:24) is difficult to determine: is it Israel or Israel's enemies? We argue it is Israel based on the clarification that the sinners are in Zion (v. 14). Israel's best efforts were fruitless (i.e. the images of *chaff* and *straw*) in the end. In fact, the breath they expended in making treaties with Assyria and Egypt would have the opposite effect – these countries would be the source of their destruction (*your breath is a fire that consumes you*).

This punishment will destroy the wicked, both in Israel (v. 11) and among the nations (lit. *peoples*, v. 12). The thoroughness of their destruction is pictured as being *burned to ashes* (lit. 'lime', 4x) or burned like dry *thorn-bushes*. Our feeble attempts to deliver ourselves will likewise come to nothing; we must rely on the Sovereign of the universe to save us.

13–16. God calls all nations, both those *far away* and those *near*, to acknowledge his sovereign might and power, which was demonstrated in his punishment of Israel. *The sinners in Zion are terrified* because they realize that only the righteous can stand before his cleansing fire.

Verses 14b–16 follow an ancient liturgical form in which a 'who' question is followed by the response 'the one who' (see Ps. 15:1–5). The question is who can enter the newly restored Jerusalem: *Who of us can dwell with the consuming fire / . . . with everlasting burning?* (*môpĕdê* [pl.], occurs only here). The phrases *consuming fire* and *everlasting burning* stress God's cleansing of Zion (see 4:4).

The participles in the question's response (v. 15) indicate the continuous nature of the actions God expects from his people – those who (1) *walk righteously* (lit. 'in righteousnesses' [pl.]); (2) *speak what is right* (lit. 'in truths' [pl.]); (3) *reject gain from extortion* (lit. 'extortions' [pl.] or 'unjust gains' [pl.], 2x); (4) *keep their hands from accepting bribes* (lit. 'who shakes out his palms from grasping onto the bribe'); (5) *stop* [*'āṭam*, 10x] *their ears against plots of murder* (lit. 'bloods' [pl.]); and (6) *shut* [*'āṣam*, 3x with this meaning] *their eyes against contemplating evil* (lit. 'from looking into evil', with the sense of avoiding participation in evil).

This summary of how to live a righteous life results in being able to live with a holy God. The people (lit. 'he himself [emphasis]') *will dwell upon the heights* (i.e. a place of safety, free from enemy attacks) in the safety of a *mountain fortress* (*mĕṣādôt*, 'strongholds of the cliffs') whose supply of food and water *will not fail* (lit. 'is given faithfully'). In this case it probably refers to living in Zion with a holy God (v. 16; see Hab. 3:19).

17–18. The description of the blessings of those living a righteous life continues: *your* [singular suffix = each individual will see him] *eyes will see the king in his beauty* (lit. 'a king in his beauty your eyes will envision'; inverted syntax for emphasis), referring to the true king, Yahweh, whom Isaiah saw in chapter 6. This interpretation does not rule out an intermediary king described in Isaiah 9; 11; and 32, but verse 17 primarily refers to Yahweh (see also v. 22). They will also *view a land that stretches afar* (pl. = emphasizing its distance), where God dwells. This land is either very large (i.e. *stretches afar* [NIV]) or away in the distance (NASB). The grammar favours the latter (i.e. 'distant land' rather than a 'great land'), which in turn implies that the kingdom is still some time off.

They will not fear or even consider war (lit. *terror*, v. 18), as indicated by the rhetorical questions: (1) *Where is that chief officer?* (lit. 'the one who counts'; i.e. to determine the number of soldiers, horses, weapons, etc., needed); (2) *Where is the one who took the revenue?* (lit. 'the one who weighs out'; i.e. weighing out the amount of money needed for battle or for tribute payment); and (3) *Where is the officer in charge of the towers?* (lit. 'the one who counts the towers'; i.e. to determine the number that need to be built to protect the city or to be torn down to use the rocks to strengthen the wall; see 22:10). Here the NASB may be more correct in its translations of the preparations for war.

19–20. They will never need to worry about *arrogant* [*yāʿaz*, 'to be insolent', occurs only here] *people* (lit. 'an arrogant people you will not see' = emphatic Hebrew order) or foreign invaders, *people whose speech is obscure* [lit. 'deeps', i.e. 'incomprehensibles (pl.) of lip', 2x], / *whose language is strange* [lit. 'stammering of tongue'] *and incomprehensible* [lit. 'there is not understanding'].

What is the reason for this freedom from worry? God will restore Zion so that they can envision Jerusalem as their undisturbed habitation, safe and secure for ever. The permanent nature of this city is conveyed in the imagery of a tent that can neither be moved (*its stakes will never be pulled up* [*sāʿan*, 'to travel', occurs only here]) nor broken (*nor any of its ropes broken*), both common occurrences when moving a tent.

21–22. The *kî ʾim* that begins verse 21 indicates a strong contrast with verse 20 (Williams §447): [But] *there the LORD will be our Mighty One* (*ʾaddîr*). In an interesting play on the word 'mighty' (*ʾaddîr*), the author explains that because God the *Mighty One* will protect them, they will live in peace without fear of attack. For example, there will be no military vessels (*mighty* [*ʾaddîr*] *ship*) on their waterways because such defence will no longer be needed, *For the* LORD *is our judge /... our lawgiver /... our king; / it is he who will save us.*

Notice that the author includes himself once again with the people. God is not only their *lawgiver*, the one who sets standards and laws, but also their *judge*, the one who decides legal matters. The phrase *the* LORD *is our king* recalls 6:1–3 and its ultimate fulfilment here when he lives among his people.

23–24. Their battleships, being no longer needed, eventually fall into disrepair so that they are no longer fit to sail: *your rigging* [lit. 'ropes'] *hangs loose* [*nāṭaš*, 'forsaken']: / *the mast is not held secure, / the sail* [*nēs*][22] *is not spread*. Even though the ships are derelict, there will be great plunder to divide: *Then an abundance of spoils will be divided.*

The phrase *'ad-šālāl* (lit. 'unto plunder', v. 23) could be translated several ways: (1) the 'spoil [*'ad*] of plunder' (see Gen. 49:27; Zeph. 3:8; but this is redundant and seems unlikely); (2) 'blind will divide plunder', a corruption of *'iwwēr šālāl ḥillēq* (this corresponds to the parallel phrase); (3) 'then until much plunder is divided'; or (4) 'then it [i.e. the loot] was divided until plunder was great' (the grammar and the parallel phrase suggest that this is the most likely option). No matter the translation, they will gather great plunder despite having dilapidated ships. It will be so easy to collect that even the lame will be able to gather it up.

God will provide full protection, both physically from illness (*No one living in Zion* [referring back to v. 20] *will say, 'I am ill'*) and spiritually from sin (*the sins of those who dwell there will be forgiven*; lit. 'lifted up, carried away'; see 65:17–25). These promises await their ultimate fulfilment in a still-future day (see Roberts 1979: 240–253).

Meaning
Having many of the same elements as the earlier oracles, this 'woe oracle' also speaks of God defeating the Assyrians and then restoring his nation. The author sees this deliverance as part of the greater deliverance that God will accomplish for his people; yet it

---

22. The word *nēs* generally means 'standard' or 'ensign'; only here and in Ezek. 27:7 does it have this meaning.

is clear that only a remnant, not everyone in Israel, will be restored (see v. 14: *The sinners in Zion are terrified*).

In that day, the righteous will be protected and nurtured by God, but the wicked will be destroyed. God will dwell with his people, who never again need to fear or worry about war and sickness. Most importantly, their iniquity (i.e. inward crookedness or waywardness) will be forgiven and fellowship with God will be restored. This ultimate restoration remains a future event even though there would be victory over the Assyrians in 701 BC. A glorious future still awaits God's true children, those whose sins are forgiven.

iv. The coming judgment and restoration (34:1 – 35:10)

The message in this fourth section of the palistrophe that spans Isaiah 13 – 39 is consistent with the rest of Isaiah: there will be a time of punishment, called a *day of vengeance* (34:8), for all the nations that have rebelled against God by rejecting him and his people, as well as a time of restoration for God's people who will be brought to live in Zion. Isaiah 34:8 refers to these two acts as *a year of retribution, to uphold Zion's cause.*

It is often maintained that chapters 34–35 were written by Second Isaiah (Scott 1933: 178–191; Pope 1952: 235–243). Several recent scholars argue that they form a redactional diptych (i.e. the contrasting prophecies of these two chapters are complementary) that serves to bridge the first part of Isaiah with the second part (Beuken 1992: 78–102; Childs 2001: 253). In our view this diptych serves to parallel chapters 24–27 (the 'Little Apocalypse') in the palistrophe of chapters 13–39, in that both sections describe eschatological, future events relative to God's prophecy, some very similar to those of the New Testament book of Revelation (see Figure 0.9 on p. 23).

a. Yahweh's day of vengeance (34:1–17)

Context

Chapter 34 is an oracle of judgment that God will pour out on the wicked. Four reasons are given for this judgment, each beginning with a *kî* ('for'; vv. 2, 5, 6, 8) clause. Like the 'Little Apocalypse',

Isaiah 34 – 35 should be considered proto-apocalyptic rather than apocalyptic literature, since it pictures God's punishment and restoration in the context of this present world, as opposed to the establishment of a new heaven and a new earth in the future age to come.

Comment

1–3. This unit begins with a general call to the nations that God's punishment is about to be poured out upon them: *Come near, you nations . . . Let the earth hear.* The vocabulary reflects an all-inclusive destruction: *you nations*; *you peoples*; *the earth . . . and all that is in it; the world, and all that comes out of it* (*ṣeʾĕṣāʾîm*, 11x; 7x in the book of Isaiah). The terms *earth* (*ʾereṣ*) and *world* (*tēbēl*) are a common word pair (see Ps. 90:2) signifying the entirety of the earth.

There is a sense of urgency here. Both God's *anger* and his *wrath*, a common word pair to describe his attitude towards sin and judgment (see Jer. 32:37), will be held back no longer. The MT presents destruction and death as having already taken place (the perfective sense); however, the context suggests they are future events. Thus, the verbs are probably to be understood as 'prophetic perfects' (as accomplished facts in the author's mind; Williams §165). Note that the NIV simply translates the verbs as incomplete action: *He will totally destroy* [*ḥāram*, lit. 'to put under a ban'] *them* [i.e. his foes], / *he will give them over to slaughter.* When something was put under a ban, it was 'devoted to the LORD' as an offering, which usually meant that it would be totally destroyed.

The severity of the devastation is described in verse 3: (1) *Their slain will be thrown out* (*šālak*; commonly used to refer to the disposal of a dead body); (2) *their dead bodies will stink* (*bēʾš*, 3x); and (3) *the mountains will be soaked* [*māsas*, 'to melt, become weak'; only place with this meaning] *with their blood.* The magnitude of their humiliation is demonstrated in the fact that not one will receive a respectable burial (see 1 Kgs 16:4) – perhaps none of their loved ones will be left to bury them.

4–7. The images in verse 4 picture the breadth of this destruction, which affects even creation: (1) *All the stars in the sky* [lit. 'the hosts of the heavens'] *will be dissolved* (lit. 'to rot, melt, decay') (i.e. either the stars and planets will no longer give light, or their light is significantly lessened). (2) The majestic expanse of *the heavens* [will be] *rolled up like a scroll* (i.e. they will come to an end). (3) The stars will fall from the sky, like *withered leaves* on a vine or *shrivelled figs* on the tree. For similar images concerning future judgments, see Matthew 24:29; Revelation 6:12–14.

While many consider these images to be poetic hyperbole, the unmistakable point is that the devastation will be so extensive as to affect all of creation. Later in Isaiah 65 God is said to create a new heaven and a new earth, a clear reversal of what is happening here.

Verse 5 describes a future time of judgment when (*kî*; Williams §445) God's *sword has drunk its fill* [lit. 'to be satiated'] *in the heavens*, which means that his judgment on the heavens has been satisfied. This destruction *in the heavens* could be to erase humanity's sinful mark upon them (i.e. just as the earth was destroyed in the flood); but it is more likely to be a reference to the heavenly hosts (v. 4), including the fallen angels (i.e. demons; Matt. 25:41; Rev. 12:7–9), for human impact on the heavens is minor compared with that on earth.

Once God's punishment is finished in the heavens, he will return to the earth to totally destroy *Edom*, described as 'the people devoted to my destruction' (*ḥermî*; NIV reads *the people I have totally destroyed*). The word *ḥermî* is the noun form of the verb (*ḥāram*) used in verse 2 to describe God's wrath being poured out against all nations. The term suggests that Edom is representative of all nations that have revolted against God and/or harmed his people (see v. 8: *a year of retribution, to uphold Zion's cause*).

There are several points that highlight the importance of God's punishment on Edom: (1) The word *hinnēh*, 'behold, see', serves to catch the audience's attention that something significant is about to take place (*see, it descends in judgment on Edom*). (2) The inverted syntax (lit. 'upon Edom will it [i.e. 'my sword'] come down . . . for judgment') underscores that God's judgment is certain. (3) The parallel phrase emphasizes that God's judgment on Edom is their destruction. It uses the same Hebrew preposition to equate Edom with the people God is destroying (lit. 'upon [*'al*] Edom . . . even upon [*'al*] the people devoted to my punishment'). (4) There is an interesting wordplay between the similar-sounding words *ḥarbî*, 'my sword', and *ḥermî*, 'my destruction'.

The people of Edom, though descendants of Esau, did not allow their relatives the Israelites to pass through their land during the wilderness wanderings (Num. 20:14–21). Tensions continued throughout much of their history, reaching a climax when Edom encouraged Babylon to destroy Jerusalem (Ps. 137:7). They even appear to have profited from Judah's downfall (see Obad. 11–14).

The image of God's *sword* (*ḥereb*) is picked up again in verse 6 to describe Edom's punishment in sacrificial terms: *bathed in* [lit. 'is filled with'] *blood, / it is covered* [lit. 'drips'] *with fat –* / *the blood of lambs and goats, / fat from the kidneys of rams. / For the* LORD *has a sacrifice in Bozrah* (lit. 'for a sacrifice to the LORD [is] in Bozrah'; v. 6). Bozrah was a chief city of the Edomites situated 27 miles south of the Dead Sea.

The image of *wild oxen* (v. 7), known for their strength and power, represents other nations that will fight alongside Edom and be destroyed with them. The phrases *bull calves* (an image of young warriors) and *great bulls* (a reference to mature, seasoned commanders) form a merism that represents Edom's entire army. Edom will be filled with blood and sweat from the battle: *the* [lit. 'their'] *dust will be soaked with fat* (lit. 'be greasy with fat').

8–11. The LORD inflicts this destruction to take revenge (*nāqām*, 'revenge, retribution, recompense'; v. 8) on Zion's behalf (i.e. *to uphold Zion's cause* [*rîb*, 'legal case']). The parallel phrases, God's *day of vengeance* (*nāqām*) and his *year of retribution* (*šillûmîm*, 'compensation, payment'), are directed towards Edom for the cruelty that they showed to Zion (i.e. ridiculing God's chosen people and profiting from their downfall; Ps. 137:7; Obad. 11–14).

Edom's land will become entirely useless, having been changed into *pitch* (*zepet*, 3x) and *burning sulphur* (*goprît*, v. 9); similar terms are used in describing Sodom and Gomorrah's destruction (Gen. 19:24–29). Edom's punishment will be unending: (1) the fires of destruction *will not be quenched night or day*; (2) *its smoke will rise for ever* (lit. 'for ever its smoke will rise up'; the inverted syntax is for emphasis); (3) *from generation to generation it will lie desolate* (*ḥārab* may be related to the noun *ḥereb*, 'sword'); and (4) *no one will ever* [lit. 'for forever and forevers'] *pass through it again* (v. 10). The land will remain uninhabited except for wild birds. The terms *qā'at* (*desert owl*; 5x), *qippôd* (*screech owl*; 3x) and *yanšôp* (*great owl*; 3x) are all conjectural

(v. 11). There is more consensus regarding the meaning of *'ōrōb*, *raven*, largely because of Proverbs 30:17 and Song of Solomon 5:11. Similar imagery of land that is cursed can be seen in Psalm 102:6 and Zephaniah 2:14.

The *measuring line of chaos* [*tōhû*, 'wasteland'] / *and the plumb-line* [*'abnê*, lit. 'stones'] *of desolation* (*bōhû*, 'emptiness') that God will *stretch out over Edom* (v. 11) pictures Edom's destruction in terms reminiscent of the pre-creation chaos (*tōhû wābōhû*) in Genesis 1:2. Edom was destroyed by the Assyrians, Babylonians, Greeks and finally the Maccabees. Today Jordan occupies much of the area once inhabited by the Edomites.

12–15. Edom's *nobles* and *princes* will have nothing to rule over (lit. 'there is not there a kingdom'). Her citadels and strongholds lie uninhabited, in ruins. The land will revert to a wilderness filled with *thorns* (*sîrôt*, 6x), *nettles* (*qimmôś*, 3x) and *brambles* (*ḥôaḥ*, 9x). It will be fit only for *jackals*, *owls* (lit. 'daughters of ostriches'; see Mic. 1:8), *desert creatures*, *hyenas*, *wild goats* and even (*'ak*, emphatic) *night creatures* (*lîlît*, occurs only here, v. 14; in later Jewish literature this word was a female demon believed to abduct children and seduce men). In the solitude of the land, the *owl* and the *falcon* will feel perfectly at home to mate and raise their young (v. 15).

The actions described in verse 15a seem to suggest that the rare word *qippôz* (*owl*, occurs only here) may mean 'tree snake', but the context suggests some type of bird that will (1) build a *nest* (i.e. each time *qānan* occurs, it is with a bird); (2) *lay eggs* (*mālaṭ*, possibly 'flee for safety'; but if it means to lay eggs, this is the only occurrence with this meaning); (3) *hatch* [lit. 'break'] *them*; and (4) *care for* [*dāgar*, 'to gather', 2x] *her young* / *under the shadow of her wings* (lit. 'under her shadow').

16–17. The Israelites are told to *Look* [lit. 'seek'] *in the scroll* [*sēper*] *of the LORD* (v. 16) to confirm that this prophecy happens exactly as it was recorded. Much debate has focused on the phrase *the scroll of the LORD*, but the context suggests it refers to the scroll upon which the prophecy was written (see 30:8). Some scholars believe that it is a scroll containing Isaiah's earlier prophecies (Childs 2001: 257; Roberts 2015: 437).

The accuracy of the prophecy will be verified by the fact that *None of these* [i.e. the animals just mentioned] *will be missing, / not one will lack her mate* (lit. 'a woman and her mate'). After all, it is God himself (lit. *his mouth*) *that has given the order,* / *and his Spirit* [i.e. himself = emphatic] *will gather them* [i.e. the animals in v. 15] *together.*

The phrase *He allots their portions* reads literally 'he casts down a lot for them' (v. 17). The idea here is that God has 'cast the lot' or determined the prescribed territories for the animals, each receiving its portion of Edom's land. Roberts refers to this as 'traditional Israelite terminology for the communal distribution of property' (2015: 437; see Num. 26:55–56). The parallel phrase *distributes them by measure* (lit. 'his hand parcels the land out by measuring line') indicates that God makes the distributions with accuracy. The animals will live in their inherited land for ever, *from generation to generation*. This is the judgment that God will render.

Meaning
God will administer his judgment upon the whole of creation (i.e. the heavens and the earth) in a way that is fair and consistent with his righteous standards of punishment for sin (i.e. *a year of retribution, to uphold Zion's cause,* v. 8). Edom, a perennial enemy of Israel, is representative of those who deserve God's judgment (i.e. *The LORD is angry with all nations,* v. 2). One wonders if Edom is only the 'firstfruits' of God's judgment, just as Jericho was *ḥāram*, 'dedicated to destruction' and offered up to Yahweh (Josh. 6:17–19). Its punishment was to be so extensive and thorough that Edom would never be rebuilt. The Edomites would never again have an opportunity to rebel.

b. Zion's future blessing (35:1–10)

Context
While chapter 34 speaks of the far-reaching effects of the day of vengeance when God pours out his judgment on all those who rebel against his righteous standard, the structure of chapter 35 is a song of praise (see vv. 1–2), a bright beacon of hope and joy for those who turn to God and are spared this judgment.

Recent scholars (Beuken 1992: 78–102; Childs 2001: 253) have argued that Isaiah 34 and 35 are a redactional diptych (i.e. a literary structure that contains two contrasting but complementary units) that bridge two parts of the book of Isaiah, chapters 1–33 and 36–55. Evidence cited in support of a diptych structure includes lack of any connecting markers between chapters 34 and 35; the contrasting content of the two chapters; and 35:4 (*your God will come, / he will come with vengeance; / with divine retribution / he will come to save you*), which links the themes of judgment and deliverance.

While we agree with the concept of a diptych structure, we view its function in terms of the palistrophe pattern (shown in Figure 0.9 on p. 23), in which it corresponds to the future events of the 'Little Apocalypse' (Isa. 24 – 27). The palistrophe structure thus accounts for the fact that the two passages (i.e. Isa. 24 – 27 and 34 – 35) refer to future events. These two chapters contain the contrasting themes of retribution on God's enemies and restoration for God's remnant (34:8/35:4). Other specific images of reversals include 34:9/35:6b–7a; 34:2/35:2.

Zion is pictured as a peaceful and safe refuge (i.e. no predatory animals, v. 9), a place of *everlasting joy* (v. 10), where only the *redeemed* will live. Certain images in this chapter also appear later in Isaiah: *highway* (35:8; 40:3); *water . . . in the wilderness* (35:6; 43:19; 44:3). Edom will be a burnt, smouldering wasteland, whereas Israel will be a verdant region well supplied with water.

Comment

1–2. The last reason given for the destruction in Isaiah 34:8 is also the reason why the Arabah will rejoice: God will come to Zion's rescue. The word translated as *will be glad* (*yĕśuśûm*) ends with a *mēm* which most probably means 'them', continuing on from chapter 34 in which 'them' (v. 17) refers to the desert animals; this adds weight to the concept of a diptych structure.

The terms *desert*, *parched land* and *wilderness* all refer to the land of Israel after God's purging but before his restoration. When God restores the land, the desert will demonstrate its joy by blossoming, like the beautiful purple desert crocus (*ḥăbaṣṣelet*, 2x) that opens with the spring rains.

Israel's rejuvenation is pictured in terms of its lush coastlands (v. 2): *the glory of Lebanon* (lit. 'the Lebanon', known for its towering cedars); *the splendour of Carmel* [lit. 'the Carmel', a mountain range known for its vegetation and productivity] *and Sharon* (lit. 'the

Sharon', a plain along the Mediterranean Sea coast, also known for its lush vegetation and productivity).

These same regions that were languishing in 33:9 are now bursting into bloom. The words *glory* and *splendour*, which had just been used to describe the restoration of the land, are now applied to the LORD, for they (i.e. these regions) *will see the glory* and *the splendour of our God* (v. 2).

3–4. These imperatives exhort listeners to encourage those who are weak (i.e. those with *feeble* [*rāpôt*, 4x] *hands* and *knees that give way* [lit. 'stumble']) and afraid, to tell them to rejoice, for *he will come to save you* [pl.] (v. 4). God's vengeance or retribution must be understood against the backdrop of his holiness and justice. God would not be righteous if he did not punish sin, which is wilful rebellion against him. God is the only one who can mete out proper justice, for he is the only truly perfect judge.

5–8. As a result of that day, *the eyes of the blind* and *the ears of the deaf* (*ḥērēš*, 11x; 5x in Isaiah) will *be opened*; they will now see and hear the truth. The change is so complete that those who were lame will *leap* [*dālag*, 4x] *like a deer*. Those who lacked the faculty of speech (i.e. *the mute* [ʾillēm, 6x; 2x in Isaiah] *tongue*) will *shout for joy*.

Even nature will be transformed so that wilderness and desert areas will *gush forth* with abundant *water* and *streams*. The burning sand (*šārāb*, 'scorched ground', 2x) will be turned into 'pools of water' (*ʾăgam*, 8x; 6x in Isaiah), and *the thirsty ground* (*ṣimmāʾôn*, 3x) will be changed to *bubbling springs* (*mabbûʿê*, 3x). Places that were formerly *haunts* for *jackals* (which are known to inhabit barren wildernesses; see 34:13) will sprout *grass* (*ḥāṣîr*, 3x), *reeds* and *papyrus* (*gōmeʾ*, 4x). Both reeds and papyrus grow only in or near water; thus it is another picture of a well-watered land.

The imagery of verse 8 clarifies that this restoration is only for the righteous. There will be a roadway called *the Way of Holiness* upon which those who return to Zion will walk: *it will be for those who walk on that Way* (lit. 'but it [is] for him walking the way', i.e. the ones walking in righteousness). Those who are *unclean* (i.e. 'morally and religiously impure') and *wicked fools* will not be able to hinder them, for they will not be allowed access to the road.

The *fool* is a morally corrupt person who despises wisdom and discipline (see Prov. 1:7), and mocks those who are morally pure

(Prov. 14:9); such a person is typically hardened and resistant to improvement (Prov. 27:22).

These metaphors portray a renewed condition of true spirituality in the nation of Israel, instead of their former insensitivity to God. Jesus picked up the Isaianic themes of spiritual hardness versus renewal in his teachings to the Israelites of his day (Matt. 13:14–16).

9–10. This highway will also be safe in the absence of dangerous animals (*no lion* [one of the most dangerous animals in Israel] ... *nor any ravenous* [*pĕrîṣ*, 'violent', 6x] *beast*, v. 9). It will be for the sole use of *the redeemed* (v. 9) and *those the LORD has rescued* (lit. 'ransomed', v. 10), both terms that describe the remnant who *will enter Zion* (see 2:2). The sorrow they once knew will be replaced by *gladness and joy* that is *everlasting* (v. 10). The words of verse 10 are repeated in 51:11, both referring to a time in the far distant future.

Meaning
In contrast to chapter 34's description of the future of Edom, and by extension of all those who go against God, we see in chapter 35 the deliverance, restoration, joy and blessing that God will bestow on his people, the remnant who return to Zion. Those who are redeemed will walk unhindered and in safety on their way to Zion, through land that has been restored with lush vegetation and abundant water. As they enter Zion, they will receive the comfort and eternal joy that only God can provide.

v. The Isaianic Narratives; SEAM (36:1 – 39:8)

Excursus: the Isaianic Narratives in their literary and historical setting

Peter Ackroyd argues that chapters 36–39 are a redactional bridge between First and Second Isaiah, linking the message of punishment in First Isaiah with the message of restoration in Second Isaiah (1982: 3–21), a view that was quickly picked up by many others. While we agree that there are no clear literary links or natural flow between chapter 35 and the material that follows in Isaiah 36 – 39, the Isaianic Narratives continue the similar themes of judgment followed by restoration begun in chapters 28–33 and continued into chapters 34–35. The imminent threat of judgment can be seen in chapters 36–37, but then 37:14 turns towards the theme of restoration when Hezekiah lays out Sennacherib's letters before God, who in turn promises to destroy the Assyrians (37:36–38).

The whole of Isaiah 13 – 35 has stressed God's sovereignty over the nations, and here God's sovereignty is demonstrated over the most powerful nation of the time. Yet Israel demonstrate neither gratitude for his gracious deliverance nor remorse for their sinful behaviour. Instead they disregard God's deliverance, saying to one another, *Let us eat and drink . . . for tomorrow we [may] die!* (see 22:12–14). God therefore warns of further punishment for the nation of Israel at the hands of the Babylonians (39:6–7), which will eventually necessitate deliverance from the Babylonian exile (described in chs. 40–48).

We argue that the Isaianic Narratives (chs. 36–39) are the final section of the palistrophe in Isaiah 13 – 39, and that this section is parallel to the so-called Oracles to the Nations (chs. 13–23). Both sections, Isaiah 13 – 23 and 36 – 39, describe God's punishment on nations that have harmed God's people (see Figure 0.9 on p. 23).

The link between the two sections is the short oracle against Assyria (14:24–27), which encapsulates what God will do to nations that go against God's people. Verse 26 is key, stipulating that all those who go against God's people will be punished like Assyria: *This is the plan determined for the whole world; / this is the hand stretched out over all nations.* Isaiah 36 – 37 then describes in detail Assyria's ruthlessness towards Israel, followed by the destruction of Assyria.

There has been significant debate regarding the relationship between 2 Kings 18 – 20 and Isaiah 36 – 39. The historical events of Isaiah 36 – 39 are found in 2 Kings 18:13 – 20:21, except that Isaiah's account leaves out 2 Kings 18:14–16, referred to as the A-account (Childs 1967: 70–73), which shows Hezekiah in an unfavourable light, having surrendered to Sennacherib and taken the gold from the temple doors to pay tribute (see Figure 36.1).

PARALLEL PASSAGES

Isaiah 36:1 – 39:8 and 2 Kgs 18:13 – 20:21 are parallel passages, with only slight variations:

- The 2 Kings narrative more commonly uses the shortened form of Hezekiah's name (*ḥizqîyâ*). Isaiah consistently uses the longer form, *ḥizqîyāhû*.
- Hezekiah's surrender appears only in 2 Kings 18:14–16.
- Hezekiah's prayer is only in Isaiah 38:10–20.
- Only 2 Kings 18:17 mentions that the *supreme commander* (*tartān*) also came.

Figure 36.1 The parallel passages Isaiah 36:1 – 39:8
and 2 Kings 18:13 – 20:21

Initially there was wide consensus that 2 Kings 18 – 20 was the original story and that the Isaiah account borrowed from it. This allowed Stade (1886: 156–192) and Duhm (1922: 227–240)[23] to argue that the A-account was the original version around which the rest of the narratives were developed. These redactional narratives are usually divided into two accounts (i.e. B¹ = 2 Kgs 18:13 – 19:9a; B² = 2 Kgs 19:9b–37).

More recently, Smelik (1986: 70–92), and to some extent Seitz (1993a: 47–57), has questioned this view, suggesting the priority of the Isaiah passage over the 2 Kings account, largely because Marduk-Baladan's visit coincides so well with the context of Isaiah 36 – 39. It is now fairly well agreed that the slight differences between the accounts in 2 Kings 18 – 20 and Isaiah 36 – 39 can be attributed to a third source that the authors/editors of 2 Kings and Isaiah both used in shaping their narratives (Childs 2001: 262; Roberts 2015: 443).[24]

---

23. Clements argues that the A-account reflects the actual events, as confirmed by Assyrian records, and that the B-account is a later midrashic expansion that turned the defeat into Yahweh's victory (1980b).

24. There are minor differences between the text of this account in Isaiah and that in 2 Kings, but since our purpose is to interpret the account in

John Bright and others have even argued that there were two campaigns, one in 701 BC and another later one (2000: 298–309), that were combined in the biblical account; however, this argument has very little evidence in support.

There has also been much debate about the date of and relationship between Isaiah 36 – 39. While chapters 36 and 37 contain a clear chronological flow of thought, chapters 38 and 39 are only loosely connected to the events of 701 BC (i.e. *in those days*). For example, *Marduk-Baladan* (Marduk-apal-iddina II), who is mentioned in chapter 39, led the Babylonian opposition against Assyria in 703–702 BC, but in 702 BC was defeated and fled to Elam; thus his visit to Hezekiah must have preceded this date.

The most plausible sequence of events in these chapters is as follows:

1. Chapter 38, which describes Hezekiah's illness and recovery, begins with a general statement of its connection with the events around 701 BC. Hezekiah's prayer (Isa. 38:9–20; not found in the 2 Kings passage) disrupts the chronology of the narrative.

2. Marduk-Baladan visits Hezekiah, having heard that he has been sick and has now recovered (Isa. 39). The phrase *at that time* makes a clearer connection between chapters 38 and 39. It is plausible that Marduk-Baladan used this visit to encourage Hezekiah to rebel against Sennacherib, which led to the invasion by Sennacherib.

3. Sennacherib begins his assault on Judah; Hezekiah surrenders and pays a tribute (2 Kgs 18:14–16).

4. Sennacherib sends his messengers to Jerusalem the first time to demand from them unconditional surrender in addition to the tribute they have already paid (2 Kgs 18:17–37; Isa. 36:2–22).

5. Hezekiah sends a message to Isaiah requesting prayer on behalf of Jerusalem that God might deliver them. God responds that Sennacherib will return to Assyria, where he will die (2 Kgs 19:1–7; Isa. 37:1–7).

(note 24 *cont.*) Isaiah we will bring in parallels from 2 Kings only to highlight important differences in the accounts.

6. Sennacherib, receiving word that Egypt is advancing against him, again sends messengers to Jerusalem with a letter demanding Hezekiah's complete surrender (2 Kgs 19:8–13; Isa. 37:8–13).

7. Hezekiah himself takes this letter to God. Isaiah communicates God's response that Sennacherib will not harm the city but will return home the same way he came (2 Kgs 19:14–34; Isa. 37:14–35).

8. Sennacherib defeats Egypt and brings his troops to Jerusalem.

9. God sends his angel to kill 185,000 Assyrian soldiers, whereupon Sennacherib returns to Assyria and later dies (2 Kgs 19:35–37; Isa. 37:36–38).

The connection between chapters 36–39 is therefore literary, not chronological. The warning regarding Judah's deportation was placed at the end of Isaiah 1 – 39 to serve as a bridge to Isaiah 40 – 66, which describes the return from Babylon. We believe that the date of chapters 36–39 generally fits the context of 701 BC and that it is not necessary, as Roberts argues, to date these narratives much later than the events they record (2015: 444). However, there is still no clear consensus as to how this material was arranged and why. Our view is that a lengthy palistrophe (chs. 13–39) accounts for the position of these chapters in the book.

Historical setting[25]

After the death of Sargon in 705 BC, a wave of rebellions flowed throughout the Assyrian Empire. Sennacherib met the challenge head-on, systematically putting them down. After suppressing the Babylonian rebellion led by Marduk-Baladan, Sennacherib headed west towards the Mediterranean Sea and then south, conquering Sidon and the mainland of Tyre. Others submitted quickly to his authority, including several Phoenician cities, Ashdod, Ammon, Moab and Edom.

Sennacherib then went on to attack Ashkelon, Ekron and Judean strongholds. A coalition army of Philistines, Egyptians and Ethiopians met Sennacherib at Eltekeh (south of Ekron) but was

---

25. See also the detailed historical setting in the Introduction.

decisively defeated. Sennacherib then turned to Judah to finish their destruction. By this time most of Judah's strongholds had been destroyed; Jerusalem was one of the few remaining cities (*ANET* 287–288).

a. The deliverance of Jerusalem (36:1 – 37:38)

Context

As noted, the Isaianic Narrative is not presented in chronological sequence. Rather, the narrative starts from the point of the arrival of the Assyrian forces and their defeat. This focuses initial attention on how these chapters demonstrate Yahweh's authority over the nations before returning to the events which led up to the events reported here.

Comment

1–3. In response to Hezekiah's decision to stop tribute payments, Sennacherib arrived in Judah during the fourteenth regnal year of King Hezekiah (see Figure 36.2). Sennacherib began attacks on *all the fortified cities of Judah* (v. 1; *ANET* [288] says forty-six cities), systematically capturing them. After exacting an exceptionally heavy tribute from Hezekiah, he sent three of his high officials with a *large* [lit. 'heavy'] *army* from Lachish to Jerusalem to coerce Hezekiah and his army into full surrender. According to 2 Kings 18:17, these three officials were Tartan (the 'supreme commander', the highest-ranking official under the king), Rab-saris (the 'chief officer', the second-highest-ranking official) and Rabshakeh (the 'field commander').

Why would he do this when Hezekiah had paid the required tribute? No doubt Sennacherib recognized that Hezekiah capitulated only under duress and would probably rebel again if given the chance. Also, Sennacherib was in a better position to negotiate full surrender now that he had defeated the Egyptians. Even though Tartan was the highest Assyrian official present, the Isaiah 36 account mentions only the *field commander (rab-šāqēh)*, most probably because his knowledge of Hebrew meant that he did all the speaking.

The field commander came from Lachish (the last fortified city Assyria captured before turning its army towards Jerusalem) and

---

Different Dates for Hezekiah's First Year of Reign

2 Kgs 18:1 – Hezekiah began to reign in the third year of Hoshea
= 727 BC
Hezekiah began his co-regency with Ahaz in 727 BC

2 Kgs 18:13 – Sennacherib came to attack Jerusalem in 701 BC,
the fourteenth year of Hezekiah's reign = 715 BC
Hezekiah began his sole reign in 715 BC

Figure 36.2 When did Hezekiah begin to reign?

stood by *the aqueduct of the Upper Pool, on the road to the Launderer's Field* (lit. 'field of washers', v. 2), which was one of Jerusalem's primary water supplies (Isaiah had met Ahaz here about thirty years earlier in 735 BC; see 7:3).

Hezekiah sent several officials out to meet the field commander (v. 3): (1) *Eliakim son of Hilkiah*, the highest official, who was overseer of the palace (lit. 'over the household') and had recently replaced Shebna (see 22:15–25); (2) *Shebna the secretary*, who issued public decrees and documents (possibly the same Shebna); and (3) *Joah son of Asaph*, the recorder (*hammazkîr*, lit. 'the rememberer').

4–6. In his message Sennacherib, referred to as *the great king, the king of Assyria*, taunts Hezekiah: *on what are you* [sing.] *basing this confidence* [*biṭṭāḥôn*, 3x] *of yours?* (v. 4). The second person singular form *you* indicates that the field commander, who declares Sennacherib's message in Hebrew, is addressing Hezekiah specifically, calling into question the wisdom of rebelling against Sennacherib, the implication being that he should know better (see 10:7–13). There is little doubt that Hezekiah underestimated the power of the new king Sennacherib, who quickly defeated the nations that revolted against Assyria following Sargon II's death.

Verse 5 continues to jab at Hezekiah: *You say* [lit. 'I say'] *you have counsel and might for war – but you speak only empty words* (lit. 'only words of lips'; inverted syntax for emphasis). There are two views regarding the identity of the speaker at this point: (1) according to the MT, Sennacherib is speaking (*'āmartî*, lit. 'I say . . .'); (2) *BHS*, 1QIsaᵃ, several other Hebrew manuscripts and 2 Kings 18:20

support the NIV reading *you say*, referring to Hezekiah. We argue that the context supports the MT's reading, for two reasons: (1) The words of the last phrase of verse 5, *that you rebel against me*, are clearly those of Sennacherib: the commander is simply his messenger. (2) The immediate verbs in context are second person singular; a scribe would have had little reason to change these verbs to first person singular forms, because that would result in a more difficult reading of the text here.

Sennacherib's commander challenges Hezekiah, knowing that the Israelite army alone cannot withstand the Assyrian forces sent to quell the rebellion: *I know you* [sing.] *are depending* [lit. 'behold you trust'] *on Egypt, that splintered* [lit. 'crushed'] *reed of a staff* (v. 6; see Ezek. 29:6–7). Egypt is compared to a staff that is so brittle it splinters apart, like a reed that punctures the hand when someone leans upon it.

A *splintered reed* is a fitting picture of Tirhakah who, when he came out in force against Sennacherib, was easily defeated and thus was of no help to Hezekiah (see 2 Kgs 19:9; Isa. 37:9). Tirhakah, of Nubian or Cushite origin, was pharaoh of Egypt from about 690 to 664 BC, but he may have been called *Pharaoh* here since he represents the pharaoh. Before that he was a renowned army general who may well have come to Hezekiah's aid once before.

7–8. The commander also questions whether Israel's God will be willing and able to lend support. Assyrian spies must have informed Sennacherib that Hezekiah had destroyed the worship sites on the high places (lit. 'his high places') and instructed all of Judah to worship at the altar in Jerusalem: *You must worship before this altar.* Sennacherib assumed that Hezekiah's actions would be offensive to Yahweh, turning Yahweh against him.

The subtle change between the singular and plural forms in the phrase *if you* [sing.] *say to me, 'We are depending on the* LORD *our God'* (v. 7) suggests that the field commander is trying to cause division between the people and their king (Roberts 2015: 453). Sennacherib's challenges are like other Assyrian propaganda of the time period (Machinist 1982: 719–737).

What he did not know was that Hezekiah was following what God had prescribed in the law and that Yahweh detested the idol worship on the high places that were destroyed (see 2 Kgs 18:3–6).

The Assyrian mindset was that any truly great god should be honoured by building many beautiful temples and altars – the more idols or representations of the god, the greater the god (see 10:10). Seen through an Assyrian lens, Hezekiah's actions would have been tantamount to blasphemy.

The commander appears to plead with Hezekiah to submit to Sennacherib: *make a bargain* [*hit'āreb*, 2x with this meaning] *with my master*, and then appears to indulge in some derisive taunts of his own: *I will give* [lit. 'let me give'] *you* [sing. = Hezekiah] *two thousand horses – if you* [sing.] *can put riders on them!* (v. 8). The commander even uses the particle of entreaty (*nā'*, 'please, I pray') to exhort him to take the horses. The implication is that Hezekiah should take his offer so that his army will not be completely slaughtered by the Assyrians.

9–10. The commander continues his mocking tone: *How then can you repulse one officer* [*peḥâ*, 'governor', not to mention one of his professional soldiers] *of the least of my master's officials* [*'abdê*, 'servants'] *...?* The implication is that Sennacherib's troops are so well trained that they would overpower Israel even if a substantial supply of horses and chariots were given to them.

As the climax to his argument, Sennacherib claims to have the LORD's approval: *The LORD himself told me to march against this country and destroy it* (v. 10). It was a common custom to confer with the gods before ever launching an attack, to ensure that the gods condoned and would support the action. Presumably there was an omen interpreted as being favourable, from which Sennacherib assumed that Yahweh condoned this battle.

11–12. The Israelite envoys ask the commander to address them (lit. 'speak, please, to your servants') in *Aramaic* (*'ărāmît*), not *Hebrew* (*yĕhûdît*, most probably Judean Hebrew; see Neh. 13:24), so that the *people on the wall* (v. 11) will not be intimidated by what they are hearing (lit. 'in the ears of the people') and lose the will to fight. Aramaic was the trade language used by officials; commoners were less likely to know it. However, this shows the naïveté of the Israelite envoys, for it was clearly the commander's goal to intimidate both Hezekiah and everyone within hearing: *Was it only to your master and you that my master sent me . . . and not to the people sitting on the wall – who . . . will have to eat their own excrement* [*here'*, 3x] *and* *drink their own urine?* (v. 12). The syntax in Hebrew highlights the irony of such a question. The word *urine* (*šayin*, 2x) appears only here and in the parallel passage, 2 Kings 18:27, but the *qērê* reading (i.e. 'what is to be read') is a euphemism for urination (lit. 'waters of the feet'). Both passages may have intentionally recorded the more vulgar original terms of Rabshakeh to emphasize their desperate plight but included the *qērê* reading so that it would be somewhat less offensive.

Assyria's reputation for being merciless and cruel lent credence to his words. Cutting off the food and water supplies of their victims during a siege to coerce surrender was common. Fortunately, Jerusalem was able to maintain a steady water supply thanks to Hezekiah's tunnel (see 2 Chr. 32:3–4), so the bigger problem was that the food supply would eventually run out.

13–15. The commander's final ploy was to sow seeds of doubt regarding Israel's leadership by suggesting that Hezekiah had misled them about their ability to successfully throw off Assyrian rule: *do not let Hezekiah deceive you* (pl., v. 14). His goal was to convince them that war with Assyria was futile and that if they surrendered, Sennacherib would be merciful. However, the commander makes a serious mistake when he mocks not only Hezekiah (i.e. *He cannot deliver you!*, v. 13) but Hezekiah's God as well (*Do not let Hezekiah persuade you to trust in the* LORD).

The field commander seems confident that Hezekiah was the main motivator behind the people's trust in Yahweh. He conjectures what the king must have said to persuade his people: *The* LORD *will surely deliver us,* and *this city will not be given* [lit. 'will never be given'] *into the hand of the king of Assyria* (i.e. stated emphatically).

16–17. The commander puts the best possible spin on surrender: *make peace with me* [lit. 'make with me a blessing'] . . . *Then each of you will eat fruit from your own vine . . . and drink water from your own cistern* (v. 16). Once they surrender, they can continue to prosper in their own land, *until I come and take you to a land like your own* (v. 17).

Even when he tells them that they will be deported to Assyria, he pictures it similarly to the Promised Land: *a land of corn and new wine, a land of bread and vineyards* (v. 17). Second Kings 18:32 adds the phrases 'a land of olive trees and honey. Choose life and not death!'

If threats proved ineffective, then certainly this appeal ought to persuade them into surrendering.

18–20. When there is no response from the people, the commander continues to undermine their reliance on the LORD, likening him to all the other gods: *Have the gods of any nations ever delivered their lands from the hand of the king of Assyria?* (v. 18).

The commander then lists the cities whose gods had failed to protect them from capture by the Assyrians (v. 19): *Hamath* (734 BC), *Arpad* (705 BC), *Sepharvaim* (about 705 BC), *Samaria* (722 BC). The 2 Kings 18:34 account adds 'Hena' and 'Ivvah' to the list. He specifically cites Samaria, perhaps knowing that they professed to worship the same God as Judah. His concluding remark turns from mockery to blasphemy: *How then can the LORD deliver Jerusalem from my hand?* (v. 20).

21–22. The people remained silent because Hezekiah had commanded them not to answer the Assyrian (v. 21); nevertheless, the commander's words probably had their desired effect. When the officials went to report Sennacherib's message to Hezekiah, they had torn their clothes (v. 22), a sign of grief and distress.

37:1–4. Upon hearing the report of his officials, Hezekiah tears his robe as well and puts on sackcloth (lit. 'covered himself with the sackcloth', a clear demonstration of sorrow). Hezekiah is in dire straits: the Assyrians had arrived, ready to attack, but there would be no help from Egypt. Having nowhere else to turn, he enters *the temple* [*bêt*, 'the house'] *of the LORD* (v. 1) to consult God. He also sends Eliakim, Shebna and the elders of the priests (pl.) in sackcloth to ask Isaiah to pray that the remnant left in Jerusalem might survive.

Hezekiah refers to this terrible crisis facing the nation as *a day of distress and rebuke and disgrace* (v. 3) as terrible as death in childbirth: *as when children come to the moment of birth* [lit. 'breaking forth'] *and there is no strength to deliver them* (Roberts suggests this may be a common proverb; 2015: 456). It was because of Hezekiah that the nation was in this disastrous position, and he lacked the power to deliver them.

Despairing of help (*'ûlay*, 'perhaps', at the beginning of v. 4 highlights his uncertainty), Hezekiah calls on Isaiah in hopes that the prophet's God (*the LORD your God*, v. 4) will have heard the Assyrian field commander's ridicule of the living God and *will rebuke him* (*hôkîaḥ* often has a legal sense to it, v. 4). The verb *to ridicule* (*ḥāraṗ*) means 'to taunt, insult' and is used in parallel with

the word 'to blaspheme' (*gādap*; see 2 Kgs 19:22//Isa. 37:23).
Perhaps God will act to show the Assyrian how wrong he was in
his estimation of God's power.

Hezekiah appeals to Isaiah to *pray* [lit. 'lift up a prayer'] *for the
remnant that still survives* (v. 4). He is referring to Jerusalem, for the
other cities had already been defeated. Hezekiah realizes that Isaiah
had been right all along (see Isaiah's message to Ahaz in 8:7).

5–7. An apparent awkwardness in the sequence of events
surfaces in verse 5, which states, *When King Hezekiah's officials came
to Isaiah*, even though in verse 3 the officials had already arrived and
were speaking to Isaiah (*They told him*). This same awkwardness
appears in the parallel account in 2 Kings 19:3–5. Roberts believes
that the narrator gets ahead of himself (2015: 456) when recording
the account of Hezekiah's officials delivering his message to Isaiah
(vv. 3–4). An even better option is to read the *wāw* as a resumptive
wāw, resuming the train of thought from the preceding clause,
which could still be translated similarly to the NIV (Williams §440).

God has indeed heard the Assyrian's ridicule and responds
through Isaiah: *do not be afraid of what you have heard . . .* [for the]
underlings [lit. 'lads, youths'] [of Sennacherib] *have blasphemed* [*gādap*,
7x] *me* (v. 6). To refer to the Assyrian messengers as *underlings* (*na'ărê*,
'lads, youths', and not as 'servants' [*abdê*]) belittles their positions
of power in the Assyrian kingdom (see 3:4 where the same term is
used of Judah's leaders, *nĕ'ārim*, 'lads, youths').

God will cause Sennacherib to become fearful (lit. 'I will put a
spirit [*rûaḥ*] in him') concerning a report or rumour that causes him
to return *to his own country* where he will be *cut down with the sword* (v.
7). The Annals of Esarhaddon mention that his brothers had
spread rumours about him to their father; this may be the rumour
referred to here (see *ANET* 289). Whatever the rumour, the divine
initiative is clearly fulfilled in verses 37–38.

8–9. The assumption in the narrative is that Isaiah's message
gave Hezekiah the encouragement he needed not to surrender to
Sennacherib. The commander left Jerusalem to deliver his response
to Sennacherib, who had captured Lachish and was now attacking
Libnah, 7 miles to the north. It was common for the Assyrian army
to capture a fortified city like Lachish first and then seize the
weaker cities around it.

While at Libnah, Sennacherib received a report regarding hostile manoeuvres by *Tirhakah, the king of Cush* (v. 9). This Nubian king is generally dated to 690–664 BC, thus making mention of him as *king* an anachronism. More probably his father, Shebitku, the Nubian king in 701 BC, sent him as commander of the army to fight against Sennacherib at Eltekeh. He is referred to as 'king' simply because he later became king and that is how the readers would know him. But before the battle, Sennacherib sends his emissaries to Jerusalem one more time to urge their surrender.

10–13. The commander blasphemes Yahweh yet again, hoping to weaken Hezekiah's trust in him: *do not let the god you depend on deceive you* (v. 10). Again, the message from Sennacherib comes in letter form (see v. 14), recapitulating much of the first message: Hezekiah should not let his God *deceive* him (lit. 'give him false hopes'). At this point Sennacherib is hoping to secure Jerusalem's full surrender before facing off in battle against Tirhakah.

Once again, he declares that Assyria has destroyed every other country it set out to attack: *Surely [hinnēh] you have heard what the kings of Assyria have done to all the countries, destroying [ḥāram, 'devoting them to destruction']* them completely . . . *Did the gods of the nations that were destroyed by my predecessors deliver them . . . ?* He then lists specific cities that surrendered: *Gozan* (Adad-nirari III, 808 BC), *Harran* (Sargon II), *Rezeph and the people of Eden who were in Tel Assar* (Tiglath-pileser III). The emphasis of this verse is that the gods of these nations could not protect their cities from the Assyrians.

He then personalizes the message for King Hezekiah by asking the whereabouts of the kings of several other city-states he had defeated: *Hamath* (totally destroyed about 720 BC by Sargon II); *Arpad* (destroyed about 740 BC by Tiglath-pileser III); *Lair* (uncertain); *Sepharvaim* (destroyed about 720 BC by Sargon II); *Hena* (uncertain); and *Ivvah* (uncertain). Of the cities we can identify, their kings were either killed or captured and the cities themselves destroyed. Hezekiah would probably have been familiar with these Assyrian conquests.

The reference to *Lair* (*lāʿîr*) is complicated; the NIV reading lists it as a separate city-state, whereas some translations read it together with Sepharvaim (lit. 'to the city of Sepharvaim'; LXX; NASB; NRSV; ESV). Roberts argues that *Lair* is the Assyrian city Laḥīru, which is possible, but there were multiple cities with the name Lahiru (2015: 467).

14–16. Hezekiah took the letter (*hassĕpārîm*, pl.)[26] and immediately went to the temple to lay it before the LORD (lit. Hezekiah *spread it out before the LORD*). Even though the Hebrew text switches between singular and plural letter(s), there was most probably one letter for each visit (though Rabshakeh may have embellished each letter with his own thoughts), thus at this point Hezekiah can take them both before the LORD.

With faith apparently renewed, he himself calls upon God instead of asking Isaiah to intercede: *LORD Almighty* [lit. 'of hosts'], *the God of Israel, enthroned between* [lit. 'sitting (between)', but technically there is no preposition] *the cherubim* [see 1 Sam. 4:4], *you alone are God over all the kingdoms of the earth. You* [lit. 'you yourself', emphatic] *have made heaven and earth* (v. 16). The name *LORD* is the name of Israel's personal God. Hezekiah declares God's sovereignty and power: he is the creator of the world, the sovereign God over all its nations, and by implication the only true God.

17–20. Hezekiah exhorts God to listen to Sennacherib's blasphemy: *Give ear, LORD . . . listen to all the words Sennacherib has sent to ridicule the living God.* Sennacherib has insulted God by putting him in the same category as idols that cannot deliver a nation from Assyria's hand. The difference is that Yahweh is alive, listening to his mockery, and can take whatever action he then chooses.

Hezekiah uses the phrase *it is true* (*ʾāmnām*) to stress that the Assyrians have in fact demonstrated immense power, laying waste all the nations (lit. 'all the lands and their lands'; 2 Kgs 19:17 is probably the better reading: 'the nations and their lands') that Sennacherib named in his letter. Hezekiah affirms that the Assyrians were able to destroy these countries and their gods, for they were useless statues artisans had crafted from *wood and stone* with no power to repel an Assyrian invasion.

---

26. Both Isa. 37:14 and 2 Kgs 19:14 contain the plural form 'letters' in this verse. Later the 2 Kings passage refers to 'them' (pl.), whereas the Isaiah passage says 'it' (sing.). A few words after this, both Isaiah and 2 Kings refer to the 'letters' as 'it' (sing.; *spread it out before the LORD*).

In the second part of verse 19 the Hebrew text places the phrase *and destroyed them* at the very end of the sentence for emphasis. However, Hezekiah knows he is appealing to the only living God, entreating him to deliver Jerusalem *so that all the kingdoms of the earth may know that you, LORD, are the only God*. This is a very compelling argument (see Ps. 115:1–18): deliverance here would not only spare Israel, it would confirm to the Assyrians and to all the nations of the earth that Yahweh is truly different from other gods.

The MT reads *you, LORD, are the only God* (lit. 'you alone are Yahweh', v. 20), whereas 2 Kings 19:19 is even more emphatic, literally 'you, you alone, Yahweh, are God'. Hezekiah is calling upon God to uphold his glory, like Moses' appeal in Exodus 32:11–12. It is important to God that his name, and thus his sovereignty, be honoured among the nations, so that they have no reason not to trust him.

21–25. After Hezekiah prays, God launches into a declaration of Sennacherib's offences, which include blasphemy, and the judgment he will incur as a result (vv. 22–29). Notice that God continues to speak through his messenger Isaiah instead of speaking directly to Hezekiah, as was typical when God wished to communicate with the king in the pre-classical period (Holladay 1970: 29–51).

In the next few verses God explains four reasons why he will punish Assyria, although there is some debate as to how to translate God's declarations against Assyria (i.e. *him* = the king) in verse 22:

1. Assyria has mocked Israel: literally 'She [i.e. Assyria; the feminine form indicates the nation as a whole] despises you [i.e. Israel], thus mocking you, Virgin Daughter [of] Zion.' This idea is reinforced in the parallel phrase: literally 'She [i.e. Assyria] wagged her head behind you [i.e. in derision; see Ps. 109:25], Daughter of Jerusalem' (v. 22).

2. When Sennacherib mocked Israel, he was actually mocking their God: *Who is it you have ridiculed and blasphemed? / . . . Against the Holy One of Israel!* (i.e. the one who protects them; v. 23). Not only has he mocked *the Holy One of Israel* by assuming his impotence and speaking proud words in defiance of him, but Assyria's attack on God's city Jerusalem is a personal affront to him.

3. Assyria has even allowed its messengers to mock God: *By your messengers* [lit. 'through the hand [sing.] of your servants'] / *you have*

ridiculed the Lord, v. 24). The prophet now refers to them as 'servants', not 'lads' as he did in verse 6. God holds the king responsible for allowing his servants to mock the living God.

4. The king has made some grandiose claims about Assyria's mighty power: (a) mountains have been no obstacle to his large chariot forces; (b) he has pillaged Lebanon of its natural resources, felling its choicest cedar and juniper trees, no matter how remote; and (c) he has taken the water supplies of nations for his own use, either by digging wells or, as in the case of Egypt, by claiming to dry up its entire irrigation system.[27] Drying up the streams of Egypt *with the soles of my feet* is a reference either to the method of opening dirt irrigation channels with one's foot or to some type of delivery gate opened with one's foot to direct water from the Nile to crops.

26–29. Sennacherib operated under the false assumption that he had determined and accomplished all these things by his own wisdom and might (vv. 24–25). How mistaken he was! Speaking in the first person, God informs Hezekiah that it was he who had decreed the Assyrian's actions long ago: *In days of old* [lit. 'from days before'] *I planned it; / now I have brought it to pass* (v. 26).

The phrase *days of old* may refer to God's plan from eternity past (see 51:9) or to Isaiah's earlier prophecies (*c.*740 BC; see Lam. 2:17). Sennacherib may have *turned* [*šā'â*, 'laid waste', 7x] *fortified cities / into piles of stone* (v. 26), but his actions were all part of God's larger plan.

The next phrases in verse 27 describe the outcomes of his conquests:

> *Their people, drained of power* [lit. 'short of hand'],
>   *are dismayed and put to shame.*
> *They are like plants in the field,*
>   *like tender green* [*yereq*, 8x] *shoots,*
>   *like grass sprouting on the roof,*
> [they are = ellipsis] *scorched*[28] *before it grows up.*

Chiasm

---

27. Sennacherib defeated Egypt in Palestine but never advanced into Egypt itself, so there is no substance to this exaggerated claim.

28. The word *šĕdēmâ*, 'fields', makes little sense here. The reading *šĕdēpâ*, 'scorched', in the parallel passage in 2 Kgs 19:26 makes more sense.

It was God who had drained these cities of power so that Sennacherib could seize them; it was he who allowed them to be humiliated by the Assyrians. Assyria efficiently and effectively carried out God's plan, not their own plan on their own initiative, nor in their own strength (see 10:13–15).

Nothing falls outside of Yahweh's omniscience and providence: *But I know where you are* [lit. 'your sitting'] / *and when you come and go* / *and how you rage* [lit. 'how you excite yourself'; *hithpael* stem, only 2x; see Gen. 45:24] *against me* (v. 28). Therefore, *because* of Sennacherib's *insolence* (*ša'ănān*, 10x; 5x in Isaiah; but elsewhere it means 'peaceful or at ease'), God will lead him back to Assyria the same way he came (lit. 'in the way which you came in it', v. 29): *I will put my hook* (*ḥāḥ*, 8x; 5x in Ezekiel) *in your nose* / *and my bit in your mouth.*

The Assyrians placed hooks in the cartilage of the nose or in the lower lip of their captives to physically subdue them and lead them into exile (see Amos 4:2–3), similar to rings used to lead oxen. These images portray God bringing the unruly country of Assyria into submission, leading its ruler Sennacherib back to his own land. There was only one main route back to Assyria: the Great Trunk Road along the River Euphrates back to Nineveh (about 700 miles).

30–32. God provides a *sign* (*'ôt*) so that Hezekiah will know the timing. A sign does not have to be miraculous, and this one is not: *This year you will eat what grows by itself* [*sāpîaḥ*, 'self-seeding plants' (4x); implies that they will not have time to plant crops], *and the second year what springs from that* [*šāḥîs*, 'self-seeding plant'; occurs only here].[29] The sign means that they will not be able to plant because the battle rages across the crop cycles of two years, but in the third year they can resume the usual sow–reap crop cycle. The implication of the sign is that Israel will soon be able to resume normal life because the Assyrians will no longer be a threat.

According to Sennacherib's annals, his siege of Jerusalem lasted for only one year. Thus, if it began in the spring as is normal for battles, the Israelites would not have been able to plant crops that year. Then the battle lasted for one year into the next spring so that

---

29. The parallel account in 2 Kgs 19:29 reads *sāḥîš*, the only occurrence of that word.

they could not plant crops, but in the third year they could freely sow and harvest once again (v. 30).

The imagery then shifts from literal to figurative. God promises that *a remnant* [*pĕlêṭat*] *of the kingdom* [lit. 'house'] *of Judah* will prosper (*will take root below and bear fruit above*, v. 31). This remnant (called both a *remnant* [*šĕ'ērît*] and *a band of survivors* [*pĕlêṭâ*, 'escaped ones']) will come from Jerusalem. They are spared because of the promises God made to David (v. 32; see 2 Sam. 7) and confirmed to Isaiah (see Isa. 4:2–6).

The phrase *The zeal* [i.e. the enthusiasm towards a cause] *of the* LORD *Almighty / will accomplish this* occurs only three times in the Old Testament, each in association with God's deliverance of Israel from the Assyrians (2 Kgs 19:31; Isa. 9:7; 37:32). Here it serves to confirm this good news and to encourage Hezekiah to trust God.

33–35. Sennacherib's annals claim: 'Himself [Hezekiah] I made a prisoner in Jerusalem, his royal residence, like a bird in a cage. I surrounded him with earthworks in order to molest those who were leaving his gate' (*ANET* 288). Earthworks (mounds of earth surrounding a city) were erected to block provisions and supplies from entering the city and to hinder people from leaving it. This supports the biblical account in verse 33: *He will not enter this city / or shoot an arrow here. / He will not come before it with shield / or build* [lit. 'to pour out'] *a siege ramp* [*sōlĕlâ*, lit. 'an assault ramp', 11x] *against it.*

Sennacherib appears to have taken the first step in the process of conquering the city by building earthworks but he did not reach the next step of building siege ramps. Siege ramps were constructed of earth next to the city's walls so that a siege machine could be brought close enough to break through the walls of a city (see Ezek. 4:2 for the various stages of a siege); this was one of the final stages of a city's capture.

God then reiterates that he will send Sennacherib home *by the way that he came*, adding that Sennacherib will not even enter Jerusalem (v. 34). God will protect Jerusalem for his own sake and for David's sake. Notice he does not say for Hezekiah's sake; this promise of deliverance goes back much further, to its foundation in God's promise to David.

Some have dismissed this as a late, unhistorical story (Clements 1980a: 287–288) based upon apparent discrepancies with the account in the Assyrian annals, but there are several good reasons to question the Assyrian account: (1) historical annals do not record defeats of a king; (2) the description of Sennacherib's so-called victory over Jerusalem is rather feeble compared with how other Assyrian kings describe their victories (see Roberts 2015: 472); (3) Hezekiah remained on the throne even after inciting a rebellion against the Assyrians, which was not usual Assyrian protocol; (4) Sennacherib's annals never say that Jerusalem was captured – only that he made Hezekiah a prisoner in Jerusalem (*ANET* 288); and (5) reliefs showing the capture of Lachish, a city of secondary importance, and not Jerusalem, the capital city, adorn the walls of Sennacherib's palace in Nineveh.

36–38. These verses narrate the details of Sennacherib's rout and the destruction of his army. The angel of the LORD put to death 185,000 soldiers from the Assyrian camp while they slept (v. 36). The phrase 'and it came about in that night', which suggests suddenness, is recorded in 2 Kings 19:35. The unexpectedness of this mass slaughter is characterized by the phrase (lit.) 'behold, all of them were dead bodies'.

The text here is not explicit as to how the angel of the LORD destroyed the Assyrian army, but there is other evidence: (1) In Herodotus's description of Sennacherib's defeat in Egypt, field mice nibbled his armies' quivers, bowstrings and shield handles during the night (*Hist.* 2.141). The next day the army fled. While there are clearly difficulties with his account (e.g. there is no evidence that Sennacherib ever went into Egypt), this record may be an embellished account of Sennacherib's defeat at Jerusalem (Montgomery and Gehman 1951: 497–498). (2) Isaiah 10:16 refers to a *wasting disease* (*rāzôn*, 3x; see Ps. 106:15) among Assyria's stout warriors (see esp. Roberts 2015: 471–474) and a fire burning up its glory (i.e. could refer to a high fever). (3) Isaiah 10:18 likens the destruction to *when one who is ill wastes away*. This evidence suggests something like a plague, possibly bubonic plague, which is transmitted by infected fleas carried by rodents. Without treatment the plague is fatal in about 30–90 per cent of cases.[30]

---

30. Bubonic plague is often thought to be the cause of the Black Death in the fourteenth century that killed about 50 million Europeans

Sennacherib *broke camp and withdrew*, returning to Nineveh, where he remained (v. 37) until he was eventually killed by two of his sons, Adrammelek (possibly *Adramilissu*) and Sharezer (possibly *[Nabu]-shar-uṣur*), while worshipping in the temple of *Nisrok* (possibly Ninurta) about twenty years later in 681 BC (see the Babylonian Chronicle 3.34–38; *ANET* 309). In the end his god was helpless to protect him. Sennacherib's two sons fled to *Ararat* (Urartu), and Esarhaddon (Akk. *Aššur-aḫ-iddina*, 'the [god] Aššur has given a brother') became king.

Meaning

This section describes the events surrounding 701 BC when God stepped in to protect his precious children. The focus of the passage is on one pagan ruler's excessive pride versus the one true God who is sovereign over the world. God's reputation and his promise to David (2 Sam. 7) were in jeopardy. His response to the Assyrian challenge was therefore severe, decimating Sennacherib's troops (see Isa. 10:19) and causing the king to retreat in disgrace to Nineveh. God not only spares Jerusalem, but Sennacherib learns that any verbal attack that seeks to diminish God's glory and sovereignty is blasphemy and will be met with severe punishment.

b. Hezekiah's sickness and recovery (38:1–22)

Context

While the narrative of chapter 37 concludes with the rout of Sennacherib and his subsequent murder, chapter 38 takes the reader back in time to Hezekiah's illness sometime before God delivered Judah from the Assyrian siege.

As noted earlier, Hezekiah's sickness and healing are chronologically among the first things to occur in chapters 36–39. The account of Hezekiah's healing is slightly more detailed in the 2 Kings passage than in the Isaiah account, whereas Hezekiah's song of thanksgiving (vv. 10–20), which is a prominent feature in

---

(note 30 *cont.*) ('Bubonic Plague', Wikipedia, <https://en.wikipedia.org/wiki/Bubonic_plague>, accessed 4 February 2020).

the Isaiah account, does not appear in 2 Kings. Not only is this song of thanksgiving plagued with rare words and readings that are difficult to interpret, but there are also chronological difficulties in the narrative itself.

It is worth noting that Hezekiah's prayer for an extension of life had an unintended consequence: Manasseh, who would prove to be Judah's most wicked king, would be born during this fifteen-year period.

Comment

1–3. This section begins with a general reference to time, *in those days*, making it difficult to determine the exact chronology of these events. Miracle- or sign-stories are sometimes linked together even though they are not strictly in chronological order (see Elisha stories in 2 Kgs 2:19–25; 4:1–44).

We are told that *Hezekiah became ill* [*ḥālâ*, 'to be sick, weak'] *and was at the point of death* (lit. 'Hezekiah was sick enough to die' [infinitive construct of degree; Williams §275]), which is an interesting contrast with Hezekiah's name, 'Yahweh has strengthened me'. Isaiah told him to put his *house in order* (lit. 'command to your house', v. 1) and prepare to die. God graciously provides Hezekiah time to choose a successor, since he had no son at the time.

Hezekiah turned his face to the wall and prayed to the LORD (v. 2). The phrase 'turning his face to the wall' implies the desire to be alone with God and tune out other distractions. Hezekiah reminds God of his devotion up until this moment: *Remember* [lit. 'I beseech you,'[31] remember, I pray'], LORD, *how I have walked before you faithfully* [lit. 'in truth'] *and with wholehearted devotion* [lit. 'with an undivided heart'] *and have done what is good in your eyes* [lit. 'the good in your eyes I have done', emphatic order, v. 3]. Hezekiah stresses his piety in this verse, reminding God of his faithful and wholehearted devotion. His prayer contains no mark of penitence in the face of death. God's honour appears to be at stake: how could a righteous and loving God not listen to such a godly servant of his?

---

31. This verse begins with *'ānnâ*, which often precedes a fervent request (see Neh. 1:5).

The intensity of his request is underscored by the words *'annâ* ('I beseech you') and *nā'*, 'I pray', both particles of entreaty (v. 3a), and by his copious tears. The action of 'weeping bitterly' is emphasized with (1) the addition of an extra Hebrew noun 'weeping' (lit. 'he wept weeping' = NIV he *wept bitterly*); and (2) the addition of *gādôl*, 'great' (i.e. 'with great weeping').

4–6. God's response demonstrates that he listens to the prayers of a righteous person and, according to 2 Kings 20:4, he answers quickly: 'Before Isaiah had left the middle court'[32] of the palace, God gave him a message to deliver to the king. The title *the LORD* [Yahweh], *the God of your father David* underscores that God is keeping his promises to Hezekiah's forefather, David.

In God's response we can see the personal attention he gives to Hezekiah's request: *I have heard your prayer and seen your tears; I will add fifteen years to your life*. God's heart was moved by Hezekiah's grief, prompting him to respond with two assurances: (1) he will give Hezekiah fifteen more years of life and by implication heal him, something that is explicitly stated in 2 Kings 20:5; and (2) he will deliver Jerusalem from the Assyrians (vv. 5–6).

The inverted syntax at the beginning of verse 6 is emphatic: *And I will deliver you and this city from the hand* [lit. 'palm'] *of the king of Assyria*. For additional emphasis, God repeats the assurance: *I will defend* [*gānan*, 8x; four are in this context – see 37:35] *this city* (v. 6), which indicates that God had not yet delivered Jerusalem.

7–8. At this point the parallel passages depart from each other. In 2 Kings 20:7 Isaiah instructs the servants to 'Prepare a poultice of figs' (which will be discussed at Isa. 38:21), but the Isaianic account describes the sign and then proceeds to Hezekiah's song of praise to God for his healing (38:9–20). The obvious difficulty in the Isaiah narrative is that Hezekiah requests the sign (v. 22) after Isaiah has already declared what it will be (vv. 7–8), suggesting that

---

32. 'Middle court' reflects the *qērê* reading, whereas 'city' follows the *kĕthîb* reading. We favour the *qērê* reading because the rare word *tîkōnâ* suggests 'middle' not 'midst', and the context implies that the response came quickly.

Hezekiah's song was inserted into the narrative (see the *Context* section of 38:1–22 for further discussion of the chronology).

Verse 7 clearly states that the sign's purpose is to confirm that God will do what he has promised: to extend Hezekiah's life and protect Jerusalem. The sign itself involved the miraculous movement of a shadow on Ahaz's stairway in a direction opposite to the normal movement of the sun. Clements suggests that a solar eclipse caused this unusual sign on 11 January 689 BC (1980a: 291); however, this eclipse would be too late, and it is difficult to see how it could have caused the shadow to return up the steps.

The parallel passage in 2 Kings 20:10 includes the detail that Hezekiah is given the choice as to which direction the shadow should move. As with a sundial, the sign of the shadow moving down the steps has to do with the normal passage of time (i.e. similar to the shadow on a sundial).[33] But it would go against the laws of nature for the shadow to return up the stairs: '*It is a simple matter for the shadow to go forward ten steps . . . Rather, have it go back ten steps.*' The implication is that God will add time onto the day by having the shadow move back up the ten steps it had already descended. Thus, the sign corresponds to what God will do for Hezekiah, lengthening his life just as he lengthens the day on which the sign is given.

9–11. This song of thanksgiving to God is identified as *a writing of Hezekiah* [i.e. a *lāmed* of agent or authorship; Williams §280] *king of Judah after his illness and recovery* (v. 9). The opening words of verse 10, *I said* (lit. emphatic 'I myself said'), probably mean 'I said to myself' or 'I thought'. Hezekiah laments the knowledge that he is about to die, feeling that his life is being taken prematurely or stolen from him (i.e. *robbed* [a rare use of the root *pāqad*] *of the rest of my years*; lit. 'in the middle [*dĕmî*, occurs only here] of his life'). The word *dĕmî* may be related to *dāmâ*, 'likeness', suggesting that one part of life is 'like' the other (i.e. the midway point in a person's

---

33. For an example of an Egyptian sundial, see 'History of Timekeeping Devices in Egypt', Wikipedia, <https://en.wikipedia.org/wiki/History_of _timekeeping_devices_in_Egypt>, accessed 4 February 2020.

life). This is a poetic expression for dying far too early in life rather than a specific reference to the exact time of his death.

Hezekiah pictures the changes that death will bring: (1) leaving the present world to be shut behind the *gates of death* (Sheol); (2) forfeiting any aspirations he had for the rest of his life (*be robbed of the rest of my years*); (3) seeing the Lord from the vantage point of Sheol, not earth; and (4) being cut off from interaction with those who continue to live on earth (*no longer will I look on my fellow man*). Death is pictured as being imprisoned behind the *gates of* Sheol; for similar phrases see 'gates of death [*māwet*]' (Job 38:17), 'deep in the realm of the dead' (Jon. 2:2) and 'gates of Hades' (Matt. 16:18).

He thinks (lit. *I said*) that his next glimpse of *the Lord himself* (lit. *Yāh*, shortened form of Yahweh; occurs twice here) will not be *in the land of the living* (v. 11); by implication, Sheol is a place of the dead where one is taken out of the stream of daily life on earth. The two phrases *I will not again see the Lord* (i.e. Yah) and [the Lord (i.e. Yah)] *in the land of the living* are arranged in stair-step parallelism, with the second phrase modifying the first (Watson 1994: 150–156). This does not mean that the Lord is not in Sheol, but that Hezekiah will not see the Lord again in the land of the living (i.e. he is about to die).

Similarly, the phrase *no longer will I look on my fellow man* is not saying he will not see his fellow human beings in Sheol, but that he will no longer live with them in the present world. The last word in verse 11, *ḥādel* (lit. 'ceasing'), is an example of metathesis (i.e. two letters that have been reversed due to a copyist error) and should read *ḥāled* (*world*).

12–14. Hezekiah continues his lament: *my house* [*dôrî*, lit. 'my dwelling place', occurs only here] *has been pulled down and taken* [lit. 'exiled'] *from me* (v. 12). He pictures the shortness of his life in the following images: (1) like a *shepherd's tent* that is never long in one place as it is moved along with the herd (v. 12); and (2) like when a *weaver* removes the work from the loom at the end of the day (*qippadtî, I have rolled up* [occurs only here] *my life*) and cuts it *off from the loom* (*dallâ*, lit. 'threads hanging from a weaving', 2x; see Song 7:6, lit. 'the hair of your head').

The verb *šālam* (*end*) in the phrase *day and night* [lit. 'from day unto night'] *you made an end of me* (v. 12) has a wide range of meanings, but in this context means 'to finish' (see 1 Kgs 9:25).

The first phrase of verse 13, *I waited patiently* [*šāwâ*] *till dawn*, is difficult to translate; nowhere else does *šāwâ* have the meaning 'wait patiently' as the NIV has translated it. A better translation is 'I settled myself down', like Psalm 131:2 'I have calmed and quietened myself'. Regardless, the end of the next verse makes it clear that Hezekiah longs for God to take away his agony and come to his aid (lit. 'become a pledge for me', v. 14; see Gen. 44:32), meaning to be his protection as God has claimed he will be (v. 5).

Knowing that death is imminent, Hezekiah expresses his sorrow in several images: (1) just as *a lion* breaks all of its victim's bones before killing him, so God has broken his bones (i.e. not literally, but figuratively 'broken his health', v. 13); and (2) he likens his cries/moans (*'ăspṣēp*, 'I cried', 4x, all in the book of Isaiah; see 29:4) to the shrill or plaintive cries of a *swift* (*sûs*), a *thrush* (*'āgûr*) (both terms occur 2x; see Jer. 8:7) and a *mourning dove* (*yônâ*, v. 14).

The next phrase is also difficult: *My eyes grew weak* [*dālal*, 'to become tiny'; this is the only place where this verb refers to eyes] *as I looked to the heavens* (lit. 'to [the] heights'). Hezekiah appears to be calling out to God in his weakened state.

15–17. Hezekiah realizes that God has ordained this sickness and he has no say in the matter: *But what can I say? . . .* [God] *himself has done this* (v. 15). Many emendations have been suggested for the next phrase, *I will walk humbly all my years*. The form of the word *walk* in the MT could mean 'to walk slowly or in procession' (occurring only here and in Ps. 42:4, 'how I used to go [along in procession] to the house of God'), or it could be an exhortation of the more common verb 'to wander about' (i.e. 'I wander about' *all my years*). Both possibilities offer a reasonable translation. In any case, the final phrase of verse 15 suggests that the anguish he has endured (i.e. *because of this anguish* [lit. 'bitterness'] *of my soul*) has humbled his soul.

Verse 16, while also difficult to translate, explains that trials like Hezekiah's cause people to turn to God and be restored (*ḥālam*, 2x with this meaning; see Job 39:4): *by such things* [lit. 'on account of these (things)'] *people live; / and my spirit finds life in them too* (v. 16). This is why Hezekiah can say, *Surely* [*hinnēh*] *it was for my benefit* [*lĕšālôm*, 'for my peace'] / *that I suffered such anguish* [lit. 'bitterness', v. 17]. Because of God's *love* (*ḥāšaq*, commonly used of God's love for Israel; see Deut. 7:7), he was delivered from the *pit of destruction* (*bĕlî*, 'wearing out') and his sins were forgiven: *you have put* [lit. 'cast'] *all my sins / behind your back* [*gēw*, 6x]. This figurative expression means that God no longer holds Hezekiah's sins against him.

18–20. Hezekiah appeals to God that those who die cannot praise him (lit. 'not Sheol thank you'; inverted syntax for emphasis), because at that point it is too late to hope for God's deliverance from sickness or death: *those who go down to the pit / cannot hope* [*śābar*, 10x; 5x in the book of Psalms] *for your faithfulness* (v. 18).

To Hezekiah Sheol is equivalent to the grave, a place where departed spirits reside who can no longer enjoy and praise God for his blessings as they did when they were alive. Hezekiah thus pleads for a longer life: *The living,* [indeed] *the living – they praise you, / as I am doing today* (v. 19).

Hezekiah also points out the need for parents to pass on to the next generation knowledge *about your* [God's] *faithfulness* (lit. 'fathers declare to sons concerning your faithfulness', v. 19), even though he himself was not successful in passing this message on to his son Manasseh. Moses also appealed to God's desire to maintain his reputation (Exod. 32:11–14). God does care what people think of him and will not give anyone reason to question his righteousness and his faithfulness; thus, people have no excuse not to trust him.

Hezekiah's affirmation in verse 20 that *The* LORD *will save* [lit. 'is ready to save'] *me* shows his renewed confidence in God. He promises to join others *in the temple* (lit. 'house of the LORD') to sing and make music *with stringed instruments* (lit. 'we will play my music for stringed instruments on stringed instruments') all the remaining days of his life. The verb *nāgan* ('to play on stringed instruments') is related to the noun *nĕgînâ* ('music played on stringed instruments', v. 20).

21–22. Verses 21–22 revert to an earlier point before Hezekiah is healed. Their placement after Hezekiah's song of praise in response to having been healed is therefore awkward (see the parallel narrative in 2 Kings 20 for a more consistent chronology of events). One way translators have attempted to smooth this apparent discrepancy, although the end result is still unsatisfactory, is to read the verbs in the past perfect tense, as though recalling something previously left out of the narrative: 'Isaiah *had said* . . .' and 'Hezekiah *had asked* . . .' (NIV, NASB, NRSV, etc.).

Instead, we argue that the sequence of the sign immediately after the two promises in 2 Kings 20 (i.e. Hezekiah's healing and Jerusalem will be spared, v. 6) suggests that the sign is given to confirm both promises and may reflect a condensed recounting of the events. The account in Isaiah suggests that the two are separate events and that the sign he asks for responds to *that I will go up to the temple of the LORD* (38:22), something specifically mentioned at the end of Hezekiah's song of praise (*we will sing . . . all the days of our lives / in the temple of the LORD*, v. 20).

Smith points out that Hezekiah's skin disease would have made him unclean (Lev. 13:18–23) and therefore restricted him from entering the temple (2007: 652), thus the importance of the sign. Seitz has recognized that chapters 37 and 38 have a similar structure, with the sign following a prayer and a prophetic response (i.e. 37:30–32; 38:20–21) (1991: 166–169). It is more likely that Isaiah 36 – 39 contains a palistrophe with Hezekiah's song of praise in the middle (see Figure 38.1).

Assyrian threat (36 – 37)	Hezekiah's healing and sign (38:1–8)	Hezekiah's praise (38:9–20)	Hezekiah's healing and sign (38:21–22)	Babylonian threat (39)

Figure 38.1 Structure of Isaiah 36 – 39

Isaiah delivers the instruction to *Prepare a poultice* [*dĕbēlâ*, 'lump of pressed figs', occurs only here] *of figs and apply* [*māraḥ*, occurs only here] *it to the boil* (*šĕḥîn*, 'ulcer, inflamed spot'). Figs are known to have therapeutic value; such a poultice would have drawn out the pus and relieved the inflammation.

Meaning

God was exceedingly gracious to give Hezekiah a warning to set his house in order before he died, since he apparently had no son at the time who could succeed to the throne. When Hezekiah pleads with God to remember his devotion and faithful service, God extends Hezekiah's life, allowing him to live through one of the most difficult periods in Israel's history. Hezekiah would be able to look back at his miraculous healing and be encouraged to have faith during the even more terrifying Assyrian assault in 701 BC when many people's lives hung in the balance. However, Hezekiah's request for a longer life also made possible the birth of Manasseh, the most wicked king in all of Judah's history. Granting Hezekiah's request was thus a double-edged sword.

c. The envoys from Babylon (39:1–8)

Context

This chapter (see also 2 Kgs 20:12–19), the final section of the Isaianic Narratives (Isa. 36 – 39), is placed out of chronological order, as indicated by verse 1 which links Hezekiah's illness and recovery to a visit from envoys of the king of Babylon, Marduk-Baladan (Marduk-apal-iddina II, lit. 'Marduk has given me an heir'). This visit would have taken place sometime before 703–702 BC, his final regnal year, which conceivably led up to the events of the Assyrian siege of 701 BC. The account serves as a background for the return from the Babylonian exile (Isa. 40 – 48), linking the two sections together.

We know that Marduk-Baladan's visit in chapter 39 took place before the siege, for two reasons: (1) Hezekiah shows him all his great wealth. However, around 701 BC Hezekiah would be forced to pay Sennacherib a tribute so large that it would remove the silver from the temple and treasuries and the gold from the temple doors (2 Kgs 18:14–15). (2) Historically, Marduk-Baladan had already stirred up rebellion in Babylon and reclaimed the throne in 703–702 BC so he needed allies to fight against Assyria. No doubt his aim in sending emissaries to visit Hezekiah was to establish an alliance to fight against Assyrian dominance. As a result, Hezekiah withheld tribute from Sennacherib, precipitating the siege of 701 BC.

Isaiah's rebuke for showing the Babylonians Israel's great wealth should have been sufficient to keep Hezekiah from joining forces with Babylon against Assyria. Since that did not happen, Hezekiah and the nation were warned that someday Babylon would turn on Israel and take them captive. Isaiah 40 then describes the return from Babylonian captivity in 539 BC, about 150 years later. Chapters 39–40 would thus take on significantly more meaning to future generations who, having been exiled to Babylon, would see the fulfilment of these prophecies as a demonstration of the power and sovereignty of God.

Comment

1–2. The timing of this important visit by the emissaries of the king of Babylon is not entirely clear (i.e. *at that time*).[34] Upon hearing of Hezekiah's illness and subsequent recovery, *Marduk-Baladan son of Baladan king of Babylon sent* him *letters and a gift* (v. 1).

Marduk-Baladan was king of Babylon from about 722 to 710 BC and then for nine months in 703–702 BC. It was sometime during these nine months that he sought an ally to resist Assyria's expansion. He would have been very interested to hear of a God who displayed great power in giving Hezekiah a sign and healing him from so grave an illness (see 2 Chr. 32:31). Forming an anti-Assyrian alliance with Hezekiah, who had the help of this powerful God, would be very useful.

Upon their arrival in Jerusalem, *Hezekiah received the envoys gladly* (lit. 'rejoiced concerning them') and showed them his house of treasures (*bêt někōtōh*, occurs only here and in the parallel passage, 2 Kgs 20:13). The narrative gives special attention to the fact that Hezekiah showed the Babylonian envoys everything, from silver, gold, spices and precious oils (lit. 'the good oil') to the *entire armoury* (lit. 'house of vessels'; see 22:8) and his treasuries: *There was nothing in his palace or in all his kingdom that Hezekiah did not show them* (v. 2; see the parallel account in 2 Chr. 32:24–31). The obvious implication is that Hezekiah was proud of his kingdom and wished to impress the envoys; perhaps he desired that Marduk-Baladan might know just how valuable an ally Judah could be.

3–4. Isaiah comes to Hezekiah with a message from God. He poses a series of questions to draw out from Hezekiah's own lips

---

34. The adjective *hahî* ('that', used 197 times in the Pentateuch and here) displays elements of both the masculine and feminine forms, possibly indicating the uncertainty of the gender of the word it modifies.

information that will incriminate him (e.g. *What did those men say, and where did they come from?*). Hezekiah evades the first question, simply responding that they came from Babylon. From his response to the question *What did they see in your palace?* we see Hezekiah's pride (see 2 Chr. 32:25, 31) and injudicious decision to impress a distant foreign ruler with the extent of his wealth. He confesses to having shown the entire collection of his treasures (*There is nothing among my treasures that I did not show them*, stated again to underscore that Hezekiah showed them everything).

5–7. Isaiah then declares to Hezekiah a message from *the LORD Almighty* (lit. 'hosts'; v. 5). He first gains Hezekiah's full attention, 'behold' (*hinnēh*), then tells him that a day will come (lit. 'days are coming') when Babylon will carry off Judah's treasure and its people. The name *Babylon* is placed at the very end of the phrase for emphasis. Then there is a description of how thoroughly Babylon will pillage Judah's wealth: (1) *everything in your palace* (lit. 'your house'); (2) *all that your predecessors* [lit. 'your fathers'] *have stored up* [*ʾāṣar*, 5x] *until this day*; and (3) *nothing will be left* (lit. 'not a thing will remain', v. 6).

The consequences then become even more personal. Hezekiah's own descendants (stated three different ways for emphasis) will be affected: *some of your* [pl.] *descendants* [lit. 'sons'], *your own flesh and blood* [lit. 'that which comes forth from you'] *who will be born to you*, will be exiled to Babylon and made eunuchs (i.e. high officials) in the king's palace. It is evident that Hezekiah never anticipated the devastating consequences of his pride. The prophecy would be fulfilled over time by several invasions (605, 598 and 586 BC; see 2 Kgs 24:10–17). Daniel and his friends would be part of this prophecy's fulfilment when they were carried into exile and trained to serve in the Babylonian kingdom (Dan. 1:1–6).

8. Upon hearing the prophecy, Hezekiah responds, *The word of the LORD you have spoken is good* (lit. 'good is the word of the LORD which you have spoken'; emphasis on the word 'good'). His reasoning is that *There will be peace and security in my lifetime.* This response might lead one to conclude that Hezekiah is callous and self-serving, seemingly unaffected by the judgment he has brought down upon the nation; his only emotion appears to be relief that it will not happen during his lifetime. However, there is another way to view his assessment that the prophecy Isaiah has given is *good*.

The word *good* (*ṭôb*) means 'suitable' or 'fitting'. In this case Hezekiah reasons that, because he has been faithful and wholehearted in his devotion to God (i.e. 38:3), it is only fair and just that the nation not be punished and sent into captivity during his time as king. The last phrase in 2 Kings 20:19 lends support to this interpretation: 'Will there not be peace and security in my lifetime?' (lit. 'Should there not be peace and truth in my days?').

Chapter 39 serves as a useful bridge to chapters 40–48. There is little mention of Babylon in the first part of Isaiah, which focuses on Assyria, their main enemy at the time. The narrative of chapter 39 thus prepares for the events of Isaiah 40 – 48 and Israel's return from Babylonian captivity about 150 years in the future.

Meaning

The events of chapter 39 are among the earliest chronologically in the Isaianic Narratives (Isa. 36 – 39) and set the stage for the rest. It is likely that the envoys sent by Marduk-Baladan were there to encourage an alliance with the Babylonians against Assyria. Hezekiah seeks to impress them with his great wealth and weaponry.

Isaiah points out what a mistake it was for Hezekiah to act in pride instead of seeking Yahweh's counsel before showing the Babylonian envoys all that was in his palace (see similar sin in Josh. 9). How true is the statement that 'Pride goes before destruction' (Prov. 16:18).

2. COMFORT (40:1 – 66:24)

There is unanimous agreement that the second part of the book of Isaiah, chapters 40–66, addresses an entirely different set of historical and interpretational issues from those of the first thirty-nine chapters. Instead of emphasizing punishment of the wicked that would lead to the Babylonian exile, there is a clear message of encouragement to a righteous remnant who would return from exile around 539 BC, almost 150 years after Isaiah. For further discussion on the unity, date and authorship of the book, see the Introduction.

A. The promise of deliverance (40:1 – 48:22)

Chapters 40–48 emphasize that God is sovereign over all peoples in that he can use even Cyrus, the pagan king of Persia, to deliver his people from the Babylonian exile. The Assyrians and Babylonians sought to assimilate conquered peoples by resettling them within their empire so that over time they would eventually adopt the local way of life and religion. Cyrus, on the other hand, sought to unify his empire by reversing these policies. He also sought to appease and curry favour with as many deities as possible by permitting exiles to return to their homelands and rebuild their places of worship.

Isaiah 40 – 48 begins with a message of comfort for God's people who will be able to return home, then ends with a seam that reiterates the major themes of the book: (1) Israel has been judged (48:17–19); (2) Israel will be delivered (48:20–21); and (3) the wicked will be punished (48:22). Restoration of a remnant is no longer a major theme, since God is dealing only with believing Israel at this point. Punishment for the wicked is stressed with the refrain, *'There is no peace,' says the LORD, 'for the wicked'* (48:22). This restoration, therefore, is only for the believing remnant. The section contains nine units, one of which is the first Servant Song (42:1–7; see Figure 0.10 on p. 26).

i. A message of comfort to the exiles (40:1–31)
The captives would be in Babylon for at least forty-seven years (for some it was even longer) before being allowed to return to Jerusalem. However, only about fifty thousand of the Israelites would return in 538 BC (see Kaiser and Wegner 2016: 571–587). Some would stay in Babylon, unwilling to sacrifice all they had acquired during the decades of exile to return to Israel and start over. Since the primary reason for returning to Jerusalem was to rebuild the temple, those who chose to leave Babylon were a God-fearing, righteous remnant who cared more about God and his temple than about their own welfare.

Chapter 40 begins the second half of the book of Isaiah by encouraging the Israelites that God still has a plan for them. In fact, their captivity is about to end, and they will be allowed to return home. Because the hope of deliverance had grown dim for many, the prophet reassures them of two realities: (1) God still loves them and is willing to deliver them; and (2) this same God, who created the world and reigns over all creation, is able to deliver them from captivity.

This chapter comprises two units: one that portrays a day when God will bring his righteous remnant back to Jerusalem (vv. 1–11); and a second that centres around three disputation oracles (vv. 12–20, 21–26 and 27–31) that affirm the greatness of Israel's God

and are meant to provide convincing evidence to the Israelites that
he will indeed bring them back to the land.

a. The announcement of God's return with his remnant (40:1–11)

Context

This section is to encourage the exiles that their captivity is nearly
over, and that their God will display both his power as a great
warrior and his gentleness as a shepherd to bring them home. They
need not doubt this deliverance for *the word of our God endures for ever*
(v. 8): once he has declared it, it will happen.

Comment

1–2. Finally, after all the stern warnings of punishment in
chapters 1–39, God gives a message of comfort: *Comfort, comfort*
[repeated for emphasis] *my people*. The narrator uses the plural form
of the verb *comfort* in addressing God's messengers who will carry
out his commands. At first glance it appears that God is speaking
here, but the phrase *says your God* implies an unnamed spokesperson.

The vocabulary of these verses stresses God's loving attitude
towards his people: he speaks *tenderly* (lit. 'unto the heart'; see
Gen. 34:3), calling them *my people* and referring to himself as *your
God*. The context gives clear indications that the people God
addresses are the remnant who have come through the
purification process: (1) *Her hard service has been completed* (lit. 'filled
up') and the exile is over. The phrase *hard service* may be better
translated 'compulsory labour' since, as Smith notes, there is little
evidence that Israel was forced to do hard labour during the
Babylonian exile (2009: 94). (2) The phrase *her sin* [lit. 'iniquity']
has been paid for means that the punishment she deserved for
rebelling against God is finished. (3) *She has received from the LORD's
hand double* [*kiplayim*, 'twofold', 3x] *for all her sins*. The image here
is of a balanced scale where the weights on both sides are equal.
In other words, Israel has suffered no more than she deserved,
nor was her guilt minimized by paying less than she deserved (i.e.
either would suggest an unjust God). The full punishment for
Israel's sins has now been satisfied.

This oracle of salvation predicts a future deliverance, but the verbs here picture the deliverance as completed action (i.e. prophetic perfects). God's messengers needed to speak persuasively, for it would be a difficult task to convince the despondent nation that God would now comfort them.

3–5. The unidentified speaker (*a voice is calling*) is one of God's messengers who acts as a herald or forerunner announcing the preparations necessary for the coming king, God; use of heralds was common in the Ancient Near East. These preparations entail clearing all obstacles (lit. 'turn back the way'), raising valleys and lowering hills (v. 4).

The way back to Israel is through the *wilderness* (*midbār*) or *desert* (*ʿărābâ*). This could be a literal reference to the waste areas between Israel and Babylon, but is more probably a figurative reference to difficulties of the journey. Usually travellers in the Ancient Near East would skirt around deserts by following rivers, but this journey is pictured as heading directly across the desert on a *highway* (*mĕsillâ*; usually raised above the surrounding land) expressly built for this purpose.

The announcement suggests the LORD's coming cannot be far behind. The two phrases *the rough ground* [*ʿāqōb*, only occurrence with this meaning] *shall become level,* / *the rugged places* [*rekāsîm*, occurs only here] *a plain* convey that nothing can stop God's arrival. His glory will be revealed to all (lit. 'all flesh will see it together') when the nations see that Yahweh has delivered the remnant. His coming is guaranteed by the LORD himself (*the mouth of the LORD has spoken*).

Whybray and others believe that verses 3–8 represent Second Isaiah's call and commission (1975: 48). However, these verses differ significantly from other call narratives (see Oswalt 1998: 48; Childs 2001: 295–297).

6–8. The identity of the speaker is vague at the beginning of verse 6; a voice is heard to say *Cry out*. This could be the voice of the messenger who called out in verses 3–5, or the singular imperative *Cry out* may indicate that the prophet is to proclaim God's message. The next phrase reads *and I said* (lit. 'and he said', v. 6b) in the NIV, which agrees with LXX and 1QIsaᵃ; however, the MT reading that refers back to the indefinite, unidentified speaker is to be preferred. The reference to *our God* in verse 8 is the best indication that the speaker is the prophet throughout these verses, or there is a change in the speaker back to the prophet.

The prophet then proclaims the message that God's word can always be trusted (it *endures* [lit. 'stands'] *for ever*), unlike humans, who are as transient and perishable as *grass* and *flowers of the field*, especially when the breath of the all-powerful LORD *blows* upon them (i.e. testing them). This is an important message for the exiles. The impressive Babylonian Empire is about to fade away, as human powers do, but God's message of deliverance will come true; he can always be trusted.

9–11. The NIV translates the first phrase of verse 9 as *You who bring good news to Zion*, but the Hebrew text suggests that Zion is the bearer of good news. Like a military herald who announces (lit. 'raise up your voice with strength') the good news of victory, Zion proclaims, *Here is your God!* (lit. 'behold your God') to the cities of Judah.

With the interjection *See* (*ḥinnēh*) to gain his audience's attention, the prophet then declares the vision of the arrival of the *Sovereign LORD* in Jerusalem, bringing his remnant, called his *reward* (*śĕdārô*, 'reward, hire, wages') and *recompense* (*pĕ'ullātâ*, 'recompense, work'). Here he reigns *with power*, having won a great victory (i.e. both *reward* and *recompense* refer to the spoils of war) by bringing his remnant home from enemy territory. Yahweh is pictured as both a great warrior who rules with *a mighty arm* (metonymy for his power, v. 10) and a gentle shepherd leading his flock back to the fold (v. 11), carrying the lambs in his arms *close to his heart* (the NIV conveys the proper nuance) – a wonderful image of God's gentle care for his people.

Meaning

In a major shift from judgment to restoration, God now turns his attention to bringing his children back to Jerusalem. Pictured as both a mighty warrior and a loving shepherd, he will prove that he keeps his promise to deliver the righteous remnant of Israel.

b. God is able and willing to restore his chosen nation and bring them home (40:12–31)

Context

Three disputation oracles (vv. 12–17, 18–26 and 27–31) in this section exhibit the greatness of Israel's God and are meant to provide convincing evidence to the Israelites that he will indeed bring them back to the land. A disputation oracle is a form of argumentation that begins on ground common to both sides, then proceeds to prove a disputed point by means of rhetorical questions. The author builds his case here with a series of rhetorical questions (vv. 12, 13, 14, 18, 21, 25, 27, 28), addressing two primary questions: (1) 'Is God able to deliver us?' (vv. 12–26); and (2) 'Is God willing to deliver us?' (vv. 27–31).

Comment

(1) The greatness of God (40:12–17) (first disputation oracle)

12. The prophet begins by laying the common ground between himself and his contemporaries. First, his rhetorical questions establish agreement that God is the creator of the universe: *Who has measured the waters . . . marked off the heavens . . . held the dust of the earth . . . weighed the mountains . . . ?* The obvious answer is 'only God', the one who created the universe. That which is vast from a human perspective is easily measured and manipulated in the hands of God.

Like an artisan fashioning a tiny universe on a workbench, God measures the oceans *in the hollow* [šōʻal, 'palm', 3x] *of his hand* and the heavens with *the breadth of his hand* (lit. 'span', equal to the length between the tips of the thumb and little finger, or half a cubit [about 23 cm]), and carries the *dust of the earth in a basket* (šāliš, 'a third', equal to a third of an ephah [about 12 litres]). He can even weigh the vast mountains on scales (*peles*, 2x; see scales pictured in *ANEP* 639).

13–14. Verse 13 shifts from God's omnipotence to his limitless wisdom (*Who can fathom* [tāḵēn, 'to estimate, determine'] *the Spirit of the LORD* [i.e. his thought processes]). God needs no *counsellor*; not only is he the architect of the world, but he is the ultimate origin of all knowledge, wisdom and justice.

In the creation myth known as the *Enuma Elish* (*ANET* 60–72), Marduk the creator-god could not create the world on his own but needed his father Ea's help. Yahweh, however, did not consult with anyone, nor did anyone teach him wisdom (*bîn*, 'discernment', and *těbûnōt* [pl.], 'understandings') or righteousness (lit. 'the way of justice'). We can only marvel at this great God.

15–17. *Surely* (*bēn* = emphatic) even the combined power and resources of the nations of the earth are as nothing in comparison with God. They are merely *a drop* [*mar*, occurs only here] *in a bucket* [*dělî*, 2x] or like *dust* [*šahaq*; only occurrence with this meaning] *on the scales.* Even the earth's innumerable islands are as insignificant as *fine dust* (*daq*, similar in sound and meaning to the previous word for 'dust') in comparison with God.

Verse 16 turns our gaze to his infinite worthiness: even the vast cedar forests of Lebanon with all their animals cannot provide a sacrifice suitable (lit. 'there is not enough') for him. Compared with God, the mighty nations on this earth are as nothing; they are *worthless* [*'epes*, 'nothing'] / *and less than nothing* [*tōhû*, 'empty']. The implication is that if creation is merely a tiny product of Yahweh's hands, then God can surely rule over the Babylonians and bring about this great deliverance.

(2) God has no rivals (40:18–26) (second disputation oracle)

18–20. The next question addresses the assumption that Yahweh is merely one of a number of gods: *With whom, then, will you compare God?* [*'ēl* = common Semitic name for God]. Polytheism, the norm for the nations surrounding Israel, had lured away many Israelites over the years. The prophet once again begins his argument by laying out common ground: this time it is Israelite tradition, namely that God is greater than any idol (see Ps. 97:9).

The prophet ridicules the idea of placing one's trust in anyone other than Yahweh. Every other so-called god is merely an *image* (*děmût*) or *idol* (*pesel*), an inanimate statue, crafted (lit. 'engraved') by a person at every stage. First the base is cast (lit. 'poured out'), usually of bronze; then it is overlaid with gold or silver (see 41:7), and silver chains are fashioned (lit. 'smelt') to adorn it. The more ornate the idol, the greater was its supposed potency.

If a person could not afford (*mĕsukkān*, 'one who is too poor'; occurs only here) gold or silver, a *skilled* (lit. 'wise') artisan (lit. 'engraver') could be hired to carve an idol of wood (v. 20; this verse contains several difficult issues [see Williamson 1986: 1–20], but the overall meaning is clear).

In that case, the person would first find a solid piece of wood that would not rot (*rāqab*, 2x), and hire a wood carver to fashion it into a stable statue that would not *topple* (lit. 'totter'). What could be worse than a god that easily fell over and was unable to get up off the ground? The clear irony reinforces the absurdity of comparing such an object with the living God.

21–24. There is a reproachful tone in the rhetorical questions of verse 21: *Do you not know? / Have you not heard?* (lit. 'Surely you know, don't you? Surely you have heard, haven't you?'). The author wonders how they could fail to know that Yahweh sovereignly rules over the earth (vv. 21–26), since this is a truth that has been declared *from the beginning* [lit. 'from the head'] . . . *since the earth was founded* [lit. 'foundations (*môsādâ*, 6x) of the earth'], meaning 'from the beginning of time'.

The prophet goes on to proclaim the traditions he alluded to in verse 21. Creation openly displays God's glory (see Ps. 19) as he sits *enthroned above the circle of the earth* (v. 22). Here the word *circle* (*ḥûg*, 'vault, horizon') refers to the firmament (Gen. 1:6) or the horizon that appears to encircle the earth.

To Yahweh, who has stretched out the heavens like a curtain (*dōq*, occurs only here) or *spreads* [*mātaḥ*, occurs only here] *them out like a tent*, the inhabitants of the earth look *like grasshoppers* (*ḥăgābîm*, 'a type of locust'). Their insignificance is in stark contrast to the greatness and majesty of God. His sovereignty extends over all the governments of this world. He establishes rulers (lit. 'dignitaries' and 'judges'), then reduces them to nothing (*'ayin*, 'nothing', and *tōhû*, 'emptiness') with merely a breath (vv. 23–24).

The fragility of their rule is pictured as seedlings beginning to sprout (*no sooner* [*'ap bal*, lit. 'never yet'] *are they planted* highlights the speed of the destruction). The young plants are extremely vulnerable: *then he blows* [*nāšap*, 2x] *on them and they wither.*

25–26. The prophet repeats the question asked in verse 18, now phrased as though Yahweh is speaking: *'To whom will you* *compare me . . .?' says the Holy One.* Holiness is part of God's essential character, something of which an unholy person is acutely aware when in his presence (see 6:3–5). The emphasis here is that God has no equals.

The people are to look to the heights (*mārôm* = 'heavens'), for God has *created* (*bārā'*, 21x in Isaiah, more than in any other OT book) the *starry host one by one* [lit. 'by number'] . . . *not one of them is missing* [lit. 'unaccounted for']. The sense here is that God created and keeps record of each and every star; by contrast, humans cannot even count the stars (see Gen. 15:5). God marshals the bodies of heaven every day like a well-disciplined army, calling them each by name to give them their marching orders. Because of his mighty power not one of them dares to miss being 'on parade'. Again, the emphasis is that if Yahweh can sustain all of heaven, he can certainly take care of his people.

Many of the gods of Babylonia were associated with the heavenly bodies;[1] this would therefore have had special significance for them. The fact that Yahweh has these heavenly bodies at his beck and call, and places the sun, moon and stars in their designated positions, shows them to be subordinate to him.

(3) God watches over his people (40:27–31) (third disputation oracle)

27–28. The prophet continues his rhetorical questions: *Why do you complain . . . ? / Why do you say . . . / 'My way is hidden from the LORD . . . '?* The parallel terms *Jacob* and *Israel* must refer to the nation of Israel as a whole, or rather to the remnant that remains, for the northern kingdom had been deported long ago.

Israel's complaint is that Yahweh is ignoring their perceived legitimate claim to covenantal protection: *My way is hidden from the LORD; / my cause* [lit. 'justice'] *is disregarded* [lit. 'passed over'] *by my God*. This complaint is easy to understand in the context of the Babylonian exile. It is not God's competence which is being questioned here, but his willingness to step in and deliver Israel.

---

1. The 'Triad of Heaven' included the supreme god An, associated with the sky; Enlil, the god associated with wind, air, earth and storms; and Enki, the god of water, knowledge, mischief, crafts and creation.

The prophet responds (v. 28) in rhetorical fashion, similar to verse 21: 'Surely you know, don't you? Surely you have heard, haven't you?' He then reminds them of the Israelite tradition that Yahweh, the creator of this universe, never grows tired (Ps. 121:3–4) and that the depths of his wisdom cannot be fathomed (lit. 'there is no searching of his understanding'). Apparently, Israel has forgotten who God is and his true nature. God is not limited in power that he should grow tired of watching over Israel, nor is he bound by time to act. God continued to care for his nation and would deliver them at the proper time.

29–31. God possesses two attributes that enable him to keep his promises: omnipotence and omniscience. Therefore, Israel merely need wait upon Yahweh, who can give them the strength to endure. Even the strongest of them (i.e. the young and vigorous) would tire and find it difficult to endure during the Babylonian exile, *but those who hope in the* LORD / *will renew their strength* (lit. 'will have their strength renewed'). God's strength is revealed through people's weaknesses (see 2 Cor. 12:9).

The word *hope* (*qāwâ*) means 'to wait with confidence and trust'. This hope would allow them to *soar on wings like eagles, run and not grow weary, walk and not be faint,* all images of tireless strength (see 58:11). Sometimes God allows us to experience circumstances beyond our control; we simply must wait until God brings about a change (see a similar message in Hab. 3).

Meaning

The prophet masterfully answers two vital questions that he anticipates the Israelites will have: Is God able to deliver them? Is God willing to deliver them? The answer to both is an emphatic 'Yes!' After more than forty years in the Babylonian exile, it would have been easy for the Israelites to give up hope, but the prophet assures them that those who wait on God will be given unparalleled strength to rise above their circumstances and trust God to bring them home.

ii. The case for God's deliverance (41:1–29)

Context

This chapter is the second section of the palistrophe (see Figure
0.10 on p. 26) and is parallel to 'The case for God's punishment' in
Isaiah 46 – 47. The chapter is typically divided as follows: (1) a trial
(vv. 1–7); (2) two salvation oracles (vv. 8–13, 14–16); (3) a communal
promise (vv. 17–20); and (4) a trial for false gods (vv. 21–29).

In the language of trial speeches, God answers the complaint
voiced in 40:27 by declaring his plan. The coastlands, even the
entire world (40:5), will stand in awe when they see how he will
deliver his special nation. Only an all-powerful God could use a
pagan king to deliver his people; who would have imagined such a
thing?

Comment

a. God will use Cyrus to bring back the Israelites (41:1–4) (first trial speech)
   1–2. The *islands* (i.e. distant shores around the Mediterranean
Sea; parallel to the word *lĕ'ummîm, nations*) are implored to listen in
silence to Israel's defence: *Let them come forward and speak* [i.e. lay out
their defence]*; / let us meet together at the place of judgment.*

The words *Be silent before me* suggest that the evidence will be so
convincing that they do not need to say a word. They will gain new
understanding of God's plan, which will empower them (lit. *renew
their strength* [*kōaḥ*, includes both physical and intellectual strength]).
The people have been gathered together to listen carefully to what
God has to say, so that they can determine if God's judgment is fair.

Verse 2 describes the lightning-swift career of Cyrus in the years
shortly before the fall of Babylon (539 BC), when God used him to
bring down many nations. God would raise up (lit. 'awaken') Cyrus
from the east, *calling him in righteousness.* God's calling of Cyrus was
a righteous and fitting decision, for Cyrus was a just and fair ruler
whom God would use to punish the Babylonians for their
exceptional cruelty towards those who rebelled against them, and
especially for their excessively harsh treatment of Israel.

Cyrus subdued kings, decimating the nations *with his sword* and
with his bow (metonymy for his whole army) until they were like *dust*

(see 2 Sam. 22:43). They would flee before him like *wind-blown* [*nādap*, 8x] *chaff*.

3–4. Cyrus proceeds to conquer new territory (lit. '[in] a path with his feet he did not go') efficiently and without harm to himself (lit. 'in peace'), as God directs his movements. The author then poses the rhetorical question *Who has done this and carried it through . . . ?* God himself answers: *I, the LORD – with the first of them / and with the last – I am he* (see 44:6). All of this has been God's plan from the beginning.

Yahweh was at the very beginning (lit. 'head') and will continue to exist even after the last human generation comes to an end (i.e. *with the first of them / and with the last*). The phrase *I am he* means he is the only eternal God; therefore, it is he alone who has planned everything (see 43:10, 13).

b. God will bring about an extraordinary deliverance (41:5–16)

5–7. The nations come from the ends of the earth to marvel at what this God has done, and yet they approach with fear. Their fear is legitimate, for they realize God could send Cyrus against them as well. The nations therefore encourage each other to work together (lit. 'one helps his friend') and to *be strong* (*ḥāzaq*).

The artisans (i.e. *the metalworker*, lit. 'engraver'; *the goldsmith*, lit. 'the smelter'; *the one who smooths with the hammer* [*paṭṭîš*, 3x]; and *the one who strikes the anvil* [*paʿam*, only occurrence with this meaning]) encourage each other as they fashion more and finer idols in order to curry favour with their gods and secure their help to repel Cyrus. When setting up the idols, they nail them down so that the idols cannot be accidently knocked over (lit. 'totter'; v. 7; see 40:18–20). The irony here is glaring: even though the nations are addressed by the true and living God, they turn instead to idols made with their own hands, idols that have no power to keep themselves from being toppled over, much less to deliver others.

8–9. In this oracle of salvation (vv. 8–20) Yahweh turns from the nations to reassure Israel that their fate is different from that of the surrounding nations. He uses several terms of endearment to communicate his care, calling them (1) *Israel, my servant*; (2) *Jacob, whom I have chosen* (i.e. their relationship to God is unique among the nations); and (3) *descendants of Abraham my friend* (lit. 'my loved one').

In the Ancient Near East a friendship between two parties was often honoured and continued by their descendants, thus Israel would receive the same preferential treatment that God had accorded Abraham, his friend.

God was confirming to the nation of Israel that he would gather (lit. 'seize') them *from the ends of the earth, / from its farthest corners* (occurs only here; i.e. the Babylon exile) and return them to their land. This assurance is reinforced with additional endearing terms: *'You are my servant'; / I have chosen you and have not rejected you.* The phrases *my servant* and *I have chosen you* are repeated in these two verses for emphasis. God had not rejected Israel even though their current circumstances had caused many to believe that he had (see 40:27).

10–12. Because Israel has been chosen by God, he tells them, *do not fear* and *do not be dismayed* (*šāta'*, 2x, both in this passage; see vv. 10, 23), a phrase characteristic of oracles of salvation). God gives the following additional personal assurances: (1) *I am with you*; they have no need to fear when the almighty God is at their side. (2) *I am your God*; they have God's individual attention. (3) *I will strengthen you and help you*; God will provide them with strength and power. (4) *I will uphold you with my righteous right hand*; he will support them.

God's *righteous right hand* speaks of his power (the right hand was thought to be the stronger), as well as his justice and equity. With God as their protector, Israel's enemies will entirely disappear from the scene (lit. 'men of strife will be as nothing; men of war against you as non-existent'). There will be no-one left to wage war against them, a picture of complete deliverance.

13–14. The reason (*kî, for*) why they need not fear their enemies is reiterated (cf. v. 10): God himself will take hold of Israel's right hand to help them. God tells them twice not to fear, for he will help them. Yet he also acknowledges the truth of their weakness and diminutive size (i.e. *you worm Jacob*), which drew the scorn of other nations (see Ps. 22:6). There has been significant discussion about the translation of the parallel phrase *little Israel* (lit. 'men [*mětê*] of Israel', v. 14): (1) Some understand *mětê* to mean 'few', similar to Genesis 34:30 where it means 'men of number', an idiomatic expression meaning 'few people'. (2) Others emend the text to *rimmâ*, 'maggot', assuming a *rēsh* has been lost; this provides a reasonable parallel phrase. Since there is little textual evidence for a change, the MT reading should probably be favoured; thus the phrase 'men of Israel' parallels 'worm of Jacob' to signify their low point.

There is an interesting change in gender for the nation of Israel from masculine in verse 13 (probably emphasizing Israel as a people group: God will uphold each one of them) to feminine in verse 14 (probably emphasizing Israel as a country: he will protect them as a country). The Holy One of Israel is her redeemer (*gōʾēl*, 'near relative', whose duty it was to help and protect another relative in desperate circumstances [see Lev. 25:47–49]). Thus, Israel has nothing to fear, for God considers himself under obligation to protect her.

15–16. The word *see* (*hinnēh*) introduces an unexpected development: Yahweh will make Israel like a new, sharp *threshing-sledge* (*môrag*, 3x), made even more dangerous because of its *many teeth* (*baʿal pîpîyôt*, 'lord of mouths'; *pîpîyôt* may be a duplication of the word for mouth), able to slice mountains into tiny particles of chaff that will be blown away by the wind, leaving nothing behind. The metaphor is clear: all obstacles, obstructions or enemies will be removed. Israel will be able to rejoice in her Lord, *the Holy One of Israel*, whose holy and just deeds have shown him to be worthy of all her praise.

Additional note: threshing-sledge

A threshing-sledge consisted of a board affixed with nails or blades that served as teeth. As it was dragged along the threshing-floor by donkeys or oxen, the straw was cut without damaging the grains of wheat. The grain and straw were then winnowed, using wind to blow away the straw and husks, leaving behind the heavier grain.

c. The homeward march of the exiles (41:17–20)

17–18. This section is reminiscent of Israel's exodus from Egypt when Yahweh supplied the nation with water on several occasions (see Exod. 15:22–25; etc.). The phrase *the poor and needy* refers to the Israelites in the Babylonian exile, longing for help. It should remind them of their ancestors who wandered in the desert, longing for water. The phrase *search for water, / but there is none* can be read either figuratively or literally. Thirst is a common metaphor for extreme anguish and/or spiritual distress (see Ps. 42:1), thus it could be a reference to spiritual suffering during the exile (see Isa. 55:1). Alternatively, it could be a literal reference to lack of water for the returnees.

Either way, God will abundantly provide for the needs of the nation, as he did for their ancestors in the wilderness: *I will make rivers flow* [lit. 'open up'] *on barren heights, / and springs within the valleys / . . . pools of water, / and . . . springs* [lit. 'goings forth of water']. Taken together, these different sources of water represent abundance.

19–20. God will also provide shade from a variety of trees – *cedar, acacia, myrtle* and others, most of which do not naturally grow in the desert. The path through the desert is oasis-like, with shade and water. Because of God's abundant provision, the eyes of the nation will be opened; Israel will *see and know* that this is from the hand of God. They will *consider* [lit. 'take it to heart'] *and understand* [lit. 'have insight'] the greatness of Yahweh who has done all of this.

d. God's final argument: he is the true God, for he predicts the future (41:21–29) (second trial speech; see 41:1–4)

21–23. These verses, which return to the trial scene portrayed in verses 1–7, help frame the oracles of deliverance in verses 8–20 (Childs 2001: 320). Yahweh delivers his final and strongest challenge to false idols, defying them to *present* [lit. 'bring near'] [their] *case* and *set forth* [their] *arguments* [*ʾăṣumôt*; occurs only here]. The prophet here refers to God as *Jacob's King* to remind the Israelites that he is fighting for them.

God then challenges the idols to talk about past events (*former things*; see 42:9; etc.) *so that we may consider them* [lit. 'let us put them to our hearts'] / *and know their final outcome* [lit. 'end']. In other words, he wants them to both identify those events in history in which the god(s) played a part, and then explain the purpose of those events and the role they play in their overall plan.

He also challenges them to *declare . . . the things to come*; only truly divine beings can control or guide history and thus predict future events. God scornfully goads them to take action – any action, whether for good or for evil (i.e. *so that we will be dismayed* [*šāta'*, 2x]) – knowing full well that they are inanimate objects with no power to perform even the slightest of movements.

Whybray notes the heavy sarcasm in this verse: 'any proof that they are really alive at all will be welcome!' (1975: 69). By contrast, Yahweh had just revealed his plan, specifically pointing out that he will send a deliverer in order to bring back the nation of Israel to their land (see 41:2–4).

24–26. The silence of the gods is telling evidence against them. The word *but* (*hēn*, 'behold') at the beginning of verse 24 heightens the conclusion God draws as he declares his verdict. Yahweh is God and the idols *are less than nothing* (lit. 'from nothing'); their works *are utterly worthless* (*'āpa'*, occurs only here; *BHS* suggests it is a copyist error for *'epes*, 'nothing', which is a possibility).

After hearing the evidence and God's verdict, anyone who chooses to seek out and worship idols *is detestable* (lit. 'an abomination has been chosen by you'). The Hebrew word 'abomination' is positioned as the first word in the final phrase for emphasis and refers to something morally repulsive; thus, it is an abomination to spurn the true God in order to put faith in worthless entities.

As the gods continue to remain silent, Yahweh then reviews his case: he had foretold that he would bring someone from the north and the east to deliver Israel. Yahweh bases his claim to divinity on his ability to predict these historical events (e.g. Cyrus), events which no-one other than their orchestrator could have known.

Several points serve as evidence that the phrases *one from the north* and *one from the rising sun* refer to Cyrus: (1) Cyrus did indeed come from the north and east. Armies from the east that travelled west followed the northern route along the River Euphrates and then came down into Israel. (2) The word *rulers* (*sĕgānîm*, v. 25) is an Akkadian loanword referring to the 'provincial governors' of Babylon (Saggs 1959: 84–87), whom Cyrus defeated. (3) Cyrus quickly and thoroughly defeated the Babylonians, which fits the image of *a potter treading the clay* (*tît*, 2x; v. 25). (4) Verse 27 indicates that Cyrus's coming was both good news for Israel and unwelcome news for Babylon.

The phrase *who calls on my name* (v. 25) is possibly a reference to
Cyrus's instructions to rebuild the temple of the LORD and
recommence worship of him (2 Chr. 36:23; Ezra 1:2–3). However,
the verse may be better translated as 'he will be called by my name'
(see 'his name will be called', 9:6), meaning he will do God's
service. Cyrus never exclusively worshipped Yahweh; as a good
pagan he feared all the gods. Isaiah 45:5 makes it clear that Cyrus
did not know (NIV reads *acknowledge*) Yahweh.

Verse 26 asks the question *Who told of this from the beginning, so that
we could know?* The three clauses that follow all begin with 'surely
there was no-one' (*'ap 'ēn*), meaning that no-one else could do this.
God alone could foretell it and then bring it about (i.e. *No one told
of this, / no one foretold* [lit. 'proclaimed'] *it*). To hold the view that
Yahweh is not foretelling these events undercuts God's claims to
be superior to the false gods.

27–29. Verse 27 provides the answer to the rhetorical questions
in verse 26: *I was the first to tell Zion, 'Look, here they are!'* (lit. 'behold,
behold them'), meaning the events God had foretold about 150
years in advance so that Israel would know who had caused them
to happen.

Verses 27 and 28 are related: the message of deliverance from
Babylon would be *good news* (v. 27b), but when God looks among
them (lit. 'even from them'; i.e. 'among the people') for a leader (lit.
'counsellor') to deliver the nation, none are fit. The NIV reads *no one
among the gods to give counsel*; however, the literal reading of the
Hebrew text is 'there is not a *man* even from among them'. This
would suggest that God is looking for a deliverer from within the
nation of Israel, not the gods. When God does not find one, he will
look to Persia and raise up a deliverer from there.

Before each of the Servant Songs (except for 49:1–9, which
begins a new section), there is a statement similar to verse 28
confirming that no-one else can do whatever God says he will do
(i.e. 41:28; 50:2; 51:18; possibly even 59:16): *I* [God] *look but there is no
one* (lit. 'no man'), so God brings his own deliverer.

In wartime a counsellor was often sought in order to provide
sound advice, but here God could find *no one to give answer* [lit. 'could
return a word'] *when I ask*[ed] *them*. At an earlier point, false
prophets had declared peace and good news for Israel (see Mic. 3:5).

Yahweh declares them all to be false; only he himself can deliver them.

Meaning

What an astounding turn of events for the Jewish people living throughout the Babylonian Empire: they will be allowed to return home. Apparently, no-one from among the Israelites could deliver them from exile. Yet who could have imagined that God would raise up the pagan king Cyrus to not only allow his people to return to their homeland, but even provide the financial means to rebuild their temple? Certainly no idol or false prophet could have foretold this, let alone accomplish it; only the true and living God could.

Excursus: the Servant Songs

Isaiah 42:1–9; 49:1–12; 50:4–11; and 52:13 – 53:12 have often been categorized as Servant Songs even though debate continues about the accuracy of labelling these as separate units. From about the 1940s, others have viewed these songs as belonging to the context of Isaiah 40 – 55 and not as separate units within those chapters (Snaith 1944–5: 79–81; Blenkinsopp 2002: 76). Some also consider them to have been written by another author (i.e. Second Isaiah [Whybray 1975: 71]; or a later author/redactor [Blenkinsopp 2002: 209–212]).

These songs describe how God will deliver his people by means of a servant, although there is debate as to whether they all refer to the same person. The servant has been variously identified as Israel; a remnant of Israel; a royal figure (Cyrus, Jehoiakim, Future David); the prophet (Isaiah, Second Isaiah); Second Moses; and/or Messiah (see survey in Rowley 1965: 7–20).

Israel is said to be God's servant in several passages (see 41:8; etc.), but elsewhere the servant's identity is less clear (see 42:1–7; 49:5–7; etc.). Identifying the servant in the Servant Songs as Israel can lead to apparent contradictions. For example, the 'bruised reed' that the servant will not break in 42:3 refers to Israel who are languishing in the Babylonian exile and thus cannot also be the servant who delivers them. Similarly, 49:5 says that the servant's task is to bring Israel back to God: how can Israel bring themselves back to God? It is therefore our view that the identity of the servant does not remain constant throughout the second part of the book (see Figure 42.1).

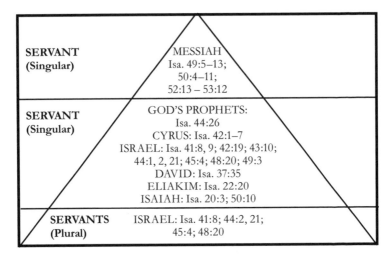

Figure 42.1 Uses of the word 'servant'

We believe that the first Servant Song points to Cyrus, someone outside Israel who would deliver them. However, the next three Servant Songs refer to both a physical and a spiritual deliverer. Cyrus was able to restore the Israelites to their land, as well as provide the means for them to restore the temple; yet he could not restore their hearts. God would have to look elsewhere to find a deliverer who could also bring Israel back to himself; thus the final three Servant Songs refer to the deliverance that the coming Messiah would bring. It is possible for the Servant Songs to have different referents since the context of each (chs. 40–48 and 49–57) is significantly different.

iii. God explains his plan (42:1 – 44:5)

Isaiah 42:1 – 44:5, the third section of the palistrophe, explains in more detail God's plan to deliver Israel and is parallel to Isaiah 45:18–25, which revisits the same theme (see Figure 0.10 on p. 26). Chapter 42 begins with what many refer to as a Servant Song (vv.

1–9), the only Servant Song in chapters 40–48. Even though it better aligns with an oracle of deliverance, we will maintain this terminology since the four Servant Songs have similar characteristics.

This rather long section from 42:1 to 44:5 consists of at least three separate oracles: (1) a Servant Song (42:1–9); and (2) two oracles of salvation, each with the same structure (42:10 – 43:13; and 43:14 – 44:5). Once again God's plan concerning how he will deliver his people Israel is declared. His sovereignty will be demonstrated when he accomplishes their deliverance and the restoration of his temple by means of the pagan king Cyrus.

a. First Servant Song (42:1–9)

Context

In this first Servant Song, God empowers his servant to bring deliverance and justice upon the earth. The servant in this passage has been variously identified as the Messiah, Cyrus, Isaiah, Israel, a remnant, and so on.[2] Some have suggested that this is a commissioning of Second Isaiah (see Blenkinsopp 2000: 207, 212; etc.), whereas others identify him as a royal figure (Williamson 1994: 132–134; etc.). Matthew quotes the first four verses of this first Servant Song (i.e. 42:1–4) and then explains that Jesus 'filled up' this scripture during his ministry (Matt. 12:15–22).

In chapter 42, Israel is represented by the *bruised reed* and *smouldering wick* (v. 3) as they languish in exile. Because Cyrus released the exiles and Isaiah 40 – 48 as a whole focuses on what God accomplishes through Cyrus, there is good reason to assume that the servant who will deliver Israel in chapter 42 is Cyrus as well (see also 41:9 where Cyrus is specifically called *my servant*).

This song is made up of two parts: (1) the description of the servant (42:1–4); and (2) how the servant is used to reveal God's greatness (42:5–9).

---

2. For good bibliographies related to this passage and the other Servant Songs, see Oswalt 1998: 113–115; Childs 2001: 409–410; Smith 2009: 152–156.

Comment

(1) Description of the servant (42:1–4)

1–2. God formally presents the servant in verse 1: *Here is* [lit. 'behold'] *my servant*. The title *my servant* is applied to several people in the Old Testament, each being called by God for a special purpose (Abraham, Gen. 26:24; Moses, Num. 12:7; etc.).

God upholds (lit. 'to grasp, take hold of') his *chosen one* and delights in him, causing his spirit to rest upon him (see 11:2; 61:1). The thought here is that the spirit of God empowers him to perform a special task. The phrase *he will bring justice to the nations* is probably a reference to Cyrus's decree that allowed exiled peoples to return home, reversing previous unjust policies of deportation.

The fact that the servant will not *raise his voice in the streets* suggests that he will bring about justice in a quiet manner, without ostentation. Cyrus did not need to manufacture support for his reign. In fact, when he rode into Babylon two weeks after having taken the city, the people cheered him, for they were again allowed to serve Marduk, the patron god of Babylon.

3–4. Two images depict the servant's gentleness: (1) *A bruised* [rāṣûṣ, 'crushed, bruised'] *reed he will not break* (šābar conveys more serious damage than rāṣûṣ). A 'crushed reed' often represented fragility (see 36:6), thus handling a *bruised reed* would require great care. (2) *A smouldering* [kēheh, 'dim, weak', 7x, but only once with this meaning] *wick* [pištâ, 3x] *he will not snuff out*. Both images depict the low condition of the nation of Israel during the Babylonian exile; however, God will not allow the nation, nor the dim remains of their faith, to be extinguished.

God will use the servant to effect Israel's deliverance and *bring forth justice*, a reference to verse 1. God will not allow him to *falter* [lit. 'grow weak'; related to the word 'dim' in the previous verse] *or be discouraged* (lit. 'be bent'; related to the word 'crushed reed' in v. 3) until he has accomplished all that God intends and established justice on the earth. This concept of 'establishing justice' may refer specifically to allowing exiles to return to their homelands (see Figure 42.2), or more generally to the fairness of Persian laws. The phrase *In his teaching* [tôrâ] *the islands will put their hope* [lit. 'will wait expectantly'] supports the latter interpretation.

> **Cyrus's Decree**
>
> As far as Ashur and Susa, Agad, Eshnunna, the towns of Zamban,
> Me-Turnu, Der as well as the region of the Gutians, I returned to
> [these] sacred cities on the other side of the Tigris, the sanctuaries of
> which have been ruins for a long time, the images which [used] to
> live therein and established for them permanent sanctuaries . . . May
> all the gods whom I resettled in their sacred cities ask daily Bel and
> Nebo for a long life for me and may they recommend me [to him];
> to Marduk, my lord . . .
> (*ANET* 316).

Figure 42.2   Cyrus's decree

(2) The servant is used to reveal God's greatness (42:5–9)

5–7. Before Yahweh's message is delivered, the next three
phrases describe why he has the authority to make this declaration:
(1) He is *God* (*hā'ēl*, '*the* God'), the article suggesting that he is
superior to any other so-called god. The word *'ēl* is the general
term for deity throughout the Ancient Near East, whereas *the*
LORD (Yahweh) is God's personal, covenant name. (2) He created
everything there is; he 'stretched out' the heavens and literally
'beat, pounded out' the earth. (3) He gave *breath* (*nĕšāmâ* = 'breath
of life'; see Gen. 2:7) and *life* (lit. 'spirit') to all its people. It is this
creative, sovereign God who has called forth the servant in
righteousness.

The introductory phrase *This is what God the* LORD *says* has
prompted some scholars to identify this as a new unit. We would
argue instead that the phrase is an affirmation that Yahweh has the
ability to do what he has just promised. The use of the singular *you*
in verse 6 to refer to the servant (*I, the* LORD, *have called* you [sing.]
in righteousness . . . I will keep you *and will make* you) confirms that the
servant song is continuing.

If this passage does indeed refer to Cyrus, God has already proclaimed to the nations that Cyrus will deliver Israel from the
Babylonian exile (see 41:2–4, 25). Thus, when the nations see this
taking place, they will know that Yahweh is a powerful God who
delivers his nation in a miraculous way.

The words *I, the LORD* and *I am the LORD* (vv. 6, 8, respectively) bracket the servant's commission: (1) *I . . . have called you in righteousness*, meaning that it was proper for God to call upon Cyrus, who will properly dispense God's justice. (2) God will support and direct him (*I will take hold of your hand*, v. 6). (3) God will guard/protect him (*I will keep* [lit. 'watch over'] *you*). (4) God has made an agreement to deliver his people through him (*I . . . will make you / to be a covenant for the people,* lit. 'give him as an agreement'; see also 49:8). The servant (i.e. Cyrus) will fulfil an agreement between God and his people that he will deliver them. (5) Once the servant delivers Israel, he will be *a light for the Gentiles* that Yahweh is the true God. The servant will be the means by which their spiritually blind eyes are opened. (6) He will free those imprisoned in *darkness* (v. 7; see 49:9; 61:1). Notice the contrast between *darkness* and *light* in verses 6–7. Gentile nations will now have good reason to believe that Yahweh is the sovereign God who can be trusted (vv. 6b–7) and will be drawn to serve him (see God's promise to Israel in Deut. 4:5–8).

In 49:9, the Jewish exiles are called *captives* and *those in darkness*, thus the reference here is most probably to a literal release from the bondage of exile. Yet their literal release is also a picture of release from spiritual bondage, namely unbelief that had imprisoned them. They are now free to experience renewed spiritual closeness with their God. The reversal of their dire straits is dramatically pictured by the opening of blind eyes and the release or escape from the dark confines of prison (lit. 'house of confinement', v. 7).

In 42:18–19, God's servant Israel is said to be *deaf* and *blind*, making the nation a poor servant. The servant of 42:1–9 will help open Israel's blinded eyes; his deliverance will help them to see that God still loves and cares for them.

8–9. As the climax to this section, God emphatically reminds the nation of who he is: *I am the LORD; that is my name!* He will deliver them and assert his right to receive all of the praise and glory for this action. He will not share his glory with anyone (lit. 'my glory to another I will not give'; the syntax of this phrase is highly emphatic), especially not with worthless *idols* (*pĕsîlîm,* 'carved images').

Yahweh is the one who declared the *former things* which have now come to pass (i.e. God's people were punished). He now declares *new things* (i.e. God's people will be delivered) before they take place (*before they spring into being*). The implication is that it was necessary for deliverance through Cyrus to be decreed before it took place.

Meaning

As already promised in several earlier passages, God is going to use his servant to bring justice to the nations. God's plan is so remarkable that only he can bring it about, but he will need to convince Israel that he is capable. God will use this servant, Cyrus, to deliver his people, thereby demonstrating his power and bringing himself glory. He will deal gently with the exiles (i.e. not breaking a bruised reed) and will allow them to return to their lands.

b. Two oracles of salvation (42:10 – 44:5)

The salvation oracles build upon the Servant Song in 42:1–9 and encourage the nation that God can indeed bring about this great deliverance. They begin with a declaration that Yahweh is one who triumphs over his enemies (42:10–13; 43:14–21), followed by a description of Israel's lack of obedience and God's chastening (42:14–25; 43:22–28). After the chastening is completed, the phrase *but now* (*wĕʿattâ*) introduces the climax when God intervenes to deliver his people (43:1–13; 44:1–5). In each oracle, God encourages his people not to be afraid (43:1, 5; 44:2, 8) by declaring their exquisite value in his sight: he created them, called them his own, and promises to be with them (43:1–2; 44:21). They are precious in God's sight because he loves them and will redeem them (43:1, 4, 7; 44:22–23).

Westermann calls the song 42:10–13 an 'eschatological hymn of praise' (1967: 102); however, it makes better sense as a hymn of praise for something that will take place relatively shortly (i.e. their release from the Babylonian captivity).

Two unique elements are found in the salvation oracles. The first is that the Israelites will serve as God's witnesses when he delivers them (43:10–13); the second concerns God's ownership of Israel (44:5).

(1) First oracle of salvation (42:10 – 43:13)

Context

The proper response to God's deliverance proclaimed in the Servant Song is for the nation to sing *a new song*. The old song was one of sadness and punishment; this new song will be one of deliverance and blessing. God had been silent for a long time, but it is now time for him to come to the aid of his people.

Comment

(a) Sing to the LORD a new song (42:10–13)

10–12. The people are to *sing to the LORD a new song*, a common exhortation in 'hymns of praise'; see Pss 33:3; 40:3; etc.), for he has clearly demonstrated that he deserves their praise.

The author expects this new song of God's praise to be spread to the uttermost *ends of the earth*: (1) towards *the sea* and the *islands* (see 41:1) in the west, and (2) to the *wilderness* (*Kedar* is a tribe of the Syro-Arabian desert; cf. 21:17), *Sela* ('rock'; may refer to Petra) and the *mountaintops* in the east. The Hebrew text of verse 12 is arranged as a chiasm with the following literal translation:

A Let them give
    B to the LORD glory
    B' and his praise in the coastlands
A' Let them declare

13. Yahweh is portrayed as both *champion* (*gibbôr*, 'a military hero') and *warrior* (lit. 'a man of wars'; see Exod. 15:3) who will go to battle with zeal. He will raise a war cry and will *triumph* [*gābar*; related to *gibbôr*] *over his enemies*. The emphatic nature of his crying out is lost in the NIV's translation. A literal reading is 'he will cry out, surely he will roar' (*ṣāraḥ*, 2x).

(b) God has long been silent, but now he will come in power (42:14–17)

14–15. This section further describes the *former things* and the *new things* of 42:9. God begins a divine monologue: *For a long time* [*mē ʿôlām*, 'from long before'] *I have kept silent* [*ḥāšâ*], / *I have been quiet* [*ḥāraš*, similar sounding to *ḥāšâ*] *and held myself back* (lit. 'I controlled myself'). While the nation was being punished in exile, God did not allow himself to come to Israel's aid. But now he will no longer be silent; he will not hold himself back.

He likens the suddenness and intensity with which he will now act to that of a woman in labour, for it will come on suddenly and cannot be restrained (lit. 'but now, like the woman giving birth I will groan [*ep̄ʿeh*, occurs only here], I will both pant [*ʾešōm*, occurs only here] and gasp [*ʾeš̆ʾap*, 4x with this meaning]'). Something new, Israel's deliverance, is about to be born.

Any impediment to the return of the exiles will be removed: God *will lay waste* [lit. 'dry up'] *the mountains . . . dry up* [lit. 'cause to wither'] *all their vegetation* [i.e. vegetation can also hinder travel]; / *. . . turn rivers into islands / and dry up the pools.*

16–17. Because the exiles will be in a helpless and hopeless state, God says he *will lead the blind by ways* [lit. 'in a way'] *they have not known.* God's special care and protection will be unlike any they have ever known: he will make the dark and rough way before them both light and smooth. *These are the things* God *will do.*

Verse 17 is not a redactional expansion as Childs suggests (2001: 333), but a natural outcome. The structure of the Hebrew sentence forces readers to wait until the second part of the verse to find out to whom it refers: that is, those Israelites who continue to trust (the verbs are participles here) in idols. However, once Israel experience God's great deliverance, they will be ashamed of having put their trust in worthless idols (see 41:21–29) and will turn to Yahweh, the true God.

(c) The prophet rebukes Israel, hoping to turn them back towards Yahweh (42:18–25)

18–20. God exhorts the blind and deaf to see and hear, then identifies them as Israel: *Who is blind but my servant, / and deaf like the messenger I send?* Although Israel has the privileged position of being *in covenant* with God (lit. 'one who was at peace [with me]', v. 19), they have become *blind* and *deaf* by not living according to it.

Israel had seen many things that God had done but continued in unbelief; had heard much but still lacked obedience (lit. 'opening ears but will not listen', v. 20b). They will therefore be held more culpable than other nations. What a paradox: Yahweh is served by a blind servant and a deaf messenger.

21–22. God's plan, which has always been based upon his right-eousness (*for the sake of his righteousness*, v. 21), was to exalt his *law* (or 'instruction') and make it *great and glorious*. God's law was always for the well-being of his people: following his guidelines would allow them to be prosperous and to lead meaningful lives. And yet, despite being given every opportunity, Israel did not submit to God's plan and were therefore punished.

God's people are described as being *plundered and looted* (historically they were *plundered and looted* by Sennacherib in 701 BC and Nebuchadnezzar in 586 BC); and *trapped* [*pāḥaḥ*, occurring only here] *in pits* [*ḥur*, 'holes', 2x] and *prisons* (lit. 'houses of confinement'). These latter terms suggest imprisonment and figuratively corres-pond well with the Babylonian exile.

The people of Israel became *plunder with no one to rescue them.* There was no-one to stand up for them and say, *Send them back.* This was the case when King Nebuchadnezzar, a strong warrior and sovereign ruler over the Babylonian Empire, removed the Israelites from their land.

23–25. The prophet asks rhetorical, penetrating questions: *Which of you* [lit. 'who among you' (pl.)] *will listen* to the message that Israel will be plundered with none to deliver them (v. 23)? Then he asks, *Who handed . . . Israel to the plunderers* [*mĕšissâ*, 6x]*?* (v. 24). The answer to this last question should be obvious: Yahweh did. The questions are related and intended to get them thinking: Israel had persisted in disobedience by not obeying God's law (lit. 'they were not willing to walk in his ways'), a deliberate choice (v. 24); thus God had to punish them.

Even when God *poured out on them his burning anger* (lit. 'the wrath of his anger', v. 25) and they were completely consumed by the *violence* [*ʿĕzûz*, 5x] *of war*, they gave no heed to their punishment (lit. *did not take it to heart*). Even amid devastating punishment the Israel-ites remained hard-hearted towards God.

(d) God will deliver Israel (43:1–13; contains third trial speech, 43:8–13)[3]

1–2. At the end of chapter 42 Israel continues to disobey so that God must punish them, yet this is not the final word. In a major shift (*But now, this is what the LORD says*) God now speaks reassuringly to Israel, heaping up statements regarding his love for the nation: (1) he is Israel's creator and the one who *formed* them, who took special care in making them into his nation; (2) Israel has no need to fear because (*kî*) God has redeemed them; that is, he has reclaimed the nation as his own; (3) Israel is his chosen nation: *I have summoned you* [sing.] *by name; you* [sing.] *are mine*; and (4) God will protect them even in dire circumstances (*when you pass through the waters*). The singular forms throughout this passage indicate the close relationship between God and each Israelite.

The image of 'passing through' flooding water and burning fire conveys well the Babylonian captivity, but it gives hope that they will not be entirely overwhelmed (*the rivers . . . will not sweep over you*) or destroyed (*you will not be burned* [*kāwâ*, 3x]). God continues to show his lovingkindness even though Israel has turned its back on him.

3–4. A second reason (*kî*) why Israel need not fear is that Yahweh will give other nations in exchange for them: *I give Egypt for your ransom* [i.e. price paid for Israel's release], / *Cush* [south of

---

3. Goldingay and Payne have argued for a chiastic structure in 43:1–7 (really, an extended chiasm called a palistrophe):

    1 Yhwh as one who creates, calls, shapes ('fear not')
      2 Yhwh's promise regarding a journey ('I am with you')
        3a Yhwh in relationship with Israel
          3b Yhwh is one who gave up people for Israel
            4a Yhwh is Israel's lover
          4b Yhwh is one who gave up people for Israel
        5a Yhwh in relationship with Israel ('fear not, I am with you')
      5b-6 Yhwh's promise regarding a journey
    7 Yhwh as one who creates, calls, shapes

This structure explains the significant repetition (2006: 271–272).

Egypt] *and Seba* [part of Ethiopia] *in your stead.* In fact, Cyrus's successor, Cambyses, would ultimately be the one to conquer Egypt. The three names *your God, the Holy One of Israel* and *your Saviour* emphasize his close relationship with Israel.

The imagery of ransom comes from Israel's civil law stipulating that a payment could sometimes be given in exchange for the life of a person (see Exod. 21:30). Here God gives a *ransom (kōper)* for Israel. In this context the word *kōper* (16x), meaning either a 'bribe' (see Amos 5:12) or a 'ransom' (see Ps. 49:7), highlights both the high cost of Israel's deliverance and their high value in God's sight (Childs 2001: 335). God makes it clear that he has never abandoned them and has the power to protect them. He is still Israel's Saviour (which correlates to their rescue from exile) even though the nation has rebelled against him.

God repeats his assurances that he will give others in *exchange* for Israel, because of his great love for them: *since you are precious and honoured in my sight* [lit. 'in my eyes'], / *and because I* [lit. 'I myself'] *love you* (v. 4).

5–7. Verse 5 begins with the temporary prohibition *Do not be afraid* [now], because God's presence is promised to Israel. God's special love for his people, whom he calls *sons* and *daughters* (v. 6), and his covenant relationship compel him to respond to their situation and deliver them. Whybray notes that 'The idea of Yahweh as the father of Israel was not new (e.g. Hos. 11:1); but here, and even more explicitly in verse 7, there is a more personal note: each Israelite is Yahweh's own son or daughter' (1975: 83; see Exod. 4:22).

He will gather Israel's offspring *from the ends of the earth*, which suggests that this return is not limited to the return from the Babylonian exile. He created Israel for his *glory* (v. 7), and thus his glory will be displayed by their deliverance.

8–10. As the trial speech continues, God says to *Lead out those* [lit. 'a people'] *who have eyes but are blind* [i.e. Israel], / *who have ears but are deaf.* Childs argues that 'lead out' is a technical term in the legal setting that means to bring out for judgment (see Gen. 38:24; 2001: 335). Even though Israel is *blind* and *deaf,* they should still be able to serve as *witnesses* to testify to the other nations how Yahweh delivered them. God assembles the nations to hear their testimony: that no other God could deliver Israel (v. 10).

God challenges the nations to identify which of their gods could have foretold Israel's release, and to bring witnesses to prove it (v. 9). Their silence testifies to the fact that neither the nations nor their gods are able to do what God had done in foretelling and accomplishing Israel's deliverance.

God's declaration *I am he. / Before me no god was formed, / nor will there be one after me* is a clear statement of monotheism. In most Ancient Near Eastern religions the gods created other gods; but this is not the case with Yahweh. He alone is the sovereign God: no God existed before him, and none will come after him (v. 10).

11–13. Yahweh makes the declaration 'I am the LORD' (or similar) about eighteen times in Isaiah 40 – 48 (41:4, 13; 42:6; etc.). His emphatic declaration *I, even I, am the LORD* (Yahweh) underscores that he alone is the one who delivered Israel *and not some foreign god among you* (v. 12). God's closing statement summarizes his plan: (1) *I* [lit. 'I, myself'] *have revealed* (i.e. prophesied [it]); (2) *and saved* (i.e. the actual deliverance); (3) *and proclaimed* (i.e. declared to Israel that he was the one who accomplished it). The strongest statement of God's divinity and sovereignty is in verse 12: *I am God* (*'ēl*), using the general Semitic word for the supreme God.

Again, he reminds Israel that they are to serve as *witnesses* to all these facts. *From ancient days* [lit. 'from a day'; i.e. from the first day] *I am he*; in other words, his eternality confirms his power. Because Yahweh is the true God, his actions cannot be thwarted or reversed: *No one can deliver out of my hand. / When I act, who can reverse it?* The answer to this rhetorical question is clearly 'No-one'. God had challenged the so-called gods to demonstrate their divinity, and their silence proves his case: he is the true God, and the nation of Israel is his evidence and his witness. No-one else could have foretold the deliverance of Israel and then brought it about.

Meaning

This oracle of salvation further describes God's plan: only an all-powerful, sovereign God would be able to deliver Israel from Babylon through Cyrus, the Persian king. God will accomplish this amazing feat so that Israel might understand that he is the true God (43:10). The people of Israel, who are currently blind to God, will have the ability to be his witnesses once they are delivered from Babylon (43:10–13), and to proclaim God's power and faithfulness to the other nations. They need not worry, for Yahweh their God is the only all-powerful, eternal God whose plans no-one can thwart.

(2) Second oracle of salvation (43:14 – 44:5)

Context
These verses describe the fitting conclusion to the trial scene in 43:8–13: the captor, Babylon, will become the captive. As with the earlier oracle of salvation, this one also begins with the announcement of the defeat of Yahweh's enemy, Babylon (43:14–21), followed by the description of Israel's disobedience and God's punishment upon her (43:22–28). But the passage ends with Yahweh exhorting Israel not to fear, for he is about to deliver her (44:1–5).

Comment

(a) God will deliver Israel (43:14–21)
14–15. Not only will Yahweh defeat the Babylonians, but they will be taken away in the very ships for which they were renowned. The name 'Chaldeans' (typically translated as *Babylonians* in the NIV) is used eighty times in the Old Testament (7x in Isaiah) to refer to a people who settled in lower Mesopotamia and founded the Neo-Babylonian Empire.

God will go to Babylon and chase their people out as fugitives. There has been much debate about the meaning of the rare word *bārîḥîm*. Being related to the more common verb *bāraḥ*, 'to flee', and the adjective *bārîaḥ*, 'fleeing' (see 27:1), it is most likely to mean *fugitives* (4x; see 15:5).

God will punish the Babylonians for their cruelty to Israel because of his special relationship to Israel. This relationship is highlighted in the wording throughout these two verses: (1) *your Redeemer, the Holy One of Israel*; (2) *for your* [Israel's] *sake*; and (3) *I am the LORD, your Holy One, / Israel's Creator, your King.*

16–18. The language of verses 16–21 implies a second exodus motif: just as God *made a way through the sea* for Moses and the people (Exod. 14) and destroyed Pharaoh and his great army, so God will once again demonstrate his great power when he delivers his children from exile. God defeated Egypt's well-supplied army with its *chariots, horses*[4] and *reinforcements*. The Babylonian forces will be felled, *never to rise again*, having been destroyed (*snuffed out like a wick*, v. 17) just as Pharaoh's forces were destroyed in the crossing of the Reed Sea. God instructs the nation of Israel not to *dwell on the past* and to forget the *former things* (i.e. the punishments mentioned in 42:9; 43:9; etc.).

19–21. Instead of Israel focusing on the misery of their exile, God now directs their attention (*see, hinnēh*) to the *new thing* he is about to do, that is, bringing them back to their homeland. Indeed (*'ap* = emphatic; present in MT, but absent in the NIV), he will prepare their route and supply their needs by *making a way in the wilderness / and streams in the wasteland*. During the first exodus God did not construct a literal road to lead his people through the wilderness, but he did 'make a way' in the figurative sense of leading and guiding them clearly with a 'pillar of cloud' by day and a 'pillar of fire' by night (Exod. 13:21).

The phrase *streams in the wasteland* may be a figurative expression of blessings or spiritual renewal, but during the exodus from Egypt God supplied literal water when Israel was in need. The next phrase, *wild animals honour me, / the jackals and the owls* (lit. 'daughters of ostriches' [i.e. just two examples of wild animals; see 34:13]), / *because* [*kî*] *I provide water in the wilderness*, may be read two ways: (1) figuratively, as referring to the nations that observe God's provision for Israel (similar to Josh. 2:9–11); or (2) literally, in the sense that even the wildlife of the desert will benefit from God's supply of water to his people. The latter explanation probably corresponds better to the first exodus.

Israel, the nation God formed for himself, will be delivered and, as a natural outcome, will finally declare God's praise (see 41:16b).

---

4. In Codex Leningradensis the phrase 'the chariots and the horses' contains an error: either the *maqqeph* (i.e. 'the chariots *of* horses') or the *wāw* (i.e. 'the chariots *and* the horses') between the words should be deleted. The *maqqeph* is most likely to be the problem.

(b) Israel's disobedience and her punishment (43:22–28)

22–25. Verse 22 begins a new argument which Whybray suggests is a trial speech, 'one in which Yahweh summons, not the heathen gods and their worshipers, but his own people, to defend himself against their claim that their punishment has been undeserved' (1975: 89; see 43:26).

The very people whom God created to proclaim his praise in verse 21 do not call on him in verse 22 (lit. 'yet not to me have you called' = emphatic order). Instead of calling out to God for deliverance, they blame him for their exile and complain that they are tired of his treatment – these charges are completely unfounded. God then describes Israel's unfaithfulness with the phrase 'they have become weary [*yāga'*, 29x, 12x in Isa. 40 – 66] of following Yahweh' (corresponding to the NASB; the NIV incorrectly inserts a negation that does not appear in the Hebrew text: *you have not wearied yourselves for me*).

God addresses the Israelites' complaints head-on, making it clear that he had not put heavy burdens on any of them while they were in Babylon: *I have not burdened you with grain offerings / nor wearied you with demands for incense* (v. 23; i.e. there was no temple in which to offer sacrifices to Yahweh). The *incense* (*lĕbōnâ*, probably 'frankincense', v. 23) and *fragrant calamus* (lit. 'spice reed', v. 24; this was an imported product) were, according to Jeremiah 6:20, unnecessary extravagances that Yahweh had not requested. There is a wordplay here: *You have not bought [qānâ] any fragrant calamus [qāneh] for me.*

They had not *lavished on me* [i.e. God] *the fat of* [their] *sacrifices* [lit. 'and with the fat of your sacrifices you have not satisfied me'; the inverted syntax is for emphasis]. God had requested a portion of the fat from the sacrifices (see Exod. 29:13, 22), not necessarily the excessive amount implied here (i.e. *hiphil* of *rāwâ*, 'to cause to drench').

The wording suggests that they were giving these extravagant sacrifices to the gods of Babylon. Thus instead of offering God their best (which he deserved), they were offering God their worst (i.e. their sins): *But you have burdened me with your sins / and wearied me with your offences.* These sins were an affront to God.

Even though Israel did nothing to show that they deserved forgiveness, God nevertheless forgave a remnant of them: *I, even I* [i.e.

highly emphatic], *am he who blots out* [participle implying continual action of blotting out sin] / *your transgressions*. He does so for his own sake, because of his mercy, and not based upon anything they have done. The syntax of the last phrase lends emphasis: *'your sins* I will never remember' (a permanent prohibition; Williams §396).

26–28. In these verses Yahweh is willing to listen to their counter-arguments in support of their innocence: *Review the past for me* [lit. 'cause me to remember'] / . . . *state the case for your innocence* (lit. 'recount you in order that you may be justified'). When no rebuttal is forthcoming, God himself reviews the facts of the case that justify the punishment they have received.

From as far back as Jacob, Israel's *first father* from whom all Israelites are descended, there had been a steady progression of sin (see Hos. 12:2–4). Even those whom God had sent to lead the people closer to him (*those I sent to teach* [*mĕlîṣîm*, 4x, all with different meanings] *you*) rebelled against him (i.e. his priests, Levites, some prophets, etc.).

In the absence of counter-arguments, Yahweh acted on the evidence he presented: he *disgraced* [*ḥālal*, 'to profane'] *the dignitaries* [lit. 'princes'] *of* [their] *temple* (*qōdeš*, 'holy place' = leaders of the Jerusalem priesthood). To 'profane the princes' means to take away their consecrated status before God. He also *consigned Jacob to destruction* [*ḥērem*] / *and Israel to scorn* [*giddûpîm*, 'defamation, abuse', 2x].

(c) Israel's deliverance: a salvation oracle (44:1–5)

1–2. The words *But now* (v. 1) signal a transition from the rehearsal of Israel's past sins to this salvation oracle which revisits themes Isaiah has already addressed (see 41:8, 9; 43:10; etc.).

God assures the Israelites that they are his servants (*Jacob, my servant*, v. 1) and that he has chosen them from the womb (see Jer. 1:5). Therefore *Jeshurun* (= the nation of Israel) need not fear, for God has chosen them. The term *Jeshurun* (*yĕšurûn*, 'upright', 4x; all the rest in Deuteronomy) is parallel to *Jacob* (Israel) and probably refers to the remnant returning from Babylon.

Israel's situation in Isaiah 44:2 corresponds well with Deuteronomy 33:26. The events that gave rise to Moses' praise correspond to the historical context of Isaiah 44. With one rare title for God, Isaiah effectively reminds them of the time God delivered them from Egypt, protected them through the wilderness wanderings and settled them in the Promised Land. Thus, the name is intended to encourage Israel that this same God will deliver them from Babylon, bring them through the wilderness and return them to their homeland. Both contexts are suitable reasons to praise God.

3–5. The author uses the images of *water* poured on *the thirsty land* and *streams* [*nōzĕlîm*, 'flowings'] *on the dry ground* to picture God's spirit (i.e. his power) being poured out on the remnant of the nation: they *will spring up like grass* [lit. 'sprout up in between the grass'] *in a meadow, / like poplar trees by flowing streams*. These two images suggest that the remnant will thrive vigorously while scattered among the nations. This blessing will extend even to succeeding generations of their offspring (*my blessing on your descendants*).

Verse 5 distinguishes two possible groups within this remnant: (1) One group comes by assent (i.e. *I belong to the LORD*), such as Gentiles who believe in Yahweh. Upon seeing Israel's prosperity, some Gentiles will desire to become proselytes. (2) Another group comes by assent but also belongs to Israel – those who *call themselves by the name of Jacob*, who *take the name Israel* (*yĕkanneh*, 'to give someone a name of honour' [*HALOT* 2.483]) and are true believers. They will demonstrate loyalty and true devotion to the LORD either by proclaiming *I belong to the LORD* or by writing on their hand the words *The LORD's* (see 56:3, 6–8). While not certain, it appears that the writing on the hand is to be taken literally, just as their verbal proclamation would be literal; in any case, their dedication is the most important issue. That people will be honoured to be associated with Israel and especially her God is a new element in the salvation oracles.

Meaning

In the second salvation oracle (43:14 – 44:5) God's deliverance is so remarkable that his people will forget their former punishment. He uses terms that should remind them of their exodus from Egypt (i.e. *he who made a way through the sea* [43:16]; *who drew out the chariots and horses* [43:17]) and contrasts their fate with the fate of Babylon: Israel will not be a snuffed-out wick (see 42:3) as Babylon will be (see 43:17). God will pour out his spirit on Israel and will raise up a righteous remnant who willingly declare their allegiance to God (44:5).

iv. A true God cannot be created by people (44:6–23)

Context
Isaiah 44:6–23 again concerns the delusion that people can create gods – a common theme in the book of Isaiah. The unit forms a contrasting parallel in the palistrophe to 45:8–17, which presents Yahweh as the one true God who created all people (see Figure 0.10 on p. 26). In this trial scene Yahweh challenges the nations concerning their idols; he states three times that any nation that foolishly trusts in idols will be put to shame. Like the two previous oracles of salvation, witnesses are called upon to confirm that God's promises have been fulfilled and that they need not fear, for God will protect them.

This is the third passage in Isaiah 40 – 48 that describes the worthlessness of idols. This description of idols implies that the recipients of this oracle believe that their idols are the actual embodiment of the gods and not merely representations of them. Here the folly of idolatry is positioned between declarations of God's greatness; the first presents God's pre-eminence: *Is there any God besides me? / . . . I know not one* (44:8); the second highlights his care: *Israel, I will not forget you* (44:21).

Comment

a. The LORD, not idols (44:6–8)
6–7. God first declares who he is: *the LORD* (yhwh), which is his personal name; *Israel's King and Redeemer*, a name that expresses his role by choice; *the LORD Almighty* (lit. 'Lord of hosts'), a name that conveys his omnipotence; and *the first and . . . the last*, a name expressive of his eternality (see 41:4). He is the only God who exists (*apart from me* [*bil'āday*, 'beside me, apart from me', 16x; 6x in the book of Isaiah] *there is no God*), the only one who foretold Israel's deliverance and set in motion all that would take place.

Once again God challenges all so-called gods to defend their divinity by doing what he has done in declaring what has happened and what will happen: *Who then is like me? . . . / Let him declare and lay out* [lit. 'arrange it'] *before me / what has happened . . . / and what is yet to come* (lit. 'the coming things even which will come'; see 41:22–23). Yahweh has been directing Israel (i.e. *my ancient* ['*ōlām*] *people*) from the time that he established them as his people. They should have been able to attest to his actions from their beginning as a nation.

8. Because God has been directing and guiding their way, the Israelites need not be *afraid* (*tirhû*, 'to be paralysed with fear' [*HALOT* 2.437]; occurs only here). Earlier they were called to be Yahweh's witnesses that there is no other God than he (i.e. 43:10, 12). He now asks them once again to confirm that he is the only God because he declared *long ago* (lit. 'from that time', meaning long before the event) that he would deliver them. Then once again he declares himself to be the sole divinity: *Is there any God* ['*ĕlôah*, 60x] *besides me?* God is their only *Rock* (*ṣûr*, 'rock, cliff'), an immovable foundation upon which they can rely.

b. The futility of idolatry (44:9–20)

9–11. The primary theme of 44:9–20 is the condemnation of those who fabricate idols (lit. 'shapers of idols'); these image-makers are *nothing* (*tōhû*, 'emptiness, nothing'). Having made the idol with their own hands from inanimate materials, they of all people should know that an idol has no intrinsic divine status, nor anything that should compel one's worship. In contrast to idols, Yahweh has just proven that he is the only God, by declaring future events and bringing Israel out of the Babylonian exile, something no-one ever expected.

Yet the nation of Israel blindly and shamefully clung to their idols: *the things they* [Israel] *treasure are worthless* [lit. 'they do not profit']. Their *craftsmen are only human beings* (implied = how could human beings create divinity?). Those who endorse idols (lit. 'their own witnesses') *are blind; / they are ignorant* [i.e. blinded by their own ignorance, choosing to believe a lie]*, to their own shame.*

'Behold' (*hēn*) at the beginning of verse 11 draws attention to the conclusion. The outcome for all idol-makers (lit. 'and their companions') is the same: they will be *put to shame* and suffer humiliation because they put their faith in something that could not help them (vv. 9, 11).

12–17. The entire description of idol-making is meant to illustrate the absurdity that something made by humans could be believed to have divine capabilities. God examines step by step the idol-making process, focusing on the limitations of the creators of idols (i.e. mere humans), by means of tools wielded by their own hands and from materials they themselves have mined or grown.

First, an idol is made by artisans: *The blacksmith takes a tool* [lit. 'blacksmith iron axe'; *ma'ăṣād*, 2x] / *and works with it in the coals* [*peḥām*, 3x]; / *he shapes an idol with hammers* [*maqqābôt*, 4x with this meaning]. As we were reminded in verse 11, artisans are mere humans, the implication being that they possess no extraordinary powers. In fact, as the artisans work, they get hungry, lose strength and grow faint (v. 12). As soon as they stop eating and drinking, the process comes to a halt (v. 12), for it all depends on human strength.

The carpenter (lit. 'an engraver of woods') measures a piece of wood with a *line* (*qaw*), outlines it with a 'stylus' (*śered*, occurs only here), cuts it with a 'carving knife' (*maqṣu'â*, occurs only here) and marks it with a *compass* (*mĕḥûgâ*, occurs only here). In subtle irony, the worker shapes the wood into a *human form in all its glory*, yet it has no life, let alone supernatural power. It is a statue that merely 'sits' *in a shrine* (lit. 'house', v. 13).

The artisans use ordinary materials. The blacksmith pounds out metal, a material mined by workers. The carpenter uses wood from trees that were planted and grown by workers in Israel (v. 14), such as cypress, oak and 'fir' (*'ōren*, occurs only here); cedar was sometimes imported from Lebanon for special idols.

The word *'ap*, 'even', is used twice in verse 15 to create irony: the same person who 'even' *kindles* [*nāśaq*, 3x] *a fire . . . bakes bread . . .* [and] *roasts his meat* (vv. 15, 16) from some of the wood is also the one who 'even' *fashions a god* (*'ēl* or *pesel*, 'idol') from the rest of it and then *worships it*. The final phrase of verse 15, *and bows down* [*sāgad*, 4x] *to it*, is used only in Isaiah, mainly in this passage.

The contrast here is striking: the same wood that could be burned for warmth (*'ûr*, 'fire', 5x with this meaning, all but one in Isaiah), to bake bread and to prepare meals (lit. 'flesh he eats [emphatic order], he roasts [*ṣālâ*, 3x] a roast') was also wood that was worshipped and entreated to provide protection: *Save me! You are my god!* (v. 17).

All of this is strikingly different from what Yahweh declared about himself to the Israelites in verse 6: *I am the first and I am the last; / apart from me there is no God*. How could a human create out of earth's natural, physical materials something supernatural – a deity?

18–20. Why cannot people see the absurdity of these actions? Because both eyes and hearts are *plastered over* (*ṭāḥaḥ*, 'besmeared from seeing', occurs only here); in other words, they are unable or unwilling to perceive and understand.

The idolaters do not take time to reflect on their actions (*No one stops to think*, lit. 'no-one returns it to his heart'). The implication is that if they would only take a moment to reflect, they would realize that the wood they use to cook food is the same wood they make into an idol, *a detestable thing* (lit. 'an abhorrence'). The latter phrase expresses moral outrage: it is an abomination to fall down and worship a block of wood, especially when they could be serving the living God.

Those who worship idols cannot resist doing so and do not even realize they are being deceived (v. 20): *Such a person feeds on ashes* (i.e. worthless residue); such people are misled (lit. 'deceived') by their hearts. They cannot perceive, let alone renounce, the lie they believe (*he cannot save himself, or say, / 'Is not this thing in my right hand a lie?'*).

c. Wake up, Israel (44:21–23)

21–23. Picking up the theme of Israel's relationship to God begun in 43:10, God pleads with the nation not to be deceived by idolatry any longer and to remember what is critical: (1) *you, Israel, are my servant* (2x); (2) *I have made* [lit. 'formed'] *you*; (3) *I will not forget* [*nāšâ*, 6x] *you* (lit. 'you will not be *forgotten* by me' = emphatic order); (4) *I have swept away your offences like a cloud*; and (5) *I have redeemed* [lit. 'to reclaim as one's own'] *you*. The repetition in the first phrase is for emphasis, but the wording of each phrase is slightly different: (1) 'my servant you are', emphasizing ownership; and (2) 'a servant to me you are', emphasizing their role as servants of God (i.e. 'to me').

God then urges Israel to return to him (v. 22). Two images represent how thoroughly he blots out their sins, redeeming them so that they can return to him: *I have swept away* [lit. 'blotted out'] *your offences like a cloud* (lit. 'dark cloud') and like a *morning mist* (lit. 'cloud'), both of which blot out or cause the sun to disappear.

Verse 23 is a song of praise to God, similar to 42:10–12 and other psalms of praise. Creation is summoned to break forth (*pāṣaḥ*, 8x, all but one in Isaiah) in resounding praise to God. The word *kî*, 'for', signals the reason for this great joy: God has redeemed Israel, thereby displaying his glory (lit. 'glorified himself in Israel'). This deliverance is described in prophetic perfects; that is, the author is so certain of this outcome that he describes it as completed action.

Meaning

Yahweh is the only one worthy to receive the name 'God' – there is no other. His people are the best witnesses of this fact. When God says *I know not one*, his statement is all the more remarkable when we remember his omniscience. This one true God has proven he knows the future; thus his people need never worry.

Yet our blindness can be incredibly persistent. The illustration of idol-makers is meant to teach us that nothing in the earth, especially nothing that people have made, could ever approach or supersede God. This God reminds Israel of his great love for them and that he has not forgotten them. He is willing to clear away their sins so that they can once again experience a close relationship with him: *Return to me, / for I have redeemed you* (44:22).

v. The LORD is sovereign (44:24 – 45:7)

Context

Isaiah 44:24 – 45:7, positioned in the middle of the palistrophe (see Figure 0.10 on p. 26), showcases the power and sovereignty of Yahweh, noting many of his greatest achievements (i.e. *I, the LORD, do all these things*, 45:7; *the Maker of all things*, 44:24; *makes fools of diviners*, 44:25; *fulfils the predictions of his messengers*, 44:26; and brings Cyrus to deliver Israel, 44:28).

Idols are mentioned thirteen times in Isaiah 40 – 48: six are before this section (40:18–20; 41:5–7, 21–24, 29; 42:17; 44:9–20) and six appear after it (45:16, 20–21; 46:1–2, 5–7; 47:12–15; 48:5). At the heart of this section God declares, *I am the LORD, and there is no other; / apart from me there is no God* (45:5–6), which he reiterates three times in this section (45:5, 6, 21). Idols are incapable of bringing about Israel's deliverance.

Similarly, of the seven times when God is said to bring Cyrus to deliver his people, three appear before the section 44:24 – 45:7 (41:2–4, 25–26; 42:1–9) and three after it (45:13; 46:11; 48:14–15); but the most detailed description is found at the heart of this section (44:28 – 45:4). The palistrophe builds to this climactic point when Cyrus is specifically mentioned by name as the servant whom God will use to deliver his nation.

Comment

a. Jerusalem will be inhabited (44:24–28)

24. The LORD, the personal, covenant-keeping name for God, reiterates in a song of praise that he is Israel's *Redeemer* (used 13x in Isa. 40 – 66), the one who has bought them back and delivered them. He knows them intimately, having formed them *in* [lit. 'from'] *the womb*, and was preparing Israel even before their birth to be his nation. Their history went all the way back to God's call to Abraham and his development of Israel as a nation in Egypt, but the birth here probably signifies entering into the covenant with Yahweh at Mount Sinai.

God makes the pronouncement *I am the LORD* (or God) ten times in Isaiah 44 – 45 (44:24; 45:3, 5, 6, 7, 8, 18, 19, 21, 22) to stress that only he can do these amazing things. Verse 24 also notes the greatness and power of God, as demonstrated in creation. God alone is the *Maker of all things*; he *stretches out the heavens* above and *spreads out* [lit. 'beating out'] *the earth* beneath.[5] Taken as a whole, this verse serves to reassure Israel that Yahweh can be trusted.

25–28. Moving from his role in creation, Yahweh then describes his activity in history. He *foils* [*pārar*, 'to break, destroy'] *the signs of false prophets* (*baddîm*, 2x with this meaning), making them look like fools[6] (v. 25). By contrast, he confirms *the words of his servants* (lit.

---

5. We agree with the NIV's choice to follow the *kĕthîb* reading of v. 24b: *who spreads out the earth by myself*. This reading, not the *qĕrē* reading 'from me', corresponds well with the parallel unit.

6. To arrive at the NIV's translation *and turns it into nonsense*, the MT's reading *śākal* ('to have success') must be emended to *sākal*, 'to act

'word of his servant' = Isaiah; v. 26) and the plan (*ʿaṣat*, 'counsel') *of his messengers*.

With the word *hāʾōmēr*, 'the one who says', God confirms the certainty of the promises that Isaiah prophesies: (1) Jerusalem will be inhabited and the rest of Judah's cities rebuilt (i.e. the exiles will return, v. 26). (2) At God's command *the watery deep* (*ṣûlâ*, occurs only here) will dry up. This is a reference to the unhindered return of the exiles from Babylon and recalls their miraculous exodus from Egypt (v. 27). (3) Cyrus will rebuild Jerusalem and its temple. According to Josephus (*Ant.* 10.1–2), Cyrus was shown this passage in Isaiah, causing him to initiate the return of the exiles to Jerusalem; however, this is unlikely given the circumstances. The phrase *Let its foundations be laid* (v. 28) is synecdoche, referring to the whole temple.

Cyrus is specified by name for the first time in 44:28. He is called *my shepherd*, a phrase that was often used in the Ancient Near East of a benevolent ruler. Here it suggests that Cyrus will carry out God's good intentions for his people (*my shepherd . . . will accomplish all that I please* [lit. 'my desire']), even though he is a pagan ruler, a concept that would have shocked the Israelites.

Additional note: Cyrus II (the Great) (*c.*559–530 BC)

Cyrus II (the Great) (Hebrew/Aramaic *kôreš*) was the founder of the Persian Empire under the Achaemenid dynasty. He controlled most of the known world during his lifetime, his empire stretching from Egypt and the Aegean Sea (Hellespont) in the west to the River Indus (which flows from the Himalayas through Pakistan to the Arabian Sea) in the east.

He ascended the throne following the death of his father, Cambyses I, in 559 BC. About 550 BC he conquered Astyages (king of the Median Empire from 585 to 550 BC), who was his overlord, and then began the remarkable feat of uniting the two countries into a single, powerful empire that the biblical authors referred to

---

(note 6 *cont.*) foolishly'. This change is quite plausible, for sometimes sibilants are interchanged, as Gesenius notes (GKC §6k).

as 'the Medes and the Persians' (see Dan. 5:28). He employed several strategies to accomplish this task: (1) he respectfully observed Median culture; (2) he established one of his royal residences in Ecbatana in Media; and (3) he appointed various Medes to high positions in his provincial government. Cyrus respected the customs, cultures and religions of the lands he conquered and is said to have followed the dictum 'Diversity in counsel, unity in command' (Roberto 2013: 304, pl. 3).

Cyrus went on to conquer Croesus king of Lydia and even marched through Assyria, but it was not until 539 BC that he finally defeated the Babylonian Empire. According to Herodotus, the Persians, led by Gobryas, entered Babylon by diverting the River Euphrates (*Hist.* 1.189–191) and were able to capture the city in one night (16 [12?] Oct. 539 BC) with little resistance from the Babylonian army (*ANET* 316), although some have questioned this account. Seventeen days later, when Cyrus himself entered the city, he was met with cheers and jubilation, for the Babylonians had grown discontented under Nabonidus, who openly favoured the god Sin over Marduk, the traditional god of Babylon.

The Edict of Cyrus (538 BC) allowed captives to return to their homelands and worship their gods; thus, the Israelites returned to Jerusalem to rebuild their temple to Yahweh (2 Chr. 36:22–23; Ezra 1:1–3; *ANET* 316).

b. God uses Cyrus to deliver his people (45:1–7)

1–3. At the core of the section 44:24 – 45:7 is a royal oracle (45:1–5) in which God addresses Cyrus: *This is what the LORD says to his anointed, / to Cyrus.* 'Anointing' typically refers to a special equipping for a specific task that God has given. Those who were anointed include priests (Exod. 28:41), prophets (1 Kgs 19:16) and kings (1 Sam. 10:1). However, as Childs points out, nowhere else is a foreign king designated in this way (2001: 353). In the Cyrus Cylinder Cyrus claims to have been chosen and appointed by Marduk (*ANET* 315–316).

Cyrus will be guided and directed by God to bring about his purposes (i.e. *Cyrus, whose right hand I take hold of*). The right hand was considered the place of honour (see Ps. 110:1) and strength (see Ps. 80:17). God will *subdue nations before him / and ... strip kings of their armour* (lit. 'I will open the loins of kings', meaning that he will disarm them). He will also *open doors before him / so that gates will not be shut* (v. 1); that is, God will allow Cyrus to enter regions, seize power and rule sovereignly over them.

Starting in verse 2 God speaks to Cyrus, informing him that he will go before him to smooth his way (lit. 'make straight the mountains' [*hădûrîm*, occurs only here]). God will *break down gates of bronze / and cut through bars of iron*, a reference to the hundred bronze gates which were said to line the walls of Babylon (Herodotus, *Hist.* 1.179). God will also give Cyrus the great riches hidden away in Babylon's storehouses: *I will give you hidden treasures* [lit. 'treasures of darkness'], */ riches stored in secret places* (v. 3). All these blessings will be bestowed upon Cyrus to confirm to him that he is being used of God (i.e. *who summons you by name*).

4–5. God has singled out Cyrus, summoning him by name and bestowing on him *a title of honour* (*kānâ*, 4x), though Cyrus did not return the honour (*though you do not acknowledge me*). God's purpose in doing this is to bring deliverance to his chosen people (*for the sake of Jacob my servant*, v. 4).

An important lesson to draw from these verses is that God can use people to accomplish his purposes even when they are unaware of him doing so. He can do this because he is *the LORD, and there is no other*. God's declaration that he is *the LORD* occurs in each of verses 5, 6 and 7 (vv. 5 and 6 include *and there is no other*, then v. 7 concludes *I, the LORD, do all these things*).

Cyrus typically credited his gods with his victories, so it is doubtful that he understood that Yahweh was guiding him. But Cyrus did desire to appease as many gods as possible in order to curry favour with them (see the Cyrus Cylinder).

6–7. The ultimate purpose (i.e. *so that*) of bringing deliverance to Israel is to (1) demonstrate God's glory across the world (*from the rising of the sun / to the place of its setting* = a merism meaning 'everywhere'); and (2) show the nations that no god can compare with Yahweh (*so that . . . people may know there is none besides me. / I am the LORD, and there is no other*; v. 6).

The passage then concludes as it started, proclaiming God as the creator (v. 7). Mentioned among his creative powers is his ability to create circumstances that are both good (*šālôm*, 'peaceful'; a reference to what Cyrus and Israel would experience) and disastrous (rā', 'evil', 'calamity'; the outcome for Babylon). Because this verse can also be translated 'God creates evil', it often raises the question of whether a morally pure God could create evil. But verse 7 merely states that God can create circumstances that are either favourable or difficult. How a person chooses to respond to the circumstances will be either morally 'good' or 'evil'; for example, Adam and Eve were in ideal circumstances, and yet they chose to disobey God.

Meaning
Isaiah 44:28 – 45:7 brings to a climax God's argument: God is greater than any other so-called god because he will deliver Israel through Cyrus, the pagan king of Persia. Even though Yahweh guided and protected Israel throughout their history, they continued to rebel against him and follow other gods. But God is adamant that no idol or god can compare with him. He existed from the beginning and will continue to exist into the future. He has directed human events and will continue to do so. His use of Cyrus is one of the strongest arguments that none can compare with him.

vi. The true God is the creator (45:8–17)

Context
After the climax in Isaiah 44:28 – 45:7, God once again points out the folly of relying on anyone other than him. This section, 'The true God is the creator', 45:8–17, corresponds to the earlier section 'A true God cannot be created by people', 44:6–23, and has a similar theme (see Figure 0.10 on p. 26). Idols could never bring Cyrus to deliver the Israelites; only an all-powerful, all-knowing God could do that, and he will not be required to give Cyrus any payment or reward.

Comment

a. God's supreme power (45:8–13)
   8–10. Having just affirmed that he can do anything (i.e. *I bring prosperity and create disaster*, v. 7), God reveals that his ultimate plan

is to bring righteousness upon this earth. The heavens are exhorted to *rain down* (lit. 'drip or trickle down') God's righteousness. The earth is to *let salvation spring up* [and] *righteousness flourish* (v. 8). The whole of creation will be filled with God's righteousness and salvation because God *created* [*bārā'*] *it* (note that grammatically speaking the 'it' at the end of the verse in the Hebrew text must refer to *salvation* [*yeša'*]).

In contrast to this wonderful picture of righteousness and salvation that fill the earth (v. 8), two woe (*hôy*) oracles follow (vv. 9, 10). They each contain examples of the folly and presumption of people who argue against their Maker: *Woe to those who quarrel* [lit. 'to the one who is contending'] *with their Maker* [lit. 'the one who formed him'].

The contender is likened to *potsherds* [*ḥereś*, 'earthenware vessel, potsherd' (sing.)] *among the potsherds on* [lit. 'of'] *the ground*. The phrase *ḥereś ḥarśê 'ădāmâ*, 'earthenware jar among <u>jars of earth</u>' (the NIV reads *potsherds* for 'jars') occurs nowhere else, but the construct chain (the words underlined) indicates the material out of which the jar is made (i.e. clay). Whether one translates *ḥereś* as 'earthenware jar' or 'potsherd', the image remains the same: this is an average person who has no special strength or power among the others to back up his or her boastful claims.

The image continues with the clay pots (i.e. humans) questioning the judgment of the potter (God), saying, *What are you making?* or *The potter has no hands* (lit. 'your work [say] there are not hands to it' [the sing. suffix could refer to 'your work' or to God]). The cryptic nature of the latter phrase allows for a variety of interpretations: (1) the dual form of *hands* (*yādayim*) may represent the skilled work of the potter; thus the 'clay' is questioning the potter's ability; or (2) *hands* may be equivalent to 'handles' (on a pot) or 'feet' (on a basin/bowl); thus the 'clay' is questioning how the potter has chosen to fashion it.

Because the dual form of *hands* only ever refers to physical, human hands, the first option seems the most plausible. But the parallelism favours the second idea that the clay is questioning how the potter formed the vessel:

Will the clay say to the potter, 'What are you making?'
Or your work [say to the potter], 'There are no hands to it'?

Either way, God's creatures are complaining about his actions, without being specific. They could be dissatisfied that God has brought salvation to a remnant of Israel and not to all of them; or more probably they are protesting about how he did it, choosing Cyrus, who also destroyed many of them (see Childs 2001: 351). There could even be some from among the remnant who question God's choice in using a pagan to deliver them.

The second woe (v. 10) continues the same complaints against God as the woe in verse 9: *Woe to the one who says to a father, / 'What have you begotten?'* [lit. 'caused to be born'] / *or to a mother, / 'What have you brought to birth?'* Just as the clay questioned the actions of the potter, so the parents are being questioned for giving the child life. Once again, some are questioning God's actions in how he chose to deliver his nation.

11–13. Even though 'woes' have been pronounced upon the people who challenge God's actions, he now graciously offers them an explanation (*concerning things to come, / do you question me about my children . . . ?* lit. 'they question me about the things coming concerning my children'). There is some debate regarding whether God's people are posing questions or making statements, but the context favours questions.

God's titles reveal that he has the character (i.e. *the Holy One of Israel*) and the authority (i.e. *its Maker*) to produce righteousness in his nation. The first step is to deliver them from Babylon. God declares his capability, emphatically stating that he created the earth, humanity, the heavens and all that is in them (lit. 'I commanded all of their hosts', which means everything in the heavens). Therefore, he can surely raise up one individual, Cyrus, in order to set his people free: *I will raise up Cyrus in my righteousness* (lit. 'in righteousness', v. 13). The latter phrase either means 'to bring about righteousness' or is a reference to God's righteous plan.

God will *make all his* [Cyrus's] *ways straight* (i.e. unhindered) so that he can accomplish Yahweh's plan to rebuild Jerusalem (lit. 'he himself will build my city') and bring back the exiles (v. 13). Cyrus will accomplish all this with no thought of asking God for *a price* (lit. 'not in exchange for a payment') or *reward* (lit. 'present, bribe'). The word *reward* calls to mind King Ahaz who thought himself exceedingly wise for paying the Assyrians to destroy the

Syro-Ephraimite coalition. But in the end, they not only received this substantial payment from Ahaz, but they also were able to seize control of Judah. And yet, when God later used Persia to deliver Israel, there were no strings attached; God had no special tribute to pay for their release.

b. Because Yahweh has proven himself to be the true God, the wise will turn to him (45:14–17)

14–15. Verses 14–17 extend into the more distant future and will not be fulfilled merely by Israel's deliverance through Cyrus. Once again, from this prophetic perspective the prophet cannot distinguish how short or extended the time is between events. God will enrich his people with the *products* [lit. 'product'] *of Egypt and the merchandise of Cush*, as well as Sabean servants. The Sabeans are described as 'people of measurement' (i.e. 'unusual measurement'), an expression that implies they are tall in stature.

These same three nations were promised to Cyrus in 43:3–4 as a ransom instead of Israel, but ultimately they will come in subservience to Israel and will honour their God: (1) *they will trudge behind you* [Israel]; (2) *coming over to you in chains* [*ziqqîm*, 'fetters', 4x]; and (3) *they will bow down before you / and plead with you*; thus Israel will be a mediator between these nations and God. The terminology here implies captivity and subservience to Israel, not co-captivity with Israel in Babylon, as Childs suggests (2001: 351–352). They will acknowledge Yahweh as the one who brought about Israel's deliverance: *Surely God is with you . . . there is no other god* (v. 14).

The phrase *you are a God who has been hiding himself* (v. 15) could mean that (1) he 'hid his face' (reflexive) when Israel forsook him and persisted in sin (see Deut. 31:16–17); or (2) he was 'not visible' (passive) to Israel during their captivity, but at the right time he became visible to them again by acting on their behalf. Both are true.

16–17. While those who relied on idols (lit. 'engravers of idols' [*ṣîr*, 'idols', only here with this meaning]) will be put to shame and humiliated (lit. 'and even be humiliated', emphatic), those who rely on Yahweh will never (*to ages everlasting*, lit. 'for ever', emphatic) be put to shame. Instead, *Israel will be saved by the* LORD / *with an everlasting salvation*.

The phrase *everlasting salvation* (lit. 'deliverance forevers' [pl.], v. 17) means 'always delivered' and is parallel to *never be put to shame . . . to ages everlasting* (lit. 'until forevers [pl.] for ever' = 'for all times').

Meaning

It is a foolish thing to question the way God chooses to act, but those who complain in this passage have done just that. God defends his actions by declaring that it is he who created the universe, including humanity. He can therefore use Cyrus as his servant to accomplish all that he intends (e.g. free the exiles and rebuild his city and temple). God is not obligated to pay or reward Cyrus for his service because servants merely obey their masters out of duty.

But Israel's deliverance from Babylon is just the beginning: God will do something even greater. The Egyptians, Cushites and Sabeans will see the mighty works of Israel's God and come in submission to Israel. Those who rely on Yahweh will never be humiliated or put to shame. This is just as true today as it was back then.

vii. God further elaborates his plan (45:18–25)

Context

This section corresponds to 42:1 – 44:5, which also describes God's plan for delivering Israel (see Figure 0.10 on p. 26). His plan is declared publicly and is founded on righteousness so that other nations will see the greatness of Israel's God and come to him. A new element, only hinted at earlier, is explicitly introduced in this section: God's plan of deliverance is far broader than Israel alone. It will extend to the whole world (45:22), such that one day every person will bow before God and acknowledge him as the only God (45:23–24).

This section also contains a disputation speech (see v. 21) wherein God once again challenges the nations to entreat their gods to demonstrate that they can determine the future as he himself has done. God then reiterates that he is the only God and will one day be acknowledged as such.

Comment

18–19. The introduction to this section (v. 18) corresponds to the introduction of its corresponding section in the palistrophe (i.e. 42:5 in the section 42:1 – 44:5). The two introductions describe God as the creator of the world in very similar terms:

Isaiah 42:5   *This is what God the Lord says –*
the Creator of the heavens,
who stretches them out,
who spreads out the earth with all that springs from it,
who gives breath to its people, and life to those who walk
   on it.

Isaiah 45:18   *For this is what the LORD says –*
he who created the heavens, he is God;
he who fashioned and made the earth, he founded it;
he did not create it to be empty, but formed it to be
   inhabited –
he says: 'I am the LORD, and there is no other . . . '

The word *kî* (*for*) at the beginning of this section should most probably be translated as 'truly, indeed' (Williams §449) to stress the certainty of the statement that follows. Yahweh, the creator of the heavens and earth, has had a purpose for all of creation from the very beginning: *he did not create it* [i.e. creation] *to be empty* [*tōhû*, lit. 'a waste place'; see Gen. 1:2], / *but formed it to be inhabited*. He stresses the fact that creation was *created, fashioned, made* and *founded* by him. He therefore has a right to declare its purpose (he *formed it to be inhabited*). To make clear that no-one else has this right, he again declares that there is no other god; he alone is the LORD.

God did not perform any of his actions *in secret* [*sēter*, occurs only here], *somewhere in a land of darkness,*[7] but openly so that all nations might see that Yahweh keeps his promises (i.e. *I, the LORD, speak the truth*; v. 19).

---

7. The parallel phrase *Seek me in vain* [*tōhû*] should be read 'Seek me in a waste place [i.e. 'uninhabited place']', like the previous verse.

20–22. The NIV divides verse 20 into two sentences to make the meaning consistent with previous prophecies: God gathers up the true remnant from all nations (sentence 1), but there are still those who trust worthless idols (sentence 2). The grammar in the MT, which combines these phrases, suggests that they refer to the same group; thus God is summoning *fugitives* (lit. 'survivors'; i.e. those who have survived the Persian onslaught) from all the nations who still cling to worthless idols *that cannot save.*

The next verse (v. 21) proclaims how futile it is to carry around a wooden idol that cannot see, hear or deliver (v. 20). By contrast, there is great wisdom in trusting Yahweh; he declared his intentions long ago and his plans have been fulfilled.

God then asks the rhetorical question *Who foretold this* [i.e. Israel's deliverance; see v. 17] *long ago . . . ?* (lit. 'from before', v. 21). He answers his own question, declaring that he is the one who foretold this deliverance which has transpired. Yahweh has proven that he has no rivals (*And there is no God* [lit. 'there is not again a God'] *apart from me*), that he is indeed a righteous God and a true Saviour. He then addresses all people everywhere (*all you ends of the earth*, v. 22), urging them to turn to him (i.e. in belief) and be saved, for he is the only true God. The word *saved* (*yāšaʿ*) means 'to be rescued', opening up the possibility of a spiritual rescue later. In this major step into a new age, even Gentiles can turn to Yahweh (v. 22).

23–25. In the strongest words possible, *By myself I have sworn* (i.e. God is declaring by irrevocable oath, with inverted syntax for emphasis), Yahweh confirms that one day every knee will bow to him and every person will confess that he is the only God (see Dan. 7:13–14). If the nations will examine his oracles of the past, they will clearly see that Yahweh keeps his word. As a result, all people will have to acknowledge that he is the only true God and that only in the LORD is there righteousness ('righteousnesses', pl.; NIV, *deliverance*) and strength.

The next phrase further clarifies who will acquiesce to him: *All who have raged against him / will come to him and be put to shame* (v. 24). They will be forced to acknowledge that he is the true God, even if they do not necessarily accept him as their spiritual deliverer. Salvation is not, therefore, universal, but only for those who make the appropriate choice.

However, *all the descendants of Israel*, meaning those who have relied on the LORD, will be vindicated. They too will see and acknowledge that he is the one true God and will boast about their sovereign God who has delivered them. His people will at last be a light to the nations. They too will now see that this amazing, all-powerful God has delivered them. Even though only the believing remnant cared enough about serving God to take advantage of this deliverance from Babylon, the offer was open to all the exiled Israelites. The remnant's physical deliverance is a picture of their spiritual deliverance as they chose to step out in faith to return and rebuild Jerusalem and the temple so that they could offer the sacrifices God required.

Meaning

God created the world with a purpose and has been working out his plan throughout history. Because this plan has not been declared in secret, everyone will be held accountable for knowing it. God makes a universal call to the nations to turn to him and be delivered (v. 22), for there is no other God. Even the *fugitives from the nations* who follow idols will one day acknowledge Yahweh as the only true God: *before me every knee will bow; / by me every tongue will swear* (v. 23).

Those who have rebelled against God will one day be ashamed, but how encouraging this section is for those who have relied upon Yahweh! They will be vindicated and boast about their all-powerful God who keeps his promises and delivers his people.

viii. The case for God's punishment: the gods of Babylon versus the God of Israel (46:1 – 47:15)

Context

Isaiah 46 – 47 describes the downfall of Babylon's gods. In the palistrophe it is parallel to the description of Yahweh's case for delivering his people in 41:1–29 (see Figure 0.10 on p. 26). In contrast to the previous section in which Yahweh is acknowledged to be the only true God and even offers deliverance to all nations, here these false gods will be shamefully carried off to captivity on the backs of beasts and cattle (46:1–2). How degrading for Yahweh to be compared to such impotent idols.

Isaiah 46 – 47 begins as a disputation speech whose tone is more condemnatory than persuasive (Childs 2001: 359) but by chapter 47 sounds more like a lament. Nevertheless, the hope is that the truth will convince some Israelites of the error of relying on mere idols.

Scholars have questioned the historical accuracy of chapters 46–47 since certain details do not coincide with the events of 539 BC. For example, 46:1–2 states that *their idols are borne by beasts of burden* (lit. 'their images are for the animals and beasts') and are taken off into captivity; yet we know that Persia allowed the Babylonians to continue to worship their gods. However, it is possible that, as in other prophecies, the author combines events from various periods, not realizing the time difference between them. Nabonidus's own records describe how Sennacherib carried off Marduk, who remained in Ashur for twenty-one years (*ANET* 309). Nabonidus also mentions that during his own reign he brought his god Sin to Babylon, thereby replacing the worship of Marduk (*ANET* 312). Cyrus claims that Nabonidus set up imitations of the gods (*ANET* 315) in place of the originals, which may have been sent off to storage.

Another apparent discrepancy is the prediction of Babylon's destruction in 47:11; however, the city was captured, not decimated, in 539 BC. The word *šōʾâ*, 'destruction or ruin' (v. 11), would be better translated as *a catastrophe* (as in NIV) in this context. Historically, the Persian conquest of Babylon certainly qualifies as a catastrophic event. It is also possible that the poetic nature of these chapters allows for a figurative interpretation of these two events.

Chapter 46 divides into three sections: verses 1–2 describe the humiliation of the idols Bel and Nebo; the other two sections, verses 3–11 and 12–13, both begin with the exhortation *Listen to me* and encourage Israel to trust that God will deliver them. Chapter 47 has four sections: the first two (vv. 1–4, 5–7) begin with images of Babylon 'sitting' forlornly before going off into captivity; the next two (vv. 8–11, 12–15) describe the charges against Babylon. Isaiah 46 – 47 then concludes with the ominous warning to Babylon that *there is not one that can save you.*

Comment

a. The example of the Babylonian gods (46:1–4)

1–2. The opening of this section laments the sad situation of the chief Babylonian gods, who have been humiliated: *Bel* [*bēl*] *bows down, Nebo stoops low* (*qāras*, 2x, both in this context). This is similar to 2:9–22 where everything that has been lifted up will be brought low (i.e. humbled) before the majesty of Yahweh.

Bel is typically identified with Marduk, the patron god of Babylon and the head of the pantheon during the Neo-Babylonian period. *Nebo* (usually written as *Nabū*, the son of Marduk) was worshipped in Babylon's sister city Borsippa. He was the god of writing and wisdom, and keeper of the Tablets of Destiny, which conferred authority upon certain gods. The royal names Nebuchadnezzar and Nabonidus both contain the divine name Nebo.

These so-called gods, being defeated and humbled, were carried by *beasts of burden* (lit. 'they are for the animal and beast'). They had become a *burden for the weary*. The word *weary* may refer to the heavy load that tires a pack animal, or to the idol worshippers who have lost faith in the ability of these idols to deliver them from the Persians.

With tragic irony these so-called gods were unable to deliver themselves from being carried away (*unable to rescue* [lit. 'escape'] *the burden*), much less protect those who worshipped them. This shameful march into captivity contrasts significantly with the triumphal Babylonian New Year (*Akitū*) procession when Bel was paraded through the streets and then returned to his temple.

3–4. With the words *Listen to me*, God redirects Israel's attention away from Babylon's impotent, degraded idols to himself, with the assurance that he has constantly supported them: *I have upheld* [you] [lit. 'the one carrying you as a load'] *since your birth* [lit. 'from the belly'; i.e. 'womb', v. 3]. He then promises to rescue and sustain them throughout their lives (*even to your old age*, v. 4), although the promise does not extend to all of Israel but merely to a remnant.

The contrast is unmistakable: the Babylonian gods are 'being carried' (*nāśā'*) around by the beasts of burden because they have no power to act for themselves or others (vv. 1–2), whereas Yahweh has been carrying (*nāśā'*) the nation of Israel since their birth (vv.

3–4). God repeats for emphasis the promise *I* [lit. 'I myself', emphatic] *will sustain you* (v. 4).

b. Yahweh has no equals (46:5–13)

5–7. Yahweh once again challenges his people with the question *To whom will you liken me . . . ?* (see 40:25). Three different words for 'to liken' are used in this sentence to create emphasis: *dāmâ*, 'to be like'; *šāwâ*, 'to make like'; and *māšal*, 'to compare'.

Verse 6 describes the expense involved in making an idol: (1) *Some pour out* [*hazzālîm*, 'lavish'; occurs only here] *gold from their bags* [lit. 'from a bag', *kîs*, 6x, most often to hold 'weights'; see Deut. 25:13]; (2) [they] *weigh out silver on the scales* (*qāneh*, 'reed, rod', used in measurement, but in this verse the reed/rod is the beam that holds the scale pans); and (3) *they hire a goldsmith* [lit. 'refiner'] *to make it into a god* [*'ēl*]. Once the idol is made, they *bow down* (*sāgad*, 5x, all in the book of Isaiah; however, its Aramaic equivalent occurs 11x), and even (*'ap*, highlighting the incredibility of their actions) worship it. As mentioned above, the idol being carried on people's shoulders may be a reference to the Babylonian *Akitū* festival.

Perhaps because the Israelites fell into idolatry over and over again, God wishes to drive home the truth that people can make, carry and worship costly idols of silver and gold (vv. 6–7; see 44:12–20), but no matter how much time and money are lavished upon them, idols will never be able to respond to their *cries* for help or *save them from their troubles* (v. 7).

8–11. Verses 8–11 continue the disputation speech wherein God accuses the Israelites of having a long history of being *rebels* (lit. 'transgressors') and following after idols despite their covenant relationship with the only true God. God urges Israel to *Remember this, keep it in mind* (*wĕhit'ōšāšû, keep it in mind*, occurs only here), that idols cannot deliver anyone.

The word *remember* often has the connotation 'to take appropriate action', which in this case would be to give up their idols and serve God wholeheartedly. They are urged to recall that God had brought to pass *the former things, those of long ago* (i.e. their punishments; v. 9; see 43:18–19) that he had foretold. Just as certainly as those events took place, so their deliverance will come, a concept that has been repeated several times to encourage belief and trust.

Based upon that confirmation, there follows a statement to which both parties ought to be able to agree: *I am God, and there is no other* (lit. 'there is not any besides'). His pre-eminence is affirmed by the fact that he makes known everything from the beginning to the end and does not deviate from accomplishing his purpose (*My purpose* [i.e. plan] *will stand, / and I will do all that I please*, v. 10).

This is the sixth, and final, time in Isaiah 40 – 48 that God explains his plan to use Cyrus to deliver his people: *From the east I summon a bird of prey* ['*ayit*, 6x] . . . *a man to fulfil my purpose* (lit. 'a man of my plan', v. 11). The word 'surely' (*'ap*) is used three times in verse 11 for emphasis (the NIV does not include any of them), highlighting that Yahweh will use Cyrus to carry out the events he has previously ordained (*What I have said . . . what I have planned . . . I will do*, v. 11).

12–13. God delivers the stubborn, rebellious people of Israel *who are now far from my righteousness*, but he will bring his *righteousness near* and *grant salvation* to Israel. *Righteousness* and *salvation* are linked here in the sense that he is bringing salvation to Israel because of his righteousness. Verse 13 forms a chiasm:

A *I am bringing my righteousness near, it is not far away;*
 B *and my salvation will not be delayed.*
 B' *I will grant salvation to Zion,*
A' *my splendour to Israel.*

The word *splendour* in the final phrase describes God's *righteousness* in the first phrase. The phrase *I am bringing my righteousness near* means that, despite Israel's persistent pursuit of unrighteousness, God will continue to fulfil his plan to deliver Israel – what a gracious God!

c. A taunt song regarding Babylon (47:1–15)

1–3. Following the Ancient Near Eastern convention of referring to a city as female, Babylon is personified in verse 1 as *Virgin Daughter Babylon*. Presumably she is considered 'inviolate' or a *virgin* in the sense of never having been conquered, but that was about to change; thus the taunt *No more will you be called / tender or delicate*. Because of her extreme pride and her cruel oppression of Israel, she will be humiliated (i.e. removed from her throne and made to sit in the dust on the ground, v. 1).

Babylon is commanded to take off her *veil* (*ṣammâ*, a sign of virginity, 4x) and prepare for slave labour – that of grinding grain. According to Ridderbos, grinding grain with *millstones* (lit. 'hand mill') was 'one of the most arduous tasks performed by slave girls' (1986: 422). As a further degradation, Babylon is told to *Lift up your skirts* [*šōbel*, 'long flowing dress', occurs only here], *bare your legs* [*šōq*, 'thigh', an immodest sight], / *and wade through the streams* (a reference to deportation). Babylon is to be conquered, deported and subjected to hard labour, but she will experience even greater humiliation: her *nakedness will be exposed* as she is led off into captivity (v. 3). The queen has now been utterly humbled.

Whybray argues that this ridicule, intended to undermine the nation, was written before the destruction actually took place since it is not accurate: Cyrus did not totally destroy the city when he captured it (1975: 118–119). However, the taunt never mentions a 'total destruction'; the figurative images merely portray humiliation and defeat.

The phrase *I will spare no one* (lit. 'I come to an understanding with no-one' [*HALOT* 3.910]) indicates that the entire nation, from its leaders to its workers, will be punished when God takes vengeance (v. 3) on Babylon for her cruelty to God's people. Once again there is a contrast with the nation of Israel who were captives in Babylon, but who one day will be elevated in status to royalty (see 49:23).

Similar to elsewhere in Isaiah, the point of view here changes from verse to verse, making it difficult to know who is speaking. For example, the first person pronoun in 47:3b and 6 refers to Yahweh, whereas verse 4, written in the third person, reflects the words of the author.

4–7. The taunt flows right into a prophetic oracle. The author combines three titles in his description of God's punishment of Babylon: *our Redeemer*; *the LORD Almighty* (lit. 'hosts'); and *the Holy One of Israel* (v. 4).

Babylon, the *queen city* (lit. 'daughter') of the *Babylonians* (lit. 'Chaldeans'[8]), will *go into darkness* (lit. 'the darkness', v. 5), an image suggestive of captivity, and will *no more ... be called / queen* [lit. 'mistress, queen mother'] *of kingdoms* (i.e. will no longer rule other nations). First Babylon is told to *sit in silence* (*dûmām*, 2x), meaning that she is to take her rightful punishment without complaining or arguing.

God then cites two primary reasons for Babylon's punishment. First, when he used the Babylonians to punish his people, they were crueller and harsher than was necessary: *you showed them no mercy* [*raḥămîm*, 'mercies' (pl.), v. 6; see Ps. 137:8–9]. *Even on the aged / you laid a very heavy yoke* (*'ōl*, 'an animal's yoke'; this image came to represent a 'burden' or 'hard work'). It was considered excessively cruel in the Ancient Near East to place those who were aged into forced labour, as Israel's aged were compelled to do.

Second, Babylon's unmitigated arrogance led her to blaspheme, falsely claiming that she would be queen for ever over all her enemies and therefore rival to Yahweh's eternal sovereignty: *I am for ever – the eternal queen!* (v. 7; see also vv. 8, 10). Yahweh will hold her responsible for her actions and her boasts. Yet Babylon *did not consider these things* [lit. 'you did not take these things to your heart'] *or reflect on what might happen* (v. 7). It never crossed her mind that God could punish her and remove her from her position of power.

8–9. The words *now then* (v. 8) introduce God's further condemnation of Babylon: (1) God accuses her of being a *lover of pleasure* (*'ădînâ*, 'pleasure-seeking, self-indulgent', occurs only here). (2) She mistakenly considers herself secure, thinking none would dare to attack her (lit. 'dwelling securely'). (3) She is under the delusion that none could challenge her ultimate power: *I am, and there is none besides me* (v. 8; see also v. 10 and God's claim in 44:6; 47:7). This boast was another challenge to Yahweh's claim to sovereignty.

---

8. Marduk-apal-iddina II (the biblical Marduk-Baladan), leader of the district known as Bit-Yakin, took control of Babylon in 721–710 BC and 703–702 BC. Because he was a Chaldean king, at this time the country of Babylon was sometimes referred to as Chaldea, and its people the Chaldeans (*IBD* 1.258).

(4) She thinks herself immune to loss and defeat: *I will never be a widow / or suffer the loss of children*. In the Ancient Near East a widow who was childless (*šĕkôl*, 2x) was effectively bereft of material support, protection and honour.

God declares that the very thing Babylon, once called the *queen of kingdoms* (v. 5), never expected will come upon her quickly; she will be captured *in a moment, on a single day*. Her punishment will come *in full measure* (lit. 'completely'), meaning it will be severe, with nothing and no-one to spare her. None of her *many sorceries* (*kešep*, 5x) and *potent spells* (*ḥeber*, 4x with this meaning) will bring relief.

10–11. Babylon thought she could act with impunity, being deceived in her thinking (i.e. *your wisdom and knowledge mislead you* [lit. 'lead you astray']). She assumed that her actions would go unnoticed (*No one sees me*) and unchallenged (*I am, and there is none besides me* [lit. 'and no-one else']). Her blasphemous *I am* boast is strikingly similar to God's own legitimate claims (see 43:11; 44:6, 8). Yet Yahweh was well aware of her wickedness, especially in her cruel treatment of Israel, and would most certainly hold her accountable. His judgment could not be averted, either by 'conjuring' (*šaḥrāh*) it away (although disputed, this is the most likely meaning here, v. 11) or by offering a *ransom* (lit. 'to atone' in this context may carry the nuance 'to pacify'; see Gen. 32:20).

Their punishment, described as *disaster* (lit. 'evil'), *calamity* (*hôwâ*, 2x) and *catastrophe* (*šô'â*, 'trouble, ruin'), would come upon them suddenly. The Persians did in fact take Babylon quickly – in a single night (see Herodotus, *Hist.* 1.189–191).

12–13. The author taunts Babylon with the uncertainty and futility of calling upon her many gods (i.e. *Perhaps you will succeed, / perhaps you will cause terror*, v. 12). Their *magic spells* and *sorceries* might cause fear among the other nations, but would have no effect on Yahweh, the true God. The author urges them to consult their astrologers (lit. 'the ones seeing by the stars'), who were renowned for their special powers, knowing that nothing they said or did could avert the impending judgment.

14–15. The word *surely* (*hinnēh*) draws attention to the conclusion. Babylon's astrologers are as powerless as *stubble* burned up in a fire; *They cannot even save themselves / from the power of the flame* (v. 14). These are not flames that provide the comforts of warmth and light (lit.

'These are not coals [*gaḥelet*, 2x] for their warmth; this is not a fire to sit before it'). This is a terrible consuming fire that will annihilate them, leaving nothing: *there is not one that can save you* (v. 15).

Meaning

While God has protected Israel and brought her a deliverer, the gods of Babylon are powerless to rescue her people. The contrast could not be more striking: on the one hand, Israel's God controls history, even using a pagan king to do his will; on the other, man-made idols are so entirely powerless that they cannot even save themselves from being carried away on the backs of donkeys.

Powerful and invulnerable Babylon cannot in fact resist God, thus demonstrating to Israel the greatness of her God.

ix. Israel's faithlessness is rebuked, but deliverance is promised (48:1–22)

Context

Chapter 48, the final section of the palistrophe in Isaiah 40 – 48, centres once again on Yahweh's promise of deliverance for Israel, the main theme of chapter 40 as well (see Figure 0.10 on p. 26). At the end of this chapter lies another of the book's seams (48:17–22), which summarizes three main themes of Isaiah: (1) Israel has been judged (past) (48:17–19); (2) Israel will be delivered (48:20–21); and (3) the wicked will be punished (48:22). The theme of a remnant that appears in the seams of chapters 1–39 no longer appears in the seams of chapters 40–66, since God is speaking only to the believing remnant (i.e. those returning to Israel).

The seam ends with a refrain that closes the first section of Isaiah 40 – 66 and summarizes much of the book's message: *'There is no peace,' says the* LORD, *'for the wicked'* (48:22; see 57:21; 66:24). The introductory statement to the seam in verse 17 is almost identical to the introduction of the salvation oracle that begins in 43:14. Both contain three of God's names: *the* LORD, *your Redeemer* and *the Holy One of Israel*, each of which is an important reminder of God's relationship to Israel.

There are three sections in chapter 48: (1) a disputation oracle that begins with the word *šāmaʿ* ('hear' or 'listen') (vv. 1–11); (2) a trial speech that also begins with *šāmaʿ* (vv. 12–16); and (3) a divine declaration, introduced by the words *This is what the* LORD *says* (vv. 17–22). Chapter 48 pushes the Israelites to realize that God had announced his plan long ago, a plan that began with judgment (i.e. the *former things*, v. 3) and ends with restoration (i.e. the *new things*, v. 6). God laments that if only Israel had obeyed initially, they would have been spared much punishment. The good news is that they will one day receive unending peace and righteousness (v. 18). We also often have reason to lament the 'if only's in our lives.

Comment

a. Israel's obstinacy (48:1–11)

1–2. The author begins this oracle with a summons to all Israel: *you who are called by the name of Israel / and come from the line* [*mimmê*, 'waters', possibly suggesting seminal fluids] *of Judah.*[9] A more likely reading of this phrase is *and come* 'from the loins' [*mimmēʿê*, i.e. a change in one letter] *of Judah*, following 1QIsaᵃ, *BHS* and Mishnah. Even though Israel split from Judah in 931 BC, their similar origin is emphasized in both readings. The author criticizes their hypocritical behaviour, saying they *take oaths in the name of the* LORD and *invoke* [*zākar*, 'profess, praise'; see 26:13] *the God of Israel – / but not in truth or righteousness.*

The Israelites claim to believe in the LORD, calling themselves *citizens* [lit. 'from'] *of the holy city.* They *claim to rely on the God of Israel – / the* LORD *Almighty* (lit. 'LORD of hosts'), but all their religious words and activities are a mockery, for they refuse to obey Yahweh. It is as though they want all the benefits of the covenantal relationship without a commitment to obey him.

3–5. God reminds Israel that he declared the *former things* (i.e. punishment for their rebellious ways) long ago, knowing that it would be hard for them to obey him (see God's warnings in Deut. 28:15–28). Even though God had long warned of the *former things* (i.e. punishments), when the time came to act it would seem to

---

9. There are no other examples of the phrase 'waters of Judah/Israel'; thus, it appears that the Hebrew letter *ʿayin* has fallen out.

come suddenly: *then suddenly I acted and they* [i.e. 'the things', meaning the judgment] *came to pass* (v. 3).

God likens Israel's obstinacy to the strongest-known metals at the time: *your neck muscles were iron, / your forehead was bronze* (v. 4). He announced his actions well in advance so that he could undercut any claims they might make that their idols (*'ōṣeb*, 'false god' [only occurrence with this meaning]; *pesel*, 'divine image'; *nesek*, 'metal statue') had brought about these punishments (v. 5).

6–9. In spite of the nation's rebelliousness since inception (*Well do I know how treacherous you are*, v. 8), God explains to Israel that *From now on I will tell you* [lit. 'I have caused you to hear'] *of new things, / of hidden things* [lit. 'guarded things'] *unknown to you* regarding their deliverance from Babylon through Cyrus. God had warned Israel of punishment for their rebellion since the time of their entry into Canaan, but the message of deliverance was revealed only during the time of Isaiah.

God had *hidden* these *new things* (i.e. *You have neither heard . . . your ears have not been open*) regarding the details of their deliverance so that they would not be able to deceive themselves into thinking they had known God's plan all along (v. 7) or that their idols had revealed it to them, for God knew how treacherous they were (lit. 'because I knew you would deal very deceptively' [emphatic word order]). The phrase *new things* (pl.; v. 6) refers to all the events surrounding Israel's deliverance and return to Israel under Cyrus. The statement that these *hidden things . . . are created now, and not long ago* (vv. 6–7) does not mean God is initiating a new plan, but rather that God's plan is only now taking shape.

The unusual switch between second person singular and plural forms in verse 6 highlights that each person (sing.) has now heard about the deliverance so that collectively they (pl.) can declare it.

Israel's persistent rebellion throughout their history was reason enough for Yahweh to destroy them; however, God demonstrated his great patience (*I delay my wrath*, lit. 'made long my anger', and the parallel phrase *I hold it back* [*ḥāṭam*, 'to restrain', occurs only here] *from you*, v. 9) towards the nation for his *own name's sake* (i.e. his reputation, v. 9; this phrase does not appear elsewhere in Isaiah, but see Ezek. 20:8–9) and to allow them to continue as a nation (lit. 'so as not to cut you off').

God gave Israel every chance to turn to him, something that only a remnant would do. This remnant would demonstrate their faith in God by leaving their families, homes, and so on, to return to a destroyed land and rebuild the temple to offer the sacrifices required by God. If God could bring a remnant of rebellious Israelites to true repentance, then he truly is a gracious and awesome God.

10–11. The interjection *see* (*hinnēh*) lends emphasis to Yahweh's patient work of refining the nation, not with fire as is done with silver, but through afflictions and trials. In the clause *I have tested you in the furnace of affliction* (v. 10), the MT's reading *běḥartîkā*, 'I chose you', should be read as *běḥantîkā*, 'I tested you' (i.e. a change of one Hebrew letter). This reading is supported by 1QIsa^a and is parallel to the preceding phrase. God states that he does so *for my own sake* (repeated for emphasis, v. 11), so as not to be dishonoured (*How can I let myself* [lit. 'it' = my name] *be defamed?*).

Apparently, God's name had been defamed for allowing his people to be taken off into exile (see Moses in the wilderness, Exod. 32:11–14). He will now lead them out of exile to restore the glory of his name (i.e. *I will not yield* [lit. 'give'] *my glory to another*, v. 11). God jealously guards his glory so that other nations will not question his abilities and goodness, thinking him a feeble, indecisive God.

b. The promise of deliverance (48:12–16)

12–14. At the beginning of this oracle God repeats the call to *listen* to what he declares about himself: *I am he;* / *I am the first and* [lit. 'even I am'] *the last.* In other words, he is the eternal God who knows the outcomes throughout all of history. The phrase *I am he* (v. 12) implies that he is the one who sovereignly controls all things (see 41:4; 43:13), having created the world: [*'Even', 'ap*] *my own hand laid the foundations of the earth,* / *and my right hand spread out* [*ṭāpaḥ*, occurs only here] *the heavens* (v. 13).

In verse 14 the author interrupts God's first-person narration to explain to Israel (i.e. *all of you*) that God would use Cyrus to carry out his plan against the Babylonians. They are to *listen* and reflect on the rhetorical question 'Who among them [the gods] has declared these things?' (i.e. the *new things* of v. 6; NASB). The implied response is that no-one else could have done this.

Even though he is not mentioned by name, this is the seventh time that Cyrus is introduced. The context makes clear who is being referred to: *The LORD's chosen ally* [lit. 'loves him'] who *will carry out his purpose* [lit. 'his delight'] *against Babylon; / his arm will be against the Babylonians* (lit. 'Chaldeans').

15–16. God's power and truthfulness are underscored in his statement *I, even I, have spoken.* Cyrus will indeed *succeed in his mission* (lit. 'his way') to punish the Babylonians and release the exiles to return to their homelands (v. 15).

There is a shift in person when the *Sovereign LORD* is referred to in the third person at the end of verse 16: *And now the Sovereign LORD* [lit. 'the Lord (*ădōnāy*) LORD (*yĕhwih*)'] *has sent me, / endowed with his Spirit.* Opinion varies regarding the identity of the speaker (i.e. *me*): (1) Isaiah, (2) Cyrus or (3) another prophet. Ridderbos argues for another prophet (1986: 431), yet there is no mention in Isaiah of another prophet.

Each phrase in verse 16 could easily pertain to Isaiah: (1) God's spirit comes upon Isaiah to empower him to exhort the people to *come near* and *listen* (cf. v. 14); (2) his messages were publicly declared (i.e. *I have not spoken in secret*); (3) he declared Yahweh's message about Cyrus and could confirm its veracity (i.e. *at the time it happens, I am there*); and (4) he declared God's messages on numerous occasions: *And now the Sovereign LORD has sent me, / endowed with his* [God's] *Spirit* (see Firth and Wegner 2011: 233–244). Other examples of an abrupt change in speaker between Isaiah and God include 5:2–3; 6:8; 8:1–3; 10:12.

Some scholars have argued that verse 16 is a statement of the Trinity in the Old Testament (Chafer 1948: 1.301; Grudem 2020: 271–272), but this is clearly not what Isaiah would have meant. At this point in God's revelation the concept of the Trinity was not yet revealed. *His Spirit* was a reference to the power that emanated from God; at least this is how the Old Testament author would have understood it. The phrase is therefore best translated as 'the LORD has sent me [Isaiah], empowered by his spirit [God's power]' (Firth and Wegner 2011: 233–244).

*c. A message of remorse and restoration; **SEAM** (48:17–22) (Refrain: 'There is no peace,' says the LORD, 'for the wicked')*

17–19. Verse 17 marks the beginning of the seam that ends this section (Isa. 40 – 48). The messenger of verse 16 now delivers Yahweh's message in the first person. Once again God refers to himself using the same three names, *the LORD* [Yahweh], *your Redeemer, the Holy One of Israel*, as in 43:14 (see also 44:24; 45:11), in order to emphasize his relationship to Israel. He is the one who knows what is best for the nation and directs them (v. 17).

If only (*lû'* particle, indicating a hypothetical past condition, but emphasizing God's desire) Israel *had paid attention to* and obeyed God's commands, they would have been greatly blessed with endless *peace* (*šālôm*) and 'righteousness' (*ṣidāqâ*; NIV, *well-being*); many descendants, as numberless as the *grains* (*mā'â*, occurs only here) of sand; and the unending protection of God's presence (i.e. *their name would never be blotted out . . . before me*). The images of a *river*, the incessant movement of *the waves of the sea*, offspring as numerous as the grains of sand, and Israel constantly being in God's presence – all convey the abundance Israel forfeited by their disobedience.

Rather than being oppressive, the law supplied the guidelines needed to allow them to prosper. Choosing not to follow God's commands led them into sin, idolatry, and ultimately captivity.

20–22. This section (chs. 40–48) ends where it began, with Israel fleeing the Babylonian captivity: *Leave Babylon, / flee from the Babylonians!* (lit. 'Chaldeans',[10] v. 20). When the Babylonians were defeated by Cyrus, the Israelites left with *shouts of joy* under Cyrus's more favourable policy of allowing captives to return to their home country.

Verses 20–21 are a song of deliverance that describes how Yahweh *redeemed* the nation of Israel (v. 20). Verse 21 reminds Israel that God had provided them with abundant provisions during their journey through the desert; their experience is likened to the first exodus when God brought water from a rock (Exod. 17:6).

The first part of Isaiah 40 – 66 closes with the refrain *'There is no peace,' says the LORD, 'for the wicked'* (v. 22), which in this context

---

10. About 626 BC they became synonymous with the Neo-Babylonian Empire, as this verse notes.

means that there will be no deliverance for the wicked of Israel. As this refrain progresses further in the book (i.e. 57:21; 66:24), it appears to take on a broader meaning regarding the final destruction of the wicked. The essence of deliverance has a spiritual dimension: only those who fear and reverence Yahweh will be delivered.

The similar refrain in 57:21 uses a different name for God ('Yahweh', 48:22; 'my God' [*ʾĕlōhîm*], 57:21). It is possible that the use of the name Yahweh, God's covenantal name, was meant to emphasize that he would deliver them based upon his covenantal relationship with Israel.

Meaning

Chapter 48 concludes this section of Isaiah by highlighting the Lord's constant reminders that he would care for the Israelites, including both punishment for disobedience and blessing for obedience (Deut. 8). The Israelites demonstrated time and again that they were a stubborn people who continued to wander off into idolatry and sin. God longed for them to exhibit a change of heart. He laments that if only they had been obedient, their experience could have been very different (vv. 18–19).

When they did not repent, his justice demanded punishment, and they were carried off into exile in Babylon. God describes this as their being tested in the furnace of affliction (v. 10). Yet to prevent his name from being disgraced among the nations, he would use Cyrus to deliver his people. Then all nations would know that God is the true Redeemer of Israel (vv. 17, 20).

Nevertheless, there will be some who continue to rebel against him; God declares that there will be no peace for them. The phrase *no peace* has two dimensions: (1) in the short term, they will not be delivered from Babylon; and (2) on a spiritual level, they will forfeit their relationship with God and thereby experience eternal punishment.

Once Israel has been punished sufficiently for her sins (40:2), Yahweh will deliver a remnant from exile and bring them back to the land (40:10–11). To accomplish Israel's deliverance Yahweh will call Cyrus, a pagan king, who will achieve God's purposes without payment or reward (see 45:13). Cyrus could be considered a 'messianic figure', for Yahweh called him (41:2; 46:11) to bring about his purpose (44:28; 48:14–15) of deliverance for Israel (44:28; 45:13).

God did not declare this deliverance previously, for rebellious Israel would think that they already knew about it or that their idols had delivered them. Instead this deliverance would be so amazing that no-one would be able to doubt it was the work of a sovereign, all-powerful God. Yet not every Israelite will obey, and for those who do not there will be *no peace*.

God shows unparalleled patience towards Israel, not forcing or coercing them to obey. Nevertheless, he uses discipline, which he had clearly outlined in the law, to bring them back to himself. Israel could have escaped all the harsh treatment and punishment if only they had lived obediently (see 48:18–19).

B. Zion is restored through Yahweh's servant (49:1 – 57:21)

Isaiah 49 – 57 again describes God's deliverance of a remnant of Israel, except that this section goes beyond the deliverance from Babylon when it states that eunuchs and foreigners (56:3–8) can also have a part in it. These chapters open with the second Servant Song and form the second major section of Isaiah 40 – 66 (see Figure 0.11 on p. 29). God had turned his back on Israel for a short time, but now he is ready to deliver them. In addition, the destruction that was directed towards Israel in the first part of Isaiah is now directed against their enemies.

God will use his 'servant' to deliver Israel, but the identity of this servant is somewhat vague. Since no-one in Israel could serve as their deliverer (see 50:2a; 51:18), Yahweh would have to bring his own.

The seam (57:15–21) at the end of this section begins with *For this is what the high and exalted One says* (v. 15) and includes the same three elements as other seams in the book: (1) Israel has been judged (57:16–17); (2) Israel will be delivered (57:18–19); and (3) the wicked will be punished (57:17, 20–21). The refrain *'There is no peace,' says my God, 'for the wicked'* (57:21) once again marks the end of a section in the book, except that this time the title *my God* is used instead of *the LORD*. The author's reference to *my God* in chapter 57 emphasizes his close relationship with this powerful God.

This new section (chs. 49–57) contains another set of oracles concerning the restoration and glorification of Zion. One of the most significant differences between this section and Isaiah 40 – 48 is that some themes prevalent in chapters 40–48 (e.g. Cyrus, the capture of Babylon and idolatry) are no longer mentioned. The exodus from Babylon is still alluded to as a demonstration of God's amazing power, but the name 'Babylon' is no longer used (see 52:11). The theme of the 'servant' will culminate in this section and cease to be referred to after it.

i. God will restore Zion (49:1–26)
Context

Chapter 49 consists of two parts: (1) the second of Isaiah's Servant Songs (vv. 1–13); and (2) a disputation oracle in which Israel claims that God has forgotten her, but Yahweh assures her that he has not (vv. 14–26). In this interesting Servant Song Israel is chosen first to be God's servant until she realizes that she cannot accomplish his deliverance; God must then send another servant, the Messiah.

When in the disputation oracle that follows (v. 14) Zion laments that God has forgotten her, God compellingly reassures her that he will never forget her (v. 15). He then declares that the world's nations will bring Zion's children back to her (v. 22) – so many, in fact, that she will soon become cramped for space (v. 20). God will also fight on her behalf, seeking retribution against her former oppressors (vv. 25–26).

Comment
a. The second Servant Song (49:1–13)
(i) Yahweh's servant is a light to the nations (49:1–6)

1–3. As the song opens, the servant entreats the Gentiles (*you islands; you distant nations*) to *listen* to his important message: he has been called by the Lord to be his servant. The Lord formed a special plan for this servant even before he was born (*before I was born the Lord called me; / from my mother's womb* [lit. 'loins'] *he has spoken* [lit. 'remembered'] *my name*). Similar terminology regarding the servant's calling is used for Israel (43:1), Cyrus (45:4), Jeremiah (Jer. 1:5) and even Paul (Gal. 1:15).

Verses 2–3 confirm the servant's commissioning: the images of a *sharpened sword* (i.e. both precise and deadly) and a *polished* [*bārûr*, 'chosen, selected, sharpened'] *arrow* (i.e. a weapon prepared for God's use) suggest that he is specially equipped to be Yahweh's mouthpiece. He is made all the more effective having been hidden in *the shadow of his* [God's] *hand* and concealed *in his quiver* until an appointed time. Isaiah 51:16 uses similar terminology to refer to Israel (*I have put my words in your mouth / and covered you with the shadow of my hand*).

We learn in verse 3 that *Israel* is the servant (*You are my servant, / Israel*)[11] through whom God's *splendour* will be displayed (see 44:23). From among all the nations in the world God has prepared a specific servant, the nation of Israel. God's quiver holds many arrows (i.e. nations), but this one is special because it will be used to draw the other nations to himself, to be a kingdom of priests (a priest is God's intermediary between himself and the people; Exod. 19:5–6).

4–6. Despite God's clear calling of the servant and his promise to work through him (v. 3), the servant looks back over his work and declares that it has accomplished nothing; that he has not been able to do what God required of him: *But I said, 'I have laboured in vain* [*rîq*, 'for nothing, empty']*; / I have spent my strength for nothing at all* [*tōhû*, 'emptiness, nothing']*'* (v. 4). Yet he is confident that God will, in due course, deliver him (*my reward is with my God*, v. 4). One of the most common evangelical interpretations of this song is that it refers to the Messiah, even though it is unlikely he would claim to have spent his strength in vain. As we have already noted, verse 3 identifies the servant as Israel.

Once Israel realizes that it cannot fulfil this calling, God moves to the next step in his plan, introduced by the words *And* [i.e. 'so'] *now the* LORD *says* (v. 5a): he will raise up another servant, the

---

11. Of the several translations proposed for v. 3, the reading 'And he said to me, "You are my servant, O Israel, through you I will be glorified"' is preferred because of the order of the Hebrew phrases and normal Hebrew grammar. The difficulty of this translation is that in v. 5 the servant's job is to bring Israel back to God.

Messiah, in order *to bring Jacob* [i.e. Israel] *back to him* (v. 5). There are multiple interpretations of this verse. (1) Some suggest the servant is Israel (Muilenburg 1956: 565); Childs agrees that the servant is Israel, now embodied in a suffering, individual figure (2001: 387). Williamson suggests that it is a remnant of Israel (Williamson 1994: 150–152). (2) Others identify the servant as Second Isaiah (Whybray 1975: 138; Blenkinsopp 2000: 300) or all the prophets merged into a single prophet (McKenzie 1968: 105). (3) Smith proposes that Israel (either the land or the people) is where God will be glorified (2009: 346). (4) Some suggest the servant will function as Israel, to be God's special messenger (Oswalt 1998: 291; Motyer 1999: 309).

The servant's call and commission appear in verses 5–6: (1) *he who formed me in the womb to be his servant* (parallel to v. 1; the phrase also suggests a special relationship with God); and (2) *to bring Jacob back to him / and gather Israel to himself.*[12] God will honour him (v. 5b) and enable him to complete his assigned task (*my God has been my strength*).

This new servant will be tasked with an even greater assignment than bringing the preserved (*nĕṣîrê*) ones of Israel (i.e. a remnant) back to God; he will be a witness to the Gentiles: *I will also make you a light for the Gentiles* [lit. 'nations' (pl.)], / *that my salvation may reach* [lit. 'to be my salvation'] *to the ends of the earth* (see 52:10). The servant is to *be* the salvation (i.e. to be God's means) and not merely a witness to God's salvation. The mission to which Israel was initially called, namely to bring other nations to God, will actually be accomplished by this servant.

(2) Two further oracles concerning the servant (49:7–13)

7. The prophet's message here further explains the earlier message concerning the servant. This message comes from *the LORD* who is called *the Redeemer* and *the Holy One of Israel* (see 48:17), two titles that reflect God's intimate relationship to his people. The message is directed to the servant, who is described in terms of

---

12. The phrase should be translated as 'and gather Israel to himself', using the *qĕrê* reading *lô*, 'to him', rather than the *kĕthîb* reading *lōʾ*, 'not'.

several seemingly contradictory statements: he was *despised and abhorred by the nation* [sing.] of Israel (see also 53:3), but *kings* and *princes* from other nations will honour him; he is said to be a *servant of rulers*, and yet kings and princes will *bow down* to him.

The phrase *the servant of rulers* does not appear to align with the rest of the sentence: if kings and princes will show him honour,[13] how can he be a servant to them? This is one of the puzzling aspects of the servant. He will serve and aid leaders, but not in a way they would expect: he will die for their sins, as we will see later in 53:4–9.

God has chosen the servant to accomplish his goals. He will succeed and be honoured by the nations because of the LORD's faithfulness. This promise is confirmed by *the LORD, the Holy One of Israel, who is faithful.* This is the only place in the book of Isaiah that explicitly affirms that the LORD is faithful. Israel need have no fears regarding their deliverance.

8–13. The second oracle (vv. 8–13), which opens with the familiar phrase *This is what the LORD says,* assures the servant that God will use him to restore the nation of Israel (*I will help you*). At a suitable time planned by God (*the time of my favour*), God will bring the servant *to be a covenant for the people* [*'am* sing.], most probably Israel or a remnant of Israel; see 42:6].

Apparently, the servant will be the manifestation of this covenant (*běrît*, 'agreement'), meaning he will be the guarantee between God and Israel that God will restore to them their lands, including areas destroyed in 586 BC. In 42:6 Cyrus is also said to be a covenant for the people, yet he only partially completed the task of deliverance when he allowed them to return to Israel and build their temple.

This servant will not only provide release from captivity (v. 9), he will also protect them (v. 10), ensure they have ample provisions (v. 10) and bring them back from many places, not only Babylon (v. 12). Those who return (i.e. *Come out; Be free*) are pictured as flocks who are abundantly provided for along the way. They will easily

---

13. Notice that kings show honour to the servant by standing and princes by bowing down.

find food during the journey to Israel (*will feed beside the roads / and find pasture on every barren hill*, v. 9). He will *lead them beside springs* [*mabbû'ê*, 3x] *of water* (v. 10).

He will protect them under the harshest of conditions (*šārāb*, 'the sun's scorching heat', 2x) as they travel through the hostile, barren hills of the desert. The figurative language of verse 11 depicts the lengths to which God will go to remove all obstacles on the long route home, turning his *mountains into roads* and raising up the low valleys (*my highways will be raised up*). The image of returning on highways is repeated in, for example, 11:16; 19:23.

But the most startling aspect of this return from exile is how far reaching it is in scope. The exiles come not only from Babylon, but from other regions as well (v. 12): *from afar*, from the *north*, from the *west* (lit. 'the sea') and *from the region of Aswan* (lit. *Sînîm*).

The word *Sînîm* occurs only here and may refer to any of the following regions: (1) an area in the south called Sin ('Pelusium', Ezek. 30:15); (2) Syene (possibly a corruption of *sĕwēnîm* = Egyptian *Swn* or modern *Aswān*; see 1QIsaᵃ; Ezek. 30:6); or (3) Sin in the Sinai Desert (Exod. 16:1). We favour Syene, a district on the southern frontier of ancient Egypt (Blenkinsopp 2000: 303–304; Smith 2009: 355). Regardless of the exact locations, the key here is that exiles will come from all points of the compass, well beyond the return from Babylon.

The oracle ends with a glorious outburst of praise to Yahweh (v. 13). The heavens and earth are exhorted to *burst* [*pāṣaḥ*, 8x; 6x in the book of Isaiah] *into song* because of the 'comfort' (*nāḥam*) and *compassion* (*rāḥam*; the two words sound similar in the Hebrew) which the LORD displays for his people, *his afflicted ones*.

b. Zion's restoration (49:14–26)

(1) God has not forgotten his people Israel (49:14–21)

14–15. Turning from the prospect of deliverance to their current condition in exile, we now hear a complaint from Israel: *But Zion said, 'The LORD has forsaken me'* (v. 14). The Israelites exiled in Babylon wondered whether God had forgotten them and would ever again act on their behalf (see 40:27). The LORD immediately reassures them that this is not the case; that his love for his nation is much too strong for him to abandon them: *Can a mother forget the baby at her breast* ['*ûl*, 'suckling', 2x] . . . *?* / *Though she may forget, / I* [myself = for emphasis] *will not forget you!* (v. 15). God affirms that even if a mother could forget her baby (something highly unlikely), he could never forget Israel. God's love far exceeds every form of human love.

16–17. The dramatic imagery of verse 16 underscores God's love for Jerusalem and how personally invested he is: *See* [*hinnēh* = indeed], *I have engraved you on the palms of my hands* [the inside hollow or flat of the hand]*; / your walls are ever before me* (see *ANEP* fig. 749). In this context 'engraving' implies cutting with a sharp object. Even though Israel was forbidden from tattooing and self-mutilating by cutting (see Lev. 19:28), God uses this image to reinforce how permanent is his love for them. His engraved hands and Israel's walls serve as a constant reminder to God of Israel – he could never forget them.

The imagery of verses 16–17 is progressive, moving from God's ever-present care of Zion's walls, to Zion's sons[14] who <u>hurry back</u> to rebuild them, and finally to the departure of those who <u>destroy</u> and <u>devastate</u> Zion's walls. In Hebrew, the underlined words 'hurry back' (***mihărû***) and 'destroy/devastate' ('your destroyers' = ***mĕharsayik***; 'your devastators' = ***mahăribayik***) sound similar.

18–21. Zion is directed to *Lift up your eyes* (v. 18; downcast eyes indicate sadness) in anticipation of restoration, ready to watch her scattered inhabitants be gathered back from all directions. The LORD confirms with an oath (*As surely as I live*) that he will restore Zion, that her children will return to her. These children, born to Zion during her *bereavement* (the time when her land was *ruined, made desolate* and *laid waste*), will be so numerous that the land will now be too small an area to hold them (*now you will be too small for your people*, v. 19). They will ask Zion to make room for them (lit. 'draw near to me that I will dwell [here]', v. 20).

---

14. 1QIsaᵃ, Aquila (a Greek translation) and Vulg. read 'your builders' will come quickly. However, the MT's reading 'sons' makes good sense, since it will more than likely be the sons who do the rebuilding. Either way, there is little difference in the overall meaning.

Zion will wonder where they have all come from: *'Who bore me these? / I was bereaved and barren; / I was exiled and rejected'* (v. 21). Her God-fearing children (some of whom are Israelites by birth, others of whom are adopted as Israelites because their hearts are obedient to God) will be as jewels that ornament Zion, the bride, to enhance her beauty (v. 18). Not only will her offspring be numerous, but those who had destroyed (lit. 'swallowed') the land will be so far removed that the Israelites will have nothing to fear upon their return to rebuild the ruins of Jerusalem (v. 19).

This return of Israel's children began during the reign of Cyrus, but because the large number of offspring here does not correspond to the small remnant that returned from Babylon, a return that continues into the future is suggested (see 19:23–25). This return is a fulfilment of God's promise to the servant in 49:6.

(2) Yahweh has restored Zion's children (Isa. 49:22–26)

22–23. While the familiar phrase *This is what the Sovereign LORD* [lit. 'the Lord (*'ădōnāy*) LORD (*yĕhwih*)'] *says* (v. 22) marks the beginning of a new unit, its content is largely the same as that of the previous unit. God will beckon to the Gentile nations, lifting up both his hand and his banner to signal that they should bring his remnant back to their land: *I will lift up my banner* [*nissî*; see 11:12] *to the peoples; / they will bring your sons in their arms* [lit. 'in their bosom' (*ḥōṣen*, 4x)] / *and carry your daughters on their hips* [*kātēp*, 'shoulder, side'; v. 22], both phrases suggesting nearness. Kings and princesses will be their caretakers (*'ōmĕnayikĕ*, 'your guardians'), an image of the extravagant care the remnant will receive.

These Gentile rulers will be so impressed with the greatness of Israel's God that they will show honour by bowing down to the Israelites: *They will bow down before you with their faces to the ground; / they will lick the dust at your feet* (v. 23), acts that convey submission and deference (see *ANEP* fig. 355).

The remnant will learn two things as a result of their deliverance from exile and the events that follow: (1) Yahweh is a majestic God who rules supremely over all his works (*Then you will know that I am the LORD*, v. 23). (2) They can certainly place all their hope and trust in the LORD (*those who hope in* [lit. 'wait on'] *me will not be disappointed* [lit. 'will not be put to shame', v. 23]).

24–26. The rhetorical questions of verse 24 begin a new argument that this restoration will occur no matter how strong the enemy forces are. The NIV follows the preferable variant reading *fierce* (*'ārîṣ* [supported by v. 25, 1QIsaᵃ, Peshitta and Vulg.] instead of *ṣaddîq*, 'righteous') in verse 24b.

The rewording of these rhetorical questions as statements of reassurance in verse 25 (i.e. 'captives of the mighty one' and 'prey of the fierce') confirms that no nation can hinder God's promised deliverance because he himself will fight for their release: *I* [myself = emphatic] *will contend with those who contend with you, / and your children I* [myself] *will save* (v. 25).

The image of Israel's oppressors eating *their own flesh* and drinking *their own blood* in verse 26 is suggestive of internal conflicts that will weaken the nations. This is precisely the infighting that took place in Babylon which allowed the Persians to conquer them and Cyrus to be cheered as their deliverer (infighting was also partially to blame for the downfall of the Persian Empire). Yahweh's deliverance of Israel will confirm to all people that he truly is the almighty God of Israel: *Then all mankind will know / that I, the LORD, am your Saviour, / your Redeemer, the Mighty One of Jacob.* Each title for God highlights his close relationship to Israel (v. 26).

Meaning

The Servant Song which begins this section highlights that God will use the servant to deliver Israel. This servant will bring not only a remnant of Israel back to God, but also a remnant from the other nations. The same two questions posed in Isaiah 40 – 41 are answered, though in reverse order: (1) Is God willing to deliver Israel? The response is in 49:11–21. (2) Is God able to deliver Israel? The response is in 49:22–26. Once again, the answer to both questions remains an unequivocal 'yes!'

God chooses powerful imagery to prove to Israel how much he loves them: (1) his love for them is greater than a nursing mother's care for her child; and (2) he has inscribed Zion on his very hands so that she remains always before him. Israel will experience God's blessing – so much so that they will wonder where the great number of their inhabitants have come from. They will be a remnant of God-fearers, including Gentiles, who come from nations around the world to serve Yahweh – a fulfilment of 49:6 where the servant will be *a light for the Gentiles*. Then all nations will know that Yahweh is the almighty God.

ii. Israel's disobedience (50:1–11)

Context
Following the reassurance to Israel that God is able and willing to deliver her, the second part of the second section (i.e. Isa. 49 – 57) returns to the theme of her disobedience (see Figure 0.11 on p. 29), once again as a disputation oracle. Isaiah 50:1–11 can be broken into two units: (1) in verses 1–3 God will never permanently break his relationship with Israel (i.e. the imagery of divorce), but rather will send her away for a time due to her many transgressions; and (2) verses 4–11 constitute a third Servant Song.

A messenger formula, *This is what the LORD says*, marks the beginning of the first unit. The start of the second unit is signalled by a change in speaker to the first person. In verses 4–9 the servant speaks of his hope in God's deliverance. He then calls Israel to make a choice in verses 10–11: either trust in the LORD and be delivered, or trust in themselves (i.e. *walk in the light of your fires*; may refer to the fire of their false sacrifices) and receive punishment.

We believe that this Servant Song also describes the Messiah (as in 49:5–12) whom God will use to deliver a remnant of his people.

Comment

a. Yahweh did not reject Israel, but Israel rejected Yahweh (50:1–3)
 1. In the context of Israel's mournful cry that God has forgotten her (see 49:14) Yahweh asks Israel two questions that have strong disputation overtones: *Where is your mother's* [i.e. Israel's] *certificate of divorce / with which I sent her away?* (see Deut. 24:1–4 which describes how a marriage can be dissolved by the husband issuing a certificate of divorce). The implied response is that there is none. The rare phrase *certificate* [sēper, 'scroll'] *of divorce* [kĕrîtût, possibly related to the verb kārat, 'to cut'] appears only three times: Deuteronomy 24:1–4; Isaiah 50:1; and Jeremiah 3:8. God is pictured here as the husband

of Israel (an image used frequently by the prophets; see Ezek. 16; Hos. 1 – 3), who could take Israel back since he had not formally divorced her by issuing a certificate of divorce.

The second question relates to payment of a debt: *Or to which of my creditors / did I sell you?* In the Ancient Near East it was possible for a husband to sell himself, his wife or his children in payment of an outstanding debt (see Exod. 21:7; 2 Kgs 4:1). Once again, the implied answer is that God has no creditors; therefore, Israel has not been sent away in payment of a debt.

The reason (introduced by the word *hēn*, 'behold'; left untranslated in the NIV) Israel was *sent away* (*šullĕḥâ*; verb often used of divorce) is *because of* her transgressions. The problem was of Israel's own making; she had separated herself from God because of her many iniquities, particularly in following other gods (see 42:24–25). Yahweh would gladly take her back if only she would forsake her sins.

2–3. The disputation oracle continues in these verses with God posing several rhetorical questions, all suggesting that Israel had given up on him: *When I came, why was there no one? / When I called, why was there no one to answer?* Then he asks two absurd questions: *Was my arm too short to deliver you? / Do I lack the strength to rescue you?* These questions will set the stage for the third Servant Song in verses 4–11. Since there was no-one in Israel upon whom God could call to draw the nation back to himself, he would have to bring his own servant.

But before God reveals how he will deliver the nation, he makes it very clear that he has the power to deliver them. He directs their attention (*hinnēh*, 'behold, indeed') to previous miracles he accomplished for his people: the crossing of the Reed Sea (v. 2; see Exod. 14:15–31) and the great darkness (*qadrût*, occurs only here) he brought over Egypt (v. 3; see Exod. 10:21–23). The word *covering* (*kĕsût*) in the parallel phrase sounds similar to *qadrût*, 'darkness'. Certainly a God with this kind of power could perform a new exodus to bring them out of the Babylonian captivity. Many times during their long history God had protected and delivered the nation, yet they spurned him.

b. The third Servant Song (50:4–11)

4–5. Nevertheless, not everyone doubted God's ability to deliver. The abrupt change in speaker marks the beginning of the third Servant Song, which opens with the servant's declaration of trust in and total submission to Yahweh. He is attuned to God, listening and following his instructions, unlike the rest of the nation (he *wakens my ear to listen like one being instructed*). While the term *servant* is not mentioned until verse 10, there is little doubt that the passage refers to him. This Servant Song responds to God's questions in 50:2 and describes another of God's miraculous interventions to deliver Israel.

Again, the servant in this passage has been variously identified as (1) the Messiah; (2) a prophet (generally thought to be Second Isaiah); (3) Israel; or (4) a remnant of Israel (see discussion on 49:1–7). We believe that the servant here refers to the coming Messiah (as do the other Servant Songs in chapters 49–57). God has empowered this servant with *a well-instructed tongue* (lit. 'tongue of disciples' [*limmûdîm*, 'learned ones, disciples'], referring to the servant's obedience). He is used by the *Sovereign* [*ʾădōnāy*] LORD [*yĕhwih*] (lit. 'the Lord LORD'; see vv. 4–5, 7, 9) to comfort and sustain (*ʿût*, only time with this meaning) the weary ones with his instruction, similar to Jeremiah's ministry in Jeremiah 31:25–26.

Every morning God wakes and teaches his servant, who listens attentively to divine instruction (*He . . . wakens my ear*, v. 4; *opened my ears*, v. 5) and obeys him (*I* [lit. 'I myself', emphatic] *have not been rebellious*, v. 5). His obedience contrasts with the rebellious actions of the nation (see especially v. 2, *When I called, why was there no one to answer?*).

6–7. He even submitted himself (lit. *I offered* myself, v. 6) to hostile treatment for the sake of Yahweh. He was beaten, mocked and spat upon (lit. 'my face [emphatic order] I did not hide from mocking and spitting'; see Deut. 25:9) and his beard was pulled out in order to humiliate him (see Neh. 13:25). Jesus was subjected to similar types of punishment (beating: Matt. 26:67; 27:26, 30; etc.; mocking: Matt. 27:27–31, 33–44; etc.; spitting: Matt. 27:30; Mark 14:65; etc.). Each verb in verse 6 is out of order syntactically to express emphasis.

In the face of disgrace and humiliation, the servant explains how his trust in and reliance upon God helped him through: *Because the Sovereign LORD* [lit. 'the Lord (*'ădōnāy*) LORD (*yĕhwih*)'] *helps me, / I will not be disgraced. / Therefore have I set my face like flint* [*ḥallāmîs*, 5x; i.e. one of the hardest-known rocks at the time], / *and I know I will not be put to shame* (v. 7; see Jer. 1:18–19). The servant did not suffer for wrongdoing and therefore is not ashamed. He knows that in the end he will be vindicated (i.e. declared innocent).

8–9. The servant knows that Yahweh (lit. 'the Lord [*'ădōnāy*] LORD [*yĕhwih*]'), the true judge, is near (lit. 'near is my vindicator', emphatic order) and able to step in at any time. The servant therefore challenges his opponent (his *accuser*, lit. 'lord of my judgment') to a trial, for he is confident that any charges brought against him will not stand. His enemies will all be destroyed when Yahweh comes to vindicate him: *They will all wear out like a garment* eaten by moths (*'āš*, 8x; v. 9).

10–11. The servant delivers two parting messages, one for the godly and one for the ungodly: *Who among you* [pl.; an indirect question] *fears the LORD* 'and is continuing to obey' (the nuance of the participial form) *the word of his servant?* (v. 10). Those who can respond in the affirmative have a true relationship with God. They need to prepare to walk for a period *in the dark* (lit. 'darknesses'; the plural form suggests 'intense darkness' or 'adversities') while maintaining their trust in God. This is probably a reference to those who were forcibly exiled to Babylon because the nation refused to obey God, a truly dark time with little hope.

But now (*hēn*) at the beginning of verse 11 signals a contrast with those who do not rely on God. The image of light also features in the message to the wicked, who light torches for themselves (lit. 'they gird themselves with flaming torches' [*zîqôt* (fem. pl.), occurs only here]; see similar masc. form in Prov. 26:18). Light is usually a symbol of deliverance in the Old Testament, but the wicked walk in artificial light, created so that they can walk in darkness while rejecting God's light. Fires were probably part of their worship rituals to their false gods who had no power to deliver them. They will instead experience God's power and justice, causing them to *lie down in torment* (*ma'ăṣēbâ*, occurs only here; v. 11).

Meaning

This section begins by reminding the Israelites that their sins took them away from God, though he had not abandoned them. They had acted wrongly in turning their backs on him; however, he will deliver Israel as he has done in the past.

While the identity of the servant is debated, his mission is quite clear: Yahweh will use him to deliver Israel. Even though they will suffer adversity for a time, those who obey the servant's instruction will be delivered by trusting in the LORD their God. By contrast, those who reject his instruction and rely on their own power or their false idols for deliverance will be punished.

iii. God brings deliverance (51:1 – 53:12)

This passage is the third unit of the second section (Isa. 49 – 57) of Isaiah 40 – 66 (see Figure 0.11 on p. 29). It is generally agreed that 51:1 begins this section and that the fourth Servant Song closes it. Isaiah 51:1 – 53:12 contains seven oracles that take up the theme of Zion's restoration and are directed towards the God-fearing remnant who were addressed earlier in 50:10. Each oracle opens with an exhortation (51:1, 4, 7, 9, 17; 52:1, 11).

a. Yahweh will bring comfort to Zion (51:1 – 16)

Context

The first three oracles begin with exhortations for Israel to look to Yahweh their redeemer: (1) *Listen to [šim'û,* 'hear'] *me, you who pursue righteousness / and who seek the* LORD (51:1); (2) *Listen [haqšîbû,* 'give attention'] *to me, my people; / hear me ['ēlay ha'ăzînû,* 'give ear to me'], *my nation* (51:4); and (3) *Hear [šim'û] me, you who know what is right* (51:7). Each of these oracles is exhorting the remnant (i.e. *who pursue righteousness,* v. 1; *my people,* v. 4; *who know what is right,* v. 7) to look to their God for deliverance. The climax of the section is reached in the fourth oracle, which is addressed to Yahweh, urging him to rouse himself *as in days gone by*: *Awake, awake ['ûrî,* twice for emphasis], *arm of the* LORD, / *clothe yourself with strength!* (51:9).

Comment

(1) Look to your past (51:1–3)

1–3. Yahweh issues an impassioned call to the remnant of Israel who seek righteousness (50:10) to come to him for comfort and renewal: *Listen to me, you who pursue* ['actively pursue' = participle] *righteousness* (v. 1). He exhorts them to return to their spiritual roots: *look to the rock from which you were cut / and to the quarry* [lit. 'mouth (maqqebet,* only occurrence with this meaning) of a cistern'] *from which you were hewn* (v. 1).

Ultimately *the rock* or *quarry* is Yahweh; but in the context here *rock* refers to Abraham and his descendants who became the nation of Israel, and *quarry* refers to Sarah's womb from which Israel emerged. Yahweh encourages the remnant, who undoubtedly were discouraged that so few sought to obey the LORD. He reminds them that even though Abraham *was only one man* (v. 2) when God called him, an entire nation was born from him. What Yahweh did with a single person he can surely do for the small, believing remnant.

Three terms in verse 3 highlight that Zion had become a wilderness: (1) *ḥarbôt,* 'waste places'; *midbār,* 'wilderness'; and *ʿarbôt,* 'desert plains'. But now God will look with favour upon Zion, restoring the devastated land to look like *Eden . . . the garden of the LORD* (see Ezek. 36:35) and filling it with *joy, gladness, thanksgiving* and *the sound of singing* (*zimrâ,* 'melody', 4x). In that day Israel will praise and thank God for this great deliverance.

(2) Remember God's promises (51:4–6)

4–6. Yahweh directs the remnant to listen attentively and then tenderly reminds them that they are 'his people' and that their promised deliverance is both imminent (vv. 4–5) and certain (v. 6). God's *instruction* (v. 4) and his justice will be witnessed by all nations and will serve to enlighten them about the righteousness of God (*my justice will become a light to the nations*). Once the nations see this, they too will long to have this deliverance (*The islands will . . . wait in hope for my arm* [metonymy for power], v. 5).

Isaiah 51:4–6 is like 42:1–4, except that here God himself establishes justice and his law, whereas in chapter 42 it is the servant who does so. The two passages are complementary: 51:4–6 emphasizes the certainty that Yahweh's universal sovereignty will be manifest, and 42:1–4 emphasizes the agent who brings it about, namely the servant.

God directs those to whom the oracle is given in verse 4 to *Lift up your* [pl.] *eyes to the heavens* (*šāmayim*, probably initially the dual ending designating the upper heavens [i.e. beyond the sky where God dwells] and lower heavens [i.e. the sky we see]). He then encourages them that when the heavens, the earth and all earth's inhabitants have been destroyed (i.e. *vanish* [*mālaḥ*, 'to scatter', occurs only here] *like smoke, wear out like a garment, die like flies* [*kĕmô-kēn*, 'like thus'; i.e. 'in like manner']), God's salvation and righteousness will continue to endure for eternity (lit. 'my righteousness will not be shattered', v. 6). He is the only one upon whom they can rely.

(3) Remember God's character (51:7–8)

7–8. Once again Yahweh exhorts the remnant (*Hear me*), those who *know what is right* (lit. 'who are knowing righteousness') and have God's law in their hearts (v. 7). They are not to *fear the reproach of mere mortals* nor *their insults* (*niddûpâ*, 'abuse', occurs only here; see a similar form in Ezek. 5:15), because the wicked will perish, pictured once again as cloth that is destroyed by moths or their larvae (*the worm will devour them like wool*; moth larvae eat fabrics made from animal fibres, such as silk, wool and cashmere, because they contain keratin). Why can they be confident that the wicked will meet their end? Because God's righteousness and his salvation are for ever (lit. *lĕʿôlām*, 'for a generation of generations', vv. 6, 8) and therefore can always be relied upon.

(4) Trust your redeemer (51:9–16)

9–11. The repeated exhortation to *awake* (three times in v. 9) is a tacit accusation that God has not been at work on behalf of the Israelites. The phrase *arm of the LORD* is a synecdoche for his strength or power, emphasizing in this verse Yahweh's role as a warrior (see Ps. 93:1). The prophet appeals to God (similar to the corporate laments of Ps. 44:1–3, 23; etc.) to act as he did in days of old when he destroyed *Rahab* (v. 9) or when he *dried up the sea . . . so that the redeemed might cross over* (an exodus motif; v. 10).

The rhetorical question *Was it not . . . ?* serves as a strong affirmation: of course it was God who performed the miracles. The Israelites are called *the redeemed*, for God was reclaiming his own property from Egyptian bondage. The name *Rahab*[15] is a metaphorical reference to Egypt (see esp. 30:7); thus, in the context of God's power displayed in the crossing of the Reed Sea (v. 10), the cutting up of *Rahab* represents the defeat of Egypt by the LORD as they sought to recapture the Israelites at the outset of the exodus. The parallel structure suggests that *Rahab* and the *monster* are the same entity.

Elsewhere, the terms *Rahab* and *monster* (*tannîn*, also translated as 'dragon' or 'sea monster'; see Gen. 1:21; Job 26:12) are a reference to forces of chaos associated with primeval ocean waters (Oswalt 1998: 341–342; Blenkinsopp 2000: 332–333). Their combined appearance in chapter 51 may suggest both primeval chaos and defeat of the Egyptians. It is not unusual for a biblical author to demythologize a popular Ancient Near Eastern image familiar to his audience.

Verse 11 is a nearly identical repetition of 35:10. The prophet has recalled these times of victory to encourage the remnant, referred to as *the redeemed* (*gĕʾûlîm*, v. 10) and the *rescued* (*pĕdûyê*, v. 11), to have faith that what Yahweh has done in the past he will do again. They will be rescued and will return from Babylon to Zion. But there is an aspect that continues into the more distant future: *everlasting joy will crown their heads.*

12–16. Verses 12–16, Yahweh's response to the appeal of verses 9–10, draw a comparison between what God did in the past at creation and what he will do by delivering his people from the Babylonian exile. The phrase *I, even I* (stated twice for emphasis, v. 12), which corresponds to the double imperative that Yahweh *awake*, emphatically refutes the charge that he has been inactive. The participle in the phrase *who comforts* [lit. 'continues to comfort'] *you* indicates that he has never stopped comforting them. The word

---

15. 'Rahab' is spelled as *rāḥāb* in Joshua (see Josh. 2:1, 3; etc.), *rāḥab* in
    Job and some Psalms (see Job 9:13; etc.), and *raḥab* in Isaiah (see 30:7;
    etc.).

comforts (v. 12) goes far beyond the idea of soothing words. Similar to its use in 40:1 it refers to the end of suffering that Yahweh will bring about for his nation.

God reproaches his people for being afraid of mere humans (i.e. even those who oppress them) whose lives fade away as quickly as grass, and for forgetting his sovereignty and power as creator of heaven and earth (v. 13). Oswalt summarizes it thus: 'to live in fear of humans is to have effectively forgotten God' (1998: 346). The remnant are reminded that they need not fear humans when this powerful God is on their side (v. 13; see 2:22), something that the exiles would be prone to forget – something we are prone to forget as well.

The remnant are referred to in these verses in second person masculine and feminine singular forms, as well as masculine plural forms. This shift in person and number is frequently seen, even within a single passage, in the Psalms and the Prophets.

Verse 14 confirms that the exiles (*ṣōʿeh*, 'stooped ones', 4x; refers to being bent over by the weight and shame of fetters) will soon be set free and no longer suffer the deprivations of their captivity: *they will not die in their dungeon, / nor will they lack bread*. These common images for captivity suggest malnourishment from ill-treatment, or are a more generalized reference to privations typically associated with captivity.

The oracle in verses 12–16 concludes by confirming that the God who controls creation (*who stirs up the sea so that its waves roar*, a reference back to verse 10; see Jer. 31:35b) is the same God who has called the nation of Israel out of captivity. They can count on this deliverance because (1) his name is the LORD Almighty (*ṣĕbāʾôt*); (2) he is the God of creation, *the LORD your God, who stirs up the sea* (v. 15); (3) he has given them his laws; and (4) he has protected them with his hand (v. 16).

Verse 16 highlights God's covenant relationship with and great love for Israel. He takes care to remind them that he has (1) taught them how to live by providing his decrees to follow (*I have put my words in your mouth*); (2) shielded them like shadows that protect from the blazing Near Eastern sun (lit. 'with the shadow of my hand covered you'); and (3) selected them to be his people (lit. 'my people you are'); in both cases the inverted syntax denotes emphasis.

The oracle concludes with a description of God similar to that in verse 13 (*I who set* [lit. 'planted'] *the heavens in place, / who laid the foundations of the earth*), except that it concludes with the declaration *You are my people* (v. 16) instead of a description of Israel cowering in fear (v. 14).

Meaning

This section prepares the way for the fourth Servant Song in chapter 52. The remnant need to know that the Babylonian exile was Israel's own fault, not God's. But now their punishment has come to an end and it is Babylon's turn to feel God's wrath.

Israel need not worry that the remnant is indeed small, for as a nation they began with only one person, Abraham, whom God blessed and multiplied. Israel also need not fear, for their God, the God who made creation, will soon bring about their deliverance.

b. Yahweh delivers his people (51:17 – 52:12)

Context

Following Yahweh's affirmation that he will come and bring deliverance to Israel, the section 51:17 – 52:12 is composed of three additional oracles, each beginning with repeated commands for emphasis to urge Israel into action: (1) *Awake, awake!* [lit. 'rouse yourself'] / *Rise up, Jerusalem* (51:17), for her judgment is complete and her oppressors will now be punished (51:17–23); (2) *Awake, awake, Zion, / clothe yourself with strength!* (52:1), for she is to prepare for her deliverance (52:1–10); and (3) *Depart, depart, go out from there* (52:11), for Israel will leave exile (52:11–12).

Comment

(1) Yahweh's cup of wrath has been appeased (51:17–23)

17–18. Now that the prophet has demonstrated that Israel is the one at fault, not Yahweh as originally claimed (v. 9), he once again cries out, *Awake, awake!* However, this time he calls to the nation, represented by its chief city Jerusalem (*Rise up, Jerusalem*), to rouse themselves from the hopelessness of their long exile (i.e. *who have drunk from the hand of the* LORD / *the cup of his wrath*, v. 17; see

vv. 22–23). It is time for them to trust Yahweh, for he will deliver them.

The parallel phrase reads literally 'the chalice [*qubbaʿat*, 2x] of the cup [*côs*] of reeling'. This *cup* causes reeling or staggering (*tarʿēlâ*, 3x) like one who is drunk. The implication is that they are being overcome by the weight of their punishment. Drinking *the cup of his wrath* is a common image for judgment in the Old Testament (e.g. Jer. 25:15–27); thus, drinking *to its dregs* (lit. 'you have drunk, you have drained' is a hendiadys meaning 'to drink to the last drop') implies receiving the full extent of God's punishment.

Verse 18 is an introduction to the fourth Servant Song (52:13 – 53:12). Note that this verse continues to refer to Jerusalem even though there is an unexpected change from second person singular (v. 17) to third person singular (v. 18), as is common in prophetic literature. The image of Jerusalem as a mother, drunk and staggering without the assistance of any of her children (*among all the children she brought up / there was none to take* [lit. 'to seize'] *her by the hand*) is a dismal picture of her wretched condition. It was a common responsibility in the Ancient Near East for children to care for inebriated parents (see *Tale of Aqhat, ANET* 150). There was no leader to guide them through God's punishment and towards deliverance (i.e. *there was none to guide her*). The fourth Servant Song reveals the solution.

19–20. In verse 19 the author states that *double calamities* have befallen the city of Jerusalem: (1) the *ruin and destruction* of its buildings and walls, and (2) the decimation of its population by *famine* [*hārāʿāb*] *and sword* [*haḥereb*] – similar-sounding words. These word pairs describe almost complete destruction; none are left to *comfort* (*nûd*, 'show sympathy for'; see Jer. 15:5; etc.) her as she endures God's righteous punishment that she brought upon herself. The NIV's reading of the parallel phrase *who can* [third person] *console you* (lit. 'How will I comfort you?') is preferable, for it closely aligns with *who can comfort you* earlier in the verse, and is the reading that appears in the versions and 1QIsaᵃ.

Her sons are helpless (*Your children have fainted / . . . like antelope* [*tēʾô*, 2x] *caught in a net* [lit. 'antelope of a net'], v. 20) under the full weight of God's punishment (*They are filled with the wrath of* [i.e. from] *the LORD*). Antelopes are among the world's fastest animals but are virtually helpless once captured.

21–23. God has another announcement, one of hope, for those in exile: *Therefore hear this, you afflicted one, / made drunk* [*šĕkurâ*, occurs only here, but is related to *šēkar*, 'strong drink'], *but not with wine* (v. 21). Note that drunkenness once again expresses how the many decades of exile have caused the nation to stagger under the weight of this punishment. The *Sovereign LORD* (lit. 'Lord [*ădōnāy*] LORD [*yĕhwâ*]') their God, who is also called the one *who defends his people*, has taken the cup of wrath out of their hands and put it into their oppressors' hands (vv. 22–23). It is unclear whether the phrase *who said to you, / 'Fall prostrate that we may walk on you'* (v. 23b) is a literal or figurative reference to subjugation; however, Assyrian rock reliefs depict this brutal treatment (*ANEP* 345). The important message is that Israel's punishment is over. Even more importantly, they *will never drink again* the goblet (lit. 'chalice of the cup') of God's wrath. Not only that, their oppressor, Babylon, will undergo punishment next.

(2) Prepare for deliverance (52:1–12)

1–2. Once again, the prophet uses the double imperative *Awake, awake* (see 51:9, 17) for emphasis. He calls Zion (called *šĕbîyâ*, 'captive', occurring only here; v. 2) to shake off the dusty rags of her captivity and put on her queenly attire, her *garments of splendour* (v. 1) that she wore as a free person. The word *šĕbî* can be read as 'captive' (NASB) or *sit enthroned* (NIV), but 'captive' seems preferable in this context. Jerusalem will be restored to a position of strength and honour as *the holy city*.

The *uncircumcised and defiled* (v. 1), a reference to the Babylonians at the very least, will never spoil or desecrate her again. The city is told to leave behind the humiliation of her captivity: *Shake off your dust* [lit. 'shake yourself from the dust']; *rise up* [and] *free yourself from* [lit. 'rid yourself of'] *the chains* [*môsēr*, 'fetters', 3x; see a similar form, *mûsar*, 'shackles', Job 12:18] *on your neck* (v. 2).

3–4. The author shifts from balanced poetic phrasing (vv. 1–2) to prose (see NASB) as he explains the reasons why Yahweh will deliver the nation. Some scholars consider verses 3–6 to be a later prose addition (Whybray 1975: 165; Blenkinsopp 2002: 340; etc.), inspired as a reflection upon the poem. However, it is preferable and equally plausible to argue that the author first presents a poetic oracle, which he then develops and explains in prose.

The *kî* clause beginning verse 3 introduces the reasons behind the directives of verses 1–2: Israel is in bondage and God will redeem her. Verse 3 takes up the theme of 50:1 with a twist: because God had not sold Israel when he sent her into exile, he could redeem her *without money*. As noted above, in Hebrew society debtors could sell themselves, their wives or their children as bondservants to appease their creditors, but enslavement of fellow Jews was prohibited by the law in Leviticus 25:39–40, although that was not always followed (see Neh. 5:4–5). Bondservants worked until the debt was fulfilled, they were redeemed, or they were released in the Year of Jubilee. God was free to redeem Israel because he owed no debt to anyone.

God then reviews their history. Before the first exodus, the Israelites went down to Egypt of their own accord, having left their land because of a severe famine. Pharaoh's harsh treatment of the Israelites after the death of Joseph caused God (lit, 'the Lord [*'ădōnāy*] LORD [*yĕhwih*]') to lead the people out of Egypt. Later, *Assyria . . . oppressed them* by taking them captive. The phrase 'oppressed them for nothing' (*bĕ'epes 'āšāqô*, 'for nothing', v. 4; omitted in the NIV) can be understood several ways: (1) 'For nothing', as in 'having no reason'; the Assyrians had no good reason to take the Israelites captive. (2) 'For nothing', as in 'without payment of money'; thus, in this context Yahweh had no debt that would cause him to sell his nation to Assyria. (3) 'Without limits', meaning that both the Assyrians and the Babylonians set no limits to the severity of their treatment of the Israelites. The context favours the second option that no money was exchanged for sending them into or redeeming them from exile (v. 3).

5–6. Verse 5 begins with a question that is awkwardly worded in Hebrew: literally, 'And now what to me here?' The LORD is posing the rhetorical question, What should I do now, given that *my people have been taken away for nothing* [*ḥinnām*, 'without compensation']? Their captors, the Babylonians, provoked God's anger by harming and mocking (see Ps. 137:3) God's children. He will not tolerate such an affront.

Some scholars suggest emending the unusual form *yĕhêlîlû* (lit. 'they howl' [see NASB]) to *yhllû*, 'to boast', or *yhllû*, 'are profaned' (see *BHS*). The parallel phrase (*my name is constantly blasphemed*) strongly suggests the form should be *wĕhêlîlû*, from the verb *hālal*, 'to mock, deride' (see NIV, NEB; similar meaning in Ps. 102:8; Isa. 44:25); confusion could easily have arisen because of similarities between the Hebrew letters.

Verse 6 contains two conclusions based on verse 5, each beginning with *therefore* (*lākēn*): (1) *Therefore my people will know my name*, meaning they will know the character of their God by his actions; and (2) [therefore they will know] *that it is I who foretold it. / Yes, it is I*. In other words, they will know that God keeps his word. The NIV correctly assumes an ellipsis here.

7–10. These verses form a song of praise to God for his deliverance from the Babylonian captivity. The declaration *Your* [Israel's] *God reigns!* is both a testimony that this deliverance is proof of God's sovereignty, and a fitting conclusion to the hope of deliverance first introduced in Isaiah 40.

Verse 7 begins with the exclamation *How beautiful* [*nā᾽â*, 3x] *on the mountains / are the feet of those who bring good news*. The first phrase *those who bring good news* is then intensified in the next phrase as *who bring good tidings* (lit. 'who brings good news of happiness' [*tôb*]). This highly poetical language expresses just how much the people esteem the anonymous messenger (the messenger is singular in the Hebrew) because of the joy that his message brings (see also 40:9–11). His announcement of *peace* (*šālôm*) and *salvation* (*yĕšû῾â*, better translated as 'victory') calls to mind a military runner carrying to Zion a message of victory that Yahweh has just delivered his people from exile in Babylon.

The exclamation *Your God reigns!* (*mālak ᾽ĕlōhāyik*, v. 7), a declaration like those found in so-called 'enthronement psalms' (e.g. Pss 93:1; 96:10), reminds Israel that Yahweh is their true King and the ruler over all the earth. The implication is that their hopes and expectations are finally about to become reality. The remnant may also have believed that their deliverance from Babylon would signal the inauguration of Yahweh's kingdom and the hopes associated with 2:2–4 and 4:2–6.

The *watchmen* would be the first to see a messenger coming with good news. They break forth (*pāṣaḥ*, 8x; 6x in Isaiah) into joyful singing before the rest of the people join in (v. 9). Verse 8 provides the first reason (*kî*, 'for') for their praise: *When the LORD returns to* [or more likely 'restores'] *Zion, / they will see it with their own eyes.*

The second reason for this great joy is found in verse 9: for *he has redeemed* [lit. 'bought them back'; i.e. to take legal possession of] *Jerusalem* and comforted them from the sorrow of their captivity. Even those who live in the ruins of Jerusalem will have reason to sing, for the LORD has delivered his people in the sight of all nations. The figurative phrase *bare his holy arm* (i.e. pulling up one's garment in order to have the full use of one's limbs) means to prepare to act. This great deliverance would serve to teach the rest of the nations how great is the God of Israel (*the ends of the earth will see / the salvation of our God*).

11–12. The section concludes with the Israelites' triumphal departure from the land of their captivity: *Depart, depart* [lit. 'turn aside', repeated for emphasis], *go out from there!* These verses echo the theme of sanctity in 52:1–6, which refers to Jerusalem as *the holy city* where *the uncircumcised and defiled / will not enter . . . again* (v. 1). This new exodus will be different from the exodus from Egypt: (1) They will not leave *in haste* (*ḥippāzôn*, 3x; see Exod. 12:11) or flee (*mĕnûsâ*, 2x). (2) They are to *touch no unclean thing*, to *come out . . . and be pure*; that is to say, they are not to bring anything from Babylon that would defile them (see Exod. 12:35–36).

This journey back to Jerusalem will be both a sacred religious processional (i.e. the sacred vessels will be carried by ceremonially purified priests; *Come out from it and be pure*, v. 11) and the victory march of a conquering army on its return home (*the LORD will go before you, / [and] will be your rear guard*, v. 12). The sacred vessels that had been brought to Babylon by Nebuchadnezzar (see 2 Kgs 25:14–15) will now, under Cyrus, be returned to the temple to restore its functioning (see Ezra 1:7–11; 5:14–15). During the return journey, they will enjoy the same degree of safety as in the first exodus, for Yahweh will lead his people and serve as their rear guard (lit. 'your gathering'; see Exod. 14:19).

Meaning

Once Israel's punishment is complete, she will never again have to
drink from *the goblet of* God's *wrath* (51:22); instead it will be given
into the hand of Israel's tormentors (51:23). Israel is to shake off the
dust of captivity and clothe herself in beautiful garments, for she
will return to Zion, where God will reign (52:7). All the ends of
the earth will be able to see this amazing deliverance and acknowledge the greatness of Israel's God. Israel's deliverance from
Babylon will be different from their deliverance from Egypt in
that (1) they will be purified and thus will bring the vessels of the
LORD's house out with them; and (2) they will not depart in haste,
nor as fugitives.

This future deliverance, however, will have elements that were
not true of the people's return from Babylon: (1) the sky will vanish,
the earth wear out, and inhabitants die (51:6); and (2) the
uncircumcised and the unclean will be barred from ever again
entering Zion (52:1). This passage is thus another example of the
'prophetic perspective' wherein deliverance from Babylon is
pictured against a distant future deliverance. The prophet perceives
them as one panoramic picture with little time difference between
the two events. This future deliverance, which will have both physical and spiritual aspects, will be orchestrated by God, but he will
have to send someone from outside Israel (i.e. 50:2; 51:18) to carry
it through to completion.

*c. The fourth Servant Song: the servant of the LORD is humiliated then
exalted (52:13 – 53:12)*

Context

This song continues the theme of the deliverance of God's people
(see Figure 0.11 on p. 29). The introduction in 51:18 indicates that
there was no-one within Israel who could deliver the nation,
therefore necessitating that God bring his own servant. The fourth
so-called Servant Song in 52:13 – 53:12 goes into much further
detail about the servant than do the other songs, even stating that
it will be necessary for the servant to suffer and die for the nation
in order to deliver a remnant. Just as God's use of Cyrus to deliver
the Israelites came as a complete surprise to them, so too this *man*

of suffering (53:3), this 'suffering servant', was someone they had never foreseen.

Most scholars view 52:13–15 as an integral part of the fourth Servant Song, though others consider it an editorial unit separate from Isaiah 53 (Whybray 1975: 169; etc.). There are two reasons, however, why the poem in 52:13 – 53:12 is more likely to be a single unit: (1) the servant is referred to in both 52:13 and 53:11; and (2) third person masculine singular verbs and pronouns are used consistently throughout. Oswalt notes that this passage has a clear literary structure of 'five stanzas of three verses each (52:13–15; 53:1–3, 4–6, 7–9, 10–12)' (1998: 376).

Similarities with the third Servant Song (50:4–11) are evident. The servant is (1) obedient to Yahweh (50:4–5//53:10–12); (2) beaten and humiliated (50:6//52:14; 53:3, 8–10); and (3) helped by God (50:7, 9//53:12). While the identity of the servant is not specified, he is most commonly seen as a prophet (Isaiah, Second Isaiah; see Whybray 1975: 169; Blenkinsopp 2002: 356; etc.); Israel or a remnant of Israel (Davidson 1903: 437–439; Childs 2001: 422; etc.); or the Messiah (Young 1965–72: 3.348; Oswalt 1998: 407–408; etc.).

The second person singular pronouns in 52:13–15 could refer to Israel as a collective entity. However, 53:3–6 distinguishes the servant from Israel: *he was despised, and we held him in low esteem . . . and the LORD has laid on him / the iniquity of us all*. For this reason, it is preferable to view the servant as an individual – either the prophet or the Messiah. The predominant view since the time of the early Church Fathers onwards has been that he is the Messiah, particularly since several New Testament passages quote this poem in reference to Christ (see Matt. 8:17; Rom. 15:21; etc.).

Comment

13–15. There is a clear change in person and content at this point as God, speaking in the first person, directs the audience's attention to the servant: *See [hinnēh], my servant will act wisely [śākal]*. The verb *śākal* has a wide range of meanings: 'to have success, have insight, understand, teach' (*HALOT* 3.1328–1330). Its meaning is clarified by the parallel unit *he will be raised and lifted up and highly exalted*, meaning that he will be held in high regard; thus, the servant is one who will be successful and highly esteemed in the eyes of the people.

Verses 14–15 are a sharp contrast with the description of the servant in verse 13 and must therefore refer to a different time or aspect of his life. A two-part comparison is drawn in verses 14–15 with the words *just as* [*ka'ăšer*] . . . *so* [*kēn*]: *Just as* [*ka'ăšer*] *there were many who were appalled at him* [lit. 'you', i.e. Israel, not the servant as the NIV suggests] / [so] [*kēn*, not translated in the NIV] *his appearance was so disfigured* [*mišḥat*, occurs only here] *beyond that of any human being* (v. 14); and *so* [*kēn*] *he will sprinkle many nations* (v. 15). In other words, just as the nations were appalled to watch the Israelites being driven from their land into exile, so in the same way they will be stunned at the appearance of the servant and his ability to cleanse (*sprinkle*) many nations. While it is unclear how or why the servant became disfigured, this is a development of the theme introduced in 50:6, an earlier Servant Song.

Some scholars who question the referent of the singular pronoun 'you' (v. 14) follow the LXX and Syriac reading 'him' (the NIV does as well). However, the reading 'you' (i.e. Israel) is preferable, for two reasons: (1) the second person singular forms often refer to Israel elsewhere in the near context (51:13, 15–17, 19–23; 52:1–2, 7–8); and (2) the nations were stunned at Yahweh's poor treatment of Israel.

The Hebrew preposition *mîn* (*beyond that*) that occurs in the last two phrases of verse 14 should be read in the comparative sense (Williams §317): *beyond* [lit. 'more than'] *that of any human being*; and *his form marred beyond* [lit. 'more than'] *human likeness*, emphasizing the severe disfigurement of the servant.

Despite disagreement on whether to translate *yazzeh* (from the root *nāzâ*) as 'to sprinkle' (NIV) or 'to startle' (*HALOT* 2.683), of the twenty-four times it appears in the Old Testament it never means 'to startle', but rather 'to sprinkle' in the sense of ritual cleansing (see Exod. 29:21; Lev. 4:6, 17; etc.). The translation 'to startle' is often suggested because of (1) the reaction of the kings who *shut* [*qāpaṣ*, 7x] *their mouths* in surprise (see Ps. 107:42) in the parallel unit; and (2) the LXX's reading 'to marvel, wonder at'.

Verse 15b explains the reason (*kî*) for the surprised reaction of the kings: *For what they were not told, they will see, / and what they have not heard, they will understand.* They are startled because of what the servant will do: he *will sprinkle* or cleanse *many nations.* Paul picks up

52:15 in Romans 15:21 and applies it to his preaching of the gospel to the Gentiles.

53:1. There is now a change in speaker as the prophet poses the rhetorical question *Who has believed our message?* The ones who believed the message are the ones in the parallel phrase to whom *the arm of the LORD* (i.e. his strength) had been revealed. Thus, the ones who believed God would experience his deliverance.

The phrase *our message* may refer to the message of all the prophets, but later in the passage the plural forms (*we*) refer at least to Israel and the prophet (see vv. 2–3). Then in verse 6 the plural form may open up the message to include all believers, whether Jew or Gentile: *We all, like sheep, have gone astray* [i.e. everyone has strayed from God], / *each of us has turned to our own way; / and the LORD has laid on him / the iniquity of us all* (v. 6).

Childs correctly points out the skilful weaving together of 52:15 to 53:1 with terms related to 'seeing' and 'hearing' (2001: 413):

> *For what they were not told, they will see,*
> *and what they have not heard, they will understand.* (52:15)
> *Who has believed our message and to whom has the arm of the LORD*
>   *been revealed?* (53:1; emphasis added)

This structure suggests that what the kings heard and saw was the message that the servant would *sprinkle* (or cleanse) many nations. The parallel unit refers to God's power (*the arm of the LORD* [has] *been revealed*). Thus, God's power has been revealed by sending his servant to cleanse many nations.

2–3. The opening conjunction, best translated in the explicative sense as 'namely, even' (Williams §434), directly links verse 2 to verse 1 and continues the message regarding the servant God sent: *He grew up before him* [i.e. the LORD, the nearest antecedent in v. 1] *like a tender shoot* [*yônēq*]. The word *yônēq* (11x) is related to the Hebrew verb meaning 'to give suck', but this is the only time the word refers to a sapling.

The phrase *He grew up before him* implies that God's eye is on the servant; he is under God's special care. The servant is likened to a *tender shoot* that pushes up from the *dry ground*, an apt image in that

God could find no deliverer in the spiritually barren land of Israel until he himself caused a deliverer to spring up (see 51:18).

There was nothing remarkable in the servant's outward appearance (*He had no beauty* [*tō'ar*, 'form'; see lit. 'man of form' in 1 Sam. 16:18] *or majesty to attract us to him*, v. 2). Nothing in the servant's appearance suggested his exceptional nature. Instead, he was *despised and rejected* [*ḥādēl*, 'to refrain from others', 3x] . . . *like one from whom people hide their faces*. While the Hebrew of this latter phrase is difficult (lit. 'like hiding faces from him'), the general idea is that people spurn and reject the servant, holding him *in low esteem* (lit. 'we did not regard him'), for he is not the type of deliverer they expect.

The servant is also described as a *man of suffering*, meaning he had suffered enough both physically and emotionally to be *familiar with pain* (lit. 'knowing of sickness'). The terminology here is like that of a song of lament in which the psalmist expresses the pain, suffering and rejection by others that this servant experiences (see Ps. 22).

4–6. A contrast is drawn between the servant (*he*) and the people (*we*) who realize that the servant bore their *pain* (lit. 'our sicknesses') and *suffering* (lit. 'our pain'). It is not unusual for a prophet to identify with his listeners as he does here (note the plural forms).

Whybray argues against this being 'vicarious atonement', something unparalleled in the rest of the Old Testament and, according to him, contrary to its teaching (1975: 171; see Smith's counterargument, 2009: 448–449). The particle (*'ākēn*, 'surely') and the inverted syntax of verse 4 heighten the contrast between the two clauses: (1) *Surely he* [himself] *took up our pain / and bore our suffering*; versus (2) *yet we* [ourselves] *considered him punished by God, / stricken by him, and afflicted*. The grammar therefore argues against Whybray's position that the people did not understand that he was struck for them. The unique phrase 'smitten of/by God [*'ĕlōhîm*]' may be understood as a superlative, meaning he was 'terribly struck'; however, the passive form clearly favours that God inflicted the punishment.

The vocabulary of the servant's description powerfully expresses the vicariousness of the suffering and the extent of the punishment that *brought us peace* (v. 5): he was *pierced* [or 'wounded'] *for* [*mîn*, 'on account of'; Williams §319] *our transgressions*, and *crushed for [mîn] our iniquities*. Whybray maintains that the passage refers to Second Isaiah and does not refer to vicarious atonement:

> If the author had intended to imply such a transference of guilt, he would almost certainly have used the particle *bĕ*, which denotes an exchange. The fact that he chose instead the particle *mîn* [*for* in the NIV] indicates that he regarded the Servant's ill treatment as the result of the people's sin but not as a substitute for the punishment which they had deserved.
>
> (1975: 175)

While the preposition *bĕ* can suggest 'in exchange for' (Williams §246) as Whybray notes, the preposition *mîn* can also mean 'because of, on account of' (Williams §319), which in this context is just as effective a way to convey vicariousness (i.e. 'he was pierced because of our iniquities').

The servant was chastened on behalf of the nation, yet the affliction he endured was not in vain, for the nation was healed *by his wounds* (v. 5). Notice that the progression of this verse indicates spiritual healing of sin, not physical healing: *he was pierced for our transgressions . . . crushed for our iniquities . . . the punishment that brought us peace . . . by his wounds we are healed*. A theological problem arises if this is understood as physical healing in that, based upon the completed work of Christ's atonement, God would be required to heal us when we request it. Scripture makes it clear that God is able to heal us physically but is under no obligation to do so (see 2 Cor. 12:7–9).

The waywardness of the whole nation is confirmed in verse 6: *we all* (lit. 'all of us', including the speaker) wandered into sin, aptly pictured as sheep that wander off. Notice that it was the LORD who then placed their sin upon the servant: *the LORD has laid on* [lit. 'cause to fall upon'] *him / the iniquity of us all*. Childs points out that 'What occurred was not some unfortunate tragedy of human history but actually formed the center of the divine plan for the redemption of his people and indeed of the world' (2001: 415).

Verse 6 clearly goes beyond anything that any prophet (Isaiah, Jeremiah, Ezekiel, etc.) could have carried out and is a beautiful illustration of what Jesus alone could accomplish (see Luke 23:2–4, 13–16).

7–9. All this suffering (*oppressed* [*nāgaś*] suggests physical brutality and *afflicted* [*ʿānâ*] emotional agony) was endured by the servant without a word of complaint: *led like a lamb to the slaughter*. The rest of verse 7 forms a chiasm (literal wording):

> A but he did not open his mouth [*wĕlōʾ yiptaḥ-pîw*];
>   B like a lamb that is led to slaughter,
>   B′ and like a sheep that is silent before its shearers,
> A′ so he did not open his mouth [*wĕlōʾ yiptaḥ-pîw*].

Compare Jesus' similar attitude during the time leading up to his unjust crucifixion (see Matt. 26:63; 27:12–14). The servant was also treated harshly and judged when he was arrested: *By* [*min*, 'on account of'; Williams §319] *oppression* [*ʿōṣer*, 2x with this meaning] *and judgment he was taken away* (i.e. led away to punishment, v. 8).

The prophet asks, *Yet who of his generation protested?* (lit. 'and with his generation, who considered it?'; NEB: 'who gave a thought to his fate?'; v. 8). No-one from his generation seemed to even care that the servant was killed on behalf of God's people who themselves deserved to die.

Whybray suggests that the phrase *cut off from the land of the living* refers to a near-death experience (Lam. 3:54). In other words, 'The Servant was regarded as being "as good as dead"' (1975: 177). The phrase 'to cut off' occurs 177 times in the Old Testament, almost all of which mean 'to die' or 'to kill someone'. Thus, Smith comments, 'Only dead people are cut off from the living' (2009: 454), an observation that is further supported by mention of the servant's grave in verse 9.

The final phrase in verse 8 is difficult to interpret: *for the transgression of my people he was punished* (lit. 'because of the transgression of my people a stroke was to him'). A literal reading of the phrase *he was punished* is either (1) 'a stroke [was] to it', where 'it' is a collective singular noun referring to 'my people', the nearest possible antecedent; or (2) 'a stroke [was] to him', where 'him' refers to the servant (i.e. the subject of the sentence).

The first translation implies that the nation was guilty and deserved the punishment it received, whereas the second implies that, although the nation was guilty, the servant received the punishment. Since the servant is the subject of the sentence, we can infer that it was he who received the punishment and that the concept of substitution is thus implied here.

There is some question as to whether the first two phrases in verse 9 are synonymous parallelism (NIV, NRSV, ESV) or antithetical parallelism (NASB). The argument hinges on whether *the rich* were considered wicked in the Old Testament. The first pair of parallel phrases describes the location of the servant's grave site: *He was assigned* [lit. 'given'] *a grave with the wicked* [*rĕšāʿîm*], / *and* [or 'but'] *with the rich* [*ʿāšîr*] *in his death.* There is a possible play on words between *wicked* and *rich* which have similar letters, simply reversed.

The rich are often viewed as corrupt in Scripture (see Jer. 22:13–17; etc.), but it is unlikely that wealthy Joseph of Arimathea would have been considered wicked (Mark 15:43). Even though he was a member of the Council, he 'had not consented to their decision and action' regarding Jesus (Luke 23:51).

The second pair of parallel phrases explains why he did not deserve to be buried with the wicked: *though* [ʿal, a subordinating word that signals a concession to the verse's main idea; Williams §288b] *he had done no violence* [*ḥāmās*, 'violence or wrong'], / *nor was any deceit* [*mirmâ*, 'fraud or deception'] *in his mouth.* The word *mouth* is synecdoche for his whole person. Since these two phrases are clearly synonymous parallelism, the former two are also probably synonymous, and not antithetical, parallelism.

It is unclear why the MT retains the plural form 'in his deaths' (*bĕmōtāyw*) unless it was intended to signify an exceptionally violent death (i.e. *HALOT*, 'to the extreme death' [2.563]).

10–12. Verse 10 contrasts with verse 9b and highlights the results of the servant's suffering; even though he had done nothing wrong, it was actually the LORD's desire that he should suffer. He would be 'crushed' (*dakkĕ'ô*, 'beaten') and 'wounded' (*heḥĕlî*, 'he caused [him] to be sick'), and would offer his life as a 'guilt offering' (*'āšām*, v. 10).

As a result of this offering (1) the LORD will be 'pleased' in the sense that the suffering has accomplished a purpose; (2) *he* [i.e. the servant] *will see his offspring* [i.e. the righteous remnant]; (3) God will *prolong his days*, either by resurrection (most likely; Young 1965–72: 3.355) or by progeny that further his lineage; and (4) God's plan will have progressed (*the will of the LORD will prosper in his hand*, v. 10). As Westermann observes, 'There is no doubt that God's act of restoring the Servant, the latter's exaltation, is an act done upon him after his death and on the far side of the grave' (1969: 267).

According to Leviticus 4 – 5, the *'āšām* ('guilt offering') was to be offered for an unintentional sin. When made aware of his or her guilt, a person would offer this sacrifice (see Lev. 5:2–7). This is the exact sacrifice the Messiah needed to make on behalf of sinners, who may not recognize their sin until the Holy Spirit reveals it to them.

Yahweh is once again the speaker in verse 11. Verses 11 and 12 each contain three parallel units that form two chiasms that refer to what the servant's work accomplishes. A literal translation of the complex structure of the Hebrew text follows:

¹¹A Because of the anguish of his soul,
   B he will see,
   B′ he will be satisfied
  A′ by his knowledge;
Result: The righteous one, my servant, will justify the many
     and their iniquities he himself will bear.
¹²A Therefore [*lākēn*] I will apportion to him a part
   B with the many,
   B′ and with the strong
  A′ he will divide plunder; because he emptied himself to the
    death and was reckoned with the rebellious ones;
Result: and he himself carried the sins of the many and
    interceded for the transgressors.

Verse 11 explains that the servant will be satisfied with the results of what *he has suffered* (lit. 'because of the anguish of his soul'; the phrase carries the nuance of 'being toilsome and laborious'). LXX and 1QIsa^a add the word 'light' (Hebrew *'ôr*) after the verb 'he will see', which is the reading that the NIV follows: *he will see the light of life and be satisfied*. It is possible that a later copyist added *'ôr* to finish what he believed to be an incomplete sentence.

The last part of verse 11 states the consequence of the servant's hard work: *by his knowledge* [he] *will justify* [lit. 'make righteous'] *many* [lit. 'the many'; even though intentionally vague, it refers to those who accept this forgiveness for their sins] by bearing their iniquities on their behalf (i.e. once again, the substitutionary concept). *By his knowledge* must refer to his understanding that God's plan for him was to carry away sins.

The word *therefore* (*lākēn*) at the beginning of verse 12 introduces the results of the servant's faithful work (v. 11): *I* [i.e. God] *will give* [*ḥālaq*] *him a portion among the great, / and he will divide* [*ḥālaq*] *the spoils with the strong* (lit. 'with the strong, he will divide spoils' [emphatic order]). If his *spoils* (which usually refers to plunder taken in battle) are a metaphor for those whom he has freed from their sins, then the *great* and the *strong* may refer to Satan and his minions who held these captives until they were freed by the servant.

Verse 12 concludes with four reasons why the servant is successful: (1) *he poured out his life unto death* [lit. 'the death']; (2) [he] *was numbered with the transgressors* (i.e. he was considered to be one of them); (3) *he* [himself] *bore the sin of many*; and (4) [he] *made intercession for the transgressors*. Each reason is forcibly expressed by the inverted Hebrew syntax.

These images call to mind the sacrificial system wherein the death of an animal symbolically served as a substitute for the human, who deserved death; however, because it was only symbolic, it could not fully substitute for a human life. What was required to remove sin was a righteous (i.e. sinless) human (i.e. the servant) to die in place of the sinful. The servant then could 'intercede' on behalf of the transgressors. While the prophets did play an intermediary role of intercession for the people (see Jer. 14:10–16), they fell far short of being able to *justify many* (v. 11). Oswalt states it succinctly: 'This man, by what he has done, will make people righteous!' (1998: 404).

Meaning

This song is the climax of the preceding oracles which describe God's deliverance for his people, a deliverance which began with the return from exile but will be complete only when the nation is spiritually restored. Even though the servant of the fourth Servant Song has been identified in various ways, the New Testament authors understood this passage to refer to Jesus the Messiah (e.g. Isa. 52:15 = Rom. 15:21; Isa. 53:1 = John 12:38; etc.).

This servant would cleanse many nations (52:15); bear the griefs and sorrows of the many (53:4); be pierced for sins (53:5); remove iniquities (53:6); suffer and die for those who are guilty (53:8), though he himself had committed no violence or deception (53:9); justify many by his death (53:11); and intercede for transgressors (53:12). No other servant did all of these things. The apostle John said it best: 'Look, the Lamb of God, who takes away the sin of the world!' (John 1:29).

iv. Zion's glorious future (54:1–17)

Context
Following the description in the last section of the servant who will suffer and die for many, this section speaks of the glorious future for Zion that results from the servant's death (see Figure 0.11 on p. 29). The *many* of 53:11 refers to Zion's offspring, those whom the servant will justify by removing their sins.

This passage is generally divided into two units, verses 1–10 and 11–17, with themes similar to those of 49:14–23 (i.e. a promise of numerous children, 49:21//54:1–3; Zion's need to expand to accommodate her offspring, 49:20–21//54:2–3; assurance of God's love for Israel, 49:14–19//54:7–8; a promise of restoration, 49:17–19//54:9–10; etc.). Verses 1–10 constitute a song of praise that begins with imperatives (i.e. commands to do something), followed by the reasons why (*kî*, 'for'). For example, in verse 1 they are commanded to sing *because* [*kî*] *more are the children of the desolate woman / than of her who has a husband*.

At the time of the prophecy, Zion is pictured as a barren woman who has been forsaken by her husband (vv. 1, 6) and afflicted (vv. 7–9), a metaphor for the Babylonian exile. Yet one day, as Yahweh promises, he will so bless her that she will forget her shame and humiliation. The prophet looks into the future and sees the nation gloriously restored – her walls covered with *precious stones* and her gates with *sparkling jewels*, and all her enemies defeated.

Even when read in a figurative sense, this great restoration far surpasses Jerusalem's restoration following the Babylonian exile. This is an example of the 'prophetic perspective' wherein the prophet glimpses both the nation's return to Jerusalem from Babylon and a future, far more glorious restoration, without having an awareness of the interval of time between the two. The conclusion to the oracle in verse 17 assures Zion of her glorious restoration: *This is the heritage of the servants of the LORD, / and this is their vindication from me.*

Comment

a. Yahweh's covenant of peace with Zion (54:1–10)

1. The exhortations to *sing* (*piṣḥî*, 'burst into song', 7x) and *shout for joy* (*ṣaḥălî*, 7x) signal a song of praise (vv. 1–10) that commences a new section. Zion should *shout for joy* because the sons of the 'barren one' (NIV = *desolate woman*) will be more numerous than the sons of *her who has a husband*. The LORD compares two different periods of Zion's life: as a married woman prior to exile and as a 'barren woman' while in exile (v. 1; see 49:21). Yet Zion will be repopulated; in fact, her inhabitants (i.e. *children of the desolate woman*) will be more numerous than before.

Galatians 4:27 quotes Isaiah 54:1 and applies it to a future time of blessing under the new covenant when the new Jerusalem will be more densely populated than ever before. The Babylonian exile had a purging effect, allowing God to bring a believing remnant back to Zion. New Testament believers are a continuation of the believing remnant of the Old Testament.

2–3. In order to accommodate all her children, Zion is encouraged to *enlarge the place of* [her] *tent*. Women in the Ancient Near East were typically responsible for erecting and maintaining the family tent. Zion is to expand hers generously and substantially: *stretch your tent curtains wide, / do not hold back; / lengthen your cords, / strengthen your stakes* (v. 2). Zion will *spread out* [*pāraṣ*, 'break out'] *to the right and to the left* (signifying 'in all directions', v. 3), for her descendants will be numerous (see Gen. 28:14). Zion will need to act in faith since she is barren at the time.

The phrase *and settle in their desolate cities* (v. 3) could mean that Zion's children will (1) conquer other nations and occupy the cities whose inhabitants they have destroyed; or (2) drive out other nations from Israel's land and resettle in their cities following the Babylonian exile. The latter is preferable, for the remnant would 'inherit' the land that their ancestors owned prior to the seventy years of exile.

4–5. Zion will have no reason to be afraid. She will forget the shame of her youth (i.e. her sinful past) and *the reproach* [i.e. 'disgrace'] *of her widowhood* [*'almānût*, 4x] that in this context probably refers to the Babylonian exile. Zion will be so blessed that she will forget the humiliation of these earlier times. Yahweh, her *Maker*, will be her *husband*.

Both *Maker* and *husband* are 'honorific plurals' (Williams §8), whereas God's name *the LORD Almighty* (lit. 'of hosts') is singular. *Maker*, *husband*, *Redeemer* and *the Holy One of Israel* are familiar terms used for Israel's God in earlier chapters. These names reflect his special relationship with Israel. It is their God who controls the whole earth and who can therefore be trusted.

6–8. Yahweh will call back (lit. 'has called', a prophetic perfect – pictured as already accomplished) to himself Israel in her distress, poignantly portrayed as a rejected, deserted young wife (lit. 'a woman of youth', v. 6). The rejection of a young wife at the age when she is most desirable is particularly heartbreaking.

Yahweh admits that he rejected the nation for a short while (lit. 'a little moment', i.e. during the Babylonian exile; v. 7). The books of Jeremiah (chs. 2; 5) and Ezekiel (chs. 8 – 11; 16) record just how justified God was in rejecting them. Yet he will demonstrate the magnitude of his overwhelming compassion for Israel (*deep compassion*, lit. 'great compassions' [pl.]) by taking the initiative to bring them back (lit. 'I will gather you back', v. 7).

Verse 8 likens God's momentary rejection (lit. *I hid my face from you*) to a brief outburst of anger (lit. 'with a flood [*šeṣep*, occurs only here; suggests that God's anger was intense] of wrath') that will be followed by *everlasting kindness* (*'ôlām ḥesed*) and *compassion* (*rāḥam*) that only God can demonstrate. Graciously gathering up a chastened Israel in his arms, he reminds her that he is her redeemer (i.e. 'the one who bought her back').

9–10. Yahweh, seeking to reassure Israel that he will not abandon her again, gives two reasons (*kî*) why he can be trusted. First, he equates the oath he makes here with the one he made to Noah when he promised that he would never again flood the earth (lit. 'for the waters of Noah [is] this', v. 9); in the same way he will never again be angry with Israel. *The days of Noah* (lit. 'waters of Noah') were a time like the exile when people were subjected to severe punishment from Yahweh. The MT reads 'waters of Noah'; however, a slight change in word division creates the more favourable reading *like the days of Noah*, which is supported by 1QIsaᵃ. The oath, one of the most compelling means of confirming the truthfulness of a statement, was meant to unequivocally assure them that their punishment was now finished.

Second, God can be trusted because he gives his word not to revoke his *covenant of peace* (v. 10). Even though the mountains, an image of stability and permanence, may tremble (*mûṭ*) and be removed (*mûš*; these two verbs sound similar), God's *unfailing love ... will not be shaken* (*mûš*, lit. 'be removed'), nor will his *covenant of peace* with Israel *be removed* (*mûṭ*, lit. 'be shaken'). This covenant corresponds to the 'covenant of peace' in Ezekiel 37:26 and the 'new covenant' in Jeremiah 31:31–34. God's *unfailing love* (*ḥeṣed*) and *compassion* (*rāḥam*) are the ultimate benefits of this covenant of peace.

b. The new Jerusalem (54:11–17)

11–12. The description of Zion as an *afflicted city, lashed by storms and not comforted* (see 51:21), describes her plight during the Babylonian captivity. The phrase *not comforted* refers to the period when God turned away from or abandoned her, thus allowing her overthrow and the forceful removal of her inhabitants from Israel, pictured as being *lashed by storms*. The word *hinnēh* ('behold', omitted in the NIV) in verse 11b signals a shift: God promises to restore Zion's glory (vv. 11b–13) and protection (vv. 14–17).

In verse 11b God himself promises to *rebuild* (lit. 'set down') Zion *with stones of turquoise* (lit. 'your stones in antimony [*bappûk*]'; certain passages suggest it is a pigment used to adorn eyes [see 2

Kgs 9:30], thus in this context it may refer to stones that are painted to make them stand out); *foundations with lapis lazuli* (*sappîr*, 'some type of blue stone'; see Exod. 24:10); *battlements* [*šimšôt*, 'suns'; only occurrence with this meaning] *of rubies* [*kadkōd*, 2x]; *gates of sparkling jewels* (*'eqdāḥ*, 'stones of sparkling', occurs only here); and *walls* [*gĕbûl*, 'boundary'] *of precious* [lit. 'delightful'] *stones*. Scholars are divided as to whether to read this description of the city's great worth and/or beauty in a figurative or literal sense. The theme of Zion glorified with precious and semi-precious stones is picked up in later literature (see Tobit 13:16–18; Rev. 21:19–21).

13–17. The description now turns from the beauty of the city to the well-being of her children, who *will be taught by* [lit. 'of'] *the* LORD and experience great peace (v. 13). Whybray suggests they are taught the skills required for building the city (1975: 188), yet this seems far too narrow given the context. According to 48:17, where the theme of being *taught by the* LORD is first introduced, the emphasis is on being taught about the LORD, not by the LORD; thus, it is reasonable to assume that the phrase *taught by the* LORD in 54:13 also means to be taught about him. This deep spiritual knowledge will then bring them *peace* (*šālôm*).

Verses 14–17 describe Yahweh's protection of restored Zion, which is established in righteousness and called once again by the descriptive name 'city of righteousness' (see 1:26). She will no longer be oppressed and *will have nothing to fear* (i.e. terror [*mĕḥittâ*, 4x with this meaning]), for Yahweh will never again incite a nation against her (v. 15). Any attack (*gûr*, 4x with this meaning) upon restored Zion will be doomed to fail; the attacker will surrender to the inhabitants of Zion (lit. 'will fall beside you' [Williams §286] or 'because of you' [Williams §291]), for Yahweh is her protector.

Zion need never fear because Yahweh himself created (lit. 'I myself have created', stated emphatically) both the blacksmith ('the one who fans the coal' [*peḥām*, 3x]) who makes dangerous weapons (lit. *a weapon fit for its work*, v. 16) and the warrior (lit. *the destroyer*) who uses these weapons. No *weapon* (*kĕlî*, 'utensil') will ever triumph over his people, nor will anyone ever be able to condemn them in court (lit. 'any tongue that rises up against you for judgment you will cause to be condemned', v. 17).

The final phrases of verse 17, *This is the heritage* [or 'inheritance'] *of the servants of the LORD* / . . . *their vindication* [lit. 'righteousness'] [is] *from me*, form a conclusion to the chapter as a whole. Because God has vindicated his people, they no longer need fear being captured or exiled. Verse 17 is a further development of 53:10 in which the suffering servant is said to have offspring; here it shows that those offspring will be protected and vindicated by God.

Meaning

Following Isaiah 53, which pictures the servant dying for the nation, Yahweh promises that he will prosper and bless his people. Twice in this chapter Yahweh is called Israel's *Redeemer* (vv. 5, 8), emphasizing the deliverance that he will initiate. Even though they endured a long exile in Babylon, one day they will never again fear being subjected to shame and punishment.

Now that the punishment is over, they can look forward to the blessings. In fact, the number of children Israel ultimately has during this time of blessing will be far greater than the number before the exile. This chapter thus describes God's plan for Zion and his people which begins in exile but ends with a glorious restoration.

v. God's gracious mercy (55:1 – 56:8)

Context

Yahweh's servant has prepared the way of glorious deliverance for God's people (Isa. 53), which has been described in Isaiah 54. Now it is time to offer this deliverance to those who desire it (Isa. 55 – 56; see Figure 0.11 on p. 29), not only to Israel but to all who are willing to seek the LORD. The rest of the book of Isaiah will highlight the transformations that can occur because of the servant's sacrifice. Oswalt summarizes the purpose of chapters 56–66: 'These chapters are about the internalization of the law by means of an intimate relationship with the God who alone can enable people to live holy lives' (1998: 453).

While many scholars argue that chapter 56 begins a new section whose tone is entirely different from that of chapters 49–55, there are at least four points that run counter to this view:

1. The pattern of the refrains in the book of Isaiah suggests that a major break occurs at 57:21 (see also 48:22 and 66:24) and not after chapter 55.

2. Three aspects of Isaiah 55 continue into Isaiah 56: (a) the prophet is the narrator in both; (b) God is speaking in first-person forms ('my', 'me' and 'I'; 55:8–9, 11; 56:1); and (c) the benefits of seeking the LORD (i.e. 55:6), each marked by (*kî*, 'for'), continue into the next chapter: *for he will freely pardon* (55:7b); *For my thoughts are not your thoughts* (55:8); [for] *my ways* [are] *higher than your ways / and my thoughts than your thoughts* (55:9); [for] *it will not return to me empty, / but will accomplish what I desire / and achieve the purpose for which I sent it* (55:11); [For] *you will go out in joy and be led forth in peace* (55:12); *for my salvation is close at hand / and my righteousness will soon be revealed* (56:1); *For . . . I will give . . . a memorial . . . an everlasting name / that will endure for ever* (56:4–5); *for my house will be called / a house of prayer for all nations* (56:7b).

3. The themes of chapters 55 and 56 are similar: God's deliverance (i.e. 'for you will go out with joy' [55:12]//'for my salvation is about to come' [56:1]); and the gathering of a remnant (i.e. *and nations you do not know will come running to you* [55:5]//*Let no foreigner who is bound to the LORD say . . .* [56:3]).

4. Two promises in Isaiah 55 are fulfilled in Isaiah 56: the promise that *nations you do not know will come . . . to you* (55:5) is fulfilled in 56:6 when *foreigners . . . bind themselves to the LORD* (56:6); and the promise of deliverance in 55:11 (*it* [my word] *will not return to me empty*) is said to be about to be revealed in chapter 56 (*my salvation is close at hand / and my righteousness will soon be revealed* [56:1]). In other words, the offer of salvation is merely described in chapter 55, but how to access it is described in chapter 56.

This section is generally divided into three parts: 55:1–5; 55:6–13; and 56:1–8. The first oracle (55:1–5) is a universal call of deliverance encouraging any who are thirsty to come to God, ending with a startling conclusion: *nations you do not know will come running to you.*

The second oracle (55:6–13) warns to seek God while he may be found, the implication being that there may be a time when he cannot be found and, therefore, they may miss his deliverance. It then concludes with the glorious promise that Israel will be delivered.

The final oracle (56:1–8) begins and ends with a declaration from the LORD that his deliverance is coming soon, but at the end there is a startling statement similar to that at the end of 55:5: *I will gather still others to them / besides those already gathered.*

Comment

a. Yahweh offers an everlasting covenant (55:1–5)

1–2. Yahweh seeks the listeners' attention with the interjection *hôy*, 'woe' (untranslated by the NIV), and then, in a series of imperatives (*come, buy, eat*), offers deliverance (pictured as *water, wine* and *milk*) to anyone who thirsts for it (v. 1). The imagery is reminiscent of lady wisdom in Proverbs 9:1–9, who calls out to the 'simple' to come and gain insight: 'Come, eat my food / and drink the wine I have mixed' (v. 5). It also echoes the cries of Ancient Near Eastern water-sellers, with one crucial difference: the water, wine and milk here are offered without cost, thus deliverance is free. This offer extends to *all . . . who are thirsty* (v. 1) and not just those returning from Babylon.

Israel (= *you*) had often laboured for and spent money (lit. 'weighed out silver') on things that did not satisfy. The LORD offers that which truly satisfies – 'water' and 'bread' that represent true spiritual food. The LORD urges (*Listen, listen* [lit. 'continually listen'; Williams §206], v. 2) the people to accept his offer, for it is far better than what they currently have (*you will delight in the richest of fare,* lit. 'you will enjoy yourself in the fatness of your soul').

3–5. God exhorts the people yet again to listen and grasp the importance of his offer of life (i.e. *that you* [lit. 'your soul'] *may live,* v. 3). He then announces that he *will make* [lit. 'cut'] *an everlasting covenant with you, / my faithful love promised to David* (v. 3). It is uncertain how these two phrases relate to each other since there is no indication in the Hebrew; however, if the NIV's translation is correct, then the *everlasting covenant* is described as God's *faithful love* [lit. 'faithful mercies', pl.] *promised to David.*

The phrase *everlasting covenant* (*běrît ʿôlām*) is used twelve times in the Old Testament (see 24:5; etc.) and is likened to 'the kind mercies shown to David' (Williamson 1978: 31–49) when God established him and his descendants as an everlasting ruling dynasty (see 2

Sam. 7:8–17). God focuses on the Davidic covenant with its abundant mercies (suggested by the plural form *ḥasdê*, 'kind mercies') and promise of an everlasting relationship with the LORD. The covenant was ultimately fulfilled by the Messiah who came through the line of David (see Matt. 1).

The repetition of the word *see* (*hēn*, 'behold') at the beginning of verses 4 and 5 (omitted in v. 5 in the NIV) draws attention to God's plan. At one time God had worked through David to display his glory to the nations (*I have made him a witness to the peoples*, v. 4), but now God will use this restored nation to bring other nations to himself (*Surely you* [sing.] *will summon nations you know not*, v. 5) – all because God has *endowed you* [i.e. the remnant] *with splendour.*

Notice that David is not called a 'king' but rather a *witness* (*'ēd*), *ruler* (*nāgîd*) and a *commander* [*mĕṣawwēh*] *of the peoples* (v. 4). These terms may have been used to reflect the fact that David was merely the viceroy of the true king, Yahweh. David was a *witness* in the sense that (1) each time David conquered a nation, the victory displayed the strength of his God to them (see Ps. 18:43–50); and (2) David's alliances allowed him to influence many nations.

No matter how David's role is understood, the author makes clear that the exiles, and later the righteous remnant, will be a witness for God to the nations (see 44:8): *nations you do not know will come running to you* (v. 5). Gentile nations will be drawn to this righteous nation that has been glorified by its God. Both of God's names – *the LORD your God* and *the Holy One of Israel* – call attention to his special relationship to Israel.

b. A solemn invitation (55:6–13)

6–7. A sense of urgency is now added to the invitation of verse 1: *Seek* [pl.] *the LORD while he may be found; / call on him while he is near.* This assumes that there is a time when he cannot be found and is not near. While this call is directed primarily to the exiles, verse 5a lets us know it is also for the nations that Israel brings to God. The exhortation to *call on him while he is near* signals that the time of deliverance has arrived.

The exiles must now indicate on an individual basis their readiness to be delivered by forsaking their wicked ways and turning to the LORD, for *he will freely pardon* (lit. 'will make great to forgive', v. 7). Those who refuse to do so will forfeit their chance to take part in this deliverance. Not every Israelite chose to return to Israel under Cyrus's policy of repatriation: only about fifty thousand made that choice, and, in so doing, had to give up their relative prosperity in Babylon. The only thing the Israelites truly lacked in Babylon was a temple to worship Yahweh. The journey home would be long, and resettlement of the devastated land would require time and considerable labour. Only those who cared enough about following God and were willing to make these sacrifices would return; thus they are called a righteous remnant.

8–11. Beginning with the word 'for' (*kî*), verse 8 provides God's reason why he is willing to abundantly pardon those who turn to him (see end of v. 7): because God is gracious and sees the bigger picture, he knows the most suitable way to accomplish his goals and bring the best possible outcomes of their disobedience. *The wicked* (v. 7) are urged to forsake their *ways* and *thoughts* and trust in him:

A *For my thoughts*
 B *are not your thoughts,*
 B′ *neither are your ways*
A′ *my ways.*
(v. 8)

In this chiasm God challenges the wicked on two fronts. (1) He reminds them that his ways are different from theirs; thus, the way in which he brings deliverance will truly amaze the exiles. Just as the heavens seemingly reach infinitely high above the earth (v. 9), so God's thoughts are infinitely higher than our thoughts – compelling confirmation that Yahweh will indeed accomplish his promise of deliverance for the nation of Israel. God's *ways* and *thoughts* together form the totality of his actions. Human beings do not have the capacity to fully understand them, for we are neither omnipotent nor omniscient. (2) Just as (*ka'ăšer*) rain and snow water the earth so that seeds can sprout and flourish (similar imagery in 40:8), so (*kēn*) God's word will not return without accomplishing all that he intended: [it] *will accomplish what I desire* (v. 11).

12–13. The *kî* (i.e. 'with the result that') at the beginning of verse 12 signals the result of the preceding verse (Williams §450): there will be an exodus from Babylon of those who have turned towards God. Their departure will be marked by great joy and peace; even nature will *burst into song* and *clap* [*māḥā'*, 3x] [its] *hands* because Yahweh has delivered the exiles.

The highly figurative language continues in verse 13 with images of God's renewal: the *thorn-bush* (*naʿaṣûṣ*, 2x) and *briers* (*sirpād*, occurs only here) will be transformed into trees (*juniper, myrtle* [*hădas*, 6x; 3x in Zech. 1]), implying a reversal of the curse to which the ground was subjected in Genesis 3:18.

The fruitfulness of the land will be a sign of God's reputation (*for the* LORD'*s renown*; lit. 'for a name'), which will *endure for ever* (lit. 'not be cut off'). Deliverance from Babylon is seen as a first step: if God can accomplish the first deliverance, then he can bring about the restoration of the whole earth.

c. The true people of God (56:1–8)

1–2. God's promised deliverance is about to come, but only those who have a proper heart attitude will benefit from it. Those whose hearts follow God will choose to return to Jerusalem and rebuild the temple. The messenger formula of verse 1 states, *This is what the* LORD *says: / 'Maintain justice* [i.e. attitude] / *and do what is right'* [lit. 'righteousness', i.e. action]. God's blessing will be poured out on those who follow these two positive commands. God then explains why obeying them is so urgent: *for my salvation is close at hand / and my righteousness will soon be revealed* (v. 1). He expects his children to be ready for him, and to show their readiness by displaying his righteousness.

God then gives two negative commands: to keep *the Sabbath without desecrating it* and to keep *their hands from doing any evil* (v. 2). It is easy to see how keeping the Sabbath might take on great significance following the exile since the nation had been restricted from temple worship for so long. It was important to remind the Israelites that it was still an essential part of God's laws (Sabbath-keeping continued to be a problem during the post-exilic period; see Neh. 10:31; 13:16–22). The next command to keep *their hands from doing any evil* is an all-encompassing summary of the negative requirements of the law.

Obedience to these four commands demonstrates true right-eousness, involving both a proper heart attitude and obedience to God's law.

3–8. Foreigners (lit. 'son of a foreigner'; see the prohibition against the Ammonites and Moabites in Deut. 23:3) and eunuchs (see Deut. 23:1), who were considered second-class members and were forbidden to enter the assembly of the LORD, are now welcomed. The Ammonites and Moabites had been forbidden because of their ill-treatment of Israel during the exodus (Num. 21 – 22). These and other foreigners had thought, *The LORD will surely exclude me from his people*, because they were not Jewish.

The eunuch thought he would be excluded because he could neither reproduce nor perpetuate his name: *I am only a dry tree*. Eunuchs, whether voluntary or not, may have been deemed unfit to serve God because of their castration, just as maimed animals were considered unfit to be offered as sacrifices to God. Both groups had thought themselves permanently excluded; however, anyone committed to Yahweh from these two groups will be openly accepted in God's restored kingdom.

Eunuchs are to demonstrate their commitment to Yahweh by (1) keeping the Sabbath; (2) choosing what pleases God; and (3) holding fast to (lit. 'grasping') God's covenant (i.e. the Mosaic covenant at this point, v. 4; see Jer. 50:4–5). Foreigners are similarly to demon-strate their commitment to Yahweh by (1) binding *themselves to the LORD / to minister to him* (vv. 3, 6); (2) loving *the name of the LORD*; (3) being *his servants*; (4) keeping *the Sabbath without desecrating it*; and (5) holding fast to (lit. 'grasping') his covenant (v. 6). Notice that eunuchs do not show their devotion to God by ministering to him as the foreigners do; apparently, while they are able to have a restored relationship to God, they are still bound by physical limitations.

Because the eunuch cannot reproduce, he will be given some-thing greater than descendants: a *memorial* (*yād*, 'a hand') within the temple (lit. 'my house')[16] and an *everlasting name* (v. 5), perhaps

---

16. For an example of a memorial set up in the temple or its precincts, see
  Yadin 1972: 71–74.

written on the memorial (see 2 Sam. 18:18). This memorial will be even better than offspring, for it will *endure for ever* (lit. 'which will not be cut off').

Whether Israelites, foreigners or eunuchs, their correct heart attitude towards God is a prerequisite to acceptable worship, which God approves by (1) bringing them to his *holy mountain* (i.e. Zion); (2) giving them joy in his *house of prayer* (this phrase is used only here); and (3) accepting *their burnt offerings and sacrifices* (v. 7). The acceptance of foreigners and eunuchs would no doubt have stunned law-abiding Israelites, but they had already been informed that *nations you do not know will come running to you* (55:5).

Their true worship has a further wonderful result, introduced by the word *for* in verse 7 (Williams §450): *my house will be called / a house of prayer for all nations* (quoted in Matt. 21:13; Mark 11:17; Luke 19:46). The passage concludes with Yahweh's solemn declaration (*the Sovereign LORD* [lit. 'the Lord (ʾădōnāy) LORD' (yĕhwih)] *declares*, v. 8) that he has not yet finished gathering people: *I will gather still others to them* [i.e. the exiles of Israel] */ besides those already gathered.* The implication is that the remnant will be numerous and from many nations.

Meaning

Once God has described his plan to deliver Israel, not only from the Babylonian captivity but also spiritually (i.e. *In righteousness you will be established*, 54:14), which he calls *the heritage of the servants of the LORD* (54:17), he then offers this deliverance to anyone who will accept it (55:1–2). This general call to those who are thirsty is a figurative appeal to anyone willing to accept this spiritual deliverance from God. The plan demands that they agree to the covenant (most probably the new covenant, 55:3) that the LORD is offering them. If they do, then they will see God's faithful mercies, just as he had shown to David.

Initially the context of this passage is the return from the Babylonian exile, but it extends to a time in the distant future when God will gather a righteous remnant from many nations, those who will serve him obediently and glorify him. They must turn to him while the opportunity is available, for there is a point when it will be too late to 'call to God' (55:6).

Because of Israel's constant wandering into sin, God must remind them how to be righteous in his eyes. He also wants to make it clear that this righteousness is not for Israel alone, but for all who will turn to him in obedience. Even foreigners and eunuchs, who previously could not participate in cultic worship, would now be accepted wholeheartedly by God, whose house will be a *house of prayer for all nations*. The only requirement is a sincere relationship with God. The concept that God's deliverance is open to more than the nation of Israel is one of the most exciting developments in the second part of the book of Isaiah.

vi. No hope for evil leaders (56:9 – 57:21)

Context

For the urgent call to repent in 55:6 (*Seek the* LORD *while he may be found; / call on him while he is near*) to truly make sense, the author must also describe the consequences for those who do not do so, which are now set forth in this final section of this part of Isaiah (chs. 49–57; see Figure 0.11 on p. 29). The call to come and eat of the good things from God (55:1–2) is contrasted with a call to the beasts of the field to come and devour those who have rejected God's offer (56:9).

These wicked people (the passage alternates between the wicked leaders and the wicked in general) will indeed eat and drink, but they will not be satisfied. Blinded by their sin, they are deluded into thinking they need never suffer the consequences of their sins, that life will continue as it always has (*tomorrow will be like today, / or even far better,* 56:12).

But according to chapter 57, this is not correct: the wicked who have relied on their idols will receive little help from them (v. 13), while the righteous will enter into peace (v. 2). Indeed, God was angry with his people for a little while, but ultimately he will deliver them.

This section then ends with a seam similar to those of the other sections (48:17–22 and 66:1–24). It begins with a declaration, *For this is what the high and exalted One says*, and then summarizes the key themes of the book: (1) Israel has been judged (57:16–17); (2) Israel will be delivered (57:18–19); and (3) the wicked will be punished

(57:17, 20–21). The seam concludes with a refrain common to the Isaianic seams of the second half of the book, *'There is no peace,' says my God, 'for the wicked'* (see 48:22 and an extended version in 66:24).

Isaiah 56:9 – 57:21 comprises two units: (1) the sins of the nation of Israel (56:9 – 57:14); and (2) Yahweh will bring deliverance for the humble (57:15–21).

Comment

a. The sins of the nation of Israel (56:9 – 57:14)

9–12. Verse 9 marks an abrupt change, returning to the theme of punishment for Israel's indolent leaders (called *watchmen*, v. 10) who will be destroyed (*come and devour, all you beasts of the forest!*). The beasts are a symbolic reference either to God's punishment in general or to the enemies he will use to destroy them. These degenerate leaders no longer possess the necessary qualities to serve as the nation's *watchmen* (see Ezek. 3:17–21), being instead (1) *blind*, in the sense that *they all lack knowledge* of how to follow God (v. 10); (2) *mute* [*'illēm*, 6x] *dogs* that are unable to warn of imminent danger (i.e. [who] *cannot bark* [*nābaḥ*, occurs only here], v. 10); (3) indolent people who *lie around and . . . love to sleep* (*nûm*, 6x; v. 10); (4) greedy, like *dogs with mighty appetites* (lit. 'mighty of throat'), who *never have enough* (lit. 'they do not know fullness', v. 11); (5) corrupt, lacking in *understanding* (lit. 'they do not know how to discern', v. 11); (6) unrepentant (*they all turn to their own way* instead of to God); and (7) self-serving (lit. 'each one to his own gain out of its end', v. 11).

Leaders are often pictured as shepherds in the Old Testament (Num. 27:17; Ezek. 34:5; etc.) and prophets are often portrayed as watchmen (Jer. 6:17; Ezek. 3:17; etc.). Both were corrupt at this point, unlike the picture Ezekiel paints of God, Israel's true shepherd (Ezek. 34).

Instead of declaring warnings to repent, these leaders call out to their friends, inviting them to carouse: *'Come,'* each one cries, *'let me get wine! / Let us drink our fill of beer!'* (v. 12). Without vision or direction, they are unable to lead the people in any beneficial direction (see Prov. 29:18). Even worse, they are entirely blind to the punishment God is preparing and assume that life will continue as it is: *And tomorrow will be like today, / or even far better* (lit. 'the rest will be much greater', v. 12).

57:1–2. As a result of Israel's failed leadership, *the righteous* [the syntax here puts emphasis on 'the righteous'] *perish, / and no one takes it to heart* (lit. 'there is not a man that puts [it] upon his heart', v. 1). The nation has sunk so low that no-one is concerned that the number of righteous persons (lit. 'men of *ḥesed* ['kindness']') is dwindling, and that as they die the number of evildoers increases: *the righteous are taken away / to be spared from evil* (lit. 'for from the presence of evil the righteous are gathered', v. 1).

For the righteous, death is pictured as going to a place of *peace* and *rest* (*they find rest as they lie in death* [lit. 'going straight ahead of him'] away from all the evil, v. 2).

3–4. There is a vehemence in the contrast drawn between the *righteous* of verses 1–2 and the idolaters portrayed in verses 3–13a: *But you* [lit. 'yourself' = emphasis] – *come here, you children of a sorceress, / you offspring of adulterers and prostitutes!* Yahweh summons the idolaters to appear before him and give an account of themselves. He accuses them of being what he utterly despises: those who blatantly rebel by engaging in sorcery and sexual rites associated with idolatry.

The Israelites were adulterers in the sense that they displayed unfaithfulness to God, with whom they were in a covenant relationship, by having joined themselves to the gods of foreign nations. Similarly, they had prostituted themselves by giving their worship to idols (including engaging in cult prostitution), supposedly in order to receive their help.

The openly rude gestures of the wicked, 'sneering' (lit. 'you make wide the mouth') and 'sticking out their tongues' (lit. 'you make long a tongue', v. 4) as they mock Yahweh, are manifestations of how far they have wandered from God's laws. They are a *brood* [lit. 'children'] *of rebels* who are the *offspring of liars* [*šāqer*, 'deception']; that is, they pretend to be righteous while brazenly practising idolatry.

5–8. Their idolatrous practices included both fertility rites and child sacrifice, both of which were condemned by the exilic prophets. The phrases *You burn with lust among the oaks* (*'ayil*, 'mighty tree', 3x with this meaning, all in Isaiah; v. 5) and *You have made your* *bed on a high and lofty hill* (v. 7) refer to ritual prostitution in Baal worship that was meant to ensure the fertility of the land.

The hilltop sites of idol worship were typically planted with luxuriant gardens to promote the belief that Baal caused the land to be fertile, hence the references to *among the oaks* (the word *bāʾēlîm* could also be translated 'among the gods', but this is unlikely here) and *every spreading* [lit. 'luxuriant'] *tree* (v. 5).

Child sacrifice was also practised *in the ravines* [lit. 'wadis'] / *and under the overhanging* [*sāʿîp*, 4x] *crags* (v. 5), particularly during the reigns of Ahaz and Manasseh, who sacrificed children in the Valley of Ben Hinnom. This kind of apostasy is particularly detestable to Yahweh (see Jer. 7:31).

God is therefore justified in giving them over to the consequences of pursuing idol worship (see Rom. 1:18–32): *The idols among the smooth stones of the ravines are your portion.* There is a wordplay between the similar-sounding words *smooth stones* (*ḥallĕqê*) and *your portion* (*ḥelqēk*).

The *smooth stones* (v. 6) probably refer to the 'standing stones' or 'pillars' (*maṣṣēbah*) that represented Baal (see Exod. 34:13; Smith 2009: 552) and to which they offered sacrifices: *to them* [i.e. *the smooth stones*] *you have poured out drink offerings / and offered grain offerings.* God pauses in his recital of their sins to pose the rhetorical question *In view of all this, should I relent* [lit. 'have compassion']? The answer is clearly 'no!', for these acts of wickedness demanded judgment.

Next on the list of their sins is the statement *You have made your bed on a high and lofty hill* (v. 7), both a figurative and a literal reference to their idolatry, which included spending the night worshipping before the gods on hilltops (i.e. high places). There is little evidence that these idolatrous practices occurred during the post-exilic period (Ezra 9 – 10; Neh. 9 – 10), as some have suggested (see Whybray 1975: 202). More probably it is a pre-exilic projection of what sins in this future time would be like.

The people have also brought pagan worship into their homes: *Behind your doors and your doorposts / you have put your pagan symbols* [*zikrônēk*, 'your memorial, remembrance', v. 8]. Verses 8b–9a speak figuratively of their adulterous pursuit of any and all idols, forming intimate relationships with them instead of with God (i.e. *forsaking me*).

They have (1) *uncovered, climbed into* and *opened . . . wide* their beds, suggesting intimacy with many gods; (2) *made a pact with those whose beds* [they] *love*, a reference to their alliances and treaties with countries that worshipped these foreign gods (alternative translation: 'you cut yourself on account of them', a common practice to gain the pity of the gods; see 1 Kgs 18:28); and (3) *looked with lust on their naked bodies* (lit. 'hand', a euphemism for sexual parts, thus the readings 'manhood' [NASB], *naked bodies* [NIV] or 'nakedness' [ESV]), an image portraying the sexual nature of their false religions.

9–10. In forming alliances with other *far away* nations, Israel often also accepted their gods. Israel sent envoys to the far nations of Egypt (2 Kgs 19:9; Isa. 37:9) and Babylon (Ezek. 23:14–17, 40) to request aid. Some scholars suggest repointing *melek* (lit. 'to the king' in the MT) to *Molek*, a Canaanite deity, thus the translation *You went* [*šāpal*, 'went down', 3x with this meaning] *to Molek* (NIV) with gifts of appeasement (i.e. *olive oil and . . . perfumes*, v. 9). However, Oswalt points out that Canaan was not a 'far away' nation (1998: 480).

Verse 9 states that the Israelites sent their envoys *to the very realm of the dead* (lit. 'Sheol'), hyperbole for either a very long distance or that Israel's leaders caused their envoys to incur guilt equal to their own for relying on humans instead of on God. Even though they wearied themselves with all their travels in pursuit of false gods who had no ability to act on their behalf, they refused to give up the practice (*you would not say, 'It is hopeless'* [*yā'aš*, 6x], v. 10). Somehow, they found renewed energy (lit. 'you found life in your hand') to continue their sinful pursuit – the sin nature is indeed a powerful force.

11–14. The NIV captures the nuance in God's question to Israel: *Whom have you so dreaded* [*dā'ag*, 7x] *and feared / that you have not been true to me* [emphatic statement, lit. 'that *me* they did not remember'], */ . . . nor taken this to heart?* (i.e. taken God seriously, v. 11). Israel often feared human kings so much that they forgot to fear God. They mistook God's long-suffering patience (lit. 'silence') for an inability to act, and thus did not revere him (lit. 'that *me* you did not fear', v. 11b).

Ironically, they still went through the motions of offering sacrifices and pretending righteousness. God would expose them for the chronic idolaters that they were: *I* [lit. 'I, myself', emphatic] *will expose your righteousness and your works* (v. 12). In that day when they *cry out for help*, God will mockingly reply, *let your collection of idols save you!* (v. 13). Their idols are powerless and unable to act – *a mere breath will blow them away* – but the outcome is entirely different for those who rely upon the LORD.

The promise of deliverance in verses 13b–14, as in 40:3–5, describes the preparation necessary to bring God's people home: *Build up, build up* [repeated for emphasis], *prepare the road!* Every obstruction (*miksôl*, i.e. 'hindrance') is to be removed from the path (v. 14), so that those who *take refuge* in God can return to Zion (*my holy mountain*), the land they are to inherit (v. 13).

b. Yahweh will bring deliverance for the humble; *SEAM* (57:15–21)
(Refrain: 'There is no peace,' says my God, 'for the wicked')

15–17. This seam in verses 15–21 begins with a declaration from *the high and exalted One* and concludes the section (Isa. 49 – 57) with the phrase *says my God*. As with the other seams, it summarizes the key themes of Isaiah: (1) Israel has been judged (57:16–17); (2) Israel will be delivered (57:18–19); and (3) the wicked will be punished (57:17, 20–21).

God's character traits described at the beginning of verse 15 serve to confirm his ability to keep his word. He is *the high and exalted One*, a phrase taken from 6:1 that describes his transcendence, who *lives* [*šōkēn*, 'is enthroned'] *for ever* (a reference to his perpetuity) and *whose name is holy* (a reference to his sacredness). God then provides two reasons (*kî*, 'for') why the people can be assured that he will act on their behalf to deliver them. First, he has the authority to do so: *I live in a high and holy place*, either heaven or a restored Zion, though the two terms may be synonymous. Second, his love for his people is confirmed by the fact that he also dwells with the *contrite* [lit. 'crushed'] *and lowly* [lit. 'humble'] *in spirit*.

The latter phrase refers to those whose hearts are penitent towards God, those who show sorrow for having done wrong. God's presence will encourage them: he will *revive* [lit. 'bring to life'] *the spirit of the lowly* and *revive the heart of the contrite* by forgiving their sins. Both God's encouragement and his forgiveness are necessary if these people are to possess God's holy mountain (v. 13b).

Yahweh understands the limitations of human beings, for he is their creator (i.e. *the very people* [lit. 'breaths'] *I* [lit. 'myself'] *have created*, v. 16). He knows when to contend with his people and when to step back; thus, his anger will subside when necessary. Though God displayed his legitimate anger (lit. 'I was angry and I struck him; I hid [my face] and I struck [him]', v. 17), they still continued pursuing their *sinful greed* (representative of their sin) and *wilful ways* (lit. 'the ways of his heart'). Nevertheless, God must limit his punishment, otherwise they *would faint away* (i.e. be overcome and die).

Only an all-knowing God could know the limitations of his creatures, but only an all-loving God would care enough not to exceed their limitations.

18–19. Israel's sin did not thwart God's love and his plans for them: *I have seen their ways, but I will heal them.* Because they will not be able to deliver themselves, God will step in to *restore comfort* to his people and stir them to praise him (*creating praise* [*nûb*, occurs only here] *on their lips*); all this will cause them to forget the former punishments.

Some think the 'healing' refers to the reunification of God's people so that the nation is no longer severed and scattered. But since the context indicates that healing occurs after God has seen their actions (i.e. *I have seen their* [lit. 'his'] *ways, but I will heal them* [lit. 'him']), it is more likely to refer to spiritual healing from their wicked ways. God will restore their *comfort* (*niḥumîm*); this rare plural noun (3x) signifies the abstract nature of comfort (Williams §7).

The announcement of *Peace, peace* (v. 19; the repetition is either for emphasis or to express a superlative 'perfect peace'; Williams §16) is for those *far and near*. The latter phrase should be read in a literal, physical sense, such that *near* refers to the Israelites living in Jerusalem or in Babylon just prior to their return to Jerusalem, and *far* refers to both Israelites and Gentiles who are scattered across the Ancient Near East. God's assurance that he *will heal them* is confirmed by the repetition of this phrase at the beginning (v. 18) and at the end (v. 19) of his statement.

20–21. While there will be peace for the remnant, the wicked are pictured as a storm-tossed (*gāraš*, 3x with this meaning) sea *which cannot rest*, whose churning waters bring up mud and mire. The imagery vividly portrays what the familiar refrain expresses: *'There is no peace,' says my God, 'for the wicked.'* The author clearly dissociates himself from the wicked when he says *my God* (v. 21). This refrain closes the second section (chs. 49–57) of the second part of the book of Isaiah.

Meaning

Following the earlier call of God for them to come and have their spiritual thirst quenched (55:1 – 56:8), the author now describes what will happen to those who reject this offer. He begins with the *watchmen* (leaders) who should know better but are blind and mute. They seek after false gods, bringing them into their homes, and even offering up their children to them. Because they refuse to look to the true God, when punishment comes they will be taken away by it (57:13).

God's plan, which has been consistent throughout Israel's history, is summarized in 57:13b: *But whoever takes refuge in me / will inherit the land / and possess my holy mountain.* When Israel wandered from God, they were removed from the land. Yet God protected and guarded those who were truly 'contrite and lowly of heart' (v. 15), never abandoning them. God's plan had a clear goal that took all this into account. For those who surrender and choose to obey God, they will find refuge in him and be incorporated into the righteous remnant; but for those who continue to rebel against God, they will never find *peace*, experiencing instead his continued displeasure.

C. The glory of Zion (58:1 – 66:24)

The final nine chapters of the book of Isaiah reiterate the key elements of God's plan in its entirety one last time, with an emphasis on the future glory of Zion (see Figure 0.12 on p. 30). Isaiah 58 describes the marks of true righteousness that characterize God's people (e.g. *Is not this the kind of fasting I have chosen: / to loose the chains of injustice / and untie the cords of the yoke, / to set the oppressed free / and break every yoke?*, 58:6). This is contrasted in chapter 59 with a description of the many sins of his people. However, the chapter ends with a heartfelt confession of these sins which makes their redemption possible (i.e. *The Redeemer will come to Zion*, 59:20). Chapters 60–62 then portray the deliverance that the LORD will bring for his people: *good news to the poor / . . . freedom for the captives / and release from darkness for the prisoners* (61:1). Zion will ultimately be restored and protected by Yahweh and will be called 'My [God's] Delight Is in Her' (62:4; *Hephzibah*).

In contrast with the glories of restored Zion, chapter 63 pictures the day when the LORD pours out his vengeance on all who have rejected him (63:1–6). Following the punishment, the remnant pray to God in chapter 64, pleading for him to act on their behalf and display his great power: *Oh, that you would rend the heavens and come down . . . !* (64:1). God responds in chapters 65–66 by reassuring his people that he has always loved them and has an incredible plan for them; but for those who choose to reject God there is an equally terrifying outcome.

The final seam of the book, Isaiah 65 – 66, is also an extended explanation of God's plan. It contains similar themes to those found in the earlier seams: (1) Israel has been judged (65:1–16), with emphasis given to God's repeated calls to the nation of Israel, yet they continually defy him. (2) A remnant of Israel will be delivered (65:8–15, 17–25; 66:7–14, 19–23); most remarkably, this remnant will be gathered from many distant nations (66:19–20) and will serve alongside the remnant from Israel (66:21). (3) The wicked will be punished (65:6–7, 11–15; 66:3–6, 14b–17, 24). This theme is greatly expanded in the refrain detailing the terrifying promise of eternal judgment: *And they will go out and look on the dead bodies of those who rebelled against me . . . and they will be loathsome to all mankind* (66:24).

i. Call for true repentance (58:1–14)

Context

The final section of the book of Isaiah (Isa. 58 – 66) clearly describes God's plan for delivering Israel and punishing those who reject him. Chapter 58 attributes the delay in their deliverance to their hypocrisy; their empty, ritualistic fasting would accomplish nothing. God responds only to true fasting, which requires heartfelt humility.

Debate continues as to whether Isaiah 58 is a unified whole or separate units (vv. 1–3a; 5–9a; and a later interpolation, vv. 3b–4) that have been joined by a redactor. Either way there is a clear flow to the chapter, beginning with an accusation against the people (vv. 1–4) arising from their complaint in verse 3, followed by an explanation of what God intended true fasting to be (vv. 5–9a), and concluding with two conditional sentences (vv. 9b–12, 13–14) which state that God will bring his promised deliverance once the people have demonstrated a true change of heart.

Comment

1–4. Yahweh exhorts the prophet to *shout . . . aloud* (lit. 'call with your throat') in declaring the sins of his people, *the descendants of Jacob*. The call is urgent and specific, for the people are remarkably blind to their transgressions (*piš'ām*, suggesting 'inward rebellion') and *sins*, which need to be cleansed. The prophet's voice is to be 'as piercing as a trumpet' (*Raise your voice like a trumpet* [*šôpār*, 'ram's horn']) to grab the people's attention and alert them to the need for drastic action.

Verses 2–3a describe the religious activity of God's people, who claim to (1) seek him diligently (lit. 'me they seek day by day', with inverted syntax for emphasis); (2) delight in God's *ways*; (3) follow his laws; (4) seek God's justice (*They ask me for just decisions*; lit. 'judgments of righteousness'); and (5) desire his nearness. All this and yet God is not responsive. The NIV reading conveys the lack of genuineness in their actions: *they seem eager to know my ways* (v. 2). For a similar theme of hypocrisy, see 29:13: *These people come near to me with their mouth / and honour me with their lips, / but their hearts are far from me.*

The problem persisted into Jesus' day, for he accused the Pharisees of being 'blind guides' (Matt. 15:14) and 'whitewashed tombs' (Matt. 23:27). When the people complain that God has not noticed or responded to their fasting, he immediately counters that fasting has not changed their lives at all; it is merely empty ritual. As proof, he cites the fact that on fast days they do as they please (lit. 'you find [your] delight'), exploiting (lit. 'oppress') their *workers* (lit. 'hard labourers', v. 3).

Instead of leading to humble repentance, their fast days resulted in quarrels, *strife* (*maṣṣâ*, 3x with this meaning) and fist fights (*striking each other with wicked fists* [*'egrōp*, 2x]). Yahweh tells them plainly how objectionable their actions are: *You cannot fast as you do today / and expect your voice to be heard on high* (i.e. by God). It is evident that they fasted in hopes of manipulating God instead of using it to align their hearts to his.

5–7. In the disputation that follows, Yahweh describes the kind of attitude and actions he expects when they fast (lit. 'is this not like the fast that I choose?', v. 5; the rhetorical question presupposes an affirmative answer). True fasting requires people to *humble themselves* inwardly (lit. 'a day of humbling a man's soul', v. 5), and to outwardly demonstrate this humility in some form, whether by (1) *bowing* [*kāpap*, 5x] *one's head like a reed* (v. 5); (2) *lying* [*yāṣaʿ*, 'to make one's bed', 4x] *in sackcloth and ashes* (a common sign of repentance); (3) loosening *the chains* [*ḥarṣōb*, 'bonds', 2x] *of injustice* (i.e. treating everyone justly; v. 6); (4) untying (*nātar*, 3x) *the cords* [*'ăguddâ*, only time with this meaning] *of the yoke* (i.e. releasing those in bondage); or (5) sharing their food, providing shelter to the homeless (i.e. *wanderer* [*mĕrûdîm*, 3x]) and giving clothes to *the naked* (v. 7).

The phrase *Is it not to* (*hălôʾ*) at the beginning of verse 7 suggests they knew they were to extend these concrete marks of compassion to anyone in need, whether foreigner or family (lit. 'do not hide yourself from your own flesh', v. 7), but ignored doing so. Israel was to be an example to the other nations in the Ancient Near East and so demonstrate the kindness of its God. Self-denial for the sake of others is difficult and rare, but God expected it from his people (i.e. 'love your neighbour as yourself', Lev. 19:18).

8–9a. This kind of righteous, compassionate behaviour has other profound, positive ramifications (introduced by the word *'āz*, then, v. 8) for God's children. (1) Their *light will break forth like the dawn*; this figurative expression indicates that God will bring deliverance to them. The word *dawn* (*šaḥar*, v. 8) is often used as an image to represent deliverance and victory (see 9:2). (2) Their *healing will quickly appear* (lit. 'will sprout up quickly'). God will restore health, both spiritual and physical, to his people. (3) Their *righteousness will go before* them, to lead and smooth their way. (4) *The glory of the* LORD *will be your* [i.e. the Israelites'] *rear guard* (lit. 'will gather you'), a phrase to be understood in the sense that God will keep them together, bringing stragglers along as he guides them back from exile. (5) God will answer their cries and be present with them (i.e. *here I am*, v. 9a).

9b–12. The if–then statements of verses 9b and 10 reiterate the characteristics of true fasting given in verses 6–7, with similarly impressive results. They are to *do away with* (1) *the yoke* [i.e. burden] *of oppression* (see 9:4); (2) *the pointing finger* (i.e. passing the blame onto someone else, or perhaps pointing out another's errors or faults); and (3) *malicious talk* (lit. 'speaking wickedness', referring to the broad spectrum of sin carried out by one's words). They are also to give aid to the hungry (lit. 'offer your soul for the hungry') and afflicted. The NIV reading *spend* [*pûṣ*, 'to offer', only occurrence with this meaning] *yourselves* implies more than simply giving money or material goods. It carries the idea of working on behalf of the hungry and afflicted in order to reduce poverty in general.

The next two phrases, *your light will rise in the darkness, / and your night will become like the noonday* (v. 10b), are a figurative reference to divine deliverance, of being rescued from fear and adversity, similar to Psalm 23:4. Isaiah 58:10b corresponds closely to verses 7–8 with the same result of light conquering darkness and gloom being converted to midday light, meaning that God's deliverance will guide and protect them, which is further described in the next couple of verses.

Verses 11 and 12 continue to enumerate the results of tending to the needs of the poor and oppressed. (1) They will have assurance of God's continual guidance. (2) God will provide for their needs (lit. 'he will satisfy in the sun-scorched [*ṣaḥṣāḥôt*, occurs only here, but is related to *ṣiḥēh*, 'parched', 5:13] regions of your soul') so abundantly that they will be *like a well-watered* [*rāweh*, 3x] *garden, / like a spring whose waters never fail* [lit. 'lie']. The image of water, so vital to life in a land as dry as Israel, was a sign of blessing that would certainly have resonated with the people. (3) God will give his strengthening power to transform and rejuvenate (lit. 'he will reinvigorate your bones'; see 66:14). (4) Jerusalem and other cities that had been destroyed will be rebuilt (*rebuild the ancient ruins . . . raise up the age-old* [lit. 'generations and generations'] *foundations*, v. 12).

Notice it is God's people (lit. 'some from among you [*mimmekā*]'; i.e. the remnant, v. 12), not God himself, who are called *Repairer of*

Broken Walls and *Restorer of Streets with Dwellings* (possibly 'paths to dwellings'). The phrases suggest that the city had been destroyed for quite some time, but God will empower his people to rebuild Jerusalem. The walls of Jerusalem were rebuilt during Nehemiah's lifetime about 445–433 BC, but the mention of returning it to its former glory is more likely to be a reference to their future, ultimate restoration.

13–14. The concluding if–then statement highlights the import- ance of keeping the Sabbath, setting it apart to Yahweh: *keep your feet from breaking the Sabbath / and from doing as you please* [lit. 'turn your foot from what pleases you'] *on my holy day* (see Num. 15:32–36). Verse 13 makes it clear that to honour the Sabbath meant to refrain from doing what they pleased and instead do what honoured God. Observing the Sabbath was to serve as a sign of the people's dedication to Yahweh (see Ezek. 20:12, 20). There would have been little incentive to observe the Sabbath during the many long years of exile, so it is easy to see why honouring God this way in the post-exilic period would bring 'delight' to the LORD.

Verse 14 explains that once the people learn to truly obey and honour God, they will experience *joy in the LORD*. God tells them, *I will cause you to ride in triumph on the heights of the land* [a quotation from Deut. 32:13] */ and to feast on the inheritance of your father Jacob*. The latter two images picture a life that is blessed by God, enjoying the abundance of the land of Israel, as was promised to Jacob long ago (see Gen. 35:12). All these blessings are confirmed by the word of Yahweh.

In the first half of this chapter the people made an outward show of delighting in God (v. 2; NIV reads *seem eager*) though their hearts were far from him. They now know what truly delights God (vv. 6–14).

Meaning
God informs Israel of what it means to truly worship him: it must come from the heart and be manifested in one's actions. It was easy for them to lapse into outward observance of God's required laws, rituals and sacrifices without an inner obedience of the heart, but God demands more. These sacrifices, when performed regularly with the proper attitude, were meant to make their spiritual life

living and vibrant. God continues to link his blessings to obedience and a proper heart attitude. Once Israel learns to maintain an attitude that manifests itself in caring for the poor and oppressed, then it will be a witness for God to all nations.

ii. God will bring deliverance (59:1–21)

Context

God once again reminds Israel of the glorious heritage he has given them in his covenant (v. 21), but their sins have separated them from him (v. 2). As a result, they are reminded of the true elements of repentance. This chapter is crucial to the message of Isaiah 58 – 66, for without true repentance the glorification of Zion mentioned in later chapters cannot occur, for it demands a softened, receptive heart towards God.

Even though there is a logical progression in chapter 59, many scholars argue that it is made up of three distinct units (Whybray 1975: 220; Childs 2001: 484; Blenkinsopp 2003: 186) that reflect changes in literary forms and unexpected changes in speakers. Nevertheless, the prophets often change speakers and literary forms within their works. In verses 1–8, the prophet encourages the Israelite community that God is capable of delivering the nation, though he has temporarily withdrawn his saving hand because of their iniquities. Verses 9–15a are the confession or lament of a group of Israelites who acknowledge the fact that the sins of the people have caused the suffering and misery they are experiencing. The prophet speaks again in verses 15b–21, reassuring the people that Yahweh has seen their sad plight and will bring about their desperately needed deliverance.

Comment

a. Israel's sins have alienated them from God (59:1–8)

1–2. Just as the people complained that God did not respond to their fasting (58:3), so the prophet addresses their complaint that God is not acting on their behalf: *Surely* [*hēn*] *the arm of the* LORD *is not too short to save* [lit. 'from saving'], / *nor his ear too dull to hear* [lit. 'too heavy from hearing'].

The prophet sharply rebukes the idea that God's inactivity shows his incapability – he awaits only their repentance (cf. 50:1–3) before springing into action. The issue here is that their sins have divided them from Yahweh so that he refuses to respond to their cries: *But* [*kî ʾim*; Williams §447] *your iniquities have separated you from your God* (v. 2a). The emphatic syntax of verse 2b reads literally: 'your sins have caused [his] face to hide from hearing from you', meaning that God will not respond to their cries. This is a crucial theological theme throughout the Bible: sin separates us from God (Mic. 3:4). Childs observes that 'the accusations in verses 1–8 probe to a new theological depth in exploring the essence of Israel's evil' (2001: 488).

3–4. The enumeration of the people's sins in verses 3–8 could fit almost any period of Israel's history, for they continually reverted to their old ways. Their hands are *stained* [lit. 'defiled'] *with blood* (i.e. they are guilty of bloodshed). There is an interesting narrowing in specificity in the parallelism of verse 3, going from *hands* to *fingers*, a reference to their 'actions', and from *lips* to *tongue*, that is, their 'words'.

The 'sins of their lips' (vv. 3b–4) include the sin of omission in addressing matters of justice and integrity, as well as the sin of commission in the lies that served to further their own evil designs (*they utter lies . . . and give birth to evil*, v. 4). Their constant contemplation of evil gives birth to even more trouble and evil. The phrase *They rely on empty arguments* (lit. 'trusting upon emptiness' [*tōhû*]; GKC §119aa) is broader in meaning than the NIV reading suggests; it includes trusting in any other sources for deliverance rather than in God.

5–6. Two images in the phrase *They hatch the eggs of vipers* [*sipʿônî*, 3x] / *and spin a spider's web* illustrate the premeditation and danger of their sins. The image of adders' eggs hatching carries the idea of evil plans made and carried out. Those who participate in the plans of these evildoers will die (*Whoever eats their eggs will die*).

Similarly, evildoers weave sinful plans as carefully as a spider spins its web. These plans have no useful purpose (i.e. they are *useless for clothing*, v. 6) other than to advance their evil purposes and promote violence. Whybray comments that 'the plots of the wicked catch both the unwary who do not perceive the danger and also those who attempt to crush it' (1975: 221–222).

The imagery here depicts how dangerous their sin is – to themselves, to others and to society as a whole. The prophet is purposeful in choosing the images of 'viper' and 'spider', creatures feared for being hard to detect and difficult to differentiate between poisonous and non-poisonous varieties. Clearly, the vipers and spiders referred to here fall into the 'harmful' category.

7–8. The eagerness with which sinful Israel pursues sin is described in verses 7–8. The people *rush into sin*, are *swift* to kill those who are innocent (lit. 'to pour out innocent blood'), and plan out and pursue sin (*they pursue evil schemes,* lit. 'their thoughts are thoughts of iniquity', v. 7). Their lives are so marked by violence (lit. 'violence and destruction are in their highways', v. 7) that they do not even know the *way of peace* (*šālôm,* 'peace, goodwill, God's blessing', v. 8); the NIV captures the emphatic tone of the Hebrew syntax in the entire verse.

Four different Hebrew words refer to the patterns of their sinful behaviour: *their ways* (*mĕsillôt,* 'highways', v. 7), *way* (*derek,* v. 8), *paths* (*ma'gĕlôt,* 'track, ruts', v. 8) and *roads* (*nĕtîbôt,* v. 8). The intractable nature of their sin is so regular and persistent that it hardens their hearts like a path that is created and packed hard by continual treading.

Those who walk in the ways of wickedness will never know peace, a theme that is highlighted at the beginning and end of verse 8. The people have become so hardened by sin that they can no longer remember what it is like to act in ways that are pleasing to God (i.e. *the way of peace*).

b. Acknowledgment of their sins (59:9–15a)

9–10. The word *so* (*'al-kēn,* v. 9) links verses 9–15a to the description of the people's sin in the preceding section; thus, the people's condition as described here is the direct result of their sinfulness. This passage is a corporate confession of sin in which the author includes himself among those who are suffering as a result of their sinful condition. *Justice* and *righteousness* evade them – a truth marking the beginning and end of this section (vv. 9, 14).

Verses 9b–10 are filled with figurative language that contrasts the respite they hoped for with the punishment they received: *light/ darkness, brightness/shadows, midday/twilight, the strong/the dead.* They are seeking relief, but all they get is more pain: *We look* [lit. 'we hope'] *for light* [*něgōhôt*, 'gleams of light', occurs only here; i.e. deliverance], *but all is darkness*[es] (the plural forms suggest that they searched repeatedly for light and found only darkness). They remain in darkness like the blind who *walk in deep shadows* (lit. 'gloom'). Even in broad daylight they stumble around uselessly: *among the strong* [*ʾašmannîm*, occurs only here], *we are like the dead*.

11–12. They *growl like bears* (12x; see Hos. 13:8) and *moan mournfully like doves*, lamenting their distress. They languish in a state that is far from justice, righteousness and *deliverance* (i.e. God's saving activity).

The word *kî* at the beginning of verse 12 introduces the reason for the people's lament: their sin. What follows is a formal confession in which all three Hebrew words for sin are used: (1) *offences* (*pěšāʿēnû*, lit. 'our rebellion'), (2) *sins* (*ḥaṭṭōʾwtênû*, lit. 'our falling short of God's standard') and (3) *iniquities* (*waʿăwōnōtênû*, lit. 'our inward crookedness'). These three words also appear in Psalms 32:1–2 and 51:2–3.

Even though they knew and acknowledged their sins (i.e. *our sins testify* [lit. 'answer'] *against us*; *we acknowledge our iniquities*, v. 12), at this point they had not yet fully repented; knowledge of sin alone does not constitute repentance. Because justice and righteousness continue to elude them (vv. 9, 14), the implication is that despite their awareness of their sin, they refuse to turn from it and live righteously.

13–15a. There is a shift from the first person to infinitive absolutes that specifically delineate the sins of the nation: *rebellion and treachery* [lit. 'denying knowledge of him'] *against the LORD, turning our backs on our God, inciting revolt and oppression* (i.e. planning oppression against others) and *uttering lies our hearts have conceived* (lit. 'uttering from [the] heart words of deception').

They have effectively driven out of the nation all justice, righteousness and truth, and anyone who even attempts to pursue these (*So justice is driven back, / and righteousness stands at a distance*, v. 14). This illustrates the truth of 2 Corinthians 6:14: 'what fellowship can light have with darkness?' Then, when Israel was at its worst, God stepped in.

c. God determines to deliver a remnant of the nation (59:15b–21)

15b–16. At this point, when the nation is thoroughly corrupt, Yahweh assesses the situation: *The LORD looked and was displeased* [lit. 'it was evil in his eyes'] / *that there was no justice* (v. 15b). Though he searched each and every heart, God *was appalled that there was no one to intervene* (v. 16; see Ezek. 22:30). He could find no leader willing or able to lead the people away from sin and injustice. If the people were to be delivered, only he himself could do it. Here Yahweh is pictured as the divine warrior, a common Isaianic image (see 42:13; 52:10), whose *own arm* (synecdoche for God himself and his great power) and whose *own righteousness* (i.e. the essence of his character) empower him.

Some think that 59:15b–16 was borrowed from 63:5 because of their similarities and their contexts; they argue that Yahweh's warlike actions fit the context of fighting foreign nations (ch. 63) better than that of fighting Israel (ch. 59; Duhm 1922: 463; Whybray 1975: 226). However, Israel's wickedness was similar to that of the foreign nations. In fact, Israel was so corrupt that God searched four times for someone to deliver his people, but could find no-one (see 41:27–28; 50:2; 51:18; 59:15b–16).

We have argued that each of the first three of these passages introduces a Servant Song. God could find no-one among the Israelites to deliver the nation, the implication being that he himself would need to provide a deliverer. The Servant Songs that follow then describe the servant whom he would send. Isaiah 59:15b–16 also states in similar terms that he could find no deliverer, which could suggest that it introduces another (a fifth) Servant Song in 61:1–3. However, unlike the other introductions, there is a large gap between 59:15b–16 and the supposed song in 61:1–3. More significantly, 59:16b states that God himself steps in to deliver the nation: *his own arm achieved salvation for him.* A Servant Song describing a servant delivering the nation is therefore unnecessary in this case.

17–19. As God prepares to act, he is pictured as dressing for battle. His protective power derives from his *righteousness*, depicted as a *breastplate* (*širyôn*, 8x), and *salvation*, pictured as a *helmet* (*kôbaʿ*, 6x; v. 17). That he clothes himself with *vengeance* and *zeal* (lit. 'he wrapped himself in zeal like a robe' [*mĕʿîl*]) shows his readiness to act quickly to vindicate his name, which has been trampled even by his own people. Vengeance can indeed be attributed to God when we realize that he is just and must deal with devastating sin by administering punishment that is just, proportionate and balanced.

The verbs change from completed action in verses 15b–17 to incomplete action in verses 18–20 because of God's decision to act in verse 18 (*According to what they have done, / so will he repay*). God will dispense justice on any enemy, whether from within Israel (v. 16) or among the Gentiles (v. 18): *he will repay the islands* [lit. 'coastlands'] *their due* [lit. 'dealings'], judging people according to their deeds. The repetition of *kĕʿal* (i.e. *according to*) in verse 18 underscores the precision with which God will act ('*according to what they have done, so he will repay*'; see *HALOT* 2.827). By punishing his enemies (i.e. those who have gone against his people), God will vindicate himself to his people and to the nations as the one true sovereign God to whom all people are accountable.

When God acts, he will do so with power and speed (*he will come like a pent-up* [*sār*, 'bound-up'] *flood*). As a result, nations far and wide will fear him (*from the west* to *the rising of the sun*, v. 19). God will be glorified through his deliverance of Israel.

20–21. Yahweh will come to the nation of Israel to deliver only a remnant of his people, those who turn from their sins (*those in Jacob who repent of their sins*, v. 20).

The prose statements, beginning with the words *As for me* [lit. 'but I'], *this is my covenant with them*, depart from the poetry of the preceding verses, prompting some to label them a later addition regarding God's relationship to the remnant (Whybray 1975: 228). However, narrative expansions frequently appear in the book of Isaiah (44:9–20; 45:18; etc.; see NASB) and are not necessarily the work of later redactors. In fact, God's covenant with his remnant has already been mentioned several times and is a central part of God's deliverance (see 54:10; 55:3; etc.).

Two key concepts are conveyed in verse 21: (1) the spirit of God will be upon this remnant, meaning that God's power will guide them (see 61:1); and (2) they will obey his commandments (*my words that I have put in your mouth will always be on your lips*; see 51:16).

Notice that the third person masculine plural form indicating to whom the covenant is given (*my covenant with them*) is followed by second person singular forms as the remnant is addressed and each of the specific blessings is described (*My Spirit, who is on you* [masc. sing.], *will not depart from you* [masc. sing.], *and my words that I have put in your* [masc. sing.] *mouth . . .*).

Whybray thinks this verse speaks of 'a promise of the gift of prophecy to all God's people such as is found in Jl. 2:28–29, with perhaps the additional concept that the Spirit guides the people of God, which we find in 63:14' (1975: 229). However, we think the verse speaks of the new covenant's promise of the spirit that will come to live within believers (i.e. the remnant), a promise confirmed in Acts 2 when the Holy Spirit comes at Pentecost (see Acts 2:1–21 where Joel 2:28–32 is said to be fulfilled).

The phrase *my words that I have put in your mouth will always be on your lips* refers to new-found obedience to the law which Yahweh gives to them (see Josh. 1:8) that will last *from this time on and for ever* (v. 21).

Meaning

The key to this chapter appears in verse 1: God declares that he is powerful and listening. The implication is that people should get ready, for he will act. Much of this chapter describes the corrupt state of God's people. Then, in verses 9–15, the Israelites, along with the author, confess their sins, at which point God declares that he will deliver them.

However, God will have to bring about this deliverance, since there is no-one morally fit within the nation to lead them back to him. God himself, pictured as a divine warrior, comes to their aid. He will redeem his people just as he had promised (see 2:1–4 and 4:2–6), but he will also justly and righteously repay all his enemies, including both Israelites and foreigners. This will be no temporary deliverance, but one that will last from that point on, displaying God's glory and honour to such an extent that other nations will observe this mighty display of his power and fear him as well (v. 19).

iii. The redemption of Zion (60:1 – 62:12)

Chapters 60–62 contain a much more detailed description of the deliverance of God's people mentioned in the previous chapter (see Figure 0.12 on p. 30). Even though the Israelites thought themselves forsaken by God, the prophet foresees a time (see 60:10; 61:4) when the prosperity and glory of Jerusalem will be obvious to all. Conspicuously absent are any words of condemnation – there are only promises regarding Jerusalem's wonderful future.

a. The future glory of Zion (60:1–22)

Context

Many scholars view Isaiah 60 as a unity, or at least a redactional unity, describing the glorious transformation of Zion that echoes the restoration of Zion portrayed in 49:14–23. The chapter comprises the following sections: (1) an introduction (vv. 1–3); (2) a description of the nations bringing the remnant and their wealth to Zion (vv. 4–9, with a concluding statement in v. 9b); (3) a depiction of the nations honouring Zion (vv. 10–16, with a concluding statement in v. 16b); and (4) a description of Zion's future glory (vv. 17–22, with a conclusion in v. 22b).

It is not clear when this restoration of Jerusalem takes place, but its description goes well beyond the city's restoration in the sixth century BC, to merge with a future restoration: (1) foreigners and kings (pl.) (v. 10) will participate in the reconstruction efforts; (2) nations will come to Zion's light (v. 3); (3) great wealth will be brought to Zion (vv. 5–9, 11); and (4) the LORD's presence will be in Zion (vv. 19–20).

Chapter 60 mentions four times (vv. 10b, 14, 15, 20) that Jerusalem endured a previous period of affliction that has now ended. There will be an ingathering to Jerusalem of a remnant (*your sons come from afar*, v. 4), whose wealth (vv. 5, 17), flocks (vv. 6–7) and honour (vv. 13–16) will be restored. They will enjoy God's protection (v. 12) and therefore peace (v. 18) because he is present with them (vv. 2b, 19b–20).

Comment

(1) The announcement of Zion's physical restoration (60:1–9)
1–3. The prophet urges Jerusalem to *arise* and *shine* for *your light* [i.e. deliverance, the saving action of God] *has come.* While the physical deliverance of Zion is primarily emphasized, spiritual

deliverance is also included (see v. 21). Physical and spiritual blessings are often linked in the Old Testament. The parallel phrase clarifies that this *light* is *the glory of the* LORD (v. 1b; repeated in similar terms in v. 2b), a theophany similar to that in 40:5.

Jerusalem will not only receive Yahweh's light, but will also reflect his light (i.e. *your dawn* [*zeraḥ*, 'light shining forth', occurs only here, v. 3). While the nations lie in *thick darkness*, an image of spiritual blindness, Israel (i.e. the remnant) will be a beacon drawing the nations to the one true God. Jerusalem will finally fulfil Yahweh's original purpose of drawing the nations to him (see 2:2–4).

4–9. Continuing the theme of drawing the nations, Zion's 'children' (i.e. the remnant; v. 4) gather to return to her (see 49:18a) and are supported by the nations on their journey (*your daughters are carried* [*'āman*, 'looked after', possibly 'nursed'] *on the hip*, v. 4).

Zion will become the repository of great wealth as nations bring their tribute (*to you the riches of the nations will come*, v. 5) by sea and by travelling caravans (vv. 5–6) to honour Israel's God. Whybray argues: 'The note of nationalism – albeit of "religious nationalism" – is unmistakable' (1975: 231).

A personified Jerusalem experiences great joy as a result (v. 5): (1) *you will look and be radiant* (*nāhar*, 3x with this meaning); (2) *your heart will throb* (*pāḥad*, 'tremble with awe'); (3) *and swell* [lit. 'be wide'] *with joy*. With a sense of eager anticipation of 'coming home' (i.e. *Who are these that fly along . . . like doves to their nests?*, v. 8), the nations bring so much wealth to Zion that the country is literally teeming with abundance: *Herds* [lit. 'a vast number'] *of camels will cover your* [Israel's] *land* (v. 6). Camels from *Midian* (i.e. east of the Gulf of Aqaba), *Ephah* (i.e. about midway down the east coast of the Gulf of Aqaba) and *Sheba* (i.e. the southern region of Saudi Arabia; see 1 Kgs 10) will bring gold and frankincense. Frankincense is a costly aromatic resin used for incense and perfumes that has been traded in the Arabian Peninsula for over five thousand years. Those bringing tribute proclaim *the praise of the* LORD as they come (v. 6).

Flocks from *Kedar* and *Nebaioth* in northern Arabia will be driven to Jerusalem and offered as sacrifices to Yahweh (v. 7). The *ships of Tarshish* (most probably located in south-western Spain) were renowned for transporting exceptional gold and wealth. All this wealth will be dedicated to *the LORD your God, / the Holy One of Israel* (the latter title occurs 30x in the OT, 25x in the book of Isaiah; v. 9). With it, God *will adorn* [his] *glorious temple* (lit. 'I will beautify my house of splendour'; v. 7). All of these wonderful things will come about because Yahweh has glorified his people (i.e. *you*, v. 9).

(2) The announcement of Zion's political restoration (60:10–14)

10–14. The city that had been trampled by pagan nations will now be restored by them under Israel's direction, as God demonstrates his kindness (*rāḥam*, 'love, compassion') to her. *Foreigners* (lit. 'sons of a foreigner', v. 10) will rebuild the walls that had been destroyed in the Babylonian destruction of 586 BC; however, these future walls will no longer be needed for protection. In fact, their gates will now stand open continually so as not to hinder the great influx of gifts (*so that people may bring you the wealth of the nations*, v. 11).

Kings in tribute procession will be led (passive participle) into the city as they acknowledge their submission to Israel and her God, similar to Assyrian, Babylonian and Roman customs, *for* (*kî*) nations that do not submit will be destroyed (lit. 'will be utterly in ruins', v. 12). Some emend the passive participle to an active participle, but Oswalt is correct in arguing that some may be coming voluntarily and some involuntarily (1998: 547).

Childs says that there is wide consensus that verse 12 is a later interpolation written in prose (2001: 494), but there is little reason to see it as narrative, as he states. The verse is more probably parallelism (with ellipsis) that translates literally as follows:

> For the nation or kingdom that will not serve you will perish;
> the nations [that will not serve you] will be utterly ruined.

Whybray seeks to make a distinction here between worship of Yahweh and service of Israel: 'Here the reference is not to the worship of Yahweh but to the service of Israel' (1975: 235). While he is technically correct, it is difficult to distinguish between the two. Serving God's people is an act of serving Yahweh; thus, *the nation or kingdom that will not serve you* [i.e. Israel] *will perish* (v. 12).

God's temple (lit. 'the place of my sanctuary') will be adorned with cedar (lit. *the glory of Lebanon*), *juniper, fir* [*tidhār*, possibly 'elm',

2x] and *cypress*, all trees from that region, known for their beauty and fragrance.

The phrase *I will glorify the place for my feet* (v. 13) indicates that God will be present in Zion (see Ezek. 43:7). Later in Isaiah 66:1 God claims that heaven is God's throne and the earth his footstool, all figurative language for God's omnipresence. In other words, 'throne in heaven' and 'footstool on earth' is a merism representing everything from heaven to earth. Thus, the primary implication of this verse is that the city is now suitably holy for the holy God who wishes to dwell there (see vv. 19–20). Jerusalem's restoration in 539 BC prefigures only a fraction of the glory that awaits it, as pictured in this passage.

All nations, even those that afflicted Israel, will acknowledge Yahweh as the sovereign king. God's justice will be made manifest when *The children of your* [Israel's] *oppressors will come bowing before you* (v. 14; see 49:23). Yet the honour Israel receives is only because of her relationship with God.

(3) The announcement of Zion's spiritual restoration (60:15–22)

15–17. The theme of Jerusalem's transformation from her wretched and forsaken state (see 54:6) to one of *everlasting pride* (*lig'ôn*, 'splendour') is repeated and expanded. When Jerusalem lay in ruins, no-one passed through her, for there was nothing of value to see or take; but Yahweh will make her once again a place of pride and joy visited by caravans and other travellers.

The phrases *You will drink the milk of nations / and be nursed at royal breasts* refer to the sustenance and wealth that Zion will receive from the nations and their rulers. The Ancient Near Eastern idea of being suckled by a goddess may be the intended background of this image (Oswalt 1998: 552). Note that her physical wealth is also accompanied by spiritual wealth. The miraculous transformation of the city will reawaken the Israelites to the fact that Yahweh is their powerful deliverer and that they have a special relationship with him (*Then you will know that I, the LORD, am your Saviour, / your Redeemer, the Mighty One of Jacob*).

The physical abundance and great blessing that Jerusalem will enjoy is portrayed in the superior, more valuable materials of her reconstruction: *Instead of bronze ... gold, / and silver in place of iron. /*

Instead of wood . . . bronze, and so on. (v. 17). Even the political governance of Jerusalem will be totally renewed: *peace* [will be] *your governor* [lit. 'supervisor'] *and well-being* [lit. 'righteousness'] *your ruler* [lit. 'overseer']). The implication is that peace and righteousness will be so pervasive that they take the place of governors and rulers; after all, God will be present as their ruler.

18–22. God's presence and the transformation of his people mean that violence and destruction will have no place in the land. The naming of Jerusalem's walls *Salvation* and her gates *Praise* reflects the new character of the city.

God's presence will provide *everlasting light* (*ʾôr ʿôlām*, 2x in vv. 19–20) so that there will be no need for the sun and moon [lit. 'your moon will not be gathered']; this is an image of spiritual well-being (see Zech. 14:7). *Your God will be your glory* suggests a renewed relationship with Yahweh in which his people rely on him. Physical and spiritual darkness will be no more, nor will there be *days of sorrow* (i.e. sorrow and mourning will be things of the past, v. 20).

In verses 21–22 the author turns from describing the changes in the city to the changes occurring in the people. They will all be *righteous* (*ṣaddîqîm* [pl.], possibly an abstract plural [Williams §7], v. 21) and will possess the land for ever. Sin is the primary reason cited in the Old Testament for God's people not possessing the land. But now that the people are righteous, there will be no reason why they cannot take and keep possession of it.

The term *shoot* (*nēṣer*, 'branch, sprout', v. 21) may be a reference to Messiah (see 11:1). In this context, however, the remnant is the *shoot* planted by God (lit. 'his planting'[17]), an image of growth and permanence. Just like a shoot, Israel needed God's tenacious nurturing for it to become a reality. It was in constant danger of dying because of the people's sin and the oppression of other

---

17. The *kĕthîb* reading is 'the shoot of his planting', but the *qĕrê* reads 'my plantings'. The first person singular ending of 'my plantings' seems to be favoured by the next phrase, 'work of my hands', but the plural 'plantings' is difficult. It could possibly refer to one planting when they arrived from Egypt and another when they arrived from Babylon.

nations. But this restoration that God achieves will bring him glory.

The remnant will greatly increase during this time of peace, for even the smallest family will become a clan and a mighty nation (v. 22; the opposite is pictured in 30:17). There will be no delay in the fulfilment of this promise. When it is the appropriate time (lit. *in its time*), God will act *swiftly* (v. 22).

Meaning

This chapter pictures the fulfilment of Isaiah 4:2–6 when God wonderfully restores his nation and sets up his kingdom. He glorifies his people, showering them with the blessings of numerous children (v. 4), abundant wealth (v. 5), increased flocks and herds (vv. 6–7), the rebuilding of Zion by foreigners (v. 10), protection (v. 12), honour (vv. 13–16), peace (v. 18) and his own presence (vv. 19–20). The people themselves will be characterized by righteousness (v. 21) and so demonstrate to the rest of the world the greatness of their God.

b. Good news for the afflicted (61:1–11)

Context

Once the nation repents and turns back to God (Isa. 59), he can pour out his blessings on the nation and restore Jerusalem (Isa. 60). Chapter 60 describes the restoration and concludes with the declaration *I am the LORD; / in its time I will do this swiftly* (60:22). Chapter 61 then explains how God will bring about this restoration.

Isaiah 59:16 is the context for Isaiah 61:1–3: God has determined to deliver his people, but there is no-one in Israel capable of bringing about physical and spiritual deliverance. Only the Messiah would be able to accomplish it, but, in the meantime, Isaiah will declare God's message of deliverance until Messiah comes. Jesus picks up verses 1–2 and says that he has filled them up (*plēroō*) (see Luke 4:18–19); thus the message that Isaiah was to announce (i.e. *to proclaim good news to the poor / . . . to bind up the broken-hearted, / to proclaim freedom for the captives*, 61:1) will ultimately be fulfilled by Jesus. Notice that Jesus ended his quote before the phrase *and the day of vengeance of our God* (also known as the Day of the LORD), which was reserved for a future date not within Jesus' lifetime.

Early in the twentieth century, it was argued that verses 1–3 were a fifth Servant Song (Cannon 1929: 284–288). But after Zimmerli's article discussing the linguistic differences between Second and Third Isaiah (1950: 110–122), these verses began to be viewed as a justification of the call to ministry of Third Isaiah. More recently Beuken (1989: 411–442) and Childs (2001: 503) have argued that the speaker of Isaiah 61:1–3 is the embodiment of the suffering servant of Isaiah 53, 'who can be an individual as well as a collective entity'. However, only the Messiah, not a collective entity, could die to take away sin.

This chapter is commonly thought to be a single unit comprising three sections: verses 1–7, 8–9 and 10–11. The primary difficulty is determining the speaker(s) of the first and last sections. To clarify the speaker's identity, Targum adds the phrases 'The prophet said' to verse 1 and 'Jerusalem has said' to verse 10. However, it seems most likely that the first person singular forms should be understood to refer to the same person.

Comment

(1) The prophet's call and message (61:1–3)

1–3. There is a sudden change in theme and pronouns (i.e. first person singular forms) at the outset of chapter 61: *The Spirit of the Sovereign LORD is on me, / because the LORD has anointed me / to proclaim good news to the poor.* The title *the Sovereign LORD* (lit. 'Lord' [*ădōnāy*] 'LORD' [*yĕhwih*]), which appears at the beginning and end of chapter 61, is used twenty-three times in the book of Isaiah (12x in chapters 40–66). Whybray notes similarities between the speaker in this passage and the servant described elsewhere:

> The speaker claims, like the Servant, to have received Yahweh's Spirit
> (cf. 42:1) in order to bring a message of hope to his people, and to
> restore their fortunes (cf. 49:6). Those who regard the second Servant
> Song as extending beyond 49:6 will also note two further similarities:
> the year of the LORD's favour, and the day of vengeance of our God
> (verse 2), corresponds to the 'time of favour' and the 'day of salvation'

of 49:8, and the proclaiming of liberty to the captives, and the opening
of the prison (verse 1) corresponds to 49:9*a*.

(1975: 239–240)[18]

While the speaker remains unidentified, he claims to have been
anointed by God and given his authority for a specific purpose – to
proclaim good news (v. 1; see 42:1; 45:1). His anointing may be
understood literally (prophets [1 Kgs 19:16] and kings [1 Sam. 16:13]
were sometimes anointed to the office) or figuratively (i.e. anointing
in the sense that God endowed him with his power and sent him
with a specific message).

The word *because* (v. 1) draws a close connection between his
anointing and God's deliverance of the remnant. Verses 1b–3
delineate the mission of the speaker in five infinitive phrases: (1) *to
proclaim good news to the poor* (i.e. to act as a herald); (2) *to bind up the
broken-hearted* (lit. 'broken of heart'; i.e. to heal those discouraged or
humbled); (3) *to proclaim freedom* [*děrôr*, 'liberty', 6x] *for the captives /
and release from darkness* [*pěqaḥ-qôaḥ*, lit. 'opening'] *for the prisoners*;
(4) *to proclaim the year of the* LORD's *favour / and the day of vengeance of our
God* (notice that the time of favour is for a longer period ['a year']
as compared with the time of vengeance ['a day']); and (5) *to comfort
all who mourn.*

The word translated as *release from darkness* (*pěqaḥ-qôaḥ*, occurring
only here, v. 1b) may be (1) the word *pěqaḥqôaḥ*, meaning 'opening'
(see 1QIsaᵃ); (2) dittography (i.e. repetition of the last part of the
word); or (3) a rare verb form (*HALOT* 3.960). In view of the
parallel phrase just before, it probably means 'liberation' *for the
prisoners. The year of the* LORD's *favour* (and *day of* his *vengeance*) is
generally thought to be the Day of the LORD when he delivers his
people and pours out his wrath on the wicked (see Joel 2:11; Isa.
34:8).

The three images in verse 3 describe the coming blessings for
those *who grieve in Zion*: (1) *to bestow on them a crown* [*pě'ēr*, 'headdress';
a sign of gladness in 61:10] *of beauty / instead of ashes* ['*pr*, a sign of

---

18. A number of scholars think this passage refers to Messiah (Oswalt
    1998: 562–563; Childs 2001: 503; Smith 2009: 630–633; etc.).

mourning; this is a wordplay on *p'r* (*crown*), which has the same Hebrew letters but in a different order]; (2) *the oil of joy* [i.e. the regular practice of anointing oneself with fragrant oils; see Ps. 45:7] / *instead of mourning*; and (3) *a garment* [*ma'ăṭēh*, occurs only here] *of praise / instead of a spirit of despair*; the garment pictured here wraps the entire body; thus, one is so entirely enveloped in praise that there is no room for discouragement.

The result (Williams §179) of this great transformation is that *They* [i.e. the inhabitants of Zion] *will be called oaks of righteousness, / a planting of the LORD*. Trees were a sign of permanence and stability, but these trees are characterized by righteousness and are planted by the hand of the LORD; thus the citizens of Zion will be founded and rooted in righteousness so as to exhibit God's glory (*his splendour*, v. 3).

(2) A description of their deliverance (61:4–9)

4–7. The spiritual restoration of the remnant in verse 3 is followed by the physical restoration of Jerusalem in verse 4: *They will rebuild the ancient ruins, renew the ruined cities* (lit. 'cities of desolation') and restore cities that have been *devastated for generations* (lit. 'generations and generations'). The *ancient ruins* and *places long devastated* (v. 4) most probably refer to the Babylonian destruction of Israel. It remained *devastated for generations* (v. 4b) until its *ruined cities* were restored by a remnant. Here we see a prophetic perspective in which the prophet envisions the rebuilding of Jerusalem after the Babylonian exile (*c.*538 BC), as well as its restoration in the distant future when Zion will be glorified and its inhabitants purified (vv. 4–9).

Foreigners (lit. 'sons of a foreigner'; also called *strangers*, v. 5) who once devastated Israel will now perform Israel's manual labour, tending their flocks, fields ('*ikkār*, 'farmers', 7x) and vineyards (*kōrēm*, 'vine dresser', 5x).

The restored remnant themselves will be honoured as *priests of the LORD* (v. 6) and supported by foreign nations (lit. 'in their riches you will boast' [*tityammārû*, 2x with this meaning], with inverted order for emphasis), similar to the priests of the Old Testament who did not own property and were supplied with food by the rest of the nation. They will serve as mediators and intercessors for the nations, a fulfilment of Exodus 19:5–6: 'you will be for me a kingdom of priests and a holy nation'.

Another important reversal is that Israel will no longer pay tribute to other nations for protection. Instead, the wealth of the nations will flow back to them (*You will feed on the wealth of nations*, v. 6).

Again, contrasts are drawn between Israel's former shame and their glorious restoration (v. 7). Their *shame* will be forgotten in the light of the *everlasting joy* they experience upon receiving a *double portion* (v. 7) of their inheritance.

This is the only occurrence of the phrase *double portion* in the book of Isaiah, but throughout the Old Testament it means something that is 'doubled' or 'twofold' (*mišneh*; see Exod. 16:22). The firstborn son typically received a 'double portion' of the inheritance; Israel is said to be God's firstborn (see Exod. 4:22).

8–9. The LORD briefly summarizes the rationale for his actions: *For* [*kî*] *I, the LORD, love justice; / I hate* [lit. 'hating'] *robbery and wrongdoing.* Israel deserved judgment and the resultant shame that God had brought upon them. The NIV and ESV reading *I hate robbery and wrongdoing* (*bĕʿawlâ*, lit. 'in iniquity') is problematic because it leaves untranslated the *bĕ* ('in', 'by', etc.) at the beginning of the word 'wrongdoing'.

If the MT is correct, then the phrase 'I hate robbery in the burnt offering' (i.e. not offering God what is rightfully his) is a reasonable interpretation. It may also be synecdoche, referring to any action that displeases God (see 1:13). Either reading fits the context well.

Following the punishment that God had dispensed (i.e. *instead of your shame*, v. 7), God can declare that because he loves justice and is faithful, he will now *reward* (*pĕʿullātām*) his people (v. 8). The word *reward* sometimes carries the idea of 'recompense' or 'compensation', as it does here. He seals his promises by making an *everlasting covenant* with them.

Covenants served to confirm promises, in this case a promise that this restoration is to last for ever (*ʿôlām*; see 55:3). Oswalt holds that this refers to the Abrahamic covenant because the promise in Genesis 12:1–3 was later confirmed by the Abrahamic covenant (1998: 573). However, given the context's future aspect (*I will reward . . . and make*, v. 8), it is more likely to refer to the new covenant that God is yet to make with them.

Now that the remnant has been restored, Yahweh can pour out upon them blessings in the form of descendants (*zeraʿ*, 'seed', and *ṣeʾĕṣāʾ*, 'offspring', 11x; 7x in Isaiah). In the Ancient Near East children were a sign of God's blessing (Ps. 127:3). Nations will not only know of these descendants (i.e. to *be known among the nations* suggests that they are important and renowned), but will recognize that they are a mark of God's blessing upon Israel (*All ... will acknowledge / that they are a people the* LORD *has blessed*, v. 9).

(3) A song of thanksgiving (61:10–11)

10–11. Just as this chapter began with first person singular forms, so it ends with these forms in this individual song of thanksgiving for God's great deliverance. While some scholars contend that the person speaking is the Messiah (Motyer 1999: 380; Childs 2001: 506; etc.), it is more common to argue that the speaker is Zion or the remnant personified (Oswalt 1998: 574; Blenkinsopp 2003: 230–231; etc.). The Targum suggests 'Jerusalem', but it seems more likely that these verses refer to the same speaker as the first person singular forms in verses 1–3 (i.e. Isaiah [or the author]).

If the prophet is the speaker, then the remnant will be the ones who benefit from his message (see esp. v. 1, *to proclaim freedom for the captives / and release from darkness for the prisoners*). They are referred to in the third person and second person plural forms in verses 4–9. The prophet not only announces this deliverance to the remnant, but he rejoices greatly when the LORD accomplishes it (v. 10).

The prophet delights *greatly* [emphatic form] *in the* LORD, praising and thanking God, *for* [*kî*, v. 10b] *he* [God] *has clothed me with garments of salvation / and arrayed* [*yāʿaṭ*, occurs only here] *me in a robe of his righteousness.* The prophet is being covered or enveloped in salvation and righteousness.

The prophet likens his garments to those of *a bridegroom* and *a bride.* The phrase *as a bridegroom adorns his head like a priest* (lit. 'as a bridegroom he acts as a priest a turban [*pĕʾēr*]') is awkward. *HALOT* suggests reading the MT as *yĕkônēn*, 'to set up', and that 'to put on a turban' would fit within this verb's range of meanings (2.465). This suggestion requires the change of only one Hebrew letter and thus seems most reasonable. A bridegroom putting on a turban and a bride adorned with jewels (lit. 'ornaments', most probably of precious metals; see Gen. 24:53) suggest being prepared for marriage, just as the prophet is prepared for his ministry.

The *for* (*kî*) at the beginning of verse 11 gives yet another reason for this great joy: not only has God (lit. 'the Lord [*ădōnāy*] LORD [*yĕhwih*]') clothed them with salvation and righteousness, he has also caused *righteousness and praise* to sprout up so that all the nations will see it. The arrival of this spiritual reawakening is likened to plants naturally sprouting from the fertile earth, a fulfilment of 60:21.

Meaning

Israel has seen significant affliction and punishment because of their sins, but their repentance, manifested in Isaiah 59, allows for the blessings of restoration portrayed in chapters 60–62. The speaker in 61:1–3 appears to be the prophet who has prophesied this great restoration. No matter who is identified as the speaker, the message is clear: he has been anointed and sent by God to proclaim deliverance for his people.

This restoration will include two facets: blessing (proclaiming *the year of the LORD's favour*) as well as punishment (*the day of vengeance of our God*). But Zion's mourning will be turned to gladness as God pours out blessing upon them. This deliverance is pictured as bringing good news to the afflicted, binding up the broken-hearted, proclaiming liberty to the captives and allowing prisoners to go free. They will be an example to all nations of the abundant blessings a nation can experience when it turns to God.

In Luke 4:16–21 Jesus claims that he fills (*plēroō*) Isaiah 61:1–3 with more meaning. Thus, the prophet's message of God's deliverance that began in 539 BC, with the return of the remnant and the rebuilding of Zion, took on a further spiritual dimension by the coming of the Messiah.

c. The vindication of Zion (62:1–12)

Context

The glorification of Zion is a primary theme in the last part of Isaiah. Here in chapter 62 God will fulfil his covenant relationship to Israel by providing for her as a husband provides for his wife (i.e.

continuing the theme of 61:10–11); she will never again lack anything.

While some have questioned the unity of this chapter, more recently most scholars agree it is a unit composed of three parts, but disagree as to its specific divisions. We suggest the following divisions: (1) the prophet will continue to plead for Zion's restoration (vv. 1–7); (2) Yahweh's commitment to Jerusalem is confirmed by an oath (vv. 8–9); and (3) preparation for God's deliverance (vv. 10–12).

Comment

(1) The prophet continues to plead for Zion's restoration (62:1–7)

1–5. Based upon the prophet's divinely bestowed endowments of salvation and righteousness (i.e. *garments of salvation . . . a robe of righteousness*, 61:10), he determines to take action: *For Zion's sake* [lit. 'on account of Zion'; Williams §366] *I will not keep silent*. He will not rest until her salvation and glorification are complete and she is fully restored to her God.

Identifying the speaker in verses 1 and 6 encounters the same difficulties as in Isaiah 61. Some scholars argue that the first person singular forms of verses 1 and 6 refer to Yahweh, for it makes sense that God would post sentinels to protect Jerusalem (see Whybray 1975: 246–247; Oswalt 1998: 578). However, it would be unusual for God to be referred to in the first person singular in verses 1 and 6, and yet be called by the names LORD in verses 2, 3 and 4 and God in verses 3 and 5.

Instead, scholars now tend to argue that there is little indication in the context of a change in speaker from chapter 61, whom we have argued is the prophet Isaiah. Thus the prophet (i.e. the first person singular forms) states that he will not keep silent until Yahweh brings deliverance to Zion, and then reiterates that Zion's righteousness will be a light to the nations that will bring glory to God: *The nations will see your vindication* (lit. 'righteousness', v. 2; see 60:1–3).

Zion will be honoured as a beautiful *crown* and a *royal diadem* (ṣānôp, 'crown, turban', 4x); similarly, a Babylonian inscription refers to Borsippa as the tiara of Bel (Marduk) (*ANET* 331).

Yahweh will hold Zion in his hand, an image that signifies his protection, guidance and care of her (v. 3; notice that Yahweh is not wearing this crown). While crowns were said to be worn by deities in the Ancient Near East, Whybray suggests that the idea of Yahweh wearing a crown like the pagan deities may have been unacceptable to the Jews (1975: 247).

The LORD will even give Jerusalem *a new name* that will signify her new nature (see vv. 2, 4), similar to her new name/character in 60:18b. She will no longer be referred to as *Deserted* (lit. 'Forsaken') but will be called *Hephzibah* (lit. 'My Delight Is in Her'); and her land which was called *Desolate* (as in ravaged, with no-one to care for it) will be changed to *Beulah* (lit. 'Married').

Her former names, *Deserted* and *Desolate*, are apt descriptions of Zion following 586 BC after her inhabitants were forced to abandon her. By contrast, her new name signifies that she is the LORD's cherished wife: 'My delight is in her.' In the Old Testament a new name often signified a radical change of fortune or status; for example, Abram ('Exalted Father') was changed to Abraham ('Father of a Multitude', Gen. 17:5) following God's covenant with him.

Yahweh will express his delight in his new bride, a relationship confirmed by his covenant with her (see 54:5): *As a young man marries a young woman* [lit. 'virgin'], / *so will your Builder* [lit. 'your sons'] *marry you*.

Notice that the literal reading 'your sons' would be odd in this context. It would mean that Zion's sons marry Zion, which does not align well with the parallel phrase *so will your God rejoice over you* (v. 5). For this reason, the editors of *BHS* suggest emending the pointing (but not the consonants) to read *bōnayik*, 'your builder', a designation also used of Yahweh in Psalm 147:2.

6–7. The unity of verses 1–7 is supported by the continuation of first person singular forms and the theme of Jerusalem's special relationship with God. The prophet continues speaking, delivering an urgent call to prayer on behalf of Jerusalem in verse 6. He creates emphasis in two ways: (1) through inverted syntax, placing the phrase *on your walls* before the verb; and (2) in his choice of vocabulary (i.e. *give yourselves no rest* [*dŏmî*, 2x], lit. 'all the day and all the night'). He has *posted watchmen* (lit. 'keepers'; perhaps similar to modern-day 'prayer warriors') on the walls of Jerusalem with the purpose of inundating God with prayers for the speedy deliverance of the nation (*You who call on the LORD, / give yourselves no rest, / and give him no rest*, vv. 6–7).

What an endearing prophet: he cares so much about Jerusalem's deliverance that he enlists others to bombard heaven on her behalf, until God *makes her the praise of the earth*.

(2) Yahweh's commitment to Jerusalem is confirmed by an oath (62:8–9)

8–9. In the Ancient Near East an oath was one of the strongest means of confirming the truthfulness of a statement. Here God swears by his omnipotence (*by his right hand / and by his mighty arm*) in order to substantiate his claim that there will be an end to Israel's punishment.

God is promising that no nation will ever again come to attack and plunder Israel, or take her crops away (lit. 'I will surely never give your grain away') as Midian, Syria, Assyria and Babylon (and others) had done in the past, in accordance with the covenant curses of Deuteronomy 28:30–33. Instead, they will be able to harvest their crops and praise God for their food and drink *in the courts of my* [God's] *sanctuary*. This is reminiscent of the harvest celebrations when the Israelites offered gifts and sacrifices in the temple (see Exod. 23:16). The fact that the covenant curses will no longer be carried out suggests that the covenant will never again be broken on the part of Israel.

(3) Preparation for God's deliverance (62:10–12)

10–12. With emphatic repetition the prophet exhorts both God and the remnant to take the first steps towards this deliverance. He tells the remnant to *pass through the gates*, and urges God to *prepare* [lit. 'clear away'] *the way, build up* [lit. 'pile up'] *the highway* (i.e. a road made firm with stones and fill), *remove the stones* (lit. 'stone from stone') and *raise a banner* (*nēs*, 'standard'); see 49:22. During the return from Babylon God's *reward* and *recompense* were the Israelites, but the author now applies these phrases to the remnant returning from the nations.

Like the double imperatives of 52:11 when the exiles are told to *Depart, depart* from Babylon, the repeated imperatives here serve to emphasize and confirm what will soon happen. Yahweh is about to keep his promise; therefore those in Jerusalem are to prepare for the remnant's return. Again, the prophetic perspective allows the prophet to envision the second return as a continuation of the first.

The banner is a sign to the nations to begin bringing back the remnant scattered among them just as they had been gathered up from the Babylonian exile (49:22; the similarity here is intentional).

The LORD addresses his child, *Daughter Zion*: *See, your Saviour comes! / See, his reward is with him, / and his recompense accompanies him.* His proclamation is reminiscent of 40:10 with one interesting change: instead of *the Sovereign LORD* (lit. 'Lord' [*'ădōnāy*] LORD [*yĕhwih*]), it is *your Saviour* (lit. 'your salvation') who comes.

All the nations that saw Israel's defeat will now see its restoration. The returning exiles will be called *the Holy People* and *the Redeemed of the LORD* (v. 12a). Zion will also be referred to as *Sought After* and the *City No Longer Deserted*, both much more favourable than her former names *Deserted* and *Desolate* (v. 4). Again, the change of name brings into focus the change of circumstances for the remnant.

Meaning

This chapter is a wonderful confirmation of the prophet's role as God's messenger. Not only does he continue to proclaim Jerusalem's deliverance until it happens (v. 1), he even exhorts watchmen to constantly bombard God with prayers concerning his promises and his commitment to Zion until deliverance becomes a reality.

Because God has already sworn that the remnant will never again be plundered (vv. 8–9), the prophet now exhorts them to get ready for God's deliverance.

The prophet uses terminology very similar to that regarding Israel's return from Babylon in order to remind them that just as God kept his promise then, so he will do the same in this future deliverance. This prophetic perspective allows the prophet to view this future return of the remnant as a continuation of the return from Babylon. Nations will see it and glorify the God who keeps his word and delivers his people even when they do not deserve it.

iv. Yahweh's day of vengeance upon the nations (63:1–6)

Context

Chapters 61–62 describe the year of the LORD's favour, and this is followed by the day of his vengeance in 63:1–6. Zion was exhorted to prepare for God's deliverance in 62:10–12, and now in the first part of chapter 63 he comes (see Figure 0.12 on p. 30) to destroy Edom, who had shown particular animosity towards Jerusalem during its destruction by Babylon (see Ps. 137:7; Ezek. 25:12; Joel 3:19; Obad. 13–14).

As descendants of Esau, God held Edom guilty of a breach of familial relationship and punished them accordingly, thereby delivering Israel from their perennial enemy. This section highlights the thoroughness of Edom's destruction. The Edomites had become Israel's enemies par excellence, not only for their cruelty towards Judah following Jerusalem's destruction by Babylon, but also for their long history of oppression beginning well before Edom refused to allow Israel to pass through their land on the way to the Promised Land (see Num. 20:14–21).

Isaiah 63:1–6 is generally considered a unit containing two parts: (1) verses 1–3 pose several questions (vv. 1a, 2) to which Yahweh responds (vv. 1b, 3); and (2) verses 4–6 provide Yahweh's explanation of his actions. Some have pointed out similarities between this passage and 59:15b–20, but 63:1–6 expands upon the punishment of Edom that is mentioned in 34:6, the only other place where the two names Edom and Bozrah are used together in the book of Isaiah.

Comment

1–3. Like a sentinel who challenges those who approach, the speaker in verse 1 asks the identity of the one who is approaching Israel: *Who is this coming from Edom, / from Bozrah, with his garments stained crimson* [ḥāmûṣ, occurs only here and functions as a play on the word ḥāmôṣ, 'oppressor']?

The second part of the question in verse 1 (i.e. *striding forward* [lit. ṣōʿeh, 'fettered, tilted, lying down', but should more probably read ṣōʿēd, 'striding solemnly'] *in the greatness of his strength*) parallels the first (i.e. *Who is this, robed in splendour . . . ?*, lit. 'the one honoured in his clothing') and emphasizes his power and majesty. The traveller responds: *It is I, proclaiming victory* [lit. 'speaking in righteousness'], / *mighty to save*. The NIV reads *victory* here, but the translation 'in righteousness' better captures the fact that the punishment was well deserved.

This figure, pictured as a warrior *robed in splendour*, is Yahweh, though not explicitly identified. He comes from the direction of *Bozrah*, the ancient capital of Edom, which was located about 30 miles south-east of the Dead Sea.

The sentry poses a second question (v. 2), this time about the bloodstains on his garment that look like red wine. The irony of the stains is that Edom, once known for its cultivation of vineyards and its presses for crushing grapes, is now crushed itself, leaving the marks of Yahweh's recent victory.

Yahweh gives a lengthy reply to the sentry in verses 3–6, explaining that he has been destroying Israel's (and therefore his) enemies, and emphasizing that he alone punished Edom: *I have trodden the winepress* [*pûrâ*, 2x; see Hag. 2:16 where it indicates a measurement, i.e. 'fifty *pûrâ*'; thus, it may refer to the trough or tub of the winepress (see Smith 2009: 659)] *alone*. The word *alone* suggests that God is not making use of an intermediary like Cyrus (i.e. *from the nations no one was with me*). God can display *wrath* against the wicked for their cruel treatment of his children and their continual rejection of him. The thoroughness of their destruction is pictured by Yahweh's completely *stained* clothing (lit. 'all my clothing I have stained').

4–6. God's punishment, called *the day* [signifying a short time] *of vengeance*, was to avenge Israel because of Edom's cruelty. It is literally said to be 'in my [God's] heart', meaning something that God had considered seriously. Even though *the year* (i.e. a long time) of redemption for his remnant was about to begin, the prophet speaks of it as being completed (i.e. *bāʾâ*, 'has come'; see Williams §165); this is another example of a prophetic perfect (see the similar phrase *the year of the LORD's favour*, 61:2).

Verse 5 takes up the recurring theme that God surveyed the nation of Israel but found no righteous person who could deliver them (*I looked, but there was no one to help*; see also 41:27–28; 50:2; etc.). He is disappointed (*appalled*, v. 5) that Israel was so thoroughly corrupt that no-one could aid in this judgment against Edom; only Yahweh's own righteousness and power could carry it out (see 59:16). God demonstrated great power (*my own arm achieved salvation for me*) and determination (*my own wrath sustained me*) in carrying his plan through to completion. In this context the phrase *salvation for me* refers to God's vindication: he will be exonerated of any accusations that he mistreated his people or was unjust in destroying the wicked.

God's judgment was thorough, extending beyond Edom to the other *nations* (lit. 'peoples'): *I trampled the nations in my anger* (v. 6). The word *trampled* (*rāmas*, 'to tread') is typically used of nations destroying other nations. It is now the nations' turn to receive their just punishment (see 14:25; 41:25) and to feel the full consequences of God's justice: he *poured their blood on the ground* (lit. 'and I brought down their juice of the grapes to the ground'). Ultimately God and his people will be vindicated, and justice fulfilled. Both the Old and the New Testament speak about the Day of the LORD when this will be accomplished.

Meaning

Yahweh is portrayed as the divine warrior (see Hab. 3:3–15) who directs punishment towards Edom for their ill-treatment of Israel, a recurring Old Testament theme (see Ps. 137:7; Isa. 34:5–6; etc.). The Edomites were related to the Israelites through Esau (see Gen. 36:1), yet they refused to come to Israel's aid during the exodus from Egypt (Num. 20:18). But this was only the start of their hostility, for they also encouraged Babylon in its destruction of Jerusalem (Ps. 137:7) and displayed cruelty towards their relatives (Joel 3:19; Obad. 13–14). Because of their constant animosity towards Israel, Edom becomes a picture of Israel's perpetual enemies. Thus, in verse 6 God extends the punishment beyond Edom, as he pours out his wrath on the *nations* (pl.).

God had given the nations ample time and opportunity to repent, yet, because he is truly righteous, he could not for ever hold off his judgment, called *the day of vengeance*. The word *day* emphasizes that this judgment is a short period of punishment, as compared with the longer *year for me to redeem* (i.e. to reclaim as his own). There should be satisfaction in knowing that someday in the future, perhaps even soon, wickedness will be judged, and the remnant will be delivered.

v. Communal lament: asking for God to display his great mercy (63:7 – 64:12)

Context

Many consider 63:7 – 64:12 a communal lament song (Westermann 1969: 386–387; Whybray 1975: 255; etc.), though somewhat loosely structured, containing four basic elements (see Figure 0.12 on p. 30):

1   Introduction: a historical account of Yahweh's past gracious acts towards his people (63:7–14)
2   An appeal for Yahweh's help (63:15 – 64:5a)
3   A confession of sin (64:5b–7)
4   A final appeal for Yahweh's help (64:8–12)

Oswalt points out the seeming discrepancy that gives rise to this passage: 'If he [God] has the power to destroy Israel's enemies with a single blow [i.e. his destruction of Edom in 63:1–7] . . . why does Israel remain enslaved to its unrighteousness?' (1998: 603).

Comment

a. Introduction: a historical account of Yahweh's past gracious acts towards his people (63:7–14)
Throughout their history, Israel rebelled and grieved God's holy spirit (v. 10) so that they became his enemy (vv. 7–14). This historical account sets out the crucial turning points in God's relationship with Israel: (1) his election of Israel as a nation (63:7–9); (2) their rebellion and punishment (63:10); (3) their deliverance when God parted the Reed Sea (63:11–12; see Hoffmeier 1999: 214); and (4) his protection and provision in leading them through the wilderness (63:14).

7–9. The communal lament begins with the author's personal comment (*I will tell of* [lit. 'remember'] *the kindnesses* [*ḥasdê*, pl.] *of the Lord*), but then he quickly shifts to the first person plural form *us* so as to include himself with Israel. Verse 7 begins and ends with a reference to God's 'lovingkindnesses' (NASB), also designated as *many good things* and *compassion* (lit. 'compassions'). He had been extremely patient and gracious towards the nation.

In view of the mercy that God had poured out on Israel, he declares in a tone of irony, *'Surely they are my people, / children who will be true to me'; / and so he became their Saviour*, the one who would deliver them. God had high expectations for his children, the Israelites, especially given the great mercy he had showered on them. In the Ancient Near East it was a disgrace for children not to obey their parents, thus he expected their obedience; but they habitually failed to live up to these expectations.

Because of the covenant relationship, Yahweh suffered when they suffered: *In all their distress he too was distressed* (lit. 'to him was distress', v. 9). The MT reads literally 'in all their distress, no [*lōʾ*] distress', but the *qērê* reading 'in all their distress, distress was to him [*lô*]' seems much more likely. The two readings *lōʾ*, 'no', and *lô*, 'to him', sound alike in Hebrew and are frequently mistaken for each other. Time after time God delivered them: (1) *the angel of his presence* [lit. 'of his faces'] *saved them*; (2) *in his love and mercy he redeemed them*; and (3) *he lifted them up and carried them / all the days of old* (v. 9).

The phrase *angel of his presence* refers either to the angel sent by God to lead the Israelites in the wilderness (see Exod. 23:20–23; 33:14) or to the angel of the LORD who often appeared in times of trouble (e.g. to Gideon, Manoah). Yahweh tenderly cared for the nation, at times even lifting them up and carrying them (see 46:3) like a good shepherd.

10–14. The syntax of verse 10 highlights the wilfulness of Israel's rebellion: literally 'yet they themselves rebelled' and thereby *grieved his Holy Spirit* (lit. 'spirit of his holiness'). God's discipline therefore became more severe; *he himself fought against them* by turning them over to their enemies.

It should not have surprised Israel that their wickedness would cause their righteous God to punish them further. At the same time God's righteous judgments showed his faithfulness and love towards Israel, just as parents show true love by reproving their children when necessary (see Prov. 3:12).

The phrase *his Holy Spirit* occurs only three times in the Old Testament (Isa. 63:10, 11; Ps. 51:11) and would not have been

understood as referring to the third person of the Trinity (see
Childs 2001: 524), but as a power emanating from God that demonstrated his holiness. God placed his holy character in their presence
(pictured as his presence on the mercy seat of the Ark of the Covenant, or in the pillar of cloud and pillar of fire; Exod. 13:21); thus
when they sinned it grieved him. The nature of the Holy Spirit will
be more fully developed later in the New Testament, but this verse
lays an important foundation.

In verses 11–14 the people look back, recalling *the days of old*
[*ʿôlām*, v. 11], beginning with the days of Moses[19] and the parting of
the Reed Sea: *who sent his glorious arm of power / to be at Moses' right
hand, / who divided the waters before them* (v. 12). God's 'mighty arm'
(synecdoche for his power and strength) was sent to empower
Moses (lit. *be at Moses' right hand*). God supplied water, manna, quail
and protection at Moses' request, but his most memorable feat was
the parting of the Reed Sea. Other nations marvelled at Israel's
God, who gained for himself *everlasting renown* (lit. 'an everlasting
name') by parting the waters and destroying kingdoms (see Josh.
2:9–11).

Two similes describe how the Israelites went through the sea
(*tĕhōmôt*, depths, vv. 13–14): (1) *Like a horse in open country* [lit. 'wilderness'], / *they did not stumble*, meaning the Israelites were sure-footed
and agile; and (2) *like cattle that go down to the plain, / they were given rest
by the Spirit of the LORD*, a picture of passing through a place of
provision and rest (i.e. the Promised Land). It was the spirit of the
LORD (i.e. his power) that gave them this rest and protection. God's
gracious provision and care for his people also gained the respect
and fear of other nations.

---

19. In the phrase *where is he who brought them through the sea, / with the shepherd*
   [lit. 'shepherds'] *of his flock . . . ?* (v. 11), the singular word 'shepherd'
   would refer to Moses (who is mentioned multiple times in the passage)
   and the plural 'shepherds' to Moses and the other leaders (i.e. elders,
   etc.). It was common during Moses' time to refer only to Moses, even
   though Aaron, his spokesperson, was usually in the background (cf.
   Exod. 12:1 with v. 21).

b. An appeal to Yahweh for help (63:15 – 64:12)

The tone and intensity of the lament song change in verse 15 with the prophet's appeal to God to have pity on his children. He bases his appeal on three grounds: (1) Yahweh's father–son relationship with Israel (63:15–17); (2) his love for his temple and his people (63:18–19); and (3) his reputation (64:1–5).

(1) An appeal based upon Yahweh's father–son relationship with Israel (63:15–17)

15–17. The author has just recounted the glorious deeds of the past and now requests similar acts from God in the present. He entreats Yahweh to look down from heaven (*zĕbul*, 'lofty residence of God', 5x) and see the plight of his children (see Ps. 80:14–15): *Where are your zeal and your might* [lit. 'mighty deeds', pl.]? / *Your tenderness* [lit. 'mercies'] *and compassion* [lit. 'compassions'] *are withheld* [*'āpaq*, 'to restrain oneself', 6x with this meaning] *from us* [lit. 'from me', v. 15]. Childs argues that 'the prophet's "me" is encompassed within the community's "we"' (2001: 524), a view supported by the next verse (v. 16). However, we think it more likely that the prophet is speaking for the nation, as he did in verse 7, or that he appeals to God's compassion on behalf of the sinful nation based upon his own obedience to God.

The lament implies that Yahweh has been indifferent to the Israelites' plight. The prophet pleads with God based upon the covenant relationship (i.e. the Mosaic covenant) which is often described in father–son terms (see Deut. 32:19–20). The author twice claims an intimate father–son relationship between God and his *servants* even though their forefathers, *Abraham* and *Israel* (Jacob), would not have recognized them because of their disobedience: *But* [*kî*] *you are our Father, / though* [*kî*, used concessively; Williams §448] *Abraham does not know us / or Israel acknowledge* [lit. 'recognize'] *us*. He goes on to claim the same promises that were given to the patriarchs: *our Redeemer* [i.e. 'the one who claimed them for his own'] *from of old* [*'ôlām*] *is your name*. God's name represents his reputation and character. The *Redeemer from of old* who delivered his people in the past is also our redeemer today.

Both questions in verse 17a accuse God of hardening their hearts and letting them wander from him: *Why, LORD, do you make us wander from your ways / and harden [qāšaḥ, 2x] our hearts so we do not revere you?* The author believes so strongly in divine sovereignty that every action is under God's hand.

God can indeed harden hearts, as noted in 6:9–11, but he does so only for the greater purpose of bringing glory to himself (e.g. Pharaoh's heart was hardened to bring greater glory to God when he delivered his people from Egypt). God's ways are high above our ways (55:9), but they are always right and for our ultimate benefit. Thus, the author appeals to God to once again come to their aid, for they are his *servants* and the tribes of his *inheritance*.

(2) An appeal based upon his love for his temple and his people (63:18–19)

18–19. The author continues his appeal based upon Yahweh's love for (1) his temple, which Israel possessed for only *a little while* (*miš'ār*, 4x) before it was destroyed by their *enemies*, a reference to the events of 586 BC (v. 18);[20] and (2) his people, whose special relationship with Yahweh has been from days of old (*We are yours from of old* ['ôlām]), whereas these enemies have never had this special relationship with him (*they have not been called by your name* [lit. 'your name has not been called over them', signifying a lack of relationship]).

One would have expected God to react in fury when his holy temple was trampled, yet the author sees no evidence of his stepping in to correct the problem. According to this final lament, Yahweh is being accused of abandoning his people.

(3) An appeal based upon God's reputation (64:1–5)

1–2.[21] Hoping to spur God into action, the author pleads, *Oh,* [*lû'* = optative, expressing a strong desire; Williams §460] *that you*

---

20. Verse 18a appears to be missing the phrase 'your holy sanctuary' (lit. 'for a little while your [holy people] possessed . . . '), thus scholars typically suggest emending the text. However, it may be a purposeful ellipsis; that is, the author intended that the phrase 'your holy sanctuary' be assumed from v. 18b.

21. In the Hebrew Bible Isaiah 64:1 = 63:19; the entire chapter reflects this misalignment in verse numbers.

would rend the heavens and come down (v. 1). According to the Ancient Near Eastern worldview, the gods resided in heaven, located above the visible sky. In this verse the clouds separate Yahweh from people, so that Yahweh need only tear through this insubstantial partition in order to display his deliverance (see Ps. 18:9).

The author further exhorts Yahweh to demonstrate his power (*that the mountains would tremble before you* [v. 1]; *cause the nations to quake before you* [v. 2]) so that his enemies might experience first-hand his mighty acts that have been recounted through the ages (*come down to make your name known to your enemies*).

The author likens Yahweh's deliverance to a fire that *sets twigs* [*hămāsîm*, occurs only here] *ablaze* or that *causes water to boil* (lit. 'churn', v. 2). In the same way, he wants the sight of God's deliverance to cause the nations to tremble before Yahweh, as they see his power and respond in reverence before him.

3–5. The author appeals to Yahweh to perform his prior awesome acts (*nôrā'ôt*, 'acts that produced fear and reverence') that also brought glory to his name because they far surpassed anything the Israelites ever expected. Even more impressive is the fact that this all-powerful God *acts on behalf of those who wait for him* (v. 4; by contrast, other gods in the Ancient Near East were generally thought to be capricious and callous) and helps *those who gladly do right* [lit. 'rejoicing and doing righteousness', a hendiadys, v. 5], / *who remember your ways* (lit. 'they remember you in your ways'). A God who protected and provided for his people was unique: to see this mighty God at work would be an incredible teaching tool for the nations.

The Israelites found themselves in a well-deserved but hopeless situation: *But* [*hēn* is often emphatic; *HALOT* 1.251] *when we continued to sin* [lit. 'but we continued to sin a long time' ('*ôlām*; not 'for ever' in this passage)] *against them* [i.e. 'your ways'], / *you* [lit. 'you yourself'] *were angry.* The phrase *How then can we be saved?* is difficult to translate, but the context points to a question being posed here (see Oswalt 1998: 625); the assumed answer is 'we can't be saved.'

(4) Confession of sin (64:6–7)

6–7. Fully cognizant of the extent to which the nation has sinned, the author describes sin's pervasiveness with the emphatic words *all* (used three times) and *no one* (lit. 'there is not one who calls'): (1) *All of us* have become like one who is unclean and therefore must be separated from God. The word *unclean* is often used of ceremonial impurity (see Lev. 11:4–38), but sometimes refers to other uncleanness, like that of leprosy (see Lev. 13:11) or sexual emissions (see Lev. 15:16–17). (2) *All our righteous acts are like filthy rags*, a reference to garments worn during menstruation; even their righteous acts are utterly sinful. (3) *We all shrivel up like a leaf* (see opposite in Ps. 1:3). (4) *Like the wind our sins sweep us away*, meaning their sins control them and will in the end lead to their punishment. (5) *No one* seeks after God; he therefore has *given us over to our sins*.

With the pronoun *us* the author includes himself among those lost in sin and deserving of punishment. He realizes that on their own they have no hope, for even their supposedly righteous deeds are appalling.

The Israelites do not even care enough about their sinful condition to call out to God (*No one calls on your name*, v. 7), so that Yahweh is fully justified in 'hiding his face' from them. When God is said to 'turn his face towards' Israel, it signifies his pleasure and blessing upon them. But when he 'turns his face away', the opposite is true, and they can expect punishment. He is therefore turning them over to the power of iniquity (lit. 'over to the hand of our iniquities', v. 7). Sin is a powerful master that can do irreparable damage to one's life (see Rom. 1:18–32). In this case, however, the author has hope for at least a remnant of his people (v. 8).

(5) A final appeal (64:8–12)

8–12. The hopelessness of their situation is tempered by the author's undying faith that should be an example to Israel: *Yet* [lit. 'but now'] *you, LORD, are our Father. / We are the clay* (v. 8). They are to view Yahweh as the all-powerful God who made a covenant with Israel, and themselves as subservient to him, like clay that a potter shapes into vessels for different uses (see 45:9).

Though the nation has sinned against Yahweh, the author maintains faith that God will take care of his children. Thus he pleads with God on behalf of the entire nation to relent in his wrath: *Do not be angry beyond measure* [lit. 'until very much'], *LORD; / do not remember our sins for ever* [lit. 'do not until for ever remember our sins';

the inverted syntax is emphatic] / . . . *for we are all your people* (lit. 'your people all of us', v. 9).

Once again the author takes up the theme of the nation's desperate condition (see 63:18): its *sacred cities have become a wasteland* [i.e. since Israel is God's chosen nation, its cities are all set apart to God] / . . . *Jerusalem* [is] *a desolation* (v. 10). Even worse, the temple which was the centre of worship lies in heartbreaking ruin: *Our holy and glorious temple* [lit. 'house'], *where our ancestors praised you, / has been burned* [lit. 'was for a burning'] *with fire, / and all that we treasured* [*maḥămaddênû*, 'our precious objects'; i.e. the temple along with its vessels and Zion itself] *lies in ruins* (v. 11). What the prophet foresees is the destruction of Jerusalem and the temple in 586 BC.

In his final appeal the author asks two questions: (1) Can God simply sit back and let these things happen to his people and his holy nation? (2) Will God continue to punish Israel? The author pleads for God to relent and not punish them *beyond measure* (lit. 'will you afflict us until greatness?', v. 12).

So much had already been destroyed (i.e. *after all this*, lit. 'will you in spite of this' [Williams §288b]); surely at some point Yahweh must turn from his wrath, which the author describes as 'keeping silent', and have pity on them. In the next chapter Yahweh responds to these final two questions (v. 12) that conclude the lament.

Meaning

The communal lament song of 63:7 – 64:12 provides much of the justification for why Yahweh rises up to deliver his people. Chapter 63 opens with a beautiful portrayal of Yahweh as the divine warrior coming to punish the enemies of his people (pictured as Edom). The rest of the lament then lays out the reasons why God should deliver his people: he has a special relationship with Israel as their father and redeemer; their enemies had destroyed his temple; and so on.

When God looks on Israel's deplorable condition, with his holy cities (the prophet sees all the cities of Israel as dedicated to God, 64:10) lying in ruins and his temple destroyed, he must surely decide to come to their rescue. The prophet confesses that Israel has greatly sinned, wandering far from God; but he also believes that God will still keep his promises to the nation and bring them back to himself.

The communal lament ends with two heart-wrenching questions – *After all this, L*ORD, *will you hold yourself back?* / *Will you keep silent and punish us beyond measure?* – both of which must be answered 'No! Of course not.' It is thus time for Yahweh to act.

vi. God's ultimate plan will bring himself glory; SEAM (65:1 – 66:24)

Earlier form-critical scholars saw Isaiah 65 – 66 as a compilation of smaller units consisting of a variety of genres and settings. More recently, however, the trend is to read them as a redacted literary unit. Several scholars have noted the similarity of themes between Isaiah 1 and 65 – 66, which points to editorial shaping towards a thematic unity of the book (see Introduction). Many of the themes in Isaiah 65 – 66 are also found at the end of the book of Revelation (e.g. new heaven and new earth; tears wiped away by God; destruction of the wicked). (See Figure 0.12 on p. 30.)

In Isaiah 65 – 66 God responds to the lament of the previous section (63:7 – 64:12), especially the two final questions in 64:12. To the first question regarding whether God will continue the severe punishment under which they languish, God responds that he had made the first moves towards reconciliation but the people rebuffed him (*I revealed myself to those who did not ask for me*, 65:1). While claiming to be Yahweh's people (*Oh, look upon us . . . / for we are all your people*, 64:9), they continued to make sacrifices to pagan deities and observe abhorrent rituals: [they] *continually provoke me / to my very face, / offering sacrifices in gardens / and burning incense, keeping secret vigil* and eating *the flesh of pigs* (65:3–5).

In response to the second question as to whether God's punishment will continue *beyond measure*, God responds that the extent of their punishment will be in just proportion to the extent of their sin and that, for the present, they have not yet been sufficiently punished: *I will not keep silent but will pay back in full* (65:6); *I will measure into their laps / the full payment for their former deeds* (65:7).

The message of Isaiah 65 – 66 in which God calls to his nation but they fail to respond (see 65:1, 12) was a consistent problem throughout Israel's history. Yahweh's plan as stated at the beginning of Isaiah is about to be fulfilled: *Zion will be delivered with justice / . . . and those who forsake the L*ORD *will perish* (1:27–28).

While there is little agreement among scholars concerning the details and arrangement of the units of Isaiah 65 – 66 (see Smith 2009: 665–667), it is nevertheless organized in parallel units, whose climax is reached at the beginning of chapter 66:

1. God called but few responded (65:1–7)
2. God delivers a remnant (65:8–25)
   3. GOD IS SOVEREIGN (66:1–2a)
1'. God called but few responded (66:2b–6)
2'. God delivers a remnant (66:7–24)

Scholars have noted that these last two chapters form the final section of the book, but we believe they also function as the final seam of the book, which contains the same themes as the other seams, with an interesting new twist: (1) Israel has been judged (65:1–16) and given fair punishment for their constant defiance against God. (2) God demonstrates exceptional treatment in delivering a remnant (65:8–15, 17–25; 66:7–14, 19–23), in contrast to the plight of the wicked (65:13–16). The remarkable twist is that this remnant will be gathered from many distant nations (66:19–20) and will serve alongside the remnant from Israel (66:21). (3) The wicked will be punished (65:6–7, 11–15; 66:3–6, 14b–17, 24). The familiar refrain is presented in a greatly expanded form: *And they will go out and look on the dead bodies of those who rebelled against me . . .* (66:24).

a. God will preserve his remnant (65:1–25)

Context
As chapter 65 opens, God speaks in the first person, declaring the charge he brings against his people (vv. 1–7). He makes it clear that he must punish the nation for their wickedness (i.e. *a people who continually provoke me to my very face*, v. 3), otherwise he would not be a just God. Thus verses 6–7 conclude with a warning of impending punishment.

The next section (vv. 8–25) opens and closes with similar phrases (*This is what the LORD says*, v. 8; *says the LORD*, v. 25) and sets forth God's intention to spare a righteous remnant: *I will not destroy them all* (v. 8). Thus God will make a distinction between his true servants (*my people who seek me*, v. 10) for whom he will provide and the rest (*you who forsake the* LORD, v. 11) who will receive their just punishment.

Beginning in verse 17, God describes the blessings that he will bestow on 'his servants': he will create for them a new heaven and earth, one that will no longer have the problems associated with the present heaven and earth (i.e. no more sorrow or weeping, v. 19; no infant mortality, v. 20; no premature death, v. 20; no enemies, v. 22; etc.).

Comment

(1) Israel's rebellion will be punished (65:1–7)

1–2. Yahweh's first response to the pleading questions at the end of chapter 64 is that he has already shown Israel great mercy: *I revealed myself* [lit. 'I allowed myself to be sought out'] *to those who did not ask for me* (v. 1). In each phrase of verse 1, God takes the initiative, calling Israel to himself even though they did not 'call on his name'. The context suggests they wilfully rejected God's help, turning instead to false gods. Yet God stands holding out (lit. 'stretched out') his *hands* (v. 2), eagerly and repeatedly imploring them to turn to him: *Here am I, here am I* (repeated for emphasis).

The picture is a profound one: the sovereign God, the creator of the world and all humanity, the one who chose Israel and entered into a covenant relationship with them, does not force them to respond to his loving entreaties to return to him (Exod. 19:1–9) and serve him whole heartedly. He offers his help and invites them into a relationship, but Israel was an obstinate people (v. 2) who followed their own devices (i.e. their *own imaginations*, thinking they knew what was best) and walked in ways that were not *good* for them (paths that led them into further sinfulness and ultimately punishment). God, whose ways are best, longed to spare them this suffering. The apostle Paul applies 65:1–2 to the offer of salvation to the Gentiles because the Israelites continued to rebel (see Rom. 10:19–21).

3–7. The Israelites blatantly show their contempt for Yahweh in their worship of foreign deities, provoking him to his very face (v. 3). The participles of verses 2b–5 indicate the continuing nature of their sin: (1) *offering sacrifices in gardens* (lit. 'the gardens'; often in the form of fertility rites to ensure a good harvest), sacrifices that were continually condemned by the pre-exilic prophets (see 1:29); (2) *burning incense on altars of brick* (lit. 'offering incense upon the bricks'; most probably an altar of bricks heated to burn the incense), a practice that was condemned as early as Leviticus 26:30; (3) spending the night in secret vigils (lit. 'in the kept things') in graveyards, either to consult the dead (i.e. necromancy, a practice Isaiah condemned in 8:19) or to seek an oracle from a god or demon by means of a dream (a practice referred to as 'incubation'); and (4) eating pork (*haḥăzîr*, 'the pork', 7x) and other *impure meat*, a practice specifically forbidden in the law (see Lev. 11:7) but generally allowed in other Ancient Near Eastern religions (Hess 2007: 188, 217–218).

To add insult to injury, those who commit these forbidden acts consider themselves more holy than those who do not (i.e. *Keep away; don't come near me, / for I am too sacred for you* [lit. 'I am holier than you', v. 5]). These sins are a continual offence to God, like irritating smoke from *a fire that keeps burning all day* (v. 5). God will mete out the punishment they deserve in full measure: *I will not keep silent but will pay back in full* [i.e. 'make a full recompense', v. 6]*; / I will pay . . . back into their laps* [lit. 'bosom', suggesting a nearness from which they cannot escape] . . . *the full payment for their former deeds* (v. 7). They will not be able to skirt this punishment to be doled out in full measure, for God is just.

The inevitability of judgment lies in the fact that *it stands written before me* [God], which may be a reference to (1) a heavenly book in which sins are recorded (see Dan. 7:10; Rev. 20:11–15); (2) the prophecies of the book of Isaiah which will stand as a record against them (see 8:1–16; 30:8); or (3) the curses in Deuteronomy 27 – 28 for breaking their covenant with Yahweh. God *will not keep silent* (v. 6), a reference to the question in 64:12b; however, his response probably was not necessarily what the author was expecting, for God will 'speak' by bringing punishment on the wicked.

Israel had not learned from their punishments. Their sins had accumulated over the years, their ancestors having demonstrated similar wickedness (i.e. *both your sins and the sins of your ancestors*, v. 7);

for example, Solomon was criticized for offering sacrifices on the high places (1 Kgs 3:3). God considers the worship of false gods (the burning of *sacrifices on the mountains*, v. 7) a direct affront to him (lit. 'they have reproached me').

(2) God will bring deliverance (65:8–16)

8–10. With the introductory words *This is what the* LORD *says*, God is now ready to address the author's second question in 64:12. While the nation will indeed be punished (64:12 assumes that they are already in the midst of this punishment) for their rebellion, not everyone will be destroyed. Yahweh will spare those who submit to him: *so will I do on behalf of* [lit. 'for the sake of'] *my servants; / I will not destroy them all* [lit. 'the whole'; v. 8].

The illustration of grapes (v. 8) originates in the harvest process when clusters left on the vine after the main harvest were later gleaned because they still had value: *As* [*ka'ăšer*] *when juice* [*hattîrôš*, 'new wine'] *is still found in a cluster of grapes / and people say, 'Don't destroy it, / there is still a blessing in it'*, in the same way (*kēn*) God will act on behalf of the remnant (lit. *my servants*, vv. 8–9) to preserve them – the grammatical structure *ka'ăšer* ['just as'] ... *kēn* ('so') signals a strong comparison (Williams §264). New wine can be drunk after about a month of fermentation, but generally improves in flavour the longer it ages.

The phrases *my servants* (65:8, 9, 13, 14–15), *his servants* (56:6; 66:14), *your servants* (63:17) or *servants of the* LORD (54:17) become common expressions for the righteous remnant in the latter part of Isaiah and are distinct from the singular form.

Verse 9 further explains what God means at the end of verse 8 when he says, *I will bring forth descendants from Jacob*. The promises to the patriarchs will be realized in the remnant. Those descendants of *Jacob* (i.e. Israel) and *Judah* (i.e. *my servants*) will inherit the land, which is portrayed as a pastoral idyll of rest and peace (*Sharon will become a pasture for flocks, / and the Valley of Achor a resting-place* [*rēbeṣ*, 4x] *for herds*, v. 10).

Sharon is the fertile coastal plain along the Mediterranean Sea known primarily for its pasturing flocks (see 1 Chr. 5:16). The *Valley of Achor* is the more barren land near Jericho on the far eastern side of Israel. The two extremities taken together indicate that the whole land is a place of peace and rest for those who seek after Yahweh. The name *Achor* 'trouble' (see Josh. 7:24–26) serves as a wordplay, since it will be transformed into a place of peace and rest (see Hos. 2:15).

11–12. Attention is now turned from the remnant towards those who continue to rebel against Yahweh: *But as for you who forsake the* Lord. They are described as forsaking God's *holy mountain* (i.e. Zion), instead holding sacred feasts to foreign gods: (1) they *spread a table for Fortune*, the personal name of the Syrian and Phoenician god Gad (the article on this word suggests it is a personification of 'good fortune'; see the names Baal-gad [see Josh. 11:17] and Migdal-gad [see Josh. 15:37]); and (2) they *fill bowls of mixed wine for Destiny*, who is most probably the god Meni, 'the god of fate'; again the article suggests it is a personification of 'fate'.

Those who continue to pursue false gods will be destined (*mānâ*, a wordplay on the god's name *Destiny* [*měnî*, occurs only here]) by God *for the sword*, because they have refused his appeal to return to him: *I called but you did not answer, / I spoke but you did not listen* (v. 12). The parallel phrase in verse 12 reads literally 'you will bow down to the slaughter', implying that if they do not bow down in worship to God, they will be killed. These phrases reiterate that God pursued Israel, but they wilfully rejected him, choosing instead that which is evil (lit. 'the evil in my eyes'), thereby incurring his displeasure.

13–15. Based upon (i.e. *therefore*) their response to the *Sovereign* Lord (lit. 'the Lord [*ădōnāy*] Lord [*yěhwih*]'), God declares contrasting outcomes for the righteous remnant (i.e. *my servants*), who will eat, drink, rejoice and sing for joy, and the wicked (i.e. *but you* [second person plural]), who will know intense despair, being hungry, thirsty and put to shame, and crying in anguish (lit. 'from pain of heart' and 'from a crushed spirit'; v. 14). The fact that this punishment of the wicked comes from the *Sovereign* Lord adds weight to the certainty of the pronouncement.

The names of the wicked will be used only as a curse by God's (lit. 'the Lord [*ădōnāy*] Lord [*yěhwih*]') *chosen ones* (see Jer. 29:22), whereas his servants will receive a new name (see Isa. 62:4; Rev. 22:4) that represents their new character (this is a common theme in the second part of Isaiah; see 56:5; 62:2).

16. God will reign supreme; his actions and character will no longer be hidden but will be made manifest to all. They will be obvious to all for the following two reasons: (1) whoever invokes a blessing or an oath in the land will do so by Yahweh *the one true God* (lit. 'God of truth'); and (2) the troubles of the past will be entirely forgotten and hidden from God's sight (i.e. he will not remember their former deeds against them again).

(3) The blessings of the righteous: a new heaven and a new earth (65:17–25)

17–19a. The *kî* ('for') at the beginning of verse 17 links it to the previous verse, providing the reason why the *past troubles will be forgotten* (Williams §444). The word *see* directs attention to God's new creative work (v. 17), which he undertakes after the heavens and earth are destroyed (see 51:6). Some suggest that *ḥādāš*, 'new', means 'renewed', though most contexts suggest 'new' in the sense of not existing before (e.g. Exod. 1:8; Josh. 9:13; etc.). Either way the author speaks of a complete transformation of the world that the remnant will enjoy.

In context *the former things* refers to *the past troubles* (v. 16) that will no longer be remembered. A verbal link joins verses 16–17; verse 16 states in positive terms that troubles are forgotten, and verse 17 states the same concept in negative terms. These troubles have been superseded in memory by God's remarkable new creation whose focal point is Jerusalem and its inhabitants (lit. 'for behold I am creating Jerusalem'; same terminology as v. 17a).

God will rejoice over the city and his people who have been made new: *I will rejoice over* [lit. 'because of'; Williams §247] *Jerusalem / and take delight in* [lit. 'because of'] *my people*. The only way God can rejoice his people is if they are cleansed (see 4:2–6). This new creation will be free from the curse of the former one (Gen. 3:17).

19b–25. New Jerusalem will enjoy the following characteristics: (1) In contrast to the pain and sorrow the Israelites had experienced all too often, weeping will now be absent: *crying will be heard in it* [Jerusalem] *no more* (v. 19b). (2) Infant mortality, which was prevalent in the Ancient Near East, will no longer exist: *Never again will there be in it / an infant* [lit. 'a suckling'] *who lives but a few days* [lit. 'an infant of days'; v. 20]. (3) Longevity will be the norm: *the one who fails to reach a hundred* [lit. 'a son of a hundred years'] / *will be considered accursed* (v. 20; see Ps. 90:10). In Israel a long life was a sign of God's blessing, whereas a shortened life was often attributed to sin, thus suggesting the restriction if not elimination of sin on this new earth. The remnant's lives are likened to the life of a tree which is long and healthy (v. 22). The patriarchs would plant a tree when they desired a long-lasting reminder of God's promises or an event (see Gen. 21:33). (4) There will be no fear of invasion: *No longer will they build houses and others live in them, / or plant and others eat* (v. 22; see Judg. 6). (5) They will enjoy immediate access to God: *Before they call I* [lit. 'I myself'; emphatic] *will answer; / while they are still speaking I* [lit. 'I myself'; emphatic] *will hear* (v. 24). This calls to mind the Israelites' complaints that Yahweh had not heard their laments (see 40:27; 49:14; etc.); however, the imagery of God's responsiveness far surpasses anything that they could have imagined. (6) Nature will be at peace: *They* [animals] *will neither harm nor destroy / on all my holy mountain* (v. 25).

Similar to 62:8, verses 21–22 are a reversal of the curse in Deuteronomy 28:30: *my chosen ones will long enjoy* [lit. 'will wear out'] / *the work of their hands* (i.e. they will make full use of the results of their labours, v. 22). *They will not labour in vain* (lit. 'for the emptiness or vanity'; v. 23). Whybray notes that 'the ideal life as conceived by the ancient Jews was not one of idleness but of satisfying work' (1975: 278).

Their children will not be *doomed to misfortune* (*behālâ*, 'disaster, ruin, horror', 4x; lit. 'born for (the) disaster'), meaning they will not experience the terror of sudden, unexplained death, which was thought to be a punishment from God. Both terms *in vain* and *misfortune* include the article, which indicates a 'well-known substantive' (Williams §85). God will bless them and their descendants with prosperity and protection.

Verse 25 is a condensation of 11:6–9, which lacks only the phrase *and dust will be the serpent's food*, a paraphrase of Genesis 3:14. Oswalt argues that this phrase means the serpent will eat only dust, and 'When that happens, the curse will be totally broken' (1998: 662). However, since it is a figure of speech for the serpent's humiliation in Genesis 3:14, the same is probably true here. Thus the inclusion of the phrase *and dust will be the serpent's food* suggests that the curse on the serpent, the one who started the rebellion against God, will remain.

The expression *on all my holy mountain* appears five times in chapters 56–66, but only once in chapters 1–39. It refers to Mount Zion, signifying the realm over which Yahweh rules, which in this case is the whole new creation. The final phrase, *says the LORD*, adds certainty to the prophecy.

Meaning

Isaiah 65 is the most important chapter for describing God's plan regarding his righteous remnant. While God had initially chosen the entire nation of Israel (v. 1), they were a rebellious people who continued to provoke him (v. 3). Therefore, God chose to use punishment (v. 7) to bring forth a purified nation that would serve him. He likens this righteous remnant to a *cluster of grapes* that remains on the vine after harvest and is gathered, for they still have value.

God will provide for and bless his remnant, whom he calls *my servants*; but the rest will suffer his punishment. He will make new heavens and a new earth where his servants will live, enjoying what God intended from the very beginning.

The author shapes the passage to envision the eschatological hope of future Zion in contrast to what it had just been through. Childs points out, 'The promise in chapter 65 is not an apocalyptic flight into an imaginative world of fantasy, but the fulfillment of God's will taking shape throughout the entire book of Isaiah' (2001: 538).

b. The LORD sovereignly directs his creation (66:1–24)

Context

While the structure of this chapter has been debated, the climax of Isaiah 65 – 66 is reached in 66:1–2 when God declares his sovereignty. The beginning and end of this declaration are marked by the phrases *This is what the LORD says* and *declares the LORD*, respectively. Even though he is sovereign over all creation, he chooses to show favour to those who are repentant and fear him.

Again, there is significant debate as to how to divide this
chapter. We separate chapter 66 into the following units: (1) verses
1–6, in which God calls but few respond; and (2) verses 7–24,
describing God's deliverance of a remnant.

Comment

(1) God calls but few respond (66:1–6)

1–2. In these verses God assures his remnant that the changes
mentioned in the previous section (see 65:17–25) will occur. They
can know this with certainty for two reasons: (1) God is
omnipresent and omnipotent; nothing in his present, vast creation
can contain him. (2) He has chosen to show favour to his righteous
remnant, those who are *contrite in spirit* and who *tremble at my* [God's]
word (see 57:15).

The phrase *This is what the* Lord *says* (lit. 'thus says the* Lord',
v. 1) introduces a statement regarding the exceeding greatness of
Yahweh: *Heaven* [lit. 'the heavens'] *is my throne, / and the earth is my
footstool* (see Ps. 103:19). These places are where God's sovereignty is
on display but, as the two rhetorical questions that follow suggest,
they can in no way contain him: (1) *Where is the* [lit. 'this'] *house you
will build for me?* and (2) *Where will my resting-place* [lit. 'this place of my
resting?'] *be?* The implied answer to both is that nothing can possibly be built that can hold God. Verse 2 provides the rationale for
why this is so: he made everything (lit. 'all these things my hand
has made' [emphatic order]); the Creator cannot be contained by
anything he himself has created.

Turning from God's omnipresence and omnipotence, verse 2b
shifts focus to his sovereignty. While he is all-powerful and all-
knowing, he can choose to shower his attention on whomever he
pleases. Then God emphatically declares two characteristics of
the persons he will favour (lit. 'but this one I will look upon with
pleasure' [emphatic order]): (1) those with a *humble* [i.e. the
opposite of proud and haughty] *and contrite* (lit. 'broken', meaning
one who shows remorse) inner attitude; and (2) those who
outwardly demonstrate an attitude of awe and reverence for God
and his word (*who tremble* [*ḥārēd*, 'to be frightened at', 6x; twice in
this passage, 66:2, 5] *at my* [God's] *word*). These are the people

who seek God (65:10) and whom God calls *my servants* (65:9, 13–15).

3–4. God's disputation shifts from his sovereignty and special regard for those who are humble and repentant to those Israelites who demonstrate the opposite: *They have chosen their own ways, / and they delight in their abominations* (v. 3b). The Hebrew of the preceding four pairs of participial phrases is difficult, but the outwardly religious acts of these Israelites are likened to practices that are detestable to God. The first part of each phrase mentions a sacrificial action that was part of the worship prescribed by God; the second part of the phrase then likens it to a heathen sacrificial practice that is abominable to God.

The first phrase pair likens the person who sacrifices a bull to someone who kills another person (lit. 'the one who is slaughtering the bull, the one who strikes a person'). The latter may refer to human sacrifice, but at the very least is an allusion to Exodus 21:12. The relationship between the paired phrases is somewhat uncertain since the word *like* found in most English translations is absent in the Hebrew text.

The second phrase pair, *whoever offers a lamb* [lit. 'sacrifices the lamb'] / *is like one who breaks a dog's neck*, probably refers to the sacrifice of dogs, a practice unknown among the Israelites but included in the cultic practices of other Ancient Near Eastern cultures (Sasson 1976: 199–207; Lobell and Powell 2010: 26–35).

In the third phrase pair, *whoever makes a grain offering* [lit. 'gift, tribute, offering'] / *is like one who presents pig's blood*, the words that are underlined have been added to smooth the translation and do not appear in the Hebrew. Pigs were unclean according to the Mosaic law (see Lev. 11:7) and were not to be offered to God.

The fourth and final phrase pair, *whoever burns memorial* [lit. 'the one who is remembering'] *incense / is like one who worships* [lit. 'blesses'] *an idol* [*āwôn*, 'sin, iniquity']. The word *incense* (*lĕbōnâ*) probably means frankincense, an aromatic resin from Oman, Yemen and the Horn of Africa. The wording here (lit. 'the one who is remembering incense') is indeed unusual, for one usually burns or offers up incense.

The NIV reading *memorial incense* is unlikely, for two reasons: (1) in the syntax of this sentence the participle serves as 'the subject who does something . . . ' (i.e. '*the one who* kills the bull'), parallel to the other phrases of the verse; and (2) the word *memorial* (*'azkārâ*) also appears in Leviticus 24:7, where it is spelled differently. A better translation would be: 'the one who remembers [to offer] incense' or 'the one who remembers [the purpose] for incense' (i.e. to worship God). Either way the appearance of *'azkārâ* in the first part of the phrase suggests it is something that God had commanded.

The last two phrases of verses 3 and 4 form a wordplay that describes the people's sin: they *chose* their own ways and their souls *delighted* in their abominations (v. 3); they *chose* that which did not *delight* God (NIV reads *what displeases me*; v. 4). Both word pairs suggest that Israel's worship had become syncretistic. Yahweh will bring on each of these wicked persons the punishment they deserve and fear. God had done his part to call them to repentance: *when I called, no one answered, / when I spoke, no one listened* (v. 4).

5–6. With the phrase *Hear the word of the LORD*, the author seeks to gain the attention of the remnant (*you who tremble at his word*). The author makes a sharp distinction between those who make up their own rules (v. 4) and the righteous remnant who fear God. Because they have trembled at God's word (v. 2), responding with obedience to what he has said, they will have no need to tremble at his punishment.

The righteous ones are hated by their neighbours (lit. 'your brothers') and are excluded from their fellowship for remaining faithful to Yahweh (lit. 'on account of my name'). The wicked mock them, saying, *Let the LORD be glorified, / that we may see your joy!* (lit. 'let us appear with your joy'). The wicked do not believe that God will deliver the remnant; but if he does, they expect to be delivered as well because they consider themselves equally God's children. But God emphatically affirms that the mockers will be put to shame and will not take any part in the joy of the remnant.

No sooner does he mention that the mockers will be put to shame than the punishment begins: *Hear that uproar from the city / . . .* [and] *the temple! / It is the sound of the LORD / repaying his enemies all they deserve.* The three phrases of verse 6 each begin with *qôl*, 'sound' (lit. 'a "sound" of uproar from a city', 'a "sound" from a temple', 'the "sound" of Yahweh making recompense to his enemies').

Those who had mocked the righteous and forbidden them to worship in the temple now experience God's wrath, which emanates from the temple.

(2) Yahweh delivers a remnant (66:7–24)

(a) Zion will be populated (66:7–9)

7–9. As judgment of the wicked gets underway, so too restoration of the righteous begins, described in terms of childbearing. This is not the first time in the book that Zion is pictured as a mother receiving children during the restoration (see 49:18–23; 54:1–3). What is different here, however, is not the great number of children who arrive, but the unprecedented speed with which they arrive. This speed is emphasized in verses 7–8, particularly in the repetitive language of verse 7, the rhetorical questions of verse 8, and the summary sentence at the end of verse 7: *she delivers* [*mālaṭ*] *a son* [lit. 'a male'] – this is the only time *mālaṭ*, 'to escape, rescue', means 'to give birth to'.

The rhetorical question *Can a country be born in a day / or a nation be brought forth in a moment* [lit. 'at one time']? assumes the answer 'No, a country cannot be brought into existence fully and completely in a day.' And yet the context suggests that what God will do will truly amaze his people.

The restoration of the nation will not depend on the long process of growth through the naturally occurring births of its citizens. Instead, a remnant will be gathered from other nations (vv. 18–20), allowing God's kingdom to be established and populated very quickly.

God concludes in verse 9 with a double affirmation that these events will take place: *Do I* [lit. 'myself'] *bring to the moment of birth* [lit. 'cause to break'] / *and not give delivery?* The author, stunned by the remarkable nature of these events, exclaims: *Who has ever heard of such things* [lit. 'like the this'; v. 8]?

(b) The conclusion of God's plan (66:10–24) (Final refrain: *And they will go out and look on the dead bodies of those who rebelled against me; the worms that eat them will not die, the fire that burns them will not be quenched, and they will be loathsome to all mankind*)

This section builds to a climax in verse 14 wherein *the hand of the* L*ORD* *will be made known to his servants* and the righteous will rejoice and prosper, *but his fury will be shown to his foes.* The four *kî* ('for') phrases (vv. 15, 16, 18, 22) that follow then describe what this means.

10–14a. The author now widens his audience from Israel alone to all who love Israel: *Rejoice with Jerusalem and be glad for* [lit. 'with'] *her,* / all you who love her. The only ones who would *love* or *mourn over* Jerusalem are those who care about God and his people – in other words, the remnant from both Israel and the Gentiles (vv. 18–19).

The remnant will find peace and rest in restored Jerusalem, their needs being bountifully *satisfied* (lit. 'be satisfied from her comforting [*tanḥûm,* 5x] breasts') by their loving God: *for* [lit. 'with the result that'; Williams §368] *you . . . will drink deeply / and delight in her* [i.e. Jerusalem's] *overflowing* [*mizzîz,* occurs only here] *abundance* (i.e. lavish supply).

Verses 12–14a refer back to the peace and prosperity God will bring to the restored nation. Her peace will be as endless as an ever-flowing river. *The wealth* [lit. 'glory'] *of nations* will pour into her just as *a flooding stream* fills the land. God will treat his remnant like a loving mother caring for her child, providing sustenance (*feed*), protection (*carried on her arm / and dandled* [lit. 'to play, to take delight in'] *on her knees*; v. 12) and comfort (*so will I* [myself; emphatic] *comfort you*; v. 13).

When God's servants experience this restoration (*When you see this,* v. 14), they will rejoice and prosper (*you* [lit. 'your bones'] *will flourish* [lit. 'sprout'] *like the grass*) because of this demonstration of his power. Occasionally in the Old Testament bones are seen as the seat of the emotions (see Jer. 20:9).

One would expect the book to end with the climactic deliverance of God's remnant, but it does not, concluding instead with a final message of judgment. We argue that this is because each of the seams must incorporate each of the three key themes of the book, including judgment on the wicked.

14b–17. There is a sudden and chilling contrast at the end of verse 14, as Yahweh declares his intention to destroy his enemies: *but his fury will be shown to his foes.* The rare verb *zāʿam* ('to curse, scold') in the MT should be changed to the more common noun *ẓaʿam* ('indignation, fury') which requires only a change of vowel pointing.

Then beginning with verse 15 God introduces four *kî* ('for') phrases (vv. 15, 16, 18, 22) that describe God's plan for this final restoration, though some of the *kî* phrases are not translated as such in the NIV (only vv. 16, 18 are).

In the theophany beginning in verse 15, God comes riding in a chariot, brandishing both fire (mentioned three times in vv. 15–17) and sword as he unleashes judgment: *See* [lit. 'for behold'], *the LORD is coming with fire, / and his chariots are like a whirlwind* [*sûpâ*, 'strong storm' or 'gale']. The unusual syntax here (lit. 'for behold the LORD with fire he will come') lends emphasis.

Chariots at this time were considered an invincible weapon that could quickly inflict great damage. Yahweh rides his chariot in other theophanies as well (see Ps. 68:17), and he is often said to use fire (see Gen. 19:24) and the sword (see Ps. 7:12) as his weapons.

This judgment will be administered quickly (*like a whirlwind*; Jer. 4:13 uses this phrase to refer to the Babylonian army) and fiercely (lit. 'with fury'). Verse 15 describes God's judgment in a chiasm:

A *See, the LORD is coming with fire,*
　B *and his chariots are like a whirlwind;*
　B' *he will bring down his anger with fury,*
A' *and his rebuke with flames of fire.*

The second *kî*, at the beginning of verse 16, emphasizes the thoroughness of his judgment: *the LORD will execute judgment on all people* [lit. 'all flesh'], / *and many will be . . . slain* (v. 16). Verse 17 further identifies the *many* who will feel the blow of Yahweh's sword: (1) they worship the gods of fertility on the high places (*who consecrate* [lit. 'dedicate themselves'] *and purify themselves to go into the gardens* [i.e. to worship their false gods]); and (2) they follow the example of those who eat unclean things (lit. 'the flesh of the pigs, the rats, and the other unclean things'; see 65:4). Their clear defiance of God's law results in their destruction as a group: *they will meet their end together with the one they follow* (lit. 'to the gardens after one in the midst'), which suggests that they are led astray by a false leader.

Although it is sometimes argued that verse 17 is a later narrative addition, there is little evidence to support this.[22] Early in their history the Israelites worshipped idols on high places. The purpose of this verse is to make plain the reason for this swift and decisive judgment, whose finality is sounded in the closing words, *declares the LORD.*

18–21. The third *kî* spells out how God's plan will bring him glory. The narrative takes a step back to state what God will do just before destroying the wicked: *And I, because of what they* [i.e. the wicked] *have planned and done . . .* [will] *gather the people of all nations and languages, and they will come and see my glory* (v. 18).

The phrase *they will come and see my glory* is readily understood. However, the first part of this verse contains two difficulties: (1) Something appears to be missing in the literal reading: 'and I, their works and their thoughts coming [feminine singular participle] . . . ' The NIV attempts to solve this by adding the words [*because of what*] *they have planned and done* and translating the nouns as verbs (i.e. 'their works' as 'they have done' and 'their thoughts' as 'they have planned'). A number of scholars add the word 'knowing', resulting in the reading 'But I, knowing their deeds and their thoughts'. (2) The verb *bāʾâ*, 'is coming', in the next clause is a feminine singular *qal* participle (or a third person feminine singular *qal* perfect) that would require a feminine subject. To resolve this issue, some scholars add the word 'time', *ʿēt* [fem.], or 'it' (is coming), though there is nothing in the context that is feminine to which it refers.

Since there is such strong support for the present reading of the Hebrew text, it would be beneficial to arrive at a translation with as little emendation as possible. First, to resolve the apparent omission in the first phrase, we suggest dividing the word *wĕʾānōkî* ('and I') into two words, *wĕʾānî* + *kî* ('And I because'), which is a very plausible reading of 1QIsaᵃ, to yield the translation: 'And I, because of their deeds and their thoughts . . .'

Second, to resolve the apparent gender disagreement in the next phrase, we suggest reading *bāʾâ* as the masculine participial form of *bô'* ('to come, go') plus a paragogic *hē* ending or an archaic *hē* ending (GKC 90f). Examples of *bā'â* as a masculine form appear in the following passages: Jeremiah 43:11, *He* [Nebuchadnezzar] *will come* [*bā'â*, the *kĕthîb* reading, and *bā'*, the *qērê* reading]; Ezekiel 7:6, 10; 30:9.

If both of these suggestions are correct, then the resulting literal translation would be 'And I, because of their works and thoughts, am about to come [imminent action of the participle; Williams §214] to gather all nations and tongues and they will come and see my glory' (similar to NIV). In the context, the phrase 'to see God's glory' is equated with punishment; that is, they will see God's power displayed in the punishment and consequently honour this powerful God.

Specifics are not given concerning this punishment except to say that some will survive to proclaim God's glory to the nations: *I will set a sign among them, and I will send some of those who survive to the nations . . . They will proclaim my glory among the nations* (v. 19). As a result, even those distant nations that have not heard of God will hear about the greatness of Israel's God. The nature of this sign ('*ôt*) is not specified, but it stands as a reminder of Yahweh's power or activity.

The mention of survivors (*pĕlêṭîm*, 5x; v. 19) implies that there is some type of punishment from which the nations will flee. Those survivors who turn to God in repentance will be able to serve as witnesses of his power and justice. God's glory is not simply his judgment, but also the restoration of his remnant.

These survivors will be sent to the far reaches of the known world: *to Tarshish* [seaport of western Spain], *to the Libyans* [MT reads *pûl*, but the word is more probably *pût*, 'Libyan'] *and Lydians (famous as archers), to Tubal* [northern area] *and Greece.* The NIV's reading *famous as archers* (*mōšĕkê qešet*, lit. 'drawers of a bow') follows the reading in Jeremiah 46:9 that describes the Lydians as being able to 'handle [lit. 'to grasp'] and bend the bow' (NASB).

Since none of the other names in the list has a descriptor, some suggest emending *mōšĕkê qešet* to read Meshek (*mešek*) and Rosh (*wĕrō'š*), similar to Ezekiel 38:2, 3; 39:1 (see NASB); however, this would require significant emendation, for which there is little evidence.

The commonality between these nations is that they have not yet heard about Yahweh's glory, something to which the survivors will soon testify. They will also *bring all your* [i.e. the remnant's] *people* [lit. 'brothers'] back to *Jerusalem* [*as*] *an offering to the* LORD. To do this, they will use nearly every means of transportation available, including horses, chariots, wagons, mules and camels (*kitkārôt*, occurs only here). The phrase *your people* (lit. 'brothers') could refer to the remnant of Israelites alone, but in 56:3–8 we learned that the believing remnant would also include eunuchs and Gentiles.

Isaiah 66:21 says that *I* [God] *will select some of them* [lit. 'and even from them'; i.e. from the nations] *also to be priests and Levites*. The word *also* (*gam*) implies that these are selected by God 'in addition to' other priests and Levites who make up part of the remnant (Williams §378). Verse 21 contains an amazing new opportunity: the roles of priests and Levites, which were initially limited to a select few Israelites, have now been opened up to the Gentiles. The role of the priest was to function as an intermediary between God and the people. Levites were to teach others about God's requirements. Nothing could better demonstrate the removal of barriers between Jew and Gentile.

The arrival in Jerusalem of this believing remnant, brought from other nations by those who survive the judgment (v. 20), is likened to a 'grain offering' [*minḥă* = an offering of homage; *HALOT* 2.605] *to the* LORD. Again, equality of status between the two groups (Jews and Gentiles) is implied here. Oswalt observes that 'it is hard to imagine what more precious offering could be given to him [God]' (1998: 689).

The notation that the offerings are brought *in ceremonially clean vessels* may indicate one of several things: (1) They are brought according to God's regulations. That is, the people who return to Jerusalem are doing so in obedience to a command from God, who had prophesied that this righteous remnant would come to him. (2) Just as grain offerings were brought in ceremonially clean vessels, so the believing remnant from other nations would now be 'clean' or righteous. (3) The grain offering represents the remnant and the *clean vessels* are the means by which they arrive (i.e. horses, chariots, etc.). This third option is supported by the phrase in/on *clean vessels*.

These modes of transportation are said to be *ceremonially clean* in that they are sanctified for the express purpose of carrying God's holy objects; see a similar concept in Zechariah 14:20–21a.

22–24. The book concludes with the fourth *kî* (absent in the NIV) describing a dramatic contrast between the righteous and the wicked. First, the righteous remnant (vv. 22–23) will endure before God, as do the new heavens and new earth: *As [ka'ăšer, lit. 'just as'] the new heavens and the new earth that I make will endure before me . . . so [kēn] will your name and descendants endure.* God assures the remnant that both their name (i.e. reputation) and offspring (i.e. lineage) will endure before him.

In this new creation Yahweh is regularly worshipped, both weekly and monthly, by 'all flesh' (*kol bāśār*; see Num. 28:9–15). These regular pilgrimages to Zion for worship would remind the remnant of the former regulations that God had established to maintain a close spiritual relationship with him. Now everyone who is left in the land will have a close relationship with God.

Second, as a continuation of the thought of verse 23, the remnant will be shown *the dead bodies of those who rebelled against me* (i.e. God; v. 24). This gives the believing remnant the opportunity to see the outcome for those who did not believe. The statement serves as a conclusion to the entire book of Isaiah and a reminder of the punishment for those who rejected God. The judgment that was announced in verses 17–18 (*they will meet their end together . . . they will come and see my glory*) is now completed in verse 24.

The word for *dead bodies* (*bĕpigrê*, lit. 'on the corpses') could be somewhat misleading, for the rest of the verse suggests a continual, never-ending state of misery, or a continual state of punishment with no conclusion: *the worms that eat them* [lit. 'their worm'] *will not die, the fire that burns them will not be quenched.* The worms will not die, and the flame will not go out, because they will always have a constant source of food; thus their bodies will be subject to a continual state of punishment (see Rev. 20:10).

The rest of humanity (i.e. the righteous remnant) will find them loathsome to look upon. The word *loathsome* (*dērā'ôn*, 'abhorrence') appears only here and in Daniel 12:2, where it speaks of 'everlasting contempt' in the context of final punishment, similar to the context here.

Later rabbinic tradition concerning worship in the synagogue required that verse 23 be repeated after verse 24 in public readings so that the book did not end on such a negative note. Many critical scholars think that verse 23 is the true conclusion to the book and that verse 24 is an unfortunate later addition (see Childs 2001: 542). We consider verse 24 to be a crucial part of the final seam of the book with its expanded version of the refrain 'there is no peace for the wicked'. This negative image at the book's end has the rhetorical effect of prompting the reader to realize a choice needs to be made.

Meaning

The final section (i.e. chapters 65–66) begins by highlighting that God initiated the relationship between himself and his people. God called out to those who grievously rebelled against him, yet they did not repent and would therefore undergo punishment, out of which God would bring a remnant for himself. This remnant is referred to as the gleanings of God's vineyard, 'God's servants', who will live in a new heaven and new earth where joy and blessing are the standard. It will be a time of prosperity and peace marked by an extended lifespan and a peaceful state in nature. There is an interesting similarity between the effects that the future deliverer brings upon this earth (Isa. 11) and life during the period of a restored heaven and earth.

Chapter 66 begins by reminding readers that the sovereign God, who cannot be contained by anything in his own creation, has chosen to have regard for those who turn to him and obey his commands. By contrast, he will punish those who pursue their own ways and have no regard for his commands. Yahweh's glory will be proclaimed to all the nations so that a remnant, incorporating both Israelites and Gentiles, will be brought from all the nations. Some of the Gentiles will even become priests and Levites. This remnant will serve Yahweh and regularly come to worship him. The remnant will be able to observe the fate of those who rebelled against God: their corpses will never be consumed (like the final judgment in Rev. 20).

The book of Isaiah begins by calling out to Israel to repent and believe, and ends with the assurance that some will indeed repent (i.e. the remnant in vv. 20–23), whereas the wicked will be punished (v. 24). These two themes recur throughout the book and are ultimately fulfilled in the book of Revelation.